CHILDREN'S WRITER'S & ILLUSTRATOR'S MARKET

2019

Includes a one-year online subscription to **Children's Writer's & Illustrator's Market** on

Where & How to Sell What You Write

THE ULTIMATE MARKET RESEARCH TOOL FOR WRITERS

To register your *Children's Writer's & Illustrator's Market 2019* and **start your one-year online subscription**, scratch off the block below to reveal your activation code*, then go to WritersMarket.com. Find the box that says "Purchased a Deluxe Edition?" then click on "Activate Your Account" and enter the activation code. It's that easy!

UPDATED MARKET LISTINGS
EASY-TO-USE, SEARCHABLE DATABASE • RECORD-KEEPING TOOLS
PROFESSIONAL TIPS & ADVICE • INDUSTRY NEWS

Your purchase of *Children's Writer's & Illustrator's Market* gives you access to updated listings related to literary agents (valid through 12/31/19). For just $9.99, you can upgrade your subscription and get access to listings from all of our best-selling Market Books. Visit **WritersMarket.com** for more information.

WritersMarket.com
Where & How to Sell What You Write

Activate your WritersMarket.com subscription
to get instant access to:

- **UPDATED LISTINGS IN YOUR WRITING GENRE:** Find additional listings that didn't make it into the book, updated contact information, and more. WritersMarket.com provides the most comprehensive database of verified markets available anywhere.

- **EASY-TO-USE, SEARCHABLE DATABASE:** Looking for a specific magazine or book publisher? Just type in its name. Or widen your prospects with the Advanced Search. You can also search for listings that have been recently updated!

- **PERSONALIZED TOOLS:** Store your best-bet markets, and use our popular recording-keeping tools to track your submissions. Plus, get new and updated market listings, query reminders, and more every time you log in!

- **PROFESSIONAL TIPS & ADVICE:** From pay-rate charts to sample query letters, how-to articles to Q&As with literary agents, we have all the resources writers need.

YOU'LL GET ALL OF THIS WITH THE INCLUDED SUBSCRIPTION TO

◄ 31ST ANNUAL EDITION ►

CHILDREN'S WRITER'S & ILLUSTRATOR'S MARKET

2019

Robert Lee Brewer, Editor

WD
WRITER'S DIGEST
BOOKS
WritersDigest.com
Cincinnati, Ohio

Children's Writer's & Illustrator's Market 2019. Copyright © 2018 F + W Media, Inc. Published by Writer's Digest Books, an imprint of F+W Media, Inc., 10151 Carver Road, Suite 300, Blue Ash, Ohio 45242. Printed and bound in the United States of America. All rights reserved. No part of this book may be reproduced in any form or by any electronic or mechanical means including information storage and retrieval systems without permission in writing from the publisher, except by a reviewer, who may quote brief passages in a review.

Writer's Market website: www.writersmarket.com
Writer's Digest website: www.writersdigest.com

Distributed in the U.K. and Europe by F&W Media International
Pynes Hill Court, Pynes Hill, Rydon Lane
Exeter, EX2 5AZ, United Kingdom
Tel: (+44) 1392 797680, Fax: (+44) 1626-323319
E-mail: postmaster@davidandcharles.co.uk

ISSN: 0897-9790
ISBN-13: 978-1-4403-5440-3
ISBN-10: 1-4403-5440-5

Attention Booksellers: This is an annual directory of F + W Media, Inc. Return deadline for this edition is December 31, 2019.

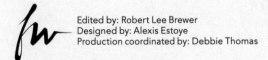

Edited by: Robert Lee Brewer
Designed by: Alexis Estoye
Production coordinated by: Debbie Thomas

CONTENTS

BUSINESS & PROMOTION

MARKETS

FROM
THE EDITOR

//

In this edition of *Children's Writer's & Illustrator's Market*, I wanted to squeeze in as many listings as I possibly could for writers and illustrators of children's books and stories. But I also wanted to share great articles on the craft, business, and promotion side of things as well.

For the craft, there are articles on writing effective dialogue, unleashing your storytelling superpower, and creating unforgettable characters. Plus, there are interviews with the likes of Leigh Bardugo, Melissa de la Cruz, Marieke Nijkamp, E. Lockhart and more. Also, we've packed in a plethora of business and promotion articles.

Of course, the listings are still "where it's at" with *Children's Writer's & Illustrator's Market*, and I tried to pack as many into this year's book as possible. You'll find listings for book publishers, literary agents, magazines, contests, and more.

Also, be sure to take advantage of the webinar for *Children's Writer's & Illustrator's Market* readers. Learn more at www.writersmarket.com/2019-cwim-webinar.

Until next we meet, keep writing and marketing what you write.

Robert Lee Brewer

Senior Content Editor

Children's Writer's & Illustrator's Market

http://writersdigest.com/editor-blogs/poetic-asides
http://blog.writersmarket.com
http://twitter.com/robertleebrewer

HOW TO USE CHILDREN'S WRITER'S & ILLUSTRATOR'S MARKET

///

As a writer, illustrator, or photographer first picking up *Children's Writer's & Illustrator's Market*, you may not know quite how to start using the book. Your impulse may be to flip through the book and quickly make a mailing list, then submit to everyone in hopes that someone will take interest in your work. Well, there's more to it. Finding the right market takes research. The more you know about a market that interests you, the better chance you have of getting work accepted. We've made your job a little easier by putting a wealth of information at your fingertips. Besides providing listings, this directory has a number of tools to help you determine which markets are the best ones for your work. By using these tools, as well as researching on your own, you raise your odds of being published.

USING THE INDEXES

This book lists hundreds of potential buyers of material. To learn which companies want the type of material you're interested in submitting, start with the indexes.

Subject Index

But let's narrow the search further. Take your list of young adult magazines, turn to the **Subject Index**, and find the **Fashion** subheading. Then highlight the names that appear on both lists (**Young Adult** and **Fashion**). Now you have a smaller list of all the magazines that would be interested in your teen fashion article. Read through those listings and decide which seem (or look) best for your work.

Illustrators and photographers can use the **Subject Index** as well. If you specialize in painting animals, for instance, consider sending samples to book and magazine publishers listed under **Animals** and, perhaps, **Nature/Environment**. Because illustrators can simply send general examples of their style to art directors to keep on file, the indexes may be more helpful to artists sending manuscript/illustration packages who need to search for a specific subject. Always read the listings for the potential markets to see the type of work art directors prefer and what type of samples they'll keep on file, and obtain art or photo guidelines if they're available online.

Age-Level Index

Age groups are broken down into these categories in the Age-Level Index:

- **PICTURE BOOKS OR PICTURE-ORIENTED MATERIAL** are written and illustrated for preschoolers to eight-year-olds.
- **YOUNG READERS** are for five- to eight-year-olds.
- **MIDDLE READERS** are for nine- to eleven-year-olds.
- **YOUNG ADULT** is for ages twelve and up.

Age breakdowns may vary slightly from publisher to publisher, but using them as general guidelines will help you target appropriate markets. For example, if you've written an article about trends in teen fashion, check the **Magazines Age-Level Index** under the **Young Adult** subheading.

USING THE LISTINGS

Some listings begin with symbols. Many listings indicate whether submission guidelines are indeed available. If a publisher you're interested in offers guidelines, get them and read them. The same is true with catalogs. Sending for and reading catalogs or browsing them online gives you a better idea of whether your work would fit in with the books a publisher produces. (You should also look at a few of the books in the catalog at a library or bookstore to get a feel for the publisher's material.)

A Note for Artists & Photographers

Along with information for writers, listings provide information for illustrators and photographers. Illustrators will find numerous markets that maintain files of samples for possible future assignments. If you're both a writer and an illustrator, look for markets that accept manuscript/illustration packages and read the information offered under the **Illustration** subhead within the listings.

If you're a photographer, read the information under the **Photography** subhead within listings to see what format buyers prefer. For example, some want the highest resolution .jpg available of an image. Note the type of photos a buyer wants to purchase and the procedures for submitting. It's not uncommon for a market to want a résumé and promotional literature, as well as sample URLs linking to previous work. Listings also note whether model releases and/or captions are required.

QUICK TIPS FOR WRITERS & ILLUSTRATORS

//

If you're new to the world of children's publishing, reviewing this edition of *Children's Writer's & Illustrator's Market* may have been one of the first steps in your journey to publication. What follows is a list of suggestions and resources that can help make that journey a smooth and swift one:

1. MAKE THE MOST OF *CHILDREN'S WRITER'S & ILLUSTRATOR'S MARKET*. Be sure to take advantage of the articles and interviews in the book. The insights of the authors, illustrators, editors, and agents we've interviewed will inform and inspire you.

2. JOIN THE SOCIETY OF CHILDREN'S BOOK WRITERS AND ILLUSTRATORS. SCBWI, more than 22,000 members strong, is an organization for both beginners and professionals interested in writing and illustrating for children, with more than seventy active regional chapters worldwide. It offers members a slew of information and support through publications, a website, and a host of Regional Advisors overseeing chapters in almost every state in the U.S. and a growing number of locations around the globe. SCBWI puts on a number of conferences, workshops, and events on the regional and national levels (many listed in the **Conferences & Workshops** section of this book). For more information, visit www.scbwi.org.

3. READ NEWSLETTERS. Newsletters, such as *Children's Book Insider*, *Children's Writer*, and the *SCBWI Bulletin*, offer updates and new information about publishers on a timely basis and are relatively inexpensive. Many local chapters of SCBWI offer regional newsletters as well.

4. READ TRADE AND REVIEW PUBLICATIONS. Magazines such as *Publishers Weekly* (which offers two special issues each year devoted to children's publishing and is available on newsstands as well as through a digital subscription) offer news, articles, reviews of newly published titles, and ads featuring upcoming and current releases. Referring to them will help you get a feel for what's happening in children's publishing.

5. READ GUIDELINES. Most publishers and magazines offer writers' and artists' guidelines that provide detailed information on needs and submission requirements, and some magazines offer theme lists for upcoming issues. Many publishers and magazines state the availability of guidelines within their listings. You'll often find submission information on publishers' and magazines' websites.

6. LOOK AT PUBLISHERS' CATALOGS. Perusing publishers' catalogs can give you a feel for their line of books and help you decide where your work might fit in. If catalogs are available, visit publishers' websites, which often contain their full catalogs. You can also ask librarians to look at catalogs they have on hand. You can even search Amazon.com by publisher and year. (Click on "book search" then "publisher, date" and plug in, for example, "Lee & Low" under *publisher* and "2016" under *year*. You'll get a list of Lee & Low titles published in 2016, which you can peruse.)

7. VISIT BOOKSTORES. It's not only informative to spend time in bookstores—it's fun, too! Frequently visit the children's section of your local bookstore (whether a chain or an independent) to see the latest from a variety of publishers and the most current issues of children's magazines. Look for books in the genre you're writing or with illustrations similar in style to yours, and spend some time studying them. It's also wise to get to know your local booksellers; they can tell you what's new in the store and provide insight into what kids and adults are buying.

8. READ, READ, READ! While you're at that bookstore, pick up a few things, or keep a list of the books that interest you and check them out of your library. Read and study the latest releases, the award-winners and the classics. You'll learn from other writers, get ideas, and get a feel for what's being published. Think about what works and doesn't work in a story. Pay attention to how plots are constructed and how characters are developed, or the rhythm and pacing of picture book text. It's certainly enjoyable research!

9. TAKE ADVANTAGE OF INTERNET RESOURCES. There are innumerable sources of information available online about writing for children (and anything else you could possibly think of). It's also a great resource for getting (and staying) in touch with other writers and illustrators through listservs, blogs, social networking sites, and e-mail, and it can serve as a vehicle for self-promotion.

10. CONSIDER ATTENDING A CONFERENCE. If time and finances allow, attending a writers conference is a great way to meet peers and network with professionals in the field of children's publishing. As mentioned earlier, SCBWI offers conferences in various locations year round. (See scbwi.org and click on "Events" for a full conference calendar.) General writers' conferences often offer specialized sessions just for those interested in children's writing. Many conferences offer optional manuscript and portfolio critiques as well, giving you feedback from seasoned professionals. See the **Conferences** section of this book for information on conferences.

11. NETWORK, NETWORK, NETWORK! Don't work in a vacuum. You can meet other writers and illustrators through a number of the things listed earlier—SCBWI, conferences, online. Attend local meetings for writers and illustrators whenever you can. Befriend other writers in your area (SCBWI offers members a roster broken down by state)—share guidelines, share subscriptions, be conference buddies and roommates, join a critique group or writing group, exchange information, and offer support. Get online—subscribe to listservs, post on message boards and blogs, visit social networking sites and chatrooms. Exchange addresses, phone numbers, and e-mail addresses with writers or illustrators you meet at events. And at conferences, don't be afraid to talk to people, ask strangers to join you for lunch, approach speakers and introduce yourself, or chat in elevators and hallways.

12. PERFECT YOUR CRAFT AND DON'T SUBMIT UNTIL YOUR WORK IS AT ITS BEST. It's often been said that a writer should try to write every day. Great manuscripts don't happen overnight; there's time, research, and revision involved. As you visit bookstores and study what others have written and illustrated, really step back and look at your own work and ask yourself, *How does my work measure up? Is it ready for editors or art directors to see?* If it's not, keep working. Join a critique group or get a professional manuscript or portfolio critique.

13. BE PATIENT, LEARN FROM REJECTION, AND DON'T GIVE UP! Thousands of manuscripts land on editors' desks; thousands of illustration samples line art directors' file drawers. There are so many factors that come into play when evaluating submissions. Keep in mind that you might not hear back from publishers promptly. Persistence and patience are important qualities in writers and illustrators working toward publication. Keep at it—it will come. It can take a while, but when you get that first book contract or first assignment, you'll know it was worth the wait. (For proof, read the "Debut Authors Tell All" article later in this book!)

BEFORE YOUR FIRST SALE

If you're just beginning to pursue your career as a children's book writer or illustrator, it's important to learn the proper procedures, formats, and protocol for the publishing industry. This article outlines the basics you need to know before you submit your work to a market.

FINDING THE BEST MARKETS FOR YOUR WORK

Researching markets thoroughly is a basic element of submitting your work successfully. Editors and art directors hate to receive inappropriate submissions; handling them wastes a lot of their time, not to mention your time and money, and they are the main reason some publishers have chosen not to accept material over the transom. By randomly sending out material without knowing a company's needs, you're sure to meet with rejection.

If you're interested in submitting to a particular magazine, see if it's available in your local library or bookstore, or read past articles online. For a book publisher, obtain a book catalog and check a library or bookstore for titles produced by that publisher. Most publishers and magazines have websites that include catalogs or sample articles (websites are given within the listings). Studying such materials carefully will better acquaint you with a publisher's or magazine's writing, illustration, and photography styles and formats.

Many of the book publishers and magazines listed in this book offer some sort of writers', artists', or photographers' guidelines on their websites. It's important to read and study guidelines before submitting work. You'll get a better understanding of what a particular publisher wants. You may even decide, after reading the submission guidelines, that your work isn't right for a company you considered.

SUBMITTING YOUR WORK

Throughout the listings, you'll read requests for particular elements to include when contacting markets. Here are explanations of some of these important submission components.

Queries, Cover Letters, & Proposals

A query is a no-more-than-one-page, well-written letter meant to arouse an editor's interest in your work. Query letters briefly outline the work you're proposing and include facts, anecdotes, interviews, or other pertinent information that give the editor a feel for the manuscript's premise—enticing her to want to know more. End your letter with a straightforward request to submit the work, and include information on its approximate length, date it could be completed, and whether accompanying photos or artwork are available.

In a query letter, think about presenting your book as a publisher's catalog would present it. Read through a good catalog and examine how the publishers give enticing summaries of their books in a spare amount of words. It's also important that query letters give editors a taste of your writing style. For good advice and samples of queries, cover letters, and other correspondence, consult *Guide to Literary Agents 2019*, as well as *Formatting & Submitting Your Manuscript, 3rd Ed.* and *The Writer's Digest Guide to Query Letters* (all published by Writer's Digest Books).

- **QUERY LETTERS FOR NONFICTION.** Queries are usually required when submitting nonfiction material to a publisher. The goal of a nonfiction query is to convince the editor your idea is perfect for her readership and that you're qualified to do the job. Note any previous writing experience and include published samples to prove your credentials, especially samples related to the subject matter you're querying about.
- **QUERY LETTERS FOR FICTION.** For a fiction query, explain the story's plot, main characters, conflict, and resolution. Just as in nonfiction queries, make the editor eager to see more.
- **COVER LETTERS FOR WRITERS.** Some editors prefer to review complete manuscripts, especially for picture books or fiction. In such cases, the cover letter (which should be no longer than one page) serves as your introduction, establishes your credentials as a writer, and gives the editor an overview of the manuscript. If the editor asked for the manuscript because of a query, note this in your cover letter.
- **COVER LETTERS FOR ILLUSTRATORS AND PHOTOGRAPHERS.** For an illustrator or photographer, the cover letter serves as an introduction to the art director and establishes professional credentials when submitting samples. Explain what services you can provide as well as what type of follow-up contact you plan to make, if any. Be sure to include the URL of your online portfolio if you have one.

- **RÉSUMÉS.** Often writers, illustrators, and photographers submit résumés with cover letters and samples. They can be created in a variety of formats, from a single page listing information to color brochures featuring your work. Keep your résumé brief, and focus on your achievements, including your clients and the work you've done for them, as well as your educational background and any awards you've received. Do not use the same résumé you'd use for a typical job application.
- **BOOK PROPOSALS.** Throughout the listings in the **Book Publishers** section, listings refer to submitting a synopsis, outline, and sample chapters. Depending on an editor's preference, some or all of these components, along with a cover letter, make up a book proposal.

A *synopsis* summarizes the book, covering the basic plot (including the ending). It should be easy to read and flow well. The gold standard for synopsis length is one page, single-spaced.

An *outline* covers your book chapter by chapter and provides highlights of each. If you're developing an outline for fiction, include major characters, plots, and subplots, and book length. Requesting an outline is uncommon, and the word is somewhat interchangeable with *synopsis*.

Sample chapters give a more comprehensive idea of your writing skill. Some editors may request the first two or three chapters to determine if they're interested in seeing the whole book. Some may request a set number of pages.

Manuscript Formats

When submitting a complete manuscript, follow some basic guidelines. In the upper-left corner of your title page, type your legal name (not pseudonym), address, and phone number. In the upper-right corner, type the approximate word count. All material in the upper corners should be single-spaced. Then type the title (centered) almost halfway down that page, the word "by" two lines under that, and your name or pseudonym two lines under "by."

The first page should also include the title (centered) one-third of the way down. Two lines under that, type "by" and your name or pseudonym. To begin the body of your manuscript, drop down two double spaces and indent five spaces for each new paragraph. There should be one-inch margins around all sides of a full page. (Manuscripts with wide margins are more readable and easier to edit.)

Set your computer to double-space the manuscript body. From page two to the end of the manuscript, include your last name followed by a comma and the title (or key words of the title) in the upper-left corner. The page number should go in the top right corner. Drop down two double spaces to begin the body of each page. If you're submitting a novel, type each chapter title one-third of the way down the page. For more information on manuscript formats, read *Formatting & Submitting Your Manuscript, 3rd Ed.* (Writer's Digest Books).

Picture Book Formats

The majority of editors prefer to see complete manuscripts for picture books. When typing the text of a picture book, don't indicate page breaks and don't type each page of text on a new sheet of paper. And unless you are an illustrator, don't worry about supplying art. Editors will find their own illustrators for picture books. Most of the time, a writer and an illustrator who work on the same book never meet or interact. The editor acts as a go-between who works with the writer and illustrator throughout the publishing process. *How to Write and Sell Children's Picture Books* by Jean E. Karl (Writer's Digest Books) offers advice on preparing text and marketing your work.

If you're an illustrator who has written your own book, consider creating a dummy or storyboard containing both art and text, and then submit it along with your complete manuscript and sample pieces of final art (hi-res PDFs or JPGs—never originals). Publishers interested in picture books specify in their listings what should be submitted. For tips on creating a dummy, refer to *How to Write and Illustrate Children's Books and Get Them Published*, edited by Treld Pelkey Bicknell and Felicity Trotman (North Light Books), or *How to Write, Illustrate, and Design Children's Books* by Frieda Gates (Lloyd-Simone Publishing Company).

Writers may also want to learn the art of dummy-making to help them through the writing process with things like pacing, rhythm, and length. For a great explanation and helpful hints, see *You Can Write Children's Books*, by Tracey E. Dils (Writer's Digest Books).

Mailing Submissions

Your main concern when packaging material is to be sure it arrives undamaged. If your manuscript is fewer than six pages, simply fold it in thirds and send it in a #10 (business-size) envelope. For a SASE, either fold another #10 envelope in thirds or insert a #9 (reply) envelope, which fits in a #10 neatly without folding.

Another option is folding your manuscript in half in a 6x9 envelope, with a #9 or #10 SASE enclosed. For larger manuscripts, use a 9x12 envelope both for mailing the submission and as a SASE (which can be folded in half). Book manuscripts require sturdy packaging for mailing. Include a self-addressed mailing label and return postage. If asked to send artwork and photographs, remember they require a bit more care in packaging to guarantee they arrive in good condition. Sandwich illustrations and photos between heavy cardboard that is slightly larger than the work. The cardboard can be secured by rubber bands or with tape. If you tape the cardboard together, check that the artwork doesn't stick to the tape. Be sure your name and address appear on the back of each piece of art or each photo in case the material becomes separated. For the packaging, use either a manila envelope, a foam-padded envelope, or a mailer lined with plastic air bubbles. Bind nonjoined edges with reinforced mailing tape and affix a typed mailing label or clearly write your address.

Mailing materials first class ensures quick delivery. Also, first-class mail is forwarded for one year if the addressee has moved, and it can be returned if undeliverable. If you're concerned about your original material reaching its destination, consider other mailing options such as UPS. No matter which way you send material, never send it in a way that requires a signature for receipt. Agents and editors are too busy to sign for packages.

Remember, companies outside your own country can't use your country's postage when returning a manuscript to you. When mailing a submission to another country, include a self-addressed envelope and International Reply Coupons, or IRCs. (You'll see this term in many listings in the Canadian & International Book Publishers section.) Your postmaster can tell you, based on a package's weight, the correct number of IRCs to include to ensure its return. If it's not necessary for an editor to return your work (such as with photocopies), don't include return postage.

Unless requested, it's never a good idea to use a company's fax number to send manuscript submissions. This can disrupt a company's internal business. Study the listings for specifics and visit publisher and market websites for more information.

E-mailing Submissions

Most correspondence with editors today is handled over e-mail. This type of communication is usually preferred by publishing professionals because it is easier to deal with as well as free. When sending an e-mailed submission, make sure to follow submission guidelines. Double-check the recipient's e-mail address. Make sure your subject line has the proper wording, if specific wording is requested. Keep your introduction letter short and sweet. Also, editors and agents usually do not like opening unsolicited attachments, which makes for an awkward situation for illustrators who want to attach .jpgs. One easy way around this is to post some sample illustrations on your website. That way, you can simply paste URL hyperlinks to your work. Editors can click through to look over your illustration samples, and there is no way your submission will be deleted because of attachments. That said, if editors are asking for illustration samples, they are most likely used to receiving unsolicited attachments.

Keeping Submission Records

It's important to keep track of the material you submit. When recording each submission, include the date it was sent, the business and contact name, and any enclosures (such as samples of writing, artwork or photography). You can create a record-keeping system of your own or look for record-keeping software in your area computer store.

Keep copies of articles or manuscripts you send together with related correspondence to make follow-up easier. When you sell rights to a manuscript, artwork, or photos, you can "close" your file on a particular submission by noting the date the material was accepted, what rights were purchased, the publication date, and payment.

Often writers, illustrators, and photographers fail to follow up on overdue responses. If you don't hear from a publisher within their stated response time, wait another month or so and follow up with an e-mail asking about the status of your submission. Include the title or description, date sent, and a SASE (if applicable) for response. Ask the contact person when she anticipates making a decision. You may refresh the memory of a buyer who temporarily forgot about your submission. At the very least, you will receive a definite "no" and free yourself to send the material to another publisher.

Simultaneous submissions

Writers and illustrators are encouraged to simultaneously submit—sending the same material to several markets at the same time. Almost all markets are open to this type of communication; those that do not take simultaneous submissions will directly say so in their submission guidelines.

It's especially important to keep track of simultaneous submissions, so if you get an offer on a manuscript sent to more than one publisher, you can instruct other publishers to withdraw your work from consideration. (Or, you can always use the initial offer as a way to ignite interest from other agents and editors. It's very possible to procure multiple offers on your book using this technique.)

AGENTS & ART REPS

Most children's writers, illustrators, and photographers, especially those just beginning, are confused about whether to enlist the services of an agent or representative. The decision is strictly one that each writer, illustrator, or photographer must make for herself. Some are confident with their own negotiation skills and believe acquiring an agent or rep is not in their best interest. Others feel uncomfortable in the business arena or are not willing to sacrifice valuable creative time for marketing.

About half of children's publishers accept unagented work, so it's possible to break into children's publishing without an agent. Writers targeting magazine markets don't need the services of an agent. In fact, it's practically impossible to find an agent interested in marketing articles and short stories—there simply isn't enough financial incentive.

One benefit of having an agent, though, is it may speed up the process of getting your work reviewed, especially by publishers who don't accept unagented submissions. If an agent has a good reputation and submits your manuscript to an editor, that manuscript will likely bypass the first-read stage (which is generally done by editorial assistants and junior editors) and end up on the editor's desk sooner.

When agreeing to have a reputable agent represent you, remember that she should be familiar with the needs of the current market and evaluate your manuscript/artwork/photos accordingly. She should also determine the quality of your piece and whether it is salable. When your manuscript sells, your agent should negotiate a favorable contract and clear up any questions you have about payments.

Keep in mind that no matter how reputable the agent or rep is, she has limitations. Representation does not guarantee sale of your work. It just means an agent or rep sees potential in your writing, art, or photos. Though an agent or rep may offer criticism or advice on how to improve your work, she cannot make you a better writer, artist, or photographer.

Literary agents typically charge a fifteen percent commission from the sale of writing; art and photo representatives usually charge a twenty five or thirty percent commission. Such fees are taken from advances and royalty earnings. If your agent sells foreign rights or film rights to your work, she will deduct a higher percentage because she will most likely be dealing with an overseas agent with whom she must split the fee.

Be advised that not every agent is open to representing a writer, artist, or photographer who lacks an established track record. Just as when approaching a publisher, the manuscript, artwork, or photos, and query or cover letter you submit to a potential agent must be attractive and professional looking. Your first impression must be as an organized, articulate person. For listings of agents and reps, turn to the **Literary Agents & Art Reps** section.

WRITING EFFECTIVE DIALOGUE

Learn the differences between writing dialogue for early readers, middle grade, and young adult.

....

Kerrie Flanagan

Dialogue is the backbone of every great children's story. But the nuances of dialogue in different age groups are very different. When children are young and learning to read, dialogue is simple. As children get older, the conversations—and the techniques for writing dialogue—become more complex.

Dialogue serves a larger purpose than simply showing a conversation between people or characters. It creates mood, enhances setting, unveils backstory, provides insights into the characters, and propels a story forward. It adds substance to the story; the way dialogue is formatted, adds white space to a page, making the text visually appealing and easier to read.

Tag lines are important as they show the reader who is speaking: *"I wish I had a magic wand," Claire said.* The phrase "Claire said" is the tag. Understanding how to use these effectively for various age groups will help you be more successful when writing for children.

EARLY READERS

For young children who are beginning to learn how to read, dialogue is especially important. Ellen Javernick, kindergarten teacher and author of more than 100 books for early readers including, *What if Everybody Did That?* and *The Birthday Pet* says, "With little people, you want to have a lot of dialogue; very little text otherwise. It carries the story for the children and can take the place of the showing."

Say you have the following:

> Johnny saw a bowl of chocolates on the table. He got excited. He asked his mother if he could have one.

Instead of simply telling the reader what's happening, you can put it into dialogue:

> "Look at those yummy chocolates on the table," Johnny said. "Mom, can I have one?"

By making this dialogue instead of narrative, it became more active and engaging for the reader.

The tags used for young readers should be simple. Stick to the basics. "Ninety-percent of the time it will be, *said*," Javernick explains. "You can occasionally weave in a couple of others like *asked* or *yelled*, but remember, these children are just learning to read. The word said is common and one of the first one-hundred sight words taught in school."

MIDDLE-GRADE

As children grow up and move toward middle-grade books, they learn to read more words and expand their vocabulary. Laura Backes, publisher of Children's Book Insider (www.writeforkids.org), *The Children's Writing Monthly*, and co-creator of Writing-Blueprints.com, says, "You can get more sophisticated with the speech tags and verbs of speech, using words like *murmured*, *intoned*, *proclaimed* as long as they fit the dialogue and tone of the scene."

The danger can happen when writers want to avoid using the word *said* and then overuse other tags. The truth is, the word *said* becomes invisible to readers. When you begin adding too many different words, like *demanded*, *articulated*, *lamented*, it can slow down readers and distract them from the conversation. Use these types of tags sparingly, otherwise you end up with something like this:

> "Are you awake?" Chuck inquired.
> "Of course, I'm awake," Eddie chortled. "I'm talking. Are you awake?"
> "Duh. I'm talking, too," Chuck confirmed. "I wonder if the bear came back."
> "Maybe it snuck into our van and ate all our food. Let's go look!" Eddie exclaimed.

Dialogue can show how a character is feeling and even reveal something about his personality, and the choice of speech tags can go a long way toward showing state of mind:

> "Of course I'll help," Sam mumbled.

> "Of course I'll help!" Sam exclaimed.

Adding action also gives us information about that character.

> "Of course I'll help," Sam said, rolling his eyes.

> "Of course I'll help." Sam sprang off the couch, knocking over his tray table and sending his dinner flying across the living room floor.

In all of these examples, what the character is saying hasn't change, but how he is saying it, or his action following the statement, give more insight.

YOUNG ADULT

When kids become teens, their needs as readers become more sophisticated. They are looking for characters and storylines with more depth, and dialogue can play a big role in that.

Todd Mitchell, YA author of *Backwards* and *The Secret to Lying*, says dialogue should also reveal your characters' desires, especially with older readers. Your characters must want something different out of the dialogue, and work hard to get that. "Dialogue is a dance where two characters are each working to achieve their desires without directly speaking them. When done well, characters show who they are and what they really want through the words and gestures they try to hide behind."

When you move into the young adult genre, tags can be left out as long as it is clear who is talking. Adding action instead of a tag can help make that clear as well.

Here is an example from Mitchell's *Secret to Lying*. This is a phone conversation between the main character, fifteen-year-old James, who is away at boarding school, and his parents. This example not only shows that you don't need tags on every line, it also refers back to what Mitchell said about the characters wanting something different from the dialogue. Plus, we get a glimpse of the relationship between James and his mom.

> I scrambled to change the subject. "Look, about this weekend. I've got a lot of work to do. There's a chemistry study group and I need to get the notes."
> "Wouldn't you rather come home?"
> "I can't."
> Mom paused. "What's wrong with you?"
> "Nothing's wrong."
> "You don't sound right to me."
> "What am I supposed to say to that?" I asked. "I mean, really, do I sound 'right' now?"
> "No. You don't." She addressed my dad: "Does he sound right to you?"
> "How about this, Mother? Is this better? It's lovely weather out."
> "Honestly, you don't sound like yourself," she said.
> "Too bad. This is me."

Great dialogue does so much more than relay a conversation. Go to a bookstore or library and study the way authors use dialogue for various age groups. Pay attention to the tags, the type of action, and think about what each scene conveys and how it moves the story along.

A memorable book includes compelling characters and an intriguing storyline. Dialogue is a great vehicle to achieve both. Understanding how to write effective dialogue for your target age group will allow you to create stronger, more interesting stories that will resonate with readers of all ages.

KERRIE FLANAGAN is an author, writing consultant, publisher, and accomplished freelance writer with more than 18 years' experience. Her work has appeared in publications such as *Writer's Digest*, *Alaska Magazine*, *The Writer*, and six *Chicken Soup for the Soul* books. She is the author of seven books, including two children's books, *Claire's Christmas Catastrophe* and *Claire's Unbearable Campout*, all published under her label, Hot Chocolate Press. She was the founder and former director of Northern Colorado Writers and now does individual consulting with writers. Her background in teaching and enjoyment of helping writers has led her to present at writing conferences across the country, including the Writer's Digest Annual Conference, the Willamette Writer's Conference, and the Writer's Digest Novel Writing Conference. You can find her online at www.KerrieFlanagan.com, www.hotchocolatepress.com, and on Twitter at @ Kerrie_Flanagan.

CREATING UNFORGETTABLE CHARACTERS

Create characters that stick with your readers long after the story is over.

....

Debbie Dadey

Some things you never forget. Even though I've spoken at thousands of venues during the twenty-seven years since the release of my first book, *Vampires Don't Wear Polka Dots*, one school and one little boy in Evansville, Indiana, stand out in my mind. The child was sobbing in the hallway. The librarian said he was upset because I was visiting. Not exactly the thing you want to hear when you are preparing to speak to hundreds of kids. But then she followed up with, "He thought he was going to see Eddie, Melody, Howie, and Liza."

I have to admit, that made me feel much better. He wanted to meet the characters in The Adventures of the Bailey School Kids series that I wrote with Marcia Thornton Jones. To him, those characters were *real*. And isn't that what we, as writers, have to do? We have to make our characters leap off the page—we have to make them come alive to our readers. That's easy to say, but so hard to do.

Creating unforgettable characters is a pretty tall order. How is it done? Or, how can you do it better? This is something we could spend a lifetime perfecting, so let's get started learning more about developing characters together.

WHO ARE GREAT CHARACTERS?

Characters answer the question, who is this story about? Robert Newton Peck said that "When the question is 'What am I going to write about?' the answer is 'Who?'"

I believe that stories develop from characters and their reactions to a problem. In his writing reference, *On Writing*, Stephen King says, "I want to put a group of characters (perhaps a pair; perhaps even just one) in some sort of predicament and then watch them try to work themselves free."

Characters drive a story. It is through the characters' eyes, ears, words, behaviors, and emotions that readers move through the story. If we do it well, the reader will, in essence, become that character and feel his desires and pain.

There are basically three kinds of characters: the protagonist, the antagonist, and secondary characters. The *protagonist* is the main character in the story. This is the one you want to root for. This is the one everyone needs to like. The protagonist is often an ordinary person dropped into an unusual predicament. Think of normal Harry Potter, who is suddenly introduced to a world of magic.

Something to consider in creating a great protagonist: They often don't follow the rules! They also have big hearts and dreams. They want or need something universal—something that everyone can understand. They almost always have deep flaws. Why? Because *real* people have flaws. If we want our characters to become real, they can't be perfect.

The easy way to look at the *antagonist* is that he is the bad guy. He is the adversary of our main character. In some way, the antagonist makes life difficult for our main character.

And since we don't live by ourselves in the real world, our imaginary world is made up of *secondary characters*, such as co-workers, teachers, parents, and friends.

All of these characters must have a personality to come alive to our readers. They all need flaws because a good guy is not always perfect and a bad guy may have some redeeming qualities. They are more real this way. And real is what we are going for, isn't it?

It's helpful to limit the number of characters and vary the character's names and personalities. It can get confusing for any reader to read about Kim, Kane, and Kurt. Keep in mind that your characters should solve their own problems, even if you are writing for children. Adults should not ride in on a white horse and save the day. Something that helps me quite a bit are character sketches and charts.

HOW CAN WE MAKE GREAT CHARACTERS?

A simple character chart can be found on the writing page of my website, www.debbiedadey. com. The basics involve jotting down what you know about your characters so you'll have a reference. The point is to learn about your characters. You need to know what they want most, where they live, their innermost thoughts, and their best friends. You need to know how old they are, what scares them, what they hate, and what they love. You need to know their birthdays and what they do with their fingers when they are bored. You need to know if they've ever had a pet and the secrets they keep buried.

Do your characters have a favorite word or unique saying? Dialogue is very important and readers should be able to tell which character is speaking without tags. Be careful to avoid slang, but strive to make each character unique.

Before Marcia Thornton Jones and I wrote the Keyholder series for Tor, we worked for a solid year coming up with character sketches and world building. I did the same thing for six months with my newest series, Mermaid Tales. I'm currently doing character sketches for my next idea. Keep in mind that when you are filling out character charts you will not use every bit of information in your story. Some of it is for you and only you to know.

You must love your characters enough to live with them for years, perhaps even decades. My first series, The Adventures of the Bailey School Kids, spawned fifty-one numbered books, Super and Holiday specials, as well as two spin-off series. I still get fan mail, even though we are no longer adding to the series. As writers, we need to love those little guys because we may live with them for a long time. We'll be taking them with us wherever we go!

In fact, that is exactly what you should do. Take your characters throughout your day with you to see how they would react. Have a little notebook and jot down what they would pick up at the grocery store. What would scare them at the dentist office? What is their favorite tree on your street? Which house would they always avoid rather than walk past? Do they want a Hershey bar every afternoon at three o'clock? Add these to your character sketches.

HOW CAN WE MAKE CHARACTERS BETTER?

Now we know about characters and how to create them, but perhaps you've received a rejection letter that says these dreaded words: *your characters are flat* or *your characters are not developed enough* or *I don't feel like I know your characters.* One important thing to make sure that you haven't overlooked is a dogma in writing: *show don't tell.* What does this mean for characters? It is terribly easy for us to say that *Andy hated his math teacher.* That's telling. Instead, it is often better for us to show it: *Andy threw his math book across the room and screamed, "You can't tell me what to do!"*

Another example of telling is *Sara was tired.* This would be showing: *Sara propped her chin in her hand. She tried to pay attention to her history teacher's lecture on ancient Greece, but her eyes kept closing and more than once she jerked herself awake.* Which one can you visualize more: *Sara is tired* or the scene in history class?

Take a look at your story and find places of telling. See if you can bring that scene and your character to life by showing. Most of the time showing will require having your character in some sort of action. Readers love action in stories (and so do editors!). This will also keep your writing from becoming passive.

Once you've finished your character sketch and written a rough draft, you should begin to go over your story with a fine-tooth comb. It won't be easy, but it will be worth it. This can take some time, but it could be the difference between a so-so character and one that is unforgettable.

While using that fine-tooth comb, consider your character's inner conflict. You need to know what is tearing your main character apart. Aside from the main problem of the story, give them an internal problem that conflicts with the main plot, if possible. An example of internal conflict in the *Hunger Games* is that Katniss is unsure about her feelings for both Peeta and Gale. To keep her family safe she must pretend to have feelings for Peeta, which hurts Gale because he cares for her. At the same time, she isn't sure if her feelings for Peeta are real. As you can see, the reader feels for Katniss because she feels so much.

Look back at your character sketches. Have you included physical, emotional, and social traits? Is your character embarrassed by her frizzy hair or the big freckle at the end of his nose? His meddling mom? Her deadbeat dad? What does he do when he's nervous or scared?

This is also the time to be a little over the top. Have some fun with your characters and let them shine. Pick a scene to make your protagonist larger than life. You may have so much fun that you'll do it again. One way to get started is to think of something that they would never do and have them do it. Then, they have to deal with the aftermath.

While you're making your main character more realistic, don't forget about your bad guy. Give your antagonist a good quality. Even the Penguin in Batman had feelings.

Find a place where you can show feelings. Find four! Show readers what's inside, what makes your characters tick. Put yourself in their shoes—literally (find a picture or some real shoes that match your character's to put on your desk as inspiration). I once went to a Pam Conrad workshop and never forgot her lesson: Try the same exercise by thinking about your character's shoes. Or are they barefoot? Are their bare feet filthy? Bloody and bruised? Or perhaps your character has shiny brand-new patent leather shoes with a black bow on top. Shoes can tell a lot about a person's character. Are they uptight, or are their parents? Now, go up your character's legs. Are their socks dirty and scrunched around their ankles? Or pink with little sea horses dancing on them? Now, keep going to see if their knees are scratched. Is there a Sponge Bob adhesive bandage? Or perhaps your character's knees are covered with perfectly pressed pants? Don't stop now. Is your character wearing their favorite jeans or a frilly dress? Keep going. Are their elbows skinned? Fingernails bitten? Keep getting higher. Pimples? Snotty nose? Keep going higher. Are there tangles in her hair? Did she accidently singe the right side in a candle while reading late at night, like in *The Hired Girl*? If you do this with your main character, you'll know them better. But guess what? You need to do it with each person in your story.

Once when my friend Marcia Thornton Jones and I were struggling while writing a scene for a Bailey School Kids book, we peeked inside a student's desk. We wanted to know what Eddie would do when he was sitting behind Liza and her long blond ponytail. Eddie has a well-deserved reputation for creating mischief. We pulled paper wads and pencil stubs out of the desk, which went into our story. But then, eureka! Inspiration was right there as we pulled out a pair of scissors. Acting out your character's actions may just help bring them to life.

Look at all your characters—make a list of them. Which one can you get rid of? Can you combine two to make one stronger character? Relationships are important. How is your main character related to each of the supporting characters? Make sure all your characters have hobbies or quirks. This is how secondary characters can shine.

Something important must be at stake in a story for us to care. And the more heartbreakingly important it is to our character, the more we care. Look at your story to see what is at stake.

Newbery Honor winner Marion Dane Bauer said that "to find good story ideas, you must understand what makes a story. A story involves someone who has a problem he must struggle to solve or who wants something he must struggle to get. (Character and plot are inseparable. As has often been said, plot is simply character in action.) The important word in that definition is *struggle*. If your character isn't struggling—if he's simply sitting around looking at, thinking about his problem the way most of us do in real life— you don't have a story. So to find a good idea, you first have to find someone whose problem or desire feels compelling to you. Then you have to carry that someone around with you long enough to begin to know how he or she will solve his problem."

Not surprisingly, the first section in Donald Maass's *Writing the Breakout Novel Workbook* is about character development. I highly recommend this workbook—I just finished using it for my most recent revision. It isn't easy, but if you wanted easy, you wouldn't be a writer, right?

We've discussed characters, how to make them, and how to make them better. But sadly, those three things are not enough to create characters that readers can't forget.

One more thing is critical: We must do the work. We can't write a story on ideas and thinking. Those are important steps, of course, but not enough. We must be more than dreamers. We must put our rears in a chair and stay there. We must do the work. Newbery Award winner Neil Gaiman said, "This is how you do it: You sit down at the keyboard and you put one word after another until it is done. It's that easy and that hard."

DEBBIE DADEY has authored and co-authored 166 traditionally-published children's books, with sales of more than 42 million. Her newest series is called Mermaid Tales from Simon and Schuster and her newest chapter book is *Ready, Set, Goal!* This STEM friendly series is about four diverse characters and their adventures in a school under the sea. You can Like Debbie at Facebook.com/debbiedadey and follow her on Twitter.

FINDING YOUR WRITING SUPERPOWER

Want to write a unique story? It's all about finding your voice, and writing *your* story.

....

Laurel Snyder

//

There's a big difference between wanting to become a writer and wanting to become an author. And while it is possible to simultaneously strive to become both a writer *and* an author, I've found that it's difficult to focus on both goals at the same time.

In fact, I discovered, at one critical moment in my own career, that all the useful books and websites and classes designed to help me submit my work and get published actually made it much harder for me to sit down and write. This is because there is a common belief that the "best practices" of publishing (querying, formatting, submitting, etc.) are the same for everyone. And maybe they are.

But the "best practices" of writing? The best practices of writing are individual, personal. Because *you* are the only person who knows what story you have to tell, what voice you're going to use, and how to find it.

Think about it like this—imagine you're going to a party. Really picture it. Go on. Close your eyes. Okay, so you pull up to the house like everyone else. You walk in the door, clutching a bottle of wine, like everyone else. Right? Maybe you're looking around, trying to figure out where to put your coat?

So far, we're all sitting here, our eyes closed, pretty much having the same experience. So far, the "best practices for party-going" might apply to us all.

But now you step into the room, and open your mouth, and in that magical moment, you are *not* like anyone else. Because the minute you begin to speak, you're *you*—a particular person with a specific voice, and something to say. Nobody could mistake you!

Your voice might be drunk, or too loud. Your voice might be planning to make an excuse to leave early, because parties make you nervous and your favorite TV show is coming on in an hour. But the point is that on some level, you *can't* really change who you are. You can't take advice from other people on how to be *you* at the party.

What happens when you try to use a voice that isn't yours, at a party? What happens if you try to mimic someone "cool" in a way that doesn't feel natural to you? How well does that go over?

When we take a class in writing, or read a book on craft, or search helpful blogs for advice on how to get published, we are looking for advice on how to be successful. But also, we're yearning for information about what's worked for people who *aren't* us. We want to believe these things are universal, and so we talk about trends. We talk about "what's against the rules." We hear the same inspirational bits of advice. *Glue your butt to the chair. Show don't tell. Build your platform. Try to be yourself on social media.* There's so much advice.

The problem is that when we listen to those rules, we're searching for the lowest common denominators. The things that work for everyone. And that's fine. It makes us feel less alone, less lost. We all get something out of those conversations, for sure. We like the tips and best practices. We feel a sense of community, a sense of hope.

But lately, surrounded by so many of these conversations, I've been feeling the need to discuss something else—the lonely process of figuring things out by myself. I want to talk about authenticity, and finding my singular voice. Because *that* is the one thing nobody can teach you to do. You have to teach yourself to find your voice, to hunt for your own distinct story. Lowest common denominators won't get you there.

That said, while nobody can tell you what your voice is, or how to use it, I've been wondering if maybe it's possible to think of best practices for *prioritizing* that search. Maybe it's possible to set ourselves up to do that individual thinking. Maybe it's worth an essay like this to shift the focus away from the publishing "best practices" and onto the solitary act of writing.

Which begins with a sort of meditation, a reflection on *who we are*. Because it is my personal belief that *what we write* most authentically extends from *who we are*.

Take me. Who am I? *I'm Laurel, a woman who grew up with a Jewish dad and a Catholic mom, raised in Baltimore. I was the oldest kid, went through a divorce, rode lots of public buses. I had epilepsy. (Still do.) As a kid I believed in fairies and unicorns firmly, but also in progressive politics. As an adult, I waited tables for 15 years, and then had two kids,* and stopped waiting tables. I went to a small public southern college, but then a very fancy-pants graduate program with a huge chip on my shoulder about how deep down I was really a waitress. I used to be a vegetarian, but I'm not anymore. I'm kind of a slob, but my worst personal trait is that I'm a bad interrupter. I love country music and I am honest, to a fault. Though sometimes I lie by accident. (It can be hard to remember facts.)

Now, this is a fairly random list of things about me, but when I add them all together like that, they feel defining. The fact that I chose to put each detail on the list *makes* them defining. I've sculpted something here, my own personal narrative, my history. It could be much longer. It could go on forever. But even in this brief form, it's particular. Nobody else has a list quite like mine, and whether or not I write *about* the details from this list, I am always, in some way, writing *from* that set of experiences.

Am I southern? Am I religious? Am I still a waitress at heart? Sure! When it's useful. But I'm so much more complicated than any of those terms. This list is so much more useful to me than being a "Jewish poet" or a "woman writer" or anything else generalized. "Who you are" defies categorization. If you can categorize it, by definition you got it wrong.

The thing to know is that *you* have a list like that too. You should be aware of that. It's a magical device, a superpower. It's the antidote to the lowest common denominators that may never feel like they fit you. It's how you remember you're a specific person. How you understand when "The Rules" don't apply to you. And I think that maybe you'll find your best, most distinct, bravest work will come from somewhere deep in that list, if you dig down.

Here's an interesting tidbit: Did you know that Maurice Sendak's original manuscript for *Where the Wild Things Are* was called *Where the Wild Horses Are*? You should look it up. It's an odd, oddly-shaped creation, that original book. Sendak said of it:

> "I couldn't really draw horses. And I didn't, for the longest time, know what to use as a substitute. I tried lots of different animals in the title, but they just didn't sound right. Finally I lit on things. But what would 'things' look like? I wanted my wild things to be frightening. But why? It was probably at this point that I remembered how I detested my Brooklyn relatives as a small child. They came almost every Sunday. My mother always cooked for them, and, as I saw it, they were eating up all our food. We had to wear good clothes for these aunts, uncles, and assorted cousins, and ugly plastic covers were put over furniture. About the relatives themselves, I remember how inept they were at making small talk with children. There you'd be, sitting on a kitchen chair, totally helpless, while they cooed over you and pinched your cheeks. Or they'd lean way over with their bad teeth and hairy noses, and say something threatening like, 'You're so cute I could eat you up.' And I knew if my mother didn't hurry up with the cooking, they probably would. So, on one level at least, you could say the wild things are Jewish relatives."
> (from *The Art of Sendak*, Selma G. Lanes)

Now, you may not have Jewish relatives who want to eat you up like Sendak, but Sendak's "things" came from his list, for sure. Nobody else's "best practices" could have suggested them.

And somewhere on your list are the things you can dig down into, to find the brave work. The work that taps into your specific story. That vulnerable place. The story only you can tell. Which is, honestly, the only story worth your time.

So the question is … where's your vulnerable place? What are the bits of your life that make you shiver, laugh, worry, and rage? And how do you remember them, find them? How do you figure out where you should start?

The really great books, the ones we love best, dig down into the personal story. They employ that individual superpower. They bring something new, something personal. This is probably true of your favorite book, even if you don't know it. Even when it isn't obvious.

Now we think of books in the Chronicles of Narnia series as "types" of books, don't we? We think of *The Wonderful Wizard of Oz* the same way. But those books were written out of C. S. Lewis's religious journey, as a Christian convert, and also out of his memories from World War I. Baum, a newspaperman, wrote *Oz* with strong feelings about women's rights. Both of them created what now feels like a "type" of book, out of their own lists.

More recently, Rick Riordan gave us Percy Jackson, drawing on his own personal and familial experiences with learning disabilities. And Suzanne Collins has explained that *The Hunger Games* grew out of her memories of watching footage from the Vietnam War, while her father was overseas, fighting. Because this is how we produce truly innovative, startling, meaningful work—the work that connects most deeply with readers. By mining our lists, our memories, and finding our truest voices.

Which brings us to the big question—what's your story, your superpower, your voice? What's the story only you can tell? And how do you find it? Below, I've tried to generate some ideas for ways you can connect with your superpower. They may not work for everyone (or anyone), but I hope they'll yield something useful. There is no succeeding or failing here. Only a goal—that we shift away from thinking about "what worked" for other people, and into a mode of thinking deeply about ourselves.

1. **YOUR LIST.** Try making a list like mine. Keep it going, indefinitely. Think about who you are, what turf you have that's just yours. The book nobody else but you can write.

2. **JOURNALING.** It's always good to do some daily writing. One fun idea is to write down the stories you retell often. "The one about the camping trip." Or "That time you had chicken pox in Chicago." We all have stories we tell. Write them down! (Related: If you have old journals or blogs, dig them out and spend time with them.

Make photocopies and revise them. Play!)

3. **OLD PHOTOS.** What makes you cry or laugh? Who is missing from your life, and why? What happened? Take some time to free-write about the old photos you find. You might be surprised at the memories that resurface.

4. **FAVORITE BOOKS.** Not just popular trendy books, but the books that really set you on fire or spoke to you as a kid. Revisiting these old texts is a remarkable way to "wake up" childhood memories.

5. **RAW EMOTION.** When you have a big feeling, don't try to fix it. Rather, have the feeling. Let it wash over you. Heighten it if you can. Sit in the darkness, shut out the noise. You don't want to get depressed, but in a safe way, explore the feeling.

6. **DREAM BOOK.** Keep a notebook by your bed for writing down dreams, which can uncork powerful emotions. I often find that writing first thing in the morning feels dreamy and different too.

7. **OTHER SENSES.** Music is powerful for me—especially music from other chapters of my life. But for some people, baking or cooking or gardening can do this too. The trick is to be present with the senses. Be alone with them, and isolate them. (If you're listening to podcasts while you bake, or emailing while you listen to old records, it won't work the same way)

8. **KIDS.** Get some! And then listen to them. Really focus on what they say and how they say it! If you have kids, or access to kids you love, steal from them. Our feelings about children tend to be so big and authentic, and kids can awaken things in us, our own memories of childhood.

9. **DRAW (OR PAINT OR SCULPT).** Get out your art supplies. Sometimes, what you can't seem to access with words you can reach in another way. But again, you need to isolate yourself with the visual or tactile experience. The idea is to uncork something, and that won't happen if you're watching TV at the same time.

10. **IMAGINARY READER.** Sit and think about the person who will read this book. To go back to the party I talked about earlier, think about how, when you walk into the party, you look for someone you know, because it's easier to talk to them. Seriously think about this—about the audience for your book, your ideal reader. Sometimes, simply thinking about this will change your tone completely.

11. **WRITE OUT LOUD.** Keep a tape recorder in the car or your purse or backpack. Sometimes, the way you talk your words out is different, and more natural, than the way you write them down. You can go back later, and transcribe, and sometimes you'll be very surprised.

12. **GET BORED.** I think this is perhaps the single biggest thing any of us can do in this day and age. When we are consuming external voices, it's extremely hard to

channel something authentic from within. So boredom is an important part of the creative process for me. I often "work" in the bath. Or I take a walk with a notebook and pen. The critical thing is to leave my phone at home. Distraction is death to real insight. You have to spend time with yourself, and flounder and dream, to get to something good.

LAUREL SNYDER is the author of six novels for children: *Orphan Island, Bigger than a Bread Box, Penny Dreadful, Any Which Wall, Up and Down the Scratchy Mountains OR The Search for a Suitable Princess*, and *Seven Stories UP*. She has also written many picture books, two books of poems, and edited an anthology of nonfiction. A graduate of the Iowa Writers' Workshop and a former Michener-Engle Fellow, Laurel has published work in the *Utne Reader, Chicago Sun-Times, Revealer, Salon, The Iowa Review, American Letters and Commentary*, and more.

THE DNA OF CHARACTERS

Dialogue, Narrative, and Actions

....

Olivia Markham

Characterization is the creation and convincing representation of fictitious characters (Random House Unabridged Dictionary, 2nd edition). To be convincing, protagonists and villain(s) must be fully developed characters within your story world. Therefore, you must get to know your characters before you start writing, even if the details change as you draft your manuscript. The sketches you develop before you begin writing (character questionnaires, Myers-Briggs assessments, enneagrams, and so on) are like the chromosomes that define basic traits and give a character life.

After that creation comes the "convincing representation of characters" or the creation on the page, since it's the characters' *dialogue*, *narrative*, and *actions*—their *DNA*—that make them truly convincing and unique. And to engage readers emotionally, a character's DNA should generally be balanced within each scene.

DIALOGUE

Including rich details in a character's dialogue can portray a more realistic sense of the fictional world and, thus, more realistic characters. Dialogue isn't just a back-and-forth between characters; it involves what they say and how they say it, their tone and speech cadence, the phrases they use repeatedly, and their physical habits and mannerisms as they talk. These details reveal rich insights about a character: his attitudes, values, worldview, and frame of mind. Dialogue reveals character not only by what is said but *how*. It truly shines when readers can identify the speaker by the words he uses and the way he talks rather than by dialogue tags.

When long narrative passages will slow the pace too much, use dialogue to convey a character's current situation and background—her interests, the work she's doing, and her familial, friendly, and romantic relationships. These elements can flavor her speech.

In Linda Howard's novel *Drop Dead Gorgeous*, protagonist Blair Mallory engages in humorous dialogue to show the current situation and convey something about the characters. In this scene, Blair and her fiancé, Wyatt Bloodsworth, are talking.

> [Wyatt] all but whimpered. "*Please*. Just tell me why you've decided you can't marry me." …
>
> "Because *Blair Bloodsworth* is too cutesy to be bearable!" Oh, God, I was beset by B-words. "People would hear that name and think, okay, she has to be a blond nitwit, one of those people who snaps gum and twirls her finger in her hair. No one would take me seriously!"
>
> He rubbed his forehead as if he were getting a headache. "So all this is because Blair and Bloodsworth both start with a *B*?"
>
> I cast my gaze upward. "The light dawns."
>
> "That's a load of bullshit."
>
> "And the bulb just burned out." Aaargh! When would the avalanche of B-words stop? This always happens to me. When something starts bugging me (aaargh again!) I can't get away from the alliteration.
>
> "Bloodsworth isn't a cutesy name, no matter what the first name is," he said, scowling at me. "It has *blood* in it, for God's sake. As in blood and guts. That isn't cutesy."

Dialogue is also perfect for showing past influences: former relationships, transformative events, socioeconomic and educational backgrounds, and where a character grew up. It can subtly hint at a character's gender, ethnicity, and age, especially with the judicious use of dialect.

Finally, dialogue is an effective tool for creating subtext and foreshadowing. What *isn't* said, what is merely hinted at, what is avoided, and what is lied about—all are elements that generate tension and nuance within scenes.

Dialogue that describes or characterizes the protagonist or other characters can obviously come from POV characters, but it can also come from other characters as they reveal their perceptions in conversation. Opinions expressed by one character about another character can say much about both the speaker and the person being discussed.

This passage from *Pride and Prejudice* by Jane Austen is an example of how characters can reveal information about others and themselves. It also highlights how dialogue can create subtext and foreshadowing by what *isn't* said but merely hinted at. The first speaker is Mrs. Bennett as she talks with her husband.

> "Why, my dear, you must know, Mrs. Long says that Netherfield is taken by a young man of large fortune from the north of England. …"
>
> "Is he married or single?"

"Oh! Single, my dear, to be sure! A single man of large fortune; four or five thousand a year. What a fine thing for our girls!"

"How so? How can it affect them?"

"My dear Mr. Bennett," replied his wife, "how can you be so tiresome! You must know that I am thinking of his marrying one of them."

"Is that his design in settling here?"

"Design! Nonsense, how can you talk so! But it is very likely that he *may* fall in love with one of them, and therefore you must visit him as soon as he comes."

Good dialogue should be condensed as much as possible. Elmore Leonard omitted nouns at the beginning of sentences, as well as pronouns like *who* and *that* within sentences. His dialogue makes his characters' speech more authentic. His characters speak a kind of shorthand, which helps make the author's dialogue swift and snappy.

Here's an example of Leonard's dialogue from his novel *Pronto*.

Raylan said … "I'm going to shoot his nose off he don't answer me. What'd you come here for?"

"Talk to her, say hello."

"About what, Harry Arno?"

"About *her*. I see her around. You know, so I want to get to know her."

NARRATIVE

The most useful form of narrative is *interior dialogue*, in which characters, in their own point of view, express opinions internally about their lives or about action as it's happening. Interior dialogue can provide insight into a character's family relations, work life, habits, and values. It can show what she excels at, and how she reacts to bad news or criticism.

Interior dialogue is put to best use when the story is in the intimate and personal first-person point of view. Here's an example from *Drop Dead Gorgeous*, in which Blair Mallory has just been hit by a car in a parking lot.

Well, for pete's sake, where *was* someone? Were all those people going to stay in the frickin' mall until midnight? How long would I have to lie there before someone saw me and came to help? I'd almost been smashed to a pulp! I needed a little concern here, a little *something*.

I was getting very indignant. Hello … a body lying in the parking lot, and no one notices? Yes, it was night, but the parking lot was lit by those huge vapor lights, and I wasn't lying between two cars or anything. I was … I opened my eyes and tried to get my bearings.

My vision was blurred; all I could see were black shadows and patches of light, and those swam and ran together.

Interior dialogue is also useful for introducing intermediate characters who are neither minor (extras or walk-ons) nor protagonists, such as a sister or best friend whose story affects the protagonist's arc. Examples of intermediates are the hero's sister in Julie

James' *Suddenly One Summer*, and Elizabeth Bennett's best friend, Charlotte, in *Pride and Prejudice*, by Jane Austen. Here's an example from *Suddenly One Summer*. Author Julie James introduces the hero's sister using the hero's interior dialogue, and gives readers another reason to like the guy.

> "Fine. I'm worried about Nicole, too," he admitted, despite being firmly of the belief that his mother didn't need to be thinking about this today.
>
> It wasn't exactly a secret that his twenty-five-year-old sister, Nicole, had been struggling as a single mom ever since giving birth to her daughter, Zoe, four months ago. As a part-time actress and a full-time instructor at a local children's theater, she worked days, evenings, and some weekends, yet still barely made enough to support herself in the city.

Expositional narrative, or summary narrative, on the other hand, should be used somewhat sparingly. In the maxim "Show; don't tell," summary narrative is the telling. Telling is acceptable when it is used to summarize minor events or provide mundane but necessary information. A change of setting can be summarized in this way, and an example of this appears in *Love Irresistibly* by Julie James.

> Promptly at seven a.m. on Sunday morning, Cade, Vaughn, and Huxley rode the elevators that would take them to the entrance of Sogna. A hostess desk, made of dark mahogany wood, stood empty before a set of wide etched glass doors—doors that were open.

Summary narrative can be used to quickly describe or tell readers something without using dialogue or actions. This is illustrated in the chapter-two opening of Linda Howard's novel *Up Close and Dangerous*.

> Cameron Justice gave the small airfield and parking lot a swift, encompassing glance as he pulled his blue Suburban into his allotted slot. Though it wasn't yet six-thirty in the morning, he wasn't the first to arrive. The silver Corvette meant his friend and partner, Bret Larsen—the L. of J&L. Executive Air Limo—was already there, and the red Ford Focus signaled the presence of their secretary, Karen Kaminsky.

Summary narrative can also appear as backstory, which helps readers understand the characters' choices, and as character descriptions, which develop mood, theme, and foreshadowing. Here is an example of minor character description from *Pride and Prejudice*, in which author Jane Austen gives her perspective of how her heroine, Elizabeth Bennett, would assess Mr. Bingley's sisters.

> Elizabeth listened in silence, but was not convinced; [the Bingley's sisters'] behavior at the assembly had not been calculated to please in general; and with more quickness of observation and less pliancy of temper than her sister, and with a judgement too unassailed by any attention to herself, she was very little disposed to approve them. They were in fact very fine ladies; not deficient in good humour when they were pleased, nor in the power of making themselves agreeable when they chose it, but proud and conceited.

THE DNA CHECKLIST

- I've used a balance of dialogue, narrative, and actions to bring the character to life on the page.
- I've revealed character through the choices they make when they're under pressure— their actions and reactions.
- I've written rounded, whole main characters rather than characters that fulfill a convenient function or stereotype within the story.
- My protagonist's characterizations reflect the particular internal issue he is struggling with in the novel. The plot is built around the way the protagonist works through that issue and resolves it.
- In general, I've used straight exposition less than dialogue or actions, since it invariably slows or kills the pace.
- I've used dialogue, rather than long passages of summary exposition or description, to convey details, history, and background. Strong details in dialogue give a more realistic sense of the fictional world, and the characters in it.
- I've omitted from my characters' dialogue any repetitious information (things the characters should already know) and anything unrealistic or unnecessary. Dialogue should not be written as though directed to the readers; it should read as if it is being spoken between the characters within a scene.

However, exposition that appears in scene sequels explains the character's conflicts *after you've dramatized them* and offers a different perspective—on the conflict, on the character's reactions to it, and on the characters involved. When you want to focus on something important, something that is key to the story or the character, you can use narrative-only scenes—or dialogue- or action-only scenes—to direct the readers' attention to specific characteristics, events, or actions.

An excellent example of this kind of scene sequel can be found in James Patterson's novel *1st to Die*. Chapter eleven contains mostly narrative, covering Lindsay Boxer's reactions to some very bad news about her health. This approach allows the reader to stay at a distance as the character comes to terms with the news. Lindsay takes her dog for a walk, thinks about her doctor, showers and assesses herself in the mirror, puts on a CD, cooks dinner, and drinks some wine. She thinks about her divorce, her mother's death, and her father—the few times she's seen him—and then on the terrace, with a view of the bay, she sits down to eat with the dog at her feet. For the second time that day, she realizes she's crying.

In general, straight exposition, or summary exposition, should be used less than dialogue or actions, since it invariably slows or kills the pace. Though sections that contain *only* interior dialogue can be used more in the young adult and romance genres, keep in mind that it can bring the action to a grinding halt.

ACTIONS

The maxim "Show; don't tell," applies chiefly to a character's actions. As the author, you decide which experiences the character will have and how he will grow, but that character is defined by what he chooses to do in the face of the problems you throw at him and based on the background and physical, mental, spiritual, and emotional makeup you've given him. The only way readers can ever fully know a character is through the choices he makes while under pressure. The greater the pressure, the deeper the revelation.

Actions reveal character through what they do, how they do it, and with whom; through how they treat themselves and others; and through physical reactions to obstacles, complications, and reversals—when progress is made but the situation then regresses to a previous status. In real life, how a person reacts to something can reveal quite a lot about who she is and her circumstances. Just as you and I are defined by our reactions to events in our lives, so it is with our characters.

Knowing your characters means you can gauge how they would react when faced with obstacles or frustrations. For instance, does your character react to events with humor, anger, or silence? Actions or reactions reflect decisions, attitudes, goals, background, and experiences—all of which are mirrored in how characters deal with obstacles, other people, and situations. Those actions reflect opinions and interpretations of people and events, as well as their unique worldview. Who they are drives the choices they make when faced with those obstacles. For example, in the novel *The Book Thief*, protagonist Liesel can't read or write. Her fellow students surround her and chant the word *dummkopf* ("stupid head") to mock her. She responds by thoroughly beating up the main instigator, which reveals quite a bit about her character.

In Julie James' *Love Irresistibly*, the protagonist, General Counsel Brooke Parker, decides how she will respond to a request from Assistant U.S. Attorney Cade Morgan.

> He'd come here, to *her* office, to ask for *her* help. Now he was threatening her with obstruction of justice charges—and most annoyingly, he was doing it with a smile.
>
> So she returned the favor. "That is nice, Mr. Morgan. Because in response to your tough-guy speech, I, in turn, would've had to give you my tough-*girl* speech, about where, exactly, federal prosecutors who come to my office looking for assistance can stick their obstruction of justice threats." She smiled ever so charmingly. "So I'm glad we were able to sidestep that whole ugly business. Whew."

Although her attention was focused on Cade, out of the corner of her eye, Brooke could see Agents Huxley and Roberts looking at the wall and ceiling, seemingly trying to hide their smiles.

Whether through dialogue, narrative, or actions, the details you include about your character must serve a purpose. If a character's traits don't imply or reveal an internal issue that drives your plot, she'll be lifeless and uninteresting—merely a list of details. Most character traits are better revealed in scenes that drive the plot forward and appeal to the senses. When you happen upon the right balance of dialogue, narrative, and action, your characters will leap to life, and readers won't be able to resist following them on their journey.

....

This is **Olivia Markham**'s second article on craft for the Writer's Market series. The first one, "Voice Lessons," appeared in the 2016 edition of *Novel & Short Story Writer's Market*. Olivia welcomes writing projects—articles, books, etc.—and also offers ghostwriting and collaborative writing services for books. She is also a freelance editor. Her website is OliviaMarkham-Editing.com.

....

UNLEASH YOUR STORYTELLING SUPERPOWER

....

Gabriela Pereira

Some say that at the heart of every story is a compelling character. I agree, but with one crucial caveat: Characters aren't just a necessary ingredient for your story—they *are* your story. Without them you have nothing more than a sequence of plot points. Characters humanize your story and give readers someone to root for. It's one thing to watch a newsreel or read a news report of a dramatic event, but when you experience that story through a character, it suddenly becomes more personal and powerful.

Compare, for example, Stephen Crane's newspaper account "The Sinking of the *Commodore*" (*The New York Press*, 1897) with his short story "The Open Boat," published in *Scribner's* magazine the following year. The former gives a sequence of events summing up what happened and when, who died, and how. The short story puts us in the boat, standing shoulder to shoulder with the desperate men as they bail the rising water and eventually abandon ship. Both accounts are from the same author, who was aboard the ship as it went down, but the short story is far more engaging. In it we see the events unfold as those sailors would have experienced them. When we craft stories around a character, we're not just telling it to our readers. We're showing them what it feels like to be there.

CHARACTER TYPES AND DESIRES

Every writer is drawn to a character archetype that she is particularly adept at bringing to life on the page. When it comes to the protagonist (or main character of your story), there are four such types. But before we dive into the particulars of each one, it's important to understand where these archetypes come from.

The protagonist is the focal point for your story. Who this character is and what she wants will drive the plot from beginning to end. The archetypes for this main character come from the intersection between her personality type and what she wants.

What Is Your Protagonist's Type?

Every character in literature falls into one of two types. No matter how nuanced or multifaceted your protagonist may be, at her most basic she is either an *everyman* or a *larger-than-life hero.*

The everyman protagonist—or what I like to call the ordinary Joe (or Jane)—is a regular guy going about his regular life, until something happens that turns his world upside down. The ordinary Joe is an unlikely hero caught in extraordinary circumstances. Though he is out of his league, he eventually rises beyond his ordinariness and does something astonishing. While at first glance the everyman might not be anything special, with the right motivation he can become a hero.

At the other end of the scale we have the larger-than-life hero. This character is so powerful and amazing, she seems almost perfect. We already know all the incredible things this character can do, so instead the key with bringing this character to life is to show a hint of vulnerability, a chink in the armor. After all, even Superman has his kryptonite.

Keep in mind these two personality types are not separate categories so much as they are opposite ends of the same spectrum. Most characters fall somewhere in the middle of two extremes, and as the story progresses they shift toward the opposite pole. I call this concept the "Opposite is Possible" theory. As writers it is our job to show that our main characters can become the opposite of how they appear at the beginning of the story. This is not about making your protagonist behave in ways that seem outlandish or *out of character.* Rather, the goal is to show the potential for change and plant the right hints, so when your everyman or larger-than-life hero does begin to shift, it doesn't force the reader out of the story. Remember that in every story, your protagonist must change in some way. Regardless of whether this change is extreme or subtle, you need to craft that main character with that possibility for change already baked into the narrative.

What Does Your Character Want?

"Make your character want something!" If you have taken a writing class or read any books about the craft, you have likely heard this advice. But it's not enough to make your protagonist want just anything. It has to be something so important to your character that the pursuit of that desire will keep your story moving. Making your character want a glass of water is not that compelling if he can simply get up and walk to the kitchen. But if your character is stranded on a raft in the middle of the ocean, then a glass of water takes on a whole new level of significance.

Just as there are two types of protagonists, there are also only two fundamental things your character can want. On one hand, your character might want to change something, whether in himself or the world around him. Or his most fervent desire might be the preservation of the status quo. Of course, no story is ever quite that simple, and often your character will want many different, sometimes contradictory things. When you consider all these desires, however, you will usually find that your character leans toward one type over the other. As with the character types, what your character wants exists on a spectrum rather than as two binary extremes.

At this point we have established that the protagonist's personality and desire fall on two distinct spectrums, but what does any of this have to do with us as writers? That's where the concept of the storytelling superpower comes in.

UNDERSTANDING YOUR STORYTELLING SUPERPOWER

When you intersect the protagonist's personality type with what she wants, you get one of four archetypes: the underdog, the disruptor, the survivor, and the protector. The storytelling superpower matrix shows how we get each of these archetypes from looking at character type and desire. The underdog is an everyman character who wants to change something in himself or the world around him. The disruptor also wants to effect change, but in this case the character is in the larger-than-life category. The survivor and protector, on the other hand, both want to preserve something in their lives or their world, with the survivor as the everyman type and the protector as a larger-than-life hero.

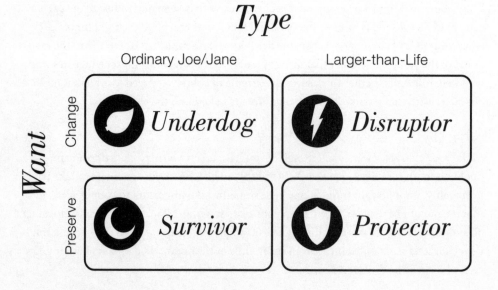

As writers, we each tend to gravitate toward one of these archetypes over the other three. Look at stories you've written or ones you love to read. Chances are, one of these archetypes keeps coming up again and again. Think also about how you view yourself, and it's likely that the archetype you most like to write (or read about) is the one you identify with the most. This is not to say that you never identify with the other types, but it's likely that one of these resonates with you more than the others. I call this preferred archetype your *storytelling superpower.*

Identifying your storytelling superpower isn't meant to set limitations or compartmentalize your creativity. Rather, when you understand your natural tendencies and preferences, it allows you to play to your strengths and stretch yourself beyond your comfort zone. After all, if one archetype tugs at your heartstrings more than the others, you'll likely pour more passion and creative energy into crafting that character, which in turn will make your writing shine.

The Three Layers of Character Development

As you'll soon discover, each archetype has positive qualities as well as weaknesses. Understanding these pros and cons will help you ratchet up the stakes and increase the conflict in your story. You will also learn to identify aspects of your character that can be off-putting to your readers, making them want to stop reading altogether. Training yourself to identify these red flags will help you craft characters and stories your readers can't help but love.

To understand each storytelling superpower archetype, you need to consider three layers of that character: her internal state, her external situation, and how readers will relate to her. In business, a *SWOT analysis* assesses an idea based on its strengths, weaknesses, opportunities, and threats. We'll do a similar analysis here, adding an extra layer to consider the reader relationship. (See the opposite page.)

Strengths and weaknesses are positive or negative traits within your character. Who is your character at his core, and what does he believe in? Every protagonist carries some internal baggage, and these qualities will affect how he reacts to various events. These internal qualities are also somewhat fixed and consistent across different situations, which means that when your character finally *does* experience a transformation at this internal layer, it will feel significant to the reader.

The external layer—opportunities and threats—are situations that happen around or to your character. What scenarios bring out the best in your character? Which situations cause her to misbehave? And, even more interesting, what environments can you create to generate more conflict and tension for your protagonist? Conflict is what makes your story interesting, and while in some rare circumstances the character's internal state might be enough to create that tension, often the juiciest conflict arises from

Character Analysis

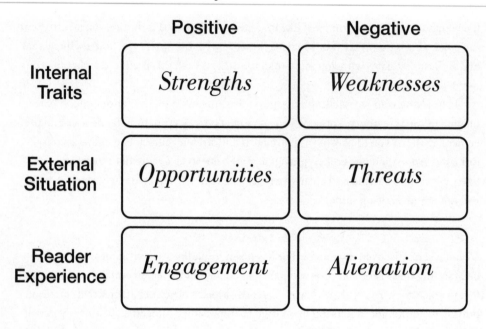

a mismatch between your protagonist's internal qualities and the environment where she finds herself.

Finally, you must also consider the relationship your character has with your reader. Which of your character's internal qualities will your readers find engaging, and which will alienate them? Does the character make choices or react to external situations in ways that resonate with readers, or are his behaviors repellent? There are also certain signature stories (e.g., rags to riches, fish out of water, etc.) that tend to work better with some archetypes than the others. Knowing what these signature stories are will help you determine if you are crafting the best narrative for your character.

MEET THE ARCHETYPES

The Underdog

The quintessential underdog is a relatable character with a deep desire to change something in herself or in the world around her. From Katniss Everdeen in Suzanne Collins's *The Hunger Games* to Marty McFly in the Back to the Future film series, underdogs are regular people caught in extraordinary circumstances but who manage to rise to the occasion and do something heroic. Underdogs have a lot of pluck and determination, and they're not afraid to do whatever it takes to reach their goals. However, these characters may sometimes feel like they have something to prove, so they pick battles they cannot win. And while their "bring it on" attitude might be inspiring and may get them through challenging circumstances, underdogs don't cope well with situations that demand retreat.

In terms of reader engagement, this archetype is one of the most compelling because people love rooting for underdogs. When readers see an underdog come out on top, it makes them think, *If he can do it, maybe I can, too.* But if taken too far, the underdog can seem self-righteous, like they have a chip on their shoulder. And when underdogs stubbornly make bad choices or pick the wrong battles again and again, readers may stop feeling sympathy for the character.

Signature underdog stories include rags-to-riches narratives, epic David-and-Goliath-style battles, and classic comebacks in which a character who used to be on top needs to earn back his former glory. Because the underdog is so relatable and these stories often have such high stakes, underdogs are compelling characters that readers find irresistible.

This is one of the most prevalent archetypes in short fiction, in part because the scope of the short story favors everyman characters over their larger-than-life counterparts. Also, it's easier to convey a character's transformation within a condensed word count if the protagonist is already seeking out change in the first place, as is the case with underdogs. To see the underdog in action, look at Mrs. Mallard in Kate Chopin's "The Story of an Hour," the nameless narrator in "The Yellow Wallpaper" by Charlotte Perkins Gilman, or Pinky in Claire Davis's story "Labors of the Heart."

The Disruptor

Disruptors are larger-than-life characters who rebel against the status quo. They will do whatever it takes to change their societies, overcome all odds, and defeat tyranny. From Elizabeth Bennet in *Pride and Prejudice* by Jane Austen, to the title character in F. Scott Fitzgerald's *The Great Gatsby*, to Tris Prior in Veronica Roth's Divergent series, disruptors take on many different forms. They are charismatic leaders who know how to persuade and inspire the people around them, though they sometimes focus so much on their mission that they wind up hurting the people around them. And, like underdogs, disruptors may concentrate so much on instigating change that despite their larger-than-life qualities they might pick fights they cannot win.

This archetype is especially powerful if you want to infuse your writing with a broader message. Because disruptors possess a strong vision, they can serve as a vessel to communicate your own opinions or ideals from behind the scenes. The danger is that if you make the allegory or satire too heavy-handed, you may end up sounding preachy and alienating your readers. Also, with all that passion and charisma comes narcissism and a lack of empathy. Disruptors don't always play well with others, and there is a fine line between being a rebel and a bully. To make your disruptor a sympathetic or even likable character, you need to make her motivations clear to your readers and have her show at least some vulnerability.

This may be the reason why disruptors are far less common in short stories than in book-length literature. It takes time to tease out a character's motivations and show her weaknesses. Short fiction may not give you the necessary space to give your disruptor the depth she needs to engage your readers. This is where supporting characters can be useful in making a disruptor protagonist seem less bad by comparison. For instance, in Flannery O'Connor's "A Good Man Is Hard to Find," the grandmother is clearly unlikable—at the beginning of the story, it is hard for readers to sympathize with her. But when The Misfit holds the family captive and begins killing people, suddenly the grandmother doesn't seem quite as terrible, and we almost feel sorry for her. Similarly, Neddy Merrill in "The Swimmer" by John Cheever is a vapid, entitled snob, but as we see his life slowly deteriorate, we can't help but feel compassion for him.

The Survivor

Until now, we have looked at characters who want to change something either in themselves or in the world around them. Now we shift gears to archetypes driven by a desire for preservation. True to his name, a survivor character will do whatever it takes to preserve his life as he knows it. This may be a literal battle for survival or simply a desire not to shake up the status quo, but to the character it feels like a life-and-death struggle. Whether he is stranded on a desert island, kidnapped by an evil genius, or fighting to beat a terminal illness, readers will admire a survivor for his pluck, determination, and sheer creative willpower.

Like underdogs, survivors are of the everyman type, so readers see a part of themselves reflected in these characters and feel inspired when they persist against all odds. There is also something inherently hopeful in this archetype. Despite the doom and gloom that often follows these characters, they hold fast and persist even if all seems lost. Taken to the extreme, survivors can become self-reliant to a fault, often isolating themselves and failing to ask for help even when they desperately need it.

As writers, we also need to be careful not to let the character's struggle derail the story and make the issue or problem the story's only raison d'être. It's one thing to craft your narrative around a character who overcomes a trauma, but there has to be more to the story than the trauma alone. A beautiful example is the short story "Everyday Use," in which author Alice Walker explores issues of race, culture, and what it means to honor your heritage. While these themes are very present throughout, this is not a "racial heritage story" but is instead a story in which the theme comes to light in how differently the two main characters interpret and understand their racial heritage, and the conflict that subsequently arises between them.

The Protector

Protectors are larger-than-life heroes. Whether or not they wear capes, boots, and spandex, when the world is in danger, they are compelled to protect it and those they love. As with survivors, protectors are driven by a desire to preserve rather than to shake things up. Whether it's Iron Man, James Bond, or the nerdy and militant Dwight Schrute from the television series *The Office*, protectors show almost superhuman fortitude in their quest to defend what they believe in, prevent disasters, and stand up to the forces of evil.

Protectors are the most popular and prevalent character archetype, in part because heroic characters are powerful and inspiring. With all this power, however, often comes arrogance, and protectors can become obsessed with status and might even misuse their power. Also, these characters do not like to follow rules or be subordinate to someone else, and they detest change, especially if it undermines their authority. As with all larger-than-life characters, the way to make protectors engaging and relatable to readers is to show a hint of vulnerability and imperfection.

Protectors often are more likable than their disruptor counterparts. After all, it's easier for readers to root for a hero who is trying to *save* the world than for one who wants to *take over* the world or *change* it in his favor. However, the horror genre often features a counter-example in which the larger-than-life protector character is extremely unlikable. This can be seen in early classics from Nathaniel Hawthorne and Edgar Allan Poe. Unsympathetic protectors in these works are compelling because readers want to see them suffer. In Hawthorne's "Young Goodman Brown" and "The Birthmark," and in many of Poe's short stories, the appeal of the story isn't that the character succeeds but that he fails. And the best way to make a reader root against a character is to make that character unlikable.

YOUR CHARACTER'S TRANSFORMATION

It's important to remember that these four archetypes are not fixed categories. Remember that change is inherent in any work of fiction; if your character doesn't change in some way, then it's a static dossier, not a story. Keep in mind that this change does not have to be extreme. You do not need to push your character from one pole to its opposite. Instead, it can be a subtle shift.

Remember, too, that the character's desire needs to drive this transformation. In Flannery O'Connor's "A Good Man Is Hard to Find," we see the grandmother change from a narcissistic and manipulative matriarch into a desperate woman begging for her life. The story is so heart wrenching because she starts out trying to control and dominate everyone in her family but ends up losing all control—including over her own life. As you craft your characters, consider not only what they want and how they will transform throughout the story, but also how that desire will affect and support that change.

Your story's resolution hinges on how you resolve your protagonist's quest for what they desire. Does your character get what she wants? If so, does she still want it? The ending will depend on how you answer these two questions, but keep in mind that your character's personality, what she wants, and how she transforms in pursuit of it, are all inextricably linked. The key is to weave these threads together without tying up your story in a neat bow. Often what distinguishes a great story from a mediocre one is the artistry of the ending, which both resolves the character's quest for the thing she wants and also transforms her. When the ending feels unexpected *and* inevitable—surprising but also deeply satisfying to the reader—you know a story is truly exceptional.

Gabriela Pereira is a writer, speaker, and self-proclaimed word nerd who wants to challenge the status quo of higher education. She is the instigator of DIYMFA.com, host of the podcast DIY MFA Radio, and has an MFA in creative writing from The New School. Her book *DIY MFA: Write with Focus, Read with Purpose, Build Your Community* is out now from Writer's Digest Books. To find out your storytelling superpower and learn how to unleash its full potential, take the quiz at DIYMFA.com/STSP.

ANATOMY OF A GREAT SHORT STORY

by Jack Smith

Many writers, at least literary fiction writers, begin their writing career with the short story, sending off work to magazines and journals, trying to get published. The competition, they discover, is "maddening," to borrow from Willy Loman's comment about the business world in *Death of a Salesman*. This is the first thing a writer discovers when s/he submits stories. Magazines often taken no more than two percent of what they receive—and they receive a lot, as market blurbs reveal.

How do you compete in that world?

If you submit and submit and submit, you will eventually—if you get the craft down. Ask published writers—it's the way it is.

But outside of the matter of publication—which can become a goal in itself, robbing a writer of the joy of writing—what about the story itself? Let's start there. What makes a good short story? What makes a great one? If you're a writer, you need to put that first. As they say, the rest will follow.

What is a short story, exactly? Short stories run different lengths, some short, some long, some bordering on the novella. James Joyce's "The Dead" has been called both short story and novella. The same for William Faulkner's "The Bear."

The short story is all about compression. It's got to be a whole story, not half-baked. It's got to round things out, have a plot, have a character arc. But it affords a small space in which to pull all this off, and that's what makes it so tough—to make a work that has fullness but sparseness too.

But let's begin with the process, not the product.

THE PROCESS

Experientially, what is the act of composition like? How is it different from writing a longer work, or is it?

Peter Selgin, author of *Drowning Lessons*, winner of the Flannery O'Connor Award for Fiction, illuminates the essential nature of the short story by contrasting it with the novel. "I've heard the difference described as that between a sprint and a marathon, or a one-night-stand versus a marriage (though I prefer to think of a story not as a one-night-stand, but as something more romantic, a brief affair)." But if we move beyond the most obvious difference—time span—what else separates these two? Perhaps a difference in intensity? No, says Selgin: "Surely a novel can be just as intense, just as urgent, though obviously the urgency has to be spread over more pages, and—usually—a wider scope of time." For him, one radical difference between the two forms is the drafting process for each, and this is a matter of intensity: "I think a big part of the difference comes down to how stories are actually written, not to the intensity of subject matter, character motivation, or plot, but the intensity brought to the composition process itself, the swift concentrated attack as opposed to a process of slow deliberation." Second, the time frame it takes to complete the work also makes the process for these two quite different: "With a novel, you may hack away at the thing for months and even years," says Selgin, "whereas a story is more like a karate chop: swift and ruthless, with the effort all concentrated into what Poe called the story's 'singular effect.'" Third, the mental activity that goes into creating a novel is much different from that of a short story: "Where writing a novel might involve as much rumination as composition, with a story it's probably better to not ruminate at all, to grab hold of the thing—that initial impulse or idea or whatever—and run it down, chase it into its lair." Or, shifting metaphors, Selgin states, "You hold your nose, take the plunge. Fitzgerald said, 'All good writing is swimming underwater and holding your breath.' His words apply especially to the short story, I think."

HALLMARKS OF THE GREAT STORY

In terms of artistic method, then, the short story may require an activity all its own. But what about its properties? What makes the successful short story? And how about the great one? Are there any reliable standards you can go by? Any criteria you can follow?

According to Robert Garner McBrearty, winner of the Sherwood Anderson Foundation Fiction Award and author of three story collections, it would be reductive to try to set forth criteria for such a complex work as the short story. "Because short stories come in so many different types, from flash fictions to longer, fully-developed stories, from the realistic to the surreal, there really isn't a one-size-fits-all description of a successful short story." Viewing flash fiction as a subgenre, he states, "For instance, the expectations about character development would be different in a flash fiction than they would be in a long story. In general, though, one would expect to find certain elements in most successful short stories." Bottom line? It comes down to the craft, says McBrearty, including "vivid characters and setting, lively dialogue, a strong writing style, the sense of something important at stake, and an interesting conflict building to a climax and resolution, even if there is not full resolution of the conflict." Still, you can have all the right stuff, you can handle the fictional elements masterfully, and yet the story can "still come off flat," says McBrearty. It seems a "great mystery," but he believes it has to do with three aspects that separate the successful story from the really great one: tone, voice, and vision. The great story, McBrearty believes, is not only superb in craft but equally strong in its overall vision: representing "the unique way the writer looks at the world."

Like McBrearty, other short story writers tend to judge a story's quality on a basis that includes but also exceeds technical performance. Donna Baier Stein, author of *Sympathetic People*, prefers stories that "reveal the complexities of our inner worlds, that show us how multi-faceted our minds and hearts really are." Besides a skill with language and a way of pulling one into the world of the story, for her the great short story writer "has psychological insight, a keenly observant eye." She finds these qualities in two of her favorite short story writers, Flannery O'Connor and Richard Bausch.

For Kerry Neville, author of two collections of short stories, a story's greatness depends on its memorability, which has much to do with the nature of the language. The great story, she says, "approaches the lyrical compression of poetry: it is vigilant in terms of the cadences of sentences, the collisions of words pressed against each other." With this in mind, she values James Joyce's "The Dead." She especially loves the closing line for its fine lyricism: "'His soul swooned slowly as he heard the snow falling faintly through the universe and faintly falling, like the descent of their last end, upon all the living and the dead.'" The stories that stay with Neville are the ones that raise her consciousness much like a lyric poem does: "a quick, intense illumination of an overlooked or forgotten spot of time in the world that might, in fact, change the way I understand myself in the world or the world's presence inside myself."

Melissa Pritchard is the Flannery O'Connor, O. Henry and Pushcart Prize winning author of four story collections and five novels. One seldom writes the enduring short story, she states. Though she's read a lot of "marvelous" stories, she's encountered only a few that are "deeply memorable, worth returning to, sharing and teaching." Even among favorite writers, says Pritchard, we find certain stories we admire far more than others. She found this to be true of William Trevor's short fiction. "Once, after I had made my way, reverently, through one of his volumes of collected stories, I discovered that though every one of his seventy stories was beautifully polished and brilliantly written, only a handful were what I considered masterpieces, enduring works of art." This discovery surprised her, but at the same time she found it "oddly comforting." It gave her insight into her own work: "What it said was that one must write prolifically, knowing not every story will be perfect, but that perhaps after the seventh or eighth or ninth story, the tenth might turn out to be the one with lasting magic."

But what does "lasting magic" look like? For Pritchard, "There is something rare and haunting about a masterful story. I believe it comes from the writer succeeding at what I call 'lofting' the story out of its immediate setting and dilemma of character or characters into a larger ethical question about human experience—a question that 'floats' above the story, ultimately unanswerable, but emotionally recognized by readers."

So, again, the really great story, the kind anthologized as "literature," is about more than craft. The craft must be there, of course, and much of what makes it great is attributable to its expert handling of craft. But the great short story has an even larger reach than that. Because of its distinctive vision and flash of insight, it has a staying power that haunts us long after we've finished reading it.

ACHIEVING COMPRESSION

As a literary form, the short story is known for its compression. It can usually be read in one sitting. In terms of space, it's confined, not expanded; it's a small world, not a vast, global one. And yet, restrained as it is, the short story, paradoxically, has enormous potential to achieve both depth and range. But how do you manage to pack so much into such a small space?

For McBrearty, there are many different ways of writing stories, but he usually tries to get the characters and the action moving quickly, and to watch out for bloated backstory: "Where we start the story is particularly important. Early drafts tend to contain too much background. Ask yourself: where does the story really start? Where does it start getting interesting? Start the story there! Or just before." Second, he says, watch out for excessive description. "A whole lot of physical details about a character may not be needed. There may be one or two striking details that will be more vivid if we leave out some of the other details." With setting, McBrearty's description tends to be spare and impressionistic. "I just want to give a sense, but a strong sense, of the environment where the story is taking place." He achieves further economy by bringing in setting details as characters engage in action instead of creating setting and then placing them in it. "Compressing the story," he says, "doesn't mean making it tight and restricted, but making it even livelier as we highlight the essential elements."

If you're a short story writer, says Baier Stein, you have to make every word count. This means being "very careful in what you choose to include." For this reason, she advises her creative writing students to limit their story to one protagonist and one point of view. You must find further ways to focus, she says: "Don't try to cover one character's entire life. Focus on a few hours, a day, a week." Time-frame wise, she recommends starting a story "close to its ending." There are, of course, exceptions, as she notes. For example, Alice Munro: "She may start a story with a scene that happens completely separate from the main plot's timeframe." There's much to learn from great writers, but Baier Stein does recommend that at least "in the early stories you write, you keep the parameters simple with a limited time frame."

Neville offers us an intriguing analogy: "A short story is like an arrow shot straight through the heart: direct and intentional. So, every sentence must serve this intent. No extraneous matter. Character details should not only allow us to 'see' a character in the moment, but to feel the weight of time that has come before and will come after for the character." Short stories tend to focus on the ordinary events of life, not the big ones, she says. Great short stories deal with the "ordinary moments made extraordinary through a writer's intentional caretaking."

"I think a short story must not take on too much in the way of plot,' says Selgin, "that ideally as little as possible should happen." For him, the old adage "less is more" is true. "John Gardner called it the 'rule of elegance and efficiency.'" Keeping this in mind, Selgin offers this advice: "If you can tell a story with two characters, don't have three; if you can tell it in one scene, don't write two scenes, and so on." An excellent story to read for compression, he believes, is John Cheever's "The Swimmer." "When Cheever sends Ned Merrill off on his symbolic journey across a river of swimming pools, he does so not across a distance of months, years, or decades, but on one summer day that, by a twist of suburban magical realism, turns into a lifetime." This isn't a prescription for all stories, though, because "other stories demand greater complexity," states Selgin. Still, in general, he says, "Do with as little complexity as possible. Trust simplicity."

According to Pritchard, compression is about tension and pressure. In a traditional story, she says, "you will be putting your main character under so much pressure, internally and externally, that she is forced to act, choose, to think and risk in radical ways." This applies to both the internal sphere, the character's mind, and the external, the world the character enters into, and such pressure leads to suspense, which is a must, Pritchard states, regardless of the kind of fiction you're writing. "Suspense is not confined to genre fiction—it is imperative in literary fiction as well. What is she going to do, what will she choose or refuse, how will she be transformed or changed by the wringing-out process you, the author, the creator of this story, have designed for her?"

If a short story is all about compression, there is no single way to achieve this—and certainly no single way to create the great story, the memorable one, the one with that lasting magic. For Selgin, "Every truly distinguished short story is a laboratory experiment, an engineered mutation that invents its own rules, that finds its own form."

WRAPPING UP

Every story you write can't be a great one. Even the greats may write only a half dozen or dozen really great ones in their life. But writing the truly great one can be your goal. Meanwhile, learn the craft. Learn how to handle the very demanding compression of the short story form. Read a lot of short stories, and find out what is good, and what is truly great. Which stories do you remember the most? Which ones linger on, stay with you, hold you fast? Study those. What is it about them? Where's the magic?

Jack Smith has published four novels: *Miss Manners for War Criminals*, *Being*, *Icon*, and *Hog to Hog*. Besides his writing, Smith was fiction editor of *The Green Hills Literary Lantern*, published by Truman State University, for 25 years.

CREATING AN ANTAGONISTIC SETTING

....

by DiAnn Mills

An antagonistic setting is as much a gift to the reader as an unpredictable plot. The explosion of an unforeseen or modified environment forces the protagonist to dig deep for ways to survive. When setting becomes a predator, a character's true inner landscape is revealed, one he cannot deny.

I welcome the task of increasing the stakes to provide an obscure setting. The work is worth every drop of perspiration—and your readers will love you for the professional touch.

Writers search for ways to raise the stakes for the protagonist. We mine weaknesses to make him squirm and pressure him to grow into a true hero—or heroine. Sometimes he fails and sometimes he succeeds. In each instance, the protagonist is caught off guard, and every breath is met with potential disaster.

We writers often turn to obvious means of adding stress, tension, and conflict through characterization, dialogue, plot twists, symbolism, and emotive conflict. These are powerful tools, and our stories must contain stellar treatment of each literary technique to ensure our protagonists are continuously challenged.

Why not add more to defy the protagonist's resolve?

Establishing an antagonistic setting as an additional means of growth and change requires skill. But once mastered, the method offers a new dimension to the story by creating additional stumbling points that add barriers to the character's goal.

Making life easy doesn't keep the reader engaged. I prefer keeping my readers up all night trying to figure out what will happen next.

An antagonistic setting means shaky ground for the protagonist. The problem creeps up to catch the character unaware, stalking him with devious tactics. Survival extends beyond defeating a villain, either mental, physical, or spiritual.

Mental Antagonistic Setting:

- A dream world
- An unconscious state
- A hallucination
- Altered thinking as in mental illness or depression
- A phobia

Phobias provide an ideal backdrop for a hostile setting. The person suffering from one of these fears can experience physical symptoms that can be life-threatening. Dizziness, dread, nausea, chest pains, panic attacks, and a host of other reactions can stop the character and debilitate him from moving forward.

Take a look at a few of these phobias as a possible way to heighten a weakness associated with setting:

- Acrophobia - fear of heights
- Astraphobia - fear of storms
- Claustrophobia - fear of being stuck in a small space
- Ophidiophobia - fear of snakes
- Pteromerhanophobia: fear of flying
- Social Phobia - fear of interacting with people

To ensure a tight, high-stakes scene, use inner and outer fears against him. This intimidates the character to not only struggle but also face an inner and outer antagonist: fear and setting. Watch plot twists emerge that will add levels to the story line. Seek ways to ensure the he faces one difficult situation after another with paralyzing fright.

Physical Antagonistic Setting:

- An unexpected storm
- A rough and foreign terrain
- A natural disaster
- An explosive work or home life
- An otherwise harmonious situation that turns hostile
- A limitation of mobility

Spiritual Antagonistic Setting:

- A belief system that supports superiority of a single race, creed, or culture
- A religious conviction that practices persecution of others

- An ideology presented in childhood has the potential to instill prejudice and strong biases that can be difficult to overcome. An aversion to others who embrace other forms of faith.

An unanticipated change in an environment reveals the true inner self by displaying strengths or weaknesses. Does he run or stand and fight? Sometimes fleeing is a form of courage. The adversity can be obvious or hidden but include the deception in ways that compel him to make tough decisions and then accept responsibility for the consequences.

A wise writer shows enough setting for the reader to envision the story world—and no more. Information overload cheats the reader of vicariously living the adventure of the character and closes the door on imagination. Readers today crave a story of adventure, growth, and unforeseen events.

How does a writer accomplish an antagonistic setting? View the location's description as though it were a characterization sketch. Concentrate on an antagonist's personality traits and use them to disguise what looks like an enticing environment:

- Determination
- Power
- Beauty
- Charm
- Manipulation
- Deception

Setting is vital and full of spirit. Let the character's surroundings whisper, "Be careful for what is ahead." Associate the location with sensory perception, for in the depths of the five senses lie emotions and memories that have the ability to paralyze.

Sight - What does he perceive around him that can alter reality?

A man dreamed of one day living in the mountains. He spent his entire savings building a cabin. During a wildfire, he was forced to evacuate and couldn't find his dog. How does this memory affect his choices today: where will he live or will he ever own another dog?

Smell - What smells trigger pleasant or unpleasant memories? If the smell is unfamiliar, how does the character react?

A twelve-year-old girl was sent to her grandparents' farm at the beginning of summer. She loved helping her grandmother pick strawberries and make preserves. She learned the reason for the visit was so her parents could work out details of a divorce. To this day, the smell of strawberries makes her ill.

Taste - What tastes draw the character to the past? Can a unique taste shake his conscious or unconscious reaction to what is going on around him?

Consider a man who was celebrating his birthday at a restaurant. The meal was served, a steak cooked to perfection, and he received a call that his mother had died. How would he view his birthday, the restaurant, or steak in the future?

Hear - What sounds soothe or disturb the character? Where did the sounds originate to pinpoint the reaction?

A woman's father worked as a professional organist. He played in churches, theaters, and private events, entertaining and inspiring everyone he met. The woman is involved in a high-stress law firm, and the only way she can relax is by listening to organ music.

Feel - How was the character touched in the past that evokes positive or negative memories?

A man was never touched as a child. He was born premature, abandoned in the hospital, and later placed in a foster care home where he didn't receive affection. As he grew, he sought inappropriate means for attention. Now he's considering a serious crime.

When plotting with setting in mind, a writer chooses at least one of the following scenarios to create a story with visceral impact:

- Man vs. man
- Man vs. animal
- Man vs. nature
- Man vs. society
- Man vs. survival
- Man vs. technology
- Man vs. God

Every situation above requires a distinct setting in which the writer can harvest the gems of antagonism. The opposition is often more than one scenario. Write the scene in the point of view of the character who has the most to lose, using staggering conflict. Use dialogue that anchors voice and responses.

A character who is familiar with a particular setting will not make the same observations or mistakes as a novice.

- A veteran police officer understands the demands and evolving nature of his job better than a rookie, who can be either nervous, apprehensive, or overconfident.
- A seasoned teacher welcomes the new school year with experience and wisdom. A new teacher is fearful about her first teaching position. Is she too strong a disciplinarian? Are her students learning? Is she offering them exciting teaching venues?

The following are instances of an antagonistic setting in a few popular genres.

Contemporary: A beautiful afternoon in a park for a family reunion is interrupted when a young girl brings her fiancé, a man who is of a different race and culture. Her father is enraged, and a fight breaks out among family members. The young girl is killed when she attempts to stop the conflict.

Fantasy: In a land faraway, a kindly king is replaced by a tyrant who levies heavy taxes upon his subjects. One man chooses to free the people of the greedy king, but he must find a way to enter the heavily guarded castle.

Historical: A wagon train pulls into a peaceful valley where the weary travelers can rest before heading across a vast prairie. A pack of hungry wolves attack the horses and livestock stopping the travelers from continuing their journey.

Romance: A couple honeymoons on an exotic, deserted island. The white sandy beaches and the call of seagulls appear to be a paradise. An unexpected storm rises, bringing high winds and twenty-foot waves. The couple is trapped with no means of contacting help.

Sci-Fi: An isolated, peaceful planet is invaded by highly intelligent aliens who require the inhabitant's water supply for their own survival. Who can help the weaker people overcome insurmountable odds?

Suspense: A heroine refers to her backyard as a haven. A tall, stone wall frames nature's display of green and flowering plants. But when a killer chases her inside the garden, she is trapped by what she thought was her respite. Can anyone help her?

Thriller: An aid to a popular politician is invited to an isolated mountain retreat center with other staff members. The aid discovers the politician plans to unleash a virus on American citizens that will kill many innocent people. The politician confiscates all devices leaving the aid helpless to tell the world of the devastation to come.

Whatever the setting, the writer strives to keep characters—and the plot—moving in unpredictable directions.

Why place your hero or heroine in an idyllic environment that makes solving the goal easy and pain free? Why not muddy the waters and create an antagonistic setting that keeps readers on the edge of their seats?

DiAnn Mills is a bestselling author who believes her readers should expect an adventure. She combines unforgettable characters with unpredictable plots to create action-packed, suspense-filled novels. Her titles have appeared on the CBA and ECPA bestseller lists; won two Christy Awards; and been finalists for the RITA, Daphne Du Maurier, Inspirational Readers' Choice, and Carol award contests. Firewall, the first book in her Houston: FBI series, was listed by Library Journal as one of the best Christian Fiction books of 2014. DiAnn is a founding board member of the American Christian Fiction Writers, a member of Advanced Writers and Speakers Association, Sisters in Crime, and International Thriller Writers. She is co-director of The Blue Ridge Mountain Christian Writers Conference and The Mountainside Marketing Conference with social media specialist Edie Melson where she continues her passion of helping other writers be successful. Learn more at www.diannmills.com.

MELISSA DE LA CRUZ

by Cris Freese

When you think of young adult fiction, it's hard to think of someone more prolific than Melissa de la Cruz. Her more-than forty-five books have appeared atop a slew of best-seller's lists—*The New York Times*, *Publisher's Weekly*, *IndieBound*, *USA Today*, *Wall Street Journal*, and *The Los Angeles Times*. Her books have been published in over twenty countries.

Much of the reason for her success—and her love of fiction for young adults—is because she never wants to grow up.

That translates to optimism and idealism, which has certainly translated into her fiction. It shines brightly in her novel, Something in Between, where Jasmine de los Santos has her dreams of attending college on scholarship ripped away, as she discovers her family is in the United States illegally. The resulting fight to protect herself and her family is beautiful—and needed in today's world.

And, of course, refusing to grow up helped with The Descendants series, as de la Cruz wrote the prequels to the hit Disney television movie.

De la Cruz is also known for her Blue Bloods series—with more than three million copies in print—and The Witches of West End series, which was also turned into a two-season drama series on Lifetime.

When you look at the list of novels, you realize its de la Cruz's work ethic that's truly prolific. And as the co-director of Yallfest and co-founder of Yallwest, she's constantly giving back to young adult readers and writers—interacting with more than 30,000 people every year.

A former fashion and beauty editor, de la Cruz has written for *The New York Times*, *Marie Claire*, *Harper's Bazaar*, *Glamour*, *Cosmopolitan*, *Allure*, *The San Francisco Chronicle*, *McSweeney's*, *Teen Vogue*, *CosmoGirl!*, and *Seventeen*.

De la Cruz grew up in Manila and moved to San Francisco with her family. She now lives in West Hollywood with her husband and daughter.

She took some time out of her busy schedule to answer a few questions for *Children's Writer's & Illustrator's Market*.

How did you get started writing? Who or what inspired you?

I've always wanted to be a writer. Ever since I can remember. But I was eleven years old when I read about the Sweet Valley High ghostwriters in the newspaper—Francine Pascal created the series, but the books were written by young 22-year-old women. Up until then, I thought all authors were 90 years old or dead. It was the first time I thought, hey, if they can do this, I can do this too.

How did your immigration experience influence Something in Between? I read that it took 20 years for you to get your green card!

Yes, when my family was approved for a green card, my sister and I were over the age of 21, and so we were in limbo. They have changed the law now so that adult unmarried children now get green cards with their parents, but back then, there was no such law that covered people with our status. So, I got my green card when I married my husband, when I was 31.

My experience made me empathize a lot with Jasmine's plight. I totally remember what it was like to feel American in your heart and mind, but not actually be American on paper. The heart of the story has my heart in it.

....

I totally remember what it was like to feel American in your heart and mind, but not actually be American on paper.

....

Was it your intention to maintain a sense of ever-optimism throughout Something in Between? Jasmine strikes me as someone who never gives up, and always sees the best in the world and people.

Yes, I'm a pretty optimistic person and I gave that to Jasmine. I think immigrants have an innate optimism—only people who have a lot of hope and faith and grit leave everything they ever know and move to a foreign country. Sometimes, when I think about how my parents did this, it takes my breath away. And their kids want so much to make it all "worth it." That kind of sacrifice is a huge responsibility.

What drove you to branch out into something very different with this novel? Did you feel like readers needed this story in today's climate?

Seventeen magazine and Harlequin asked me to write a story about immigration, and I felt I could not say "no," since I knew this experience intimately.

How much of you is in Jasmine?

I'm actually more like Royce, who wants to be a writer, who was spoiled and privileged. I modeled Jasmine after friends I knew from honors summer camps—[those] girls who were perfect: cheerleaders and class presidents and plucky, poor immigrant kids.

What was the most difficult part about writing Something in Between, a story that so obviously hits close to home?

The emotional arc of the story was really difficult, and the helplessness and despair were really hard to feel again.

You're prolific, in terms of the number of novels you've published. How are you able to keep spinning new ideas and pumping out more stories?

Ideas are the easiest part, writers have so many ideas and interests. I think, as creative people, we are open to the world and when we discover something that fascinates us, we want to delve into it more. I don't have hobbies; I just like working and reading and being with my family. I'm not distracted by entertainment—I watch very little television, and I read a ton of books.

Is it more difficult to work with and develop your own idea, or to build off of and adapt an existing idea, like with Descendants?

It's so much easier to be in a world you've created. I enjoy working in other people's universes, but I prefer to work on my own.

How did your relationship with Disney come about?

We did 15 books together before *Blue Bloods*. They asked me to lend my talents to the Descendants world, and I loved the idea. I'm a huge Disney kid; I know those characters and movies like my own and it was an honor to add to the story.

Talk about your writing process. Are you a plotter? How do you keep track of multiple characters when you have multiple points of view, such as The Isle of the Lost?

I'm a huge outliner and plotter. I've always written in multiple POV—it's my preferred way to write, ever since *Au Pairs*.

Which character do you like most in The Isle of the Lost? Who do you relate to?

I love Carlos. He's my favorite, as he's the most like me—the brainy kid in the back, a little anxious, a little nerdy.

Who was the most fun to write? How were you able to dive into well-known Disney villains and develop them into realistic characters?

I looooved writing Mal and Maleficent. Always so fun to be evil! But they are real people to me. I can always find the humanity in a character.

Where did the idea of starting with The Mayflower in Blue Bloods come from? How did that develop?

It came from reading an article about the descendants of the Mayflower, they were all these famous Americans—from George Bush to Oprah to Alec Baldwin—and I thought, *What if the reason all these people are power and famous is because they're vampires?* Then *Blue Bloods* was born.

How were you able to set apart this series from other popular vampire novels?

I wanted to write my own mythology, and I was also inspired by *Paradise Lost*. Both the Mayflower and *Paradise Lost* angle—that my vampires were angels—were in my original outline.

What drives you to write for children and teens? Why those categories?

I guess, like Peter Pan, I refuse to grow up. I think my worldview is very much a kid's, I'm very optimistic, idealistic, and I still find new things in the world to be fascinated by—adulthood is very jaded. I'm pretty much the opposite of that.

Any parting advice for aspiring authors?

Keep trying. Don't give up!

Cris Freese is a former editor of *Children's Writer's & Illustrator's Market*, a freelance writer, and literary intern with Corvisiero Literary. Follow him on Twitter @crisfreese.

MARIEKE NIJKAMP

························

by Cris Freese

///

Marieke Nijkamp is not your typical *New York Times* bestselling author. She was born and raised in the Netherlands and edited the anthology *Unbroken: 13 Stories Starring Disabled Teens*. She's also the author of *This Is Where It Ends* and *Before I Let Go*.

Recently, she took time out to discuss her writing process, projects, and more for readers of *Children's Writer's & Illustrator's Market*.

Your first two novels have featured some really strong female characters. How were you able to create characters who have stood out?

I set out to create interesting, well rounded characters. It's actually one of my favorite parts of the creative process. I love discovering characters' hopes and dreams, loves and fears, nightmares and secret desires. I want all my characters to be as complex as possible. Obviously gender plays a part in that, because our gender identity informs who we are to ourselves and in the eyes of the world. Female characters are going to have different experiences than AND be read and perceived differently from male characters. And so too nonbinary characters.

One of the most impressive things about your writing is how you capture emotion. What inspired Kyra and Corey in Before I Let Go?

I wanted to tell a story about friendship and grief and what it means to be different in a place where difference isn't accepted. I wanted to write a book about responsibility and guilt and the stories we tell ourselves and the stories we tell about ourselves. I wanted to set a mystery in the deepest, cruelest Alaskan winter. *Before I Let Go* allowed me to do all of those things at once.

Have you been to Alaska before? What went to the choice of that setting?

No, alas! I would love to visit Alaska someday, and I tried to plan a research trip while writing the book, but it didn't work due to a number of reasons. Thankfully, I had a few very gracious Alaskan readers who offered advice as I worked on the book.

As for the choice of setting: I always wanted to set a story in Alaska. I love winter, and I've always found there's something magical about snow covered days. That tied into this particularly story quite well.

In many ways, I felt like Corey possessed some of the "outsider" qualities (at least upon returning to Lost Creek) that Tyler had in This is Where It Ends. (Really, I think Kyra had them too!) Was that intentional? Can you talk about your choices in creating characters rejected by society (in some ways)?

I love writing about outsiders. As a disabled, nonbinary, queer creator I feel quite drawn to characters that don't fit in well with the societal "norm" (whatever that even means). More than that too, it's the world I know best. For the longest time, I wasn't able to rhyme the world I saw in books with the world I saw around me, because one did not reflect the other. Thankfully, that's changing and I love being able to add to that. We "outsiders" deserve to have heroes.

Having said that, I don't actually feel Tyler fits that pattern. He is one of the most mainstream characters I've written: he's a white, cishet boy who is angry at the world around him. He's easily in a position of most of acceptance. Certainly he deals with trauma and hardships, and he deserved to get help for that, but so do many of the other characters in *TIWIE*. None of them resorted to picking up a gun and killing people.

You walked a line between with the supernatural in Before I Let Go. What made you make that choice when it came to Kyra's art?

Story ideas can come from the wildest places. A lot of what happens in Lost came from an article I once read, which essentially linked medieval mysticism to mental illness. And I was very curious what would happen if I took that idea as a basis for exploring mental illness (and ableism) in a modern context. So naturally it involved some mysticism too. Or a belief system, in any case. And that required certain unexplainable things.

Was it difficult to create that question of whether what was happening in Lost Creek was supernatural or not? What made you choose to have the town so accepting of Kyra?

I wanted to explore the idea of acceptance a bit in this book. Personally, I don't think the town was accepting of Kyra. Is it acceptance when it's conditional on usefulness? Is it acceptance when it chooses to ignore humanity? Kyra wanted to be loved for all she was, with all she was. As someone whose passion was stories and storytelling, who loved fiercely, who lived with bipolar disorder. Not in spite of. Unconditionally. And she deserved nothing less.

Both of these novels really deal with loss as a teenager, and comprehending and dealing with it. When approaching heavy topics, do you have a hard time writing?

Of course approaching heavy topics isn't always easy, and I definitely need to occasionally step away and go for a walk, but it helps that I try to write the books I would love to read. I write stories I'm passionate about, and that keeps me going.

What was your writing process like for both of these novels?

I'm a plotter at heart, so for both (and honestly, all my stories) I had very extensive notes and a very extensive outline before I even put pen to paper. I love knowing what the shape of the story is before I create it, what the ending is I'm working toward. I greatly admire people who can write a story by the seat of their pants, but I'm not one of them.

And just for the record, that's okay! We all have our own process. I love discovering other people's processes, but I've learned I shouldn't try to emulate them, because I can work best when I'm working my way.

How did you originally get your agent, Jennifer Udden?

A Twitter pitch contest! I was hanging out on the #PitMad hashtag to answer questions and help people with pitches, which is something I was lucky enough to do quite a lot back then. I was querying *This is Where it Ends* at the time, so I figured I'd throw in my own pitch too. Jen requested I query her when she saw it, and the rest, as they say, is history.

Did you have any reservations about querying This is Where It Ends? Particularly with the number of school shootings in the United States?

I had reservations about writing *TIWIE*, exactly because it's such a sensitive subject. I wanted to make sure I could write the story respectfully, truthfully, and without doing harm. I strongly believe it's my responsibility as a writer to always consider whether I'm the right person to write a story, because some stories quite simply do not belong to me. Once I found a way to do right by *TIWIE*, I pursued that.

By the time I started querying, I knew I wanted to work with an agent who understood that responsibility, and I'm very glad I found her.

Forget the subject matter of This is Where It Ends for a second—how difficult was it to write a story that occurs over the course of just fifty-four minutes? How did you plot that story out?

It was really tricky and I loved doing it. I had a spreadsheet that tracked all of the main characters and some of the ensemble on a minute-by-minute basis and having that structure was beautiful.

Was the story complicated by writing from four different POVs? How were you able to not only create four completely different characters, but four completely different voices? Sometimes, characters can begin to sound the same, but not in this case.

I wrote the story four times, from four different POVs. Only when I had all the ingredients did I shuffle and start blending it together. So that helped me a lot in keeping the voices separate.

Was it difficult to write a character like Tyler? What went into his development?

Oh, absolutely. Not in the least because I didn't want to create a situation wherein my one interpretation could be seen as the quintessential profile of a school shooter. That wouldn't be responsible. So I stuck to the research there is, spent a lot of time frustrated with the Dickey Amendment, and started with the common characteristics—most of the shooters are white boys, most of them are angry, and in the vast majority of cases, mass shootings aren't a result of mental illness.

From there, I recreated Tyler in a similar way as we would try to recreate our understanding of shooters in a real life situation: through other people's stories, by trying to sort out all the puzzle pieces, and interpretation.

What is the best advice you've received as a writer? What advice would you give to writers just starting out?

Write your truth. Be brave. Never stop learning.

What one or two things do you wish you'd known when you started writing?

Some no's are not-yets. Some stories are not-yets too. Both of that is perfectly fine.

....

Cris Freese is a former editor of *Children's Writer's & Illustrator's Market*, a freelance writer, and literary intern with Corvisiero Literary. Follow him on Twitter @crisfreese.

....

LEIGH BARDUGO

Unstoppable

....

by Baihley Gentry

Leigh Bardugo has always written the stories she wanted to write.

When querying her debut, *Shadow and Bone*—in which she introduced readers to a Czarist Russia-inspired world where individuals called Grisha have the mystical ability to manipulate matter—Bardugo was faced with a publishing-industry reality. Although young adult novels were popular at the time, and her premise was unique and compelling, no literary agents seemed interested in epic or high fantasy books for young readers.

She forged ahead anyway.

"I knew very little about the market. I learned that many [agents] would not even entertain the idea of that kind of book," she says. "It's wise to know what's out there, [but don't] let that hinder you. If you have an idea, pursue it. [Think] about things that make your story a story that only you could tell—those are the things that will stand out."

The strength of that story did eventually resonate with a rep, and the series was sold in a three-book deal in 2010. Within a week of its release in 2012, *Shadow and Bone* skyrocketed to the top of *The New York Times* bestseller list—as did her six books after that: 2013's *Siege and Storm* and 2014's *Ruin and Rising*, which rounded out the Grisha trilogy; 2015's *Six of Crows* and 2016's *Crooked Kingdom*, a "heist-con" duology Bardugo likens to "*Ocean's 11* meets *Game of Thrones*"; and her two latest stand-alones in 2017: *The Language of Thorns*, her first short story collection, and *Wonder Woman: Warbringer*, about the superhero's teen years.

In sum, her books have sold more than 1 million copies combined internationally, and have earned such accolades as RT Reviewers Choice Awards in 2012 and 2015, and multiple starred reviews from *Publishers Weekly*, *Kirkus Reviews* and *School Library Journal*. Bardugo regularly writes short stories for Tor.com, and she has appeared in various anthologies, including *Last Night a Superhero Saved My Life* with notable names like Jodi

Picoult and Neil Gaiman, and *Slasher Girls & Monster Boys* alongside Jonathan Maberry and Kendare Blake.

Despite the impressive trajectory of her career, the path from aspiring author to bestseller was a circuitous one.

Born in Jerusalem and raised in Southern California, Bardugo's lifelong aspiration to be a writer led her to earn a degree in journalism from Yale. While struggling for years to finish a first draft of a novel ("I didn't know yet that I was an outliner, and how badly I needed structure in order to work"), she took jobs in copywriting, advertising and as a Hollywood makeup and special effects artist.

It wasn't until she brushed off "some pretty wonky ideas" espoused by media, TV and film about what it meant to produce creative work that Bardugo was able to embrace a "terrible, messy, ugly first draft." That experience taught her something valuable: "Let go of the idea that somehow you can outsmart a first draft," she says. "Because I have never met anybody who can."

The YA fantasy maestro took a break from promoting *The Language of Thorns* and *Wonder Woman: Warbringer* to talk world-building, personal perseverance and more.

The runaway success of a debut can put a lot of pressure on subsequent follow-ups. How did you manage to cope with that so gracefully?

When a book lists, there's the illusion of runaway success. My [first book] listed, but it's not as if you hit *The New York Times* bestseller list and all of a sudden they give you the keys to a magical clubhouse and you've suddenly arrived. That's one book, and a book does not make a career. Certainly, I had a wonderful push from my publisher and got very lucky. I'm very aware of what it means to have a publisher back you. But your job as a writer, no matter what else is happening, is to continue to produce work—whether you're succeeding or failing. [You have to put] aside ideas about sales or success or ambition, and just work.

You know, I think I have a journey that looks smooth from the outside. And I'm always a little hesitant to talk about it because I don't want people to get a false impression about what it takes to get published. But [up until the point of publishing *Shadow and Bone*], I did face plenty of rejection, and even after I signed with [my agent], every single one of those rejections stung. Because the marvel of the information age is that you're still getting email rejections months and months after you sent them. [Laughs]. And so, until *Shadow and Bone* came out, I would read those rejections—because, of course, I had to read every single one of them—and I would think, *Well, maybe they're right and everybody else is wrong.* Part of the journey is that horrific balance of, you know, delusions of grandeur and abject humility that I think writers walk the line of all the time.

You've talked about losing faith in your ability to become a professional writer. What would you tell others who are struggling with that same feeling?

I want to be really clear about something: I think we kind of fetishize the creative life. We have the vision of what it means to be an author, where you sit in your garret or looking out at your view and you give everything to your art and you commit fully to it. But the reality is that most of us have bills to pay. We have loans to pay off. We have educations to pay for. Some of us have children to take care of or other relatives or dependents or responsibilities.

And the idea that somehow you're not a real writer if you are pursuing taking care of yourself and your life, as you pursue your art, is an incredibly damaging one. Very few people have the wherewithal or the safety net to be able to pursue writing full time from moment one. And I want people to understand that you can absolutely work a job, sometimes two jobs, and have those responsibilities—and still write. I didn't fail to become a writer, and therefore had to take a job. I had to take a job to keep a roof over my head because I had student loans to pay off. And that's the way it works.

For writers trying to balance life and art, how would you encourage them to stay motivated in pursuing their passion?

Set realistic goals. Sometimes that means doing something like NaNoWriMo, or it means saying, "I'm just going to write 500 words a day, but I'm going to write 500 words a day." Or "I'm going to do writing sprints for 30 minutes before work." Or in the 45 minutes when my kid is napping, or whatever it is. Carve out a time, find a process that works for you and don't compare yourself to anybody else.

[And] get offline. Stop reading about what other authors are doing. Stop reading reviews. Let yourself be immersed in the story that you're writing.

Remember: There is no expiration date on your talent. I did not publish my first book until I was 35 years old. If you have a story to tell, it doesn't matter when you tell it. Just get it onto the page and let go of any of the ideas that somehow it's less worthwhile because it took you a little longer to get there than it took others.

Man, you're inspiring me!

[Laughs.] Oh, good. Do it. Do it.

You've said before that there is no right way to write a book. You've been publishing at least one book per year since 2012, which is an impressive output. Describe your process.

I'm an outliner. I write through a three-act structure. I build all of my books in pretty much the exact same way: I have the idea, I write it out onto a single page so that I essentially have a book that is one-page long, and then I begin to fill in all of the things that I know. I build this kind of ramshackle zero-draft, that operates as an extended outline, and that is what becomes the musculature of the book. Now, when I get into the work of actually writing the scenes and revising the book into something that it can be, that process changes a little depending on the project.

A big part of writing is the discomfort of the work not being what you want it to be and the feelings of doubt or failure that come with not being able to make the idea instantly into what you want it to be.

Everybody processes differently, but [the exact method] is something you can keep coming back to when you feel psychologically embattled. A big part of writing is the discomfort of the work not being what you want it to be and the feelings of doubt or failure that come with not being able to make the idea instantly into what you want it to be.

Your books have very elaborate, well-rounded worlds. I haven't read a book in a long time where I felt so there. When world-building, where do you typically begin?

I start with my characters and with the story, the plot. When a reader enters the first chapter of your book, they're trying to get their bearings. It's our job as authors to give them the signals they need in order to be able to navigate that world. The great challenge of world-building is not building the world. You could build a world with maps and languages and all these things [and still be missing something]. It's releasing that information to the reader. The world-building that really falls into place first is what I always describe as the sense of power—helping readers understand how power flows in the book. That could mean governmental power, personal power, magical power, whatever. But [determining how power flows] is going to determine how your characters behave on the page, and what they're able or not able to do.

You had help creating the Grisha Trilogy's Ravkan language from David Peterson, who assisted with developing the Dothraki language in HBO's Game of Thrones. What was that like?

David and I met at Worldcon several years ago. I went to a presentation of his on Dothraki. He has been kind enough to be a resource for me as we've worked through the

[Grisha] books, although we do occasionally butt heads because he wants me to be much more ambitious in my language in the book, and he's very probably right.

You write a lot of diverse characters without falling victim to stereotypes. Do you think attitudes about diversity in publishing have shifted, or does the industry still have a ways to go?

I think both of those things are true. I think that there's a new dedication to making sure that not only is representation better, but that marginalized authors and voices that maybe didn't have voices before are increasingly given platforms in publishing. And that is not only as writers, but as editors and in everything from publicity to sales. That said, I don't think there's any question that there's a long way to go because that is a long process and because until the fundamental power structures change, until the gatekeepers are different, I don't think we're going to see the kind of change that we really need to see—in the way not only that stories are told, but in the way they reach readers.

I'm sure many authors ask you what's trending in YA. What do you think is the ideal balance of writing what you're passionate about and understanding what's drawing readers in the industry?

You have to know the market. So you have to know what's selling, what isn't selling anymore, what people are fatigued by. But that doesn't mean you can say, "Oh, well, I [can't write that ever]." There was a period of time where people would say, "Oh, no more vampire books," or "no more dystopians," or no more this or that. But that is really false because what that actually meant was no more of that particular kind of story. We need a different take on vampires or we need to see a dystopian that is simply described as science fiction. YA shifts and moves faster than most other categories because so much work is being generated and consumed so quickly. And to be frank, I think if I brought *Shadow and Bone* out now, it would not have the same reception it had in 2012. Be aware of the market, but really, being aware of the market is just one part of being a storyteller and thinking about craft.

What's next for you?

Well, *King of Scars* is the first book in my upcoming duology that continues the story of the Grishaverse, and will pick up the story of Nikolai Lantsov, the young king of Ravka. And I'm [also working on] *Ninth House,* my first novel for adults. It is the start of a series set at Yale, a dark fantasy that focuses on the secret societies among East Coast elites. I've got a couple of other things cooking, but nothing I can discuss just yet.

I heard you have a band, which is probably the coolest side hustle ever. What type of music do you play?

Our lead guitarist would probably punch me for this, but I've always described it as "geek rock." It's sort of like if you put the Pixies and the New Pornographers and a little bit of They Might Be Giants in a blender. I mostly sing. Unfortunately, all of our lives got taken over by adulthood: Our guitarist had a baby. Our bassist had a baby. Our drummer bought a house. I landed my dream job. But we do occasionally meet up for band brunch and one of these days we'll have a reunion show.

I think that when you're writing, being creative in other ways is really useful and therapeutic. And whether that's creating visual art or making music—or hell, even baking—as long as you're doing something that's keeping you engaged and keeping you from chewing over reviews on Goodreads, I think you're better off.

Baihley Gentry is the associate editor of *Writer's Digest*, in which this interview originally appeared.

E. LOCKHART

....

by Cris Freese

//

If you couldn't tell by the tightly-woven plots, the twisty turns, and the extraordinary character development, E. Lockhart is a plotter.

There's no pantsing; just careful decisions, precise writing, and a lot of editing.

When you look at Lockhart's background—with a doctorate in English literature with a focus on the 19th century British novel and the history of British book illustration—it's no surprise. She's well-read, even breaking down elements of *The Talented Mr. Ripley* into the basis of *Genuine Fraud*.

That became an experiment in plot structure, telling a story backward.

And there was an experiment with flashbacks and memory loss in *We Were Liars*, leaving readers guessing until the very end.

There's a battle against the patriarchy in *The Disreputable History of Frankie Landau-Banks*.

So it also shouldn't come as a surprise that each of these novels reads very different—*Frankie* with much more of a comedic tone, while the other two read more as thrillers/mysteries.

Yet, all of them require the same kind of intensity in writing and development. These works don't come about by luck or accident. Lockhart says she rewrites each novel 15 times—that's how long it takes to produce something that's truly publishable.

There's encouragement there: Your first draft isn't going to be the one that lands you that agent, that publisher, that best-seller's list you've been dreaming of. The next draft probably won't, either.

Like anything, writing takes practice. The more you practice, the more prepared you are to deliver the real deal.

Lockhart has that down. She took some time out of her busy schedule to share her process with a few different novels, themes, her strong characters, and more.

I read that you are the child of a playwright, and used to sit in the theater and watch rehearsals. That helped lead to your love of writing. How do you feel like theater helped influence your writing style? Did you learn any specifics about storytelling?

> A scene can change hugely by shifting a couple lines. A scene seems completely different with lights, costumes, and music. A transition between scenes can make all the difference in how the second scene plays. It was a change to watch revision in action.

I imagine pulling off the storytelling and plots for We Were Liars and Genuine Fraud were a challenge. The former because of the twist, the latter because of the unconventional use of telling the story backwards. How did you come up with both concepts to plot those novels?

> Those two books had very different processes. With *We Were Liars* I started with the setting for the novel and looked for a story that was related to the setting. I worked with a five-act plot structure and created the storyline entirely from my imagination. I took a lot of time figuring out how best to use my flashbacks and the fairy tales that interrupt the story. More on *Genuine Fraud*, below.

For Genuine Fraud, did you discover the story first, or have the idea to tell it backwards?

> I started out wanting to write a backwards story, but what kind of story is best told backwards? The making of an antihero seemed like the richest choice. I found inspiration in Patricia Highsmith's novel *The Talented Mr. Ripley*, and I broke Highsmith's novel down to its most basic plot elements. I reversed those elements and began reimagining the story with contemporary characters who were women instead of men. I worked on the outline for a long time, pushing myself to depart from the source material and bringing as much of my own emotional life as I could to the story of this very difficult woman.

> ....
> # I reversed those elements and began re-imagining the story with contemporary characters who were women instead of men.
> ....

Do you write to themes, or let themes develop? I felt like I was seeing characters discover themselves in Genuine Fraud, We Were Liars, and The Disreputable History of Frankie Landau-Banks.

> Mostly themes develop as I write. I don't think a good book starts with a message, but maybe it starts with a question. *Genuine Fraud* and *Disreputable History* are both

books that come from my own questions about social class and feminism in America, particularly white people's experience of those things. Those are questions I deal with in my everyday life, too.

Would you rather write an edgier character like Jule, or someone charming and funny like Frankie? Why?

Frankie is witty, but she's very angry and pretty miserable. It's no fun to be Frankie. I most enjoy creating the scenes in which both those characters come into their full power, for good or evil. Those scenes are cathartic to write.

Any chance we see more of Jule?

Genuine Fraud is in development for film, so we'll see what happens… But I have no plans to write a sequel.

What was the inspiration behind Frankie bringing down the boys' club, so to speak?

The Loyal Order of the Basset Hound is a symbol of the old boys' network that still runs our country. Of course it's worth imagining how it would feel to try to bring it down. Especially for young people.

How did We Were Liars come about? I saw that you re-wrote it 15 times! Was the twist always a part of the original storyline?

I rewrite all my books at least 15 times. That's how long it takes for me to make something that's any good. Yes, the twist was always part of We Were Liars. I hadn't done a book of that nature before and it took a lot of work to set up the twist. I relied on critiques from writer friends. I had more help on that book than on any other.

Where does the inspiration for your standout characters come from? Frankie, Jule and Cadence are all so different.

Thank you! All of them are driven by my own emotional life, but I situate the stories differently so I can play things up in dramatic ways. For example, Cadence is an heiress, a migraine-sufferer, an amnesiac, and a drug addict. I have never been any of those things.

But she's also been dumped by her first love. That, I can relate to.

Which character do you relate to the most?

Of those three, I'm most like Frankie. But she's smarter than I am. *Dramarama* is my most autobiographical book.

Is it difficult to switch genres from novel to novel? What do you enjoy writing the most?

Comedies are more fun. But I don't like to start a novel saying, "Oh, I know how to do this." I like to be a little unsure on my feet.

What is the best advice you've received as a writer? What advice would you give to writers just starting out?

Don't try to write the Great American Novel. Don't try to write a great novel. Don't try to write a good novel. Don't try to write a mediocre novel.

Just try to write a novel. It's fine if it's terrible. It really is fine. You can fix it later.

What one or two things do you wish you'd known when you started writing?

I wish I'd known about the *Writer's Market!* It seemed impossible to break into publishing. Impossible. There was no Internet. I just asked everybody I knew to tell me anything they knew—and finally got an introduction which led to my first agent.

What's next?

I'm working on a new YA set on a college campus that's mostly abandoned for the summer. It has a complicated structure that turns out to be very difficult. But that's where the fun is.

. . . .

Cris Freese is a former editor of *Children's Writer's & Illustrator's Market*, a freelance writer, and literary intern with Corvisiero Literary. Follow him on Twitter @crisfreese.

. . . .

KWAME ALEXANDER

··

by Kerrie Flanagan

Kwame Alexander is the *New York Times* best-selling author of 24 books, including *The Crossover*, *The Playbook*, *Surfs Up*, and *Booked*. Kwame believes that poetry can change the world, and he uses it to inspire and empower young people through his Page to Stage Writing and Publishing Program. A regular speaker at schools and conferences in the U.S., he also travels the world planting seeds of literary love. He co-founded LEAP for Ghana, an International literacy program that has established student scholarship opportunities, provided literacy training for teachers, facilitated girls' empowerment workshops, and facilitated career development projects in conjunction with Ashesi University and the U.S. Embassy in Ghana.

Alexander's 23-year journey to the 2015 Newberry Medal Award for his book, *The Crossover*, was filled with many ups and downs. But his willingness to say *yes* to potential opportunities and take control over his own destiny enabled his success.

Growing up, Alexander was surrounded by books. His father was a publisher and his mother an English teacher. Despite his parents' influences, by middle school, he fell out of love with reading and his passion for books became dormant.

"I grew up with a man who had written 16 books, gotten his Ph.D. from Columbia University, forced me to read the encyclopedia and the dictionary, made me read books from the time I could walk," Alexander says. "By the time I was 12, I knew *Pedagogy of the Oppressed* by Paulo Freire, I knew *The Three Musketeers*; I knew literature, but I hated it."

When he went to college at Virginia Tech, he wanted nothing to do with literature, so he pursued a biochemistry major with the hopes of becoming a doctor. During his sophomore year, his life took a new direction down a familiar path. He enrolled in a poetry class taught by professor and award-winning poet, Nikki Giovanni.

"Taking Nikki's class woke me up and reminded me of the joy, and what can happen when you read a poem that knocks you off your feet. It was also at a time when I was meeting a lot of girls on campus. I may not know how to talk to them, but I can certainly write them a poem. Those two things conspired together and I was off to the races."

He changed his major to English and immersed himself back into the world of litera-ture. During his junior year, he started down the road to becoming a writer, saying *yes* to new opportunities.

In addition to writing love poems to some of the campus co-eds (including one whom is now his wife), he wrote a play. Alexander wanted to produce it, but needed a ven-ue and an audience. After learning about a student leadership conference that was being held at the College of William and Mary, he called the organizer to ask if she was inter-ested in having entertainment during the event. She agreed to his terms—including pay-ment—and the play was performed for about 800 students.

"After the play, during the Q&A, one of the students asked, 'Is your play going on tour?' [pause] *Yes!* Of course, it's going on tour. At the end of that night, I had bookings for eight colleges including Rutgers, Princeton, Temple, Hampton University, and so forth," Alexander recalls. "I am a junior in college, and I am understanding what this idea of saying *yes* means; of walking through a door and figuring out what is on the other side, and figuring out how to make it happen."

If opportunities he hoped for didn't pan out, Alexander didn't let that stop him. When publishers rejected his books, he self-published; when he wasn't invited to book festivals, he organized his own; and when he was turned down for a three-month writing fellowship in Brazil, he created his own, inviting eight accomplished, authors to join him for three weeks in Tuscany.

He continued with his writing—including another play—trying his hand at novels, poetry, and staying open to new opportunities. If someone asked him, "Kwame, have you ever thought about …?" and even if he hadn't, he would say, *yes*. This led to a children's show for television, reciting poetry to a church congregation in L.A., and successfully selling his children's book *Acoustic Rooster and his Barnyard Band* at farmers markets.

If opportunities he hoped for didn't pan out, Alexander didn't let that stop him. When publishers rejected his books, he self-published; when he wasn't invited to book festivals, he organized his own; and when he was turned down for a three-month writing fellowship in Brazil, he created his own, inviting eight accomplished, authors to join him for three weeks in Tuscany.

"There will be opportunities in life we don't get," Alexander says, "and we are going to feel sad and disappointed. But even when people are telling us no, we can say *yes* to ourselves."

And that is exactly what he kept doing. At an event in New York City, an editor suggested Alexander write a novel in verse for middle school boys about basketball. After 17 books and 20-plus years of writing, he went to his office (at Panera Bread) and began working on this project. He felt it was the best thing he had ever written. Alexander submitted the manuscript three times to the same agent who suggested the idea. She turned him down each time.

After sending it out and getting rejected by twenty different publishers, he decided he was going to publish it himself. But before he could start that process, he got one more response. An editor at Houghton Mifflin said she would be honored to publish *The Crossover*. The book was released in March 2014. On February 2, 2015, Alexander received a call: It had won the Newbery Medal Award.

"For 23 years of my writing career, I was a jet plane on a runway," Alexander says. "With each book and each year, I picked up speed. When I won the Newberry, the plane took off. And it soared 30,000 feet, and I haven't come down since. I don't know if I will ever get used to it. Sometimes I wake up and laugh and pinch myself. There is a new normal now."

Winning the award has provided him more opportunities to reach students and publish the books that are important to him.

"I want to save the world. I believe that words can do that, that books can do that. I believe the mind of an adult begins in the imagination of a child. And so, I want to create the most well-rounded, informed, honest, empathetic, connected imagination for children that I can. So that when they become adults, they have truly become more human."

Alexander proves persistence and openness can lead to reaching your dreams. He believes writers should always be prepared to walk through the door, because a *yes* will be there somewhere. It might not be in the way originally anticipated, but it will come.

He has noticed most writers are more than willing to put in the work to be successful at a job for an employer, but when it comes to putting in the work for themselves *as a writer*, it becomes more challenging and difficult.

"If you want to take destiny into your own hands, I think you have to treat your dream like you would a job. You have to put in work for it, you have to be consistent, and you have to be unwavering in your commitment."

He says a good support system is important: Make sure the people around you are going to be encouraging, supportive, and at least as smart, if not smarter than you. Surround yourself with other business minded people who are going to propel you forward.

During a keynote address to writers Alexander shared the following:

I was the guy who self-published poetry.

I was the guy who was told time and time again, poetry doesn't sell.

I was the guy who went to farmers markets.

I was you—I am you.

The only difference between you and me is that I just happened to win this medal thing and I got lucky. You don't get lucky unless you put yourself in a situation to get lucky. I mean, I think I wrote a good book, but we all write good books. This idea of saying *yes*—it works.

His best advice: "Do it! Tap into your life as a child. Remember what you went through. Pull from those experiences. Write about things that you want to write. Don't try to write to the audience. Remember what it was like to *be* the audience and write something you think is real and authentic and beautiful and compelling. I say do it."

KERRIE FLANAGAN is an author, writing consultant, publisher, and accomplished freelance writer with more than 18 years' experience. Her work has appeared in publications such as *Writer's Digest, Alaska Magazine, The Writer*, and six *Chicken Soup for the Soul* books. She is the author of seven books, including two children's books, *Claire's Christmas Catastrophe* and *Claire's Unbearable Campout*, all published under her label, Hot Chocolate Press. She was the founder and former director of Northern Colorado Writers and now does individual consulting with writers. Her background in teaching and enjoyment of helping writers has led her to present at writing conferences across the country, including the Writer's Digest Annual Conference, the Willamette Writer's Conference, and the Writer's Digest Novel Writing Conference. You can find her online at www.KerrieFlanagan.com, www.hotchocolatepress.com, and on Twitter at @ Kerrie_Flanagan.

KENNETH OPPEL

David McPherson

When inspiration hits Kenneth Oppel, it's like standing on a horizon and seeing all the possibilities. Inspiration first struck the award-winning children's author during his formative years; thankfully for him—and his readers—the well of creativity has flowed frequently ever since. Sure, like all authors, there are times it feels like the well is ready to run dry, but then—often inspired by a setting—his imagination takes flight and Oppel is off on a new adventure—discovering and inventing characters and the wonderful worlds they inhabit.

From an early age, Oppel chose the writing life. By the time he was 12, he knew his calling was crafting fiction. He wrote sci-fi epics, which he calls his "*Star Wars* phase"; then, he progressed to swords and sorcery tales, his "*Dungeons & Dragons* phase"; finally, during the summer holidays when he was 14, Oppel started writing a humorous story about a boy addicted to video games. The following summer, he rewrote the tale and the resulting novel—*Colin's Fantastic Video Adventure*—was published in 1985 in Britain, Canada, the U.S., and later in France.

Since this teenage debut, Oppel, 50, has written and published 20 books, many of which have won awards. His most popular titles are: The Silverwing Trilogy (*Sunwing, Firewing, Darkwing*), which sold more than 1 million copies around the world; *Airborn*, which won the Michael L Printz Honor Book (2005, ALA), Ruth and Sylvia Schwartz Children's Book Award (2005), Red Maple Award (2004, OLA), and The Governor General's Award for Children's Literature; *Half Brother*; *The Nest*; *Skybreaker*; *The Boundless*; and *Starclimber*. The author's latest, *Every Hidden Thing*, was published in the fall of 2016.

Born in Port Alberni, British Columbia—a mill town on Vancouver Island—Oppel spent his formative years in Victoria, B.C., and on the opposite coast, in Halifax, Nova Scotia. Today, the author lives in Toronto with his wife and three children, writing away the days, looking to discover new horizons, and taking readers with him on these inspirational journeys.

Here, Oppel talks about finding your voice, the role setting plays in sending his muse on creative flight, and other life lessons from a writer's life well lived.

Your story is pretty unique. Tell me about how you published your first novel back in 1985?

Yes, I was incredibly lucky. A family friend knew a famous writer, Roald Dahl, who liked my story enough to pass it on to an agent who liked it and passed it on and got me a publishing deal. It took me a while after that though to find my own voice, because I was only 14, and I was really trying to imitate Dahl's style, cadence, and dialogue. It was an apprentice piece for me, and definitely took a few years after that to really discover what kind of stories I wanted to write and to find my voice.

How does a writer find his voice?

Mimicry is how you begin. When I was starting, I wrote like Roald Dahl, [tried] *Star Wars* fan fiction, and I copied stories about video games and stories based on *Dungeons & Dragons* that I loved reading. The good thing about imitation is that it develops your skill as a writer by mimicking … you get to try out all these different styles and eventually, by practice and perseverance, you learn what is comfortable for you. It's like trying on a pair of shoes.

I'm sure that once you've found your voice, it constantly changes and evolves?

For sure your voice evolves. A writer's voice changes from book to book and over the course of a career … it's not fixed; most writers are chameleons.

Where do you get your ideas? I understand you once said that the inspiration/starting point for one of your books was from a photograph. Describe this process.

Sure, a photograph is a good way to jumpstart a creative writing workshop, but my ideas mostly come from things that I get passionate about or I'm curious about. There is no rhyme or reason to how I come across these ideas. It usually takes me about one to two years to write a book, so I need to be really engaged in the subject matter.

I understand that often a setting propels your muse and starts you on that creative journey?

Definitely. Settings inspire me. For example, the interior of the longest train in the world (*The Boundless*) or the inside of a hot air balloon (*Airborn*); these settings give me visual spaces that I can invent, populate, and play with, and that's what is most inspiring for me.

What happens once you inhabit this place?

I start thinking about who lives in these places and what characters might emerge. After I get a premise and a setting, then my mind gets to work thinking about all the possibilities that can conglomerate around this one idea. There are no rules to where the ideas come from. I write down all my ideas in a notebook—most of them are not good, but I know quickly which ones *are* good. I test them and they start sending out tendrils and shoots, that's when you know you are onto something.

I know songwriter Chip Taylor talks about how he gets chills when inspiration hits. As an author, do you experience a similar feeling when you discover a special idea?

Yes. I never tire of that moment of excitement you feel when you are on to something big. It's like standing on a horizon and seeing all these possibilities in front of you. You have those moments when you come up with an idea and you have them while writing a book. I always hope that they are frequent occurrences.

Talk about your latest novel *Every Hidden Thing*. On your website, you describe it as, "*Romeo and Juliet* meets *Indiana Jones* in this epic tale that combines the hunt for a dinosaur skeleton, bitter rivalries and a forbidden romance." Right away you've got the reader hooked. Tell us more.

It's a novel about two teenage paleontologists whose fathers are famous fossil hunters that hate each other; they've had a professional feud their entire lives and always want to destroy the others' reputation. Their kids meet at a lecture and then later out in the field in Wyoming and fall in love while searching for the same fossil they've called The Rex. They just have a tooth—but it's enormous—and that indicates the owner will have the biggest fossil find ever. I remember wondering who the first person was that found a dinosaur bone and how exciting that must have been and all the ways they used to describe what they had found: a mythological creature, biblical, etc. That excitement and mystery was my initial inspiration. Then, I read about the first paleontologists [Edward] Marsh & [Charles] Cope in the U.S. and this huge feud and rivalry they had. Those two real scientists were a huge inspiration. They were larger than life characters and I thought, "Wouldn't it be great if they each had a kid who fell in love with each other?" The story is part scientific fact, part history based on these larger-than-life figures, all mixed with a fictitious pair of star-crossed lovers.

What advice do you have for authors trying to break into children's literature?

Write the book that you most want to write and try to avoid that powerful magnetic pull to write something that might be popular, trendy, or moneymaking, because in the end no one really knows what type of book will be popular. Write the one that makes you the most excited and that you have the most to bring to … the story should call up something inside you and call up all your passions and be something only you can write. You have a far better chance of winning a publisher, agent, and audience through that strategy versus the approach of, *I'm going to write another dystopian novel.* Sure, some are successful, but I believe there are too many copycats out there, and books that are trendsetters and classics are always original.

What's the biggest lesson you've learned throughout your writing career?

The fact is, you will, as an aspiring/emerging writer, get a lot of rejections and you have to resign yourself to a certain statistical rejection. You will send your story out to many places before you get an offer of publication. Know that the reaction to your work is so subjective; it's really about lining your book up with the right reader. For a writer to achieve a certain level of expertise, you need talent, and you need to produce a polished piece of work to even get into the running. Even then, it's incredibly difficult. I know people who've written novels and sent them to 75 places before they get one offer, and the book goes on to be critically acclaimed.

Do you think it's still possible for someone to have a career as a children's author?

There is no guarantee anymore for someone to have a "writing career." It's tougher than ever to sustain a career and keep it going for a long time. There is a lot of energy in publishing dedicated to first-time novelists, but most of those don't fulfill their expectations. Then, it's hard to publish a second, third, or fourth book. It takes a lot of perseverance and discipline to write regularly.

Walk me through your typical day, knowing that no day is the same in a writer's life?

The writer's life is divided into compartments like any job. Some of it is brainstorming, note taking, researching, and fleshing out ideas to see how far they go. Once you have an idea, some writers just dive in, but I outline and try to figure out as much as possible … I need a road map. Once I start the actual writing, I try to write 1,000 words per day. The first draft is always horrible and it's torture. I skip around a lot, jump forward and backwards in the story to just get through it, then I suture it all together into a rough first draft.

What comes next after you've got a solid, rough first draft?

Revision, revision, revision. That's when the story really comes together: the breadth of the characters and what the story is really about. I never know what the story is about when I start. I just start with a premise, some characters, and a setting, which is usually the catalyst. The story comes to me in writing and rewriting. The rest of my days are spent editing, copyediting, and doing administrative stuff. I also do a lot of public speaking. Overall, it's an interesting and varied diet.

Really, when it comes down to it, you really have to want it, don't you?

For sure, you've got to want it. Like anything else that is off the typical path in terms of a career, it has to be this type of thing. First you have to think: Is there anything else I would rather be doing? Most artists say no. You have to be committed to even get to the starting line. It requires your full attention and energy; it can be, and often is, poorly paid, plus there's no pension plan, no benefits, or no matching contributions from a benevolent employer! You need to feel like this is really your calling. Basically, do not become a writer if you have another secret passion like wanting to be a dentist.

Did you always want it?

Yes. I was lucky. I decided early what I wanted to do and I didn't sway from that. I kept being what I most wanted to do. That told me that that was the thing.

What's the most rewarding part of being an author?

For me, the early stages of creation are still the most exciting and rewarding. That sense when you have this beautiful shiny thing in your hands—in your brain— and you are excited … you see all the places your story can go, just that sense of excitement of exploring it and mapping it out and creating this experience for a reader. The actual structure in creating it I find difficult, but the sense of satisfaction of holding the finished book is still a thrill for me: looking at the spine, the cover, the dust jacket, and smelling it … holding my own books and saying, "look, I made this, I brought this into the world." I love when I talk to a kid, or get a letter from an adult, and they remember what one of my books meant to them and how it was transporting, comforting, and educational. For example, when I hear from doctors, marine biologists, or pilots, who tell me my books inspired them to pursue their chosen career. To think you were this early ember in someone's imagination that sent him or her on this journey is pretty incredible.

Do you think today's do-it-yourself world of self-publishing has made it easier for new authors to break in and/or do you think there is still value in the traditional route of getting an agent/finding a publisher for your work?

I think the traditional route is still the most ideal route. I know of several notable examples where people self-published, their book caught on through word-of-mouth, attracted interest later from a legacy publisher, and then it was published traditionally, but those stories are rare. I've heard of some who do incredibly well who publish to Amazon/Kindle, etc. There are just so many options today and places to go; the market is so fragmented.

After having your own children, did fatherhood change and/or alter/influence your writing? Are they and your wife beta readers for your manuscripts these days?

Sure. I was writing well before I had kids and I have two in college now, but they were often excellent test audiences. I always read my first draft to them. They are great because they vote with their body language. You could always tell when they were bored, when they were interested, and those moments when you had them, as they would lean closer to me. When I would read aloud to them, I would make notes in the margin.

Reading your draft manuscript aloud sounds like another good tip for aspiring children's authors.

Definitely. When you read your stuff aloud you hear it and immediately know where it's sloppy or where the language is slack; it's a really good tool for editing and tightening.

For me, as a writer, reading is one of the best ways to improve and hone my skills. Do you agree? If so, do you read with an analytical mind, and who are some of your influences?

Reading. Oh yeah. Your style is inevitably influenced and tugged and pulled at by all the books you are reading. Early in my life—and throughout my life—I've learned tricks and techniques from other writers, and I steal techniques when I can. I'm now trying to read more non-fiction. As a fiction writer, I get way more ideas from nonfiction and way more stuff I can be inspired by. It's just another way to learn about the world in all its breadth and wonder. Reading about real things is more inspiring. That said, I still love fiction and I can always inhale a good story.

....

DAVID MCPHERSON is a Canadian writer and editor. As a freelance writer for the past 20 years, he's contributed to many publications, including *The National Post*, *Golf Canada*, *CAA Magazine*, *Hamilton Magazine*, PGATOUR.com, *Words + Music*, *Canadian Retailer*, and more. Reach him at david@mcphersoncommunications.com and follow him on Twitter (@mcphersoncomm).

....

DEBUT AUTHORS TELL ALL

Learn how first-time authors found success

·····

by Cris Freese

//

PICTURE BOOKS

Tara Luebbe and Becky Cattie

www.beckytarabooks.com; *I am Famous* (March 2018, Albert Whitman); *Shark Nate-O* (April 2018, Little Bee Books); Tracy Marchini, Bookends Literary

Quick Take: *I am Famous*—Kiely knows she is famous and the paparazzi (her parents) document her every move. It's exhausting being famous, but someone has to do it! Then she gets to be a headliner by singing at her grandfather's birthday. When both she and her performance fall flat, Kiely is worried she's lost her audience forever. But it turns out that no one is as loyal as the fans who love her.

Shark Nate-O—Nate loves sharks. He reads shark books every day, watches sharks on TV, and talks about them nonstop. He even likes to pretend he's a shark wherever he goes! However, there is one small problem . . . Nate can't swim. But with hard work and perseverance, Nate has a chance to get his bite back.

Writes From: Tara: Fort Mill, SC. Becky: Chicago, IL.

Pre-Book: Tara: I had worked in various areas of corporate retail and owned a toy and book store. Currently I just write. Becky: I was a casting producer for reality TV shows and am currently a recruiter for marketing and creative jobs.

Time Frame: I am Famous was a quick book for us and it was written and polished in two months. Shark Nate-O took about six months to get right.

Enter the Agent: Both of our book deals actually came via submissions from the 2015 Illinois Prairie Writers and Illustrators Day Conference. We had been querying agents at the time, so we doubled our efforts to get an agent onboard as soon as possible so he/she could guide us through the process. We connected with Tracy Marchini from Bookends literary and were thrilled when she agreed to take us as clients.

Biggest Surprise: We never could have imagined the number of people who have been helping us and supporting us through this. We were also surprised at how much better the artwork made our stories as our wonderful illustrators brought them to an entirely new level.

What We Did Right: We networked with other writers, joined SCBWI, found amazing critique partners, went to multiple conferences, and took advantage of every available critique and craft event. Because we were launching our first two books one month apart, we decided to put aside some advance money and hire an outside PR firm. This was a great investment and took some of the pressure off us.

What We Wish We Would Have Done Different: We made the rookie mistake of subbing a few manuscripts that were simply not ready. And we wish we had done more pre-launch things ahead of time, like having swag made, planning the launch parties, etc. The month leading up to launch was crazy, and if we'd taken care of some of the tasks a few months earlier, it would have reduced the stress. We also would have loved to have taken classes in Photoshop, web design, stand up comedy, and public speaking. Oh, and in elementary education and library science. And while we are at it, in publicity, video animation, marketing, door to door sales, tax accounting, and …

Platform: We are both on twitter (@T_luebbe) and (@b_cattie), and Facebook (beckytarabooks). We are new to Instagram and are trying to figure it out (taraluebbe and beckycattie). Our website is www.beckytarabooks.com. We also host a picture book mentoring program called Writing with the Stars, which provides free mentorships with published authors and illustrators.

Advice for Writers: Make sure your book has enough marketability to get through the acquisitions process, find critique partners and network with other writers, and last but not least, read in your genre obsessively.

Next Up: We have two more picture books coming out in 2019: a sequel to I am Famous titled I Used to Be Famous, also with Joanne Lew Vriethoff illustrating, and a book about a photobombing chameleon, Operation Photobomb. Both are with Albert Whitman. Conan the Librarian, about a mighty raider who becomes a mighty reader, will be published by Roaring Brook Press in 2020 and is illustrated by Victoria Maderna.

Aidan Cassie

aidancassie.com; *Sterling, Best Dog Ever* (July 2018, Farrar, Strauss and Giroux Books for Young Readers); Wendi Gu, Janklow & Nesbit Associates

Quick Take: When a homeless dog, Sterling, sees a sign on the side of the Butlery Cutlery Company advertising free shipping to homes around the world, he is determined to become the most terrific fork ever! Soon, he is delivered on time and undamaged to the Gilbert family's front door. Sterling is not what they ordered, but he may be exactly what they need.

Writes (and Illustrates) From: …from my artist studio, in the woods, on a small island in the Salish Sea, on Canada's west coast.

Pre-Book: For many years I was the Art Director for a giftware company where I designed and illustrated mass production knick-knacks (you know, snow-globes, hedgehog candle-holders and kitty-cat bookends). It wasn't meaningful work, but I loved illustrating all day for a steady salary, and I found visualizing and drawing characters in three-dimensions easy after getting my degree in animation.

Time Frame: The time between my last day job to my first book contract? Nine years! After doing giftware design, I had a baby, and when she became a preschooler I focused on building my art portfolio. At first I was just creating images, but I kept finding they were sequential. And then characters started growing their own narratives. Soon I was writing as well as drawing.

Sterling is only 375 words, but it took over four months of brooding, tweaking and rewriting. For me, half of that "rewriting" is actually redrawing; I rarely write without pictures, though I do sometimes write without words by sketching out a book dummy, the words only coming later.

Enter the Agent: I'd written a story the year before Sterling about a little raccoon and I'd sent it out to a handful of agents. It had a few agent nibbles, but no offers. When I was ready to submit Sterling I jumped into agent research as a full time job. I read oodles of agent interviews, used QueryTracker to prioritize the possibilities, and hunted for the agents of books I adored. Mike Curato's book,Little Elliot, Big City, had a tenderness that felt similar to my storytelling style. After researching his agent, Brenda Bowen at Sanford J. Greenburger Associates, I decided to query her first. A week later I heard back from her Assistant Literary Agent, Wendi Gu. She wrote to say that while Brenda wasn't able to take me on, she herself was just starting out and would love to represent me (with Brenda's blessing). Wendi was warm, passionate and communicative. I'd always thought having an experienced agent with an established reputation amongst editors would be a priority, but instead went with someone brand new and ambitious; someone who wanted me to do well as much as I did. With only a handful of other clients, she could put everything into helping edit my book, and pitched it to top publishers.

Biggest Surprise: I never dreamt I'd find the right agent on my first query. Luck is when opportunity meets hard work, but the serendipity of that connection changed the trajectory of my life. Going with my heart lead me to an agent who adores my work and brings that enthusiasm to editors. She sold my book within a couple of months, and two more of my books in the following year. When she changed agencies recently, I happily followed her to Janklow & Nesbit Associates.

What I Did Right: I had more than one manuscript ready when I first queried. And, later, I said yes to joining "Epic18", a group of other picture book authors (and illustrators) debuting in 2018. They established a website (epiceighteen.weebly.com), as well as a FB group where I've found an endless source of support. Publicly we celebrate each other's starred reviews, launches, book trailers, blog posts and giveaways. Privately we share our challenges, failures, wisdom, resources and guidance. Residing on an island means I'm physically isolated from the book world; these connections have been an unexpected joy and gift.

What I Wish I Would Have Done Different: Nothing jumps to mind, but I'm still months away from my first first book launch, so I expect I'll have plenty of blunders under my belt by the time my second book hits the shelves!

Platform: I imagine my Twitter following has been growing slow and steady because I'm in the fortunate position of being an illustrator as well as author. The artists of the #kidlitart community provide a visual feast in my feed.. I really should share more art on Instagram, but there are only so many hours in the day…

Advice for Writers: Find an agent who believes in your work and prioritizes you. Don't think you need the biggest name at an agency; find the one with whom your work will resonate the most. They will be your best champion.

Next Up: Like Sterling, that little raccoon story I mentioned also found a home with FSG. Juniper Makes it Big will be released in 2019, and a third book will follow.

Kerri Kokias

www.kerrikokias.com; *Snow Sisters!* illustrated by Teagan White(January 2018, Knopf Books for Young Readers); Sean McCarthy, Sean McCarthy Literary Agency.

Quick Take: Just like snowflakes, no two sisters are alike, but that doesn't mean they can't work together to make the perfect snow day!

Writes From: Seattle, Washington.

Pre-Book: I managed data collection for a social science research group with the School of Social Work at the University of Washington.

Time Frame: It took about a year and a half from when I started writing this manuscript till it sold, and another two and a half years until it was published.

Enter the Agent: I became friends with Tricia Lawrence through our local kid-lit community before she was an agent. Once she started representing authors on behalf of Erin Murphy Literary Agency I became one of her first picture books clients. She sold my first two books. I'm currently represented by Sean McCarthy of Sean McCarthy literary. I connected with Sean through the more traditional query route.

Biggest Surprise: The biggest and best surprise was seeing how Teagan White's illustrations brought Snow Sisters! to life.

What I Did Right: I connected with other writers through SCBWI and social media. Writing is so solitary, and publishing can have so many ups and downs, it's been sanity-saving to be part of a larger kid-lit community.

What I Wish I Would Have Done Different: I wish I would have learned how to revise earlier. Not just switch out a few words but really overhaul a story. I also wish I would have found a better balance between revising projects and creating new work earlier.

Platform: I can be found at www.kerrikokias.com or on Facebook, Twitter, or Instagram @kerrikokias.

Advice for Writers: Learn everything you can about the craft of writing but also be open to the other lessons this industry has to offer. Lessons on patience, perseverance, rejection and vulnerability, collaboration—did I mention patience and perseverance?

Next Up: I'm looking forward to my next picture book, Clever Hans: A Clever Horse Indeed, illustrated by Mike Lowery (G.P. Putnam's Sons, Summer 2020.)

Tina Cho

www.tinamcho.com; *Rice from Heaven: The Secret Mission to Feed North Koreans* (August 2018, Little Bee Books); Adria Goetz, Martin Literary Agency

Quick Take: Yoori, a South Korean girl, helps her father with a secret kindness mission to send rice in balloons over the border to impoverished families in North Korea, based on real events.

Writes From: Pyeongtaek, South Korea.

Pre-Book: I am an elementary teacher and have taught in the U.S. and now at an international school in South Korea. I also did freelance writing for educational and children's markets.

Time Frame: I wrote the first draft eight days after I participated in the rice balloon launch with a church group. That took only a day to write. However, almost a year later and 17 drafts, the book sold.

Enter the Agent: The short answer: Twitter. I simply responded to the tweet of another agent at the agency.

The long answer: I had submitted to many agents and was getting personal feedback, even had a personal phone call with one that didn't work out. Then you know that phrase, "when it rains, it pours"? Two agents had requested my manuscripts, and then I saw an interesting tweet from another agent I follow on Twitter. She announced there was a new agent at her agency, someone who would specialize in the Christian market. I started researching her. My stories weren't specifically written for the Christian market, but they could be tweaked to lean that way. I queried Adria with two stories I thought she'd like, one of which was Rice from Heaven. The next day she said to send them over. About three weeks later, she emailed saying she had read my stories that same day and hadn't been able to stop thinking about them. Then she asked for THE CALL. So that weekend after working out time zones in which to call, she offered representation. I signed the contract December 5th, 2017, after first querying her on October 30th. I'm so thankful to God for connecting Adria and me.

Biggest Surprise: My biggest surprise was receiving F&G's of my book the day before Valentine's Day. I was surprised my publisher mailed them to me in Korea! Another surprise is being included in this interview for Children's Writer's & Illustrator's Market!

What I Did Right: When I was told to make my manuscript more lyrical and dreamy, I sought the help of mentor texts and my three critique groups. The picture book that made the biggest impact was Jane Yolen's Owl Moon. I don't own it, so I listened to it on You Tube and wrote down every word. (Being in another country, I can't just check it out from my local library.) I studied it and her poetic techniques. I also made my own How to Write a Lyrical Picture Book 101 by studying blog posts from other authors and ReFoReMo (Reading for Research Month). You can read my long post about that here: https://groggorg.blogspot.kr/2017/06/how-to-write-lyrical-picture-book-self.html

Other things that helped me on my journey were being a part of SCBWI, Julie Hedlund's 12x12 for a couple years, taking picture book classes, attending webinars, participating in critique groups, and participating in the online kidlit community on Facebook.

Platform: I'm on Facebook daily and involved in many kidlit groups. I participate with Twitter & Pinterest weekly, and I'm slowly learning how to use Instagram for writers.

Advice for Writers: Be involved in critique groups and in the online kidlit community. You learn so much from each other. Reading blogs and articles is giving yourself a mini writing course. Take time to learn the craft of writing well. Revise, revise, and revise some more. Save money to take courses or to pay for critiques from editors. It's worth it to experience their expertise. Lastly, be patient. The writing journey is long and slow.

Next Up: Korean Celebrations, a nonfiction picture book about Korean holidays, will be published by Tuttle Fall 2018. I also have another picture book scheduled for January 2020, which hasn't been announced yet. Currently, my work-in-progress involves other picture books with Korean themes: Korean granny divers called haenyeo, a Korean princess, and a MG novel about North Korean escapees.

Jeanette Bradley

www.jeanettebradley.com; *Love, Mama* (January 2018, Roaring Brook); Emily Mitchell, Wernick & Pratt

Quick Take: When Mama goes on a trip, her baby penguin Kipling knows she'll return home soon—yet he still can't help but miss her. After all, Pillow Mama won't read, Picture Mama won't laugh, and Snow Mama is too cold to cuddle. But when Kipling receives a special delivery from Mama, he knows that no matter where she is, he is always loved.

Writes From: Rhode Island.

Pre-Book: I've always written and drawn pictures, from the time I could hold a crayon. I started out my professional life as an urban planner, and then became a health writer before I finally took the leap into writing and illustrating for kids.

Time Frame: It took about two years of writing and illustrating, plus time for editing and revisions.

Enter the Agent: I don't have a dramatic story. I slush-queried. But first, I spent a lot of time researching agents, and then I queried ones I thought were a good fit for my work. I sent out about 20 queries and got two offers of representation. I chose Emily Mitchell because she had more experience, but also because our first phone call made me think new thoughts, and I am always in favor of that.

Biggest Surprise: Many people cry when they read Love, Mama. Sometimes, people will share with me their own stories of missing a parent (or a child), and I'm always surprised by how deeply moving this is for me.

In the movie Shadowlands, C.S. Lewis says: "We read to know we are not alone." That quote resonated with me when I saw the movie, and has stuck with me.* I've discovered that writing this particular book was the equivalent of throwing thousands of bottles into the ocean with messages reading: "You are not alone." Occasionally, a reader sends a bottle back. Love, Mama is a book about love connecting two people across time and distance, so it seems fitting that it sparks strangers to connect with shared stories.

*It turns out the 1999 film Shadowlands invented this quote of CS Lewis. It's still a great quote, but Lewis didn't say it.

What I Did Right: I joined a debut author/illustrator group (Epic Eighteen). I have learned so much from the other members. We support each other's launches, take turns blogging on our group blog, and share cover reveals and book birthdays on social media. The other writers and illustrators have become friends, as we go through this bumpy ride of seeing our debuts into the world together.

What I Wish I Would Have Done Different: I really knew nothing about the business and marketing side of publishing before my book was released. I wish I had found a mentor prior to publication. I still have so much to learn!

Platform: I have a website, Facebook, Twitter (@jeanettebradley), and Instagram(@ jea_bradley). I also guest blog on other people's sites.

For the release of Love, Mama—which includes love notes sent from mother to child and back again—I shared a series of my own lunchbox love notes to my little ones on Instagram, using the hashtag #100daysofmamalove. My goal was to reach out beyond my usual bookish network and connect with preschool and kindergarten teachers and parents of young children. As a grassroots marketing campaign, it was fairly successful. I got enough interest from parenting Instagram that I started to receive requests to review baby products.

Advice for Writers: Read a lot of recently published books in your genre. It's impossible to read them all, but set reading goals,for yourself and try to read new books consistently.

With picture books in particular, typing out other people's books in manuscript form can help you to get a sense of the pacing of this highly constrained format.

Next Up: I have several picture books in the pipeline, but no announcements to share yet. I'll keep you posted!

Baptiste Paul

baptistepaul.net; *The Field* (March 2018, North-South Books); Karen Grencik, Red Fox Literary

Quick Take: The Field is a picture book about a pickup soccer (futbol) game and the joy of playing outside, even if things threaten to disrupt your game. Play on!

Writes From: I write from anywhere. I juggle many schedules. With children, there are always many distractions. Sometimes, I write in my basement. If you're a parent or someone who still works a full-time job, don't make excuses—I am proof it can be done. Learn to be flexible.

Pre-Book: I have worked many jobs—blasting rocks in a quarry, volunteering with homeless populations and children who were orphaned, in a college office, and, currently, retail management.

Time Frame: It took me over two years to write The Field. I kept revising it over and over again. The aha moment was making the connection that the story was not complete without adding the Creole words—Creole is my first language; I'm from the island of St. Lucia.

Enter the Agent: My wife, and picture book author, Miranda Paul was already being represented by the agent and since I was working on writing books together with her (in addition to my own books) I emailed Karen and asked her to represent me as well. Thankfully, she said yes.

Biggest Surprise: I was surprised to learn how small and interconnected the kidlit community is, at least in the United States. My wife and I live in Northeastern Wisconsin, which is far from the industry hotspots. Up here, we read lots of books by big-name authors, and imagine them to be larger than life. Then, lo and behold, we meet them at book signing events or dinners and have become friends with many people we admire. Sometimes, our kids play together. The authors and illustrators are mostly ordinary people like us, which shouldn't be a surprise, but it still is. A good surprise.

What I Did Right: I think I did a few things right—and I'm humbled that the book has already received three starred reviews (Horn Book, Kirkus, Booklist). One of the most significant things I did right, so to speak, was learn how to handle rejections and write about what I know.

What I Wish I Would Have Done Different: Absolutely nothing. I like how my life and the events in it have brought me to this point. I can be very thoughtful in my career choices as a writer.

Platform: I don't really think about platform. It's probably awful to admit that. Sure, I'm on some social media but there's not a regular method to this madness other than keep writing my next book(s). If I have a platform it's pretty much my pencil and a memo book. These are the tools I use regularly to write my thoughts, which turn into books.

Advice for Writers: Write what you know. Be visible and attend conferences. Volunteer within your local SCBWI chapters.

Next Up: I am super excited about two new books co-written with my wife, Miranda Paul. Adventures To School: Real-Life Journeys of Students from Around the World releases May 1, 2018 from little bee books (a division of Bonnier). This book features stories from thirteen countries around the world and chronicles some of the world's most extraordinary student treks to school. I Am Farmer (Millbrook/Lerner, February 2019) is a nonfiction picture book biography of Tantoh Nforba, an environmentalist from Cameroon who is cultivating an organic farming movement in addition to bringing clean, sustainable water to villages in need. The book will shine a spotlight on his good work and tour proceeds will benefit the Save Your Future Association (syfaglobal.org). These are both books I feel very proud to have worked on, and they shed light on important subjects.

MIDDLE-GRADE

Jonathan Roth

www.beepandbob.com; *Beep and Bob 1: Too Much Space!*; *Beep and Bob 2: Party Crashers* (March 2018, Aladdin); Natalie Lakosil, Bradford Literary Agency

Quick Take: Beep and Bob is a humorous and action-packed chapter book series about the new kid at space school (who's scared of space!) and the devoted little alien who won't leave his side.

Writes From: Rockville, MD

Pre-Book: By day I teach elementary art in a Maryland public school to more than 600 enthusiastic young artists a week. I've been published as a cartoonist before, but this is my first book series for kids.

Time Frame: I know the initial first draft of book one came quickly, taking about a month in 2015. But it's easy to lose track after that, given all the subsequent drafts and edits, as well more months for the rough and final illustrations, which I also do. Also, since Beep and Bob is a series, at any given point I find myself working on the words, pictures and/or edits of two or more books at the same time.

Enter the Agent: I queried my agent, Natalie Lakosil of Bradford Literary, with a middle grade novel, which she enthusiastically requested and then…rejected. But I still had a good feeling about her, and the following year I sent her my manuscript for the first Beep and Bob. After a little reworking, she took me on and sold it quickly in a four book deal. Moral of the story: don't take rejection personally by assuming they are rejecting you; some author-agent courtships take many projects and/or years.

Biggest Surprise: The industry standard, for some reason, is that most books are released on a Tuesday. And on the Tuesday when mine came out, I was a little shocked that no angels flew from the sky and no holiday was declared, and it was about as normal a Tuesday as a Tuesday can get. That's my long way of saying, yes, I may now have books in the world, but to my surprise most of existence goes on pretty much the same.

What I Did Right: I persevered. Which wasn't always easy, because my path to publication was long. I always try, though, to keep moving forward, because the road behind can quickly get littered with rejected projects and broken hopes, and it's crucial to be able to let them go. I also joined SCBWI early on, and they've been an amazing resource. And I somehow lucked out by getting involved with some super supportive and honest critique partners.

What I Wish I Would Have Done Different: I wish I would have written Diary of a Wimpy Kid before Jeff Kinney did. I was on the verge, really, same title and all. But I'll settle for my series, which I think can be pretty funny, too.

Platform: Though I'm on Facebook (and very occasionally Twitter) I put most of my networking energy into making connections with fellow teachers, writers and illustrators through events such as conferences, literary events and social gatherings. School visits are also very important to me, because I can connect with kids directly (6-9 year olds aren't on social media the way teens are). I also have a pretty sporky website (sporky=cool in Bob speak).

Advice for Writers: Many writers I meet get crippled by the messages coming out of the ether that proclaim rhyming picture books are a tough sell this year, as are dystopian tales, as are (insert just about any genre here). And so they veer from what they really love to write to chase some illusive trend or style, and then end up creating something that's been done and done better. My advice: it's all a tough sell, so please, please be true to your own vision and voice, and write the stories in your heart that only you can tell.

Next Up: Beep and Bob's ongoing mission, to boldly go where no kids' books have gone before, continue with book 3: Take Us To Your Sugar (Fall 2018) and book 4: Double Trouble (Spring 2019).

Leslie C. Youngblood

www.lesliecyoungblood.com; *Love Like Sky* (November 2018, Disney Hyperion); John Rudolph, Dystel, Goderich & Bourret

Quick Take: Meet eleven-year-old Georgie Matthews! Her little sister, Peaches, gets sick—really sick. Suddenly, Mama and Daddy are arguing like they were before the divorce, and even the doctors at the hospital don't know how to help Peaches get better. It's up to Georgie to set things right.

Writes From: The home of ALL four seasons and a thriving literary community—Rochester, NY. Raised here since I was about six years old. I've lived in Atlanta, Georgia; Greensboro, NC; Starkville, MS; Ghana, West Africa; and Jefferson City, MO. I landed my deal with Disney-Hyperion two years after moving back to Rochester. So it's good to be home.

Pre-Book: Everything from a foot messenger (yes, foot messenger), Walmart stockperson, column writer, to an assistant professor.

Time Frame: About a year and a half, for Love Like Sky. Clock still ticking on the novels on my hard drive.

Enter the Agent: Tayari Jones (American Marriage) was generous and referred me to her agent, Jane Dystel. Jane didn't think that the genre fiction I initially submitted was quite ready (she rejected it), but she gave me the opening to resubmit another work. Immediately, I submitted Love Like Sky. She passed it to John Rudolph!

Biggest Surprise: Probably that Love Like Sky is under the iconic Disney umbrella. And Disney-Hyperion found the perfect illustrator for my work, Vashti Harrison. And how much my editor, Laura Schreiber, loved my work.

What I Did Right: The conversation where my protagonist, Georgie, talks to her baby sister, Peaches, about the infinite nature of love are the least edited pages in the entire novel. I believe that the spirit of my late brother, Sammy, helped me. It was one of those rare writing moments where you say, "Wow! That's good." After I finished the passage, I pulled the title Love Like Sky from the dialogue.

What I Wish I Would Have Done Different: To change one thing would probably cause a domino effect so I wouldn't change a thing about Love Like Sky. Now, as for some other writing trials, like not knowing when to step away from a work and let it breathe, how much time you got?

Platform: I connect with readers looking for the essence of Black Girl Magic in the pages of books. Facebook is still my most comfortable platform. The relationships there are long-standing and nurturing. Twitter is a little more daunting, but followers are more interested in your brand than your personal life, which is different from Facebook. No post on Twitter about my dinner the night before. I try not to beat anyone over the head with my book and tweet about all the talented writers out there.

Advice for Writers: Read. Read. Read. It's always wise to invest in your craft with writing conferences, workshops and such. For those interested in children's literature, Kweli's Color of Children's Literature Conference was invaluable to me. It's a good idea to enter contest whenever possible. Oh, if you're going to use beta readers, go for critical readers, not just your best friend.

Next Up: Working on what is fondly known as "The Bogalusa Book." It's set in Bogalusa, Louisiana. Since I'm not big on outlines (Someone referred to me as a "pantser"), that's pretty much all I know for sure. The real title, like most titles I love, will be lifted from dialogue, which just hasn't happened yet. When it does, I'll know. And with this series, I believe there will be a Book III. My characters still have lots to say. I'm going to do my best to ensure they are heard.

Tami Charles

www.tamiwrites.com; *Like Vanessa* (March 2018, Charlesbridge); Lara Perkins, Andrea Brown Literary Agency

Quick Take: It only took 50 years for a woman of color to be crowned Miss America. Once 13-year-old Vanessa Martin witnesses this historic moment on television, there's no turning back. Vanessa will do what it takes to have her moment in the spotlight, even though her father and classmates think she doesn't stand a chance.

Writes From: New Jersey.

Pre-Book: For fourteen years, I taught third and fifth grades. I absolutely loved my students! They were the ones who gave me the green light to follow my author dreams.

Time Frame: The idea came to me in 2012. I didn't set out to fully write it until Nanowrimo, 2013. I revised through the spring and began the agent search in June of 2014. After years of rejections (for previous projects), I finally got my yes!

Enter the Agent: I found Lara Perkins the old fashioned way: I queried her. Once I received her email asking for "a call," I knew I was on to something!

Biggest Surprise: Publishing is soooooo slow. I didn't know this until I was in the thick of it. I can appreciate why, now that I am experiencing the inner workings of the industry. Another big surprise was the amount of editing involved. I'm pretty sure I revised Like Vanessa a good 62 times! Even that number feels low.

What I Did Right: This may sound cliché, but I didn't give up. I found a strength I didn't know I possessed and for that, I am thankful. The author journey will make you thick-skinned in the best ways possible.

What I Wish I Would Have Done Different: Actually, there's nothing I would've done differently. I wholeheartedly believe that I, like most writers, was meant to experience every emotion that comes with this process: the rejections, the crippling self-doubt, the pride and joy that fills you up. I'm thankful for all of it.

Platform: My favorites are Twitter (@TamiWritesStuff) and Instagram (@tamiwrites). I mostly post about bookish events, the highs (and sometimes lows) of the writing process, and funny memes, of course. I could use some more friends. Follow me on this crazy ride!

Advice for Writers: Blinders on. Don't worry about what other writers are doing. This isn't to be taken in a competitive sense because I can honestly say that the writing community has been beyond welcoming and kind. However, if you spend your time comparing your success to others, then you won't appreciate your self-worth. Success comes in all colors and packages. Celebrate yours every step of the way!

Next Up: I have a few irons in the fire! Middle grade: Definitely Daphne (Capstone, October 2018). Picture book: Freedom Soup (Candlewick, September 2019). Young adult: Becoming Beatriz (Charlesbridge, August 2019).

YOUNG ADULT

Dana L. Davis

www.DanaLDavis.com; *Tiffany Sly Lives Here Now* (May 2018, HarlequinTEEN); Uwe Stender, TriadaUS

Quick Take: After watching her mom lose a battle with cancer Tiffany is moving from Chicago to Los Angeles to live with a father she's never met before. But the day before she's set to leave, another man shows up claiming he is Tiffany's father and she has seven days before she's required to submit to court ordered paternity testing. Now Tiffany is living with a new family, and only she knows they may not be her real family.

Writes From: I currently live in Los Angeles.

Pre-Book: I'm an actress! I guess you could say that's my day job since I still do it. I voice Kelly on Star Vs. The Forces of Evil and Kit on Craig of the Creek and more to come that I can't talk about yet. My most recent on-camera was a guest spot on Fox's new hit series 911 that stars Angela Bassett.

Time Frame: It took me about a year to write Tiffany Sly Lives Here Now. But the book was completely rewritten during the submission process. So in total, it took me about a year and a half.

Enter the Agent: I wrote a fun middle grade four years ago about a little girl who fell into a magical world. I submitted that book all over and got a few responses from interested agents. Uwe at Triada US was the most passionate about my work and writing and so I signed with him! We never sold that book but Uwe has been so wonderful in helping me and guiding me as a writer. I would not be where I am today without his devotion. He is a wonderful agent who truly loves all his clients.

Biggest Surprise: I think what surprised me the most is how slow publishing is. When I sold Tiffany it was November of 2016. And now, almost two years later, the book is finally coming out!

What I Did Right: I listen! When we first put Tiffany on submission a few editors asked for changes. Rather than turn my nose in the air and act like those editors were mental…I actually took their advice! We took the book off submission and I re-wrote the entire manuscript. If my agents give me advice I generally take it to heart. If my editor makes a suggestion I consider it. I think listening and trusting those who support you makes a huge difference in your final product.

What I Wish I Would Have Done Different: I wish I would've started writing earlier! I spent so much time in my 20s watching TV, playing video games and basically wasting time. Ha! Becoming a great writer takes time and effort. The sooner you can start honing your craft the better.

Platform: I'm really passionate about writing people of color that are not stereotypes and creating stories where race is not an issue. Tiffany Sly is for anyone who can relate to tackling life after trauma and anyone who can relate to finding the light when everything seems so dark. My books are about healing, hope, love and laughter.

Advice for Writers: Read! It's the best way to become better at what you do. Take advice from people you trust. Never think your final product isn't capable of becoming something better. Always be open to revisions.

Next Up: The Voice In My Head! Coming from HarlequinTEEN next spring! It's about a girl named Indigo Phillips who thinks she may be hearing the voice of God. And the voice guides her and her family on a wild and crazy road trip to save her ailing twin sister. But is she really hearing the actual voice of God? I guess you'll have to read the book to find out!

Kelly deVos

http://www.kellydevos.us; *Fat Girl on a Plane* (June 2018, Harlequin Teen); Kathleen Rushall, Andrea Brown Literary Agency

Quick Take: Fat Girl on a Plane is the story of high school senior, Cookie Vonn, who wants to be the next great American designer but feels that the fashion industry won't accept her unless she loses weight. The book follows her across two timelines, before and after the major weight loss she falsely believes will solve all her problems. It's about the disparity between how society treats thin and fat people, and how to learn to love yourself in spite of all that.

Writes From: Gilbert, Arizona.

Pre-Book: I was originally a creative writing major in college, but later switched to graphic design because I became convinced that I wouldn't succeed as a writer. I've been lucky to have an awesome career as a graphic designer in the professional beauty industry and, for a time, in the fashion industry. But I always had a bit of a sense of being unfilled and I did regret that I didn't stick with my original plan of study. When I made the decision to get serious about writing again, I went back to school and finished my creative writing degree.

Time Frame: I wrote the first draft in about six months and then spent a couple of months revising with critique partners. I did one more round of revisions with my agent that took about a month Then I revised a bit more extensively with my editor once the book was acquired. I should add though that Fat Girl is my second book. I revised and revised and revised my first novel for two years before ultimately shelving it. When I finally started something new, my process had improved quite a bit.

Enter the Agent: My agent really intimidated me, so I really didn't think of querying her. Instead, I entered an online pitch contest and received a request from another agent at the same agency. That particular agent was really supportive of my work but didn't feel it was right for her list. I was really lucky that she passed my manuscript to Kathleen and that this led to an offer of representation.

Biggest Surprise: My biggest surprise has probably been how important, and sometimes difficult, it can be to find and develop relationships with critique partners. I always assumed that anyone with a background in creative writing could give feedback on a piece of work. To a certain extent that's true. But being critique partners is a much more complicated relationship. The two people need to have a good working knowledge each other's categories and genres and have a similar communication style. Otherwise, it can be too difficult to give and receive helpful feedback. A friend of mine compares finding the right critique partner to dating. There has to be a real rapport between the two partners.

What I Did Right: I built up an incredible support network of real-life friends and online friends such that I feel so well supported through this process. Through in-person meet ups, online contests and social media groups, I've been able to connect with so many talented writers. A lot of people comment that publishing moves very slowly, and that is definitely true. The waiting is hard, but what makes it bearable, and often fun, is being surrounded by such incredible people all the time and having early access to many of the best books being printed today.

What I Wish I Would Have Done Different: I think I made every possible mistake when I was getting started with querying agents, so I have a lot of material to pull from here. I guess wish I would have set aside my first book earlier than I did. I think it's possible, as a writer, to have a big idea that you just can't execute. I feel like where I continue to improve is in recognizing when something isn't working and moving on. I've seen Beth Revis talk about her "practice novels" and that idea really inspires me. As much as I'm sometimes frustrated with the idea of working on things that don't come to fruition, for me, I feel it's healthy to accept that some writing is just about becoming a better writer.

Platform: I'm starting to develop a real love of Instagram. Book cover design has reached a point where it is typically so good that I find myself really enjoying taking Bookstagram pics. I'm also on Twitter quite a bit and I love to meet other authors there.

Advice for Writers: My best piece of advice is to keep going. Keep going forward. Keep reading new things. Keep writing new things. Network with your peers. Make the most of all the resources for writers that are out there, some of which are free. Try not to get stuck on one idea or one way of doing things. And try, as best you can, to keep your love of storytelling alive. Most of us are writers because we fell in love with stories at a young age and I think it's so important to nurture that love. It's the love of the craft that sustains us when things are difficult.

Next Up: I'm really interested in female heroines who are trying to succeed in fields traditionally dominated by men, so I'm excited about my upcoming duology of YA political thrillers. The first book, The Survival Code, which follows a teen coder whose Doomsday-prepper father is accused of triggering a political crisis, will be published in 2019 by Harlequin Teen.

Katie Henry

katiehenrywrites.com; *Heretics Anonymous* (August 2018, Katherine Tegen Books); Sarah LaPolla, Bradford Literary Agency

Quick Take: When nonbeliever Michael transfers to a Catholic school in eleventh grade, he quickly connects with a secret support group. He and the rest of this band of misfits set out to challenge their school's hypocrisies, only to find their friendships--and their own beliefs tested.

Writes From: New York City.

Pre-Book: I got my undergrad degree in playwriting, which might not be the absolute least practical degree in the world, but it's close. I loved it. Post college, I worked in higher education administration and as a college admissions essay consultant, helping young adults tell their own stories.

Time Frame: The very first draft of Heretics Anonymous took me about four years to complete. At the time, I thought I was just a hopelessly slow writer. Looking back on it, it took exactly as long as it needed to. I wasn't the same person at 26 that I was at 22. I needed those years to grow up, have new experiences, and see the world in a different way.

Enter the Agent: Early on in my drafting process, I was lucky enough to take an in-person writing class with the brilliant Sarah LaPolla. She saw Heretics Anonymous in its earliest, messiest, most plotless incarnation. But she also saw the book it could be, long before I did. When I was finally (finally) done with my first draft, I queried her and was thrilled when she offered representation.

Biggest Surprise: How hard it is to let your book go into the world! Many authors talk about their "book babies," and there's a lot of truth in that. You've spent years nurturing this book, pouring love, sweat, and tears into it. But as soon as the first advanced reader copies are sent out, it doesn't just belong to you, anymore. It belongs to readers. And here's the big difference between book babies and real babies: it is considered socially unacceptable to write negative reviews of human children.

What I Did Right: I was open to editorial changes from my equally insightful and smart editor and agent. Coming from a theatre background, I knew embracing collaboration makes for better art, and their suggestions helped me create a better book. But I did stick to my guns on what really mattered to me. In the end, it's the author's name on the cover and no one else's. Publishing is a group effort, for sure, and that's an excellent thing. But your book is always going to be your book, and you have to be comfortable with the finished product. I incorporated as much advice and editorial direction as I possibly could, but I made sure it was still the book I wanted it to be.

What I Wish I Would Have Done Different: I wish I'd written more during slow times, definitely. There's a lot of waiting in publishing--that was another surprise--and the conventional wisdom is that while you wait for agents to respond to your query, or editors to read your manuscript, or for copy edits to come back in, you work on your next project. That's excellent advice I ignored in favor of refreshing my inbox every ten seconds. I don't recommend this approach. Keep writing!

Platform: Twitter is my main platform. I used to think I was terrible at tweeting, but then they raised the character limit from 140 to 280, and I realized I was just terrible at being succinct. I like Twitter because you can easily connect with so many other authors of so many genres, and also because I once achieved brief viral fame from a joke about a demon squirrel. That just doesn't happen on Instagram.

Advice for Writers: Find your people. Whether that means taking classes, forming your own local writers group, or just chatting with fellow authors on the social media platform of your choice, finding people who understand what you're going through is invaluable. One of the best parts of my debut experience has been the friends I've made. And I wish I'd been more involved in the writing community before I got my book deal. No matter where you are in the process of writing a novel, it can feel so confusing and isolating. Of course, you can (and should!) still lean on your family, friends, and ever-patient houseplants, but writer pals are a great source of support. I don't know what I'd do without mine.

Next Up: My second YA contemporary novel will release from Katherine Tegen Books in 2019. The title and release date are still secret, but I can tell you I'm working on it like there's no tomorrow.

Cris Freese is a former editor of *Children's Writer's & Illustrator's Market*, a freelance writer, and literary intern with Corvisiero Literary. Follow him on Twitter @crisfreese.

BLOGGING BASICS

by Robert Lee Brewer

In these days of publishing and media change, writers have to build platforms and learn how to connect to audiences if they want to improve their chances of publication and overall success. There are many methods of audience connection available to writers, but one of the most important is through blogging.

Since I've spent several years successfully blogging—both personally and professionally—I figure I've got a few nuggets of wisdom to pass on to writers who are curious about blogging or who already are.

Here's my quick list of tips:

1. **START BLOGGING TODAY.** If you don't have a blog, use Blogger, WordPress, or some other blogging software to start your blog today. It's free, and you can start off with your very personal "Here I am, world" post.
2. **START SMALL.** Blogs are essentially simple, but they can get complicated (for people who like complications). However, I advise bloggers start small and evolve over time.
3. **USE YOUR NAME IN YOUR URL.** This will make it easier for search engines to find you when your audience eventually starts seeking you out by name. For instance, my url is http://robertleebrewer.blogspot.com. If you try Googling "Robert Lee Brewer," you'll notice that My Name Is Not Bob is one of the top five search results (behind my other blog: Poetic Asides).
4. **UNLESS YOU HAVE A REASON, USE YOUR NAME AS THE TITLE OF YOUR BLOG.** Again, this helps with search engine results. My Poetic Asides blog includes my name in the title, and it ranks higher than My Name Is Not Bob. However, I felt the play on my name was worth the trade off.
5. **FIGURE OUT YOUR BLOGGING GOALS.** You should return to this step every couple months, because it's natural for your blogging goals to evolve over time. Initially,

your blogging goals may be to make a post a week about what you have written, submitted, etc. Over time, you may incorporate guests posts, contests, tips, etc.

6. **BE YOURSELF.** I'm a big supporter of the idea that your image should match your identity. It gets too confusing trying to maintain a million personas. Know who you are and be that on your blog, whether that means you're sincere, funny, sarcastic, etc.

7. **POST AT LEAST ONCE A WEEK.** This is for starters. Eventually, you may find it better to post once a day or multiple times per day. But remember: Start small and evolve over time.

8. **POST RELEVANT CONTENT.** This means that you post things that your readers might actually care to know.

9. **USEFUL AND HELPFUL POSTS WILL ATTRACT MORE VISITORS.** Talking about yourself is all fine and great. I do it myself. But if you share truly helpful advice, your readers will share it with others, and visitors will find you on search engines.

10. **TITLE YOUR POSTS IN A WAY THAT GETS YOU FOUND IN SEARCH ENGINES.** The more specific you can get the better. For instance, the title "Blogging Tips" will most likely get lost in search results. However, the title "Blogging Tips for Writers" specifies which audience I'm targeting and increases the chances of being found on the first page of search results.

11. **LINK TO POSTS IN OTHER MEDIA.** If you have an e-mail newsletter, link to your blog posts in your newsletter. If you have social media accounts, link to your blog posts there. If you have a helpful post, link to it in relevant forums and on message boards.

12. **WRITE WELL, BUT BE CONCISE.** At the end of the day, you're writing blog posts, not literary manifestos. Don't spend a week writing each post. Try to keep it to an hour or two tops and then post. Make sure your spelling and grammar are good, but don't stress yourself out too much.

13. **FIND LIKE-MINDED BLOGGERS.** Comment on their blogs regularly and link to them from yours. Eventually, they may do the same. Keep in mind that blogging is a form of social media, so the more you communicate with your peers the more you'll get out of the process.

14. **RESPOND TO COMMENTS ON YOUR BLOG.** Even if it's just a simple "Thanks," respond to your readers if they comment on your blog. After all, you want your readers to be engaged with your blog, and you want them to know that you care they took time to comment.

15. **EXPERIMENT.** Start small, but don't get complacent. Every so often, try something new. For instance, the biggest draw to my Poetic Asides blog are the poetry prompts and challenges I issue to poets. Initially, that was an experiment—one that worked very well. I've tried other experiments that haven't panned out, and that's fine. It's all part of a process.

SEO TIPS FOR WRITERS

Most writers may already know what SEO is. If not, SEO stands for *search engine optimization*. Basically, a site or blog that practices good SEO habits should improve its rankings in search engines, such as Google and Bing. Most huge corporations have realized the importance of SEO and spend enormous sums of time, energy and money on perfecting their SEO practices. However, writers can improve their SEO without going to those same extremes.

In this section, I will use the terms of *site pages* and *blog posts* interchangeably. In both cases, you should be practicing the same SEO strategies (when it makes sense).

Here are my top tips on ways to improve your SEO starting today:

16. **USE APPROPRIATE KEYWORDS.** Make sure that your page displays your main keyword(s) in the page title, content, URL, title tags, page header, image names and tags (if you're including images). All of this is easy to do, but if you feel overwhelmed, just remember to use your keyword(s) in your page title and content (especially in the first and last 50 words of your page).

17. **USE KEYWORDS NATURALLY.** Don't kill your content and make yourself look like a spammer to search engines by overloading your page with your keyword(s). You don't get SEO points for quantity but for quality. Plus, one of the main ways to improve your page rankings is when you...

18. **DELIVER QUALITY CONTENT.** The best way to improve your SEO is by providing content that readers want to share with others by linking to your pages. Some of the top results in search engines can be years old, because the content is so good that people keep coming back. So, incorporate your keywords in a smart way, but make sure it works organically with your content.

19. **UPDATE CONTENT REGULARLY.** If your site looks dead to visitors, then it'll appear that way to search engines too. So update your content regularly. This should be very easy for writers who have blogs. For writers who have sites, incorporate your blog into your site. This will make it easier for visitors to find your blog to discover more about you on your site (through your site navigation tools).

20. **LINK BACK TO YOUR OWN CONTENT.** If I have a post on Blogging Tips for Writers, for instance, I'll link back to it if I have a Platform Building post, because the two complement each other. This also helps clicks on my blog, which helps SEO. The one caveat is that you don't go crazy with your linking and that you make sure your links are relevant. Otherwise, you'll kill your traffic, which is not good for your page rankings.

21. **LINK TO OTHERS YOU CONSIDER HELPFUL.** Back in 2000, I remember being ordered by my boss at the time (who didn't last too much longer afterward) to ignore any competitive or complementary websites—no matter how helpful their content— because they were our competitors. You can try basing your online strategy on these

principles, but I'm nearly 100 percent confident you'll fail. It's helpful for other sites and your own to link to other great resources. I shine a light on others to help them out (if I find their content truly helpful) in the hopes that they'll do the same if ever they find my content truly helpful for their audience.

22. **GET SPECIFIC WITH YOUR HEADLINES.** If you interview someone on your blog, don't title your post with an interesting quotation. While that strategy may help get readers in the print world, it doesn't help with SEO at all. Instead, title your post as "Interview With (insert name here)." If you have a way to identify the person further, include that in the title too. For instance, when I interview poets on my Poetic Asides blog, I'll title those posts like this: Interview With Poet Erika Meitner. Erika's name is a keyword, but so are the terms *poet* and *interview*.

23. **USE IMAGES.** Many expert sources state that the use of images can improve SEO, because it shows search engines that the person creating the page is spending a little extra time and effort on the page than a common spammer. However, I'd caution anyone using images to make sure those images are somehow complementary to the content. Don't just throw up a lot of images that have no relevance to anything. At the same time...

24. **OPTIMIZE IMAGES THROUGH STRATEGIC LABELING.** Writers can do this by making sure the image file is labeled using your keyword(s) for the post. Using the Erika Meitner example above (which does include images), I would label the file "Erika Meitner headshot.jpg"—or whatever the image file type happens to be. Writers can also improve image SEO through the use of captions and ALT tagging. Of course, at the same time, writers should always ask themselves if it's worth going through all that trouble for each image or not. Each writer has to answer that question for him (or her) self.

25. **USE YOUR SOCIAL MEDIA PLATFORM TO SPREAD THE WORD.** Whenever you do something new on your site or blog, you should share that information on your other social media sites, such as Twitter, Facebook, LinkedIn, online forums, etc. This lets your social media connections know that something new is on your site/blog. If it's relevant and/or valuable, they'll let others know. And that's a great way to build your SEO.

Programmers and marketers could get even more involved in the dynamics of SEO optimization, but I think these tips will help most writers out immediately and effectively while still allowing plenty of time and energy for the actual work of writing.

BLOG DESIGN TIPS FOR WRITERS

Design is an important element to any blog's success. But how can you improve your blog's design if you're not a designer? I'm just an editor with an English Lit degree and no formal training in design. However, I've worked in media for more than a decade now and can share some very fundamental and easy tricks to improve the design of your blog.

Here are my seven blog design tips for writers:

26. **USE LISTS.** Whether they're numbered or bullet points, use lists when possible. Lists break up the text and make it easy for readers to follow what you're blogging.
27. **BOLD MAIN POINTS IN LISTS.** Again, this helps break up the text while also highlighting the important points of your post.
28. **USE HEADINGS.** If your posts are longer than 300 words and you don't use lists, then please break up the text by using basic headings.
29. **USE A READABLE FONT.** Avoid using fonts that are too large or too small. Avoid using cursive or weird fonts. Times New Roman or Arial works, but if you want to get "creative," use something similar to those.
30. **LEFT ALIGN.** English-speaking readers are trained to read left to right. If you want to make your blog easier to read, avoid centering or right aligning your text (unless you're purposefully calling out the text).
31. **USE SMALL PARAGRAPHS.** A good rule of thumb is to try and avoid paragraphs that drone on longer than five sentences. I usually try to keep paragraphs to around three sentences myself.
32. **ADD RELEVANT IMAGES.** Personally, I shy away from using too many images. My reason is that I only like to use them if they're relevant. However, images are very powerful on blogs, so please use them—just make sure they're relevant to your blog post.

If you're already doing everything on my list, keep it up! If you're not, then you might want to re-think your design strategy on your blog. Simply adding a header here and a list there can easily improve the design of a blog post.

GUEST POSTING TIPS FOR WRITERS

Recently, I've broken into guest posting as both a guest poster and as a host of guest posts (over at my Poetic Asides blog). So far, I'm pretty pleased with both sides of the guest posting process. As a writer, it gives me access to an engaged audience I may not usually reach. As a blogger, it provides me with fresh and valuable content I don't have to create. Guest blogging is a rare win-win scenario.

That said, writers could benefit from a few tips on the process of guest posting:

33. **PITCH GUEST POSTS LIKE ONE WOULD PITCH ARTICLES TO A MAGAZINE.** Include what your hook is for the post, what you plan to cover, and a little about who you are. Remember: Your post should somehow benefit the audience of the blog you'd like to guest post.

34. **OFFER PROMOTIONAL COPY OF YOUR BOOK (OR OTHER GIVEAWAYS) AS PART OF YOUR GUEST POST.** Having a random giveaway for people who comment on a blog post can help spur conversation and interest in your guest post, which is a great way to get the most mileage out of your guest appearance.

35. **CATER POSTS TO AUDIENCE.** As the editor of *Writer's Market* and *Poet's Market*, I have great range in the topics I can cover. However, if I'm writing a guest post for a fiction blog, I'll write about things of interest to a novelist—not a poet.

36. **MAKE IT PERSONAL, BUT PROVIDE NUGGET.** Guest posts are a great opportunity for you to really show your stuff to a new audience. You could write a very helpful and impersonal post, but that won't connect with readers the same way as if you write a very helpful and personal post that makes them want to learn more about you (and your blog, your book, your Twitter account, etc.). Speaking of which...

37. **SHARE LINKS TO YOUR WEBSITE, BLOG, SOCIAL NETWORKS, ETC.** After all, you need to make it easy for readers who enjoyed your guest post to learn more about you and your projects. Start the conversation in your guest post and keep it going on your own sites, profiles, etc. And related to that...

38. **PROMOTE YOUR GUEST POST THROUGH YOUR NORMAL CHANNELS ONCE THE POST GOES LIVE.** Your normal audience will want to know where you've been and what you've been doing. Plus, guest posts lend a little extra "street cred" to your projects. But don't stop there...

39. **CHECK FOR COMMENTS ON YOUR GUEST POST AND RESPOND IN A TIMELY MANNER.** Sometimes the comments are the most interesting part of a guest post (no offense). This is where readers can ask more in-depth or related questions, and it's also where you can show your expertise on the subject by being as helpful as possible. And guiding all seven of these tips is this one:

40. **PUT SOME EFFORT INTO YOUR GUEST POST.** Part of the benefit to guest posting is the opportunity to connect with a new audience. Make sure you bring your A-game, because you need to make a good impression if you want this exposure to actually help grow your audience. Don't stress yourself out, but put a little thought into what you submit.

ONE ADDITIONAL TIP: Have fun with it. Passion is what really drives the popularity of blogs. Share your passion and enthusiasm, and readers are sure to be impressed.

ROBERT LEE BREWER is an editor with the Writer's Digest Writing Community and author of *Solving the World's Problems* (Press 53). Follow him on Twitter @robertleebrewer.

WHAT ARE AGENTS REALLY LOOKING FOR?

Four literary agents who rep children's authors and illustrators explain what they're looking for in today's landscape.

....

Kerrie Flanagan

Earning a contract with a major publisher requires finding representation with a literary agent first. They are the gatekeepers. Your agent will be your advocate; she will want to see your book succeed as much as you do. She will help strengthen your manuscript before pitching it to editors, negotiate the contract with the publisher, act as a liaison between you and the editor, sell sub-rights (audio, dramatic, translation rights), and process the money due to you.

But what are agents really looking for? Four agents who represent children's literature, took time out of their busy day to share their insight and wisdom on queries, platform, what makes an engaging story, ideal clients, and writing for young audiences. By understanding what agents want to see in their submissions inbox and in their clients, you will have a better idea of how to approach them, and ultimately find representation.

MEET THE AGENTS

KELLY SONNACK (Andrea Brown Literary Agency) represents illustrators and writers for all age groups within children's literature: picture books, middle grade, chapter book, young adult, and graphic novels. Kelly is on the Advisory Board and faculty for UCSD's certificate in Writing and Illustrating for Children, and is a frequent speaker at conferences, including SCBWI's national and regional conferences, and can be found talking about all things children's books on Facebook (/agentsonnack) and Twitter (@KSonnack).

JOHN RUDOLPH's (Dystel, Goderich & Bourret LLC) list started out as mostly children's books, it has evolved to the point where it is now half adult, half children's authors—and he's looking to maintain that balance. On the children's side, John is keenly interested in middle-grade and young adult fiction and would love to find the next great picture book author/illustrator.

SARA MEGIBOW (KT Literary) is a literary agent with nine years of experience in publishing. Sara specializes in working with authors in middle grade, young adult, romance, erotica, science fiction, and fantasy. She represents *New York Times* best-selling authors, Roni Loren and Jason Hough, and international best-selling authors, Stefan Bachmann and Tiffany Reisz. Sara is LGBTQ-friendly and presents regularly at SCBWI and RWA events around the country. She tries to answer professional questions on twitter (@SaraMegibow) as time allows.

JENNIFER MARCH SOLOWAY (Andrea Brown Literary Agency) represents authors and illustrators of picture book, middle grade, and YA stories, and is actively building her list. For picture books, she is drawn to a wide range of stories from silly to sweet, but she always appreciates a strong dose of humor and some kind of surprise at the end. When it comes to middle grade, she likes all kinds of genres, including adventures, mysteries, spooky-but-not-too-scary ghost stories, humor, realistic contemporary, and fantasy. Jennifer regularly presents at writing conferences all over the country, including the San Francisco Writers Conference, the Northern Colorado Writers Conference, and regional SCBWI conferences. For her latest conference schedule, craft tips, and more, follow Jennifer on Twitter at @marchsoloway.

In a writer's world, once a manuscript is complete, writing a good query can be all-consuming, knowing it is the key to getting representation. But in your world, reading queries are a small part of how you spend your time. What catches your eyes when it comes to a query and what do you like to see in an effective query?

> **SONNACK:** I prefer my queries straightforward, simple, and professional. Tell me why you're querying me, what your book is about, and a little relevant information about

yourself. I never mind a compliment about something I've said that resonated with you or made you want to query me, or hearing about a client's book that you loved (if it's honest; I can smell a fake claim a mile away). Don't go overboard; think of this as a job application. And always follow the directions on the agent's website!

RUDOLPH: Professionalism. When I started out in publishing, I was taught to think of queries like a job application to work at a bank: If the manuscript is your résumé, the query letter is your cover letter. And just as you wouldn't try to be overly clever or silly when you apply for a bank job, your query should be equally serious, straightforward, and brief. If it helps, all I'm really looking for is a brief introduction stating genre and length, a one or two paragraph description of the work, and any relevant writing credits the author might have. No need to add any whistles or bells!

MEGIBOW: In short, a query catches my eye when it is well-written and succinctly describes an interesting story. To move from query to full manuscript to an offer of representation, I'm looking for submissions that I love and think I can sell.

However, let's back up a bit. You said "knowing it is the key to getting representation" and I want to clarify something—the query isn't the key to getting representation. The manuscript itself is the key to getting representation and (hopefully) a book deal. It may sound crazy, but in my 11-plus years' experience, I've found that a strong query accurately represents a strong manuscript. So, before jumping into the query slush pile, write, edit, polish, re-read, re-edit, and re-polish that manuscript!

So, how do we write an effective query? First, write a one-sentence description of your book—the pitch—and really nail it! This is the elevator pitch—the short, high-level description of your story, as you would explain it to a reader who is considering buying your book. Second, write a one paragraph description of the book and make that paragraph sound just like the back cover of a novel. That's it! A strong pitch plus an engaging paragraph of description is what makes an effective query.

Our website hosts a series of blog posts called "About My Query" in which our literary agents read and critique query letters (*with* the authors' permission). Read this blog: www.ktliterary.com/category/ask-daphne/about-my-query. Also, check out the Writer's Digest Successful Queries posts on the Guide to Literary Agents blog: (www.writersdigest.com/editor-blogs/guide-to-literary-agents/successful-queries), as well as the info on Query Shark (www.queryshark.blogspot.com). These resources are excellent for helping a writer see what works and what doesn't work in a query letter.

SOLOWAY: Because we receive so many submissions, unfortunately, we don't have that much time to spend on each one. We only get to see a small sample of the work, and we have to make a decision fast. Our submission guidelines ask for a query letter with a short pitch about the project and the first ten pages of a manuscript—or the complete text of a picture book. I personally am most interested in the writing and will often read the pages first before I read the query letter.

I find the projects that capture my interest have at least three of the following traits:

- A strong, engaging voice.
- An intriguing premise that somehow feels different from anything else I've seen.
- A dynamic opening scene filled with drama that has enough context to immediately ground me in the world and suck me into the story.
- An irresistible character with high stakes and agency.
- An additional story thread that is also compelling.

The best ones have all of the above!

However, I do think it's important to be able to pitch a project. I've found the best pitches raise a question in my mind (or better yet, two or three questions), the kind of question that is so intriguing, I just have to know the answer—so much so, that I will request the manuscript right away and stay up reading until three in the morning to find out what happens!

Let's say a writer has written a great query and you request the full manuscript. What typically keeps you reading and what is something that will stop you right away?

SONNACK: A great premise will keep me reading because I want to see where it goes. I start reading a manuscript wanting to love it and I read until I lose interest. Sometimes that's because I'm not connecting to a character. Sometimes it's because the stakes aren't high enough. Sometimes it's because the premise doesn't feel original or unique enough for today's market.

RUDOLPH: I don't think there's any one poison pill that will make me stop. Often, it's either a weak voice, a misunderstanding of the proposed genre, a plot that takes too long to get off the ground, or any and all combinations thereof—but it could also be something totally arbitrary, which is why I don't discourage multiple submissions. What keeps me reading? A good story well told.

MEGIBOW: I'm looking for a full manuscript that demonstrates superior craft. Yes, that's a tall order but (to reassure you all), the vast majority of my clients came to me via the query slush pile with a great query and superior manuscript. So, write and query—you're in great company!

Let's break it down a bit though. In a full manuscript, I want to see superior writing and a compelling story. I evaluate manuscripts by looking for strong characters, authentic narrative voice, organic world building, engaging conflict, compelling backstory, and an exciting plot. Typically, I stop reading if the manuscript starts to feel generic or the writing becomes less polished.

Need some examples? Check out the Books page on the KT Literary website: www.ktliterary.com/books. I'd point to any of these books and say, "here is an example of superior craft."

It can be hard to tell when your book is polished enough to keep an agent reading. My best suggestion is to read widely in the genre you're writing. Read recent titles (published in the past two years), especially by debut authors. Read books published by major publishing houses and ones that have won awards. Read widely and keep writing!

SOLOWAY: I love a good story, and if a project has a great hook—something that raises a question that I find compelling, I must read on—chances are I will read the entire manuscript. Most of the manuscripts I see have great potential, but those same drafts tend to be too raw and in need of more work. In those cases, I can tell the author is still writing to discover, or if they have discovered the end, they have yet to rework the beginning and middle.

Similarly, I find that many authors write for story but gloss over thoughts, feelings, and emotional depth in order to pursue the action, and I will find myself wondering how the character feels or thinks about a turn of events or other character. Those layers are often missing from the early draft, and it's those layers that make a good story great, or make an interesting character fascinating.

That's not to say the submission needs to be perfect, but it needs to be revised and reworked enough for me to help the author ready and polish the work for an editor. I am looking for projects that I feel I can provide value editorially and champion. I also want to feel a deep connection with the story, the characters, and the writing.

If I have trouble connecting with the character or the story, I will likely stop reading and pass. Rejections are the worst part of my job. I love writers, and I truly want everyone to achieve.

What is the biggest mistake adult writers make when writing for young audiences (up through middle grade)?

SONNACK: Sounding like they've been listening in on their kids' conversations. It's really obvious when a writer approaches a story because they want to teach their kids a lesson versus really remembering what it was like to be that age and writing from a kid's perspective.

RUDOLPH: Likewise, misunderstanding the proposed genre. For picture books, that could mean a text that's way too long, vocabulary and sentence structure way above age level, or adult characters without any kid appeal. Chapter books and middle grade are more flexible, but I still turn down a lot of those projects where the voice and characters are too advanced—or too young.

MEGIBOW: Great question! In my opinion, the biggest mistake adult writers make when writing for young readers is they use a narrative voice that sounds like an adult writing for a child. Young readers demand authentic books! Some adult writers "talk down" to young audiences by using silly language or by not fleshing out complex conflicts or characters. Avoid these mistakes! Write complex characters, real conflict, and always use an authentic voice.

SOLOWAY: Crafting a voice that sounds adult instead of having the perspective of a child.

There is lots of talk at conferences and in writing magazines about platform. How important is it to you that a writer has an established platform?

SONNACK: Platform is something that means a lot more for the adult nonfiction market where readers are looking for advice/information from an established source (say, you want a book about finance—you're probably going to want to buy a book written by someone who has some expertise in that field). In nonfiction for kids, this can be important too, but for kids' fiction, your readers don't really care who you are. This really only comes into play when an author has been successful and established a fan base. At that point, the child reader may follow the writer and want to read their next book(s).

Instead of platform, I like to see market awareness and engagement with the kid lit community. These things indicate that a prospective writer is more prepared for a career as a writer/illustrator. And that they're giving back and participating in the community we hope will support them once they publish.

RUDOLPH: I don't think platform is as important in children's books, or at least not at the point when I sign a client. I do like to see authors engage with the world, whether through social media, being a member of SCBWI, or writing in other genres. But that's very much secondary to the quality of the work. Once a client is signed, though, I do ask them to work on all of those things, and continue that work once their book is sold.

MEGIBOW: For a debut fiction writer, I'm not worried about platform at the point I read a query letter. Some writers query with no platform at all and some come to the slush pile with an extensive social media campaign already in place. Both of these writers' manuscripts will be reviewed equally. If a writer has an author website at the point they submit, I like to see that in the query letter—but it's not a deal-maker or a deal-breaker. If we go on to work together, there is time to build platform and branding after we get a book deal.

A smart platform is important to have in place once the publishing house starts shopping a novel to its retailers and once the agent starts shopping subsidiary rights, but that platform should be tailored to the author's personality and the genre in which they write. These are things that can be done after the query phase.

SOLOWAY: For me, a platform is less important than the quality of the writing and story, but good platforms never hurt!

What characteristics make up your ideal client?

SONNACK: Professional, creative, aware, kind, thoughtful, keyed in to the kid lit community, and in it for the long haul.

RUDOLPH: Optimism, patience, flexibility, and reasonable expectations. A good sense of humor doesn't hurt, either.

MEGIBOW: My clients are all amazing! They differ tremendously in personality and that's natural—I am honored to work for each and every one of them.

I represent introverts (lots of them!) and extroverts (a couple of them). I represent authors who write slowly and authors who write very, very quickly. I represent debut authors and experienced, multi-published authors and everything in between.

In general, when I offer representation to a writer they usually say, "I want to write a lot of books and keep writing for a long time." In my experience there are two characteristics that help authors survive for a long time in this competitive, crazy, unpredictable business. Those two characteristics are patience and discipline. Many successful authors have the patience to put up with publishing's ups and downs and the discipline to keep writing. But, those characteristics are not deal-breakers or deal-makers. At the end of the day I'm looking in the slush pile for incredible books that I fall head-over-heels in love with and think I can sell.

SOLOWAY: I am very editorial with my clients. I am looking for authors and illustrators who are open to revision and willing to put in the work necessary to make the project the best it can be. My style is detailed and encouraging; I don't like to be harsh or blunt. I see myself as their cheerleader and champion of their work. So I am looking for someone who appreciates that style and wants to work with me. I like to be transparent with my clients, and I hope they will do the same with me.

Because picture books are short, some writers think they are easy to write. What is the biggest mistake writers make when writing for this market and what makes a great picture book?

SONNACK: I think they're one of the hardest forms to execute, especially for new writers. Many writers don't take the time to explore the current landscape of picture books and what is succeeding today (which is quite different than when they were a picture book reader). They also often think the illustrations need to be a part of the submission package (which isn't true; the publisher usually selects an illustrator once they purchase the text). I also see a lot of manuscripts that aren't full stories (with a beginning, middle, and end, including conflict and resolution), or that aren't doing anything special with the writing.

RUDOLPH: I don't know if this is the biggest mistake, but not telling a story is up there. I get a ton of picture book manuscripts that aren't stories—they're glorified lists or concept books or poems—and I pass on almost all of them. Want to write a great picture book? Tell a great story!

SOLOWAY: The best picture books have wonderful language at the line level that is fun to read aloud, a full story arc, a full character arc, an additional story thread, and an unexpected twist at the end that is either funny or sweet or both—and all of that needs to happen in 500 words or less. It's quite a task, and the people who write great picture books are masters at their craft!

....

KERRIE FLANAGAN is an author, writing consultant, publisher, and accomplished freelance writer with more than 18 years' experience. Her work has appeared in publications such as *Writer's Digest, Alaska Magazine, The Writer*, and six *Chicken Soup for the Soul* books. She is the author of seven books, including two children's books, *Claire's Christmas Catastrophe* and *Claire's Unbearable Campout*, all published under her label, Hot Chocolate Press. She was the founder and former director of Northern Colorado Writers and now does individual consulting with writers. Her background in teaching and enjoyment of helping writers has led her to present at writing conferences across the country, including the Writer's Digest Annual Conference, the Willamette Writer's Conference, and the Writer's Digest Novel Writing Conference. You can find her online at www.KerrieFlanagan.com, www.hotchocolatepress.com, and on Twitter at @ Kerrie_Flanagan.

....

GETTING AN AGENT 101

by Jennifer D. Foster

Considered the "gatekeepers" to (large) publishing houses, literary agents are often your best bet to getting your foot in the door and making a name for yourself in the book (and even the motion picture, but that's another story!) world. But do you really need an agent? And exactly how do you find one? What are the tell-tale signs of a reputable (and not-so-reputable) literary agent? And how do you make the author-agent relationship work? Key insights, helpful tips and sound advice from authors, editors, publishing consultants, editorial directors, literary agents, writing instructors and heads of professional writing organizations give you the inside track.

WHAT LITERARY AGENTS DO

While the Writers' Union of Canada website states that "about 70 per cent of the books published in Canada do not have an agent-assisted contract," it's a radically different story in the United States. In her book *Publishing 101: A First-Time Author's Guide to Getting Published, Marketing and Promoting Your Book, and Building a Successful Career* (Jane Friedman, 2015), Jane Friedman reveals that "in today's market, probably about 80 per cent of books that the New York publishers acquire are sold to them by agents." But before taking the often-challenging plunge of getting a literary agent, do your homework to determine it you actually need one to get your manuscript published. And in order to figure that out, it's necessary to understand what, exactly, literary agents are and what they do. Jennifer Croll, editorial director of Greystone Books in Vancouver, explains it this way: "Agents act as both scouts and filters—they sort through what's out there and actively search to find the authors and proposals that are most likely to be published." Linden MacIntyre, award-winning journalist, internationally bestselling and Scotiabank Giller

Prize–winning author and former host of the fifth estate, concurs. "Agents know the world of publishing, who matters, and established agents are known and recognized by editors and publishers. A recommendation from a credible agent will usually assure that someone of influence in publishing will read the manuscript."

Trevor Cole, Toronto, Ontario–based, award-winning author of *The Whisky King*, *Hope Makes Love* and *Practical Jean*, further clarifies. An agent is beneficial "if you are committed to producing well-crafted book-length prose on a consistent professional basis." And, he says, "if the agent is part of a large house, they will have international contacts and sub-agents who can give your book its best chance at international distribution." Quite simply, "if an agent loves a book you've written, they will go to bat for it hard," he says, adding, "and once an editor agrees to buy the book, the agent's job is to get the best possible financial deal for you." Geoffrey Taylor, director of the International Festival of Authors in Toronto, Ontario, says that "an agent is the conduit for an author's work. This could mean anything from national to world rights. It could include all print forms, electronic and video/film platforms." He says that agents have a lot of "experience with contracts and can usually negotiate better terms and a higher cash advance against future sales." Terence Green explains further. "A book contract can easily be twenty pages or more. An agent familiar with the publishing business understands which clauses are negotiable, and to what degree, and can customize the boilerplate contracts often tendered as a matter of rote to ones that are more palatable and fair-minded to all parties." Martha Kanya-Forstner, editor-in-chief of Doubleday Canada, and McClelland & Stewart, and vice-president of Penguin Random House Canada, reveals that "it is exceptionally difficult for authors to negotiate the value of their own work, [and it is] much better to have an agent secure the best deal possible and ensure that all terms of that deal are then met."

Martha Webb, proprietor and literary agent with CookeMcDermid in Toronto, Ontario, sees the agent's role as that of career guide and activist. "We are an author's advocate throughout the life of their work, and the liaison between the author and publisher. Our goal is to find the best possible publishing arrangements for the author's work… to support and advocate for their interests throughout the process and to advise them throughout their writing career." Carolyn Forde, literary agent and international rights director for Westwood Creative Artists in Toronto, Ontario, sums up the advocate role this way: "The agent supports and advises their clients. We do many, many contracts a year, and most authors won't do more than one a year (and even that would be considered a lot), so we do know what's industry standard, what's author friendly and what isn't."

In an online interview with Authornomics, agent Katherine Sands, with the Sarah Jane Freymann Literary Agency in New York, takes it even further, explaining that "literary agent now means content manager…the work is hands-on with a role in developing and marketing an author's name and material for print, digital and other media—not just centered around a book deal." She believes "the digital age is revolutionizing everything and reinvented agents are now far more involved in creating opportunities for writing clients' content in emerging markets: for books, to be used online, with partners, in podcasts, in products, and in digital media to accrue sales. The new agent focus is on how writers can market and maximize their works across a wide slate." Lori Hahnel, Calgary-based author of *After You've Gone*, *Love Minus Zero* and *Nothing Sacred* and creative writing teacher at Mount Royal University and the Alexandra Writers' Centre Society, notes another role of the agent—that of editor. "Today more than ever, agents are taking on an editorial role. As publishers employ fewer and fewer editors, they need the manuscripts they get from agents to be in nearly publishable form when they're submitted."

Agents also handle other types of administrative and editorial-type tasks, such as checking royalty statements and hunting down overdue royalty checks; submitting books to reviewers and literary contests; and submitting future manuscripts to editors/publishers.

DETERMINING NEED

"Academic writing, and those working in less commercially successful genres likely don't need an agent," says Webb. Friedman, in her blog post "How to Find a Literary Agent for Your Book," adds that "if you're writing for a niche market (e.g., vintage automobiles) or wrote an academic or literary work, then you might not need an agent." Why? "Agents are motivated to take on clients based on the size of the advance they think they can get. If your project doesn't command a decent advance, then you may not be worth an agent's time, and you'll have to sell the project on your own." Kelsey Attard, managing editor of Freehand Books in Calgary, Alberta, says that "it depends on your goals...and also it depends on your genre. There are virtually no agents who represent poets, for example." Anita Purcell, executive director of the Canadian Authors Association, expounds further. "If you write poetry, short stories, or novellas, agents are not likely to take you on, and you have a better chance pitching directly to smaller presses that specialize in your particular genre." And, she adds, "authors who have been offered a contract with a publisher may want to get an agent to represent their interests before actually signing the contract. It is far easier to land an agent when you've got a firm offer from a publisher in hand."

Croll notes that those who want to work with an independent (indie) publisher can most likely get by without an agent. But, literary representation is essential for any writer wanting to make money by accessing most major publishing houses and editors, especially since the merging of many publishing companies has resulted in huge conglomerates with multiple imprints. "Editors often review agented submission first—and give them more consideration—because those submissions have already gone through a sort of vetting process," says Croll. And, shares Attard, "those biggest publishers typically don't accept unsolicited submissions from unagented authors." In the same online interview with Authornomics, Sands paints this picture: "Try this test at home: call a leading publisher tomorrow and try to get anyone to discuss your work. An agent has the greenlight to do this, but a civilian is unlikely to penetrate the publisher's robotic turnaround, shielding editors from unrepresented writers." And, she poses, "betcha you can't find out which newly-hired editor would really love your literotic chiller about a sexy ichthyologist who must solve eco-system crime in Namibia."

Dawn Green, British Columbia–based author of *In the Swish* and *How Samantha Became a Revolutionary*, has this perspective. "I think any author who wants to just be an author, just be writing novels full time, requires an agent who will allow them time to focus on their craft." Stephanie Sinclair, senior literary agent with Transatlantic Agency in Toronto, Ontario, shares Dawn Green's sentiment: "The contracts are often very tricky, and without an agent, the process can end up taking up so much time, the author has no time/energy left to write! My job is to help my authors, so they can just focus on the writing." Like Sands, Dawn Green also holds that "an agent needs to help a writer market and brand themselves. It's that classic difference between art and business." And, she adds, "today, it seems that more time needs to be put into the social media and networking side of things, and that is not easy for most introverted writers to do."

Taylor Brown, Wilmington, North Carolina–based bestselling author of the novels *Fallen Land*, *The River of Kings* and *Gods of Howl Mountain*, views the author-agent relationship from this lens. "Once your work has been published in book form, your agent's help only becomes that much more important. I think of an agent as a 'corner man' or woman of sorts." As well, he says, "they can do everything from giving feedback on manuscripts to helping interpret communications from your publisher to acting as a sounding board for important career changes. I could hardly imagine this career without an agent."

BEFORE THE QUERY

Most (good) literary agents receive hundreds of submissions a week from prospective clients, so time is precious, and second chances are rare. Part of doing your homework in finding an agent, before even entering the literary agent querying process, is ensuring your manuscript is the absolute best it can be. You want to be ready to hit "Send" as soon as an agent requests pages. In a guest blog post about finding a literary agent for The Writers' Workshop, novelist Harry Bingham says that means having a rock-solid product. "Write a good book. A stunning one. A dazzling one. One that echoes in the consciousness. One that makes a professional reader (i.e. agent/editor) sit up late with tears in their eyes." Sands agrees. In her book *Making the Perfect Pitch: How to Catch a Literary Agent's*

Eye (The Writer Books, 2004), she says, "Literary agents must be enchanted, seduced, and won over to take you on as a client."

But how do you ensure this? Have your manuscript professionally evaluated; give it to trusted beta readers for invaluable constructive feedback. "They will find idiosyncrasies in your manuscript that will surprise you and also offer suggestions. Then after you make the edits, send the manuscript to a copy editor. Agents can spot professionalism a mile away," says Lynne Wiese Sneyd, owner of LWS Literary Services in Tucson, Arizona, and literary consultant for the Tucson Festival of Books. Hiring a professional editor will ensure the manuscript is error-free and at-the-ready for agent consideration. Brown shares Wiese Sneyd's philosophy. "A professional editor who has a record of helping shepherd books to publication is simply invaluable. You cannot depend on the agent seeing the potential in your work. They are not looking for potential. They are looking for a book they can sell right now."

THE QUERY: SOME DOS AND DON'TS

Also, make sure your pitch to an agent is bang-on in every aspect. If you can't write an enticing query letter, you may not convince a literary agent that you can write a compelling book. Jan Kardys, a literary agent at Black Hawk Literary Agency LLC in Redding, Connecticut, and chairman of the Unicorn Writers' Conference, offers these tips for honing your query and book summary: "It is helpful for writers to study book publishers' websites and study catalogue copy. Once you study author's bio(s) and read the descriptions of their books, you get great ideas." Sinclair explains the pitch process this way: "Know who you are submitting to. When people send letters referencing some of my other clients and my taste, I know they have done their homework, which makes me immediately pay close attention." According to Sands, "it's the pitch and nothing but the pitch that gets a writer selected from the leaning tower of queries in a literary agent's office… The writing you do about your writing is as important as the writing itself." It is "part 'hello,' part cover letter, part interview for the coveted job of book author," she says. Agents, she stresses, "are looking first for a reason to keep reading, then for a reason to represent you…you want your pitch to give crystal clear answers—fast."

Some of those answers, says Croll, include being able to clearly describe the market for your book—who is going to buy it. "Selling your manuscript to a publisher is how an agent makes a living—that is their source of income. They are motivated to take on authors who will create work they can actually sell." And remember that your query letter is a form of communication, "so try to come across as a real person and not a pitching robot following a formula," advises Webb. Purcell couldn't agree more. "Always personalize your letter: make sure you use the agent's name and spell it correctly. If possible, find something you share in common, whether it's having the same birthplace, a mutual love of horror, or having met at a writers' conference." Like Webb, Purcell says "the query letter should not read like a form letter that is sent to every agent and publisher."

Hahnel, like Wiese Sneyd, suggests soliciting feedback from respected beta readers. The input will help "polish your query and your sample chapters until they shine." Purcell suggests taking it a step further. Writers "should ask experienced authors to review their query letter before submitting it." Why go to all this effort? "The bar is very, very high now, and so anything you can do to put your best foot forward is in your best interest," stresses Forde.

Hahnel also recommends having "a synopsis ready. Not all agents ask for them, but some will." As for a query letter, she says "don't clutter it with unnecessary information, such as courses you've taken or retreats you've gone on." Be polite and professional, says Hahnel, and ensure a confident and positive tone. "Don't say negative things like, 'I'm not sure if you'll like this.' or 'You probably won't want to read all of this.'" Attard recommends this: "Be brief, engaging, and also (at least for literary writing) let your manuscript be the star." Forde offers similar sound advice for a query. "Keep it short and concise—tell me about the book and about you. Don't try to be cute or memorable. Don't compare your book to the best book in the genre. If you say it's the next Harry Potter, what I hear is that you have unrealistic expectations." Purcell has this sage query-writing advice. "Agents often say that what catches their interest most is when writers manage to avoid some of the pitfalls of new writers, such as telling the agent that they're good writers (show, don't tell), or that all their family and friends loved the manuscript (of course they did, they love you), or that they've been wanting to be published authors since they were six years old (few writers haven't)." She says what also catches agents' interest is "when writers seem to have a strong understanding of their genre, as well as the distinction between commercial, upmarket, and literary writing."

A FEW WISE WORDS ON PLATFORM

Purcell says that it's all about branding right now "And writers should look at their social media platforms and their website, if they have one, with a critical eye that asks: 'What is my current brand and how appealing is that brand to a potential agent or publisher? Are there any posts or images that might turn an agent or publisher off?' And, she adds, "if they're unpublished, writers need to think about what makes them stand out as good candidates for representation by the agent. Have they won any writing competitions? Are they authorities on the subject matter?"

WHERE TO FIND AGENTS

Once your manuscript is ultra-polished and ready for publication, and you've decided to take the leap and find an agent, one way is to conduct online research. "I think a writer should be a good sleuth," says Dawn Green. "And most agents/agencies are clear on their websites about what they are looking for." She also suggests researching to see if agents have given (online) interviews and made additional comments about what they're looking for in a manuscript.

Publishers Marketplace is a helpful online research tool. For a $25 monthly membership, writers/authors can get snapshots of top literary agencies, seeing which books agents have sold and editors' buying patterns. A membership also offers industry news updates and deal reports. The "Dealmaker" lists a contact database and a rights and proposals board posting—all helpful for determining which agent to pitch and also for knowing how to entice each one. "It's one of the most extensive databases of agents," says Wiese Sneyd. "It's an amazing resource."

Word of mouth is also helpful. Ask authors (especially in your genre) you know and trust, and whose work you respect who their agent is and request a candid assessment of their professional and personal style. "Referrals from existing clients are also an excellent way to get an agent's attention, so if you are able to ask an established writer, do so," recommends Forde. With Brown, he's the one making the connection for the writer. "In several cases, I have come across an unrepresented writer whose work I admire and recommended them to my agent."

Another method is to read the acknowledgment section of books with a similar audience or vibe to yours, as well as those of your favorite authors, who often list their agent with a huge "thank you." In a *Forbes*' blog post by contributor Nick Morgan, he succinctly explains the process: "Find books that are similar to what you hope yours will be, and that you like, and read the acknowledgements. Every writer thanks her agent fulsomely in the acknowledgements, or she'll never publish again."

Writers' conferences are also another viable route to find agents who are actively seeking new titles/authors. These agents are often speakers/panelists there, offering writers the chance to meet with them one-on-one to pitch their manuscript. "Face-to-face meetings with agents can help you get a foot in the door—as long as you keep it professional and respectful," notes Purcell. Hahnel knows "two people who were able to sign with agents at 'speed-dating' sessions at conferences," but, she stresses, "I understand it's not a super-common occurrence." Taylor says to attend myriad industry events, including in-store appearances, book launches and festivals. "Talk to people. Often those in attendance are part of the book industry. Always tell people you are an author. You never know who you may be talking to."

QueryTracker.net has helped more than 2,400 authors find a literary agent. Among its many online freebies are a detailed database of more than 1,500 agent profiles, including author comments from their experience with said agent; an agent query-tracking feature; and data that lists agent reply rates, typical response times, etc. Writersdigest.com also offers a handy online feature called "New Agency Alerts" that profiles "new literary agents actively seeking writers, books, and queries now. These agents are building their client lists." Agentquery.com, which says it's "the internet's largest free database of literary agents," lets you search for agents (around one thousand of them) by category, offers an online social networking community (great for the query process) and provides agent and agency updates. Attard maintains that authors and writers should check out the deal listings on *Publishers Weekly*, and *Quill & Quire*, investigating the agents listed in those deal announcements. And annual print directories, such as the *Literary Market Place: The Directory of the American Book Publishing Industry* (which offers listings to "reach the people who publish, package, review, represent, edit, translate, typeset, illustrate, design, print, bind, promote, publicize, ship, and distribute"), are often available in your local library's reference section, says Purcell.

Brown suggests submitting to literary magazines and contests. "These publications still attract the attention of agents," he assures. He also recommends using social media. Brown "drew the attention of a couple of agents after becoming active on Twitter." Why? "I believe some of the younger literary agents monitor social media for young writers who are making waves with their essays or stories." Attard is in agreement. "Some agents are active on social media, so follow a few and get a sense of what they like and don't like, and what you should avoid doing! It can be really valuable to get a sense of how they work."

And while a seasoned, big-name agent may be able to get you an impressive advance on your book and secure an ironclad contract, don't be afraid to go with a newer literary agent, someone who's "hungry" and will most likely have more time and offer a high level of personal attention to champion not only your book, but also your literary career. Attard suggests that "if an agent is new without many prior sales, consider their history in the industry. Do they have the connections necessary to be successful?" And, cautions Webb, "a junior agent—and everyone needs to start somewhere—should be a junior agent within a reputable agency, who has the support of more senior agents behind her." In the same vein is the size of the literary agency. "This doesn't necessarily correlate with the quality of the agent or the size of the deal you can expect," verifies Friedman in her blog post "How to Find a Literary Agent for Your Book."

THE "GOOD" AGENT

What are the signs of a good literary agent? According to the website of the Canadian Authors Association, "reputable agents will be up to date on current publishing trends… and serve as experts in market sales, so they will help ensure your book gets a good cover design, and more attention from the publisher's publicity department." Purcell affirms that agents "represent you [the author], not the publisher, and will negotiate for more money, subsidiary rights, and protection clauses. Good agents are also in it for the long haul: they are as interested in building the author's career as they are in selling the first book."

MacIntyre shares the same mindset. He says that many writers aren't interested in the "bureaucracy and the fine points of the book business," so a good agent, "in addition to possessing literary instincts and professional connections, has a mercenary skill set. An agent should be a partner and a friend, but strong enough to speak truth to vanity. An agent will offer an essential service but is not a servant." He also says good agents attend myriad international book fairs; have strong professional relationships with influential editors; "play bad-cop where money matters matter; play mom/dad when the creative muse becomes petulant and sulky; pick up the tab (now and then); offer tactful commentary and advice (but not instruction) on creative issues; and know the difference between momentary insecurity and reality-based despair." MacIntyre also believes good agents have "the sensibilities and judgment of an editor; the skills of an accountant; the temerity of a union boss; a sense of humour, irony; good taste in food, drink and literature; and patience."

Kanya-Forstner stresses that "the best agents search widely and actively for new, diverse and challenging voices; for writers who bring something essential to the conversations in which they participate." She says that "the best agents are the most discerning, taking on only those clients whose work they know they can champion with the utmost integrity and confidence. The work they then submit comes with the weight of their endorsement and credibility." To Kanya-Forstner, "the best agents make it their business to be familiar with the sensibilities and interests of individual editors and with the publishing identity and strengths of individual imprints. The best agents pride themselves on being successful matchmakers."

Kardys says a "talented agent" will suggest to a writer several tactics, such as building a platform before the book deal—social media, contact lists, and doing events or writing articles/stories; provide ideas on how to market the book; and edit the writer's book summary." For her, "ideally, the best literary agents have a background as a former book editor, subsidiary rights experience at a book publisher, or the agent has started their publishing career by working for another literary agency before leaving to start their own agency."

Cole sees a good agent as "someone who seems to 'get' your work, who understands what you're writing now, and what you want to write in the future." And, adds Kanya-Forstner, since "publishing is a constantly changing business, the best agents stay on top of market trends, shifts in buying habits and retail practices." Terence Green describes the good agent in these terms: "A good agent knows editors and what they are looking for. They can provide shortcuts to editors. Many editors won't even look at unsolicited manuscripts, trusting the judgment of respected agents." So, the good agent, he says, is "in essence, the editor's first reader, winnowing the field appropriately for the editor." Friedman believes a good agent is not only an author's business manager, but also an author's "mentor and cheerleader." She shares these wise sentiments in her blog post: Literary agents are "also there to hold your hand when things go wrong with the editor or publisher. They prop you up when you're down, they celebrate your successes publicly, they look for opportunities you might not see, and they attend to your financial best interests as well as your big-picture career growth." Purcell stresses that "because the bulk of their work involves sales and negotiation, [editors] should be confident and assertive in their dealings, but always professional and respectful in their treatment of people, including you." She also believes agents should be "strategic thinkers" with strong social media skills. And "being well-organized is also a useful quality in a literary agent, since they need to juggle a variety of authors, editors and projects."

THE "BAD" AGENT

While the list of qualities and skills of a good agent is long, the list for a "bad" one is comparable. Since there is no worldwide professional organization responsible for vetting agents and maintaining agent standards, virtually anyone can hang out their "Agent" shingle. Beware of sweet-talking scammers, secretive behavior, those who don't treat you as a business partner, those who don't communicate respectfully and clearly, and those who don't reply in a timely manner. They aren't legit agents. Never, ever give a literary agent money upfront—not as a retainer, not for administrative expenses and not for a reading fee/feedback. An agent only gets paid—somewhere between 10 and 15 percent of an author's earnings—when an author gets paid and the publisher's advance is received. And 20 to 25 percent is standard for foreign sales (when translation rights are licensed to foreign book publishers), since the commission is often split between foreign and domestic agents. Cole says that "if you send a manuscript to an agent and she doesn't respond after a few months, that's an agent I wouldn't bother approaching further." And, he stresses, "if you're working with an agent, and she can't give you a list of the publishers she's sent your manuscript to, that's an agent who probably isn't working hard for you." Similarly, Taylor says that "if your agent is not directing you towards a deal, perhaps it is not the best fit."

Kardys feels the following are red flags: "A writer should not work with an agent who has no experience in the book field or hasn't offered suggested changes in the manuscript." However, she says, "if the book requires major work, an agent shouldn't sign up a writer as a client." And "if the agent doesn't know the basic points of a contract, the payment structures for an advance and the latest changes in the book marketplace, you should be cautious," she warns. Friedman, in her blog post, stresses that "if an agent passes you a publisher's boilerplate contact to sign with no changes, you may be in big trouble." Hahnel says to avoid agents with "non-existent client lists or sales history." And, she alerts, "beware of agents who only work with a few publishers."

According to a Science Fiction & Fantasy Writers of America blog post by A.C. Crispin, "real agents don't advertise. They don't have to. If you see an agency name in a sponsored Google ad or in the back of a writer's magazine, odds are they're a scam." And, says Crispin in that same post, "any agent that claims their client list is 'confidential' should be regarded with wariness, and their credentials should be investigated with extra care." Also, avoid agents who don't help with improving your query and/or proposal package. In her blog post, Friedman says only a few authors can put together a "crackerjack proposal." She stresses that "an agent should be ensuring the pitch or proposal is primed for success, and this almost always requires at least one round of feedback and revision."

Membership in the newly founded Professional Association of Canadian Literary Agents (PACLA), which only permits established literary agents to join and has a strict Code of Practice, or in the Association of Authors' Representatives, Inc. (AAR), for which its some 400 member must meet the highest standards and subscribe to its bylaws and Canon of Ethics, is a positive sign, but not necessarily a guarantee. Friedman states that "people in the industry should recognize the name of your agent." She also warns that if no online mention or reference to your agent can be found and if the agent isn't a member of the AAR, "that's a red flag. Check his track record carefully. See who he's sold to and how recently." And, forewarns Purcell, "generally speaking, if an agent is pursuing you rather than the other way around, think twice—most agents already have a stable of promising authors and rarely need to be the wooer." These are all reasons why, says, Terence Green, "one must do one's 'due diligence' in the matter, just as one would before venturing into any business investment."

HOW TO KEEP THE GOOD ONES

If you do secure a literary agent, be mindful that, like in any good relationship, the author-agent "marriage" can only thrive on mutual trust and respect, shared enthusiasm and open communication. Says Purcell: "I think it's important to have a connection with your literary agent. If there isn't a genuine and mutual feeling of respect and liking for one another, the relationship may sour over time." Sinclair thinks "it's important that you can enjoy a meal together. It's an intimate relationship in a way, so you want to be sure you like each other!" Cole advises to "be reliable, meet your deadlines and appreciate [your agent's] hard work." And Webb says to "be open to feedback and trust that your agent wants to make a success of your book and your career." But, don't' expect to sit back and let your agent do all of the legwork. "Be proactive about your career, boosting your platform whenever you can, and be someone who editors want to work with," she advises. Wiese Sneyd concurs. "Learn the business ahead of time. Respect an agent's time. Avoid excessive emails. Don't expect an agent to teach you the ins and outs of publishing. You'll have questions, of course, but enter the relationship as a savvy author."

Kardys advises to "always put in writing the obligations and duties of the writer and the agent" and to "encourage open communication and timelines." She also stresses to "listen carefully when your agent tells you to build your social media platform and make a list of email contacts, as later you will not have time to do this intense work when your book is published." Brown's suggestions are also a list of dos. Only a small percentage of writers get to have an agent represent their work, he says, and "there will be ups and downs and stressors of all kinds." But, he notes, "it's important to keep in mind that many writers only dream of having such problems! So try to enjoy the whole experience, even the worries and frustrations. They are all part of the story."

MAKING THE FINAL DECISION

Kanya-Forstner advises that "agents are only as good as the authors they represent, or for new agents, as good as the writers whose work they champion on social platforms and in public discourse about books." Refer to an agent's client list, which rights they've sold, when and in which countries, view their photograph, their (literary) likes and dislikes (Goodreads is a good resource to check), their Twitter feed, their website or their company's website, and weigh it all with any kind of gut feeling you may have to help you make your final choice. It all boils down to feelings and sensibilities—a kind of personal chemistry. MacIntyre concurs: "Basically, it will come down to a gut-level response, based on impressions and the compatibility of personalities." Author Chuck Sambuchino takes a similar stance. In his online WritersDigest.com article entitled "11 Steps to Finding the Agent Who'll Love your Book," he says that, after making your list of agents to contact, "rank agents in the likelihood of a love match."

THE SUBMISSION PROCESS IN A NUTSHELL

After doing your research into finding suitable agents, it's absolutely essential to find out what each agent wants in a submission. "Be professional, read about the formatting details the agency wants and let your story do the selling," says Dawn Green. Purcell shares in her tips, adding, "it's important to find out what their preferences are and to follow their guidelines faithfully. If they want the manuscript double-spaced in the courier font with one-inch margins, that's what you should give them. You're sending them a message if you don't." Sambuchino concurs in his online piece. "Getting through the front door is often about playing by the rules. Don't send anything less—or more—than each agent has asked for." If the agent specifies that they don't want attachments, "that means they want the query letter and up to ten pages of the manuscript imbedded in the body of the email, even if that looks ugly," says Purcell. Also, says Sambuchino, be sure you're submitting to four to eight agents only at a time, giving each agent their own separate email or mailed package. "Keep things professional. No gimmicks." And don't argue if/when you get a "no thank you" reply. "An agent is not attacking you. They know the business, they know what sells, and they are honestly trying to help your words get noticed," says Dawn Green, adding not to take agent criticism personally. Taylor suggests that if you receive a "no," be sure to "follow up with a thank you and ask if they might suggest who might be interested. Sometimes advice comes your way, or even your work gets a second look. Often publishing is luck and timing."

BEYOND THE QUERY

Be sure to keep track of your submissions and their results. Sambuchino says that "if you aren't getting any page requests, your query needs work. If you're getting partial requests but then nothing, your first draft pages aren't snagging the reader. If you're getting full requests but no nibbles, it's time to take a look at the full manuscript again." Use each rejection and any feedback you may get from an agent to fine-tune your next set of submissions. "This is not an easy business, and rejection is the norm, not the exception. I like to think of rejections as marks of honor," says Brown. "It's not how many times you get knocked down; it's how many times you get back up. Each rejection is one step closer to publication. Keep the faith. Keep going. It's worth it." And be prepared to wait for as long as it takes to find your perfect match. "My experience," clarifies Terence Green, "has always been that this is not a business for the impatient."

Perhaps the best advice to keep in mind during this journey comes from Cole: "Too many beginning writers with a half-finished manuscript think the first thing they need to do is get an agent, as if that will solve everything and ensure a flourishing writing career. It doesn't work that way," he warns. "The first thing you need to do is master your craft and produce a damn good book. An agent can't make you a good writer. An agent can't make you a success. That's up to you."

Jennifer D. Foster is a Toronto-based freelance writer, editor, and content strategist. Find her online at lifeonplanetword.wordpress.com.

SOCIAL MEDIA PRIMER FOR WRITERS

by Robert Lee Brewer

Beyond the actual writing, the most important thing writers can do for their writing careers is to build a writer platform. This writer platform can consist of any number of quantifiable information about your reach to your target audience, and one hot spot is social media.

HERE'S THE THING: It's more important to chase quality connections than quantity connections on social media.

Social media is one way to quantify your reach to your target audience. If you write poetry, your target audience is people who read poetry (often other folks who write poetry). If you write cookbooks, your target audience is people who like to cook.

In both cases, you can drill down into more specifics. Maybe the target audience for the poetry book is actually people who read sonnets. For the cookbook, maybe it's directed at people who like to cook desserts.

4 SOCIAL MEDIA TIPS

Social media is one way to connect with your target audience and influencers (like agents, editors, book reviewers, other writers) who connect to your target audience. Sites like Facebook, Twitter, LinkedIn, YouTube, Pinterest, Goodreads, Red Room, and so many more—they're all sites dedicated to helping people (and in some cases specifically writers) make connections.

Here are my four social media tips for writers:

1. **START SMALL.** The worst thing writers can do with social media is jump on every social media site ever created immediately, post a bunch of stuff, and then quit because they're overwhelmed on the time commitment and underwhelmed by the lack of response. Instead, pick one site, complete all the information about yourself, and start browsing around in that one neighborhood for a while.

2. **LOOK FOR CONNECTIONS.** Notice that I did not advise looking for leads or followers or whatever. Don't approach strangers online like a used car salesman. Be a potential friend and/or source of information. One meaningful connection is worth more than 5,000 disengaged "followers." Seriously.

3. **COMMUNICATE.** There are two ways to make a mistake here. One, never post or share anything on your social media account. Potential new connections will skip over your ghost town profile assuming your account is no longer active. Plus, you're missing an opportunity to really connect with others. The other mistake is to post a million (hopefully an exaggeration) things a day and never communicate with your connections. It's social media, after all; be social.

4. **GIVE MORE THAN YOU TAKE.** So don't post a million things a day, but be sure to share calls for submissions, helpful information (for your target audience), fun quotes, great updates from your connections (which will endear you to them further). Share updates from your end of the world, but don't treat your social media accounts as a place to sell things nonstop. Remember: Don't be a used car salesman.

ONE FINAL TIP: Focus. Part of effective platform building is knowing your target audience and reaching them. So with every post, every status update, every tweet, every connection, etc., keep focused on how you are bringing value to your target audience.

POPULAR SOCIAL NETWORKING SITES

The social media landscape is constantly shifting, but here are some that are currently popular:

- Bebo (http://bebo.com)
- Digg (http://digg.com)
- Facebook (http://facebook.com)
- Flickr (http://flickr.com)
- Google+ (http://plus.google.com)
- Habbo (http://habbo.com)
- Hi5 (http://hi5.com)
- Instagram (http://instagram.com)
- LinkedIn (http://linkedin.com)
- MeetUp (http://meetup.com)

- Ning (http://ning.com)
- Orkut (http://orkut.com)
- Pinterest (http://pinterest.com)
- Reddit (http://reddit.com)
- StumbleUpon (http://stumbleupon.com)
- Twitter (http://twitter.com)
- Yelp (http://yelp.com)
- YouTube (http://youtube.com)
- Zorpia (htttp://zorpia.com)

9 THINGS TO DO ON ANY SOCIAL MEDIA SITE

Not all social media sites are created the same. However, there are some things poets can do on any site to improve the quantity and quality of the connections they make online.

1. **USE YOUR REAL NAME.** If the point of social media is to increase your visibility, then don't make the mistake of cloaking your identity behind some weird handle or nickname. Use your real name—or that is, use your real byline as it appears (or would appear) when published.
2. **USE YOUR HEADSHOT FOR AN AVATAR.** Again, avoid concealing your identity as a cartoon image or picture of a celebrity or pet. The rules of online networking are the same as face-to-face networking. Imagine how silly it would be to see someone holding up a picture of a pet cat while talking to you in person.
3. **COMPLETE YOUR PROFILE.** Each site has different ways to complete this information. You don't have to include religious or political views, but you do want to make your site personal while still communicating your interest and experience in poetry. One tip: Give people a way to contact you that doesn't involve using the social networking site. For instance, an e-mail address.
4. **LINK TO WEBSITES.** If you have a blog and/or author website, link to these in your profile on all social media sites. After all, you want to make it as easy as possible for people to learn more about you. If applicable, link to your previously published books at points of purchase too.
5. **MAKE EVERYTHING PUBLIC.** As a poet, you are a public figure. Embrace that state of mind and make everything you do public on social media. This means you may have to sacrifice some privacy, but there are pre-Facebook ways of communicating private matters with friends and family.
6. **UPDATE REGULARLY.** Whether it's a status update or a tweet, regular updates accomplish two things: One, they keep you in the conversation; and two, they let

people you know (and people you don't know) see that you're actively using your account. Activity promotes more connections and conversations, which is what poets want on social media sites.

7. **JOIN AND PARTICIPATE IN RELEVANT GROUPS.** One key to this tip is relevancy. There are lots of random groups out there, but the ones that will benefit you the most are ones relevant to your interests and goals. Another key is participation. Participate in your group when possible.

8. **BE SELECTIVE.** Piggybacking on the previous tip, be selective about who you friend, who you follow, which groups you join, etc. Don't let people bully you into following them either. Only connect with and follow people or groups you think might bring you value—if not immediately, then eventually.

9. **EVOLVE.** When I started social media, MySpace was the top hangout. Eventually, I moved on to Facebook and Twitter (at the urging of other connections). Who knows which sites I'll prefer in five months, let alone five years, from now. Evolve as the landscape evolves. In fact, even my usage of specific sites has had to evolve as user behavior changes and the sites themselves change.

FINAL THOUGHT

If you have a blog, be sure to use it to feed your social media site profiles. Each new post should be a status update or tweet. This will serve the dual purpose of bringing traffic to your blog and providing value to your social media connections.

ROBERT LEE BREWER is an editor with the Writer's Digest Writing Community and author of *Solving the World's Problems* (Press 53). Follow him on Twitter @robertleebrewer.

FUNDS FOR WRITERS 101

Find Money You Didn't Know Existed

···

by C. Hope Clark

When I completed writing my novel over a decade ago, I imagined the next step was simply to find a publisher and watch the book sell. Like most writers, my goal was to earn a living doing what I loved so I could walk away from the day job. No such luck. Between rejection and newfound knowledge that a novel can take years to sell enough for a single house payment, I opened my mind to other writing avenues. I learned that there's no *one* way to find funds to support your writing; instead there are *many*. So many, in fact, that I felt the need to share the volume of knowledge I collected, and I called it FundsforWriters.com.

Funds are money. But obtaining those funds isn't necessarily a linear process, or a one-dimensional path. As a serious writer, you study all options at your fingertips, entertaining financial resources that initially don't make sense as well as the obvious.

GRANTS

Grants come from government agencies, nonprofits, businesses and even generous individuals. They do not have to be repaid, as long as you use the grant as intended. No two are alike. Therefore, you must do your homework to find the right match between your grant need and the grant provider's mission. Grantors like being successful at their mission just as you like excelling at yours. So they screen applicants, ensuring they fit the rules and show promise to follow through.

Don't fear grants. Sure, you're judged by a panel, and rejection is part of the game, but you already know that as a writer. Gigi Rosenberg, author of *The Artist's Guide to*

Grant Writing, states, "If one funder doesn't want to invest in your project, find another who does. And if nobody does, then begin it any way you can. Once you've started, that momentum will help your project find its audience and its financial support."

TYPES OF GRANTS

Grants can send you to retreats, handle emergencies, provide mentors, pay for conferences, or cover travel. They also can be called awards, fellowships, residencies, or scholarships. But like any aspect of your writing journey, define how any tool, even a grant, fits into your plans. Your mission must parallel a grantor's mission.

The cream-of-the-crop grants have no strings attached. Winning recipients are based upon portfolios and an application that defines a work-in-progress. You don't have to be a Pulitzer winner, but you must prove your establishment as a writer.

You find most of these opportunities in state arts commissions. Find them at www.nasaa-arts.org or as a partner listed at the National Endowment for the Arts website, www.nea.gov. Not only does your state's arts commission provide funding, but the players can direct you to other grant opportunities, as well as to artists who've gone before you. Speaking to grant winners gives you a wealth of information and a leg up in designing the best application.

Foundations and nonprofits fund the majority of grants. Most writers' organizations are nonprofits. Both the Mystery Writers of America (www.mysterywriters.org) and Society of Children's Book Writers and Illustrators (www.scbwi.org) offer scholarships and grants.

Many retreats are nonprofits. Journalist and freelancer Alexis Grant (http://alexisgrant.com/) tries to attend a retreat a year. Some ask her to pay, usually on a sliding scale based upon income, and others provide scholarships. Each time, she applies with a clear definition of what she hopes to gain from the two to five-week trips. "It's a great way to get away from the noise of everyday responsibilities, focus on writing well and meet other people who prioritize writing. I always return home with a new perspective." One resource to find writing retreats is the Alliance of Artists Communities (www.artistcommunities.org/).

Laura Lee Perkins won four artist-in-residence slots with the National Park Service (www.nps.gov). The federal agency has 43 locations throughout the United States where writers and artists live for two to four weeks. From Acadia National Park in Maine to Sleeping Bear Dunes National Lakeshore in Michigan, Perkins spoke to tourists about her goals to write a book about Native American music. "Memories of the US National Parks' beauty and profound serenity will continue to enrich my work. Writers find unparalleled inspiration, quietude, housing, interesting staff, and a feeling of being in the root of your artistic desires."

Don't forget writers' conferences. While they may not advertise financial aid, many have funds available in times of need. Always ask as to the availability of a scholarship or work-share program that might enable your attendance.

Grants come in all sizes. FundsforWriters posts emergency grants on its grants page (www.fundsforwriters.com) as well as new grant opportunities such as the Sustainable Arts Foundation (www.sustainableartsfoundation.org) that offers grants to writers and artists with children under the age of 18, or the Awesome Foundation (www.awecomefoundation.org), which gives $1,000 grants to creative projects.

Novelist Joan Dempsey won an Elizabeth George Foundation grant (http://www.elizabethgeorgeonline.com/foundation/index.htm) in early 2012. "I applied to the Foundation for a research grant that included three trips to places relevant to my novel-in-progress, trips I otherwise could not have afforded. Not only does the grant provide travel funds, but it also provides validation that I'm a serious writer worthy of investment, which is great for my psyche and my résumé."

FISCAL SPONSORSHIP

Nonprofits have access to an incredibly large number of grants that individuals do not, and have the ability to offer their tax-exempt status to groups and individuals involved in activities related to their mission. By allowing a nonprofit to serve as your grant overseer, you may acquire funds for your project.

Deborah Marshall is President of the Missouri Writers Guild (www.missouriwritersguild.org) and founder of the Missouri Warrior Writers Project, with ample experience with grants in the arts. "Although grant dollars are available for individual writers, writing the grant proposal becomes difficult without significant publication credits. Partnering with a nonprofit organization, whether it is a writing group, service, community organization, or any 501(c)3, can fill in those gaps to make a grant application competitive. Partnering not only helps a writer's name become known, but it also assists in building that all-important platform."

Two excellent groups that offer fiscal sponsorship for writers are The Fractured Atlas (www.fracturedatlas.org) and Artspire (www.artspire.org), sponsored by the New York Foundation for the Arts and open to all US citizens. Visit The Foundation Center (www.foundationcenter.org) for an excellent tutorial guide to fiscal sponsorship.

CROWD SOURCING

Crowd sourcing is a co-op arrangement where people support artists directly, much like the agricultural co-op movement where individuals fund farming operations in exchange for fresh food. Kickstarter (www.kickstarter.com) has made this funding method successful in the arts.

Basically, the writer proposes his project, and for a financial endorsement as low as $1, donors receive some token in return, like an autographed book, artwork, or bookmark. The higher the donation, the bigger the *wow* factor in the gift. Donors do not receive ownership in the project.

Meagan Adele Lopez (www.ladywholunches.net) presented her debut self-published book *Three Questions* to Kickstarter readers, requesting $4,400 to take her book on tour, create a book trailer, pre-order books, and redesign the cover. Eighty-eight backers pledged a total of $5,202. She was able to hire an editor and a company that designed film trailers. For every $750 she received over her plan, she added a new city to her book tour.

Other up-and-coming crowd sourcing companies include Culture 360 (www.culture360.org) that serves Asia and Europe, and Indiegogo (www.indiegogo.com), as well as Rocket Hub (www.rockethub.com). And nothing stops you from simply asking those you know to support your project. The concept is elementary.

CONTESTS

Contests offer financial opportunity, too. Of course you must win, place or show, but many writers overlook the importance that contests have on a career. These days, contests not only open doors to publishing, name recognition, and money, but listing such achievements in a query letter might make an agent or publisher take a second glance. Noting your wins on a magazine pitch might land a feature assignment. Mentioning your accolades to potential clients could clinch a freelance deal.

I used contests as a barometer when fleshing out my first mystery novel, *A Lowcountry Bribe* (Bell Bridge Books). After I placed in several contests, earned a total of $750, and reached the semi-finals of the Amazon Breakthrough Novel Award (www.createspace.com/abna), my confidence grew strong enough to pitch agents. My current agent admits that the contest wins drew her in.

Contests can assist in sales of existing books, not only aiding sales but also enticing more deals for future books . . . or the rest of your writing profession.

Whether writing short stories, poetry, novels, or nonfiction, contests abound. As with any call for submission, study the rules. Double checking with entities that screen, like FundsforWriters.com and WinningWriters.com, will help alleviate concerns when selecting where to enter.

FREELANCING

A thick collection of freelancing clips can make an editor sit up and take notice. You've been vetted and accepted by others in the business, and possibly established a following. The more well known the publications, the brighter your aura.

Sooner or later in your career, you'll write an article. In the beginning, articles are a great way to gain your footing. As your career develops, you become more of an expert, and are expected to enlighten and educate about your journey and the knowledge you've acquired. Articles are, arguably, one of the best means to income and branding for writers.

Trade magazines, national periodicals, literary journals, newsletters, newspapers and blogs all offer you a chance to present yourself, earn money, and gain readers for a platform. Do not discount them as income earners.

Linda Formichelli, of Renegade Writer fame (www.therenegadewriter.com) leaped into freelance magazine writing because she simply loved to write, and that love turned her into an expert. "I never loved working to line someone else's pockets." A full-time freelancer since 1997, with credits like *Family Circle*, *Redbook*, and *Writer's Digest*, she also writes articles, books, e-courses, and e-books about her profession as a magazine writer.

JOBS

Part-time, full-time, temporary or permanent, writing jobs hone your skills, pad your resume, and present avenues to movers and shakers you wouldn't necessarily meet on your own. Government and corporate managers hire writers under all sorts of guises like Social Media Specialist and Communications Specialist, as well as the expected Reporter and Copywriter.

Alexis Grant considers her prior jobs as catapults. "Working at a newspaper (*Houston Chronicle*) and a news magazine (*US News & World Report*) for six years provided the foundation for what I'm doing now as a freelancer. Producing stories regularly on tight deadlines will always make you a better writer."

Joan Dempsey chose to return to full-time work and write her novel on the side, removing worries about her livelihood. "My creative writing was suffering trying to freelance. So, I have a day job that supports me now." She still maintains her Facebook presence to continue building her platform for her pending novel.

DIVERSIFICATION

Most importantly, however, is learning how to collect all your funding options and incorporate them into your plan. The successful writer doesn't perform in one arena. Instead, he thrives in more of a three-ring circus.

Grant states it well: "For a long while I thought of myself as only a journalist, but there are so many other ways to use my skills. Today my income comes from three streams: helping small companies with social media and blogging (the biggest source), writing and selling e-guides and courses (my favorite), and taking freelance writing or editing assignments."

Formichelli is proud of being flexible. "When I've had it with magazine writing, I put more energy into my e-courses, and vice versa. Heck, I'm even a certified personal trainer, so if I get really sick of writing I can work out. But a definite side benefit to diversifying is that I'm more protected from the feast-or-famine nature of writing."

Sometimes pursuing the more common sense or lucrative income opportunity can open doors for the dream. When my novel didn't sell, I began writing freelance articles. Then I established FundsforWriters, using all the grant, contest, publisher and market research I did for myself. A decade later, once the site thrived with over 45,000 readers, I used the very research I'd gleaned for my readers to find an agent and sign a publishing contract . . . for the original novel started so long ago.

You can fight to fund one project or study all resources and fund a career. Opportunity is there. Just don't get so wrapped up in one angle that you miss the chance to invest more fully in your future.

C. HOPE CLARK manages FundsForWriters.com and is the author of several books, including *Lowcountry Bribe* and *Palmetto Poison*. Learn more at http://chopeclark.com.

THE AGENT QUERY TRACKER

Submit smarter and follow up faster with these simple spreadsheets to revolutionize your record-keeping.

....

Tyler Moss

Everyone knows the real magic of writing comes from time spent in the chair, those sessions in which your fingertips flitting across the keyboard can barely keep pace with the electric current sparking through your brain.

Those in-between periods, full of administrative tasks—the querying, the tracking of payments, the day-to-day doldrums that occupy the interstitial moments of a writer's life—become an afterthought. But when such responsibilities are given short shrift, the inevitable result is disorganization—which at best can impede creativity and at worst can have dire consequences. Missed payments, embarrassing gaffes (querying the same agent twice, or realizing you have no record of where your previous agent submitted your last novel), and incomplete records come tax time are entirely avoidable headaches.

Still, organized record-keeping takes work. Which is why we decided to do it for you.

This does not have to mean you're about to start spending more time on these tasks—in fact, quite the opposite. Once you invest in a standard process up front, each future action will require little more than filling out a few cells in a spreadsheet. (Learn to love them as I have for their clean, quadrilateral beauty.)

You can use the simple guides on the following pages to customize forms of your own, whether you're querying an agent, tracking the places your agent is submitting, or working on your freelancing career between projects.

AGENT QUERY TRACKER

AGENT	**Example:** Booker M. Sellington		
AGENCY	The Booker M. Sellington Agency		
E-MAIL	BMS@bmsagency.com		
DATE QUERIED	8/1/16		
MATERIALS SENT	Query, Synopsis, first 10 pages		
DATE FOLLOWED UP	9/1/16		
RESPONSE	Request for additional materials		
ADDITIONAL MATE-RIALS REQUESTED	Full manuscript		
DATE FOLLOWED UP	10/15/16		
RESPONSE	Offer of representation		
NOTES	Specializes in thrillers		

Few writers hit the jackpot and manage to land a literary agent on their first query. As this process can take weeks or months, and as agency guidelines vary widely, it can be helpful to keep a detailed record of whom you have contacted, what agency they work for, what materials you've sent in, and the specifics of their responses. Customize your own tracker starting from these column headings:

- **AGENT, AGENCY & E-MAIL:** Where you are sending your query
- **POLICY AGAINST QUERYING MULTIPLE AGENTS AT AGENCY:** [Optional Field] Some agencies have a no-from-one-agent-means-no-from-the-whole-agency policy; noting this saves you time and embarrassment, particularly at larger firms where multiple reps might seem like a potential fit
- **DATE QUERIED & MATERIALS SENT:** When and what you submitted, always following guidelines (query letter, first ten pages, synopsis, proposal, etc.)
- **"NO RESPONSE MEANS NO" POLICY:** [Optional Field] Agents who specify in their guidelines that no response equates to a rejection, meaning you shouldn't follow up
- **DATE FOLLOWED UP:** In the event of no response and excluding those with the policy noted above
- **RESPONSE:** A rejection, a request to see more, or any constructive feedback
- **ADDITIONAL MATERIALS REQUESTED & DATE SENT:** Typically a full or partial manuscript is requested if your query garners interest

- **DATE FOLLOWED UP:** For a full or partial, follow up after at least four weeks if there's no response (unless you have an offer for representation elsewhere, in which case you'll follow up immediately to request a decision or withdraw your manuscript from consideration)
- **RESPONSE:** The agent's final feedback or response
- **NOTES:** Any helpful info on your interaction with the agent or agency, or feedback that could be addressed before additional querying (e.g., "The protagonist often behaves erratically and inconsistently," or "The manuscript could use a proofread")

If you opt to forgo seeking representation and instead are submitting directly to publishers that accept unagented submissions, then I suggest you make a separate spreadsheet to track that information, swapping the headings **AGENT** and **AGENCY** for **ACQUIRING EDITOR** and **IMPRINT/PUBLISHER**, respectively.

ORGANIZE YOUR QUERIES

Both versions of the tracker are available for download at writersdigest.com/GLA-18.

AGENT SUBMISSIONS TO PUBLISHER TRACKER

IMPRINT/PUBLISHER	Example: Pendant Publishing		
ACQUIRING EDITOR	Elaine Benes		
DATE SENT	8/1/16		
DATE FOLLOWED UP	9/1/16		
RESPONSE	Pass		
EDITOR'S COMMENTS	Says a "book about nothing" is not right for their Spring 2018 lineup		
ADDITIONAL NOTES	Suggests changes to plot in which the judge sentences protagonist to be the antagonist's butler		

After signing with an agent, it's critical to stay in close communication as she sends your manuscript to publishers. Such records allow you to stay involved in the direction of your career, gather essential data about the imprints your agent believes you'd be best suited for, and pinpoint commonalities or contradictions in feedback. And if you must someday sever ties with your agent, you'll have what you need to help your new representation pick up right where your old representation left off. Keep record of the following details:

- **IMPRINT/PUBLISHER, ACQUIRING EDITOR & DATE SENT:** The details of exactly where and when your agent submitted your manuscript
- **DATE FOLLOWED UP:** Date on which your agent followed up with the acquiring editor if you did not receive an initial response
- **RESPONSE:** Accepted, rejected, revise-and-resubmit request
- **EDITOR'S COMMENTS:** A one-line description highlighting any relevant feedback received
- **ADDITIONAL NOTES:** Miscellaneous information about the publisher, editor or the overall interaction between agent and publishing house

---

PRO TIP: SAVE SPREADSHEETS TO GOOGLE DRIVE

Recently I read a news story in which a writer in New Orleans ran into his burning home to save the manuscripts of two completed novels stored on his computer—the only place he had them saved. Luckily, he weathered the blaze and escaped with laptop in hand. Though we can admire his dedication to his work, there are any number of digital-age options that could've prevented this horrible scenario—among them, Google Drive.

The system is ideal for uploading a fresh document of your manuscript every time you make changes, storing files online in addition to on your computer (Google Drive has an online storage function similar to services such as Dropbox and Microsoft OneDrive).

Google Drive allows you to create documents, spreadsheets, slide shows, and more, all of which can be accessed from anywhere—laptop, tablet, smartphone—by logging into a free Google account. Such items are easily shared with your co-author, agent, or publicist for more efficient record keeping or file sharing. It's also a great place to create and modify the trackers from this article.

Simply log in to your account at google.com/drive (or create one for free), hit the New button in the top left corner of the interface and click on Google Sheets. This will open a new window with a clean spreadsheet, where you can then begin entering the appropriate column headings. Title the spreadsheet by clicking "Untitled spreadsheet" at the top of the page. Once complete, you'll be able to open up your Freelance Payment Tracker or Agent Query Tracker on any device with an Internet connection—far from flames or flood.

FREELANCE PITCH TRACKER

SUBJECT	**Example:** Essay about meeting Stephen King in the waiting room at the dentist		
PUBLICATION	*Writer's Digest*		
EDITOR	Tyler Moss		
E-MAIL	wdsubmissions@ fwmedia.com		
PITCH SUBMITTED	8/1/16		
FOLLOW UP	8/15/16		
RESULT	Accepted		
DEADLINE	10/15/16		
NOTES	$0.50 cents/word for 600 words		

For freelance writers, ideas are currency—but they don't exist in a vacuum. Once you've brainstormed a solid premise and started to pitch potential markets, the resulting interactions can quickly clutter your in-box. Avoid losing track by recording your pitches in a spreadsheet with the following column headings:

- **SUBJECT:** One-line description of your story idea
- **PUBLICATION:** Name of magazine, website, or newspaper you pitched to
- **EDITOR & E-MAIL:** Where you sent your pitch
- **PITCH SUBMITTED:** When the query was sent
- **FOLLOW UP:** The date on which you plan to follow up if you haven't received a response (typically two weeks later, unless the submission guidelines specify otherwise)
- **RESULT:** Accepted, rejected, asked to rework
- **DEADLINE:** If accepted, date story is due
- **NOTES:** Additional info, based on your interactions with the editor (e.g., "Publication pays too little," or "Editor rejected pitch, but encouraged pitching again soon")

In addition to keeping track of irons currently in the fire, this spreadsheet is invaluable for later looking up contact info of editors you haven't e-mailed in a while.

If you want to track submissions to literary journals, simply switch out the column headings **SUBJECT** and **PUBLICATION** with **STORY TITLE** and **JOURNAL**, respectively, ax the **FOLLOW UP** column (journals tend to operate on slower, more sporadic schedules, sometimes without full-time staff), and replace the **DEADLINE** column with **READING FEE** (so you can evaluate and track any submission expenses where applicable).

ORGANIZE YOUR FREELANCE LIFE

Find both the freelance pitch and journal versions of this pitch tracker available for download at writersdigest.com/GLA-18.

FREELANCE PAYMENT TRACKER

ARTICLE HEADLINE	Example: Tongue Tied		
PUBLICATION/URL	*Ball & String Magazine*		
PAYMENT	$500		
DATE PUBLISHED	July 2016		
TOTAL WORDS	1,000		
$/WORD	$0.40 cents/word		
INVOICE #	#2014-1		
INVOICE SUBMITTED	8/12/16		
PAID	8/30/16		

When you've been commissioned to write a piece, it's vital to document the status of your payment. Not only will it keep you from missing a check, but it's incredibly useful for noting what a publication has paid you in the past and comparing the rates of different publications for which you freelance—which can help you prioritize your time by targeting the most lucrative outlets. It's also a lifesaver come April 15.

As depicted in the example spreadsheet above, you can use the following column headings to trace the path of your payments:

- **HEADLINE:** Title of the finished, published piece
- **PUBLICATION/URL:** Outlet that published the article and, if applicable, the URL where the article can be found online
- **PAYMENT:** Total payment received for work
- **DATE PUBLISHED:** Date article went live online, or issue month if for a print magazine or journal
- **TOTAL WORDS & $/WORD:** Length of the piece and amount you were paid per word, found by dividing the total payment by the total number of words (a common standardization for freelance payment rates)

- **INVOICE # & SUBMITTED:** Unique number of the invoice you submitted for this particular article (if applicable), and date on which it was submitted
- **PAID:** Date on which you received the payment, most commonly via check or direct deposit

Of course, you can also use this same basic format to develop a spreadsheet that covers advances, royalties, speaking honoraria, etc. Use the basic format outlined here to construct your own customized version.

TYLER MOSS is the editor-in-chief of *Writer's Digest*. Follow him on Twitter @tjmoss11.

CONTRACTS 101

....

by Cindy Ferraino

//

After you do a victory dance about getting the book deal you always dreamed about or your article hitting the top of the content list of a popular magazine, the celebration quickly comes to a halt when you realize you are not at the finish line yet. Your heart begins to beat faster because you know the next possible hurdle is just around the corner—the contract. For many, the idea of reviewing a contract is like being back in first grade. You know you have to listen to the teacher when you could be playing outside. You know you have to read this contract but why because there are terms in there that look like an excerpt from a foreign language syllabus.

Before I changed my status to self-employed writer, I was working as a grants and contracts administrator at a large medical university in Philadelphia. I helped shepherd the M.D. and Ph.D. researchers through the channels of grants and contracts administration. While the researchers provided the technical and scientific pieces that could potentially be the next cure for diabetes, heart disease, or cancer, I was there to make sure they did their magic within the confines of a budget and imposed contractual regulations. The budget process was easy but when it came to contract regulations—oh well, that was a different story. I became familiar with the terms such as indemnifications, property and intellectual rights, and conditions of payments. I was an integral part of reviewing and negotiating a grant or contract that had the best interests for every party involved.

After my son was born, I left the university and my contracts background went on a brief hiatus. Once my son went off to school, I began freelance writing. After a few writing gigs sprinkled with a few too many rejection slips, I landed an assignment for *Dog Fancy* magazine. I was thrilled and eagerly anticipated the arrival of a contract in my inbox. As I opened the document, the hiatus had lifted. I read through the contract and was able to send it back within a few hours.

For many new freelancers or writers who have been around the block, contract administration is not something that they can list as a perk on their resume. Instead of searching through the Yellow Pages for a contract lawyer or trying to call in a special favor to a writer friend, there are some easy ways for a newbie writer or even a seasoned writer to review a contract before putting a smiley face next to the dotted line.

TAKE A DEEP BREATH, THEN READ ON

Remember breaking those seals on test booklets and the voice in the background telling you, "Please read the directions slowly." As you tried to drown out the voice because your stomach was in knots, little did you know that those imparting words of wisdom would come in handy as you perspired profusely over the legal jargon that unfolded before your eyes. The same words go for contracts.

Many writers, including myself, are anxious to get an assignment underway, but the contract carrot continues to loom over our creative minds. "I'm surprised by writers who just skim a contract and then sign it without understanding what it means," says Kelly James-Enger, author of books including *Six Figure Freelancing: The Writer's Guide to Making More* (Random House) and the blog Dollarsanddeadlines.blogspot.com. "Most of the language in magazine contracts isn't that complicated, but it can be confusing when you're new to the business."

When I receive a contract from a new publisher or editor, I make a second copy. My children call it "my sloppy copy." I take out a highlighter and begin to mark up the key points of the contract: beginning and end date, conditions of payment, how my relationship is defined by the publisher, and what the outline of the article should look like.

The beginning and end date of a contract is crucial. After I recently negotiated a contract, the editor changed the due date of the article in an e-mail. I made sure the contract was changed to reflect the new due date. The conditions of the payments are important because it will describe when the writer will be paid and by what method. Most publishers have turned to incremental payment schedules or payments to be made online like PayPal. How the publisher considers your contractor status is important. If you're a freelance contract writer, the contract should reflect that as well as identify you as an independent contractor for IRS tax purposes. Finally, the contract will highlight an outline of what your article or proposal should look like.

As you slowly digest the terms you are about to agree to for your assignment or book project, you gain a better understanding of what an editor or publisher expects from you and when.

CUTTING TO THE LEGAL CHASE

Once you have had a chance to review a contract, you may be scratching your head and saying, "Okay, now what does this all mean to me as a writer?" James-Enger describes

PAYMENT TYPES

There are any number of different arrangements for publishers to pay writers. However, here are three of the most common and what they mean.

- Pays on acceptance. This means a publisher pays (or cuts a check) for the writer upon acceptance of the manuscript. This is usually the best deal a writer can hope to receive.
- Pays on publication. In these cases, a publisher pays (or cuts a check) for the writer by the publication date of the manuscript. For magazines, this could mean several months after the manuscript was accepted and approved. For books, this could mean more than a year.
- Pays after publication. Sometimes contracts will specify exactly how long after publication. Be wary of contracts that leave it open-ended.

three key areas where writers should keep sharp on when it comes to contracts—indemnification, pay and exclusivity provisions.

INDEMNIFICATION is a publisher's way of saying if something goes wrong, we are not responsible. If a claim is brought against another writer's work, a publisher does not want to be responsible for the legal aftermath but you could be the one receiving a notice in the mail. James-Enger warns writers to be on the lookout for indemnification clauses. "In the U.S., anyone can sue anyone over just about anything," she says; "I'm okay with agreeing to indemnification clauses that specify breaches of contract because I know I'm not going to plagiarize, libel or misquote anyone. But I can't promise that the publication will never be sued by anyone whether or not I actually breached the contract."

PAY is where you want the publisher "to show you the money." Writers need to be aware of how publishers will discuss the terms of payment in the contract. James-Enger advises to have "payment on acceptance." This means you will be paid when the editor agrees to accept your manuscript or article. If there is "no payment on acceptance," some publishers will pay when the article is published. "Push for payment whenever you can," she says.

EXCLUSIVITY PROVISIONS are where a particular publisher will not allow the writer to publish an article or manuscript that is "about the same or similar subject" during the time the publisher runs the piece. Because of the nature of the writing business, James-Enger feels writers need to negotiate this part of the contract. "I specialize in health, fitness and nutrition, and I'm always writing about a similar subject," she says.

CONTRACT TIPS

Even seasoned freelancers can find themselves intimidated by contracts. Here are a few things to consider with your contract:

- **KEEP COPY ON RECORD.** If the contract is sent via e-mail, keep a digital copy, but also print up a hard copy and keep it in an easy-to-find file folder.
- **CHECK FOR RIGHTS.** It's almost never a good idea to sell all rights. But you should also pay attention to whether you're selling any subsidiary or reprint rights. The more rights you release the more payment you should expect (and demand).
- **WHEN PAYMENT.** Make sure you understand when you are to be paid and have it specified in your contract. You may think that payment will come when the article is accepted or published, but different publishers have different policies. Get it in writing.
- **HOW MUCH PAYMENT.** The contract should specify exactly how much you are going to be paid. If there is no payment listed on the contract, the publisher could use your work for free.
- **TURN IN CONTRACT BEFORE ASSIGNMENT.** Don't start working until the contract is signed, and everything is official. As a freelancer, time is as important as money. Don't waste any of your time and effort on any project that is not yet contracted.

WHEN TO HEAD TO THE BARGAINING TABLE

Recently, I became an independent contractor for the American Composites Manufacturing Association (ACMA). When I reviewed the terms of the contract, I was concerned how my independent contractor status was identified. Although I am not an ACMA employee, I wanted to know if I could include my ACMA publications on my resume. Before I signed the contract, I questioned this issue with my editor. My editor told me I may use this opportunity to put on my resume. I signed the contract and finished my assignment.

Writers should be able to talk to an editor or a publisher if there is a question about a term or clause in a contract. "Don't be afraid to talk to the editor about the changes you'd like to make to a contract," James-Enger says; "You don't know what you'll get or if an editor is willing to negotiate it, until you ask."

When writers have to approach an editor for changes to a contract, James-Enger advises writers to act professionally when it comes to the negotiations. "I start out with saying—I am really excited to be working with you on this story and I appreciate the assignment, but I have a couple of issues with the contract that I'd like to talk to you about," she says. "Sure I want a better contract but I also want to maintain a good working relationship with my editor. A scorched-earth policy doesn't benefit any freelancer in the long run."

Negotiating payment terms is a tricky subject for some writers. Writers want to get the most bang for their buck but they don't want to lose a great writing assignment. Do your research first before you decide to ask an editor for more money to complete the assignment. Double check the publisher's website or look to see if the pay scale is equivalent to other publishers in the particular industry. Some publishers have a set publishing fee whereas others may have a little more wiggle room depending on the type of the assignment given. In today's economy, writers are a little more reluctant to ask for a higher rate for an article. If the publisher seems to be open to discussion about the pay scale, just make sure you approach the situation in a professional manner so as to not turn the publisher away from giving you another assignment.

WHO OWNS YOUR WRITING?

Besides payment terms, another area that writers may find themselves on the other end of the negotiation table is with ownership rights. We all want to take credit for the work that we have poured our heart and soul into. Unfortunately, the business of publishing has different ways of saying how a writer can classify their work. Ownership rights vary, but the biggest one that writers have a hard time trying to build up a good case against is "all rights." "All rights" is exactly what it means: *hope you are not in love with what you have just written because you will not be able to use it again.*

In recent months, I have written for two publications that I had given "all rights" to the company. My rationale is that I knew I would never need to use those articles again but I did make sure I was able to include those articles for my byline to show that I have publishing experience.

If you feel that you want to reuse or recycle an article that you had written a few years ago, you might want to consider negotiating an "all rights" clause or maybe going to another publisher. "We don't take all rights so there is no reason for authors to request we change the rights clause," says Angela Hoy, author and owner of WritersWeekly.com and Booklocker.com. "Our contracts were rated 'Outstanding' by Mark Levine (author of *The Fine Print of Self-Publishing*) and has also been called the clearest and fairest in the industry."

James-Enger is also an advocate of negotiating against contracts with an "all rights" clause. "I hate 'all rights' contracts, and try to avoid signing them as they preclude me from ever reselling the piece as a reprint to other markets," she says. "I explain that to editors, and I have been able to get editors to agree to let me retain nonexclusive reprint rights even when they buy all rights—which still lets me market the piece as a reprint." James-Enger also advises that "if the publisher demands all rights, then negotiate if the payment is sub-standard."

So if you are just receiving a contract in the mail for the first time or you are working with a new publisher, you should not be afraid of the legal lingo that blankets the message "we want to work with you." Contracts are meant to protect both the interests of the publishers and writers. Publishers want the commitment from writers that he or she will provide their best work and writers want to be recognized for their best work. But between those contracts lines, the legal lingo can cause writers to feel they need a law degree to review the contract. No, just sit back and relax and enjoy the prose that will take your writing to the next level.

RIGHTS AND WHAT THEY MEAN

A creative work can be used in many different ways. As the author of the work, you hold all rights to the work in question. When you agree to have your work published, you are granting a publisher the right to use your work in any number of ways. Whether that right is to publish the manuscript for the first time in a publication, or to publish it as many times and in as many ways as a publisher wishes, is up to you—it all depends on the agreed-upon terms. As a general rule, the more rights you license away, the less control you have over your work and the money you're paid. You should strive to keep as many rights to your work as you can.

Writers and editors sometimes define rights in a number of different ways. Below you will find a classification of terms as they relate to rights.

- **FIRST SERIAL RIGHTS.** Rights that the writer offers a newspaper or magazine to publish the manuscript for the first time in any periodical. All other rights remain with the writer. Sometimes the qualifier "North American" is added to these rights to specify a geographical limitation to the license. When content is excerpted from a book scheduled to be published, and it appears in a magazine or newspaper prior to book publication, this is also called first serial rights.
- **ONE-TIME RIGHTS.** Nonexclusive rights (rights that can be licensed to more than one market) purchased by a periodical to publish the work once (also known as simultaneous rights). That is, there is nothing to stop the author from selling the work to other publications at the same time.
- **SECOND SERIAL (REPRINT) RIGHTS.** Nonexclusive rights given to a newspaper or magazine to publish a manuscript after it has already appeared in another newspaper or magazine.
- **ALL RIGHTS.** This is exactly what it sounds like. "All rights" means an author is selling every right he has to a work. If you license all rights to your work, you forfeit the right to ever use the work again. If you think you may want to use the article again, you should avoid submitting to such markets or refuse payment and withdraw your material.
- **ELECTRONIC RIGHTS.** Rights that cover a broad range of electronic media, including websites, CD/DVDs, video games, smart phone apps, and more. The contract should

specify if—and which—electronic rights are included. The presumption is unspeci-fied rights remain with the writer.

- **SUBSIDIARY RIGHTS.** Rights, other than book publication rights, that should be cov-ered in a book contract. These may include various serial rights; movie, TV, audio, and other electronic rights; translation rights, etc. The book contract should specify who controls the rights (author or publisher) and what percentage of sales from the licensing of these rights goes to the author.
- **DRAMATIC, TV, AND MOTION PICTURE RIGHTS.** Rights for use of material on the stage, on TV, or in the movies. Often a one-year option to buy such rights is offered (generally for 10 percent of the total price). The party interested in the rights then tries to sell the idea to other people—actors, directors, studios, or TV networks. Some properties are optioned numerous times, but most fail to become full productions. In those cases, the writer can sell the rights again and again.

Sometimes editors don't take the time to specify the rights they are buying. If you sense that an editor is interested in getting stories, but doesn't seem to know what his and the writer's responsibilities are, be wary. In such a case, you'll want to explain what rights you're offering (preferably one-time or first serial rights only) and that you expect addi-tional payment for subsequent use of your work.

The Copyright Law that went into effect January 1, 1978, states writers are primarily sell-ing one-time rights to their work unless they—and the publisher—agree otherwise in writ-ing. Book rights are covered fully by contract between the writer and the book publisher.

CINDY FERRAINO has been blessed with a variety of assignments, including newspaper arti-cles, magazine articles, ghost-written articles, stories for books, and most recently authoring a book on accounting and bookkeeping terminology, *The Complete Dictionary of Accounting & Bookkeeping Terms Explained Simply* (Atlantic Publishing Group).

30-DAY PLATFORM CHALLENGE

Build Your Writing Platform in a Month

....

by Robert Lee Brewer

///

Whether writers are looking to find success through traditional publication or the self-publishing route, they'll find a strong writer platform will help them in their efforts. A platform is not marketing; it's the actual and quantifiable reach writers have to their target audience.

Here is a 30-day platform challenge I've developed to help writers get started in their own platform-building activities without getting overwhelmed. By accomplishing one task for one day, writers can feel a sense of accomplishment and still handle their normal daily activities. By the end of the month, writers should have a handle on what they need to do to keep growing their platform into the future.

DAY 1: DEFINE YOURSELF

For Day 1, define yourself. Don't worry about where you'd like to be in the future. Instead, take a look at who you are today, what you've already accomplished, what you're currently doing, etc.

EXAMPLE DEFINE YOURSELF WORKSHEET

Here is a chart I'm using (with my own answers). Your worksheet can ask even more questions. The more specific you can be the better for this exercise.

NAME (AS USED IN BYLINE): Robert Lee Brewer

POSITION(S): Senior Content Editor - Writer's Digest Writing Community; Author; Freelance Writer; Blogger; Event Speaker; Den Leader - Cub Scouts; Curator of Insta-poetry Series

SKILL(S): Editing, creative writing (poetry and fiction), technical writing, copywriting, database management, SEO, blogging, newsletter writing, problem solving, idea generation, public speaking, willingness to try new things, community building.

SOCIAL MEDIA PLATFORMS: Facebook, LinkedIn, Google+, Twitter, Tumblr, Blogger.

URLs: www.writersmarket.com; www.writersdigest.com/editor-blogs/poetic-asides;

http://robertleebrewer.blogspot.com/; www. robertleebrewer.com

ACCOMPLISHMENTS: Named 2010 Poet Laureate of Blogosphere; spoken at several events, including Writer's Digest Conference, AWP, Austin International Poetry Festival, Houston Poetry Fest, and more; author of Solving the World's Problems (Press 53); published and sold out of two limited edition poetry chapbooks, **ENTER** and **ESCAPE**; edited several editions of **Writer's Market** and **Poet's Market**; former GMVC conference champion in the 800-meter run and MVP of WCHS cross country and track teams; undergraduate award-winner in several writing disciplines at University of Cincinnati, including Journalism, Fiction, and Technical Writing; BA in English Literature from University of Cincinnati with certificates in writing for Creative Writing-Fiction and Professional and Technical Writing.

INTERESTS: Writing (all genres), family (being a good husband and father), faith, fitness (especially running and disc golf), fantasy football, reading.

IN ONE SENTENCE, WHO AM I? Robert Lee Brewer is a married Methodist father of five children (four sons and one daughter) who works as an editor but plays as a writer, specializing in poetry and blogging.

As long as you're being specific and honest, there are no wrong answers when it comes to defining yourself. However, you may realize that you have more to offer than you think. Or you may see an opportunity that you didn't realize even existed.

DAY 2:
SET YOUR GOALS

For today's platform-building task, set your goals. Include short-term goals and long-term goals. In fact, make a list of goals you can accomplish by the end of this year; then, make a list of goals you'd like to accomplish before you die.

EXAMPLE GOALS

Here are some of examples from my short-term and long-term goal lists:

SHORT-TERM GOALS:

- Promote new book, Solving the World's Problems.
- In April, complete April PAD Challenge on Poetic Asides blog.
- Get Writer's Market 2016 to printer ahead of schedule.
- Get Poet's Market 2016 to printer ahead of schedule.
- Lead workshop at Poetry Hickory event in April.
- Etc.

LONG-TERM GOALS:

- Publish book on platform development for small businesses.
- Raise 5 happy and healthy children into 5 happy, healthy, caring, and self-sufficient adults.
- Continue to learn how to be a better husband and human being.
- Become a bestselling novelist.
- Win Poet Laureate of the Universe honors.
- Etc.

Some writers may ask what defining your-self and creating goals has to do with plat-form development. I maintain that these are two of the most basic and important steps in the platform-building process, be-cause they define who you are and where you want to be.

A successful platform strategy should communicate who you are and help you get where you'd like to be (or provide you with a completely new opportunity). If you can't communicate who you are to strang-ers, then they won't realize how you might be able to help them or why you're impor-tant to them. If you don't have any goals, then you don't have any direction or pur-pose for your platform.

By defining who you are and what you want to accomplish, you're taking a huge step in establishing a successful writing and publishing career.

DAY 3:
JOIN FACEBOOK

For today's task, create a profile on Face-book. Simple as that. If you don't have one, it's as easy as going to www.facebook.com and signing up. It takes maybe 5 or 10 min-utes. If that.

10 FACEBOOK TIPS FOR WRITERS

Many readers probably already have a Face-book profile, and that's fine. If you have al-ready created a profile (or are doing so today), here are some tips for handling your profile:

- Complete your profile. The most checked page on most profiles is the About page. The more you share the better.
- Make everything public. Like it or not, writers are public figures. If you try to hide, it will limit the potential platform.
- Think about your audience in everything you do. When your social media profiles are public, anyone can view what you post. Keep this in mind at all times.
- Include a profile pic of yourself. Avoid setting your avatar as anything but a headshot of yourself. Many people don't like befriending a family pet or cartoon image.
- Update your status regularly. If you can update your status once per day, that's perfect. At the very least, update your status weekly. If your profile is a ghost town, people will treat it like one.
- Communicate with friends on Facebook. Facebook is a social networking site, but networking happens when you commu-nicate. So communicate.
- Be selective about friends. Find people who share your interests. Accept friends who share your interests. Other folks may be fake or inappropriate connections try-ing to build their "friend" totals.
- Be selective about adding apps. If you're not sure, it's probably best to avoid. Many users have wasted days, weeks, and even months playing silly games on Facebook.
- Join relevant groups. The emphasis should be placed on relevancy. For in-stance, I'm a poet, so I join poetry groups.

- Follow relevant fan pages. As with groups, the emphasis is placed on relevancy. In my case, I'm a fan of several poetry publications.

In addition to the tips above, be sure to always use your name as it appears in your byline. If you're not consistent in how you list your name in your byline, it's time to pick a name and stick with it. For instance, my byline name is Robert Lee Brewer—not Robbie Brewer, Bob Brewer, or even just Robert Brewer.

There are times when I absolutely can't throw the "Lee" in there, but the rest of the time it is Robert Lee Brewer. And the reasoning behind this is that it makes it easier for people who know me elsewhere to find and follow me on Facebook (or whichever social media site). Name recognition is super important when you're building your writer platform.

DAY 4:
JOIN TWITTER

For today's task, create a Twitter account. That's right. Go to www.twitter.com and sign up—if you're not already. This task will definitely take less than 5 minutes.

As with Facebook, I would not be surprised to learn that most readers already have a Twitter account. Here are three important things to keep in mind:

- **MAKE YOUR PROFILE BIO RELEVANT.** You might want to use a version of the sentence you wrote for Day 1's task. Look at my profile (twitter.com/robertleebrewer) if you need an example.

- **USE AN IMAGE OF YOURSELF.** One thing about social media (and online networking) is that people love to connect with other people. So use an image of yourself—not of your pet, a cute comic strip, a new age image, flowers, robots, etc.
- **MAKE YOUR TWITTER HANDLE YOUR BYLINE—IF POSSIBLE.** For instance, I am known as @RobertLeeBrewer on Twitter, because I use Robert Lee Brewer as my byline on articles, in interviews, at speaking events, on books, etc. Be as consistent with your byline as humanly possible.

Once you're in Twitter, try finding some worthwhile tweeps to follow. Also, be sure to make a tweet or two. As with Facebook, people will only interact with your profile if it looks like you're actually there and using your account.

SOME BASIC TWITTER TERMINOLOGY

Twitter has a language all its own. Here are some of the basics:

- **TWEET.** This is what folks call the 140-character messages that can be sent on the site. Anyone who follows you can access your tweets.
- **RT.** RT stands for re-tweet. This is what happens when someone shares your tweet, usually character for character. It's usually good form to show attribution for the author of the original tweet.
- **DM.** DM stands for direct message. This is a good way to communicate with someone on Twitter privately. I've ac-

tually had a few opportunities come my way through DMs on Twitter.

- **#.** The #-sign stands for hashtag. Hashtags are used to organize group conversations. For instance, Writer's Digest uses the #wdc to coordinate messages for their Writer's Digest Conferences. Anyone can start a hashtag, and they're sometimes used to add humor or emphasis to a tweet.
- **FF.** FF stands for follow Friday—a day typically set asides to highlight follow-worthy tweeps (or folks who use Twitter). There's also a WW that stands for writer Wednesday.

DAY 5: START A BLOG

For today's task, create a blog. You can use Blogger (www.blogger.com), WordPress (www.wordpress.com), or Tumblr (www.tumblr.com). In fact, you can use another blogging platform if you wish. To complete today's challenge, do the following:

- **CREATE A BLOG.** That is, sign up (if you don't already have a blog), pick a design (these can usually be altered later if needed), and complete your profile.
- **WRITE A POST FOR TODAY.** If you're not sure what to cover, you can just introduce yourself and share a brief explanation of how your blog got started. Don't make it too complicated.

If you already have a blog, excellent! You don't need to create a new one, but you might want to check out some ways to optimize what you have.

OPTIMIZE YOUR BLOG

Here are some tips for making your blog rock:

- **USE IMAGES IN YOUR POSTS.** Images are eye candy for readers, help with search engine optimization, and can even improve clicks when shared on social media sites, such as Facebook and Google+.
- **USE HEADERS IN POSTS.** Creating and bolding little headlines in your posts will go a long way toward making your posts easier to read and scan. Plus, they'll just look more professional.
- **WRITE SHORT.** Short sentences (fewer than 10 words). Short paragraphs (fewer than five sentences). Concision is precision in online composition.
- **ALLOW COMMENTS.** Most bloggers receive very few (or absolutely zero) comments in the beginning, but it pays to allow comments, because this gives your audience a way to interact with you. For my personal blog, I allow anyone to comment on new posts, but those that are more than a week old require my approval.

DAY 6: READ AND COMMENT ON A POST

For today's task, read at least one blog post and comment on it (linking back to your blog). And the comment should not be something along the lines of, "Hey, cool post. Come check out my blog." Instead, you need to find a blog post that really speaks to you and then make a thoughtful comment.

Here are a few possible ways to respond:

- **SHARE YOUR OWN EXPERIENCE.** If you've experienced something similar to what's covered in the post, share your own story. You don't have to write a book or anything, but maybe a paragraph or two.
- **ADD ANOTHER PERSPECTIVE.** Maybe the post was great, but there's another angle that should be considered. Don't be afraid to point that angle out.
- **ASK A QUESTION.** A great post usually will prompt new thoughts and ideas—and questions. Ask them.

As far as linking back to your blog, you could include your blog's URL in the comment, but also, most blogs have a field in their comments that allow you to share your URL. Usually, your name will link to that URL, which should either be your blog or your author website (if it offers regularly updated content).

It might seem like a lot of work to check out other blogs and comment on them, but this is an incredible way to make real connections with super users. These connections can lead to guest post and interview opportunities. In fact, they could even lead to speaking opportunities too.

DAY 7:
ADD SHARE BUTTONS TO YOUR BLOG

For today's challenge, add share buttons to your blog and/or website.

The easiest way to do this is to go to www.addthis.com and click on the Get AddThis button. It's big, bright, and orange. You can't miss it.

Basically, the site will give you button options, and you select the one you like best. The AddThis site will then provide you with HTML code that you can place into your site and/or blog posts. Plus, it provides analytics for bloggers who like to see how much the buttons are boosting traffic.

If you want customized buttons, you could enlist the help of a programmer friend or try playing with the code yourself. I recently learned that some really cool buttons on one friend's blog were created by her husband (yes, she married a programmer, though I don't think she had her blog in mind when she did so).

Plus, most blogging platforms are constantly adding new tools. By the time you read this article, there are sure to be plenty of fun new buttons, apps, and widgets available.

Here's the thing about social sharing buttons: They make it very easy for people visiting your site to share your content with their social networks via Facebook, Twitter, LinkedIn, Google+, Pinterest, and other sites. The more your content is shared the wider your writer platform.

DAY 8:
JOIN LINKEDIN

For today's challenge, create a LinkedIn profile. Go to www.linkedin.com and set it up in a matter of minutes. After creating profiles for Facebook and Twitter, this task should be easy.

LINKEDIN TIPS FOR WRITERS

In many ways, LinkedIn looks the same as the other social networks, but it does have its own quirks. Here are a few tips for writers:

- **USE YOUR OWN HEAD SHOT.** You've heard this advice before. People want to connect with people, not family pets and/or inanimate objects.
- **COMPLETE YOUR PROFILE.** The more complete your profile the better. It makes you look more human.
- **GIVE THOUGHTFUL RECOMMENDATIONS TO RECEIVE THEM.** Find people likely to give you recommendations and recommend them first. This will prompt them to return the favor.
- **SEARCH FOR CONNECTIONS YOU ALREADY HAVE.** This is applicable to all social networks. Find people you know to help you connect with those you don't.
- **MAKE MEANINGFUL CONNECTIONS WITH OTHERS.** Remember: It's not about how many connections you make; it's about how many meaningful connections you make.
- **MAKE YOUR PROFILE EASY TO FIND.** You can do this by using your byline name. (For instance, I use linkedin.com/in/robertleebrewer.)
- **TAILOR YOUR PROFILE TO YOUR VISITOR.** Don't fill out your profile thinking only about yourself; instead, think about what your target audience might want to learn about you.

LinkedIn is often considered a more "professional" site than the other social networks like Facebook, Google+, and Twitter. For one thing, users are prompted to share their work experience and request recommendations from past employers and current co-workers.

However, this site still offers plenty of social networking opportunities for people who can hook up with the right people and groups.

DAY 9:
RESPOND TO AT LEAST THREE TWEETS

For today's task, respond to at least three tweets from other tweeps on Twitter.

Since Day 4's assignment was to sign up for Twitter, you should have a Twitter account—and you're hopefully following some other Twitter users. Just respond to at least three tweets today.

As far as your responses, it's not rocket science. You can respond with a "great article" or "cool quote." A great way to spread the wealth on Twitter is to RT (retweet) the original tweet with a little note. This accomplishes two things:

- One, it lets the tweep know that you appreciated their tweet (and helps build a bond with that person); and
- Two, it brings attention to that person for their cool tweet.

Plus, it helps show that you know how to pick great resources on Twitter, which automatically improves your credibility as a resource on Twitter.

DAY 10:
DO A GOOGLE SEARCH ON YOURSELF

For today's task, do a search on your name.

First, see what results appear when you search your name on Google (google.com). Then, try searching on Bing (bing.com). Finally, give Yahoo (yahoo.com) a try.

By searching your name, you'll receive insights into what others will find (and are already finding) when they do a search specifically for you. Of course, you'll want to make sure your blog and/or website is number one in the search results. If it isn't, we'll be covering SEO (or search engine optimization) topics later in this challenge.

OTHER SEARCH ENGINES

For those who want extra credit, here are some other search engines to try searching (for yourself):

- DuckDuckGo.com
- Ask.com
- Dogpile.com
- Yippy.com
- YouTube.com

(Note: It's worth checking out which images are related to your name as well. You may be surprised to find which images are connected to you.)

DAY 11:
FIND A HELPFUL ARTICLE AND LINK TO IT

For today's task, find a helpful article (or blog post) and share it with your social network—and by social network, I mean that you should share it on Facebook, Twitter, and LinkedIn at a minimum. If you participate on message boards or on other social networks, share in those places as well.

Before linking to an article on fantasy baseball or celebrity news, however, make sure your article (or blog post) aligns with your author platform goals. You should have an idea of who you are and who you want to be as a writer, and your helpful article (or blog post) should line up with those values.

Of course, you may not want to share articles for writers if your platform is based on parenting tips or vampires or whatever. In such cases, you'll want to check out other resources online. Don't be afraid to use a search engine.

For Twitter, you may wish to use a URL shortener to help you keep under the 140-character limit. Here are five popular URL shorteners:

- bit.ly. This is my favorite.
- goo.gl. Google's URL shortener.
- owl.ly. Hootsuite's URL shortener.
- deck.ly. TweetDeck's URL shortener.
- su.pr. StumbleUpon's URL shortener.

By the way, here's an extra Twitter tip. Leave enough room in your tweets to allow space for people to attribute your Twitter handle if they decide to RT you. For instance, I always leave at least 20 characters to allow people space to tweet "RT @robertleebrewer" when retweeting me.

DAY 12:
WRITE A BLOG POST AND IN-CLUDE CALL TO ACTION

For today's task, write a new blog post for your blog. In the blog post, include a call to action at the end of the post.

What's a call to action?

I include calls to action at the end of all my posts. Sometimes, they are links to products and services offered by my employer (F+W Media) or some other entity. Often, I include links to other posts and ways to follow me on other sites. Even the share buttons are a call to action of sorts.

Why include a call to action?

A call to action is good for giving readers direction and a way to engage more with you. Links to previous posts provide readers with more helpful or interesting information. Links to your social media profiles give readers a way to connect with you on those sites. These calls to action are beneficial to you and your readers when they are relevant.

What if I'm just getting started?

Even if you are completely new to everything, you should have an earlier blog post from last week, a Twitter account, a Facebook account, and a LinkedIn account. Link to these at the end of your blog post today. It's a proper starting place.

And that's all you need to do today. Write a new blog post with a call to action at the end. (By the way, if you're at a loss and need something to blog about, you can always comment on that article you shared yesterday.)

DAY 13:
LINK TO POST ON SOCIAL MEDIA PROFILES

For today's challenge, link your blog post from yesterday to your social networks.

At a minimum, these social networks should include Facebook, Twitter, and LinkedIn. However, if you frequent message boards related to your blog post or other social networks (like Google+, Pinterest, etc.), then link your blog post there as well.

I understand many of you may have already completed today's challenge. If so, hooray! It's important to link your blog to your social media accounts and vice versa. When they work together, they grow together.

Is it appropriate to link to my blog post multiple times?

All writers develop their own strategies for linking to their articles and blog posts, but here's my rule. I will usually link to each blog post on every one of my social networks at least once. Since I have a regular profile and a fan page on Facebook, I link to each of those profiles once—and I only link to posts once each on Google+ and Linke-dIn. But Twitter is a special case.

The way Twitter works, tweets usually only have a few minutes of visibility for tweeps with an active stream. Even tweeps with at least 100 follows may only have a 30-minute to hour window of opportunity to see your tweet. So for really popular and timely blog posts, I will tweet them more often than once on Twitter.

That said, I'm always aware of how I'm linking and don't want to become that annoying spammer that I typically avoid following in my own social networking efforts.

LINKING TIPS

Some tips on linking to your post:

- Use a URL shortener. These are discussed above.
- Apply title + link formula. For instance, I might Tweet this post as: Platform Challenge: Day 13: (link). It's simple and to the point. Plus, it's really effective if you have a great blog post title.
- Frame the link with context. Using this post as an example, I might Tweet: Take advantage of social media by linking to your blog posts: (link). Pretty simple, and it's an easy way to link to the same post without making your Twitter feed look loaded with the same content.
- Quote from post + link formula. Another tactic is to take a funny or thought-provoking quote from the post and combine that with a link. Example Tweet: "I will usually link to each blog post on every one of my social networks at least once." (link). Again, easy stuff.

DAY 14:
JOIN GOOGLE+

For today's task, create a Google+ (plus. google.com) profile.

Many of you may already have G+ profiles, but this social networking site is still rather new compared to Facebook and Twitter. Plus, Google+ status updates often show up in search results on Google's search engine.

I've heard people describe Google+ as a mix between Facebook and Twitter, and I don't think that's too far off the mark. Personally, I think it's still growing, which can be a good and bad thing.

The good news is that you could still be one of the first G+-users on the block; bad news is that you have to wait (and hope) for other people to migrate over to the block. Of course, Google has a huge reach online, so there's no reason to doubt that people will migrate...eventually.

One tool I've really learned to appreciate on Google+ is the Hangouts feature, which makes it easy to record video chats with other people, including experts in your field on Google+ and then share permanently on YouTube. Since I feel video is the future of online, I think this is really cool.

As with Facebook and LinkedIn, keep these tips in mind:

- Complete your profile completely. Use your name. Provide easy to find contact information. Describe who you are.
- Use an image of yourself. Not a cartoon. Not an animal. Not a piece of art. Remember that people like to connect with other people.
- Post new content regularly. Let people know you are using your account. That means connecting with other G+'ers as well.

DAY 15:
MAKE THREE NEW CONNECTIONS

For today's task, make an attempt to connect with at least three new people on one of your social networks.

Doesn't matter if it's Facebook, Twitter, LinkedIn, or Google+. The important thing is that you find three new people who appear to share your interests and that you try to friend, follow, or connect to them.

As a person who has limited wiggle room for approving new friends on Facebook, I'd like to share what approach tends to work the best with me for approving new friend requests. Basically, send your request and include a brief message introducing yourself and why you want to connect with me.

That's right. The best way to win me over is to basically introduce yourself. Something along the lines of, "Hello. My name is Robert Lee Brewer, and I write poetry. I read a poem of yours in *XYZ Literary Journal* that I totally loved and have sent you a friend request. I hope you'll accept it." Easy as that.

Notice that I did not mention anything about checking out my blog or reading my poems. How would you like it if someone introduced themselves and then told you to buy their stuff? It sounds a bit telemarketer-ish to me.

While it's important to cultivate the relationships you already have, avoid getting stuck in a rut when it comes to making connections. Always be on the lookout for new connections who can offer new opportunities and spark new ideas. Your writing and your career will benefit.

DAY 16:
ADD E-MAIL FEED TO BLOG

For today's challenge, add an e-mail feed to your blog.

There are many ways to increase traffic to your blog, but one that has paid huge dividends for me is adding Feedblitz to my blog. As the subscribers to my e-mail feed have increased, my blog traffic has increased as well. In fact, after great content, I'd say that adding share buttons (mentioned above) and an e-mail feed are the top two ways to build traffic.

Though I have an account on Tumblr, I'm just not sure if it offers some kind of e-mail/RSS feed service.

The reason I think e-mail feeds are so useful is that they pop into my inbox whenever a new post is up, which means I can check it very easily on my phone when I'm waiting somewhere. In fact, this is how I keep up with several of my favorite blogs. It's just one more way to make your blog content accessible to readers in a variety of formats.

If I remember, this task didn't take me long to add, but I've been grateful for finally getting around to adding it ever since.

DAY 17:
TAKE PART IN A TWITTER CONVERSATION

For today's task, take part in a Twitter conversation.

Depending upon the time of month or day of week, there are bound to be any number of conversations happening around a hashtag (mentioned above). For instance, various conferences and expos have hashtag conversations that build around their panels and presentations.

Poets will often meet using the #poetparty hashtag. Other writers use #amwriting to communicate about their writing goals. Click on the hashtag to see what others are saying, and then, jump in to join the conversation and make new connection on Twitter.

DAY 18:
THINK ABOUT SEO

For today's task, I want you to slow down and think a little about SEO (which is tech-speak for search engine optimization, which is itself an intelligent way of saying "what gets your website to display at or near the top of a search on Google, Bing, Yahoo, etc.").

So this task is actually multi-pronged:

- Make a list of keywords that you want your website or blog to be known for. For instance, I want my blog to be known for terms like "Robert Lee Brewer," "Writing Tips," "Parenting Tips," "Platform Tips," "Living Tips," etc. Think big here and don't limit yourself to what you think you can actually achieve in the short term.
- Compare your website or blog's current content to your keywords. Are you lining up your actual content with how you want your audience to view you and your online presence? If not, it's time to think about how you

can start offering content that lines up with your goals. If so, then move on to the next step, which is...
- Evaluate your current approach to making your content super SEO-friendly. If you need some guidance, check out my SEO Tips for Writers below. There are very simple things you can do with your titles, subheads, and images to really improve SEO. Heck, I get a certain bit of traffic every single day just from my own SEO approach to content—sometimes on surprising posts.
- Research keywords for your next post. When deciding on a title for your post and subheads within the content, try researching keywords. You can do this using Google's free keyword tool (googlekeywordtool.com). When possible, you want to use keywords that are searched a lot but that have low competition. These are the low-hanging fruit that can help you build strong SEO for your website or blog.

A note on SEO: It's easy to fall in love with finding keywords and changing your content to be keyword-loaded and blah-blah-blah. But resist making your website or blog a place that is keyword-loaded and blah-blah-blah. Because readers don't stick around for too much keyword-loaded blah-blah-blah. It's kind of blah. And bleck. Instead, use SEO and keyword research as a way to optimize great content and to take advantage of opportunities as they arise.

SEO TIPS FOR WRITERS

Here are a few SEO tips for writers:

- Use keywords naturally. That is, make sure your keywords match the content of the post. If they don't match up, people will abandon your page fast, which will hurt your search rankings.
- Use keywords appropriately. Include your keywords in the blog post title, opening paragraph, file name for images, headers, etc. Anywhere early and relevant should include your keyword to help place emphasis on that search term, especially if it's relevant to the content.
- Deliver quality content. Of course, search rankings are helped when people click on your content and spend time reading your content. So provide quality content, and people will visit your site frequently and help search engines list you higher in their rankings.
- Update content regularly. Sites that are updated more with relevant content rank higher in search engines. Simple as that.
- Link often to relevant content. Link to your own posts; link to content on other sites. Just make sure the links are relevant and of high interest to your audience.
- Use images. Images help from a design perspective, but they also help with SEO, especially when you use your main keywords in the image file name.
- Link to your content on social media sites. These outside links will help increase your ranking on search engines.
- Guest post on other sites/blogs. Guest posts on other blogs are a great way to provide traffic from other relevant sites

that increase the search engine rankings on your site.

DAY 19:
WRITE A BLOG POST

For today's task, write a new blog post.

Include a call to action (for instance, encourage readers to sign up for your e-mail feed and to share the post with others using your share buttons) and link to it on your social networks. Also, don't forget to incorporate SEO.

One of the top rules of finding success with online tools is applying consistency. While it's definitely a great thing if you share a blog post more than once a week, I think it's imperative that you post at least once a week.

The main reason? It builds trust with your readers that you'll have something to share regularly and gives them a reason to visit regularly.

So today's task is not about making things complicated; it's just about keeping it real.

DAY 20:
CREATE EDITORIAL CALENDAR

For today's task, I want you to create an editorial calendar for your blog (or website). Before you start to panic, read on.

First, here's how I define an editorial calendar: A list of content with dates attached to when the content goes live. For instance, I created an editorial calendar specifically for my Platform Challenge and

"Platform Challenge: Day 20" was scheduled to go live on day 20.

It's really simple. In fact, I keep track of my editorial calendar with a paper notebook, which gives me plenty of space for crossing things out, jotting down ideas, and attaching Post-It notes.

EDITORIAL CALENDAR IDEAS

Here are tips for different blogging frequencies:

- Post once per week. If you post once a week, pick a day of the week for that post to happen each week. Then, write down the date for each post. Beside each date, write down ideas for that post ahead of time. There will be times when the ideas are humming and you get ahead on your schedule, but there may also be times when the ideas are slow. So don't wait, write down ideas as they come.
- Post more than once per week. Try identifying which days you'll usually post (for some, that may be daily). Then, for each of those days, think of a theme for that day. For instance, my 2012 schedule offered Life Changing Moments on Wednesdays and Poetic Saturdays on Saturdays.

You can always change plans and move posts to different days, but the editorial calendar is an effective way to set very clear goals with deadlines for accomplishing them. Having that kind of structure will improve your content—even if your blog is personal, fictional, poetic, etc. Believe me, I used to be a skeptic before diving in, and the results on my personal blog speak for themselves.

One more benefit of editorial calendars

There are times when I feel less than inspired. There are times when life throws me several elbows as if trying to prevent me from blogging. That's when I am the most thankful for maintaining an editorial calendar, because I don't have to think of a new idea on the spot; it's already there in my editorial calendar.

Plus, as I said earlier, you can always change plans. I can alter the plan to accommodate changes in my schedule. So I don't want to hear that an editorial calendar limits spontaneity or inspiration; if anything, having an editorial calendar enhances it.

One last thing on today's assignment

Don't stress yourself out that you have to create a complete editorial calendar for the year or even the month. I just want you to take some time out today to think about it, sketch some ideas, and get the ball rolling. I'm 100% confident that you'll be glad you did.

DAY 21: SIGN UP FOR SOCIAL MEDIA TOOL

For today's task, try joining one of the social media management tools, such as Tweetdeck, Hootsuite, or Seesmic.

Social media management tools are popular among social media users for one reason: They help save time and effort in managing multiple social media platforms. For instance, they make following specific threads in Twitter a snap.

I know many social media super users who swear by these tools, but I actually have tried them and decided to put in the extra effort to log in to my separate social media accounts manually each day.

Here's my reasoning: I like to feel connected to my profile and understand how it looks and feels on a day-to-day basis. Often, the design and feel of social media sites will change without notice, and I like to know what it feels like at ground zero.

DAY 22: PITCH GUEST BLOG POST

For today's task, pitch a guest blog post to another blogger.

Writing guest posts is an incredible way to improve your exposure and expertise on a subject, while also making a deeper connection with the blogger who is hosting your guest post. It's a win for everyone involved.

In a recent interview with super blogger Jeff Goins, he revealed that most of his blog traffic came as a result of his guest posting on other blogs. Some of these blogs were directly related to his content, but he said many were in completely different fields.

GUEST POST PITCHING TIPS

After you know where you want to guest blog, here are some tips for pitching your guest blog post:

- Let the blogger know you're familiar with the blog. You should do this in one sentence (two sentences max) and be specific. For instance, a MNINB reader could say, "I've been reading your Not Bob blog for months, but I really love this Platform Challenge." Simple as that. It lets me know you're not a spammer, but it doesn't take me a long time to figure out what you're trying to say.

- Propose an idea or two. Each idea should have its own paragraph. This makes it easy for the blogger to know where one idea ends and the next one begins. In a pitch, you don't have to lay out all the details, but you do want to be specific. Try to limit the pitch to 2-4 sentences.

- Share a little about yourself. Emphasis on "a little." If you have previous publications or accomplishments that line up with the blog, share those. If you have expertise that lines up with the post you're pitching, share those. Plus, include any details about your online platform that might show you can help bring traffic to the post. But include all this information in 1-4 sentences.

- Include your information. When you close the pitch, include your name, e-mail, blog (or website) URL, and other contact information you feel comfortable sharing. There's nothing more awkward for me than to have a great pitch that doesn't include the person's name. Or a way to learn more about the person.

What do I do after the pitch is accepted?

First off, congratulations! This is a great opportunity to show off your writing skills. Here's how to take advantage of your guest post assignment:

- **WRITE AN EXCEPTIONAL POST.** Don't hold back your best stuff for your blog. Write a post that will make people want to find more of your writing.
- **TURN IN YOUR POST ON DEADLINE.** If there's a deadline, hit it. If there's not a deadline, try to turn around the well-written post in a timely manner.
- **PROMOTE THE GUEST POST.** Once your guest post has gone live, promote it like crazy by linking to your post on your blog, social networks, message boards, and wherever else makes sense for you. By sending your own connections to this guest post, you're establishing your own expertise—not only through your post but also your connections.

DAY 23:
CREATE A TIME MANAGEMENT PLAN

For today's task, create a time management plan.

You may be wondering why I didn't start out the challenge with a time management plan, and here's the reason: I don't think some people would've had any idea how long it takes them to write a blog post, share a link on Twitter and Facebook, respond to social media messages, etc. Now, many of you probably have a basic idea—even if you're still getting the hang of your new-fangled social media tools.

Soooo... the next step is to create a time management plan that enables you to be "active" socially and connect with other writers and potential readers while also spending a majority of your time writing and publishing.

As with any plan, you can make this as simple or complicated as you wish. For instance, my plan is to do 15 minutes or less of social media after completing each decent-sized task on my daily task list. I use social media time as a break, which I consider more productive than watching TV or playing Angry Birds.

I put my writing first and carve out time in the mornings and evenings to work on poetry and fiction. Plus, I consider my blogging efforts part of my writing too. So there you go.

My plan is simple and flexible, but if you want to get hardcore, break down your time into 15-minute increments. Then, test out your time management plan to see if it works for you. If not, then make minor changes to the plan until it has you feeling somewhat comfortable with the ratio of time you spend writing and time you spend building your platform.

Remember: A platform is a life-long investment in your career. It's not a sprint, so you have to pace yourself. Also, it's not something that happens overnight, so you can't wait until you need a platform to start building one. Begin today and build over time—so that it's there when you need it.

DAY 24:
TAKE PART IN A FACEBOOK CONVERSATION

For today's task, take part in a conversation on Facebook.

You should've already participated in a Twitter conversation, so this should be somewhat similar—except you don't have to play with hashtags and 140-character restrictions. In fact, you just need to find a group conversation or status update that speaks to you and chime in with your thoughts.

Don't try to sell or push anything when you join a conversation. If you say interesting things, people will check out your profile, which if filled out will lead them to more information about you (including your website, blog, any books, etc.).

Goal one of social media is making connections. If you have everything else optimized, sales and opportunities will take care of themselves.

DAY 25:
CONTACT AN EXPERT FOR AN INTERVIEW POST

For today's task, find an expert in your field and ask if that expert would like to be interviewed.

If you can secure the interview, this will make for a great blog post. Or it may help you secure a freelance assignment with a publication in your field. Or both, and possibly more.

How to Ask for an Interview
Believe it or not, asking for an interview with an expert is easy. I do it all the time, and these are the steps I take.

- **FIND AN EXPERT ON A TOPIC.** This is sometimes the hardest part: figuring out who I want to interview. But I never kill myself trying to think of the perfect person, and here's why: I can always ask for more interviews. Sometimes, it's just more productive to get the ball rolling than come up with excuses to not get started.
- **LOCATE AN E-MAIL FOR THE EXPERT.** This can often be difficult, but a lot of experts have websites that share either e-mail addresses or have online contact forms. Many experts can also be reached via social media sites, such as Facebook, Twitter, LinkedIn, Google+, etc. Or they can be contacted through company websites. And so on.
- **SEND AN E-MAIL ASKING FOR AN E-MAIL INTERVIEW.** Of course, you can do this via an online contact form too. If the expert says no, that's fine. Respond with a "Thank you for considering and maybe we can make it work sometime in the future." If the expert says yes, then it's time to send along the questions.

How to Handle an E-mail Interview

Once you've secured your expert, it's time to compose and send the questions. Here are some of my tips.

- **ALWAYS START OFF BY ASKING QUESTIONS ABOUT THE EXPERT.** This might seem obvious to some, but you'd be surprised how many people start off asking "big questions" right out of the gate. Always start off by giving the expert a chance to talk about what he or she is doing, has recently done, etc.

- **LIMIT QUESTIONS TO 10 OR FEWER.** The reason for this is that you don't want to overwhelm your expert. In fact, I usually ask around eight questions in my e-mail interviews. If I need to, I'll send along some follow-up questions, though I try to limit those as well. I want the expert to have an enjoyable experience, not a horrible experience. After all, I want the expert to be a connection going forward.
- **TRY NOT TO GET TOO PERSONAL.** If experts want to get personal in their answers, that's great. But try to avoid getting too personal in the questions you ask, because you may offend your expert or make them feel uncomfortable. Remember: You're interviewing the expert, not leading an interrogation.
- **REQUEST ADDITIONAL INFORMATION.** By additional information, I mean that you should request a headshot and a preferred bio—along with any links. To make the interview worth the expert›s time, you should afford them an opportunity to promote themselves and their projects in their bios.

Once the Interview Goes Live...

Link to it on your social networks and let your expert know it is up (and include the specific link to the interview). If you're not already searching for your next expert to interview, be sure to get on it.

DAY 26: WRITE A BLOG POST AND LINK TO SOCIAL PROFILES

For today's task, write a new blog post.

In your blog post, include a call to action and link it on your social networks. Also, don't forget SEO.

Remember: One of the top rules of finding success with online tools is applying consistency. While it's definitely a great thing if you share a blog post more than once a week, I think it's imperative that you post at least once a week.

The main reason? It builds trust with your readers that you'll have something to share regularly and gives them a reason to visit regularly.

If this sounds repetitive, good; it means my message on consistency is starting to take root.

DAY 27: JOIN ANOTHER SOCIAL MEDIA SITE

For today's task, join one new social media site. I will leave it up to you to decide which new social media site it will be.

Maybe you'll join Pinterest. Maybe you'll choose Goodreads. Heck, you might go with RedRoom or some social media site that's not even on my radar at the time of this article. Everything is constantly evolving, which is why it's good to always try new things.

To everyone who doesn't want another site to join...

I understand your frustration and exhaustion. During a normal month, I'd never suggest someone sign up for so many social media sites in such a short period of time, but this isn't a normal month. We're in the midst of a challenge!

And no, I don't expect you to spend a lot of time on every social media site you join. That's not always the point when you first sign up. No, you sign up to poke around and see if the site interests you at all. See if you have any natural connections. Try mingling a little bit.

If the site doesn't appeal to you, feel free to let it be for a while. Let me share a story with you.

How I Came to Rock Facebook and Twitter

My Facebook and Twitter accounts both boast more than 5,000 followers (or friends/subscribers) today. But both accounts were originally created and abandoned, because they just weren't right for me at the time that I signed up.

For Facebook, I just didn't understand why I would abandon a perfectly good MySpace account to play around on a site that didn't feature the same level of music and personal blogging that MySpace did. But then, MySpace turned into Spam-opolis, and the rest is history.

For Twitter, I just didn't get the whole tweet concept, because Facebook already had status updates. Why tweet when I could update my status on Facebook?

But I've gained a lot professionally and personally from Facebook and Twitter—even though they weren't the right sites for me initially. In fact, Google+ is sort of in

that area for me right now. I don't use it near enough, but I started an account, because it just feels like a place that will explode sooner or later. It's not like Facebook is going to be around forever.

The Importance of Experimentation

Or as I prefer to think of it: The importance of play. You should constantly try new things, whether in your writing, your social media networks, or the places you eat food. Not only does it make life more exciting and provide you with new experiences and perspective, but it also helps make you a more well-rounded human being.

So don't complain about joining a new social media site. Instead, embrace the excuse to try something new, especially when there are only three more tasks left this month (and I promise no more new sites after today).

DAY 28: READ POST AND COMMENT ON IT

For today's task, read and comment on a blog post, making sure that your comment links back to your blog or website.

If you remember, this was the same task required way back on Day 6. How far we've come, though it's still a good idea to stay connected and engaged with other bloggers. I know I find that sometimes I start to insulate myself in my own little blogging communities and worlds—when it's good to get out and read what others are doing. In fact, that's what helped inspire my Monday Advice for Writers posts—it gives me motivation to read what others are writing (on writing, of course).

DAY 29:
MAKE A TASK LIST

For today's task, make a task list of things you are going to do on each day next month. That's right, I want you to break down 31 days with 31 tasks for each day—similar to what we've done this month.

You see, I don't want you to quit challenging yourself once this challenge is over. Of course, you get to decide what the tasks will be. So if you aren't into new social media sites, don't put them on your list. Instead, focus on blog posts, commenting on other sites, linking to articles, contacting experts, or whatever it is that you are going to do next month to keep momentum building toward an incredible author platform.

Somewhere near the end of the month, you should have a day set aside with one task: Make a task list of things to do on each day of the next month. And so on and

so forth. Keep it going, keep it rolling, and your efforts will continue to gain momentum and speed. I promise.

DAY 30:
ENGAGE THE WORLD

For today's task, engage the world.

By this, I mean that you should comment on status updates, ask questions, share answers, start debates, continue debates, and listen—that's right, don't be that person who dominates a conversation and makes it completely one-sided.

Engage the world by entering the conversation. Engage the world by having the courage to take risks and share things of consequence. Engage the world by having the courage to make mistakes and fail and learn from those mistakes and failures.

The only people who never fail are those who never try, and those people never succeed at anything except avoiding failure and success. Don't be that person. Engage the world and let the world engage you.

ROBERT LEE BREWER is an editor with the Writer's Digest Writing Community and author of *Solving the World's Problems* (Press 53). Follow him on Twitter @robertleebrewer.

BOOK PUBLISHERS

///

There's no magic formula for getting published. It's a matter of getting the right manuscript on the right editor's desk at the right time. Before you submit it's important to learn publishers' needs, see what kind of books they're producing, and decide which publishers your work is best suited for. *Children's Writer's & Illustrator's Market* is but one tool in this process. (Those just starting out, turn to the article "Quick Tips for Writers & Illustrators" in this book.)

To help you narrow down the list of possible publishers for your work, we've included several indexes at the back of this book. The **Subject Index** lists book and magazine publishers according to their fiction and nonfiction needs or interests. The **Age-Level Index** indicates which age groups publishers cater to.

If you write contemporary fiction for young adults, for example, and you're trying to place a book manuscript, go first to the Subject Index. Locate the fiction categories under Book Publishers and copy the list under Contemporary. Then go to the Age-Level Index and highlight the publishers on the Contemporary list that are included under the Young Adults heading. Read the listings for the highlighted publishers to see if your work matches their needs.

Remember, *Children's Writer's & Illustrator's Market* should not be your only source for researching publishers. Here are a few other sources of information:

- The Society of Children's Book Writers and Illustrators (SCBWI) offers members an annual market survey of children's book publishers for the cost of postage or free online at www.scbwi.org. (SCBWI membership information can also be found at www. scbwi.org.)
- The Children's Book Council website (www.cbcbooks.org) gives information on member publishers.
- If a publisher interests you, send a SASE for submission guidelines or check publishers' websites for guidelines *before* submitting. To quickly find guidelines online, visit The Colossal Directory of Children's Publishers at www.signaleader.com.
- Check publishers' websites. Many include their complete catalogs, which you can browse. Web addresses are included in many publishers' listings.

- Spend time at your local bookstore to see who's publishing what. While you're there, browse through *Publishers Weekly* and *The Horn Book*.

SUBSIDY & SELF-PUBLISHING

Some determined writers who receive rejections from royalty publishers may look to subsidy and co-op publishers as an option for getting their work into print. These publishers ask writers to pay all or part of the costs of producing a book. We strongly advise writers and illustrators to work only with publishers who pay them. For this reason, we've adopted a policy not to include any subsidy or co-op publishers in *Children's Writer's & Illustrator's Market* (or any other Writer's Digest Books market book).

If you're interested in publishing your book just to share it with friends and relatives, self-publishing is a viable option, but it involves time, energy, and money. You oversee all book production details. Check with a local printer for advice and information on cost or check online for print-on-demand publishing options (which are often more affordable).

Whatever path you choose, keep in mind that the market is flooded with submissions, so it's important for you to hone your craft and submit the best work possible. Competition from thousands of other writers and illustrators makes it more important than ever to research publishers before submitting—read their guidelines, look at their catalogs, check out a few of their titles, and visit their websites.

ABBEVILLE FAMILY

Abbeville Press, 116 W. 23rd St., New York NY 10011. (646)375-2136. **Fax:** (646)375-2359. **E-mail:** abbeville@abbeville.com. **Website:** www.abbeville.com. Our list is full for the next several seasons. *Not accepting unsolicited book proposals at this time.* **Publishes 8 titles/year. 10% of books from first-time authors.**

FICTION Picture books: animal, anthology, concept, contemporary, fantasy, folktales, health, hi-lo, history, humor, multicultural, nature/environment, poetry, science fiction, special needs, sports, suspense. Average word length 300-1,000 words.

HOW TO CONTACT Please refer to website for submission policy.

ILLUSTRATION Works with approx 2-4 illustrators/year. Uses color artwork only.

PHOTOGRAPHY Buys stock and assigns work.

ABDO PUBLISHING CO.

8000 W. 78th St., Suite 310, Edina MN 55439. (800)800-1312. **Fax:** (952)831-1632. **E-mail:** nonfiction@abdopublishing.com. **Website:** www.abdopublishing.com. ABDO publishes nonfiction children's books (pre-kindergarten to 8th grade) for school and public libraries—mainly history, sports, biography, geography, science, and social studies. "Please specify each submission as either nonfiction, fiction, or illustration. Publishes hardcover originals. **Publishes 300 titles/year.**

TERMS Guidelines online.

ABRAMS

115 W. 18th St., 6th Floor, New York NY 10011. (212)206-7715. **Fax:** (212)519-1210. **E-mail:** abrams@abramsbooks.com. **Website:** www.abramsbooks.com. **Contact:** Managing Editor. Publishes hardcover and a few paperback originals. **Publishes 250 titles/year.**

⚬ Does not accept unsolicited materials.

FICTION Publishes hardcover and "a few" paperback originals. Averages 150 total titles/year.

TIPS "We are one of the few publishers who publish almost exclusively illustrated books. We consider ourselves the leading publishers of art books and high-quality artwork in the U.S. Once the author has signed a contract to write a book for our firm the author must finish the manuscript to agreed-upon high standards within the schedule agreed upon in the contract."

ABRAMS BOOKS FOR YOUNG READERS

115 W. 18th St., New York NY 10011. **Website:** www.abramsyoungreaders.com.

⚬ Abrams no longer accepts unsolicited mss or queries.

ILLUSTRATION Illustrations only: Do not submit original material; copies only. Contact: Chad Beckerman, art director.

ALADDIN

Simon & Schuster, 1230 Avenue of the Americas, 4th Floor, New York NY 10020. (212)698-7000. **Website:** www.simonandschuster.com. Aladdin also publishes Aladdin M!X, for those readers too old for kids' books, but not quite ready for adult or young adult novels. **Contact:** Acquisitions Editor. Aladdin publishes picture books, beginning readers, chapter books, middle grade and tween fiction and nonfiction, and graphic novels and nonfiction in hardcover and paperback, with an emphasis on commercial, kid-friendly titles. Publishes hardcover/paperback originals and imprints of Simon & Schuster Children's Publishing Children's Division.

HOW TO CONTACT Simon & Schuster does not review, retain or return unsolicited materials or artwork. "We suggest prospective authors and illustrators submit their mss through a professional literary agent."

ALGONQUIN YOUNG READERS

P.O. Box 2225, Chapel Hill NC 27515. **Website:** algonquinyoungreaders.com. Algonquin Young Readers is a new imprint that features books for readers 7-17. "From short illustrated novels for the youngest independent readers to timely and topical crossover young adult fiction, what ties our books together are unforgettable characters, absorbing stories, and superior writing.

FICTION Algonquin Young Readers publishes ficiton and a limited number of narrative nonfiction titles for middle grade and young adult readers. "We don't publish poetry, picture books, or genre fiction."

HOW TO CONTACT Query with 15-20 sample pages and SASE.

ILLUSTRATION "At this time, we do not accept unsolicited submissions for illustration."

TERMS Guidelines online.

AMBERJACK PUBLISHING

P.O. Box 4668 #89611, New York NY 10163. (888)959-3352. **Website:** www.amberjackpublishing.com. Amberjack Publishing offers authors the freedom to write without burdening them with having to promote the work themselves. They retain all rights. "You will have no rights left to exploit, so you cannot resell, republish or use your story again."

FICTION Amberjack Publishing is always on the lookout for the next great story. "We are interested in fiction, children's books, graphic novels, science fiction, fantasy, humor, and everything in between."

HOW TO CONTACT Submit via online query form with book proposal and first 10 pages of ms.

Ⓐ AMULET BOOKS

Imprint of Abrams, 115 W. 18th St., 6th Floor, New York NY 10001. **Website:** www.amuletbooks.com. *Does not accept unsolicited mss or queries.* **10% of books from first-time authors.**

FICTION Middle readers: adventure, contemporary, fantasy, history, science fiction, sports. Young adults/teens: adventure, contemporary, fantasy, history, science fiction, sports, suspense.

ILLUSTRATION Works with 10-12 illustrators/year. Uses both color and b&w. Query with samples. Contact: Chad Beckerman, art director. Samples filed.

PHOTOGRAPHY Buys stock images and assigns work.

ARBORDALE PUBLISHING

612 Johnnie Dodds, Suite A2, Mt. Pleasant SC 29464. (843)971-6722. **Fax:** (843)216-3804. **E-mail:** submissions@arbordalepublishing.com. **Website:** www.arbordalepublishing.com. **Contact:** Acquisitions Editor. "The picture books we publish are usually, but not always, fictional stories with nonfiction woven into the story that relate to science or math. All books should subtly convey an educational theme through a warm story that is fun to read and that will grab a child's attention. Each book has a 4-page *'For Creative Minds'* section to reinforce the educational component. This section will have a craft and/or game as well as 'fun facts' to be shared by the parent, teacher, or other adult. Authors do not need to supply this information with their submission, but if their ms is accepted, they may be asked to provide additional information for this section. Mss should be less than 1,000 words and meet all of the following 4 criteria: fun to read—mostly fiction with nonfiction facts woven into the story; national or regional in scope; must tie into early elementary school curriculum; must be marketable through a niche market such as a zoo, aquarium, or museum gift shop." Publishes hardcover, trade paperback, and electronic originals. **Publishes 12 titles/year. 50% of books from first-time authors. 99% from unagented writers.**

FICTION Picture books: animal, folktales, nature/environment, science- or math-related. No more than 1,000 words.

NONFICTION Prefer fiction, but will consider nonfiction as well.

HOW TO CONTACT All mss should be submitted via e-mail to Katie Hall. Mss should be less than 1,000 words. All mss should be submitted via e-mail. Mss should be less than 1,000 words. 1,000 mss received/year. Accepts electronic submissions only. Snail mail submissions are discarded without being opened. Acknowledges receipt of ms submission within 1 month. Publishes book 18 months after acceptance. May hold onto mss of interest for 1 year until acceptance.

ILLUSTRATION Works with 20 illustrators/year. Prefers to work with illustrators from the US and Canada. Uses color artwork only. Submit Web link or 2-3 electronic images. Contact: Katie Hall.

TERMS Pays 6-8% royalty on wholesale price. Pays small advance. Book catalog and guidelines online.

TIPS "Please make sure that you have looked at our website to read our complete submission guidelines and to see if we are looking for a particular subject. Manuscripts must meet all four of our stated criteria. We look for fairly realistic, bright and colorful art—no cartoons. We want the children excited about the books. We envision the books being used at home and in the classroom."

Ⓐ ATHENEUM BOOKS FOR YOUNG READERS

Simon & Schuster, 1230 Avenue of the Americas, New York NY 10020. **Website:** kids.simonandschuster.com. Publishes hardcover originals.

FICTION All in juvenile versions. "We have few specific needs except for books that are fresh, interesting and well written. Fad topics are dangerous, as are works you haven't polished to the best of your ability. We also don't need safety pamphlets, ABC books, coloring books and board books. In writing picture book texts, avoid the coy and 'cutesy,' such as stories about characters with alliterative names." Agented submissions only. No paperback romance-type fiction.

NONFICTION Publishes hardcover originals, picture books for young kids, nonfiction for ages 8-12 and novels for middle-grade and young adults. 100% require freelance illustration. Agented submissions only.

TERMS Guidelines for #10 SASE.

TIPS "Study our titles."

BAILIWICK PRESS

309 East Mulberry St., Fort Collins CO 80524. (970)672-4878. **Fax:** (970)672-4731. **E-mail:** info@ bailiwickpress.com. **Website:** www.bailiwickpress. com. "We're a micro-press that produces books and other products that inspire and tell great stories. Our motto is 'books with something to say.' We are now considering submissions, agented and unagented, for children's and young adult fiction. We're looking for smart, funny, and layered writing that kids will clamor for. Authors who already have a following have a leg up. We are only looking for humorous children's fiction. Please do not submit work for adults. Illustrated fiction is desired but not required. (Illustrators are also invited to send samples.) Make us laugh out loud, ooh and aah, and cry, 'Eureka!'"

HOW TO CONTACT "Please read the Aldo Zelnick series to determine if we might be on the same page, then fill out our submission form. Please do not send submissions via snail mail or phone calls. You must complete the online submission form to be considered. If, after completing and submitting the form, you also need to send us an e-mail attachment (such as sample illustrations or excerpts of graphics), you may e-mail them to aldozelnick@gmail.com." Responds in 6 months.

ILLUSTRATION Illustrated fiction desired but not required. Send samples.

ⒶBALZER & BRAY

HarperCollins Children's Books, 10 E. 53rd St., New York NY 10022. **Website:** www.harpercollinschildrens.com. "We publish bold, creative, groundbreaking picture books and novels that appeal directly to kids in a fresh way." **Publishes 10 titles/year.**

FICTION Picture Books, Young Readers: adventure, animal, anthology, concept, contemporary, fantasy, history, humor, multicultural, nature/environment, poetry, science fiction, special needs, sports, suspense. Middle readers, young adults/teens: adventure, animal, anthology, contemporary, fantasy, history, humor, multicultural, nature/environment, poetry, science fiction, special needs, sports, suspense.

NONFICTION "We will publish very few nonfiction titles, maybe 1-2 per year."

HOW TO CONTACT Contact editor. Agented submissions only. Agented submissions only. Publishes book 18 months after acceptance.

ILLUSTRATION Works with 10 illustrators/year. Uses both color and b&w. Illustrations only: send tearsheets to be kept on file. Responds only if interested. Samples are not returned.

PHOTOGRAPHY Works on assignment only.

TERMS Offers advances. Pays illustrators by the project.

ⒶBANTAM BOOKS

Imprint of Penguin Random House, Inc., 1745 Broadway, New York NY 10019. (212)782-9000. **Website:** www.randomhousebooks.com. *Not seeking mss at this time.*

BAREFOOT BOOKS

2067 Massachusettes Ave., 5th Floor, Cambridge MA 02140. (617)576-0660. **Fax:** (617)576-0049. **E-mail:** help@barefootbooks.com. **Website:** www.barefootbooks.com. **Contact:** Acquisitions Editor. "We are a small, independent publishing company that publishes high-quality picture books for children of all ages and specializes in the work of artists and writers from many cultures. We focus on themes that support independence of spirit, encourage openness to others, and foster a life-long love of learning. Prefers full manuscript." Publishes hardcover and trade paperback originals. **Publishes 30 titles/year. 35% of books from first-time authors. 60% from unagented writers.**

FICTION "Barefoot Books only publishes children's picture books and anthologies of folktales. We do not publish novels."

HOW TO CONTACT Barefoot Books is not currently accepting ms queries or submissions. 2,000 queries received/year. 3,000 mss received/year.

ILLUSTRATION Works with 20 illustrators/year. Uses color artwork only. Reviews ms/illustration packages from artists. Send query and art samples or dummy for picture books. Query with samples or send promo sheet and tearsheets. Responds only if interested. Samples returned with SASE. Pays authors royalty of 5% based on retail price. Offers advances.

Sends galleys to authors. Originals returned to artist at job's completion.

TERMS Pays advance. Book catalog for 9x12 SAE stamped with $1.80 postage.

○ BARRONS EDUCATIONAL SERIES

250 Wireless Blvd., Hauppauge NY 11788. **Fax:** (631)434-3723. **Website:** www.barronseduc.com. **Contact:** Wayne R. Barr, manuscript acquisitions.

FICTION Picture books: animal, concept, multicultural, nature/environment. Young readers: adventure, multicultural, nature/environment, fantasy, suspense/mystery. Middle readers: adventure, fantasy, multicultural, nature/environment, problem novels, suspense/mystery. Young adults: problem novels. "Stories with an educational element are appealing."

NONFICTION Picture books: concept, reference. Young readers: biography, how-to, reference, self-help, social issues. Middle readers: hi-lo, how-to, reference, self-help, social issues. Young adults: reference, self-help, social issues, sports.

HOW TO CONTACT Query via e-mail with no attached files. Full guidelines are listed on the website. Submit outline/synopsis and sample chapters. "Nonfiction submissions must be accompanied by SASE for response." Due to the large volume of unsolicited submissions received, a complete evaluation of a proposal may take 4-6 weeks. Please do not call about the status of individual submissions. Publishes book 1 year after acceptance.

ILLUSTRATION Works with 20 illustrators/year. Reviews ms/illustration packages from artists. Query first; 3 chapters of ms with 1 piece of final art, remainder roughs. Illustrations only: Submit tearsheets or slides plus résumé. Responds in 2 months.

TERMS Pays authors royalty of 10-12% based on net price or buys ms outright for $2,000 minimum. Pays illustrators by the project based on retail price. Catalog available for 9x12 SASE. Guidelines available on website.

TIPS Writers: "We publish pre-school storybooks, concept books and middle grade and YA chapter books. No romance novels. Those with an educational element." Illustrators: "We are happy to receive a sample illustration to keep on file for future consideration. Periodic notes reminding us of your work are acceptable." Children's book themes "are becoming much more contemporary and relevant to a child's day-to-day activities, fewer talking animals. We are interested in fiction (ages 7-11 and ages 12-16) dealing with modern problems."

BEHRMAN HOUSE INC.

11 Edison Place, Springfield NJ 07081. (973)379-7200. **Fax:** (973)379-7280. **E-mail:** customersupport@behrmanhouse.com. **Website:** www.behrmanhouse.com. **Contact:** Editorial Committee. Publishes books on all aspects of Judaism: history, cultural, textbooks, holidays. "Behrman House publishes quality books of Jewish content—history, Bible, philosophy, holidays, ethics—for children and adults." **12% of books from first-time authors.**

NONFICTION All levels: Judaism, Jewish educational textbooks. Average word length: young reader—1,200; middle reader—2,000; young adult—4,000.

HOW TO CONTACT Submit outline/synopsis and sample chapters. Responds in 1 month to queries; 2 months to mss. Publishes book 18 months after acceptance.

ILLUSTRATION Works with 6 children's illustrators/year. Reviews ms/illustration packages from artists. "Query first." Illustrations only: Query with samples; send unsolicited art samples by mail. Responds to queries in 1 month; mss in 2 months.

PHOTOGRAPHY Purchases photos from freelancers. Buys stock and assigns work. Uses photos of families involved in Jewish activities. Uses color and b&w prints. Photographers should query with samples. Send unsolicited photos by mail. Submit portfolio for review.

TERMS Pays authors royalty of 3-10% based on retail price or buys ms outright for $1,000-5,000. Offers advance. Pays illustrators by the project (range: $500-5,000). Book catalog free on request. Guidelines online.

BELLEBOOKS

P.O. Box 300921, Memphis TN 38130. (901)344-9024. **Fax:** (901)344-9068. **E-mail:** bellebooks@bellebooks.com. **Website:** www.bellebooks.com. BelleBooks began by publishing Southern fiction. It has become a "second home" for many established authors, who also continue to publish with major publishing houses. **Publishes 30-40 titles/year.**

FICTION "Yes, we'd love to find the next Harry Potter, but our primary focus for the moment is publishing for the teen market."

HOW TO CONTACT Query e-mail with brief synopsis and credentials/credits with full ms attached (RTF format preferred).

TERMS Guidelines online.

TIPS "Our list aims for the teen reader and the crossover market. If you're a 'Southern Louise Rennison,' that would catch our attention. Humor is always a plus. We'd love to see books featuring teen boys as protagonists. We're happy to see dark edgy books on serious subjects."

❷ BERKLEY

Penguin Group (USA) Inc., 375 Hudson St., New York NY 10014. **Website:** penguin.com. The Berkley Publishing Group publishes a variety of general nonfiction and fiction including the traditional categories of romance, mystery and science fiction. Publishes paperback and mass market originals and reprints. **Publishes 700 titles/year.**

○ "Due to the high volume of manuscripts received, most Penguin Group (USA) Inc. imprints do not normally accept unsolicited mss. The preferred and standard method for having mss considered for publication by a major publisher is to submit them through an established literary agent."

FICTION No occult fiction.

NONFICTION No memoirs or personal stories.

HOW TO CONTACT Prefers agented submissions. Prefers agented submissions.

○ BESS PRESS

3565 Harding Ave., Honolulu HI 96816. (808)734-7159. **Fax:** (808)732-3627. **Website:** www.besspress. com. Bess Press is a family-owned independent book publishing company based in Honolulu. For over 30 years, Bess Press has been producing both educational and popular general interest titles about Hawai'i and the Pacific.

NONFICTION "We are constantly seeking to work with authors, artists, photographers, and organizations that are developing works concentrating on Hawai'i and the Pacific. Our goal is to regularly provide customers with new, creative, informative, educational, and entertaining publications that are directly connected to or flowing from Hawai'i and other islands in the Pacific region." Not interested in material that is unassociated with Hawai'i or the greater Pacific in theme. Please do not submit works if it does not fall into this regional category.

HOW TO CONTACT Submit your name, contact information, working title, genre, target audience, short (4-6 sentences) description of your work, identifies target audience(s), explains how your work differs from other books already publishing on the same subject, includes discussion of any additional material with samples. All submissions via e-mail. Responds in 4 months.

TERMS Catalog online. Guidelines online.

TIPS "As a regional publisher, we are looking for material specific to the region (Hawaii and Micronesia), preferably from writers and illustrators living within (or very familiar with) the region.", "As a regional publisher, we are looking for material specific to the region (Hawaii and Micronesia), preferably from writers and illustrators living within (or very familiar with) the region."

BETHANY HOUSE PUBLISHERS

Division of Baker Publishing Group, 6030 E. Fulton Rd., Ada MI 49301. (616)676-9185. **Fax:** (616)676-9573. **Website:** bakerpublishinggroup.com/bethanyhouse. Bethany House Publishers specializes in books that communicate Biblical truth and assist people in both spiritual and practical areas of life. Considers unsolicited work only through a professional literary agent or through manuscript submission services, Authonomy or Christian Manuscript Submissions. Guidelines online. *All unsolicited mss returned unopened.* Publishes hardcover and trade paperback originals, mass market paperback reprints. **Publishes 90-100 titles/year. 2% of books from first-time authors. 50% from unagented writers.**

HOW TO CONTACT Responds in 3 months to queries. Publishes a book 1 year after acceptance.

TERMS Pays royalty on net price. Pays advance. Book catalog for 9 x 12 envelope and 5 first-class stamps.

TIPS "Bethany House Publishers' publishing program relates Biblical truth to all areas of life—whether in the framework of a well-told story, of a challenging book for spiritual growth, or of a Bible reference work. We are seeking high-quality fiction and nonfiction that will inspire and challenge our audience."

❷ BEYOND WORDS PUBLISHING, INC.

20827 NW Cornell Rd., Suite 500, Hillsboro OR 97124. (503)531-8700. **Fax:** (503)531-8773. **E-mail:** info@beyondword.com. **Website:** www.beyondword.com. **Contact:** Submissions Department (for agents only). "At this time, we are not accepting any unsolicited queries or proposals, and recommend that all authors work with a literary agent in submitting their work." Publishes hardcover and trade paperback originals and paperback reprints. **Publishes 10-15 titles/year.**

NONFICTION For adult nonfiction, wants whole body health, the evolving human, and transformation. For children and YA, wants health, titles that inspire kids' power to incite change, and titles that allow young readers to explore and/or question traditional wisdom and spiritual practices. Does not want children's picture books, adult fiction, cookbooks, textbooks, reference books, photography books, or illustrated coffee table books.

HOW TO CONTACT Agent should submit query letter with proposal, including author bio, 5 sample chapters, complete synopsis of book, market analysis, SASE. Agent should submit query letter with proposal, including author bio, 5 sample chapters, complete synopsis of book, market analysis, SASE.

BLACK ROSE WRITING

P.O. Box 1540, Castroville TX 78009. **E-mail:** creator@blackrosewriting.com. **Website:** www.blackrosewriting.com/home. Author provides illustrations, fully-illustrated or samples. **Contact:** Reagan Rothe. Black Rose Writing is an independent publishing house that strongly believes in developing a personal relationship with their authors. The Texas-based publishing company doesn't see authors as clients or just another number on a page, but rather as individual people.. people who deserve an honest review of their material and to be paid traditional royalties without ever paying any fees to be published. Publishes fiction, nonfiction, and illustrated children's books. **Publishes 150+ titles/year. 75% of books from first-time authors. 80% from unagented writers.**

HOW TO CONTACT "Our preferred submission method is via Authors.me, please click 'Submit Here' on our website." "Our preferred submission method is via Authors.me, please click 'Submit Here' on our website." 3,500 submissions received/year. Responds in 3-6 weeks on queries; 3-6 months on mss. Publishes ms 4-6 months after acceptance.

ILLUSTRATION Must be provided by author.

TERMS Royalties start at 20%, e-book royalties 25% Book catalog online. Guidelines online.

❶ BLOOMSBURY CHILDREN'S BOOKS

Imprint of Bloomsbury USA, 1385 Broadway, 5th Floor, New York NY 10018. **Website:** www.bloomsbury.com/us/childrens. No phone calls or e-mails. *Agented submissions only.* **Publishes 60 titles/year. 25% of books from first-time authors.**

HOW TO CONTACT *Agented submissions only.* Responds in 6 months.

TERMS Pays royalty. Pays advance. Book catalog online. Guidelines online.

BOOKFISH BOOKS

E-mail: bookfishbooks@gmail.com. **Website:** bookfishbooks.com. **Contact:** Tammy Mckee, acquisitions editor. BookFish Books is looking for novel lengthed young adult, new adult, and middle grade works in all subgenres. Both published and unpublished, agented or unagented authors are welcome to submit. "Sorry, but we do not publish novellas, picture books, early reader/chapter books or adult novels." Responds to every query.

HOW TO CONTACT Query via e-mail with a brief synopsis and first 3 chapters of ms.

TERMS Guidelines online.

TIPS "We only accept complete manuscripts. Please do not query us with partial manuscripts or proposals."

BOYDS MILLS PRESS

Highlights for Children, Inc., 815 Church St., Honesdale PA 18431. (570)253-1164. **Website:** www.boydsmillspress.com. Boyds Mills Press publishes picture books, nonfiction, activity books, and paperback reprints. Their titles have been named notable books by the International Reading Association, the American Library Association, and the National Council of Teachers of English. They've earned numerous awards, including the National Jewish Book Award, the Christopher Medal, the NCTE Orbis Pictus Honor, and the Golden Kite Honor. Boyds Mills Press welcomes unsolicited submissions from published and unpublished writers and artists. Submit a ms with a cover letter of relevant information, including experience with writing and publishing. Label the package "Manuscript Submission" and include an SASE. For art samples, label the package "Art Sample Submission." All submissions will be evaluated for all imprints.

FICTION Interested in picture books and middle grade fiction. Do not send a query first. Send the entire ms of picture book or the first 3 chapters and a plot summary for middle grade fiction (will request the balance of ms if interested).

NONFICTION Include a detailed bibliography with submission. Highly recommends including an expert's review of your ms and a detailed explanation of the books in the marketplace that are similar to the one you propose. References to the need for this book (by the National Academy of Sciences or by similar subject-specific organizations) will strengthen your proposal. If you intend for the book to be illustrated with photos or other graphic elements (charts, graphs, etc.), it is your responsibility to find or create those elements and to include with the submission a permissions budget, if applicable. Finally, keep in mind that good children's nonfiction has a narrative quality—a story line—that encyclopedias do not; please consider whether both the subject and the language will appeal to children.

HOW TO CONTACT Responds to mss within 3 months.

ILLUSTRATION Illustrators submitting a picture book should include the ms, a dummy, and a sample reproduction of the final artwork that reflects the style and technique you intend to use. Do not send original artwork.

TERMS Catalog online. Guidelines online.

CALKINS CREEK

Boyds Mills Press, 815 Church St., Honesdale PA 18431. **Website:** www.boydsmillspress.com. "We aim to publish books that are a well-written blend of creative writing and extensive research, which emphasize important events, people, and places in U.S. history."

HOW TO CONTACT Submit outline/synopsis and 3 sample chapters. Submit outline/synopsis and 3 sample chapters.

ILLUSTRATION Accepts material from international illustrators. Works with 25 (for all Boyds Mills Press imprints) illustrators/year. Uses both color and b&w. Reviews ms/illustration packages. For ms/illustration packages: Submit ms with 2 pieces of final art. Submit ms/illustration packages to address above, label package "Manuscript Submission." Reviews work for future assignments. If interested in illustrating future titles, query with samples. Submit samples to address above. Label package "Art Sample Submission."

PHOTOGRAPHY Buys stock images and assigns work. Submit photos to: address above, label package "Art Sample Submission." Uses color or b&w 8×10 prints. For first contact, send promo piece (color or b&w).

TERMS Pays authors royalty or work purchased outright. Guidelines online.

TIPS "Read through our recently published titles and review our catalog. When selecting titles to publish, our emphasis will be on important events, people, and places in U.S. history. Writers are encouraged to submit a detailed bibliography, including secondary and primary sources, and expert reviews with their submissions."

❶ CANDLEWICK PRESS

99 Dover St., Somerville MA 02144. (617) 661-3330. **Fax:** (617) 661-0565. **E-mail:** bigbear@candlewick.com. **Website:** www.candlewick.com. "Candlewick Press publishes high-quality, illustrated children's books for ages infant through young adult. We are a truly child-centered publisher." Publishes hardcover and trade paperback originals, and reprints. **Publishes 200 titles/year. 5% of books from first-time authors.**

💬 *Candlewick Press is not accepting queries or unsolicited mss at this time.*

FICTION Picture books: animal, concept, contemporary, fantasy, history, humor, multicultural, nature/environment, poetry. Middle readers, young adults: contemporary, fantasy, history, humor, multicultural, poetry, science fiction, sports, suspense/mystery.

NONFICTION Picture books: concept, biography, geography, nature/environment. Young readers: biography, geography, nature/environment.

HOW TO CONTACT "We currently do not accept unsolicited editorial queries or submissions. If you are an author or illustrator and would like us to consider your work, please read our submissions policy (online) to learn more."

ILLUSTRATION "Candlewick prefers to see a range of styles from artists along with samples showing strong characters (human or animals) in various settings with various emotions."

TERMS Pays authors royalty of 2½-10% based on retail price. Offers advance.

TIPS *"We no longer accept unsolicited mss. See our website for further information about us."*

CAPSTONE PRESS

Capstone Young Readers, 1710 Roe Crest Dr., North Mankato MN 56003. **E-mail:** author.sub@capstone-

pub.com; il.sub@capstonepub.com. **Website:** www.
capstonepub.com. The Capstone Press imprint publishes nonfiction with accessible text on topics kids love to capture interest and build confidence and skill in beginning, struggling, and reluctant readers, grades pre-K-9.

FICTION Send fiction submissions via e-mail (author.sub@capstonepub.com). Include the following, in the body of the e-mail: sample chapters, resume, and a list of previous publishing credits.

NONFICTION Send nonfiction submissions via postal mail. Include the following: resume, cover letter, and up to 3 writing samples.

HOW TO CONTACT Responds only if submissions fit needs. Mss and writing samples will not be returned. "If you receive no reply within 6 months, you should assume the editors are not interested."

ILLUSTRATION Send fiction illustration submissions via e-mail (il.sub@capstonepub.com). Include the following, in the body of the e-mail: sample artwork, resume, and a list of previous publishing credits. For nonfiction illustrations, send via e-mail (nf.il.sub@capstonepub.com) sample artwork (2-4 pieces) and a list of previous publishing credits.

TERMS Catalog available upon request. Guidelines online.

CAROLRHODA BOOKS, INC.

1251 Washington Ave. N., Minneapolis MN 55401. **Website:** www.lernerbooks.com. "We will continue to seek targeted solicitations at specific reading levels and in specific subject areas. The company will list these targeted solicitations on our website and in national newsletters, such as the SCBWI Bulletin." Interested in "boundary-pushing" teen fiction. *Lerner Publishing Group no longer accepts submissions to any of their imprints except for Kar-Ben Publishing.*

ⓐ CARTWHEEL BOOKS

Imprint of Scholastic Trade Division, 557 Broadway, New York NY 10012. (212)343-6100. **Website:** www.scholastic.com. Cartwheel Books publishes innovative books for children, up to age 8. "We are looking for 'novelties' that are books first, play objects second. Even without its gimmick, a Cartwheel Book should stand alone as a valid piece of children's literature." Publishes novelty books, easy readers, board books, hardcover and trade paperback originals.

FICTION Again, the subject should have mass market appeal for very young children. Humor can be helpful, but not necessary. Mistakes writers make are a reading level that is too difficult, a topic of no interest or too narrow, or mss that are too long.

NONFICTION Cartwheel Books publishes for the very young, therefore nonfiction should be written in a manner that is accessible to preschoolers through 2nd grade. Often writers choose topics that are too narrow or "special" and do not appeal to the mass market. Also, the text and vocabulary are frequently too difficult for our young audience.

HOW TO CONTACT *Accepts mss from agents only. Accepts mss from agents only.*

TERMS Guidelines available free.

CEDAR FORT, INC.

2373 W. 700 S, Springville UT 84663. (801)489-4084. **Website:** www.cedarfort.com. "Each year we publish well over 100 books, and many of those are by first-time authors. At the same time, we love to see books from established authors. As one of the largest book publishers in Utah, we have the capability and enthusiasm to make your book a success, whether you are a new author or a returning one. We want to publish uplifting and edifying books that help people think about what is important in life, books people enjoy reading to relax and feel better about themselves, and books to help improve lives. Although we do put out several children's books each year, we are extremely selective. Our children's books must have strong religious or moral values, and must contain outstanding writing and an excellent storyline." Publishes hardcover, trade paperback originals and reprints, mass market paperback and electronic reprints. **Publishes 150 titles/year. 60% of books from first-time authors. 95% from unagented writers.**

HOW TO CONTACT Submit completed ms. Query with SASE; submit proposal package, including outline, 2 sample chapters; or submit completed ms. Receives 200 queries/year; 600 mss/year. Responds in 1 month on queries; 2 months on proposals; 4 months on mss. Publishes book 10-14 months after acceptance.

TERMS Pays 10-12% royalty on wholesale price. Pays $2,000-50,000 advance. Catalog and guidelines online.

TIPS "Our audience is rural, conservative, mainstream. The first page of your ms is very important because we start reading every submission, but good writing and plot keep us reading."

○ CHARLESBRIDGE PUBLISHING

85 Main St., Watertown MA 02472. (617)926-0329. **Fax:** (617)926-5720. **E-mail:** tradeeditorial@charlesbridge.com. **Website:** www.charlesbridge.com. "Charlesbridge publishes high-quality books for children, with a goal of creating lifelong readers and lifelong learners. Our books encourage reading and discovery in the classroom, library, and home. We believe that books for children should offer accurate information, promote a positive worldview, and embrace a child's innate sense of wonder and fun. To this end, we continually strive to seek new voices, new visions, and new directions in children's literature. As of September 2015, we are now accepting young adult novels for consideration." Publishes hardcover and trade paperback nonfiction and fiction, children's books for the trade and library markets. **Publishes 45 titles/year. 10-20% of books from first-time authors. 50% from unagented writers.**

FICTION Strong stories with enduring themes. Charlesbridge publishes both picture books and transitional bridge books (books ranging from early readers to middle-grade chapter books). Our fiction titles include lively, plot-driven stories with strong, engaging characters. No alphabet books, board books, coloring books, activity books, or books with audiotapes or CD-ROMs.

NONFICTION Strong interest in nature, environment, social studies, and other topics for trade and library markets.

HOW TO CONTACT Please submit only 1 ms at a time. For picture books and shorter bridge books, please send a complete ms. For fiction books longer than 30 ms pages, please send a detailed plot synopsis, a chapter outline, and 3 chapters of text. If sending a young adult novel, mark the front of the envelope with "YA novel enclosed." Please note, for YA, e-mail submissions are preferred to the following address; yasubs@charlesbridge.com. Only responds if interested. Full guidelines on site. Please submit only 1 or 2 chapters at a time. For nonfiction books longer than 30 ms pages, send a detailed proposal, a chapter outline, and 1-3 chapters of text. 2,000 submissions/year. Responds in 3 months. Publishes ms 2-4 years after acceptance.

TERMS Pays royalty. Pays advance. Guidelines online.

TIPS "To become acquainted with our publishing program, we encourage you to review our books and visit our website where you will find our catalog."

○ CHICAGO REVIEW PRESS

814 N. Franklin St., Chicago IL 60610. (312)337-0747. **Fax:** (312)337-5110. **E-mail:** csherry@chicagoreviewpress.com; jpohlen@chicagoreviewpress.com; lreardon@chicagoreviewpress.com; ytaylor@chicagoreviewpress.com. **Website:** www.chicagoreviewpress.com. **Contact:** Cynthia Sherry, publisher; Yuval Taylor, senior editor; Jerome Pohlen, senior editor; Lisa Reardon, senior editor. "Chicago Review Press publishes high-quality, nonfiction, educational activity books that extend the learning process through hands-on projects and accurate and interesting text. We look for activity books that are as much fun as they are constructive and informative."

FICTION Guidelines now available on website.

NONFICTION Young readers, middle readers and young adults: activity books, arts/crafts, multicultural, history, nature/environment, science. "We're interested in hands-on, educational books; anything else probably will be rejected." Average length: young readers and young adults—144-160 pages.

HOW TO CONTACT Enclose cover letter and a brief synopsis of book in 1-2 paragraphs, table of contents and first 3 sample chapters; prefers not to receive e-mail queries. For children's activity books include a few sample activities with a list of the others. Full guidelines available on site. Responds in 2 months. Publishes a book 1-2 years after acceptance.

ILLUSTRATION Works with 6 illustrators/year. Uses primarily b&w artwork. Reviews ms/illustration packages from artists. Submit 1-2 chapters of ms with corresponding pieces of final art. Illustrations only: Query with samples, résumé. Responds only if interested. Samples returned with SASE.

PHOTOGRAPHY Buys photos from freelancers ("but not often"). Buys stock and assigns work. Wants "instructive photos. We consult our files when we know what we're looking for on a book-by-book basis." Uses b&w prints.

TERMS Pays authors royalty of 7.5-12.5% based on retail price. Offers advances of $3,000-6,000. Pays illustrators and photographers by the project (range varies considerably). Book catalog available for $3. Ms guidelines available for $3.

TIPS "We're looking for original activity books for small children and the adults caring for them—new themes and enticing projects to occupy kids' imaginations and promote their sense of personal creativity. We like activity books that are as much fun as they are constructive. Please write for guidelines so you'll know what we're looking for."

CHILDREN'S BRAINS ARE YUMMY (CBAY) BOOKS

P.O. Box 670296, Dallas TX 75367. **E-mail:** submissions@cbaybooks.com. **Website:** www.cbaybooks.blog. **Contact:** Madeline Smoot, publisher. "CBAY Books currently focuses on quality fantasy and science fiction books for the middle grade and teen markets. We are not currently accepting unsolicited submissions. We do not publish picture books." **Publishes 3-6 titles/year. 30% of books from first-time authors. 80% from unagented writers.**

HOW TO CONTACT Responds in 2 months. Publishes ms 24 months after acceptance.

ILLUSTRATION Accepts international material. Works with 0-1 illustrators/year. Uses color artwork only. Reviews artwork. Send manuscripts with dummy. Send resume and tearsheets. Send samples to Madeline Smoot. Responds to queries only if interested.

PHOTOGRAPHY Buys stock images.

TERMS Pays authors royalty 10%-15% based on wholesale price. Offers advances against royalties. Average amount $500. Pays advance. "We are distributed by IPG. Our books can be found in their catalog at www.ipgbooks.com." Brochure and guidelines online.

CHRONICLE BOOKS FOR CHILDREN

680 Second St., San Francisco CA 94107. (415)537-4200. **Fax:** (415)537-4460. **Website:** www.chroniclekids.com. "Chronicle Books for Children publishes an eclectic mixture of traditional and innovative children's books. Our aim is to publish books that inspire young readers to learn and grow creatively while helping them discover the joy of reading. We're looking for quirky, bold artwork and subject matter." Publishes hardcover and trade paperback originals. **Publishes 100-110 titles/year. 6% of books from first-time authors. 25% from unagented writers.**

FICTION Does not accept proposals by fax, via e-mail, or on disk. When submitting artwork, either

as a part of a project or as samples for review, do not send original art.

HOW TO CONTACT Query with synopsis. 30,000 queries received/year. Responds in 2-4 weeks to queries; 6 months to mss. Publishes a book 18-24 months after acceptance.

TERMS Pays variable advance. Book catalog for 9x12 envelope and 3 first-class stamps. Guidelines online.

TIPS "We are interested in projects that have a unique bent to them—be it in subject matter, writing style, or illustrative technique. As a small list, we are looking for books that will lend our list a distinctive flavor. Primarily we are interested in fiction and nonfiction picture books for children ages up to 8 years, and nonfiction books for children ages up to 12 years. We publish board, pop-up, and other novelty formats as well as picture books. We are also interested in early chapter books, middle grade fiction, and young adult projects."

CLARION BOOKS

Houghton Mifflin Co., 215 Park Ave. S., New York NY 10003. **Website:** www.hmhco.com. "Clarion Books publishes picture books, nonfiction, and fiction for infants through grade 12. Avoid telling your stories in verse unless you are a professional poet. *We are no longer responding to your unsolicited submission unless we are interested in publishing it. Please do not include a SASE. Submissions will be recycled, and you will not hear from us regarding the status of your submission unless we are interested. We regret that we cannot respond personally to each submission, but we do consider each and every submission we receive.*" Publishes hardcover originals for children. **Publishes 50 titles/year.**

FICTION "Clarion is highly selective in the areas of historical fiction, fantasy, and science fiction. A novel must be superlatively written in order to find a place on the list. Mss that arrive without an SASE of adequate size will *not* be responded to or returned. Accepts fiction translations."

NONFICTION No unsolicited mss.

HOW TO CONTACT Submit complete ms. No queries, please. Send to only *one* Clarion editor. Query with SASE. Submit proposal package, sample chapters, SASE. Responds in 2 months to queries. Publishes a book 2 years after acceptance.

ILLUSTRATION Pays illustrators royalty; flat fee for jacket illustration.

TERMS Pays 5-10% royalty on retail price. Pays minimum of $4,000 advance. Guidelines online.

TIPS "Looks for freshness, enthusiasm—in short, life."

CRAIGMORE CREATIONS

PMB 114, 4110 SE Hawthorne Blvd., Portland OR 97124. (503)477-9562. **E-mail:** info@craigmorecreations.com. **Website:** www.craigmorecreations.com.

NONFICTION "We publish books that make time travel seem possible: nonfiction that explores pre-history and Earth sciences for children."

HOW TO CONTACT Submit proposal package. See website for detailed submission guidelines. Submit proposal package. See website for detailed submission guidelines.

THE CREATIVE COMPANY

P.O. Box 227, Mankato MN 56002. (800)445-6209. **Fax:** (507)388-2746. **Website:** www.thecreativecompany.us. "We are currently not accepting fiction submissions." **Publishes 140 titles/year.**

NONFICTION Picture books, young readers, young adults: animal, arts/crafts, biography, careers, geography, health, history, hobbies, multicultural, music/dance, nature/environment, religion, science, social issues, special needs, sports. Average word length: young readers—500; young adults—6,000.

HOW TO CONTACT Submit outline/synopsis and 2 sample chapters, along with division of titles within the series. Responds in 3-6 months. Publishes a book 2 years after acceptance.

PHOTOGRAPHY Buys stock. Contact: Photo Editor. Model/property releases not required; captions required. Uses b&w prints. Submit cover letter, promo piece. Ms and photographer guidelines available for SAE.

TERMS Guidelines available for SAE.

TIPS "We are accepting nonfiction, series submissions only. Fiction submissions will not be reviewed or returned. Nonfiction submissions should be presented in series (4, 6, or 8) rather than single."

CRESTON BOOKS

P.O. Box 9369, Berkeley CA 94709. **E-mail:** submissions@crestonbooks.co. **Website:** crestonbooks.co. Creston Books is author-illustrator driven, with talented, award-winning creators given more editorial freedom and control than in a typical New York house. **50%% of books from first-time authors. 50%% from unagented writers.**

HOW TO CONTACT Please paste text of picture books or first chapters of novels in the body of e-mail. Words of Advice for submitting authors listed on the site.

TERMS Pays advance. Catalog online. Guidelines online.

CURIOSITY QUILLS

Whampa, LLC, P.O. Box 2160, Reston VA 20195. (800)998-2509. **Fax:** (800)998-2509. **E-mail:** editor@curiosityquills.com. **Website:** curiosityquills.com. **Contact:** Alisa Gus. Curiosity Quills is a publisher of hard-hitting dark sci-fi, speculative fiction, and paranormal works aimed at adults, young adults, and new adults. Firm publishes sci-fi, speculative fiction, steampunk, paranormal and urban fantasy, and corresponding romance titles under its new Rebel Romance imprint. **Publishes 75 titles/year. 60% of books from first-time authors. 65% from unagented writers.**

FICTION Looking for "thought-provoking, mind-twisting rollercoasters—challenge our mind, turn our world upside down, and make us question. Those are the makings of a true literary marauder."

NONFICTION Writer's guides, on a strictly limited basis.

HOW TO CONTACT Submit ms using online submission form or e-mail to acquisitions@curiosityquills.com. 1,000 submissions/year. Responds in 1-6 weeks. Publishes ms 9-12 months after acceptance.

TERMS Pays variable royalty. Does not pay advance. Catalog available. Guidelines online.

DARBY CREEK PUBLISHING

Lerner Publishing Group, 1251 Washington Ave. N., Minneapolis MN 55401. (612)332-3344. **Fax:** (612)332-7615. **Website:** www.lernerbooks.com. "Darby Creek publishes series fiction titles for emerging, striving and reluctant readers ages 7 to 18 (grades 2-12). From beginning chapter books to intermediate fiction and page-turning YA titles, Darby Creek books engage readers with strong characters and formats they'll want to pursue." Darby Creek does not publish picture books. Publishes children's chapter books, middle readers, young adult. Mostly series. **Publishes 25 titles/year.**

"We are currently not accepting any submissions. If that changes, we will provide all children's writing publications with our new info."

FICTION Middle readers, young adult. Recently published: *The Surviving Southside* series, by various authors; *The Agent Amelia* series, by Michael Broad; *The Mallory McDonald* series, by Laurie B. Friedman; and *The Alien Agent* series, by Pam Service.

NONFICTION Middle readers: biography, history, science, sports. Recently published *Albino Animals*, by Kelly Milner Halls, illustrated by Rick Spears; *Miracle: The True Story of the Wreck of the Sea Venture*, by Gail Karwoski.

ILLUSTRATION Illustrations only: Send photocopies and résumé with publishing history. "Indicate which samples we may keep on file and include SASE and appropriate packing materials for any samples you wish to have returned."

TERMS Offers advance-against-royalty contracts.

⊘ DELACORTE PRESS

an imprint of Random House Children's Books, a division of Penguin Random House LLC, New York, 1745 Broadway, New York NY 10019. (212)782-9000. **Website:** randomhousekids.com; randomhouseteens. com. Publishes middle grade and young adult fiction in hard cover, trade paperback, mass market and digest formats.

    All query letters and manuscript submissions must be submitted through an agent or at the request of an editor.

DIAL BOOKS FOR YOUNG READERS

Imprint of Penguin Group (USA), 345 Hudson St., New York NY 10014. (212)366-2000. **Website:** www.penguin.com/children. "Dial Books for Young Readers publishes quality picture books for ages 18 months-6 years; lively, believable novels for middle readers and young adults; and occasional nonfiction for middle readers and young adults." Publishes hardcover originals. **Publishes 50 titles/year. 20% of books from first-time authors.**

FICTION Especially looking for lively and well-written novels for middle grade and young adult children involving a convincing plot and believable characters. The subject matter or theme should not already be overworked in previously published books. The approach must not be demeaning to any minority group, nor should the roles of female characters (or others) be stereotyped, though we don't think books should be didactic, or in any way message-y. No topics inap-

propriate for the juvenile, young adult, and middle grade audiences. No plays.

HOW TO CONTACT Accepts unsolicited queries and up to 10 pages for longer works and unsolicited mss for picture books. Will only respond if interested. Only responds if interested. "We accept entire picture book manuscripts and a maximum of 10 pages for longer works (novels, easy-to-reads). When submitting a portion of a longer work, please provide an accompanying cover letter that briefly describes your manuscript's plot, genre (i.e. easy-to-read, middle grade or YA novel), the intended age group, and your publishing credits, if any." 5,000 queries received/year. Responds in 4-6 months to queries.

ILLUSTRATION Send nonreturnable samples, no originals, to Lily Malcolm. Show children and animals.

TERMS Pays royalty. Pays varies advance. Book catalog and guidelines online.

TIPS "Our readers are anywhere from preschool age to teenage. Picture books must have strong plots, lots of action, unusual premises, or universal themes treated with freshness and originality. Humor works well in these books. A very well-thought-out and intelligently presented book has the best chance of being taken on. Genre isn't as much of a factor as presentation."

DUTTON CHILDREN'S BOOKS

Penguin Random House, 375 Hudson St., New York NY 10014. **Website:** www.penguin.com. Dutton Children's Books publishes high-quality fiction and nonfiction for readers ranging from preschoolers to young adults on a variety of subjects. Currently emphasizing middle grade and young adult novels that offer a fresh perspective. De-emphasizing photographic nonfiction and picture books that teach a lesson. Publishes hardcover originals as well as novelty formats. **Publishes 100 titles/year. 15% of books from first-time authors.**

    "Cultivating the creative talents of authors and illustrators and publishing books with purpose and heart continue to be the mission and joy at Dutton."

FICTION Dutton Children's Books has a diverse, general interest list that includes picture books; easy-to-read books; and fiction for all ages, from first chapter books to young adult readers.

HOW TO CONTACT Query. Responds only in interested. Query. Responds only if interested. Query. Only responds if interested.

TERMS Pays royalty on retail price. Offers advance. Pays royalty on retail price. Pays advance.

○ EDUPRESS, INC.

Teacher Created Resources, 12621 Western Ave., Garden Grove CA 92841. (800)662-4321. **Fax:** (800)525-1254. **Website:** www.edupress.com. **Contact:** Editor-in-Chief. Edupress, Inc., publishes supplemental curriculum resources for PK-6th grade. Currently emphasizing Common Core reading and math games and materials.

○ "Our mission is to create products that make kids want to go to school."

HOW TO CONTACT Submit complete ms via mail or e-mail with "Manuscript Submission" as the subject line. Responds in 2-4 months. Publishes ms 1-2 years after acceptance.

ILLUSTRATION Query with samples. Contact: Cathy Baker, product development manager. Responds only if interested. Samples returned with SASE.

PHOTOGRAPHY Buys stock.

TERMS Work purchased outright from authors. Catalog online.

TIPS "We are looking for unique, research-based, quality supplemental materials for Pre-K through 6th grade. We publish mainly reading and math materials in many different formats, including games. Our materials are intended for classroom and home schooling use. We do not publish picture books."

WILLIAM B. EERDMANS PUBLISHING CO.

2140 Oak Industrial Dr. NE, Grand Rapids MI 49505. (616)459-4591. **Fax:** (616)459-6540. **E-mail:** info@eerdmans.com. **Website:** www.eerdmans.com. "The majority of our adult publications are religious and most of these are academic or semi-academic in character (as opposed to inspirational or celebrity books), though we also publish general trade books on the Christian life. Our nonreligious titles, most of them in regional history or on social issues, aim, similarly, at an educated audience." Publishes hardcover and paperback originals and reprints.

NONFICTION "We prefer that writers take the time to notice if we have published anything at all in the same category as their manuscript before sending it to us."

HOW TO CONTACT Query with SASE. Query with TOC, 2-3 sample chapters, and SASE for return of ms. Responds in 4 weeks.

TERMS Book catalog and ms guidelines free.

ELLYSIAN PRESS

E-mail: publisher@ellysianpress.com. **Website:** www.ellysianpress.com. **Contact:** Maer Wilson. "At Ellysian Press, we seek to create a sense of home for our authors, a place where they can find fulfillment as artists. Just as exceptional mortals once sought a place in the Elysian Fields, now exceptional authors can find a place here at Ellysian Press. We are accepting submissions in the following genres: Fantasy, Science Fiction, Paranormal, Paranormal Romance, Horror, along with Young/New Adult in these genres. Please submit polished manuscripts. It's best to have work read by critique groups or beta readers prior to submission." Publishes fantasy, science fiction, paranormal, paranormal romance, horror, young/new adult in these genres. **25%% of books from first-time authors. 100%% from unagented writers.**

HOW TO CONTACT "We accept online submissions only. Please submit a query letter, a synopsis and the first ten pages of your manuscript in the body of your e-mail. The subject line should be as follows: QUERY – Your Last Name, TITLE, Genre." If we choose to request more, we will request the full manuscript in standard format. This means your manuscript should be formatted as follows: One inch margins on all sides and a non-justified right margin; 12 pt Times New Roman font; Double spaced; Either .doc or .docx is fine. Ensure that your paragraph indentations are done via the ruler. Please DO NOT use the TAB key. There are many online guides that explain how to use the ruler. We accept simultaneous submissions. We accept submissions directly from the author or from an agent. We answer every query and submission. If you do not hear back from us within one week, we most likely did not receive your query. Please feel free to check with us. We are currently accepting the following genres only: Fantasy, Science Fiction, Paranormal, Paranormal Romance, Horror, Young Adult/New Adult in these genres. Please do not submit queries for any genres not listed above. You may email queries to submissions(at)ellysianpress(dot)com. Responds in 1 week for queries; 4-6 weeks for partials and fulls. Publishes ms 12+ months after acceptance. **TERMS** Pays quarterly. Does not pay advance. Catalog online. Guidelines online.

ELM BOOKS

1175 Hwy. 130, Laramie WY 82070. (610)529-0460. **E-mail:** leila.monaghan@gmail.com. **Website:** www.elm-books.com. **Contact:** Leila Monaghan, publisher. "We are eager to publish stories by new writers that have real stories to tell. We are looking for short stories (5,000-10,000 words) with real characters and true-to-life stories. Whether your story is fictionalized autobiography, or other stories of real-life mayhem and debauchery, we are interested in reading them!"

FICTION "We are looking for short stories (1,000-5,000 words) about kids of color that will grab readers' attentions—mysteries, adventures, humor, suspense, set in the present, near past or near future that reflect the realities and hopes of life in diverse communities." Also looking for middle grade novels (20,000-50,000 words).

HOW TO CONTACT Send complete ms for short stories; synopsis and 3 sample chapters for novels.

TERMS Pays royalties.

ENTANGLED TEEN

Website: www.entangledteen.com. "Entangled Teen and Entangled digiTeen, our young adult imprints publish the swoonworthy young adult romances readers crave. Whether they're dark and angsty or fun and sassy, contemporary, fantastical, or futuristic. We are seeking fresh voices with interesting twists on popular genres."

FICTION "We are seeking novels in the subgenres of romantic fiction for contemporary, upper young adult with crossover appeal."

HOW TO CONTACT E-mail using site. "All submissions must have strong romantic elements. YA novels should be 50K to 100K in length. Revised backlist titles will be considered on a case by case basis." Agented and unagented considered.

TERMS Pays royalty.

FACTS ON FILE, INC.

Infobase Learning, 132 W. 31st St., 16th Floor, New York NY 10001. (800)322-8755. **Fax:** (800)678-3633. **E-mail:** llikoff@infobaselearning.com; custserv@infobaselearning.com. **Website:** www.infobaselearning.com. **Contact:** Laurie Likoff. Facts On File produces high-quality reference materials in print and digital format on a broad range of subjects for the school and public library market and the general nonfiction trade. Publishes hardcover originals and reprints and e-books as well as reference databases. **Publishes 150-200 titles/year. 10%% of books from first-time authors. 45%% from unagented writers.**

NONFICTION "We publish serious, informational books and e-books for a targeted audience. All our books must have strong library interest, but we also distribute books effectively to the trade. Our library books fit the junior and senior high school curriculum." No computer books, technical books, cookbooks, biographies (except YA), pop psychology, humor, fiction or poetry.

HOW TO CONTACT Query or submit outline and sample chapter with SASE. No submissions returned without SASE. Responds in 2 months to queries. Responds in 6 months to 1 year.

ILLUSTRATION Commissions line art only.

TERMS Pays 10% royalty on retail price. Pays $3-5,000 advance. Reference catalog available free. Guidelines online.

TIPS "Our audience is school and public libraries for our more reference-oriented books and libraries, schools and bookstores for our less reference-oriented informational titles."

FAMILIUS

1254 Commerce Way, Sanger CA 93657. (559)876-2170. **Fax:** (559)876-2180. **E-mail:** bookideas@familius.com. **Website:** familius.com. **Contact:** Acquisitions. Familius is all about strengthening families. Collective, the authors and staff have experienced a wide slice of the family-life spectrum. Some come from broken homes. Some are married and in the throes of managing a bursting household. Some are preparing to start families of their own. Together, they publish books and articles that help families be happy. Publishes hardcover, trade paperback, and electronic originals and reprints. **Publishes 40 titles/year. 30% of books from first-time authors. 70% from unagented writers.**

FICTION All picture books must align with Familius values statement listed on the website footer.

NONFICTION All mss must align with Familius mission statement to help families succeed.

HOW TO CONTACT Submit a proposal package, including a synopsis, 3 sample chapters, and your author platform. Submit a proposal package, including an outline, 1 sample chapter, competition evaluation, and your author platform. 200 queries; 100 mss received/year. Responds in 1 month to queries and proposals; 2 months to mss. Publishes book 12 months after acceptance.

TERMS Authors are paid 10-30% royalty on wholesale price. Catalog online and print. Guidelines online.

FARRAR, STRAUS & GIROUX FOR YOUNG READERS

Macmillan Children's Publishing Group, 175 Fifth Ave., New York NY 10010. (212)741-6900. **Fax:** (212)633-2427. **Website:** www.fsgkidsbooks.com.

FICTION All levels: all categories. "Original and well-written material for all ages."

NONFICTION All levels: all categories. "We publish only literary nonfiction."

HOW TO CONTACT Submit cover letter, first 50 pages by mail only. Submit cover letter, first 50 pages by mail only.

ILLUSTRATION Works with 30-60 illustrators/year. Reviews ms/illustration packages from artists. Submit ms with 1 example of final art, remainder roughs. Do not send originals. Illustrations only: Query with tearsheets. Responds if interested in 3 months. Samples returned with SASE; samples sometimes filed.

TERMS Book catalog available by request. Ms guidelines online.

TIPS "Study our catalog before submitting. We will see illustrators' portfolios by appointment. Don't ask for criticism and/or advice—due to the volume of submissions we receive, it's just not possible. Never send originals. Always enclose SASE."

❶ FEIWEL AND FRIENDS

Macmillan Children's Publishing Group, 175 Fifth Ave., New York NY 10010. (646)307-5151. **Website:** us.macmillan.com. Feiwel and Friends is a publisher of innovative children's fiction and nonfiction literature, including hardcover, paperback series, and individual titles. The list is eclectic and combines quality and commercial appeal for readers ages 0-16. The imprint is dedicated to "book by book" publishing, bringing the work of distinctive and outstanding authors, illustrators, and ideas to the marketplace. This market does not accept unsolicited mss due to the volume of submissions; they also do not accept unsolicited queries for interior art. The best way to submit a ms is through an agent.

TERMS Catalog online.

❶ FIRST SECOND

Macmillan Children's Publishing Group, 175 5th Ave., New York NY 10010. **E-mail:** mail@firstsecondbooks. com. **Website:** www.firstsecondbooks.com. First Second is a publisher of graphic novels and an imprint of Macmillan Children's Publishing Group. First Second does not accept unsolicited submissions.

HOW TO CONTACT Responds in about 6 weeks.

TERMS Catalog online.

FREE SPIRIT PUBLISHING, INC.

6325 Sandburg Rd., Suite 100, Minneapolis MN 55427-3674. (612)338-2068. **Fax:** (612)337-5050. **E-mail:** acquisitions@freespirit.com. **Website:** www. freespirit.com. "Free Spirit is the leading publisher of learning tools that support young people's social-emotional health and educational needs. We help children and teens think for themselves, overcome challenges, and make a difference in the world." Free Spirit does not accept general fiction, poetry or storybook submissions. Publishes trade paperback originals and reprints. **Publishes 25-30 titles/year.**

FICTION "Please review catalog and author guidelines (both available online) for details before submitting proposal. If you'd like material returned, enclose a SASE with sufficient postage."

NONFICTION "Many of our authors are educators, mental health professionals, and youth workers involved in helping kids and teens." No general fiction or picture storybooks, poetry, single biographies or autobiographies, books with mythical or animal characters, or books with religious or New Age content. "We are not looking for academic or religious materials, or books that analyze problems with the nation's school systems."

HOW TO CONTACT Query with cover letter stating qualifications, intent, and intended audience and market analysis (comprehensive list of similar titles and detailed explanation of how your book stands out from the field), along with your promotional plan, outline, 2 sample chapters (note: for early childhood submissions, the entire text is required for evaluation), resume, SASE. Do not send original copies of work. Responds to proposals in 2-6 months.

ILLUSTRATION Works with 5 illustrators/year. Submit samples to creative director for consideration. If appropriate, samples will be kept on file and artist will be contacted if a suitable project comes up. Enclose SASE if you'd like materials returned.

PHOTOGRAPHY Uses stock photos. Does not accept photography submissions.

TERMS Book catalog and guidelines online.

TIPS "Our books are issue-oriented, jargon-free, and solution-focused. Our audience is children, teens, teachers, parents and youth counselors. We are especially concerned with kids' social and emotional well-being and look for books with ready-to-use strategies for coping with today's issues at home or in school—written in everyday language. We are not looking for academic or religious materials, or books that analyze problems with the nation's school systems. Instead, we want books that offer practical, positive advice so kids can help themselves, and parents and teachers can help kids succeed."

FULCRUM PUBLISHING

4690 Table Mountain Dr., Suite 100, Golden CO 80403. **E-mail:** acquisitions@fulcrumbooks.com. **Website:** www.fulcrum-books.com. **Contact:** T. Baker, acquisitions editor. In physics, the word fulcrum denotes the point at which motion begins. We strive to create books that will inspire you to move forward in your life or to take action. Whether it's exploring the world around you or discussing the ideas and issues that shape that world, our books provide the tools to create forward motion in your life. Our mission is simple, yet profound: Publish books that inspire readers to live life to the fullest and to learn something new every day. More than thirty years ago, when Bob Baron started Fulcrum Publishing, his goal was to publish high-quality books from extraordinary authors. Fulcrum recognizes that good books can't exist without the best authors. To that end, we have published books from prominent politicians (Governors Richard Lamm and Bill Ritter, Jr., Senators Gary Hart and Eugene McCarthy), influential Native Americans (Wilma Mankiller, Vine Deloria Jr., and Joseph Bruchac), master gardeners (Lauren Springer, Tom Peace, and Richard Hartlage), and important organizations in the environmental community (Campaign for America's Wilderness, World Wilderness Congress, Defenders of Wildlife). Our books have received accolades from the likes of Tom Brokaw, Elizabeth Dole, Nelson Mandela, Paul Newman, William Sears, MD, Gloria Steinem, Dr. Henry Louis Gates, Jr., and Kurt Vonnegut. In addition, Fulcrum authors have received awards from prestigious organizations such as the American Booksellers Association, American Library Association, Colorado Center for the Book, ForeWord magazine, National Book Foundation, National Parenting Publications, New York Public Library, PEN USA Literary Awards, Smithsonian National Museum of the American Indian, Teacher's Choice, Harvey Awards, and more. **40% of books from first-time authors. 90% from unagented writers.**

NONFICTION Looking for nonfiction-based graphic novels and comics, U.S. history and culture, Native American history or culture studies, conservation-oriented materials. "We do not accept memoir or fiction manuscripts."

HOW TO CONTACT "Your submission must include: a proposal of your work, including a brief synopsis, 2-3 sample chapters, brief biography of yourself, description of your audience, your assessment of the market for the book, list of competing titles, and what you can do to help market your book. We are a green company and therefore only accept e-mailed submissions. Paper queries submitted via US Mail or any other means (including fax, FedEx/UPS, and even door-to-door delivery) will not be reviewed or returned. Please help us support the preservation of the environment by e-mailing your query to acquisitions@fulcrumbooks.com." 200 Because of the volume of submissions we receive, we can only reply to submissions we are interested in pursuing, and it may take up to three months for a reply. No editorial remarks will be supplied. We do not provide consulting services for authors on the suitability of their mss. Ms published 18-24 months after acceptance.

PHOTOGRAPHY Works on assignment only.

TERMS Pays authors royalty based on wholesale price. Offers advances. Catalog for SASE. Your submission must include: A proposal of your work, including a brief synopsis; 2-3 sample chapters; a brief biography of yourself; a description of your audience; your assessment of the market for the book; a list of competing titles; what you can do to help market your book.

TIPS "Research our line first. We look for books that appeal to the school market and trade."

GIBBS SMITH

P.O. Box 667, Layton UT 84041. (801)544-9800. **Fax:** (801)544-8853. **E-mail:** debbie.uribe@gibbs-smith.com.

com. **Website:** www.gibbs-smith.com. **Publishes 3 titles/year. 50% of books from first-time authors. 50% from unagented writers.**

NONFICTION Middle readers: activity, arts/crafts, cooking, how-to, nature/environment, science. Average word length: picture books—under 1,000 words; activity books—under 15,000 words.

HOW TO CONTACT Submit an outline and writing samples for activity books; query for other types of books. Responds in 2 months. Publishes ms 1-2 years after acceptance.

ILLUSTRATION Works with 2 illustrators/year. Reviews ms/illustration packages from artists. Query. Submit ms with 3-5 pieces of final art. Illustrations only: Query with samples; provide résumé, promo sheet, slides (duplicate slides, not originals). Responds only if interested. Samples returned with SASE; samples filed.

TERMS Pays illustrators by the project or royalty of 2% based on retail price. Sends galleys to authors; color proofs to illustrators. Original artwork returned at job's completion. Pays authors royalty of 2% based on retail price or work purchased outright ($500 minimum). Offers advances (average amount: $2,000). Book catalog available for 9×12 SAE and $2.30 postage. Ms guidelines available by e-mail.

TIPS "We target ages 5-11. We do not publish young adult novels or chapter books."

THE GLENCANNON PRESS

P.O. Box 1428, El Cerrito CA 94530. (510)455-9027. **E-mail:** merships@yahoo.com. **Website:** www.glencannon.com. **Contact:** Bill Harris (maritime, maritime children's). "We publish quality books about ships and the sea." Average print order: 500. Member PMA, BAIPA. Distributes titles through Baker & Taylor. Promotes titles through direct mail, magazine advertising and word of mouth. Accepts unsolicited mss. Often comments on rejected mss. Publishes hardcover and paperback originals and hardcover reprints. **Publishes 3-4 titles/year. 25% of books from first-time authors. 100% from unagented writers.**

HOW TO CONTACT Submit complete ms. Include brief bio, list of publishing credits. Send SASE for return of ms or send a disposable ms and SASE for reply only. Responds in 1 month to queries; 2 months to mss. Publishes ms 6-24 months after acceptance.

TERMS Pays 10-20% royalty. Does not pay advance.

TIPS "Write a good story in a compelling style."

❹ DAVID R. GODINE, PUBLISHER

15 Court Square, Suite 320, Boston MA 02108. (617)451-9600. **Fax:** (617)350-0250. **E-mail:** info@godine.com. **Website:** www.godine.com. "We publish books that matter for people who care." This publisher is no longer considering unsolicited mss of any type. Only interested in agented material.

HOW TO CONTACT Only interested in agented material.

ILLUSTRATION Only interested in agented material. Works with 1-3 illustrators/year. "Please do not send original artwork unless solicited. Almost all of the children's books we accept for publication come to us with the author and illustrator already paired up. Therefore, we rarely use freelance illustrators."

❹◯ GOLDEN BOOKS FOR YOUNG READERS GROUP

1745 Broadway, New York NY 10019. **Website:** www.penguinrandomhouse.com. "Random House Books aims to create books that nurture the hearts and minds of children, providing and promoting quality books and a rich variety of media that entertain and educate readers from 6 months to 12 years." *Random House-Golden Books does not accept unsolicited mss, only agented material.* They reserve the right not to return unsolicited material. **2% of books from first-time authors.**

TERMS Pays authors in royalties; sometimes buys mss outright. Book catalog free on request.

GOOSEBOTTOM BOOKS

Fax: (888)407-5286. **E-mail:** submissions@goosebottombooks.com. **Website:** goosebottombooks.com. **Contact:** Shirin Bridges. Goosebottom Books is a small press dedicated to "fun non-fiction" founded by Shirin Yim Bridges, author of *Ruby's Wish*. *The Thinking Girl's Treasury of Dastardly Dames* was named by *Booklist* as one of the Top 10 Nonfiction Series for Youth of 2012. *Horrible Hauntings* made the IRA Children's Choices list with a mention that it "motivated even the most reluctant reader." And *Call Me Ixchel, Goddess of the Moon* was named one of the Top 10 Middle Grade Novels 2013 by Foreword Reviews. Middle grade nonfiction and fiction. **Publishes less than 6 titles/year. 50%% of books from first-time authors. 100%% from unagented writers.**

FICTION Gosling Press is a new partnership publishing imprint for children's middle grade fiction. Any fiction for adults.

HOW TO CONTACT 1,000 submissions received/year. Responds in 1 month. Publishes ms 18 months after acceptance.

ILLUSTRATION Considers samples.

TERMS Goosebottom Books: Pays advance plus royalties; Gosling Press: Pays royalties only. Catalog online. Goosebottom Books is not accepting submissions at this time. Goosebottom Books never accepts hard copy submissions. "We like trees."

GREENHAVEN PRESS

27500 Drake Rd., Farmington Hills MI 48331. (800)877-4523. **Website:** www.gale.com/greenhaven. Publishes 220 young adult academic reference titles/year. 50% of books by first-time authors. Greenhaven continues to print quality nonfiction anthologies for libraries and classrooms. "Our well-known Opposing Viewpoints series is highly respected by students and librarians in need of material on controversial social issues." Greenhaven accepts no unsolicited mss. Send query, resume, and list of published works by e-mail. Work purchased outright from authors; write-for-hire, flat fee.

NONFICTION Young adults (high school): controversial issues, social issues, history, literature, science, environment, health.

◉ GREENWILLOW BOOKS

HarperCollins Publishers, 10 E. 53rd St., New York NY 10022. (212)207-7000. **Website:** www.greenwillowblog.com. *Does not accept unsolicited mss.* "Unsolicited mail will not be opened and will not be returned." Publishes hardcover originals, paperbacks, e-books, and reprints. **Publishes 40-50 titles/year.**

HOW TO CONTACT *Agented submissions only.* Publishes ms 2 years after acceptance.

TERMS Pays 10% royalty on wholesale price for first-time authors. Offers variable advance.

◉ GROSSET & DUNLAP PUBLISHERS

Penguin Random House, 345 Hudson St., New York NY 10014. **Website:** www.penguin.com. Grosset & Dunlap publishes children's books that show children that reading is fun, with books that speak to their interests, and that are affordable so that children can build a home library of their own. Focus on licensed properties, series and readers. "Grosset & Dunlap publishes high-interest, affordable books for children ages 0-10 years. We focus on original series, licensed properties, readers and novelty books." Publishes hardcover (few) and mass market paperback originals. **Publishes 140 titles/year.**

HOW TO CONTACT *Agented submissions only. Agented submissions only.*

TERMS Pays royalty. Pays advance.

GRYPHON HOUSE, INC.

P.O. Box 10, 6848 Leon's Way, Lewisville NC 27023. (800)638-0928. **E-mail:** info@ghbooks.com. **Website:** www.gryphonhouse.com. "At Gryphon House, our goal is to publish books that help teachers and parents enrich the lives of children from birth through age 8. We strive to make our books useful for teachers at all levels of experience, as well as for parents, caregivers, and anyone interested in working with children." Query. Submit outline/synopsis and 2 sample chapters. Responds to queries/mss in 6 months. Publishes a book 18 months after acceptance. Will consider simultaneous submissions, e-mail submissions. Book catalog and ms guidelines available via website or with SASE. Publishes trade paperback originals. **Publishes 12-15 titles/year.**

NONFICTION Currently emphasizing social-emotional intelligence and classroom management; de-emphasizing literacy after-school activities.

HOW TO CONTACT "We prefer to receive a letter of inquiry and/or a proposal, rather than the entire manuscript. Please include: the proposed title, the purpose of the book, table of contents, introductory material, 20-40 sample pages of the actual book. In addition, please describe the book, including the intended audience, why teachers will want to buy it, how it is different from other similar books already published, and what qualifications you possess that make you the appropriate person to write the book. If you have a writing sample that demonstrates that you write clear, compelling prose, please include it with your letter." Responds in 3-6 months to queries.

ILLUSTRATION Works with 4-5 illustrators/year. Uses b&w realistic artwork only. Query with samples, promo sheet. Responds in 2 months. Samples returned with SASE; samples filed. Pays illustrators by the project.

PHOTOGRAPHY Pays photographers by the project or per photo. Sends edited ms copy to authors. Original artwork returned at job's completion.

TERMS Pays royalty on wholesale price. Guidelines available online.

TIPS "We are looking for books of creative, participatory learning experiences that have a common conceptual theme to tie them together. The books should be on subjects that parents or teachers want to do on a daily basis."

HARMONY INK PRESS

Dreamspinner Press, 5032 Capital Circle SW, Suite 2 PMB 279, Tallahassee FL 32305. (850)632-4648. **Fax:** (888)308-3739. **E-mail:** submissions@harmonyinkpress.com. **Website:** harmonyinkpress.com. **Contact:** Anne Regan. Teen and new adult fiction featuring at least 1 strong LGBTQ+ main character who shows significant personal growth through the course of the story. **Publishes 26 titles/year.**

FICTION "We are looking for stories in all subgenres, featuring primary characters across the whole LGBTQ+ spectrum between the ages of 14 and 21 that explore all the facets of young adult, teen, and new adult life. Sexual content should be appropriate for the characters and the story."

HOW TO CONTACT Submit complete ms.

TERMS Pays royalty. Pays $500-1,000 advance.

❶ HARPERCOLLINS CHILDREN'S BOOKS/ HARPERCOLLINS PUBLISHERS

195 Broadway, New York NY 10007. (212)207-7000. **Website:** www.harpercollins.com. HarperCollins, one of the largest English language publishers in the world, is a broad-based publisher with strengths in academic, business and professional, children's, educational, general interest, and religious and spiritual books, as well as multimedia titles. Publishes hardcover and paperback originals and paperback reprints. **Publishes 500 titles/year.**

FICTION "We look for a strong story line and exceptional literary talent."

NONFICTION *No unsolicited mss or queries.*

HOW TO CONTACT Agented submissions only. *All unsolicited mss returned.* Agented submissions only. Unsolicited mss returned unopened. Responds in 1 month, will contact only if interested. Does not accept any unsolicted texts.

TERMS Negotiates payment upon acceptance. Catalog online.

TIPS "We do not accept any unsolicited material."

HEYDAY BOOKS

c/o Acquisitions Editor, Box 9145, Berkeley CA 94709. **Fax:** (510)549-1889. **E-mail:** heyday@heydaybooks.com. **Website:** www.heydaybooks.com. **Contact:** Gayle Wattawa, acquisitions and editorial director. "Heyday Books publishes nonfiction books and literary anthologies with a strong California focus. We publish books about Native Americans, natural history, history, literature, and recreation, with a strong California focus." Publishes hardcover originals, trade paperback originals and reprints. **Publishes 12-15 titles/year. 50% of books from first-time authors. 90% from unagented writers.**

FICTION Publishes picture books, beginning readers, and young adult literature.

NONFICTION Books about California only.

HOW TO CONTACT Submit complete ms for picture books; proposal with sample chapters for longer works. include a chapter by chapter summary. Mark attention: Children's Submission. Reviews manuscript/illustration packages; but may consider art and text separately. Tries to respond to query within 12 weeks. Query with outline and synopsis. "Query or proposal by traditional post. Include a cover letter introducing yourself and your qualifications, a brief description of your project, a table of contents and list of illustrations, notes on the market you are trying to reach and why your book will appeal to them, a sample chapter, and a SASE if you would like us to return these materials to you." Responds in 3 months. Publishes book 18 months after acceptance.

TERMS Pays 8% royalty on net price. Book catalog online. Guidelines online.

HOLIDAY HOUSE, INC.

425 Madison Ave., New York NY 10017. (212)688-0085. **Fax:** (212)421-6134. **E-mail:** info@holidayhouse.com. **Website:** holidayhouse.com. "Holiday House publishes children's and young adult books for the school and library markets. We have a commitment to publishing first-time authors and illustrators. We specialize in quality hardcovers from picture books to young adult, both fiction and nonfiction, primarily for the school and library market." Publishes hardcover originals and paperback reprints. **Publishes 50 titles/year. 5% of books from first-time authors. 50% from unagented writers.**

FICTION Children's books only.

HOW TO CONTACT Query with SASE. No phone calls, please. Please send the entire ms, whether submitting a picture book or novel. "All submissions should be directed to the Editorial Department, Holiday House. We do not accept certified or registered mail. There is no need to include a SASE. We do not consider submissions by e-mail or fax. Please note that you do not have to supply illustrations. However, if you have illustrations you would like to include with your submission, you may send detailed sketches or photocopies of the original art. Do not send original art." Responds in 4 months. Publishes 1-2 years after acceptance.

ILLUSTRATION Accepting art samples, not returned.

TERMS Pays royalty on list price, range varies. Guidelines for #10 SASE.

TIPS "We need manuscripts with strong stories and writing."

HOUGHTON MIFFLIN HARCOURT BOOKS FOR CHILDREN

Imprint of Houghton Mifflin Trade & Reference Division, 222 Berkeley St., Boston MA 02116. (617)351-5000. **Fax:** (617)351-1111. **Website:** www.houghton-mifflinbooks.com. Houghton Mifflin Harcourt gives shape to ideas that educate, inform, and above all, delight. *Does not respond to or return mss unless interested.* Publishes hardcover originals and trade paperback originals and reprints. **Publishes 100 titles/year. 10% of books from first-time authors. 60% from unagented writers.**

NONFICTION Interested in innovative books and subjects about which the author is passionate.

HOW TO CONTACT Submit complete ms. Query with SASE. Submit sample chapters, synopsis. 5,000 queries received/year. 14,000 mss received/year. Responds in 4-6 months to queries. Publishes ms 2 years after acceptance.

TERMS Pays 5-10% royalty on retail price. Pays variable advance. Guidelines online.

IMPACT PUBLISHERS, INC.

5674 Shattuck Ave., Oakland CA 94609. **E-mail:** proposals@newharbinger.com. **Website:** www.newharbinger.com/imprint/impact-publishers. **Contact:** Acquisitions Department. "Our purpose is to make the best human services expertise available to the widest possible audience. We publish only popular psychology and self-help materials written in everyday language by professionals with advanced degrees and significant experience in the human services." **Publishes 3-5 titles/year. 20% of books from first-time authors.**

NONFICTION Young readers, middle readers, young adults: self-help.

HOW TO CONTACT Query or submit complete ms, cover letter, résumé. Responds in 3 months.

ILLUSTRATION Works with 1 illustrator/year. Not accepting freelance illustrator queries.

TERMS Pays authors royalty of 10-12%. Offers advances. Book catalog for #10 SASE with 2 first-class stamps. Guidelines for SASE.

TIPS "Please do not submit fiction, poetry or narratives."

INVERTED-A

P.O. Box 267, Licking MO 65542. **E-mail:** katzaya@gmail.com. **Website:** inverteda.com. **Contact:** Aya Katz, chief editor (poetry, novels, political); Nets Katz, science editor (scientific, academic). Books: POD. Distributes through Amazon, Bowker, Barnes Noble. Publishes paperback originals.

HOW TO CONTACT Does not accept unsolicited mss. Query with SASE. Reading period open from January 2 to March 15. Accepts queries by e-mail. Include estimated word count. Responds in 1 month to queries; 3 months to mss. Publishes ms 1 year after acceptance.

TERMS Pays 10 author's copies. Guidelines for SASE.

TIPS "Read our books. Read the *Inverted-A Horn*. We are different. We do not follow industry trends."

JEWISH LIGHTS PUBLISHING

LongHill Partners, Inc., Sunset Farm Offices, Rt. 4, P.O. Box 237, Woodstock VT 05091. (802)457-4000. **Fax:** (802)457-4004. **E-mail:** submissions@turner-publishing.com. **Website:** www.jewishlights.com. "Jewish Lights publishes books for people of all faiths and all backgrounds who yearn for books that attract, engage, educate and spiritually inspire. Our authors are at the forefront of spiritual thought and deal with the quest for the self and for meaning in life by drawing on the Jewish wisdom tradition. Our books cover topics including history, spirituality, life cycle, children, self-help, recovery, theology and philosophy. We do not publish autobiography, biography, fiction, haggadot, poetry or cookbooks. At this point we plan to do only two books for children annually, and one will be for younger children (ages 4-10)." Publishes hardcover and trade paperback originals, trade paperback reprints. **Publishes 30 titles/year. 50% of books from first-time authors. 75% from unagented writers.**

FICTION Picture books, young readers, middle readers: spirituality. "We are not interested in anything other than spirituality."

NONFICTION Picture book, young readers, middle readers: activity books, spirituality. "We do *not* publish haggadot, biography, poetry, memoirs, or cookbooks."

HOW TO CONTACT Query with outline/synopsis and 2 sample chapters; submit complete ms for picture books. Query. Responds in 6 months to queries. Publishes ms 1 year after acceptance.

TERMS Pays authors royalty of 10% of revenue received; 15% royalty for subsequent printings. Book catalog and guidelines online.

TIPS "We publish books for all faiths and backgrounds that also reflect the Jewish wisdom tradition. Explain in your cover letter why you're submitting your project to us in particular. Make sure you know what we publish."

JOURNEYFORTH

Imprint of BJU Press, 1430 Wade Hampton Blvd., Greenville SC 29609. **E-mail:** journeyforth@bjupress.com. **Website:** www.journeyforth.com. **Contact:** Nancy Lohr. JourneyForth Books publishes fiction and nonfiction that reflect a worldview based solidly on the Bible and that encourages Christians to live out their faith. JourneyForth is an imprint of BJU Press. Publishes paperback originals. **Publishes 8-10 titles/year. 30% of books from first-time authors. 80% from unagented writers.**

FICTION "Our fiction is for the youth market only and is based on a Christian worldview. Our catalog ranges from first chapter books to YA titles." Does not want picture books, short stories, speculative fiction, poetry, or fiction for the adult market.

NONFICTION Christian living, Bible studies, church and ministry, church history. "We produce books for the adult Christian market that are from a conservative Christian worldview."

HOW TO CONTACT Submit proposal with synopsis, market analysis of competing works, and first 5 chapters. Will look at simultaneous submissions, but not multiple submissions. 300+ Responds in 1 month to queries; 3 months to mss. Publishes book 12-18 months after acceptance.

TERMS Pays authors royalty based on wholesale price. Pays royalty. Pays advance. Book catalog available free in SASE or online. Guidelines online.

TIPS "Study the publisher's guidelines. We are looking for engaging text and a biblical worldview. Will read hard copy submissions, but prefer e-mail queries/proposals/submissions."

JUST US BOOKS, INC.

P.O. Box 5306, East Orange NJ 07019. (973)672-7701. **Fax:** (973)677-7570. **Website:** justusbooks.com. "Just Us Books is the nation's premier independent publisher of Black-interest books for young people. Our books focus primarily on the culture, history, and contemporary experiences of African Americans."

FICTION Just Us Books is currently accepting queries for chapter books and middle reader titles only. "We are not considering any other works at this time."

HOW TO CONTACT Query with synopsis and 3-5 sample pages.

TERMS Guidelines online.

TIPS "We are looking for realistic, contemporary characters; stories and interesting plots that introduce both conflict and resolution. We will consider various themes and story-lines, but before an author submits a query we urge them to become familiar with our books."

❶ KANE/MILLER BOOK PUBLISHERS

4901 Morena Blvd., Suite 213, San Diego CA 92117. (858)456-0540. **Fax:** (858)456-9641. **Website:** www.kanemiller.com. **Contact:** Editorial Department. "Kane/Miller Book Publishers is a division of EDC Publishing, specializing in award-winning children's books from around the world. Our books bring the children of the world closer to each other, sharing stories and ideas, while exploring cultural differences and similarities. Although we continue to look for books from other countries, we are now actively seeking works that convey cultures and communities within the US. We are committed to expanding our picture book list and are interested in great stories with engaging characters, especially those with particularly American subjects. When writing about the experiences of a particular community, we will express a preference for stories written from a firsthand experience." Submission guidelines on site.

FICTION Picture Books: concept, contemporary, health, humor, multicultural. Young Readers: contemporary, multicultural, suspense. Middle Readers: contemporary, humor, multicultural, suspense. "At this time, we are not considering holiday stories (in any age range) or self-published works."

HOW TO CONTACT If interested, responds in 90 days to queries.

TIPS "We like to think that a child reading a Kane/Miller book will see parallels between his own life and what might be the unfamiliar setting and characters of the story. And that by seeing how a character who is somehow or in some way dissimilar—an outsider—finds a way to fit comfortably into a culture or community or situation while maintaining a healthy sense of self and self-dignity, she might be empowered to do the same."

KAR-BEN PUBLISHING

Lerner Publishing Group, 1241 Washington Ave. N., Minneapolis MN 55401. **E-mail:** editorial@karben.com. **Website:** www.karben.com. Kar-Ben publishes exclusively children's books on Jewish themes. Publishes hardcover, trade paperback and e-books. **Publishes 20 titles/year. 20% of books from first-time authors. 70% from unagented writers.**

FICTION "We seek picture book mss 800-1,000 words on Jewish-themed topics for children." Picture books: Adventure, concept, folktales, history, humor, multicultural, religion, special needs; must be on a Jewish theme. Average word length: picture books–1,000. Recently published titles: *The Count's Hanukkah Countdown, Sammy Spider's First Book of Jewish Holidays, The Cats of Ben Yehuda Street.*

NONFICTION "In addition to traditional Jewish-themed stories about Jewish holidays, history, folktales and other subjects, we especially seek stories that reflect the rich diversity of the contemporary Jewish community." Picture books, young readers; Jewish history, Israel, Holocaust, folktales, religion, social issues, special needs; must be of Jewish interest. No textbooks, games, or educational materials.

HOW TO CONTACT Submit full ms. Picture books only. Submit completed ms. 800 mss received/year. Responds in 12 weeks. Most mss published within 2 years.

TERMS Pays 5% royalty on NET sale. Pays $500-2,500 advance. Book catalog online; free upon request. Guidelines online.

TIPS "Authors: Do a literature search to make sure similar title doesn't already exist. Illustrators: Look at our online catalog for a sense of what we like—bright colors and lively composition."

KREGEL PUBLICATIONS

2450 Oak Industrial Dr. NE, Grand Rapids MI 49505. (616)451-4775. **Fax:** (616)451-9330. **E-mail:** kregelbooks@kregel.com. **Website:** www.kregelpublications.com. "Our mission as an evangelical Christian publisher is to provide—with integrity and excellence—trusted, Biblically based resources that challenge and encourage individuals in their Christian lives. Works in theology and Biblical studies should reflect the historic, orthodox Protestant tradition." Publishes hardcover and trade paperback originals and reprints. **Publishes 90 titles/year. 20% of books from first-time authors. 10% from unagented writers.**

FICTION Fiction should be geared toward the evangelical Christian market. Wants books with fast-paced, contemporary storylines presenting a strong Christian message in an engaging, entertaining style.

NONFICTION "We serve evangelical Christian readers and those in career Christian service."

HOW TO CONTACT Finds works through The Writer's Edge and Christian Manuscript Submissions ms screening services. Finds works through The Writer's Edge and Christian Manuscript Submissions ms screening services. Responds in 2-3 months. Publishes ms 12-16 months after acceptance.

TERMS Pays royalty on wholesale price. Pays negotiable advance. Guidelines online.

TIPS "Our audience consists of conservative, evangelical Christians, including pastors and ministry students."

● LANTANA PUBLISHING

London , United Kingdom. **E-mail:** info@lantanapublishing.com. **Website:** www.lantanapublishing.com. Lantana Publishing is a young, independent publishing house producing award-winning picture books for children. Lantana's mission is to select outstanding writing from around the world, working with prize-winning authors and illustrators from many countries, while at the same time nurturing new writing talent. Lantana's cross-cultural collaborations have so far garnered high praise, described as 'dazzling', 'delectable', 'enchanting' and 'exquisite' by bloggers and reviewers, and receiving high commendations from awards-panels both at home and abroad. Lantana Publishing is hugely proud to bring UK children's publishing one step closer towards achieving a more diverse and inclusive children's book landscape for the next generation of young readers.

FICTION "We are currently focusing on picture books for 4-8 year-olds with text no longer than 500 words (and we prefer 200-400 words). We love writing that is contemporary and fun. We particularly like stories with modern-day settings in the UK or around the world, especially if they feature BAME families, and stories that lend themselves to great illustration."

NONFICTION "We accept some nonfiction content for the 7-11 range if it has the potential to be beautifully illustrated."

HOW TO CONTACT Responds in 6 weeks.

TERMS Pays royalty. Pays advance. Guidelines online.

LEE & LOW BOOKS

95 Madison Ave., #1205, New York NY 10016. (212)779-4400. **E-mail:** general@leeandlow.com. **Website:** www.leeandlow.com. "Our goals are to meet a growing need for books that address children of color, and to present literature that all children can identify with. We only consider multicultural children's books. Sponsors a yearly New Voices Award for first-time picture book authors of color. Contest rules online at website or for SASE." Publishes hardcover originals and trade paperback reprints. **Publishes 12-14 titles/year. 20% of books from first-time authors. 50% from unagented writers.**

FICTION Picture books, young readers: anthology, contemporary, history, multicultural, poetry. Picture book, middle reader: contemporary, history, multicultural, nature/environment, poetry, sports. Average word length: picture books—1,000-1,500 words. "We do not publish folklore or animal stories."

NONFICTION Picture books: concept. Picture books, middle readers: biography, history, multicultural, science and sports. Average word length: picture books-1,500-3,000.

HOW TO CONTACT Submit complete ms. Submit complete ms. Receives 100 queries/year; 1,200 mss/year. Responds in 6 months to mss if interested. Publishes book 2 years after acceptance.

ILLUSTRATION Works with 12-14 illustrators/year. Uses color artwork only. Reviews ms/illustration packages from artists. Contact: Louise May. Illustra-

tions only: Query with samples, résumé, promo sheet and tearsheets. Responds only if interested. Samples returned with SASE; samples filed. Original artwork returned at job's completion.

PHOTOGRAPHY Buys photos from freelancers. Works on assignment only. Model/property releases required. Submit cover letter, résumé, promo piece and book dummy.

TERMS Pays net royalty. Pays authors advances against royalty. Pays illustrators advance against royalty. Photographers paid advance against royalty. Book catalog available online. Guidelines available online or by written request with SASE.

TIPS "Check our website to see the kinds of books we publish. Do not send mss that don't fit our mission."

ARTHUR A. LEVINE BOOKS

Scholastic, Inc., 557 Broadway, New York NY 10012. (212)343-4436. **Fax:** (212)343-6143. **Website:** www.arthuralevinebooks.com. Publishes hardcover, paperback, and e-book editions.

FICTION "Arthur A. Levine is looking for distinctive literature, for children and young adults, for whatever's extraordinary." Averages 18-20 total titles/year.

HOW TO CONTACT Query. Please follow submission guidelines. Responds in 1 month to queries; 5 months to mss. Publishes a book 18 months after acceptance.

TERMS Picture Books: Query letter and full text of pb. Novels: Send Query letter, first 2 chapters and synopsis. Other: Query letter, 10-page sample and synopsis/proposal.

Ⓐ LITTLE, BROWN BOOKS FOR YOUNG READERS

Hachette Book Group USA, 1290 Avenue of the Americas, New York NY 10104. (212)364-1100. **Fax:** (212)364-0925. **Website:** littlebrown.com. "Little, Brown and Co. Children's Publishing publishes all formats including board books, picture books, middle grade fiction, and nonfiction YA titles. We are looking for strong writing and presentation, but no predetermined topics." *Only interested in solicited agented material.* **Publishes 100-150 titles/year.**

FICTION Average word length: picture books—1,000; young readers—6,000; middle readers—15,000- 50,000; young adults—50,000 and up.

NONFICTION "Writers should avoid looking for the 'issue' they think publishers want to see, choosing instead topics they know best and are most enthusiastic about/inspired by."

HOW TO CONTACT *Agented submissions only. Agented submissions only.* Responds in 1-2 months. Publishes ms 2 years after acceptance.

ILLUSTRATION Works with 40 illustrators/year. Illustrations only: Query art director with b&w and color samples; provide résumé, promo sheet or tearsheets to be kept on file. Does not respond to art samples. Do not send originals; copies only. Accepts illustration samples by postal mail or e-mail.

PHOTOGRAPHY Works on assignment only. Model/property releases required; captions required. Publishes photo essays and photo concept books. Uses 35mm transparencies. Photographers should provide résumé, promo sheets or tearsheets to be kept on file.

TERMS Pays authors royalties based on retail price. Pays illustrators and photographers by the project or royalty based on retail price. Sends galleys to authors; dummies to illustrators. Pays negotiable advance.

TIPS "In order to break into the field, authors and illustrators should research their competition and try to come up with something outstandingly different."

LITTLE PICKLE PRESS

3701 Sacramento St., #494, San Francisco CA 94118. (415)340-3344. **Fax:** (415)366-1520. **E-mail:** info@march4thinc.com. **Website:** www.littlepicklepress.com. Little Pickle Press is a 21st Century publisher dedicated to helping parents and educators cultivate conscious, responsible little people by stimulating explorations of the meaningful topics of their generation through a variety of media, technologies, and techniques. Submit through submission link on site. Includes YA imprint Relish Media.

TERMS Uses Author.me for submissions for Little Pickle and YA imprint Relish Media. Guidelines available on site.

TIPS "We have lots of manuscripts to consider, so it will take up to 8 weeks before we get back to you."

ⓐ LITTLE SIMON

Imprint of Simon & Schuster, 1230 Avenue of the Americas, New York NY 10020. (212)698-1295. **Fax:** (212)698-2794. **Website:** www.simonandschuster.com/kids. "Our goal is to provide fresh material in an innovative format for preschool to age 8. Our books are often, if not exclusively, format driven." Publishes novelty and branded books only.

FICTION Novelty books include many things that do not fit in the traditional hardcover or paperback format, such as pop-up, board book, scratch and sniff, glow in the dark, lift the flap, etc. Children's/juvenile. No picture books. Large part of the list is holiday-themed.

NONFICTION "We publish very few nonfiction titles." No picture books.

HOW TO CONTACT *Currently not accepting unsolicited mss. Currently not accepting unsolicited mss.*

TERMS Offers advance and royalties.

MAGINATION PRESS

750 First St. NE, Washington DC 20002. (202)336-5618. **Fax:** (202)336-5624. **E-mail:** magination@apa.org. **Website:** www.apa.org. Magination Press is an imprint of the American Psychological Association. "We publish books dealing with the psycho/therapeutic resolution of children's problems and psychological issues with a strong self-help component." Submit complete ms. Full guidelines available on site. Materials returned only with SASE. **Publishes 12 titles/year. 75% of books from first-time authors.**

FICTION All levels: psychological and social issues, self-help, health, parenting concerns and, special needs. Picture books, middle school readers.

NONFICTION All levels: psychological and social issues, self-help, health, multicultural, special needs.

HOW TO CONTACT Responds to queries in 1-2 months; mss in 2-6 months. Publishes a book 18-24 months after acceptance.

ILLUSTRATION Works with 10-15 illustrators/year. Reviews ms/illustration packages. Will review artwork for future assignments. Responds only if interested, or immediately if SASE or response card is included. "We keep samples on file."

MARTIN SISTERS PUBLISHING COMPANY, INC

P.O. Box 1154, Barbourville KY 40906-1499. **Website:** www.martinsisterspublishing.com. Firm/imprint publishes trade and mass market paperback originals; electronic originals. **Publishes 12 titles/year. 75% of books from first-time authors. 100% from unagented writers.**

HOW TO CONTACT "Please place query letter, marketing plan and the first 5-10 pages of your manuscript (if you are submitting fiction) directly into your e-mail." Guidelines available on site. Responds in 1 month on queries, 2 months on proposals, 3-6 months on mss. Publishes ms 9 months after acceptance.

TERMS Pays 7.5% royalty/max on print net; 35% royalty/max on e-book net. No advance offered. Catalog and guidelines online.

⟳ MASTER BOOKS

P.O. Box 726, Green Forest AR 72638. **E-mail:** submissions@newleafpress.net. **Website:** www.masterbooks.com. **Contact:** Craig Froman, acquisitions editor. Publishes 3 middle readers/year; 2 young adult nonfiction titles/year; 10 homeschool curriculum titles; 20 adult trade books/year. **5% of books from first-time authors. 99% from unagented writers.**

NONFICTION Picture books: activity books, animal, nature/environment, creation. Young readers, middle readers, young adults: activity books, animal, biography Christian, nature/environment, science, creation.

HOW TO CONTACT Submission guidelines on website. http://www.nlpg.com/submissions 500 We are no longer able to respond to every query. If you have not heard from us within 90 days, it means we are unable to partner with you on that particular project. Publishes book 1 year after acceptance.

TERMS Pays authors royalty of 3-15% based on wholesale price. Book catalog available upon request. Guidelines online.

TIPS "All of our children's books are creation-based, including topics from the Book of Genesis. We look also for home school educational material as we are expanding our home school curriculum resources."

MARGARET K. MCELDERRY BOOKS

Imprint of Simon & Schuster Children's Publishing Division, 1230 Sixth Ave., New York NY 10020. (212)698-7200. **Website:** imprints.simonandschuster.biz/margaret-k-mcelderry-books. "Margaret K. McElderry Books publishes hardcover and paperback trade books for children from pre-school age through young adult. This list includes picture books, middle grade and teen fiction, poetry, and fantasy. The style and subject matter of the books we publish is almost unlimited. We do not publish textbooks, coloring and activity books, greeting cards, magazines, pamphlets, or religious publications." **Publishes 30 titles/year. 15% of books from first-time authors. 50% from unagented writers.**

FICTION *No unsolicited mss.*

NONFICTION *No unsolicited mss. Agented submissions only.*

HOW TO CONTACT *Agented submissions only.*

TERMS Pays authors royalty based on retail price. Pays illustrator royalty of by the project. Pays photographers by the project. Original artwork returned at job's completion. Offers $5,000-8,000 advance for new authors. Guidelines for #10 SASE.

TIPS "Read! The children's book field is competitive. See what's been done and what's out there before submitting. We look for high quality: an originality of ideas, clarity and felicity of expression, a well organized plot, and strong character-driven stories. We're looking for strong, original fiction, especially mysteries and middle grade humor. We are always interested in picture books for the youngest age reader. Study our titles."

MEDIA LAB BOOKS

Topix Media Lab, 14 Wall St., Suite 4B, New York NY 10005. **Website:** onnewsstandsnow.com. **Contact:** Phil Sexton, vice president and publisher. Media Lab Books is a premier imprint that partners with industry leaders to publish branded titles designed to inform, educate and entertain readers around the world. "With brand partners that run the gamut, our books are widely variable in category and topic. From John Wayne to Disney and every brand in between, our partners have loyal followings, strong media presences and amazing stories to tell. While leveraging the platforms of our brand partners, we publish highly visual, illustrated books that surprise and delight readers of all ages. From *Jack Hanna's Big Book of Why* to *The John Wayne Code*, we truly have something for everyone. In the end, our aim is to match great ideas with amazing brands. We're looking for creative nonfiction ideas from authors with a voice (and a platform). Though we specialize in creating visually dynamic books built around big brands, we're also interested in original works focusing on popular or trending topics in most nonfiction categories, but given a unique, one-of-a-kind spin that demands publication. For example, *I'm Just Here for the Drinks* by Sother Teague." Publishes cooking, children's books, games, puzzles, reference, humor, biography, history. **Publishes 25 titles/year. 20% of books from first-time authors. 20% from unagented writers.**

HOW TO CONTACT 60 Responds in 30 days. Publishes ms 12-18 months after acceptance.

TERMS Catalog available. Electronic submissions only. On the first page of the document, please include author's name and contact information. Please send full submission packet, including overview, USP (unique selling proposition), comparable titles, proposed TOC, and 1-3 sample chapters (no more than 50 pages).

TIPS "Be sure to check out the kind of books we've already published. You'll see that most of them are brand-driven. The ones that are author-driven address popular topics with a unique approach. More general books are of no interest unless the topic in question is trending and there's minimal competition in the market."

MILKWEED EDITIONS

1011 Washington Ave. S., Suite 300, Minneapolis MN 55415. (612)332-3192. **Fax:** (612)215-2550. **Website:** www.milkweed.org. Publishes 3-4 middle readers/year. 25% of books by first-time authors. "Milkweed Editions publishes with the intention of making a humane impact on society, in the belief that literature is a transformative art uniquely able to convey the essential experiences of the human heart and spirit. To that end, Milkweed Editions publishes distinctive voices of literary merit in handsomely designed, visually dynamic books, exploring the ethical, cultural, and esthetic issues that free societies need continually to address." Publishes hardcover, trade paperback, and electronic originals; trade paperback and electronic reprints. **Publishes 15-20 titles/year. 25% of books from first-time authors. 75% from unagented writers.**

FICTION Novels for adults and for readers 8-13. High literary quality. For adult readers: literary fiction, nonfiction, poetry, essays. Middle readers: adventure, contemporary, fantasy, multicultural, nature/environment, suspense/mystery. Average length: middle readers—90-200 pages. No romance, mysteries, science fiction.

HOW TO CONTACT "Please submit a query letter with three opening chapters (of a novel) or three representative stories (of a collection). Publishes YR." Responds in 6 months. Publishes book in 18 months.

TERMS Pays authors variable royalty based on retail price. Offers advance against royalties. Pays varied advance from $500-10,000. Book catalog online. Only accepts submissions during open submission periods. See website for guidelines.

TIPS "We are looking for excellent writing with the intent of making a humane impact on society. Please read submission guidelines before submitting and acquaint yourself with our books in terms of style and quality before submitting. Many factors influence our selection process, so don't get discouraged. Nonfiction is focused on literary writing about the natural world, including living well in urban environments."

○ THE MILLBROOK PRESS

Lerner Publishing Group, 1251 Washington Ave N, Minneapolis MN 55401. **E-mail:** info@lernerbooks.com. **Website:** www.lernerbooks.com. **Contact:** Carol Hinz, editorial director. "Millbrook Press publishes informative picture books, illustrated nonfiction titles, and inspiring photo-driven titles for grades K–5. Our authors approach curricular topics with a fresh point of view. Our fact-filled books engage readers with fun yet accessible writing, high-quality photographs, and a wide variety of illustration styles. We cover subjects ranging from the parts of speech and other language arts skills; to history, science, and math; to art, sports, crafts, and other interests. Millbrook Press is the home of the best-selling Words Are CATegorical® series and Bob Raczka's Art Adventures. We do not accept unsolicited manuscripts from authors. Occasionally, we may put out a call for submissions, which will be announced on our website."

MITCHELL LANE PUBLISHERS, INC.

P.O. Box 196, Hockessin DE 33009. (302) 234-9426. **Fax:** (866) 834-4164. **E-mail:** barbaramitchell@mitchellane.com; customerservice@mitchelllane.com. **Website:** www.mitchelllane.com. **Contact:** Barbara Mitchell. Publishes hardcover and library bound originals. **Publishes 80 titles/year. 0% of books from first-time authors. 90% from unagented writers.**

NONFICTION Young readers, middle readers, young adults: biography, nonfiction, and curriculum-related subjects. Average word length: 4,000-50,000 words. Recently published: *My Guide to US Citizenship*, *Rivers of the World* and *Vote America*.

HOW TO CONTACT Query with SASE. *All unsolicited mss discarded.* 100 queries received/year. 5 mss received/year. Responds only if interested to queries. Publishes ms 1 year after acceptance.

ILLUSTRATION Works with 2-3 illustrators/year. Reviews ms/illustration packages from artists. Query. Illustration only: Query with samples; send résumé, portfolio, slides, tearsheets. Responds only if interested. Samples not returned; samples filed.

PHOTOGRAPHY Buys stock images. Needs photos of famous and prominent minority figures. Captions required. Uses color prints or digital images. Submit cover letter, résumé, published samples, stock photo list.

TERMS Work purchased outright from authors (range: $350-2,000). Pays illustrators by the project (range: $40-400). Book catalog available free.

TIPS "We hire writers on a 'work-for-hire' basis to complete book projects we assign. Send résumé and writing samples that do not need to be returned."

ⓐ MOODY PUBLISHERS

Moody Bible Institute, 820 N. LaSalle Blvd., Chicago IL 60610. (800)678-8812. **Fax:** (312)329-4157. **Website:** www.moodypublishers.org. **Contact:** Acquisitions Coordinator. "The mission of Moody Publishers is to educate and edify the Christian and to evangelize the non-Christian by ethically publishing conservative, evangelical Christian literature and other media for all ages around the world, and to help provide resources for Moody Bible Institute in its training of future Christian leaders." Publishes hardcover, trade, and mass market paperback originals. **Publishes 60 titles/year. 1% of books from first-time authors. 80% from unagented writers.**

NONFICTION "We are no longer reviewing queries or unsolicited manuscripts unless they come to us through an agent,are from an author who has published with us, an associate from a Moody Bible Institute ministry or a personal contact at a writer's conference. Unsolicited proposals will be returned only if proper postage is included. We are not able to acknowledge the receipt of your unsolicited proposal."

HOW TO CONTACT *Agented submissions only.* Does not accept unsolicited nonfiction submissions. 1,500 queries received/year. 2,000 mss received/year. Responds in 2-3 months to queries. Publishes book 1 year after acceptance.

TERMS Royalty varies. Book catalog for 9×12 envelope and 4 first-class stamps. Guidelines online.

TIPS "In our fiction list, we're looking for Christian storytellers rather than teachers trying to present a message. Your motivation should be to delight the reader. Using your skills to create beautiful works is glorifying to God."

ⓐ NATIONAL GEOGRAPHIC CHILDREN'S BOOKS

1145 17th St. NW, Washington DC 20090-8199. (800)647-5463. **Website:** kids.nationalgeographic. com. National Geographic CHildren's Books provides quality nonfiction for children and young adults by award-winning authors. *This market does not currently accept unsolicited mss.*

TOMMY NELSON

Imprint of Thomas Nelson, Inc., P.O. Box 141000, Nashville TN 37214-1000. (615)889-9000. **Fax:** (615)902-2219. **Website:** www.tommynelson.com. "Tommy Nelson publishes children's Christian nonfiction and fiction for boys and girls up to age 14. We honor God and serve people through books, videos, software and Bibles for children that improve the lives of our customers." Publishes hardcover and trade paperback originals. **Publishes 50-75 titles/year.**

FICTION No stereotypical characters.

HOW TO CONTACT *Does not accept unsolicited mss. Does not accept unsolicited mss.*

TERMS Guidelines online.

TIPS "Know the Christian Booksellers Association market. Check out the Christian bookstores to see what sells and what is needed."

NIGHTSCAPE PRESS

P.O. Box 1948, Smyrna TN 37167. **E-mail:** info@ nightscapepress.com. **Website:** www.nightscapepress.com. Nightscape Press is seeking quality book-length words of at least 50,000 words (40,000 for young adult).

FICTION "We are not interested in erotica or graphic novels."

HOW TO CONTACT Query.

TERMS Pays monthly royalties. Offers advance. Guidelines online. Currently closed to submissions. Will announce on site when they re-open to submissions.

NOMAD PRESS

2456 Christain St., White River Junction VT 05001. (802)649-1995. **E-mail:** info@nomadpress.net. **Website:** www.nomadpress.net. **Contact:** Acquisitions Editor. "We produce nonfiction children's activity books that bring a particular science or cultural topic into sharp focus. Nomad Press does not accept unsolicited manuscripts. If authors are interested in contributing to our children's series, please send a writing resume that includes relevant experience/expertise and publishing credits."

🕐 Nomad Press does not accept picture books, fiction, or cookbooks.

NONFICTION Middle readers: activity books, history, science. Average word length: middle readers—30,000.

HOW TO CONTACT Responds to queries in 3-4 weeks. Publishes book 1 year after acceptance.

TERMS Pays authors royalty based on retail price or work purchased outright. Offers advance against royalties. Catalog online.

TIPS "We publish a very specific kind of nonfiction children's activity book. Please keep this in mind when querying or submitting."

NORTHSOUTH BOOKS

600 Third Ave., 2nd Floor, New York NY 10016. E-mail: submissionsb@gmail.com. **Website:** www.northsouth.com. **Contact:** Beth Terrill.

FICTION Looking for fresh, original fiction with universal themes that could appeal to children ages 3-8. "We typically do not acquire rhyming texts, since our books must also be translated into German."

HOW TO CONTACT Submit picture book mss (1,000 words or less) via e-mail.

TERMS Guidelines online.

🌑 NOSY CROW PUBLISHING

The Crow's Nest, 10a Lant St., London SE1 1QR, United Kingdom. (44)(0)207-089-7575. **Fax:** (44)(0)207-089-7576. **E-mail:** hello@nosycrow.com. **Website:** nosycrow.com. "We publish books for children 0-14. We're looking for 'parent-friendly' books, and we don't publish books with explicit sex, drug use or serious violence, so no edgy YA or edgy cross-over. And whatever New Adult is, we don't do it. We also publish apps for children from 2-7, and may publish apps for older children if the idea feels right."

FICTION "As a rule, we don't like books with 'issues' that are in any way overly didactic."

HOW TO CONTACT Prefers submissions by e-mail, but post works if absolutely necessary. Prefers submissions by e-mail, but post works if absolutely necessary.

TERMS Guidelines online.

TIPS "Please don't be too disappointed if we reject your work! We're a small company and can only publish a few new books and apps each year, so do try other publishers and agents: publishing is necessarily a hugely subjective business. We wish you luck!"

🔘 ONSTAGE PUBLISHING

190 Lime Quarry Rd., Suite 106-J, Madison AL 35758-8962. (256)542-3213. **Fax:** (256)542-3213. **Website:** www.onstagepublishing.com. **Contact:** Dianne Hamilton, senior editor. "At this time, we only produce fiction books for ages 8-18. We have added an e-book only side of the house for mysteries for grades 6-12. See our website for more information. We will not do anthologies of any kind. Query first for nonfiction projects as nonfiction projects must spark our interest. We no longer are accepting written submissions. We want e-mail queries and submissions. For submissions: Put the first 3 chapters in the body of the e-mail. Do not use attachments! We will delete any submission with an attachment without acknowledgment." Suggested ms lengths: Chapter books: 3,000-9,000 words, Middle Grade novels: 10,000-40,000 words, Young adult novels: 40,000-60,000 words. **Publishes 1-5 titles/year. 80% of books from first-time authors. 95% from unagented writers.**

FICTION Middle readers: adventure, contemporary, fantasy, history, nature/environment, science fiction, suspense/mystery. Young adults: adventure, contemporary, fantasy, history, humor, science fiction, suspense/mystery. Average word length: chapter books—4,000-6,000 words; middle readers—5,000 words and up; young adults—25,000 and up. Recently published *Mission: Shanghai* by Jamie Dodson (an adventure for boys ages 12+); *Birmingham, 1933: Alice* (a chapter book for grades 3-5). "We do not produce picture books."

HOW TO CONTACT 500 + Responds in 1-6 months.

TERMS Pays authors/illustrators/photographers advance plus royalties. Pays advance. Guidelines online.

TIPS "Study our titles and get a sense of the kind of books we publish, so that you know whether your project is likely to be right for us."

🔘 ON THE MARK PRESS

15 Dairy Ave., Napanee ON K7R 1M4, Canada. (800)463-6367. **Fax:** (800)290-3631. **Website:** www.onthemarkpress.com. Publishes books for the Canadian curriculum. **15% of books from first-time authors.**

PHOTOGRAPHY Buys stock images.

OOLIGAN PRESS

369 Neuberger Hall, 724 SW Harrison St., Portland OR 97201. (503)725-9410. **Website:** ooligan.pdx.edu. **Contact:** Acquisitions Co-Managers. "We seek to

publish regionally significant works of literary, historical, and social value.

We define the Pacific Northwest as Northern California, Oregon, Idaho, Washington, British Columbia, and Alaska. We recognize the importance of diversity, particularly within the publishing industry, and are committed to building a literary community that includes traditionally underrepresented voices; therefore, we are interested in works originating from, or focusing on, marginalized communities of the Pacific Northwest." Publishes trade paperbacks, electronic originals, and reprints. **Publishes 3-4 titles/year. 90% of books from first-time authors. 90% from unagented writers.**

FICTION "We seek to publish regionally significant works of literary, historical, and social value.

We define the Pacific Northwest as Northern California, Oregon, Idaho, Washington, British Columbia, and Alaska."

We recognize the importance of diversity, particularly within the publishing industry, and are committed to building a literary community that includes traditionally underrepresented voices; therefore, we are interested in works originating from, or focusing on, marginalized communities of the Pacific Northwest. Does not want romance, horror, westerns, incomplete mss.

NONFICTION Cookbooks, self-help books, how-to manuals.

HOW TO CONTACT Query with SASE. *"At this time we cannot accept science fiction or fantasy submissions."* Submit a query through Submittable. If accepted, then submit proposal package, outline, 4 sample chapters, projected page count, audience, marketing ideas, and a list of similar titles. 250-500 queries; 50-75 mss received/year. Responds in 3 weeks for queries; 3 months for proposals. Publishes ms 12-18 months after acceptance.

TERMS Pays negotiable royalty on retail price. Catalog online. Guidelines online.

TIPS "Search the blog for tips."

ⓐ ORCHARD BOOKS (US)

557 Broadway, New York NY 10012. **Website:** www.scholastic.com. *Orchard is not accepting unsolicited mss.* **Publishes 20 titles/year. 10% of books from first-time authors.**

FICTION Picture books, early readers, and novelty: animal, contemporary, history, humor, multicultural, poetry.

TERMS Most commonly offers an advance against list royalties.

RICHARD C. OWEN PUBLISHERS, INC.

P.O. Box 585, Katonah NY 10536. (914)232-3903; (800)262-0787. **E-mail:** richardowen@rcowen.com. **Website:** www.rcowen.com. **Contact:** Richard Owen, publisher. "We publish child-focused books, with inherent instructional value, about characters and situations with which 5, 6, and 7-year-old children can identify—books that can be read for meaning, entertainment, enjoyment and information. We include multicultural stories that present minorities in a positive and natural way. Our stories show the diversity in America." Not interested in lesson plans, or books of activities for literature studies or other content areas. Submit complete ms and cover letter.

○ "Due to high volume and long production time, we are currently limiting to nonfiction submissions only."

NONFICTION "Our books are for kindergarten, first- and second-grade children to read on their own. The stories are very brief—up to 2,000 words—yet well structured and crafted with memorable characters, language, and plots. Picture books, young readers: animals, careers, history, how-to, music/dance, geography, multicultural, nature/environment, science, sports. Multicultural needs include: Good stories respectful of all heritages, races, cultural—African-American, Hispanic, American Indian, Asian, European, Middle Eastern." Wants lively stories. No "encyclopedic" type of information stories. Average word length: under 500 words.

HOW TO CONTACT Responds to mss in 1 year. Publishes book 2-3 years after acceptance.

ILLUSTRATION Works with 20 illustrators/year. Uses color artwork only. Illustration only: Send color copies/reproductions or photos of art or provide tearsheets; do not send slides or originals. Include SASE and cover letter. Responds only if interested; samples filed.

TERMS Pays authors royalty of 5% based on net price or outright purchase (range: $25-500). Offers no advances. Pays illustrators by the project (range: $100-2,000) or per photo (range: $50-150). Book catalog available with SASE. Ms guidelines with SASE or online.

PAGESPRING PUBLISHING

P.O. Box 2113, Columbus OH 43221. **E-mail:** sales@pagespringpublishing.com. **Website:** www.pagespringpublishing.com. **Contact:** Lucky Marble Books Editor or Cup of Tea Books Editor. PageSpring Publishing publishes women's fiction under the Cup of Tea Books imprint and YA/middle grade titles under the Lucky Marble Books imprint. Visit the PageSpring Publishing website for submission details. Publishes trade paperback and electronic originals. **Publishes 4-7 titles/year. 50% of books from first-time authors. 90% from unagented writers.**

FICTION Cup of Tea Books publishes women's fiction. Lucky Marble Books specializes in middle grade and young adult fiction.

HOW TO CONTACT submissions@pagespringpublishing.com Send submissions for both Cup of Tea Books and Lucky Marble Books to submissions@pagespringpublishing.com. Send a query, synopsis, and the first 30 pages of the manuscript in the body of the email. please. NO attachments. Endeavors to respond to queries within 3 months. Publishes ms 9-12 months after acceptance.

TERMS Pays royalty on wholesale price. Catalog online. Guidelines online.

TIPS Cup of Tea Books would love to see more cozy mysteries and humor. Lucky Marble Books is looking for humor and engaging contemporary stories for middle grade and young adult readers.

PAGESPRING PUBLISHING

PageSpring Publishing, P.O. Box 21133, Columbus OH 43221. **Website:** www.pagespringpublishing.com. PageSpring Publishing is a small independent publisher with two imprints: Cup of Tea Books and Lucky Marble Books. Cup of Tea Books publishes women's fiction, with particular emphasis on mystery and humor. Lucky Marble Books publishes young adult and middle grade fiction. "We are looking for engaging characters and well-crafted plots that keep our readers turning the page. We accept e-mail queries only; see our website for details." Publishes trade paperback and electronic originals. **Publishes 4-5 titles/year. 75%% of books from first-time authors. 100%% from unagented writers.**

FICTION Lucky Marble Books publishes middle grade and young adult novels. Cup of Tea Books pub-

lishes women's fiction. Lucky Marble Books publishes middle grade and young adult novels. No children's picture books.

HOW TO CONTACT Submit proposal package via e-mail only. Include synopsis and 30 sample pages. Responds in 3 months. Publishes ms 12 months after acceptance.

TERMS Pays royalty. Guidelines online.

TIPS "Cup of Tea Books is particularly interested in cozy mystery novels. Lucky Marble Books is looking for funny, age-appropriate tales for middle grade and young adult readers."

PANTS ON FIRE PRESS

2062 Harbor Cove Way, Winter Garden FL 34787. (863)546-0760. **E-mail:** submission@pantsonfirepress.com. **Website:** www.pantsonfirepress.com. **Contact:** Becca Goldman, senior editor; Emily Gerety, editor. Pants On Fire Press is an award-winning book publisher of picture, middle-grade, young adult, and adult books. Publishes hardcover originals and reprints, trade paperback originals and reprints, and electronic originals and reprints. **Publishes 10 titles/year. 50% of books from first-time authors. 80% from unagented writers.**

FICTION Publishes big story ideas with high concepts, new worlds, and meaty characters for children, teens, and discerning adults.

HOW TO CONTACT Submit a proposal package including a synopsis, 3 sample chapters, and a query letter via e-mail. Receives 36,300 queries and mss per year. Responds in 3 months. Publishes ms approximately 7 months after acceptance.

TERMS Pays 10-50% royalties on wholesale price. Catalog online. Guidelines online.

PAUL DRY BOOKS

1700 Sansom St., Suite 700, Philadelphia PA 19103. (215)231-9939. **Fax:** (215)231-9942. **E-mail:** editor@pauldrybooks.com. **Website:** pauldrybooks.com. "We publish fiction, both novels and short stories, and nonfiction, biography, memoirs, history, and essays, covering subjects from Homer to Chekhov, bird watching to jazz music, New York City to shogunate Japan." Hardcover and trade paperback originals, trade paperback reprints.

HOW TO CONTACT "We do not accept unsolicited manuscripts." "We do not accept unsolicited manuscripts."

TERMS Book catalog online.

TIPS "Our aim is to publish lively books 'to awaken, delight, and educate'—to spark conversation. We publish fiction and nonfiction, and essays covering subjects from Homer to Chekhov, bird watching to jazz music, New York City to shogunate Japan."

PAULINE BOOKS & MEDIA

50 St. Paul's Ave., Boston MA 02130. (617)522-8911. **Fax:** (617)541-9805. **E-mail:** design@paulinemedia.com; editorial@paulinemedia.com. **Website:** www.pauline.org. "Submissions are evaluated on adherence to Gospel values, harmony with the Catholic faith tradition, relevance of topic, and quality of writing." For board books and picture books, the entire manuscript should be submitted. For easy-to-read, young readers, and middle reader books and teen books, please send a cover letter accompanied by a synopsis and two sample chapters. "Electronic submissions are encouraged. We make every effort to respond to unsolicited submissions within 2 months." Publishes trade paperback originals and reprints. **Publishes 40 titles/year. 5% from unagented writers.**

FICTION Children's and teen fiction only. "We are now accepting submissions for easy-to-read and middle reader chapter, and teen well documented historical fiction. We would also consider well-written fantasy, fairy tales, myths, science fiction, mysteries, or romance if approached from a Catholic perspective and consistent with church teaching. Please see our writer's guidelines."

NONFICTION Picture books, young readers, middle readers, teen: religion and fiction. Average word length: picture books—500-1,000; young readers—8,000-10,000; middle readers—15,000-25,000; teen—30,000-50,000. Recently published children's titles: *Bible Stores for Little Ones* by Genny Monchapm; *I Forgive You: Love We Can Hear, Ask For and Give* by Nicole Lataif; *Shepherds To the Rescue* (first place Catholic Book Award Winner) by Maria Grace Dateno; *FSP*; *Jorge from Argentina*; *Prayers for Young Catholics*. Teen Titles: *Teens Share the Mission* by Teens; *Martyred: The Story of Saint Lorenzo Ruiz*; *Ten Commandmenst for Kissing Gloria Jean* by Britt Leigh; *A.K.A. Genius* (2nd Place Catholic Book Award Winner) by Marilee Haynes; *Tackling Tough Topics* with Faith and Fiction by Diana Jenkins. No memoir/autobiography, poetry, or strictly nonreligious works currently considered.

HOW TO CONTACT "Submit proposal package, including synopsis, 2 sample chapters, and cover letter; complete ms." Submit proposal package, including outline, 1-2 sample chapters, cover letter, synopsis, intended audience and proposed length. Responds in 2 months. Publishes a book approximately 11-18 months after acceptance.

ILLUSTRATION Works with 10-15 illustrators/year. Uses color and black-and-white- artwork. Samples and résumés will be kept on file unless return is requested and SASE provided.

TERMS Varies by project, but generally are royalties with advance. Flat fees sometimes considered for smaller works. Book catalog online. Guidelines online.

TIPS "Manuscripts may or may not be explicitly catechetical, but we seek those that reflect a positive worldview, good moral values, awareness and appreciation of diversity, and respect for all people. All material must be relevant to the lives of readers and must conform to Catholic teaching and practice."

PAULIST PRESS

997 Macarthur Blvd., Mahwah NJ 07430. (201)825-7300. **Fax:** (201)825-8345. **E-mail:** submissions@paulistpress.com. **Website:** www.paulistpress.com. **Contact:** Trace Murphy, Editorial Director. Paulist Press publishes ecumenical theology, Roman Catholic studies, and books on scripture, liturgy, spirituality, church history, and philosophy, as well as works on faith and culture. Also publishes 2-3 children's titles a year. **10% of books from first-time authors. 95% from unagented writers.**

HOW TO CONTACT Accepts submissions via e-mail. Receives 400 submissions/year. Responds in 3 months to queries and proposals; 3-4 months on mss. Publishes a book 12-18 months after receipt of final, edited ms.

TERMS Royalties and advances are negotiable. Pays negotiable advance. Book catalog online. Guidelines online.

PEACHTREE PUBLISHERS, LTD.

1700 Chattahoochee Ave., Atlanta GA 30318. (404)876-8761. **Fax:** (404)875-2578. **E-mail:** hello@peachtree-online.com. **Website:** www.peachtree-online.com. **Publishes 30-35 titles/year.**

FICTION Picture books, young readers: adventure, animal, concept, history, nature/environment. Middle readers: adventure, animal, history, nature/environment, sports. Young adults: fiction, mystery, adventure. Does not want to see science fiction, romance. **NONFICTION** Picture books: animal, history, nature/environment. Young readers, middle readers, young adults: animal, biography, nature/environment. Does not want to see religion. **HOW TO CONTACT** Submit complete ms or 3 sample chapters by postal mail only. Submit complete ms or 3 sample chapters by postal mail only. Responds in 6-7 months. Publishes book 1-2 years after acceptance. **ILLUSTRATION** Works with 8-10 illustrators/year. Illustrations only: Query production manager or art director with samples, résumé, slides, color copies to keep on file. Responds only if interested. Samples returned with SASE; samples filed.

ⓐ PENGUIN RANDOM HOUSE, LLC

Division of Bertelsmann Book Group, 1745 Broadway, New York NY 10019. (212)782-9000. **Website:** www.penguinrandomhouse.com. Penguin Random House LLC is the world's largest English-language general trade book publisher. *Agented submissions only. No unsolicited mss.*

PERSEA BOOKS

277 Broadway, Suite 708, New York NY 10007. (212)260-9256. **Fax:** (212)267-3165. **E-mail:** info@perseabooks.com. **Website:** www.perseabooks.com. The aim of Persea is to publish works that endure by meeting high standards of literary merit and relevance. "We have often taken on important books other publishers have overlooked, or have made significant discoveries and rediscoveries, whether of a single work or writer's entire oeuvre. Our books cover a wide range of themes, styles, and genres. We have published poetry, fiction, essays, memoir, biography, titles of Jewish and Middle Eastern interest, women's studies, American Indian folklore, and revived classics, as well as a notable selection of works in translation." **HOW TO CONTACT** Queries should include a cover letter, author background and publication history, a detailed synopsis of the proposed work, and a sample chapter. Please indicate if the work is simultaneously submitted. Responds in 8 weeks to proposals; 10 weeks to mss. **TERMS** Guidelines online.

ⓐ PHILOMEL BOOKS

Imprint of Penguin Group (USA), Inc., 375 Hudson St., New York NY 10014. (212)414-3610. **Website:** www.penguin.com. **Contact:** Michael Green, president/publisher. "We look for beautifully written, engaging manuscripts for children and young adults." Publishes hardcover originals. **Publishes 8-10 titles/year. 5% of books from first-time authors. 20% from unagented writers.** **NONFICTION** Picture books. **HOW TO CONTACT** *No unsolicited mss. Agented submissions only.* **ILLUSTRATION** Works with 8-10 illustrators/year. Reviews ms/illustration packages from artists. Query with art sample first. Illustrations only: Query with samples. Send résumé and tearsheets. Responds to art samples in 1 month. Original artwork returned at job's completion. Samples returned with SASE or kept on file. **TERMS** Pays authors in royalties. Average advance payment "varies." Illustrators paid by advance and in royalties. Pays negotiable advance.

PIANO PRESS

P.O. Box 85, Del Mar CA 92014. (619)884-1401. **Fax:** (858)755-1104. **E-mail:** pianopress@pianopress.com. **Website:** www.pianopress.com. **Contact:** Elizabeth C. Axford, editor. "We publish music-related books, either fiction or nonfiction, music-related coloring books, songbooks, sheet music, CDs, and music-related poetry." **FICTION** Picture books, young readers, middle readers, young adults: folktales, multicultural, poetry, music. Average word length: picture books—1,500-2,000. **NONFICTION** Picture books, young readers, middle readers, young adults: multicultural, music/dance. Average word length: picture books—1,500-2,000. **HOW TO CONTACT** Responds if interested. Publishes book 1 year after acceptance. **ILLUSTRATION** Works with 1 or 2 illustrators/year. Reviews ms/illustration packages from artists. Query. Illustrations only: Query with samples. Responds in 3 months. Samples returned with SASE; samples filed. **PHOTOGRAPHY** Buys stock and assigns work. Looking for music-related, multicultural. Model/property releases required. Uses glossy or flat, color or b&w prints. Submit cover letter, résumé, client list, published samples, stock photo list.

TERMS Pays authors, illustrators, and photographers royalties based on the retail price. Book catalog online. **TIPS** "We are looking for music-related material only for the juvenile market. Please do not send non-music-related materials. Query by e-mail first before submitting anything."

PIÑATA BOOKS

Imprint of Arte Publico Press, University of Houston, 4902 Gulf Fwy., Bldg. 19, Room 100, Houston TX 77204-2004. (713)743-2845. **Fax:** (713)743-3080. **E-mail:** submapp@uh.edu. **Website:** www.artepublicopress.com. "Piñata Books is dedicated to the publication of children's and young adult literature focusing on U.S. Hispanic culture by U.S. Hispanic authors. Arte Publico's mission is the publication, promotion and dissemination of Latino literature for a variety of national and regional audiences, from early childhood to adult, through the complete gamut of delivery systems, including personal performance as well as print and electronic media." Publishes hardcover and trade paperback originals. **Publishes 10-15 titles/year. 80% of books from first-time authors.**

NONFICTION Piñata Books specializes in publication of children's and young adult literature that authentically portrays themes, characters and customs unique to U.S. Hispanic culture.

HOW TO CONTACT Submissions made through online submission form. Submissions made through online submission form. Responds in 2-3 months to queries; 4-6 months to mss. Publishes book 2 years after acceptance.

ILLUSTRATION Works with 6 illustrators/year. Uses color artwork only. Reviews ms/illustration packages from artists. Query or send portfolio (slides, color copies). Illustrations only: Query with samples or send résumé, promo sheet, portfolio, slides, client list and tearsheets. Responds only if interested. Samples not returned; samples filed.

TERMS Pays 10% royalty on wholesale price. Pays $1,000-3,000 advance. Book catalog and guidelines online.

TIPS "Include cover letter with submission explaining why your manuscript is unique and important, why we should publish it, who will buy it, etc."

PINEAPPLE PRESS, INC.

P.O. Box 3889, Sarasota FL 34230. (941)706-2507. **Fax:** (800)746-3275. **Website:** www.pineapplepress.com. **Contact:** June Cussen, executive editor. "We are seeking quality nonfiction on diverse topics for the library and book trade markets. Our mission is to publish good books about Florida." Publishes hardcover and trade paperback originals. **Publishes 21 titles/year. 50% of books from first-time authors. 95% from unagented writers.**

FICTION Picture books, young readers, middle readers, young adults: animal, folktales, history, nature/environment.

NONFICTION Picture books: animal, history, nature/environmental, science. Young readers, middle readers, young adults: animal, biography, geography, history, nature/environment, science.

HOW TO CONTACT Query or submit outline/synopsis and 3 sample chapters. Query or submit outline/synopsis and intro and 3 sample chapters. 1,000 queries; 500 mss received/year. Responds in 2 months. Publishes a book 1 year after acceptance.

ILLUSTRATION Works with 2 illustrators/year. Reviews ms/illustration packages from artists. Query with nonreturnable samples. Contact: June Cussen, executive editor. Illustrations only: Query with brochure, nonreturnable samples, photocopies, résumé. Responds only if interested. Samples returned with SASE, but prefers nonreturnable; samples filed.

TERMS Pays authors royalty of 10-15%. Book catalog for 9×12 SAE with $1.32 postage. Guidelines online.

TIPS "Quality first novels will be published, though we usually only do one or two novels per year and they must be set in Florida. We regard the author/editor relationship as a trusting relationship with communication open both ways. Learn all you can about the publishing process and about how to promote your book once it is published. A query on a novel without a brief sample seems useless."

POLIS BOOKS

E-mail: info@polisbooks.com. **Website:** www.polisbooks.com. "Polis Books is an independent publishing company actively seeking new and established authors for our growing list. We are actively acquiring titles in mystery, thriller, suspense, procedural, traditional crime, science fiction, fantasy, horror, supernatural, urban fantasy, romance, erotica, commercial women's fiction, commercial literary fiction, young adult and middle grade books." **Publishes 40 titles/year. 33% of books from first-time authors. 10% from unagented writers.**

HOW TO CONTACT Query with 3 sample chapters and bio via e-mail. 500+ Only responds to submissions if interested For e-book originals, ms published 6-9 months after acceptance. For front list print titles, 9-15 months.

TERMS Offers advance against royalties. Guidelines online.

ⓐ PRICE STERN SLOAN, INC.

Penguin Group, 375 Hudson St., New York NY 10014. (212)366-2000. **Website:** www.penguin.com. "Price Stern Sloan publishes quirky mass market novelty series for childrens as well as licensed movie tie-in books." Price Stern Sloan only responds to submissions it's interested in publishing.

FICTION Publishes picture books and novelty/board books.

HOW TO CONTACT *Agented submissions only.*

TERMS Book catalog online.

TIPS "Price Stern Sloan publishes unique, fun titles."

ⓐ PUFFIN BOOKS

Imprint of Penguin Group (USA), Inc., 375 Hudson St., New York NY 10014. (212)366-2000. **Website:** www.penguin.com. "Puffin Books publishes high-end trade paperbacks and paperback reprints for pre-school children, beginning and middle readers, and young adults." Publishes trade paperback originals and reprints. **Publishes 175-200 titles/year.**

NONFICTION "Women in history books interest us."

HOW TO CONTACT *No unsolicited mss. Agented submissions only. No unsolicited mss. Agented submissions only.* Publishes book 1 year after acceptance.

ILLUSTRATION Reviews artwork. Send color copies.

PHOTOGRAPHY Reviews photos. Send color copies.

TIPS "Our audience ranges from little children 'first books' to young adult (ages 14-16). An original idea has the best luck."

ⓐ G.P. PUTNAM'S SONS HARDCOVER

Imprint of Penguin Group (USA), Inc., 375 Hudson, New York NY 10014. (212)366-2000. **Fax:** (212)366-2664. **Website:** www.penguin.com. Publishes hardcover originals.

HOW TO CONTACT *Agented submissions only. Agented submissions only. No unsolicited mss.*

TERMS Pays variable royalties on retail price. Pays varies advance. Request book catalog through mail order department.

ⓐ RANDOM HOUSE CHILDREN'S BOOKS

1745 Broadway, New York NY 10019. (212)782-9000. **Website:** www.penguinrandomhouse.com. "Producing books for preschool children through young adult readers, in all formats from board to activity books to picture books and novels, Random House Children's Books brings together world-famous franchise characters, multimillion-copy series and top-flight, award-winning authors, and illustrators." Submit mss through a literary agent.

FICTION "Random House publishes a select list of first chapter books and novels, with an emphasis on fantasy and historical fiction." Chapter books, middle-grade readers, young adult.

HOW TO CONTACT *Does not accept unsolicited mss.*

ILLUSTRATION The Random House publishing divisions hire their freelancers directly. To contact the appropriate person, send a cover letter and résumé to the department head at the publisher as follows: "Department Head" (e.g., Art Director, Production Director), "Publisher/Imprint" (e.g., Knopf, Doubleday, etc.), 1745 Broadway New York, NY 10019. Works with 100-150 freelancers/year. Works on assignment only. Send query letter with résumé, tearsheets and printed samples; no originals. Samples are filed. Negotiates rights purchased. Assigns 5 freelance design jobs/year. Pays by the project.

TIPS "We look for original, unique stories. Do something that hasn't been done before."

RAZORBILL

Penguin Young Readers Group, 345 Hudson St., New York NY 10014. (212)414-3427. **E-mail:** asanchez@penguinrandomhouse.com; bschrank@penguinrandomhouse.com; jharriton@penguinrandomhouse.com. **Website:** www.razorbillbooks.com. **Contact:** Jessica Almon, executive editor; Casey McIntyre, associate publisher; Deborah Kaplan, vice president and executive art director, Marissa Grossman; assistant editor, Tiffany Liao; associate editor. "This division of Penguin Young Readers is looking for the best and the most original of commercial contemporary fiction titles for middle grade and YA readers. A select

quantity of nonfiction titles will also be considered."
Publishes 30 titles/year.

FICTION Middle Readers: adventure, contemporary, graphic novels, fantasy, humor, problem novels. Young adults/teens: adventure, contemporary, fantasy, graphic novels, humor, multicultural, suspense, paranormal, science fiction, dystopian, literary, romance. Average word length: middle readers—40,000; young adult—60,000.

NONFICTION Middle readers and young adults/teens: concept.

HOW TO CONTACT Submit cover letter with up to 30 sample pages. Submit cover letter with up to 30 sample pages. Responds in 1-3 months. Publishes book 1-2 after acceptance.

TERMS Offers advance against royalties.

TIPS "New writers will have the best chance of acceptance and publication with original, contemporary material that boasts a distinctive voice and well-articulated world. Check out website to get a better idea of what we're looking for."

❍ REBELIGHT PUBLISHING, INC.

23-845 Dakota St., Suite 314, Winnipeg Manitoba R2M 5M3, Canada. **Website:** www.rebelight.com. **Contact:** Editor. Rebelight Publishing is interested in "crack the spine, blow your mind" manuscripts for middle grade, young adult and new adult novels. *Only considers submissions from Canadian writers.* Publishes paperback and electronic originals. **Publishes 6-10 titles/year. 25-50% of books from first-time authors. 100% from unagented writers.**

FICTION All genres are considered, provided they are for a middle grade, young adult, or new adult audience. "Become familiar with our books. Study our website. Stick within the guidelines. Our tag line is 'crack the spine, blow your mind'—we are looking for well-written, powerful, fresh, fast-paced fiction. Keep us turning the pages. Give us something we just have to spread the word about."

HOW TO CONTACT Submit proposal package, including a synopsis and 3 sample chapters. Read guidelines carefully. Receive about 500 submissions/year. Responds in 3 months to queries and mss. Submissions accepted via email only. Publishes ms 12-18 months after acceptance.

TERMS Pays 12-22% royalties on retail price. Does not offer an advance. Catalog online or PDF available via e-mail request. Guidelines online.

TIPS "Review your manuscript for passive voice prior to submitting! (And that means get rid of it.)"

REDLEAF LANE

Redleaf Press, 10 Yorkton Ct., St. Paul MN 55117. (800)423-8309. **E-mail:** info@redleafpress.org. **Website:** www.redleafpress.org. **Contact:** David Heath, director. Redleaf Lane publishes engaging, high-quality picture books for children. "Our books are unique because they take place in group-care settings and reflect developmentally appropriate practices and research-based standards."

TERMS Guidelines online.

RIPPLE GROVE PRESS

P.O. Box 910, Shelburne VT 05482. **Website:** www.ripplegrovepress.com. **Contact:** Rob Broder. Ripple Grove Press is an independent, family-run children's book publisher. "We started Ripple Grove Press because we have a passion for well-told and beautifully illustrated stories for children. Our mission is to bring together great writers and talented illustrators to make the most wonderful books possible. We hope our books find their way to the cozy spot in your home." Publishes hardcover originals. **Publishes 3-6 titles/year.**

FICTION We are looking for something unique, that has not been done before; an interesting story that captures a moment with a timeless feel. We are looking for picture driven stories for children ages 2-6. Please do not send early readers, middle grade, or YA mss. No religious stories. Please do not submit your story with page breaks or illustration notes. Do not submit a story with doodles or personal photographs. Do not send your "idea" for a story, send your story in manuscript form.

HOW TO CONTACT Submit completed mss. Accepts submissions by mail and e-mail. E-mail preferred. Please submit a cover letter including a summary of your story, the age range of the story, a brief biography of yourself, and contact information. 3,000 submissions/year. Given the volume of submissions we receive we are no longer able to individually respond to each. Please allow 5 months for us to review your submission. If we are interested in your story, you can expect to hear from us within that time. If you do not hear from us after that time, we are not interested in publishing your story. It's not you, it's us! We receive thousands of submissions and only publish a few books each year. Don't give up! Average length of time between acceptance of a book-length ms and publication is 12-18 months.

TERMS Authors and illustrators receive royalties on net receipts. Pays negotiable advance. Catalog online. Guidelines online.

TIPS "Please read children's picture books. We create books that children and adults want to read over and over again. Our books showcase art as well as stories and tie them together in a unique and creative way."

❹ ROARING BROOK PRESS

Macmillan Children's Publishing Group, 175 Fifth Ave., New York NY 10010. (646)307-5151. **Website:** us.macmillan.com. Roaring Brook Press is an imprint of MacMillan, a group of companies that includes Henry Holt and Farrar, Straus & Giroux. *Roaring Brook is not accepting unsolicited mss.*

FICTION Picture books, young readers, middle readers, young adults: adventure, animal, contemporary, fantasy, history, humor, multicultural, nature/environment, poetry, religion, science fiction, sports, suspense/mystery.

NONFICTION Picture books, young readers, middle readers, young adults: adventure, animal, contemporary, fantasy, history, humor, multicultural, nature/environment, poetry, religion, science fiction, sports, suspense/mystery.

HOW TO CONTACT *Not accepting unsolicited mss or queries. Not accepting unsolicited mss or queries.*

ILLUSTRATION Works with 25 illustrators/year. Illustrations only: Query with samples. Do not send original art; copies only through the mail. Samples returned with SASE.

TERMS Pays authors royalty based on retail price.

TIPS "You should find a reputable agent and have him/her submit your work."

ROSEN PUBLISHING

29 E. 21st St., New York NY 10010. (800)237-9932. **Fax:** (888)436-4643. **Website:** www.rosenpublishing. com. Artists and writers should contact customer service team through online form for information about contributing to Rosen Publishing. Rosen Publishing is an independent educational publishing house, established to serve the needs of students in grades Pre-K-12 with high interest, curriculum-correlated mate-

rials. Rosen publishes more than 700 new books each year and has a backlist of more than 7,000.

SADDLEBACK EDUCATIONAL PUBLISHING

3120-A Pullman St., Costa Mesa CA 92626. (888)735-2225. **E-mail:** contact@sdlback.com. **Website:** www. sdlback.com. Saddleback is always looking for fresh, new talent. "Please note that we primarily publish books for kids ages 12-18."

FICTION "We look for diversity for our characters and content."

HOW TO CONTACT Mail typed submission along with a query letter describing the work simply and where it fits in with other titles.

SASQUATCH BOOKS

1904 Third Ave., Suite 710, Seattle WA 98101. (206)467-4300. **Fax:** (206)467-4301. **E-mail:** custserv@sasquatchbooks.com. **Website:** www.sasquatchbooks.com. "Sasquatch Books publishes books for and from the Pacific Northwest, Alaska, and California is the nation's premier regional press. Sasquatch Books' publishing program is a veritable celebration of regionally written words. Undeterred by political or geographical borders, Sasquatch defines its region as the magnificent area that stretches from the Brooks Range to the Gulf of California and from the Rocky Mountains to the Pacific Ocean. Our top-selling Best Places® travel guides serve the most popular destinations and locations of the West. We also publish widely in the areas of food and wine, gardening, nature, photography, children's books, and regional history, all facets of the literature of place. With more than 200 books brimming with insider information on the West, we offer an energetic eye on the lifestyle, landscape, and worldview of our region. Considers queries and proposals from authors and agents for new projects that fit into our West Coast regional publishing program. We can evaluate query letters, proposals, and complete mss." Publishes regional hardcover and trade paperback originals. **Publishes 30 titles/year. 20% of books from first-time authors. 75% from unagented writers.**

FICTION Young readers: adventure, animal, concept, contemporary, humor, nature/environment.

NONFICTION "We are seeking quality nonfiction works about the Pacific Northwest and West Coast regions (including Alaska to California). The literature of place includes how-to and where-to as well as history and narrative nonfiction." Picture books: activity books, animal, concept, nature/environment. "We publish a variety of nonfiction books, as well as children's books under our Little Bigfoot imprint."

HOW TO CONTACT Query first, then submit outline and sample chapters with SASE. Send submissions to The Editors. E-mailed submissions and queries are not recommended. Please include return postage if you want your materials back. Responds to queries in 3 months. Publishes book 6-9 months after acceptance.

ILLUSTRATION Accepts material from international illustrators. Works with 5 illustrators/year. Uses both color and b&w. Reviews ms/illustration packages. For ms/illustration packages: Query. Submit ms/illustration packages to The Editors. Reviews work for future assignments. If interested in illustrating future titles, query with samples. Samples returned with SASE. Samples filed.

TERMS Pays royalty on cover price. Pays wide range advance. Guidelines online.

TIPS "We sell books through a range of channels in addition to the book trade. Our primary audience consists of active, literate residents of the West Coast."

SCHOLASTIC, INC.

557 Broadway, New York NY 10012. (212)343-6100. **Website:** www.scholastic.com.

○ Scholastic Trade Books is an award-winning publisher of original children's books. Scholastic publishes approximately 600 new hardcover, paperback and novelty books each year. The list includes the phenomenally successful publishing properties Harry Potter, Goosebumps, Captain Underpants, Dog Man, and The Hunger Games; best-selling and award-winning authors and illustrators, including Suzanne Collins, Christopher Paul Curtis, Ann M. Martin, Dav Pilkey, J.K. Rowling, Pam Muñoz Ryan, Lauren Tarshis, Brian Selznick, David Shannon, Mark Teague, and Walter Wick, among others; as well as licensed properties such as Star Wars and Rainbow Magic.

❸ SCHOLASTIC LIBRARY PUBLISHING

90 Old Sherman Turnpike, Danbury CT 6816. (203)797-3500. **Fax:** (203)797-3197. **E-mail:** slpservice@scholastic.com. **Website:** www.scholastic.com/librarypublishing. **Contact:** Phil Friedman, vice president/publisher; Kate Nunn, editor-in-chief; Marie O'Neil, art director. "Scholastic Library is a leading publisher of reference, educational, and children's books. We provide parents, teachers, and librarians with the tools they need to enlighten children to the pleasure of learning and prepare them for the road ahead. Publishes informational (nonfiction) for K-12; picture books for young readers, grades 1-3." Publishes hardcover and trade paperback originals.

○ *Accepts agented submissions only.*

FICTION Publishes 1 picture book series, Rookie Readers, for grades 1-2. Does not accept unsolicited mss.

NONFICTION Photo-illustrated books for all levels: animal, arts/crafts, biography, careers, concept, geography, health, history, hobbies, how-to, multicultural, nature/environment, science, social issues, special needs, sports. Average word length: young readers—2,000; middle readers—8,000; young adult—15,000.

HOW TO CONTACT *Does not accept fiction proposals.* Query; submit outline/synopsis, resume, and/or list of publications, and writing sample. SASE required for response.

ILLUSTRATION Works with 15-20 illustrators/year. Uses color artwork and line drawings. Illustrations only: Query with samples or arrange personal portfolio review. Responds only if interested. Samples returned with SASE. Samples filed. Do not send originals. No phone or e-mail inquiries; contact only by mail.

TERMS Pays authors royalty based on net or work purchased outright. Pays illustrators at competitive rates.

❹ SCHOLASTIC PRESS

Imprint of Scholastic, Inc., 557 Broadway, New York NY 10012. (212)343-6100. **Fax:** (212)343-4713. **Website:** www.scholastic.com. Scholastic Press publishes fresh, literary picture book fiction and nonfiction; fresh, literary nonseries or nongenre-oriented middle grade and young adult fiction. Currently emphasizing subtly handled treatments of key relationships in children's lives; unusual approaches to commonly dry subjects, such as biography, math, history, or science. De-emphasizing fairy tales (or retellings), board books, genre, or series fiction (mystery, fantasy, etc.). Publishes hardcover originals. **Publishes 60 titles/year. 1% of books from first-time authors.**

FICTION Looking for strong picture books, young chapter books, appealing middle grade novels (ages 8-11) and interesting and well-written young adult novels. Wants fresh, exciting picture books and novels—inspiring, new talent.

HOW TO CONTACT *Agented submissions only.* Agented submissions and previously published authors only. 2,500 queries received/year. Responds in 3 months to queries; 6-8 months to mss. Publishes book 2 years after acceptance.

ILLUSTRATION Works with 30 illustrators/year. Uses both b&w and color artwork. Illustrations only: Query with samples; send tearsheets. Responds only if interested. Samples returned with SASE. Original artwork returned at job's completion.

TERMS Pays royalty on retail price. Pays variable advance.

TIPS "Read *currently* published children's books. Revise, rewrite, rework and find your own voice, style and subject. We are looking for authors with a strong and unique voice who can tell a great story and have the ability to evoke genuine emotion. Children's publishers are becoming more selective, looking for irresistible talent and fairly broad appeal, yet still very willing to take risks, just to keep the game interesting."

SEEDLING CONTINENTAL PRESS

520 E. Bainbridge St., Elizabethtown PA 17022. (800)233-0759. **Website:** www.continentalpress. com. "Continental publishes educational materials for grades K-12, specializing in reading, mathematics, and test preparation materials. We are not currently accepting submissions for Seedling leveled readers or instructional materials."

FICTION Young readers: adventure, animal, folktales, humor, multicultural, nature/environment. Does not accept texts longer than 12 pages or over 300 words. Average word length: young readers—100.

NONFICTION Young readers: animal, arts/crafts, biography, careers, concept, multicultural, nature/environment, science. Does not accept texts longer than 12 pages or over 300 words. Average word length: young readers—100.

HOW TO CONTACT Submit complete ms. Responds to mss in 6 months. Publishes book 1-2 years after acceptance.

ILLUSTRATION Works with 8-10 illustrators/year. Uses color artwork only. Reviews ms/illustration packages from artists. Submit ms with dummy. Illustrations only: Color copies or line art. Responds only if interested. Samples returned with SASE only; samples filed if interested.

PHOTOGRAPHY Buys photos from freelancers. Works on assignment only. Model/property releases required. Uses color prints and 35mm transparencies. Submit cover letter and color promo piece.

TERMS Work purchased outright from authors.

TIPS "See our website. Follow writers' guidelines carefully and test your story with children and educators."

SILVER DOLPHIN BOOKS

(858)457-2500. **E-mail:** infosilverdolphin@reader-link.com. **Website:** www.silverdolphinbooks.com. Silver Dolphin Books publishes activity, novelty, and educational nonfiction books for preschoolers to 12-year-olds. Highly interactive formats such as the Field Guides and Uncover series both educate and entertain older children. "We will consider submissions only from authors with previously published works."

HOW TO CONTACT Submit cover letter with full proposal and SASE.

ⓐ SIMON & SCHUSTER BOOKS FOR YOUNG READERS

Imprint of Simon & Schuster Children's Publishing, 1230 Avenue of the Americas, New York NY 10020. (212)698-7000. **Fax:** (212)698-2796. **Website:** www. simonsayskids.com. "Simon and Schuster Books For Young Readers is the Flagship imprint of the S&S Children's Division. We are committed to publishing a wide range of contemporary, commercial, award-winning fiction and nonfiction that spans every age of children's publishing. BFYR is constantly looking to the future, supporting our foundation authors and franchises, but always with an eye for breaking new ground with every publication. We publish high-quality fiction and nonfiction for a variety of age groups and a variety of markets. Above all, we strive to publish books that we are passionate about." *No unsolicited mss.* All unsolicited mss returned unopened. Publishes hardcover originals. **Publishes 75 titles/year.**

NONFICTION Picture books: concept. All levels: narrative, current events, biography, history. "We're looking for picture books or middle grade nonfiction that have a retail potential. No photo essays."

HOW TO CONTACT *Agented submissions only. Agented submissions only.* Publishes ms 2-4 years after acceptance.

ILLUSTRATION Works with 70 illustrators/year. Do not submit original artwork. Does not accept unsolicited or unagented illustration submissions.

TERMS Pays variable royalty on retail price. Guidelines online.

TIPS "We're looking for picture books centered on a strong, fully-developed protagonist who grows or changes during the course of the story; YA novels that are challenging and psychologically complex; also imaginative and humorous middle-grade fiction. And we want nonfiction that is as engaging as fiction. Our imprint's slogan is 'Reading You'll Remember.' We aim to publish books that are fresh, accessible and family-oriented; we want them to have an impact on the reader."

SKINNER HOUSE BOOKS

The Unitarian Universalist Association, 24 Farnsworth St., Boston MA 02210. (617)742-2100, ext. 603. **Fax:** (617)948-6466. **E-mail:** bookproposals@uua.org. **Website:** www.uua.org/publications/skinnerhouse. **Contact:** Betsy Martin. "We publish titles in Unitarian Universalist faith, liberal religion, history, biography, worship, and issues of social justice. Most of our children's titles are intended for religious education or worship use. They reflect Unitarian Universalist values. We also publish inspirational titles of poetic prose and meditations. Writers should know that Unitarian Universalism is a liberal religious denomination committed to progressive ideals. Currently emphasizing social justice concerns." Publishes trade paperback originals and reprints. **Publishes 10-20 titles/year. 30% of books from first-time authors. 100% from unagented writers.**

FICTION Only publishes fiction for children's titles for religious instruction.

NONFICTION All levels: activity books, multicultural, music/dance, nature/environment, religion.

HOW TO CONTACT Query. Query or submit proposal with cover letter, TOC, 2 sample chapters. Responds to queries in 1 month. Publishes book 1 year after acceptance.

ILLUSTRATION Works with 2 illustrators/year. Uses both color and b&w. Reviews ms/illustration packages from artists. Query. Contact: Suzanne

Morgan, design director. Responds only if interested. Samples returned with SASE.

PHOTOGRAPHY Buys stock images and assigns work. Contact: Suzanne Morgan, design director. Uses inspirational types of photo's. Model/property releases required; captions required. Uses color, b&w. Submit cover letter, resume.

TERMS Book catalog for 6×9 SAE with 3 first-class stamps. Guidelines online.

TIPS "From outside our denomination, we are interested in manuscripts that will be of help or interest to liberal churches, Sunday School classes, parents, ministers, and volunteers. Inspirational/spiritual and children's titles must reflect liberal Unitarian Universalist values."

❷ LIZZIE SKURNICK BOOKS

(718)797-0676. **Website:** lizzieskurnickbooks.com. Lizzie Skurnick Books, an imprint of Ig Publishing, is devoted to reissuing the very best in young adult literature, from the classics of the 1930s and 1940s to the social novels of the 1970s and 1980s. Ig does not accept unsolicited mss, either by e-mail or regular mail. If you have a ms that you would like Ig to take a look at, send a query through online contact form. If interested, they will contact. All unsolicited mss will be discarded.

SKY PONY PRESS

307 W. 36th St., 11th Floor, New York NY 10018. (212)643-6816. **Fax:** (212)643-6819. **Website:** skyponypress.com. Sky Pony Press is the children's book imprint of Skyhorse Publishing. "Following in the footsteps of our parent company, our goal is to provide books for readers with a wide variety of interests."

FICTION "We will consider picture books, early readers, midgrade novels, novelties, and informational books for all ages."

NONFICTION "Our parent company publishes many excellent books in the fields of ecology, independent living, farm living, wilderness living, recycling, and other green topics, and this will be a theme in our children's books. We are also searching for books that have strong educational themes and that help inform children of the world in which they live."

HOW TO CONTACT Submit ms or proposal. Submit proposal via e-mail.

TERMS Guidelines online.

SLEEPING BEAR PRESS

2395 South Huron Parkway #200, Ann Arbor MI 48104. (800)487-2323. **Fax:** (734)794-0004. **E-mail:** submissions@sleepingbearpress.com. **Website:** www.sleepingbearpress.com. **Contact:** Manuscript Submissions.

FICTION Picture books: adventure, animal, concept, folktales, history, multicultural, nature/environment, religion, sports. Young readers: adventure, animal, concept, folktales, history, humor, multicultural, nature/environment, religion, sports. Average word length: picture books—1,800.

HOW TO CONTACT Accepts unsolicited queries 3 times per year. See website for details. Query with sample of work (up to 15 pages) and SASE. Please address packages to Manuscript Submissions.

TERMS Book catalog available via e-mail.

SOURCEBOOKS FIRE

1935 Brookdale Rd., Suite 139, Naperville IL 60563. (630)961-3900. **Fax:** (630)961-2168. **E-mail:** submissions@sourcebooks.com. **Website:** www.sourcebooks.com. "We're actively acquiring knockout books for our YA imprint. We are particularly looking for strong writers who are excited about promoting and building their community of readers, and whose books have something fresh to offer the ever-growing young adult audience. We are not accepting any unsolicited or unagented manuscripts at this time. Unfortunately, our staff can no longer handle the large volume of manuscripts that we receive on a daily basis. We will continue to consider agented manuscripts." See website for details.

HOW TO CONTACT Query with the full ms attached in Word doc.

SPENCER HILL PRESS

27 W. 20th St., Suite 1102, New York NY 10011. **Website:** www.spencerhillpress.com. Spencer Hill Press is an independent publishing house specializing in sci-fi, urban fantasy, and paranormal romance for young adult readers. "Our books have that 'I couldn't put it down!' quality."

FICTION "We are interested in young adult, new adult, and middle grade sci-fi, psych-fi, paranormal, or urban fantasy, particularly those with a strong and interesting voice."

HOW TO CONTACT Check website for open submission periods.

TERMS Guidelines online.

SPINNER BOOKS

University Games, 2030 Harrison St., San Francisco CA 94110. (415)503-1600. **Fax:** (415)503-0085. **E-mail:** info@ugames.com. **Website:** www.ugames.com. "Spinners Books publishes books of puzzles, games and trivia."

NONFICTION Picture books: games and puzzles.

HOW TO CONTACT Query. Responds to queries in 3 months; mss in 2 months only if interested. Publishes book 6 months after acceptance.

ILLUSTRATION Only interested in agented material. Uses both color and b&w. Illustrations only: Query with samples. Responds in 3 months only if interested. Samples not returned.

SPLASHING COW BOOKS

P.O. Box 867, Manchester VT 05254. **Website:** www.splashingcowbooks.com. **Contact:** Gordon McClellan, publisher. Splashing Cow Books publishes books under three imprints: Splashing Cow (children), Blue Boot (women) and Yellow Dot (family). Publishes mass market paperback and hardcover books. We do not publish digital books. **Publishes 10 titles/year. 100% of books from first-time authors. 100% from unagented writers.**

FICTION Interested in a wide range of subject matter for children, women and families.

NONFICTION Open to any topic that would be of interest to children, women or families.

HOW TO CONTACT Please check our website for submission guidelines. We try to reply as soon as possible, but may take up to 3 months.

TERMS Pays royalties on retail price. Does not offer an advance. Catalog online. Guidelines online.

STANDARD PUBLISHING

Standex International Corp., 4050 Lee Vance View, Colorado Springs CO 80918. (800)323-7543. **Fax:** (800)323-0726. **Website:** www.standardpub.com. Publishes resources that meet church and family needs in the area of children's ministry.

TERMS Guidelines online.

STAR BRIGHT BOOKS

13 Landsdowne St., Cambridge MA 02139. (617)354-1300. **Fax:** (617)354-1399. **E-mail:** info@starbrightbooks.com. **Website:** www.starbrightbooks.com. Star Bright Books does accept unsolicited mss and art submissions. "We welcome submissions for picture books and longer works, both fiction and nonfiction."

Also beginner readers and chapter books. Query first. **Publishes 18 titles/year. 75% of books from first-time authors. 99% from unagented writers.**

NONFICTION Almost anything of interest to children. Very keen on Biographies and any thing of interest to children.

HOW TO CONTACT Responds in several months. Publishes ms 1-2 years after acceptance.

TERMS Pays advance. Catalog available.

STERLING PUBLISHING CO., INC.

1166 Avenue of the Americas, 17th Floor, New York NY 10036. (212)532-7160. **Website:** www.sterling-publishing.com. "Sterling publishes highly illustrated, accessible, hands-on, practical books for adults and children. Our mission is to publish high-quality books that educate, entertain, and enrich the lives of our readers." Publishes hardcover and paperback originals and reprints. **15% of books from first-time authors.**

FICTION Publishes fiction for children.

NONFICTION Proposals on subjects such as crafting, decorating, outdoor living, and photography should be sent directly to Lark Books at their Asheville, North Carolina offices. Complete guidelines can be found on the Lark site: www.larkbooks.com/submissions. Publishes nonfiction only.

HOW TO CONTACT Submit to attention of "Children's Book Editor." Submit outline, publishing history, 1 sample chapter (typed and double-spaced), SASE. "Explain your idea. Send sample illustrations where applicable. For children's books, please submit full mss. We do not accept electronic (e-mail) submissions. Be sure to include information about yourself with particular regard to your skills and qualifications in the subject area of your submission. It is helpful for us to know your publishing history—whether or not you've written other books and, if so, the name of the publisher and whether those books are currently in print."

ILLUSTRATION Works with 50 illustrators/year. Reviews ms/illustration packages from artists. Illustrations only: Send promo sheet. Contact: Karen Nelson, creative director. Responds in 6 weeks. Samples returned with SASE; samples filed.

PHOTOGRAPHY Buys stock and assigns work. Contact: Karen Nelson.

TERMS Pays royalty or work purchased outright. Offers advances (average amount: $2,000). Catalog online. Guidelines online.

TIPS "We are primarily a nonfiction activities-based publisher. We have a picture book list, but we do not publish chapter books or novels. Our list is not trend-driven. We focus on titles that will backlist well. "

STONE ARCH BOOKS

1710 Roe Crest Rd., North Mankato MN 56003. **Website:** www.stonearchbooks.com.

FICTION Imprint of Capstone Publishers.Young readers, middle readers, young adults: adventure, contemporary, fantasy, humor, light humor, mystery, science fiction, sports, suspense. Average word length: young readers—1,000-3,000; middle readers and early young adults—5,000-10,000.

HOW TO CONTACT Submit outline/synopsis and 3 sample chapters. Electronic submissions preferred. Full guidelines available on website.

ILLUSTRATION Works with 35 illustrators/year. Uses both color and b&w.

TERMS Work purchased outright from authors. Catalog online.

TIPS "A high-interest topic or activity is one that a young person would spend their free time on without adult direction or suggestion."

STRAWBERRIES PRESS

750 Pinehurst Dr., Rio Vista CA 94571. (707)398-6430. **E-mail:** books@strawberriespress.com. **Website:** www.strawberriespress.com. **Contact:** Susan Zhang, Executive Editor. Strawberries books are beautifully illustrated and designed to be high-quality publications that children will love and treasure. For example, our interactive picture book for train enthusiasts entitled Choo-Choo Charlie Presents Steam Locomotives provides a fun story by Charlie the Locomotive while teaching kids about steam engines and how they work, the definition of a train, the history of steam locomotives, and how to determine a locomotive's wheel configuration number. Children even get to watch a singing cartoon video of Choo-Choo Charlie the Engineer and how he uses candy to make his train run. A fun test is included at the end of each book. Just send Strawberries the completed test and your child will receive a beautifully printed Reading Certificate that he or she can proudly frame and display for all his or her friends to see. Reading traditional picture books, watching videos, visiting websites that contain asso-

ciated subjects, taking fun tests, and earning Reading Certificates represent the interactive parts of the Strawberries reading and learning concept. Publishes interactive picture books in the 8-1/2" x 11" softcover format. **Publishes 6 titles/year. 50% of books from first-time authors. 100% from unagented writers.**

NONFICTION Interested in topics that explore exciting subjects that stimulate young minds in both the fiction and nonfiction genres. For examples of subject matter and format requirements, see online catalog of picture book titles. "We only publish wholesome learning resources and educationally constructive subject matter that retains, promotes, and enhances the innocence of children. Political, immoral, antisocial, propagandist, and other age-inappropriate themes are strictly prohibited at Strawberries Press. We do not use our publications as social engineering and brainwashing tools."

HOW TO CONTACT Submit completed ms. Receives 12-20 queries/year; 12 mss/year. Responds in 1 month. Publishes mss in 3-4 months upon acceptance.

TERMS Pays for outright purchase between $250-500. Catalog available online. Guidelines available by e-mail.

TIPS "Although there are no restrictions on the number of sentences on a single page, all picture books are limited to 40 pages. For text, illustrating, and formatting examples, view our sample online picture book."

SUNSTONE PRESS

Box 2321, Santa Fe NM 87504. (800)243-5644. **Website:** www.sunstonepress.com. **Contact:** Submissions Editor. Sunstone's original focus was on nonfiction subjects that preserved and highlighted the richness of the American Southwest but it has expanded its view over the years to include mainstream themes and categories—both nonfiction and fiction—that have a more general appeal.

HOW TO CONTACT Query with 1 sample chapter. Query with 1 sample chapter.

TERMS Guidelines online.

❶ KATHERINE TEGEN BOOKS

HarperCollins, 10 E. 53rd St., New York NY 10022. **Website:** www.harpercollins.com. Katherine Tegen Books publishes high-quality, commercial literature for children of all ages, including teens. Talented authors and illustrators who offer powerful narratives that are thought-provoking, well-written, and enter-

taining are the core of the Katherine Tegen Books imprint. *Katherine Tegen Books accepts agented work only.*

THUNDERSTONE BOOKS

6575 Horse Dr., Las Vegas NV 89131. **E-mail:** info@thunderstonebooks.com. **Website:** www.thunderstonebooks.com. **Contact:** Rachel Noorda, editorial director. "At ThunderStone Books, we aim to publish children's books that have an educational aspect. We are not looking for curriculum for learning certain subjects, but rather stories that encourage learning for children, whether that be learning about a new language/culture or learning more about science and math in a fun, fictional format. We want to help children to gain a love for other languages and subjects so that they are curious about the world around them. We are currently accepting fiction and nonfiction submissions. Picture books without accompanying illustration will not be accepted." Publishes hardcover, trade paperback, mass market paperback, and electronic originals. **Publishes 2-5 titles/year. 100% of books from first-time authors. 100% from unagented writers.**

FICTION Interested in multicultural stories with an emphasis on authentic culture and language (these may include mythology).

NONFICTION Looking for engaging educational materials, not a set curriculum, but books that teach as well as have some fun. Open to a variety of educational subjects, but specialty and main interest lies in language exposure/learning, science, math, and history.

HOW TO CONTACT "If you think your book is right for us, send a query letter with a word attachment of the first 50 pages to info@thunderstonebooks.com. If it is a picture book or chapter book for young readers that is shorter than 50 pages send the entire manuscript." Receives 30 queries and mss/year. Responds in 3 months. Publishes ms 6 months after acceptance.

TERMS Pays 5-15% royalties on retail price. Pays $300-1,000 advance. Catalog available for SASE. Guidelines available.

TILBURY HOUSE PUBLISHERS

WordSplice Studio, Inc., 12 Starr St., Thomaston ME 04861. (207)582-1899. **Fax:** (207)582-8772. **E-mail:** info@tilburyhouse.com. **Website:** www.tilburyhouse.com. **Publishes 24 titles/year.**

FICTION Picture books: multicultural, nature/environment. Special needs include books that teach children about and honoring diversity.

NONFICTION Regional history/maritime/nature, and children's picture books that deal with issues, such as bullying, multiculturalism, etc. science/nature.

HOW TO CONTACT Send art/photography samples and/or complete ms to info@tilburyhouse.com. Submit complete ms for picture books or outline/synopsis for longer works. Now uses online submission form. Responds to mss in 3-6 months. Publishes ms 1 year after acceptance.

ILLUSTRATION Works with 2-3 illustrators/year. Illustrations only: Query with samples. Responds in 1 month. Samples returned with SASE. Original artwork returned at job's completion.

PHOTOGRAPHY Buys photos from freelancers. Works on assignment only.

TERMS Pays royalty based on wholesale price. Guidelines and catalog online.

TIPS "We are always interested in stories that will encourage children to understand the natural world and the environment, as well as stories with social justice themes. We really like stories that engage children to become problem solvers as well as those that promote respect, tolerance and compassion."

TOR BOOKS

Tom Doherty Associates, 175 Fifth Ave., New York NY 10010. **Website:** www.tor-forge.com. Tor Books is the "world's largest publisher of science fiction and fantasy, with strong category publishing in historical fiction, mystery, western/Americana, thriller, YA." **Publishes 10-20 titles/year.**

HOW TO CONTACT Submit first 3 chapters, 3-10 page synopsis, dated cover letter, SASE.

TERMS Pays author royalty. Pays illustrators by the project. Book catalog available. Guidelines online.

TRIANGLE SQUARE

Seven Stories Press, 140 Watts St., New York NY 10013. (212)226-8760. **Fax:** (212)226-1411. **E-mail:** info@sevenstories.com. **Website:** https://www.sevenstories.com/imprints/triangle-square. Triangle Square is a children's and young adult imprint of Seven Story Press.

HOW TO CONTACT Send a cover letter with 2 sample chapters and SASE. Send c/o Acquisitions.

TU BOOKS

Lee & Low Books, 95 Madison Ave., Suite #1205, New York NY 10016. **Website:** www.leeandlow.com/imprints/3. **Contact:** Stacy Whitman, publisher. The Tu imprint spans many genres: science fiction, fantasy, mystery, contemporary, and more. We don't believe in labels or limits, just great stories. Join us at the crossroads where fantasy and real life collide. You'll be glad you did. Young adult and middle grade novels and graphic novels: science fiction, fantasy, contemporary realism, mystery, historical fiction, and more, with particular interest in books with strong literary hooks. Also seeking middle grade and young adult nonfiction. **Publishes 6-8 titles/year. 40%% of books from first-time authors.**

◯ For new writers of color, please be aware of the New Visions Award writing contest, which runs every year from June-October. Previously unpublished writers of color and Native American writers may submit their middle grade and young adult novels. See submission guidelines for the contest at https://www.leeandlow.com/writers-illustrators/new-visions-award.

FICTION At TU BOOKS, an imprint of LEE & LOW BOOKS, our focus is on well-told, exciting, adventurous fantasy, science fiction, and mystery novels and graphic novels starring people of color. We also selectively publish realism and nonfiction that explores the contemporary and historical experiences of people of color. We look for fantasy set in worlds inspired by non-Western folklore or culture, contemporary mysteries and fantasy set all over the world starring POC, and science fiction that centers the possibilities for people of color in the future. We welcome intersectional narratives that feature LGBTQIA and disabled POC as heroes in their own stories. We are looking specifically for stories for both middle grade (ages 8-12) and young adult (ages 12-18) readers. Occasionally a manuscript might fall between those two categories; if your manuscript does, let us know. (We are not looking for picture books, chapter books, or short stories at this time. Please do not send submissions in these categories.) Manuscript Submissions: Please include a synopsis and first three chapters o f the novel. Do not send the complete manuscript. Manuscripts should be doubled-spaced. Manuscripts should be accompanied by a cover letter that includes a brief biography of the author, including publishing history. The letter should also state if the manuscript is a simultaneous or an exclusive submission. We're looking for middle grade (ages 8-12) and young adult (ages 12 and up) books. We are not looking for chapter books (ages 6 to 9) at this time. Be sure to include full contact information on the first page of the manuscript. Page numbers and your last name/title of the book should appear on subsequent pages. Unsolicited manuscripts should be submitted online at https://tubooks.submittable.com/submit. At Tu Books, an imprint of Lee & Low Books, our focus is on well-told, exciting, adventurous fantasy, science fiction, and mystery novels and graphic novels starring people of color. We also selectively publish realism that explores the contemporary and historical experiences of people of color. We look for fantasy set in worlds inspired by non-Western folklore or culture, contemporary mysteries and fantasy set all over the world starring people of color, and science fiction that centers the possibilities for people of color in the future. We welcome intersectional narratives that feature LGBTQIA and disabled POC as heroes in their own stories. We are looking specifically for stories for both middle grade (ages 8-12) and young adult (ages 12-18) readers. Occasionally a manuscript might fall between those two categories; if your manuscript does, let us know. We are not looking for picture books, chapter books, or short stories at this time. Please do not send submissions in these categories. Not seeking picture books or chapter books.

NONFICTION We selectively publish narrative nonfiction that explores the contemporary and historical experiences of people of color or Native people. We welcome intersectional narratives that feature LGBTQIA and disabled people as heroes in their own stories.

HOW TO CONTACT Submit via Submittable page. https://tubooks.submittable.com/submit Please include a synopsis and first three chapters of the novel. Do not send the complete manuscript. Mss should be doubled-spaced. Mss should be accompanied by a cover letter that includes a brief biography of the author, including publishing history. The letter should also state if the ms is a simultaneous or an exclusive submission. "We're looking for middle grade (ages 8-12) and young adult (ages 12 and up) books. We are not looking for chapter books (ages 6 to 9) at this time. Be sure to include full contact information on

the first page of the ms. Page numbers and your last name/title of the book should appear on subsequent pages." Unsolicited mss should be submitted online. Responds only if interested.

ILLUSTRATION Tu Books, an imprint of Lee & Low Books, is not interested in illustrations for picture books, but will consider artwork for graphic novels and for book covers and spot illustrations for novels aimed at older readers (ages 8-18). Artists are welcome to submit a sample with the address of their website portfolio following the guidelines below. Our books feature children and teens of color and include a variety of fantasy, science fiction, and mystery. We are particularly interested in hearing from illustrators whose cultural, ethnic, or racial backgrounds and experiences support their knowledge of diverse cultures. We are open to seeing work from professional illustrators and artists at all levels of experience. Illustrators who have worked in other fields and are interested in creating cover and spot art for novels are also welcome.

TERMS Advance against royalties. Pays advance. Catalog available online. Please see our full submissions guidelines online.

TUMBLEHOME LEARNING

P.O. Box 71386, Boston MA 02117. **E-mail:** info@tumblehomelearning.com. **Website:** www.tumblehomelearning.com. **Contact:** Pendred Noyce, editor. Tumblehome Learning helps kids imagine themselves as young scientists or engineeers and encourages them to experience science through adventure and discovery. "We do this with exciting mystery and adventure tales as well as experiments carefully designed to engage students from ages 8 and up." Publishes hardcover, trade paperback, and electronic originals. **Publishes 8-10 titles/year. 50% of books from first-time authors. 100% from unagented writers.**

FICTION "All our fiction has science at its heart. This can include using science to solve a mystery (see *The Walking Fish* by Rachelle Burk or *Something Stinks!* by Gail Hedrick), realistic science fiction, books in our Galactic Academy of Science series, science-based adventure tales, and the occasional picture book with a science theme, such as appreciation of the stars and constellations in *Elizabeth's Constellation Quilt* by Olivia Fu. A graphic novel about science would also be welcome."

NONFICTION Rarely publishes nonfiction. Book would need to be sold to trade, not just the school market.

HOW TO CONTACT Submit completed ms electronically. Receives 20 queries and 20 mss/year. Responds in 1 month to queries and proposals, and 2 months to mss. Publishes ms 8 months after acceptance.

TERMS Pays authors 8-12% royalties on retail price. Pays $500 advance. Catalog available online. Guideliens available on request for SASE.

TIPS "Please don't submit to us if your book is not about science. We don't accept generic books about animals or books with glaring scientific errors in the first chapter. That said, the book should be fun to read and the science content can be subtle. We work closely with authors, including first-time authors, to edit and improve their books. As a small publisher, the greatest benefit we can offer is this friendly and respectful partnership with authors."

ⓐ TYNDALE HOUSE PUBLISHERS, INC.

351 Executive Dr., Carol Stream IL 60188. (800)323-9400. **Fax:** (800)684-0247. **Website:** www.tyndale.com. "Tyndale House publishes practical, user-friendly Christian books for the home and family." Publishes hardcover and trade paperback originals and mass paperback reprints. **Publishes 15 titles/year.**

FICTION "Christian truths must be woven into the story organically. No short story collections. Youth books: character building stories with Christian perspective. Especially interested in ages 10-14. We primarily publish Christian historical romances, with occasional contemporary, suspense, or standalones."

HOW TO CONTACT *Agented submissions only. No unsolicited mss. Agented submissions only. No unsolicited mss.*

ILLUSTRATION Uses full-color for book covers, b&w or color spot illustrations for some nonfiction. Illustrations only: Query with photocopies (color or b&w) of samples, résumé.

PHOTOGRAPHY Buys photos from freelancers. Works on assignment only.

TERMS Pays negotiable royalty. Pays negotiable advance. Guidelines online.

TIPS "All accepted manuscripts will appeal to Evangelical Christian children and parents."

ⓐ VIKING CHILDREN'S BOOKS

375 Hudson St., New York NY 10014. **Website:** www.penguin.com. "Viking Children's Books is known for humorous, quirky picture books, in addition to more traditional fiction. We publish the highest quality fiction, nonfiction, and picture books for pre-schoolers through young adults." *Does not accept unsolicited submissions.* Publishes hardcover originals. **Publishes 70 titles/year.**

FICTION All levels: adventure, animal, contemporary, fantasy, history, humor, multicultural, nature/environment, poetry, problem novels, romance, science fiction, sports, suspense/mystery.

NONFICTION All levels: biography, concept, history, multicultural, music/dance, nature/environment, science, and sports.

HOW TO CONTACT *Accepts agented mss only. Agented submissions only.* Responds in 6 months. Publishes book 1-2 years after acceptance.

ILLUSTRATION Works with 30 illustrators/year. Responds to artist's queries/submissions only if interested. Samples returned with SASE only or samples filed. Originals returned at job's completion.

TERMS Pays 2-10% royalty on retail price or flat fee. Pays negotiable advance.

TIPS "No 'cartoony' or mass-market submissions for picture books."

WESTMINSTER JOHN KNOX PRESS

Flyaway Books, Division of Presbyterian Publishing Corp., 100 Witherspoon St., Louisville KY 40202. **Fax:** (502)569-5113. **E-mail:** submissions@wjkbooks.com. **Website:** www.wjkbooks.com. Flyaway Books is a new imprint for children's picture books that intentionally publishes diverse content, authors, and illustrators. See our website www.flyawaybooks.com for more details and submission instructions. "All WJK books have a religious/spiritual angle, but are written for various markets-scholarly, professional, and the general reader. Flyaway Books is a new children's picture book imprint that is intentionally diverse in content and authorship.

Email submissions only. No submissions by mail. No phone queries. We do not publish fiction, poetry, or dissertations. We do not return or respond to submissions received by mail and do not respond to unsolicited phone messages. Westminster John Knox is affiliated with the Presbyterian Church (U.S.A.). " Publishes hardcover and paperback originals. **Publishes 60 titles/year. 10% of books from first-time authors. 75% from unagented writers.**

◯ Looking for fresh and challenging voices writing about social justice issues (race, LGBTQI, immigration, women's rights, economic justice, etc.) from a religious, spiritual, or humanitarian perspective. Looking for biblical studies and theology texts for graduate and seminary students and core textbooks in Bible for undergraduates. See more at www.wjkbooks.com. Flyaway Books is looking for picture books for a trade, school, and progressive church audience. See more at www.flyawaybooks.com.

NONFICTION No dissertations.

HOW TO CONTACT submissions@flyawaybooks. com Submit proposal package according to the WJK book proposal guidelines found online. 1,000 submissions received/year. Responds in 2-3 months.

ILLUSTRATION Contact submissions@flyawaybooks.com.

TERMS net royalty with advance Pays royalty on net price. Pays advance. Catalog online. Proposal guidelines online.

WHITE MANE KIDS

73 W. Burd St., Shippensburg PA 17257. (717)532-2237. **Fax:** (717)532-6110. **E-mail:** marketing@whitemane. com. **Website:** www.whitemane.com. **Contact:** Harold Collier, acquisitions editor.

FICTION Middle readers, young adults: history (primarily American Civil War). Average word length: middle readers—30,000. Does not publish picture books.

NONFICTION Middle readers, young adults: history. Average word length: middle readers—30,000. Does not publish picture books.

HOW TO CONTACT Query. Submit outline/synopsis and 2-3 sample chapters. Book proposal form on website. Responds to queries in 1 month, mss in 6-9 months. Publishes book 18 months after acceptance.

ILLUSTRATION Works with 4 illustrators/year. Illustrations used for cover art only. Responds only if interested. Samples returned with SASE.

PHOTOGRAPHY Buys stock and assigns work. Submit cover letter and portfolio.

TERMS Pays authors royalty of 7-10%. Pays illustrators and photographers by the project. Book catalog and writer's guidelines available for SASE.

TIPS "Make your work historically accurate. We are interested in historically accurate fiction for middle and young adult readers. We do *not* publish picture books. Our primary focus is the American Civil War and some America Revolution topics."

ALBERT WHITMAN & COMPANY

250 S. Northwest Hwy., Suite 320, Park Ridge IL 60068. (800)255-7675. **Fax:** (847)581-0039. **E-mail:** submissions@albertwhitman.com. **Website:** www.albertwhitman.com. Albert Whitman & Company publishes books for the trade, library, and school library market. Interested in reviewing the following types of projects: Picture book manuscripts for ages 2-8; novels and chapter books for ages 8-12; young adult novels; nonfiction for ages 3-12 and YA; art samples showing pictures of children. Best known for the classic series The Boxcar Children® Mysteries. "We are no longer reading unsolicited queries and manuscripts sent through the US mail. We now require these submissions to be sent by e-mail. You must visit our website for our guidelines, which include instructions for formatting your e-mail. E-mails that do not follow this format may not be read. We read every submission within 4 months of receipt, but we can no longer respond to every one. If you do not receive a response from us after four months, we have declined to publish your submission." Publishes in original hardcover, paperback, boardbooks. **Publishes 60 titles/year. 10% of books from first-time authors. 50% from unagented writers.**

FICTION Picture books (up to 1,000 words); middle grade (up to 35,000 words); young adult (up to 70,000 words).

NONFICTION Picture books up to 1,000 words.

HOW TO CONTACT For picture books, submit cover letter and brief description. For middle grade and young adult, send query, synopsis, and first 3 chapters. Submit cover letter, brief description.

TERMS Guidelines online.

ⓐ PAULA WISEMAN BOOKS

1230 Sixth Ave., New York NY 10020. (212)698-7000. **Fax:** (212)698-2796. **Website:** kids.simonandschuster. com. Paula Wiseman Books is an imprint of Simon & Schuster Children's Publishing that launched in 2003.

It has since gone on to publish over 70 award-winning and bestselling books, including picture books, novelty books, and novels. The imprint focuses on stories and art that are childlike, timeless, innovative, and centered in emotion. "We strive to publish books that entertain while expanding the experience of the children who read them, as well as stories that will endure, including those based in other cultures. We are committed to publishing new talent in both picture books and novels. We are actively seeking submissions from new and published authors and artists through agents and from SCBWI conferences." **Publishes 30 titles/year. 15% of books from first-time authors.**

FICTION Considers all categories. Average word length: picture books—500; others standard length.

NONFICTION Picture books: animal, biography, concept, history, nature/environment. Young readers: animal, biography, history, multicultural, nature/environment, sports. Average word length: picture books—500; others standard length.

HOW TO CONTACT Does not accept unsolicited or unagented mss.

ILLUSTRATION Works with 15 illustrators/year. Does not accept unsolicited or unagented illustrations or submissions.

Ⓐ WORDSONG

815 Church St., Honesdale PA 18431. **Fax:** (570)253-0179. **Website:** www.wordsongpoetry.com. "We publish fresh voices in contemporary poetry."

HOW TO CONTACT Responds to mss in 3 months.

ILLUSTRATION Works with 7 illustrators/year. Reviews ms/illustration packages from artists. Submit complete ms with 1 or 2 pieces of art. Illustrations only: Query with samples best suited to the art (postcard, 8½ × 11, etc.). Label package "Art Sample Submission." Responds only if interested. Samples returned with SASE.

PHOTOGRAPHY Assigns work.

TERMS Pays authors royalty or work purchased outright.

TIPS "Collections of original poetry, not anthologies, are our biggest need at this time. Keep in mind that the strongest collections demonstrate a facility with multiple poetic forms and offer fresh images and insights. Check to see what's already on the market and on our website before submitting."

WORLD BOOK, INC.

180 N. LaSalle St., Suite 900, Chicago IL 60601. (312)729-5800. **Fax:** (312)729-5600. **E-mail:** service@worldbook.com. **Website:** www.worldbook.com. World Book, Inc. (publisher of The World Book Encyclopedia), publishes reference sources and nonfiction series for children and young adults in the areas of science, mathematics, English-language skills, basic academic and social skills, social studies, history, and health and fitness. "We publish print and non-print material appropriate for children ages 3-14. WB does not publish fiction, poetry, or wordless picture books."

NONFICTION Young readers: animal, arts/crafts, careers, concept, geography, health, reference. Middle readers: animal, arts/crafts, careers, geography, health, history, hobbies, how-to, nature/environment, reference, science. Young adult: arts/crafts, careers, geography, health, history, hobbies, how-to, nature/environment, reference, science.

HOW TO CONTACT Query. Responds to queries in 2 months. Publishes book 18 months after acceptance.

ILLUSTRATION Works with 10-30 illustrators/year. Illustrations only: Query with samples. Responds only if interested. Samples returned with SASE; samples filed "if extra copies and if interested."

PHOTOGRAPHY Buys stock and assigns work. Needs broad spectrum; editorial concept, specific natural, physical and social science spectrum. Model/property releases required; captions required. Submit cover letter, résumé, promo piece (color and b&w).

TERMS Payment negotiated on project-by-project basis.

WORLD WEAVER PRESS

E-mail: submissions@worldweaverpress.com. **Website:** www.worldweaverpress.com. **Contact:** WWP Editors. World Weaver Press publishes digital and print editions of speculative fiction at various lengths for adult, young adult, and new adult audiences. "We believe in great storytelling." **Publishes 6-9 titles/year. 95% from unagented writers.**

FICTION "We believe that publishing speculative fiction isn't just printing words on the page — it's the act of weaving brand new worlds. Seeking speculative fiction in many varieties: protagonists who have strength, not fainting spells; intriguing worlds with well-developed settings; characters that are to die for (we'd rather find ourselves in love than just in lust)." Full list of interests on website. Does not want giant bugs, ghosts, post-apocalyptic and/or dystopia, angels, zombies, magical realism, surrealism, middle grade (MG) or younger.

HOW TO CONTACT Not currently open for queries. Full guidelines will be updated approximately one month before queries re-open. Frequently open for submissions for themed short story anthologies. Check website for details. Responds to query letters within 3 weeks. Responses to mss requests take longer. Publishes ms 6-24 months after acceptance.

TERMS Average royalty rate of 39% net on all editions. No advance. Catalog online. Guidelines on website.

TIPS "Use your letter to pitch us the story, not talk about its themes or inception."

WORTHYKIDS/IDEALS

Worthy Publishing Group, 6100 Tower Circle, Suite 210, Franklin TN 37067. (615)932-7600. **E-mail:** idealsinfo@worthypublishing.com. **Website:** www.worthypublishing.com. "WorthyKids/Ideals is a division of Worthy Publishing Group and publishes 20-30 new children's titles a year, primarily for 2-8 year-olds. Our backlist includes more than 400 titles, including The Berenstain Bears, VeggieTales, and Frosty the Snowman. We publish picture books, activity books, board books, and novelty/sound books covering a wide array of topics, such as Bible stories, holidays, early learning, history, family relationships, and values. Our bestselling titles include *The Story of Christmas, The Story of Easter, The Sparkle Box, Seaman's Journal, How Do I Love You?, God Made You Special, The Berenstain Bears' Please and Thank You Book,* and *My Daddy and I.* Through our dedication to publishing high-quality and engaging books, we never forget our obligation to our littlest readers to help create those special moments with books."

FICTION WorthyKids/Ideals publishes fiction and nonfiction picture books for children ages 2 to 8. Subjects include holiday, faith/inspirational, family values, and patriotic themes; relationships and values; and general fiction. Picture book mss should be no longer than 800 words. Board book mss should be no longer than 250 words.

HOW TO CONTACT Editors will review complete mss only; please do not send query letters or proposals. Previous publications, relevant qualifications or background, and a brief synopsis of your manuscript may be included in a cover letter. Please send copies only—

we cannot be responsible for an original ms. Include your name, address, and phone number or e-mail address on every page. Do not include original art or photographs. We do not accept digital submissions via e-mail or other electronic means. Send complete mss to: WorthyKids/Ideals, Attn: SUBMISSIONS, 6100 Tower Circle, Suite 210, Franklin TN 37067. Due to the high volume of submissions, we are only able to respond to unsolicited manuscripts of interest to our publishing program. We cannot discuss submissions by telephone or in person and we cannot provide detailed editorial feedback.

WORTHY KIDS/IDEALS BOOKS

6100 Tower Circle, Suite 210, Franklin TN 37067. **Website:** www.idealsbooks.com.

FICTION Picture books: animal, concept, history, religion. Board books: animal, history, nature/environment, religion. Worthy Kids/Ideals publishes for ages birth to 8, no longer than 800 words.

NONFICTION Worthy Kids/Ideals publishes for ages birth to 8, no longer than 800 words.

HOW TO CONTACT Submit complete ms. Submit complete ms.

ZEST BOOKS

2443 Fillmore St., Suite 340, San Francisco CA 94115. (415)777-8654. **Fax:** (415)777-8653. **Website:** zestbooks.net. **Contact:** Dan Harmon, publishing director. Zest Books is a leader in young adult nonfiction, publishing books on entertainment, history, science, health, fashion, and lifestyle advice since 2006. Zest Books is distributed by Houghton Mifflin Harcourt.

HOW TO CONTACT Submit proposal.

ILLUSTRATION "If you are interested in becoming part of our team of illustrators, please send examples of printed work to adam@zestbooks.net."

TERMS Guidelines online.

TIPS "If you're interested in becoming a member of our author pool, send a cover letter stating why you are interested in young adult nonfiction, plus your specific areas of interest and specialties, your resume, 3-5 writing samples."

ZUMAYA PUBLICATIONS, LLC

3209 S. Interstate 35, Austin TX 78741. (512)330-4055. **Fax:** (512)276-6745. **E-mail:** business@zumayapublishing.com. **Website:** www.zumayapublications.com. **Contact:** Elizabeth K. Burton. Zumaya Publications is a digitally-based micro-press publishing mainly in on-demand trade paperback and e-book formats in an effort to reduce environmental impact. "We currently offer approximately 190 fiction titles in the mystery, SF/F, historical, romance, LGBTQ, horror, and occult genres in adult, young adult, and middle reader categories. In 2016, we plan to officially launch our graphic and illustrated novel imprint, Zumaya Fabled Ink. We publish approximately 10-15 new titles annually, at least five of which are from new authors. We do not publish erotica or graphic erotic romance at this time. We accept only electronic queries; all others will be discarded unread. A working knowledge of computers and relevant software is a necessity, as our production process is completely digital." Publishes trade paperback and electronic originals. **Publishes 10-15 titles/year. 5% of books from first-time authors. 98% from unagented writers.**

FICTION "We are open to all genres, particularly GLBT and YA/middle grade, historical and western, New Age/inspirational (no overtly Christian materials, please), non-category romance, thrillers. We encourage people to review what we've already published so as to avoid sending us more of the same, at least, insofar as the plot is concerned. While we're always looking for good mysteries, especially cozies, mysteries with historical settings, and police procedurals, we want original concepts rather than slightly altered versions of what we've already published. We do not publish erotica or graphically erotic romance at this time." Does not want erotica, graphically erotic romance, experimental, literary (unless it fits into one of our established imprints).

NONFICTION "The easiest way to figure out what we're looking for is to look at what we've already done. Our main nonfiction interests are in collections of true ghost stories, ones that have been investigated or thoroughly documented, memoirs that address specific regions and eras from a 'normal person' viewpoint and books on the craft of writing. That doesn't mean we won't consider something else."

HOW TO CONTACT A copy of our rules of submission is posted on our website and can be downloaded. They are rules rather than guidelines and should be read carefully before submitting. It will save everyone time and frustration. Electronic query only. 1,000 queries; 50 mss requested/year. Responds in 3 months to queries and proposals; 6 months to mss. Publishes book 2 years after acceptance.

TERMS Pay 20% of net on paperbacks, net defined as cover price less printing and other associated costs; 50% of net on all e-books. Does not pay advance. Guidelines online. We do *not* accept hard-copy queries or submissions.

TIPS "We're catering to readers who may have loved last year's best seller but not enough to want to read 10 more just like it. Have something different. If it does not fit standard pigeonholes, that's a plus. On the other hand, it has to have an audience. And if you're not prepared to work with us on promotion and marketing, particularly via social media, it would be better to look elsewhere."

CANADIAN & INTERNATIONAL BOOK PUBLISHERS

//

While the United States is considered the largest market in children's publishing, the children's publishing world is by no means strictly dominated by the United States. After all, the most prestigious children's book extravaganza in the world occurs each year in Bologna, Italy, at the Bologna Children's Book Fair and some of the world's most beloved characters were born in the United Kingdom (i.e., Winnie-the-Pooh and Mr. Potter).

In this section you'll find book publishers from English-speaking countries around the world from Canada, Australia, New Zealand, and the United Kingdom. The listings in this section look just like the United States Book Publishers section; and the publishers listed are dedicated to the same goal—publishing great books for children.

Like always, be sure to study each listing and research each publisher carefully before submitting material. Determine whether a publisher is open to United States or international submissions, as many publishers accept submissions only from residents of their own country. Some publishers accept illustration samples from foreign artists, but do not accept manuscripts from foreign writers. Illustrators do have a slight edge in this category as many illustrators generate commissions from all around the globe. Visit publishers' websites to be certain they publish the sort of work you do. Visit online bookstores to see if publishers' books are available there. Write or e-mail to request catalogs and submission guidelines.

When mailing requests or submissions out of the United States, remember that United States postal stamps are useless on your SASE. Always include International Reply Coupons (IRCs) with your SAE. Each IRC is good for postage for one letter. So if you want the publisher to return your manuscript or send a catalog, be sure to enclose enough IRCs to pay the postage. For more help visit the United State Postal Service website at www.usps.com/global. Visit www.timeanddate.com/worldclock and American Computer Resources, Inc.'s International Calling Code Directory at www.the-acr.com/codes/cntrycd.htm before calling or faxing internationally to make sure you're calling at a reasonable time and using the correct numbers.

As in the rest of *Children's Writer's & Illustrator's Market*, the maple leaf ✪ symbol identifies Canadian markets. Look for International ◉ symbol throughout *Children's Writer's & Illustrator's Market* as well. Several of the Society of Children's Book Writers and Illustrator's (SCBWI) international conferences are listed in the Conferences & Workshops section along with other events in locations around the globe. Look for more information about SCBWI's international chapters on the organization's website, www.scbwi.org.

ALLEN & UNWIN

406 Albert St., East Melbourne VIC 3002, Australia. (61)(3)9665-5000. **E-mail:** fridaypitch@allenandunwin.com. **Website:** www.allenandunwin.com. Allen & Unwin publish over 80 new books for children and young adults each year, many of these from established authors and illustrators. "However, we know how difficult it can be for new writers to get their work in front of publishers, which is why we've decided to extend our innovative and pioneering Friday Pitch service to emerging writers for children and young adults.

TERMS Guidelines online.

ANDERSEN PRESS

20 Vauxhall Bridge Rd., London SW1V 2SA, United Kingdom. **E-mail:** anderseneditorial@penguinrandomhouse.co.uk. **Website:** www.andersenpress.co.uk. Andersen Press is a specialist children's publisher. "We publish picture books, for which the required text would be approximately 500 words (maximum 1,000), juvenile fiction for which the text would be approximately 3,000-5,000 words and older fiction up to 75,000 words. We do not publish adult fiction, nonfiction, poetry, or short story anthologies."

HOW TO CONTACT Send all submissions by post: Query and full ms for picture books; synopsis and 3 chapters for longer fiction.

TERMS Guidelines online.

ANNICK PRESS, LTD.

15 Patricia Ave., Toronto ON M2M 1H9, Canada. (416)221-4802. **Fax:** (416)221-8400. **Website:** www.annickpress.com. **Contact:** The Editors. Annick Press maintains a commitment to high quality books that entertain and challenge. Our publications share fantasy and stimulate imagination, while encouraging children to trust their judgment and abilities. *Does not accept unsolicited mss.* Publishes picture books, juvenile and YA fiction and nonfiction; specializes in trade books. **Publishes 25 titles/year. 20% of books from first-time authors. 80-85% from unagented writers.**

FICTION Publisher of children's books. Not accepting picture books at this time.

HOW TO CONTACT 5,000 queries received/year. 3,000 mss received/year. Publishes a book 2 years after acceptance.

TERMS Pays authors royalty of 5-12% based on retail price. Offers advances (average amount: $3,000). Pays illustrators royalty of 5% minimum. Book catalog and guidelines online.

THE BRUCEDALE PRESS

P.O. Box 2259, Port Elgin ON N0H 2C0, Canada. (519)832-6025. **E-mail:** info@brucedalepress.ca. **Website:** brucedalepress.ca. The Brucedale Press publishes books and other materials of regional interest and merit, as well as literary, historical, and/or pictorial works. Accepts works by Canadian authors only. Book submissions reviewed November to January. Submissions to *The Leaf Journal* accepted in September and March only. Manuscripts must be in English and thoroughly proofread before being sent. Use Canadian spellings and style. Publishes hardcover and trade paperback originals. **Publishes 3 titles/year. 75% of books from first-time authors. 100% from unagented writers.**

HOW TO CONTACT Publishes book 1 year after acceptance.

TERMS Pays royalty. Book catalog online. "Unless responding to an invitation to submit, query first by Canada Post with outline and sample chapter to book-length manuscripts. Send full manuscripts for work intended for children." Guidelines online.

TIPS "Our focus is very regional. In reading submissions, I look for quality writing with a strong connection to the Queen's Bush area of Ontario. All authors should visit our website, get a catalog, and read our books before submitting. Except for contest entries, we do not review manuscripts sent from outside Canada."

BUSTER BOOKS

16 Lion Yard, Tremadoc Rd., London WA SW4 7NQ, United Kingdom. (020)7720-8643. **Fax:** (022)7720-8953. **E-mail:** enquiries@mombooks.com. **Website:** www.busterbooks.co.uk. **Contact:** Buster Submissions. "We are dedicated to providing irresistible and fun books for children of all ages. We typically publish black & white nonfiction for children aged 8-12 novelty titles-including doodle books."

HOW TO CONTACT Prefers synopsis and sample text over complete ms.

TIPS "We do not accept picturebook or poetry submissions. Please do not send original artwork as we cannot guarantee its safety." Visit website before submitting.

CHILD'S PLAY (INTERNATIONAL) LTD.

Child's Play, Ashworth Rd. Bridgemead, Swindon, Wiltshire SN5 7YD, United Kingdom. 01793 616286. **E-mail:** neil@childs-play.com; office@childs-play.com. **Website:** www.childs-play.com. **Contact:** Sue Baker, Neil Burden, manuscript acquisitions. Specializes in nonfiction, fiction, educational material, multicultural material. Produces 30 picture books/year; 10 young readers/year. "A child's early years are more important than any other. This is when children learn most about the world around them and the language they need to survive and grow. Child's Play aims to create exactly the right material for this all-important time." **Publishes 40 titles/year.**

○ "Due to a backlog of submissions, Child's Play is currently no longer able to accept anymore manuscripts."

FICTION Picture books: adventure, animal, concept, contemporary, folktales, multicultural, nature/environment. Young readers: adventure, animal, anthology, concept, contemporary, folktales, humor, multicultural, nature/environment, poetry. Average word length: picture books—1,500; young readers—2,000.

NONFICTION Picture books: activity books, animal, concept, multicultural, music/dance, nature/environment, science. Young readers: activity books, animal, concept, multicultural, music/dance, nature/environment, science. Average word length: picture books—2,000; young readers—3,000.

HOW TO CONTACT Publishes book 2 years after acceptance.

ILLUSTRATION Accepts material from international illustrators. Works with 10 illustrators/year. Uses color artwork only. Reviews ms/illustration packages. For ms/illustration packages: Query or submit ms/illustration packages to Sue Baker, editor. Reviews work for future assignments. If interested in illustrating future titles, query with samples, CD, website address. Submit samples to Annie Kubler, art director. Responds in 10 weeks. Samples not returned. Samples filed.

TIPS "Look at our website to see the kind of work we do before sending. Do not send cartoons. We do not publish novels. We do publish lots of books with pictures of babies/toddlers."

CHRISTIAN FOCUS PUBLICATIONS

Geanies House, Fearn, Tain Ross-shire Scotland IV20 1TW, United Kingdom. (44)1862-871-011. **Fax:** (44)1862-871-699. **E-mail:** submissions@christianfocus.com. **Website:** www.christianfocus.com. **Contact:** Director of Publishing. Specializes in Christian material, nonfiction, fiction, educational material. **Publishes 22-32 titles/year. 2% of books from first-time authors.**

FICTION Picture books, young readers, adventure, history, religion. Middle readers: adventure, problem novels, religion. Young adult/teens: adventure, history, problem novels, religion. Average word length: young readers—5,000; middle readers—max 10,000; young adult/teen—max 20,000.

NONFICTION All levels: activity books, biography, history, religion, science. Average word length: picture books—5,000; young readers—5,000; middle readers—5,000-10,000; young adult/teens—10,000-20,000.

HOW TO CONTACT Query or submit outline/synopsis and 3 sample chapters. Include Author Information Form from site with submission. Will consider electronic submissions and previously published work. Responds to queries in 2 weeks; mss in 3-6 months. Publishes book 1 year after acceptance.

ILLUSTRATION Works on 15-20 potential projects. "Some artists are chosen to do more than one. Some projects just require a cover illustration, some require full color spreads, others black and white line art." **Contact:** Catherine Mackenzie, children's editor. Responds in 2 weeks only if interested. Samples are not returned.

PHOTOGRAPHY "We only purchase royalty free photos from particular photographic associations. However portfolios can be presented to our designer." **Contact:** Daniel van Straaten. Photographers should send cover letter, résumé, published samples, client list, portfolio.

TIPS "Be aware of the international market as regards writing style/topics as well as illustration styles. Our company sells rights to European as well as Asian countries. Fiction sales are not as good as they were. Christian fiction for youngsters is not a product that is performing well in comparison to nonfiction such as Christian biography/Bible stories/church history, etc."

✿ COTEAU BOOKS

Thunder Creek Publishing Co-operative Ltd., 2517 Victoria Ave., Regina SK S4P 0T2, Canada. (306)777-0170. **Fax:** (306)522-5152. **E-mail:** coteau@coteaubooks.com. **Website:** www.coteaubooks.com. **Contact:** Geoffrey Ursell, publisher. "Our mission is to publish the finest in Canadian fiction, nonfiction, poetry, drama, and children's literature, with an emphasis on Saskatchewan and prairie writers. De-emphasizing science fiction, picture books." Publishes chapter books for young readers aged 9-12 and novels for older kids ages 13-15 and for ages 15 and up. Publishes trade paperback originals and reprints. **Publishes 12 titles/year. 25% of books from first-time authors. 90% from unagented writers.**

FICTION No science fiction. No children's picture books.

NONFICTION *Canadian authors only.*

HOW TO CONTACT Query. Submit hard copy query, bio, 3-4 sample chapters, SASE. 200 queries; 40 mss received/year. Responds in 3 months. Publishes book 1 year after acceptance.

TERMS Pays 10% royalty on retail price. Book catalog available free. Guidelines online.

TIPS "Look at past publications to get an idea of our editorial program. We do not publish romance, horror, or picture books but are interested in juvenile and teen fiction from Canadian authors. Submissions, even queries, must be made in hard copy only. We do not accept simultaneous/multiple submissions. Check our website for new submission timing guidelines."

● CURIOUS FOX

Brunel Rd., Houndmills, Basingstoke Hants RG21 6XS, United Kingdom. **E-mail:** submissions@curious-fox.com. **Website:** www.curious-fox.com. "Do you love telling good stories? If so, we'd like to hear from you. Curious Fox is on the lookout for UK-based authors, whether new talent or established authors with exciting ideas. We take submissions for books aimed at ages 3-young adult. If you have story ideas that are bold, fun, and imaginative, then please do get in touch!"

HOW TO CONTACT "Send your submission via e-mail to submissions@curious-fox.com. Include the following in the body of the email, not as attachments: Sample chapters, Résumé, List of previous publishing credits, if applicable. We will respond only if your writing samples fit our needs."

ILLUSTRATION Please submit any illustrations/artwork by e-mail.

TERMS Guidelines online.

● FAT FOX BOOKS

The Den, P.O. Box 579, Tonbridge TN9 9NG, United Kingdom. (44)(0)1580-857249. **E-mail:** hello@fatfoxbooks.com. **Website:** fatfoxbooks.com. "Can you write engaging, funny, original and brilliant stories? We are looking for fresh new talent as well as exciting new ideas from established writers and illustrators. We publish books for children from 3-14, and if we think the story is brilliant and fits our list, then as one of the few publishers who accepts unsolicited material, we will take it seriously. We will consider books of all genres."

HOW TO CONTACT For picture books, send complete ms; for longer works, send first 3 chapters and estimate of final word count.

ILLUSTRATION "We are looking for beautiful, original, distinctive illustration that stands out."

TERMS Guidelines online. Currently closed to submissions.

● DAVID FICKLING BOOKS

31 Beamont St., Oxford OX1 2NP, United Kingdom. (018)65-339000. **Fax:** (018)65-339009. **Website:** www.davidficklingbooks.co.uk. **Contact:** Simon Mason, managing director. David Fickling Books is a story house." For nearly twelve years DFB has been run as an imprint—first as part of Scholastic, then of Random House. Now we've set up as an independent business." **Publishes 12-20 titles/year.**

FICTION Considers all categories.

HOW TO CONTACT Submit cover letter and 3 sample chapters as PDF attachment saved in format "Author Name_Full Title." Responds to mss in 3 months, if interested.

ILLUSTRATION Reviews ms/illustration packages from artists. Illustrations only: query with samples.

PHOTOGRAPHY Submit cover letter, résumé, promo pieces.

TERMS Guidelines online. Closed to submissions. Check website for when they open to submissions and for details on the Inkpot competition.

TIPS "We adore stories for all ages, in both text and pictures. Quality is our watch word."

✿ FITZHENRY & WHITESIDE LTD.

195 Allstate Pkwy., Markham ON L3R 4T8, Canada. (905)477-9700. **Fax:** (905)477-2834. **E-mail:** godwit@ fitzhenry.ca. **Website:** www.fitzhenry.ca/. Emphasis on Canadian authors and illustrators, subject or perspective. "Until further notice, we will not be accepting unsolicited submissions." **Publishes 15 titles/ year. 10% of books from first-time authors.**

HOW TO CONTACT Publishes book 1-2 years after acceptance.

ILLUSTRATION Works with approximately 10 illustrators/year. Reviews ms/illustration packages from artists. Submit outline and sample illustration (copy). Illustrations only: Query with samples and promo sheet. Samples not returned unless requested.

PHOTOGRAPHY Buys photos from freelancers. Buys stock and assigns work. Captions required. Uses b&w 8×10 prints; 35mm and 4×5 transparencies, 300+ dpi digital images. Submit stock photo list and promo piece.

TERMS Pays authors 8-10% royalty with escalations. Offers "respectable" advances for picture books, split 50/50 between author and illustrator. Pays illustrators by project and royalty. Pays photographers per photo.

TIPS "We respond to quality."

● FLYING EYE BOOKS

62 Great Eastern St., London EC2A 3QR, United Kingdom. (44)(0)207-033-4430. **E-mail:** picturbksubs@no-brow.net. **Website:** www.flyingeyebooks.com. Flying Eye Books is the children's imprint of award-winning visual publishing house Nobrow. FEB seeks to retain the same attention to detail and excellence in illustrated content as its parent publisher, but with a focus on the craft of children's storytelling and nonfiction.

TERMS Guidelines online.

● FRANCES LINCOLN CHILDREN'S BOOKS

Frances Lincoln, 74-77 White Lion St., London N1 9PF, United Kingdom. (44)(20)7284-4009. **Website:** www.franceslincoln.com. "Our company was founded by Frances Lincoln in 1977. We published our first books two years later, and we have been creating illustrated books of the highest quality ever since, with special emphasis on gardening, walking and the outdoors, art, architecture, design and landscape. In 1983, we started to publish illustrated books for children. Since then we have won many awards and prizes with

both fiction and nonfiction children's books." **Publishes 100 titles/year. 6% of books from first-time authors.**

FICTION Average word length: picture books—1,000; young readers—9,788; middle readers—20,653; young adults—35,407.

NONFICTION Average word length: picture books—1,000; middle readers—29,768.

HOW TO CONTACT Query by e-mail. Query by e-mail. Responds in 6 weeks to mss. Publishes book 18 months after acceptance.

ILLUSTRATION Works with approx 56 illustrators/year. Uses both color and b&w. Reviews ms/illustration packages from artist. Sample illustrations. Illustrations only: Query with samples. Responds only if interested. Samples are returned with SASE. Samples are kept on file only if interested.

PHOTOGRAPHY Buys stock images and assign work. Uses children, multicultural photos. Submit cover letter, published samples, or portfolio.

▲● FRANKLIN WATTS

Hachette Children's Books, Carmelite House, 50 Victoria Embankment, London EC4Y 0DZ, United Kingdom. (44)(20)7873-6000. **Fax:** (44)(20)7873-6024. **Website:** www.franklinwatts.co.uk. Franklin Watts is well known for its high quality and attractive information books, which support the National Curriculum and stimulate children's enquiring minds. *Generally does not accept unsolicited mss.*

✿ KIDS CAN PRESS

25 Dockside Dr., Toronto ON M5A 0B5, Canada. (416)479-7000. **Fax:** (416)960-5437. **Website:** www. kidscanpress.com. **Contact:** Corus Quay, acquisitions.

✿ *Kids Can Press is currently accepting unsolicited mss from Canadian adult authors only.*

FICTION Picture books, young readers: concepts. "We do not accept young adult fiction or fantasy novels for any age." Adventure, animal, contemporary, folktales, history, humor, multicultural, nature/environment, special needs, sports, suspense/mystery. Average word length: picture books 1,000-2,000; young readers 750-1,500; middle readers 10,000-15,000; young adults over 15,000.

NONFICTION Picture books: activity books, animal, arts/crafts, biography, careers, concept, health, history, hobbies, how-to, multicultural, nature/environment, science, social issues, special needs, sports. Young readers: activity books, animal, arts/crafts, biography, careers, concept, history, hobbies, how-to, multicultural. Middle readers: cooking, music/dance. Average word length: picture books 500-1,250; young readers 750-2,000; middle readers 5,000-15,000.

HOW TO CONTACT Submit outline/synopsis and 2-3 sample chapters. For picture books submit complete ms. Responds in 6 months only if interested. Publishes book 18-24 months after acceptance.

ILLUSTRATION Works with 40 illustrators/year. Reviews ms/illustration packages from artists. Send color copies of illustration portfolio, cover letter outlining other experience. Contact: Art Director. Illustrations only: Send tearsheets, color photocopies. Responds only if interested.

● LITTLE TIGER PRESS

1 The Coda Centre, 189 Munster Rd., London SW6 6AW, United Kingdom. (44)(20)7385-6333. **Website:** www.littletigerpress.com. Little Tiger Press is a dynamic and busy independent publisher. Also includes imprints: Caterpillar Books and Stripes Publishing.

FICTION Picture books: animal, concept, contemporary, humor. Average word length: picture books—750 words or less.

HOW TO CONTACT "We are no longer accepting unsolicited manuscripts. We will however, continue to accept illustration submissions and samples."

ILLUSTRATION Digital submissions preferred please send in digital samples as pdf or jpeg attachments to artsubmissions@littletiger.co.uk. Files should be flattened and no bigger than 1 mb per attachment. Include name and contact details on any attachments. Printed submissions please send in printed color samples as A4 printouts. Do not send in original artwork as we cannot be held responsible for unsolicited original artwork being lost or damaged in the post. We aim to acknowledge unsolicited material and to return material if so requested within 3 months. Please include SAE if return of material is requested.

◑ MANOR HOUSE PUBLISHING, INC.

452 Cottingham Crescent, Ancaster ON L9G 3V6, Canada. (905)648-2193. **E-mail:** mbdavie@manor-house.biz. **Website:** www.manor-house.biz. **Contact:** Mike Davie, president (novels and nonfiction). Manor House is currently looking for new fully edited, ready-to-run titles to complete our spring-fall 2017 release lineup. This is a rare opportunity for authors, including self-published, to have existing or ready titles picked up by Manor House and made available to retailers throughout the world, while our network of rights agents provide more potential revenue streams via foreign language rights sales. We are currently looking for titles that are ready or nearly ready for publishing to be released this fall. Such titles should be written by Canadian citizens residing in Canada and should be profitable or with strong market sales potential to allow full cost recovery and profit for publisher and author. Of primary interest are business and self-help titles along with other nonfiction, including new age. Publishes hardcover, trade paperback, and mass market paperback originals (and reprints if they meet specific criteria - best to inquire with publisher). **Publishes 5-6 titles/year. 90% of books from first-time authors. 90% from unagented writers.**

FICTION Stories should mainly be by Canadian authors residing in Canada, have Canadian settings and characters should be Canadian, but content should have universal appeal to wide audience. In some cases, we will consider publishing non-Canadian fiction authors - provided they demonstrate publishing their book will be profitable for author and publisher.

NONFICTION We are currently looking for titles that are ready or nearly ready for publishing to be released in 2017 onward. Such titles should be written by Canadian citizens residing in Canada and should be profitable or with strong market sales potential to allow full cost recovery and profit for publisher and author. Of primary interest are Business and self-help titles along with other nonfiction, including new age. We are also open to publishing non-Canadian authors (nonfiction works only) - provided non-Canadian authors can further provide us with a very good indication of demand for their book (Eg: actual or expected advance book orders from speaker venues, corporations, agencies or authors on a non-returnable basis) so we are assured the title will likely be a profitable venture for both author and publisher.

HOW TO CONTACT Query via e-mail. Submit proposal package, clips, bio, 3 sample chapters. Submit complete ms. Query via e-mail. Submit proposal package, outline, bio, 3 sample chapters. Submit complete ms. 30 queries; 20 mss received/year. Queries and mss to be sent by e-mail only. "We will respond in 30 days if interested-if not, there is no response. Do not follow up unless asked to do so." Publishes book 6 mos to 1 year after acceptance.

TERMS Pays 10% royalty on retail price. Book catalog online. Guidelines available.

TIPS "Our audience includes everyone-the general public/mass audience. Self-edit your work first, make sure it is well written and well edited with strong Canadian content and/or content of universal appeal (preferably with a Canadian connection of some kind)."

ORCA BOOK PUBLISHERS

1016 Balmoral Rd., Victoria BC V8T 1A8, Canada. (800)210-5277. **Fax:** (877)408-1551. **E-mail:** orca@orcabook.com. **Website:** www.orcabook.com. **Contact:** Amy Collins, editor (picture books); Sarah Harvey, editor (young readers); Andrew Wooldridge, editor (juvenile and teen fiction); Bob Tyrrell, publisher (YA, teen); Ruth Linka, associate editor (rapid reads).. Only publishes Canadian authors. Publishes hardcover and trade paperback originals, and mass market paperback originals and reprints. **Publishes 30-50 titles/year. 20% of books from first-time authors. 75% from unagented writers.**

FICTION Picture books: animals, contemporary, history, nature/environment. Middle readers: contemporary, history, fantasy, nature/environment, problem novels, graphic novels. Young adults: adventure, contemporary, hi-lo (Orca Soundings), history, multicultural, nature/environment, problem novels, suspense/mystery, graphic novels. Average word length: picture books—500-1,500; middle readers—20,000-35,000; young adult—25,000-45,000; Orca Soundings—13,000-15,000; Orca Currents—13,000-15,000. No romance, science fiction.

NONFICTION Only publishes Canadian authors.

HOW TO CONTACT Query with SASE. Submit proposal package, outline, clips, 2-5 sample chapters, SASE. Query with a SASE. 2,500 queries; 1,000 mss received/year. Responds in 1 month to queries; 2 months to proposals and mss. Publishes book 12-18 months after acceptance.

ILLUSTRATION Works with 8-10 illustrators/year. Reviews ms/illustration packages from artists. Submit ms with 3-4 pieces of final art. "Reproductions only, no original art please." Illustrations only: Query with samples; provide résumé, online portfolio. Responds in 2 months. Samples returned with SASE; samples

filed. 4 to 8 copies, digital proofs, tear sheets, press sheets.

TERMS Pays 10% royalty. Book catalog for 8½x11 SASE. Guidelines online.

TIPS "Our audience is students in grades K-12. Know our books, and know the market."

PAJAMA PRESS

181 Carlaw Ave., Suite 207, Toronto ON M4M 2S1, Canada. 4164662222. **E-mail:** annfeatherstone@pajamapress.ca. **Website:** pajamapress.ca. **Contact:** Ann Featherstone, senior editor. "We publish picture books—both for the very young and for school-aged readers, as well as novels for middle grade readers and contemporary or historical fiction for young adults aged 12+. Our nonfiction titles typically contain a strong narrative element. Pajama Press is also looking for mss from authors of diverse backgrounds. Stories about immigrants are of special interest." **Publishes 15-20 titles/year. 20% of books from first-time authors. 80% from unagented writers.**

FICTION vampire novels; romance (except as part of a literary novel); fiction with overt political or religious messages

NONFICTION "Our nonfiction titles typically contain a strong narrative element; for example, juvenile biographies and narratives about wildlife rescue." Does not want how-to books, activity books, books for adults, psychology books, educational resources

HOW TO CONTACT Pajama Press considers digital queries accompanied by picture books texts or the first 3 chapters of novel length projects. Your query should include an overview of your submission and some information about your writing background. Pajama Press prefers not to look at simultaneous submissions. Please notify us if you are submitting your project to another publisher. Please e-mail your queries and submissions to annfeatherstone@pajamapress.ca. In the interest of saving trees, Pajama Press does not accept physical mss. Any mss mailed to our office will be recycled unopened. 1,000 Responds in 6 weeks. Publishes ms 1-3 years after acceptance.

TERMS Pays advance. Guidelines online.

RONSDALE PRESS

3350 W. 21st Ave., Vancouver BC V6S 1G7, Canada. (604)738-4688. **Fax:** (604)731-4548. **Website:** ronsdalepress.com. **Contact:** Ronald B. Hatch (fiction, poetry, nonfiction, social commentary); Veronica Hatch (YA novels and short stories). "Ronsdale Press is a Canadian literary publishing house that publishes 12 books each year, four of which are young adult titles. Of particular interest are books involving children exploring and discovering new aspects of Canadian history." Publishes trade paperback originals. **Publishes 12 titles/year. 40% of books from first-time authors. 95% from unagented writers.**

FICTION Young adults: Canadian novels. Average word length: middle readers and young adults—50,000.

NONFICTION Middle readers, young adults: animal, biography, history, multicultural, social issues. Average word length: young readers—90; middle readers—90. "We publish a number of books for children and young adults in the age 10 to 15 range. We are especially interested in YA historical novels. We regret that we can no longer publish picture books."

HOW TO CONTACT Submit complete MS if you are certain it is right for Ronsdale Press. Submit complete ms if you feel it is perfect for Ronsdale Press. 40 queries; 800 mss received/year. Responds to queries in 2 weeks; mss in 2 months. Publishes book 1 year after acceptance.

ILLUSTRATION Works with 2 illustrators/year. Reviews ms/illustration packages from artists. Requires only cover art. Responds in 2 weeks. Samples returned with SASE. Originals returned to artist at job's completion.

TERMS Pays 10% royalty on retail price. Book catalog for #10 SASE. Guidelines online.

TIPS "Ronsdale Press is a literary publishing house, based in Vancouver, and dedicated to publishing books from across Canada, books that give Canadians new insights into themselves and their country. We aim to publish the best Canadian writers."

○ SECOND STORY PRESS

20 Maud St., Suite 401, Toronto ON M5V 2M5, Canada. (416)537-7850. **Fax:** (416)537-0588. **E-mail:** info@secondstorypress.ca. **Website:** www.secondstorypress.ca. "Please keep in mind that as a feminist press, we are looking for non-sexist, non-racist and non-violent stories, as well as historical fiction, chapter books, novels and biography."

FICTION Considers non-sexist, non-racist, and non-violent stories, as well as historical fiction, chapter books, picture books.

NONFICTION Picture books: biography.

HOW TO CONTACT Accepts appropriate material from residents of Canada only. "Send a synopsis and up to 3 sample chapters. If you are submitting a picture book you can send the entire manuscript. Illustrations are not necessary." No electronic submissions or queries. Guidelines on site.

○ SIMPLY READ BOOKS

501-5525 W. Blvd., Vancouver BC V6M 3W6, Canada. **E-mail:** go@simplyreadbooks.com. **Website:** www.simplyreadbooks.com. Simply Read Books is current seeking mss in picture books, early readers, early chapter books, middle grade fiction, and graphic novels.

HOW TO CONTACT Query or submit complete ms.

● SWEET CHERRY PUBLISHING

Unit 36, Vulcan Business Complex, Vulcan Rd., Leicester Leicestershire LE5 3EF, United Kingdom. **E-mail:** info@sweetcherrypublishing.com. **Website:** www.sweetcherrypublishing.com. Sweet Cherry Publishing is an independent publishing company based in Leicester. "We specialize in middle-grade series. Our aim is to provide children with compelling worlds and engaging characters that they will want to revisit again and again."

FICTION We are looking for inclusive and topical children's books.

HOW TO CONTACT submissions@sweetcherry-publishing.com

ILLUSTRATION Freelance illustrators are welcome to submit via our website.

TERMS Offers one-time fee for work that is accepted. Send the first 3 chapters or 4,000 words along with a synopsis, author biography, and cover letter detailing your target audience and your plans for further books in the series.

TIPS "Submit a cover letter and a synopsis with 3 sample chapters via post or e-mail. Please note that we strongly prefer e-mail submissions."

● TAFELBERG PUBLISHERS

Imprint of NB Publishers, P.O. Box 879, Cape Town 8000, South Africa. (27)(21)406-3033. **Fax:** (27)(21)406-3812. **E-mail:** engela.reinke@nb.co.za. **Website:** www.tafelberg.com. **Contact:** Engela Reinke. General publisher best known for Afrikaans fiction, authoritative political works, children's/youth literature, and a variety of illustrated and nonillustrated nonfiction. **Publishes 10 titles/year.**

FICTION Picture books, young readers: animal, anthology, contemporary, fantasy, folktales, hi-lo, humor, multicultural, nature/environment, scient fiction, special needs. Middle readers, young adults: animal (middle reader only), contemporary, fantasy, hi-lo, humor, multicultural, nature/environment, problem novels, science fiction, special needs, sports, suspense/mystery. Average word length: picture books—1,500-7,500; young readers—25,000; middle readers—15,000; young adults—40,000.

HOW TO CONTACT Submit complete ms. Submit outline, information on intended market, bio, and 1-2 sample chapters. Responds to queries in 2 weeks; mss in 6 months. Publishes book 1 year after acceptance.

ILLUSTRATION Works with 2-3 illustrators/year. Reviews ms/illustration packages from artists. Send ms with dummy or e-mail and jpegs. Contact: Louise Steyn, publisher. Illustrations only: Query with brochure, photocopies, résumé, URL, JPEGs. Responds only if interested. Samples not returned.

TERMS Pays authors royalty of 15-18% based on wholesale price.

TIPS "Writers: Story needs to have a South African or African style. Illustrators: I'd like to look, but the chances of getting commissioned are slim. The market is small and difficult. Do not expect huge advances. Editorial staff attended or plans to attend the following conferences: IBBY, Frankfurt, SCBWI Bologna."

☯ THISTLEDOWN PRESS LTD.

410 2nd Ave., Saskatoon SK S7K 2C3, Canada. (306)244-1722. **Fax:** (306)244-1762. **E-mail:** editorial@thistledownpress.com. **Website:** www.thistledownpress.com. **Contact:** Allan Forrie, publisher. "Thistledown originates books by Canadian authors only, although we have co-published titles by authors outside Canada. We do not publish children's picture books." **40% of books from first-time authors. 40% from unagented writers.**

FICTION Young adults: adventure, anthology, contemporary, fantasy, humor, poetry, romance, science fiction, suspense/mystery, short stories. Average word length: young adults—40,000.

HOW TO CONTACT Submit outline/synopsis and sample chapters. *Does not accept mss.* Do not query by e-mail. "Please note: we are not accepting middle years (ages 8-12) nor children's manuscripts at this

time." See Submission Guidelines on Website. 150-250 Responds to queries in 6 months. Publishes book 1 year after acceptance.

ILLUSTRATION Prefers agented illustrators but "not mandatory." Works with few illustrators. Illustrations only: Query with samples, promo sheet, slides, tearsheets. Responds only if interested. Samples returned with SASE; samples filed.

TERMS Pays authors royalty of 10-12% based on net dollar sales. Pays illustrators and photographers by the project (range: $250-750). Rarely pays advance. Book catalog on website. Guidelines online.

TIPS "Send cover letter including publishing history and SASE."

☯ TRADEWIND BOOKS

202-1807 Maritime Mews, Granville Island, Vancouver BC V6H 3W7, Canada. (604)662-4405. **Website:** www.tradewindbooks.com. "Tradewind Books publishes juvenile picture books and young adult novels. Requires that submissions include evidence that author has read at least 3 titles published by Tradewind Books." Publishes hardcover and trade paperback originals. **Publishes 5 titles/year. 15% of books from first-time authors. 50% from unagented writers.**

FICTION Average word length: 900 words.

HOW TO CONTACT Send complete ms for picture books. *YA novels by Canadian authors only. Chapter books by US authors considered.* For chapter books/Middle Grade Fiction, submit the first three chapters, a chapter outline and plot summary. Responds to mss in 2 months. Publishes book 3 years after acceptance.

ILLUSTRATION Works with 3-4 illustrators/year. Reviews ms/illustration packages from artists. Send illustrated ms as dummy. Illustrations only: Query with samples. Responds only if interested. Samples returned with SASE; samples filed.

TERMS Pays 7% royalty on retail price. Pays variable advance. Book catalog and ms guidelines online.

☯☯ USBORNE PUBLISHING

83-85 Saffron Hill, London EC1N 8RT, United Kingdom. (44)207430-2800. **Fax:** (44)207430-1562. **E-mail:** mail@usborne.co.uk. **Website:** www.usborne.com. "Usborne Publishing is a multiple-award-winning, worldwide children's publishing company publishing almost every type of children's book for every age from baby to young adult."

FICTION Young readers, middle readers: adventure, contemporary, fantasy, history, humor, multicultural, nature/environment, science fiction, suspense/mystery, strong concept-based or character-led series. Average word length: young readers—5,000-10,000; middle readers—25,000-50,000; young adult—50,000-100,000.

HOW TO CONTACT *Agented submissions only.*

ILLUSTRATION Works with 100 illustrators per year. Illustrations only: Query with samples. Samples not returned; samples filed.

PHOTOGRAPHY Contact: Usborne Art Department. Submit samples.

TERMS Pays authors royalty.

TIPS "Do not send any original work and, sorry, but we cannot guarantee a reply."

○ WHITECAP BOOKS, LTD.

210 - 314 W. Cordova St., Vancouver BC V6B 1 E8, Canada. (604)681-6181. **Fax:** (905)477-9179. **Website:** www.whitecap.ca. "Whitecap Books is a general trade publisher with a focus on food and wine titles. Although we are interested in reviewing unsolicited ms submissions, please note that we only accept submissions that meet the needs of our current publishing program. Please see some of most recent releases to get an idea of the kinds of titles we are interested in." Publishes hardcover and trade paperback originals. **Publishes 30 titles/year. 20% of books from first-time authors. 90% from unagented writers.**

FICTION No children's picture books or adult fiction.

NONFICTION Young children's and middle reader's nonfiction focusing mainly on nature, wildlife and animals. "Writers should take the time to research our list and read the submission guidelines on our website. This is especially important for children's writers and cookbook authors. We will only consider submissions that fall into these categories: cookbooks, wine and spirits, regional travel, home and garden, Canadian history, North American natural history, juvenile series-based fiction. At this time, we are not accepting the following categories: self-help or inspirational books, political, social commentary, or issue books, general how-to books, biographies or memoirs, business and finance, art and architecture, religion and spirituality."

HOW TO CONTACT See guidelines. Submit cover letter, synopsis, SASE via ground mail. See guidelines online. 500 queries received/year; 1,000 mss received/year. Responds in 2-3 months to proposals. Publishes book 1 year after acceptance.

ILLUSTRATION Works with 1-2 illustrators/year. Uses color artwork only. Reviews ms/illustration packages from artists. Query. Contact: Rights and Acquisitions. Illustrations only: Send postcard sample with tearsheets. Contact: Michelle Furbacher, art director. Responds only if interested.

PHOTOGRAPHY Only accepts digital photography. Submit stock photo list. Buys stock and assigns work. Model/property releases required.

TERMS Pays royalty. Pays negotiated advance. Catalog and guidelines online.

TIPS "We want well-written, well-researched material that presents a fresh approach to a particular topic."

MAGAZINES

///

Children's magazines are a great place for unpublished writers and illustrators to break into the market. Writers, illustrators, and photographers alike may find it easier to get book assignments if they have tearsheets from magazines. Having magazine work under your belt shows you're professional and have experience working with editors and art directors and meeting deadlines.

But magazines aren't merely a breaking-in point. Writing, illustration and photo assignments for magazines let you see your work in print quickly, and the magazine market can offer steady work and regular paychecks (a number of them pay on acceptance). Book authors and illustrators may have to wait a year or two before receiving royalties from a project. The magazine market is also a good place to use research material that didn't make it into a book project you're working on. You may even work on a magazine idea that blossoms into a book project.

TARGETING YOUR SUBMISSIONS

It's important to know the topics typically covered by different children's magazines. To help you match your work with the right publications, we've included several indexes in the back of this book. The **Subject Index** lists both book and magazine publishers by the fiction and nonfiction subjects they're seeking.

If you're a writer, use the Subject Index in conjunction with the **Age-Level Index** to narrow your list of markets. Targeting the correct age group with your submission is an important consideration. Many rejection slips are sent because a writer has not targeted a manuscript to the correct age. Few magazines are aimed at children of all ages, so you must be certain your manuscript is written for the audience level of the particular magazine you're submitting to. Magazines for children (just as magazines for adults) may also target a specific gender.

Each magazine has a different editorial philosophy. Language usage also varies between periodicals, as does the length of feature articles and the use of artwork and photographs. Reading magazines *before* submitting is the best way to determine if your material is appropriate. Also, because magazines targeted to specific age groups have a natural turnover in readership every few years, old topics (with a new slant) can be recycled.

If you're a photographer, look for listings with the **Photos** subhead. Use this strategy in combination with the subject index to narrow your search. For instance, if you photograph sports, look under Sports in the Subject Index to see which accept photos.

Because many kids' magazines sell subscriptions through direct mail or schools, you may not be able to find a particular publication at bookstores or newsstands. Check your local library, or send for copies of the magazines you're interested in. Most magazines in this section have sample copies available and will send them for a SASE or small fee.

Also, many magazines have submission guidelines and theme lists available for a SASE. Check magazines' websites, too. Many offer excerpts of articles, submission guidelines, and theme lists and will give you a feel for the editorial focus of the publication.

Watch for the Canadian ○ and International ● symbols. These publications' needs and requirements may differ from their United States counterparts.

🌑 AQUILA

Studio 2 Willowfield Studios, 67a Willowfield Rd., Eastbourne BN22 8AP, England. (44)(132)343-1313. **E-mail:** editor@aquila.co.uk. **Website:** www.aquila.co.uk. *"Aquila* is an educational magazine for readers ages 8-13 including factual articles (no pop/celebrity material), arts/crafts, and puzzles." Entire publication aimed at juvenile market. Estab. 1993. Circ. 40,000.

FICTION Young Readers: animal, contemporary, fantasy, folktales, health, history, humorous, multicultural, nature/environment, problem solving, religious, science fiction, sports, suspense/mystery. Middle Readers: animal, contemporary, fantasy, folktales, health, history, humorous, multicultural, nature/environment, problem solving, religious, romance, science fiction, sports, suspense/mystery. Length: 1,000-1,150 words. Pays £90.

NONFICTION Young Readers: animal, arts/crafts, concept, cooking, games/puzzles, health, history, how-to, interview/profile, math, nature/environment, science, sports. Middle Readers: animal, arts/crafts, concept, cooking, games/puzzles, health, history, interview/profile, math, nature/environment, science, sports. Query. Length: 600-800 words. Pays £90.

HOW TO CONTACT Accepts queries by mail, e-mail.

TERMS Pays on publication. Sample copy: £5. Guidelines online.

TIPS "We only accept a high level of educational material for children ages 8-13 with a good standard of literacy and ability."

☯ ASCENT ASPIRATIONS

Friday's Poems, 1560 Arbutus Dr., Nanoose Bay BC C9P 9C8, Canada. **E-mail:** ascentaspirations@shaw.ca. **Website:** www.davidpfraser.ca. **Contact:** David Fraser, editor. E-zine specializing in poetry and visual art. *"Ascent Aspirations* magazine publishes weekly online and in print annually. The print issues are operated as contests or as anthologies of a year's accepted submissions. Please refer to current guidelines before submitting. *Ascent Aspirations* is a quality electronic publication dedicated to the promotion and encouragement of aspiring writers of poetry. For Friday's Poems we accept submissions all the time, publish 3 poems per week, and archive then after that week is over. Magazine: 3 electronic pages; photos. Receives 100-200 unsolicited mss/month. Accepts 3 mss/issue; 156 mss/year. Publishes 10-50 new writers/year. Has

published work by Taylor Graham, Janet Buck, Jim Manton, Steve Cartwright, Don Stockard, Penn Kemp, Sam Vargo, Vernon Waring, Margaret Karmazin, Bill Hughes, and spoken-word artists Sheri-D Wilson, Missy Peters, Ian Ferrier, Cathy Petch, and Bob Holdman. Estab. 1997.

NONFICTION Query by e-mail with Word attachment. Include a brief bio. "If you have to submit by mail because it is your only avenue, provide a SASE with either International Coupons or Canadian stamps only, but provide an e-mail address for notification of publication.

POETRY Submit 1-5 poems at a time. Prefers e-mail submissions (pasted into body of message or as attachment in Word); no disk submissions. "If you must submit by postal mail because it is your only avenue, provide a SASE with IRCs or Canadian stamps." Reads submissions on a regular basis year round. "We accept all forms of poetry on any theme. Poetry needs to be unique and touch the reader emotionally with relevant human, social, and philosophical imagery." Considers poetry by children and teens. Does not want poetry "that focuses on mainstream, overtly religious verse." "No payment offered at this time."

HOW TO CONTACT Responds in 1 to week to queries; 3 months to mss. Sometimes comments on rejected mss. Publishes ms 3 months or less after acceptance.

TERMS Rights remain with author. Guidelines by e-mail or on website.

TIPS "Poetry should use language lyrically and effectively, be experimental in either form or content, and take the reader into realms where they can analyze and think about the human condition. Write with passion for your material, be concise and economical, and let the reader work to unravel your story. In terms of editing, always proofread to the point where what you submit is the best it possibly can be. Never be discouraged if your work is not accepted; it may just not be the right fit for a current publication."

☾ ASK

E-mail: ask@cricketmedia.com. **Website:** www.cricketmedia.com. *"Ask* is a magazine of arts and sciences for curious kids ages 7-10 who like to find out how the world works." Estab. 2002.

NONFICTION Needs humor, photo feature, profile. *"ASK* commissions most articles but welcomes queries from authors on all nonfiction subjects. Particularly looking for odd, unusual, and interesting stories likely to interest science-oriented kids. Writers interested in working for *ASK* should send a résumé and writing sample (including at least 1 page unedited) for consideration." Length: 200-1,600.

HOW TO CONTACT Send submissions to: Art Submissions Coordinator, Cricket Media, 70 E. Lake St., Suite 800, Chicago IL 60601. Accepts queries by e-mail, online submission form.

ILLUSTRATION Illustrations are by assignment only. PLEASE DO NOT send original artwork. Send postcards, promotional brochures, or color photocopies. Be sure that each sample is marked with your name, address, phone number, and website or blog. Art submissions will not be returned.

TERMS Rights vary. Byline given. Guidelines online.

BABYBUG

Cricket Media, Inc., 7926 Jones Branch Dr., Suite 870, McLean VA 22102. (703)885-3400. **Website:** www.cricketmedia.com. "*Babybug*, a look-and-listen magazine, presents simple poems, stories, nonfiction, and activities that reflect the natural playfulness and curiosity of babies and toddlers." Estab. 1994. Circ. 45,000.

FICTION Wants very short, clear fiction. rhythmic, rhyming. Submit complete ms via online submissions manager. Length: up to 6 sentences. Pays up to 25¢/word.

NONFICTION "First Concepts," a playful take on a simple idea, expressed through very short nonfiction. See recent issues for examples. Submit through online submissions manager: cricketmag.submittable.com/submit. Length: up to 6 sentences. Pays up to 25¢/word.

POETRY "We are especially interested in rhythmic and rhyming poetry. Poems may explore a baby's day, or they may be more whimsical." Submit via online submissions manager. Pays up to $3/line; $25 minimum.

HOW TO CONTACT Send submissions to: Art Submissions Coordinator, Cricket Media, 70 E. Lake St., Suite 800, Chicago IL 60601. Responds in 3-6 months to mss. Accepts queries by online submission form.

ILLUSTRATION "Please **do not** send original artwork. Send postcards, promotional brochures, or color photocopies. Be sure that each sample is marked with your name, address, phone number and website or blog. Art submissions will not be returned."

TERMS Rights vary. Byline given. Pays on publication. 50% freelance written. Guidelines online.

TIPS "We are particularly interested in mss that explore simple concepts, encourage very young children's imaginative play, and provide opportunities for adult readers and babies to interact. We welcome work that reflects diverse family cultures and traditions."

BOYS' LIFE

Boy Scouts of America, P.O. Box 152079, 1325 W. Walnut Hill Ln., Irving TX 75015. **Website:** www.boyslife.org. **Contact:** Paula Murphey, senior editor; Clay Swartz, associate editor. *Boys' Life* is a monthly 4-color general interest magazine for boys 7-18, most of whom are Cub Scouts, Boy Scouts, or Venturers. Estab. 1911. Circ. 1.1 million.

NONFICTION Scouting activities and general interests. Query senior editor with SASE. No phone or e-mail queries. Length: 500-1,500 words. Pay ranges from $400-1,500.

HOW TO CONTACT Responds to queries/mss in 2 months. Publishes ms approximately 1 year after acceptance. Accepts queries by mail.

ILLUSTRATION Buys 10-12 illustrations/issue; 100-125 illustrations/year. Works on assignment only. Reviews ms/illustration packages from artists. "Query first." Illustrations only: Send tearsheets. Responds to art samples only if interested. Samples returned with SASE. Original artwork returned at job's completion. Works on assignment only.

PHOTOS Photo guidelines free with SASE. Pays $500 base editorial day rate against placement fees, plus expenses. **Pays on acceptance.** Buys one-time rights.

TERMS Buys one-time rights. Byline given. Pays on acceptance. 75% freelance written. Prefers to work with published/established writers; works with small number of new/unpublished writers each year. Sample copy: $3.95 plus 9x12 SASE. Guidelines online.

TIPS "We strongly recommend reading at least 12 issues of the magazine before submitting queries. We are a good market for any writer willing to do the necessary homework. Write for a boy you know who is 12. Our readers demand punchy writing in relatively short, straightforward sentences. The editors demand well-reported articles that demonstrate high standards of journalism. We follow the *Associated Press* manual of style and usage. Learn and read our publications before submitting anything."

BREAD FOR GOD'S CHILDREN

Bread Ministries, INC., P.O. Box 1017, Arcadia FL 34265. (863)494-6214. **E-mail:** bread@breadministries.org. **Website:** www.breadministries.org. **Contact:** Judith M. Gibbs, editor. An interdenominational Christian teaching publication published 4-6 times/year written to aid children and youth in leading a Christian life. Estab. 1972. Circ. 10,000 (U.S. and Canada).

FICTION "We are looking for writers who have a solid knowledge of Biblical principles and are concerned for the youth of today living by those principles. Stories must be well written, with the story itself getting the message across—no preaching, moralizing, or tag endings." Needs historical, religious. Young readers, middle readers, young adult/teen: adventure, religious, problem-solving, sports. Looks for "teaching stories that portray Christian lifestyles without preaching." Send complete ms. Length: 600-800 words for young children; 900-1,500 words for older children. Pays $40-50.

NONFICTION Needs inspirational. All levels: how-to. "We do not want anything detrimental to solid family values. Most topics will fit if they are slanted to our basic needs." Send complete ms. Length: 500-800 words On publication

HOW TO CONTACT Responds in 6 months to mss. Publishes ms an average of 6 months after acceptance. Accepts queries by mail.

ILLUSTRATION "The only illustrations we purchase are those occasional good ones accompanying an accepted story."

TERMS Pays on publication. Pays $30-50 for stories; $30 for articles. Sample copies free for 9x12 SAE and 5 first-class stamps (for 2 copies). Buys first rights. Byline given. Publication No kill fee. 10% freelance written. Sample copy for 9x12 SAE and 5 first-class stamps. Guidelines for #10 SASE.

TIPS "We want stories or articles that illustrate overcoming obstacles by faith and living solid, Christian lives. Know our publication and what we have used in the past. Know the readership and publisher's guidelines. Stories should teach the value of morality and honesty without preaching. Edit carefully for content and grammar."

BRILLIANT STAR

1233 Central St., Evanston IL 60201. (847)853-2354. **E-mail:** brilliant@usbnc.org; hparsons@usbnc.org. **Website:** www.brilliantstarmagazine.org. **Contact:** Heidi Parsons, associate editor. "*Brilliant Star* empowers kids to explore their roles as world citizens. Inspired by the principles of peace and unity in the Baha'i Faith, the magazine and website encourage readers to use their virtues to make the world a better place. Universal values of good character, such as kindness, courage, creativity, and helpfulness, are presented through fiction, nonfiction, activities, interviews, puzzles, cartoons, games, music, and art. " Estab. 1969.

FICTION "We print fiction with kids ages 10-12 as the protagonists who resolve their problems themselves." Submit complete ms. Length: 700-1,400 words. Pays 3 contributor's copies.

NONFICTION Middle readers: arts/crafts, games/puzzles, geography, how-to, humorous, multicultural, nature/environment, religion, social issues. Query. Length: 300-700 words. Pays 3 contributor's copies.

POETRY "We only publish poetry written by children at the moment."

HOW TO CONTACT Accepts queries by e-mail.

ILLUSTRATION Reviews ms/illustration packages from artists. Illustrations only; query with samples. Contact: Aaron Kreader, graphic designer, at brilliant@usbnc.org. Responds only if interested. Samples kept on file. Credit line given.

PHOTOS Buys photos with accompanying ms only. Model/property release required; captions required. Responds only if interested.

TERMS Buys first rights and reprint rights for mss, artwork, and photos. Byline given. Guidelines available for SASE or via e-mail.

TIPS "*Brilliant Star*'s content is developed with a focus on children in their 'tween' years, ages 8-12. This is a period of intense emotional, physical, and psychological development. Familiarize yourself with the interests and challenges of children in this age range. Protagonists in our fiction are usually in the upper part of our age range: 10-12 years old. They solve their problems without adult intervention. We appreciate seeing a sense of humor but not related to bodily functions or put-downs. Keep your language and concepts age-appropriate. Use short words, sentences, and paragraphs. Activities and games may be submitted in rough or final form. Send us a description of your activity along with short, simple instructions. We avoid long, complicated activities that require adult supervision. If you think they will be helpful, please provide step-by-step rough sketches of the instructions. You may also submit photographs to illustrate the activity."

CADET QUEST MAGAZINE

Calvinist Cadet Corps, 1333 Alger St. SE, Grand Rapids MI 49507. (616)241-5616. **Fax:** (616)241-5558. **E-mail:** submissions@calvinistcadets.org. **Website:** www.calvinistcadets.org. **Contact:** Steve Bootsma, editor. Magazine published 7 times/year. *Cadet Quest Magazine* shows boys 9-14 how God is at work in their lives and in the world around them. Estab. 1958. Circ. 6,000.

FICTION "Fast-moving, entertaining stories that appeal to a boy's sense of adventure or to his sense of humor are welcomed. Stories must present Christian life realistically and help boys relate Christian values to their own lives. Stories must have action without long dialogues. Favorite topics for boys include sports and athletes, humor, adventure, mystery, friends, etc. They must also fit the theme of that issue of *Cadet Quest*. Stories with preachiness and/or clichés are not of interest to us." No fantasy, science fiction, fashion, horror, or erotica. Send complete ms by mail or e-mail (in body of e-mail; no attachments). Length: 1,000-1,300 words. Pays 5¢/word and 1 contributor's copy.

NONFICTION Informational. Send complete ms via postal mail or e-mail (in body of e-mail; no attachments). Length: up to 1,500 words. Pays 5¢/word and 1 contributor's copy.

HOW TO CONTACT Responds in 2 months to mss. Publishes ms 4-11 months after acceptance. Accepts queries by mail, e-mail.

ILLUSTRATION Works on assignment only. Reviews ms/illustration packages from artists.

PHOTOS Pays $5 each for photos purchased with ms.

TERMS Buys all rights, first rights, and second rights. Rights purchased vary with author and material. Byline given. Pays on acceptance. No kill fee. Sample copy for 9x12 SASE and $1.45 postage. Guidelines online.

TIPS "The best time to submit stories/articles is early in the year (January-April). Also remember readers are boys ages 9-14. Stories must reflect or add to the theme of the issue and be from a Christian perspective."

CARUS PUBLISHING COMPANY

30 Grove St., Suite C, Peterborough NH 03458. **Website:** www.cricketmag.com. See listings for *Babybug*, *Cicada*, *Click*, *Cricket*, *Ladybug*, *Muse*, *Spider*, and *Ask*. Carus Publishing owns Cobblestone Publishing, publisher of *AppleSeeds*, *Calliope*, *Cobblestone*, *Dig*, *Faces*, and *Odyssey*.

☉ CHEMMATTERS

American Chemical Society, Education Division, 1155 16th St., NW, Washington DC 20036. (202)872-6164. **Fax:** (202)872-8068. **E-mail:** chemmatters@acs.org. **Website:** www.acs.org/chemmatters. **Contact:** Patrice Pages, editor; Cornithia Harris, art director. Covers topics of interest to teenagers and that can be explained with chemistry. *ChemMatters*, published 4 times/year, is a magazine that helps high school students find connections between chemistry and the world around them. Estab. 1983. Circ. 30,000.

NONFICTION Query with published clips. Pays $700-$1,000 for article.

HOW TO CONTACT Responds in 4 weeks to queries and mss. Publishes ms 6 months after acceptance. Accepts queries by mail, e-mail.

ILLUSTRATION Buys 3 illustrations/issue; 12 illustrations/year. Uses color artwork only. Works on assignment only. Reviews ms/illustration packages from artists. Query. Illustrations only: Query with promo sheet, résumé. Samples returned with self-addressed stamped envelope; samples not filed. Credit line given.

PHOTOS Looking for photos of high school students engaged in science-related activities. Model/property release required; captions required. Uses color prints, but prefers high-resolution PDFs. Query with samples. Responds in 2 weeks.

TERMS Minimally buys first North American serial rights but prefers to buy all rights, reprint rights, electronic rights for ms. Buys all rights for artwork; nonexclusive first rights for photos. Byline given. Pays on acceptance. 100% freelance written. Sample copies and writer's guidelines free (available as e-mail attachment upon request).

TIPS "Be aware of the content covered in a standard high school chemistry textbook. Choose themes and topics that are timely, interesting, fun, *and* that relate to the content and concepts of the first-year chemistry course. Articles should describe real people involved with real science. Best articles feature young people making a difference or solving a problem."

CICADA

E-mail: cicada@cicadamag.com. **Website:** www.cricketmag.com/cicada. "*Cicada* is a YA lit/comics magazine fascinated with the lyric and strange and committed to work that speaks to teens' truths. We publish poetry, realistic and genre fiction, essay, and comics by adults and teens. (We are also inordinately fond of Viking jokes.) Our readers are smart and curious; submissions are invited but not required to engage young adult themes." Bimonthly literary magazine for ages 14 and up. Publishes 6 issues/year. Estab. 1998. Circ. 6,000.

FICTION Realism, science fiction, fantasy, historical fiction. Wants everything from flash fiction to novellas. Length: up to 9,000 words. Pays up to 25¢/word.

NONFICTION narrative nonfiction (especially teen-written), essays on literature, culture, and the arts. Submit complete ms via online submissions manager (cricketmag.submittable.com). Length: up to 5,000 words. Pays up to 25¢/word.

POETRY Reviews serious, humorous, free verse, rhyming. Length: no limit. Pays up to $3/line ($25 minimum).

HOW TO CONTACT Responds in 3-6 months to mss. Accepts queries by online submission form.

ILLUSTRATION Send portfolio with samples to cicada@cricketmedia.com with ONLINE PORTFOLIO SAMPLE as the subject line. For comic submissions, e-mail a short pitch/sketch(es) and a link to online portfolio with COMIC SUBMISSION as the subject line. Please **DO NOT** send final art. Please allow up to 3–6 months response time.

TERMS Rights vary. Pays after publication. Sample copy available online. Guidelines available online.

TIPS "Favorite writers, YA and otherwise: Bennett Madison, Sarah McCarry, Leopoldine Core, J. Hope Stein, José Olivarez, Sofia Samatar, Erica Lorraine Scheidt, David Levithan, Sherman Alexie, Hilary Smith, Nnedi Okorafor, Teju Cole, Anne Boyer, Malory Ortberg. @cicadamagazine; cicadamagazine.tumblr.com."

CLICK

E-mail: click@cricketmedia.com. **Website:** www.cricketmag.com. Magazine covering areas of interest for children ages 3-7. "*Click* is a science and exploration magazine for children ages 3-7. Designed and written with the idea that it's never too early to encourage a child's natural curiosity about the world, *Click*'s 40 full-color pages are filled with amazing photographs, beautiful illustrations, and stories and articles that are both entertaining and thought-provoking."

○ *Does not accept unsolicited mss.*

NONFICTION Query by e-mail with résumé and published clips. Length: 200-500 words.

HOW TO CONTACT Send submissions to: Art Submissions Coordinator, Cricket Media, 70 E. Lake St., Suite 800, Chicago IL 60601. Buys print, digital, promotional rights. Accepts queries by e-mail.

ILLUSTRATION Illustrations are by assignment only. PLEASE DO NOT send original artwork. Send postcards, promotional brochures, or color photocopies. Be sure that each sample is marked with your name, address, phone number, and website or blog. Art submissions will not be returned.

TERMS Rights vary. Sample copy available online. Guidelines available online.

TIPS "The best way for writers to understand what *Click* is looking for is to read the magazine. Writers are encouraged to examine several past copies before submitting a query."

COBBLESTONE

E-mail: cobblestone@cricketmedia.com. **Website:** www.cricketmedia.com. "*Cobblestone* is interested in articles of historical accuracy and lively, original approaches to the subject at hand." American history magazine for ages 8-14. Circ. 15,000.

○ "*Cobblestone* stands apart from other children's magazines by offering a solid look at 1 subject and stressing strong editorial content, color photographs throughout, and original illustrations." *Cobblestone* themes and deadline are available on website or with SASE.

FICTION Needs adventure. Query by e-mail with published clips. Length: up to 800 words. Pays 20-25¢/word.

NONFICTION Needs historical, humor, interview, personal experience, photo feature. Query by e-mail with published clips. Length: 700-800 words for feature articles; 300-600 words for supplemental nonfiction. Pays 20-25¢/word.

POETRY Serious and light verse considered. Must have clear, objective imagery. Length: up to 100 lines/poem. Pays on an individual basis.

HOW TO CONTACT Send submissions to: Art Submissions Coordinator, Cricket Media, 70 E. Lake St., Suite 800, Chicago IL 60601. Accepts queries by e-mail.

ILLUSTRATION Illustrations are by assignment only. PLEASE DO NOT send original artwork. Send postcards, promotional brochures, or color photocopies. Be sure that each sample is marked with your name, address, phone number, and website or blog. Art submissions will not be returned.

TERMS Buys all rights. Byline given. Pays on publication. Offers 50% kill fee. 50% freelance written. Sample copy available online. Guidelines available online.

TIPS "Review theme lists and past issues to see what we're looking for."

COLLEGEXPRESS MAGAZINE

Carnegie Communications, LLC, 2 LAN Dr., Suite 100, Westford MA 01886. **E-mail:** info@carnegiecomm.com. **Website:** www.collegexpress.com. *CollegeXpress Magazine*, formerly *Careers and Colleges*, provides juniors and seniors in high school with editorial, tips, trends, and websites to assist them in the transition to college, career, young adulthood, and independence.

◯　Distributed to 10,000 high schools and reaches 1.5 million students.

TIPS "Articles with great quotes, good reporting, good writing. Rich with examples and anecdotes. Must tie in with the objective to help teenaged readers plan for their futures. Current trends, policy changes and information regarding college admissions, financial aid, and career opportunities."

CRICKET

Cricket Media, Inc., 7926 Jones Branch Dr., Suite 870, McLean VA 22102. (703)885-3400. **Website:** www.cricketmag.com. *Cricket* is a monthly literary magazine for ages 9-14. Publishes 9 issues/year. Estab. 1973. Circ. 73,000.

FICTION Realistic, contemporary, historic, humor, mysteries, fantasy, science fiction, folk/fairy tales, legend, myth. No didactic, sex, religious, or horror stories. Submit via online submissions manager (cricketmag.submittable.com). Length: 1,200-1,800 words. Pays up to 25¢/word.

NONFICTION *Cricket* publishes thought-provoking nonfiction articles on a wide range of subjects: history, biography, true adventure, science and technology, sports, inventors and explorers, architecture and engineering, archaeology, dance, music, theater, and art. Articles should be carefully researched and include a solid bibliography that shows that research has gone beyond reviewing websites. Submit via online submissions manager (cricketmag.submittable.com). Length: 1,200-1,800 words. Pays up to 25¢/word.

POETRY *Cricket* publishes both serious and humorous poetry. Poems should be well-crafted, with precise and vivid language and images. Poems can explore a variety of themes, from nature, to family and friendships, to whatever you can imagine that will delight our readers and invite their wonder and emotional response. Length: up to 35 lines/poem. Most poems run 8-15 lines. Pays up to $3/line.

HOW TO CONTACT Send submissions to: Art Submissions Coordinator, Cricket Media, 70 E. Lake St., Suite 800, Chicago IL 60601. Responds in 3-6 months to mss. Accepts queries by online submission form.

ILLUSTRATION "Please do not send original artwork. Send postcards, promotional brochures, or color photocopies. Be sure that each sample is marked with your name, address, phone number and website or blog. Art submissions will not be returned."

TERMS Byline given. Pays on publication. Sample copy available online. Guidelines available online.

TIPS Writers: "Read copies of back issues and current issues. Adhere to specified word limits. *Please* do not query." Would currently like to see more fantasy and science fiction. Illustrators: "Send only your best work and be able to reproduce that quality in assignments. Put name and address on *all* samples. Know a publication before you submit."

DEVOZINE

1908 Grand Ave., P.O. Box 340004, Nashville TN 37203-0004. **E-mail:** devozine@upperroom.org. **Website:** www.devozine.org. **Contact:** Sandy Miller, editor. *devozine*, published bimonthly, is a 64-page devotional magazine for youth (ages 14-19) and adults who care about youth. Offers meditations, scripture, prayers, poems, stories, songs, and feature articles to "aid youth in their prayer life, introduce them to spiritual disciplines, help them shape their concept of God, and encourage them in the life of discipleship."

NONFICTION Submit devotionals by mail or e-mail listed above. Submit feature article **queries** by e-mail to smiller@upperroom.org. Length: 150-250 words for devotionals; 500-600 words for feature articles. Pays $25-100.

POETRY Considers poetry by teens. Submit by postal mail with SASE, or by e-mail. Include name, age/birth date (if younger than 25), mailing address, e-mail address, phone number, and fax number (if available). Always publishes theme issues (available for SASE or online). Indicate theme you are writing for. Length: 10-20 lines/poem. Pays $25.

HOW TO CONTACT Accepts queries by mail, e-mail, online submission form.

DIG INTO HISTORY

Cricket Media, Inc., 70 E. Lake Street, #800m, Chicago IL 60601. **E-mail:** dig@cricketmedia.com. **Website:** www.cricketmedia.com. **Contact:** Rosalie F. Baker. *Dig into History* is a magazine on world history and archaeology for kids ages 10-14. Publishes engaging, accurate, educational stories about historical events and people. Its Let's Go Digging section includes articles on archaeological discoveries, as well as the people who discovered them and those who help to preserve them. Estab. 1999.

○ Kids who love DIG are seriously curious and want to immerse themselves in the world of the past. They love the thrill of being transported to ancient times and want to know more about what people did then and why they did it. They are particularly fascinated by traces of long-ago peoples and cultures that have been digging in the dirt and in historical records—and how these traces offer insights into how people live and act today.

FICTION Authentic historical and biographical fiction, adventure, and retold legends relating to the theme. Query by e-mail with brief cover letter, one-page outline, bibliography. Length: 750-1,000 words.

NONFICTION Query by e-mail with brief cover letter, one-page outline, bibliography. Length: 750-1000 words for feature articles; 250-500 words for supplemental nonfiction; up to 700 words for activities.

HOW TO CONTACT Send submissions to: Art Submissions Coordinator, Cricket Media, 70 E. Lake St., Suite 800, Chicago IL 60601. Buys print, digital, promotional rights. Three to six months Accepts queries by mail, e-mail.

ILLUSTRATION Illustrations are by assignment only. PLEASE DO NOT send original artwork. Send postcards, promotional brochures, or color photocopies. Be sure that each sample is marked with your name, address, phone number, and website or blog. Art submissions will not be returned.

TERMS Yes Pays after publication. Sample copy available online. Guidelines available online.

TIPS "We are looking for writers who can communicate world history and archaeological concepts in a conversational, interesting, informative, and accurate style for kids. Always welcome if authors can suggest where photography can be located to support their articles."

DRAMATICS MAGAZINE

Educational Theatre Association, 2343 Auburn Ave., Cincinnati OH 45219. (513)421-3900. **E-mail:** gbossler@schooltheatre.org. **Website:** schooltheatre.org. **Contact:** Gregory Bossler, editor-in-chief. *Dramatics* is for students (mainly high school age) and teachers of theater. The magazine wants student readers to grow as theater artists and become a more discerning and appreciative audience. Material is directed to both theater students and their teachers, with strong student slant. Tries to portray the theater community in all its diversity. Estab. 1929. Circ. 45,000.

FICTION Young adults: drama (one-act and full-length plays). "We prefer unpublished scripts that have been produced at least once." Does not want to see plays that show no understanding of the conventions of the theater. No plays for children, no Christmas or didactic "message" plays. Submit complete ms. Buys 5-9 plays/year. Emerging playwrights have better chances with résumé of credits. Length: 10 minutes to full length. Pays $100-500 for plays.

NONFICTION Needs how-to, profile. practical articles on acting, directing, design, production, and other facets of theater; career-oriented profiles of working theater professionals. Submit complete ms. Length: 750-3,000 words. Pays $50-500 for articles.

HOW TO CONTACT Publishes ms 3 months after acceptance. Accepts queries by mail, e-mail.

ILLUSTRATION Buys 3-8 illustrations/year. Works on assignment only. Arrange portfolio review; send résumé, promo sheets, and tearsheets. Responds only if interested. Samples returned with SASE; sample not filed. Credit line given. Pays up to $300 for illustrations.

PHOTOS Buys photos with accompanying ms only. Looking for "good-quality production or candid photography to accompany article. We very occasionally publish photo essays." Model/property release and captions required. Prefers hi-res JPG files. Will consider prints or transparencies. Query with résumé of credits. Responds only if interested.

TERMS Byline given. Pays on acceptance. Sample copy available for 9x12 SAE with 4-ounce first-class postage. Guidelines available for SASE.

TIPS "Obtain our writer's guidelines and look at recent back issues. The best way to break in is to know our audience—drama students, teachers, and others interested in theater—and write for them. Writers who have some practical experience in theater, especially in technical areas, have an advantage, but we'll work with anybody who has a good idea. Some freelancers have become regular contributors."

FACES

E-mail: faces@cricketmedia.com. **Website:** www. cricketmedia.com. "Published 9 times/year, *Faces* covers world culture for ages 9-14. It stands apart from other children's magazines by offering a solid look at 1 subject and stressing strong editorial content, color photographs throughout, and original illustrations. *Faces* offers an equal balance of feature articles and activities, as well as folktales and legends." Estab. 1984. Circ. 15,000.

FICTION Fiction accepted: retold legends, folktales, stories, and original plays from around the world, etc., relating to the theme. Needs ethnic. Query with cover letter, one-page outline, bibliography. Pays 20-25¢/word.

NONFICTION Needs historical, interview, personal experience, photo feature. feature articles (in-depth nonfiction highlighting an aspect of the featured culture, interviews, and personal accounts), 700-800 words; supplemental nonfiction (subjects directly and indirectly related to the theme), 300-600 words. Query by e-mail with cover letter, one-page outline, bibliography. Pays 20-25¢/word.

HOW TO CONTACT Send submissions to: Art Submissions Coordinator, Cricket Media, 70 E. Lake St., Suite 800, Chicago IL 60601.

ILLUSTRATION Illustrations are by assignment only. **PLEASE DO NOT** send original artwork. Send postcards, promotional brochures, or color photocopies. Be sure that each sample is marked with your name, address, phone number, and website or blog. Art submissions will not be returned.

TERMS Buys print, digital, promotional rights. Buys all rights. Byline given. Pays on publication. Offers 50% kill fee. 90-100% freelance written. Sample copy available online. Guidelines available online.

TIPS "Writers are encouraged to study past issues of the magazine to become familiar with our style and content. Writers with anthropological and/or travel experience are particularly encouraged; *Faces* is about world cultures. All feature articles, recipes, and activities are freelance contributions."

FCA MAGAZINE

Fellowship of Christian Athletes, 8701 Leeds Rd., Kansas City MO 64129. (816)921-0909; (800)289-0909. **Fax:** (816)921-8755. **E-mail:** mag@fca.org. **Website:** www.fca.org/mag. **Contact:** Clay Meyer, editor; Matheau Casner, creative director. Published 6 times/year. *FCA Magazine*'s mission is to serve as a ministry tool of the Fellowship of Christian Athletes by informing, inspiring and involving coaches, athletes and all whom they influence, that they may make an impact for Jesus Christ. Estab. 1959. Circ. 75,000.

NONFICTION Needs inspirational, personal experience, photo feature. Articles should be accompanied by at least 3 quality photos. Query and submit via e-mail. Length: 1,000-2,000 words. Pays $150-400 for assigned and unsolicited articles.

HOW TO CONTACT Responds to queries/mss in 3 months. Publishes ms an average of 4 months after acceptance.

PHOTOS Purchases photos separately. Looking for photos of sports action. Uses color prints and high resolution electronic files of 300 dpi or higher. State availability. Reviews contact sheets. Payment based on size of photo.

TERMS Buys first rights and second serial (reprint) rights. Byline given. Pays on publication. No kill fee. 50% freelance written. Prefers to work with published/established writers, but works with a growing number of new/unpublished writers each year. Sample copy for $2 and 9x12 SASE with 3 first-class stamps. Guidelines available at www.fca.org/mag/media-kit.

TIPS "Profiles and interviews of particular interest to coed athlete, primarily high school and college age. Our graphics and editorial content appeal to youth. The area most open to freelancers is profiles on or interviews with well-known athletes or coaches (male, female, minorities) who have been or are involved in some capacity with FCA."

THE FRIEND MAGAZINE

The Church of Jesus Christ of Latter-day Saints, 50 E. North Temple St., Salt Lake City UT 84150. (801)240-2210. **Fax:** (801)240-2270. **E-mail:** friend@ldschurch.org. **Website:** www.lds.org/friend. **Contact:** Paul B. Pieper, editor; Mark W. Robison, art director. Monthly magazine for 3-12 year olds. "The *Friend* is published by The Church of Jesus Christ of Latter-day Saints for boys and girls up to 3-12 years of age." Estab. 1971.

FICTION Wants illustrated stories and "For Little Friends" stories. See guidelines online.

NONFICTION Needs historical, humor, inspirational.

POETRY Pays $30 for poems.

ILLUSTRATION Illustrations only: Query with samples; arrange personal interview to show portfolio; provide résumé and tearsheets for files.

TERMS Available online.

FUN FOR KIDZ

P.O. Box 227, Bluffton OH 45817. 419-358-4610. **Website:** funforkidz.com. **Contact:** Marilyn Edwards, articles editor. "*Fun For Kidz* is an activity magazine that maintains the same wholesome values as the other publications. Each issue is also created around a theme. There is nothing in the magazine to make it out dated. *Fun For Kidz* offers creative activities for children with extra time on their hands." Estab. 2002.

NONFICTION picture-oriented material, young readers, middle readers: animal, arts/crafts, cooking, games/puzzles, history, hobbies, how-to, humorous, problem-solving, sports, carpentry projects. Submit complete ms with SASE, contact info, and notation of which upcoming theme your content should be considered for. Length: 300-750 words. Pays minimum 5¢/word for articles; variable rate for games and projects, etc.

HOW TO CONTACT Accepts queries by mail.

ILLUSTRATION Works on assignment mostly. "We are anxious to find artists capable of illustrating stories and features. Our inside art is pen and ink." Query with samples. Samples kept on file. Pays $35 for full page and $25 for partial page.

PHOTOS "We use a number of b&w photos inside the magazine; most support the articles used." Photos should be in color. Pays $5 per photo.

TERMS Buys first North American serial rights. By-line given. Pays on acceptance. Sample copy: $6 in U.S., $9 in Canada, and $12.25 internationally. Guidelines online.

TIPS "Our point of view is that every child deserves the right to be a child for a number of years before he or she becomes a young adult. As a result, *Fun for Kidz* looks for activities that deal with timeless topics, such as pets, nature, hobbies, science, games, sports, careers, simple cooking, and anything else likely to interest a child."

GIRLS' LIFE

3 S. Frederick St., Suite 806, Baltimore MD 21202. (410)426-9600. **Fax:** (866)793-1531. **Website:** www.girlslife.com. **Contact:** Karen Bokram, founding editor and publisher; Kelsey Haywood, senior editor; Chun Kim, art director. Bimonthly magazine covering girls ages 9-15. Estab. 1994. Circ. 2.16 million.

FICTION "We accept short fiction. They should be stand-alone stories and are generally 2,500-3,500 words." Needs short stories.

NONFICTION Needs book excerpts, essays, general interest, how-to, humor, inspirational, interview, new product, travel. Query by mail with published clips. Submit complete ms on spec only. "Features and articles should speak to young women ages 10-15 looking for new ideas about relationships, family, friends, school, etc. with fresh, savvy advice. Front-of-the-book columns and quizzes are a good place to start." Length: 700-2,000 words. Pays $350/regular column; $500/feature.

HOW TO CONTACT Editorial lead time 4 months. Responds in 1 month to queries. Publishes an average of 3 months after acceptance. Accepts queries by mail, e-mail.

PHOTOS State availability with submission if applicable. Reviews contact sheets, negatives, transparencies. Negotiates payment individually. Captions, identification of subjects, model releases required. State availability. Captions, identification of subjects, model releases required. Reviews contact sheets, negatives, transparencies. Negotiates payment individually.

TERMS Buys all rights. Byline given. Pays on publication. Sample copy for $5 or online. Guidelines online.

TIPS "Send thought-out queries with published writing samples and detailed résumé. Have fresh ideas and a voice that speaks to our audience—not down to them. And check out a copy of the magazine or visit girlslife.com before submitting."

⚙ GREEN TEACHER

Green Teacher, 95 Robert St., Toronto ON M5S 2K5, Canada. (416)960-1244. **Fax:** (416)925-3474. **E-mail:** tim@greenteacher.com; info@greenteacher.com. **Website:** www.greenteacher.com. **Contact:** Tim Grant, co-editor; Amy Stubbs, editorial assistant. "We're a nonprofit organization dedicated to helping educators, both inside and outside of schools, promote environmental awareness among young people aged 6-19." Estab. 1991. Circ. 15,000.

NONFICTION Multicultural, nature, environment. Query. Submit one-page summary or outline. Length: 1,500-3,500 words.

HOW TO CONTACT Responds to queries in 1 week. Publishes ms 8 months after acceptance. Accepts queries by mail, e-mail.

ILLUSTRATION Buys 3 illustrations/issue from freelancers; 10 illustrations/year from freelancers. B&w artwork only. Works on assignment only. Reviews ms/illustration packages from artists. Query with samples; tearsheets. Responds only if interested. Samples not returned. Samples filed. Credit line given.

PHOTOS Purchases photos both separately and with accompanying mss. "Activity photos, environmental photos." Query with samples. Responds only of interested.

GUIDE

Pacific Press Publishing Association, P.O. Box 5353, Nampa ID 83653. (208)465-2579. **E-mail:** guide@pacificpress.com. **Website:** www.guidemagazine.org. **Contact:** Randy Fishell, editor; Brandon Reese, designer. *Guide* is a Christian story magazine for young people ages 10-14. The 32-page, 4-color publication is published weekly by the Pacific Press. Their mission is to show readers, through stories that illustrate Bible truth, how to walk with God now and forever. Estab. 1953.

NONFICTION Needs humor, personal experience, religious. Send complete ms. "Each issue includes 3-4 true stories. *Guide* does not publish fiction, poetry, or articles (devotionals, how-to, profiles, etc.). However, we sometimes accept quizzes and other unique nonstory formats. Each piece should include a clear spiritual element." Looking for pieces on adventure, personal growth, Christian humor, inspiration, biography, story series, and nature. Length: 1,000-1,200 words. Pays 7-10¢/word.

HOW TO CONTACT Responds in 6 weeks to mss. Accepts queries by mail, e-mail.

TERMS Buys first serial rights. Byline given. Pays on acceptance. Sample copy free with 6x9 SAE and 2 first-class stamps. Guidelines available on website.

TIPS "Children's magazines want mystery, action, discovery, suspense, and humor—no matter what the topic. For us, truth is stronger than fiction."

HIGHLIGHTS FOR CHILDREN

803 Church St., Honesdale PA 18431. (570)253-1080. **Fax:** (570)251-7847. **E-mail:** eds@highlights.com (Do not send submissions to this address.). **Website:** www.highlights.com. **Contact:** Christine French Cully, Editor in Chief. Monthly magazine for children ages 6-12. "This book of wholesome fun is dedicated to helping children grow in basic skills and knowledge, in creativeness, in ability to think and reason, in sensitivity to others, in high ideals, and worthy ways of living—for children are the world's most important people. We publish stories and articles for beginning and advanced readers. Up to 400 words for beginning readers, up to 750 words for advanced readers." Estab. 1946. Circ. Approximately 1 million..

FICTION Stories appealing to girls and boys ages 6-12. Vivid, full of action. Engaging plot, strong characterization, lively language. Prefers stories in which a child protagonist solves a dilemma through his or her own resources. No stories glorifying war, crime or violence. See Highlights.submittable.com. Up to 475 words for beginning readers. Up to 750 words for advanced readers. Pays $175 and up.

NONFICTION See guidelines at Highlights.submittable.com. Up to 400 words for beginning readers. Up to 750 words for advanced readers. Pays $175 and up for articles; pays $40 and up for crafts, activities, and puzzles.

POETRY See Highlights.submittable.com. No previously published poetry. Buys all rights. 16 lines maximum. Pays $50 and up.

HOW TO CONTACT Responds in 2 months. Accepts queries by online submission form.

TERMS Buys all rights. Byline given. Pays on acceptance. 70% freelance written. Guidelines on Highlights.submittable.com.

TIPS "We update our guidelines and current needs regularly at Highlights.submittable.com. Read several recent issues of the magazine before submitting. In addition to fiction, nonfiction, and poetry, we purchase crafts, puzzles, and activities that will stimulate children mentally and creatively. We judge each submission on its own merits. Expert reviews and complete bibliography are required for nonfiction. Include special qualifications, if any, of author. Speak to today's kids. Avoid didactic, overt messages. Even though our general principles haven't changed over the years, we are contemporary in our approach to issues."

HUNGER MOUNTAIN

Vermont College of Fine Arts, 36 College St., Montpelier VT 05602. (802)828-8517. **E-mail:** hungermtn@vcfa.edu. **Website:** www.hungermtn.org. "We accept picture book, middle grade, YA, and YA crossover work (text only—for now). We're looking for polished pieces that entertain, that show the range of adolescent experience, and that are compelling, creative, and will appeal to the devoted followers of the kid-lit craft, as well as the child inside us all." Editor: Miciah Gault. **Contact:** Cameron Finch, managing editor. Annual perfect-bound journal covering high-quality fiction, poetry, creative nonfiction, craft essays, writing for children, and artwork. Four contests held annually, one in each genre. Accepts high-quality work from unknown, emerging, or successful writers. Publishing fiction, creative nonfiction, poetry, and young adult & children's writing. Four writing contests annually. *Hunger Mountain* is a print and online journal of the arts. The print journal is about 200 pages, 7x9, professionally printed, perfect-bound, with full-bleed color artwork on cover. Press run is 1,000. Over 10,000 visits online monthly. Uses online submissions manager (Submittable). Member: CLMP. Estab. 2002. Circ. 1,000.

FICTION "We look for work that is beautifully crafted and tells a good story, with characters that are alive and kicking, storylines that stay with us long after we've finished reading, and sentences that slay us with their precision." Needs experimental, humorous, novel excerpts, short stories, slice-of-life vignettes. No genre fiction, meaning science fiction, fantasy, horror, detective, erotic, etc. Submit ms using online submissions manager: https://hungermtn.submittable.com/submit. Length: up to 10,000 words. Pays $50 for general fiction.

NONFICTION "We welcome an array of traditional and experimental work, including, but not limited to, personal, lyrical, and meditative essays, memoirs, collages, rants, and humor. The only requirements are recognition of truth, a unique voice with a firm command of language, and an engaging story with multiple pressure points." Submit complete ms using online submissions manager at Submittable. Length: up to 10,000 words. Pays $50 for general fiction or creative nonfiction, for both children's lit and general adult lit.

POETRY Submit 1-5 poems at a time. "We are looking for truly original poems that run the aesthetic gamut: lively engagement with language in the act of pursuit. Some poems remind us in a fresh way of our own best thoughts; some poems bring us to a place beyond language for which there aren't quite words; some poems take us on a complicated language ride that is, itself, its own aim. Complex poem-architectures thrill us and still-points in the turning world do, too. Send us the best of what you have." Submit using online submissions manager. No light verse, humor/quirky/catchy verse, greeting card verse. Pays $25 for poetry up to 2 poems (plus $5/poem for additional poems).

HOW TO CONTACT Responds in 4 months to mss. Publishes ms an average of 1 year after acceptance. Accepts queries by online submission form.

PHOTOS Send photos.

TERMS Buys first worldwide serial rights. Byline given. Pays on publication. No kill fee. Single issue: $12; subscription: $18 for 2 issues/2 years; back issue: $8. Checks payable to Vermont College of Fine Arts, or purchase online. Guidelines online.

TIPS "Mss must be typed, prose double-spaced. Poets submit poems as one document. No multiple genre submissions. Fresh viewpoints and human interest are very important, as is originality and diversity. We are committed to publishing an outstanding journal of the arts. Do not send entire novels, mss, or short story collections. Do not send previously published work."

IMAGINATION CAFÉ

Imagination Café, P.O. Box 1536, Valparaiso IN 46384. (219)510-4467. **E-mail:** editor@imagination-cafe.com. **Website:** www.imagination-cafe.com. **Contact:** Rosanne Tolin, contact. "*Imagination Café* is dedicated to empowering kids and tweens by encouraging curiosity in the world around them, as well as exploration of their talents and aspirations. *Imagination Café*'s mission is to offer children tools to discover their passions by providing them with reliable information, resources and safe opportunities for self-expression." Estab. 2006.

NONFICTION Manuscripts are preferred over queries. Varies. Under 1,000 words.

HOW TO CONTACT Accepts queries by e-mail.

PHOTOS

JACK AND JILL

U.S. Kids, P.O. Box 88928, Indianapolis IN 46208. (317)634-1100. **E-mail:** jackandjill@uskidsmags.com. **Website:** www.uskidsmags.com. Bimonthly magazine published for children ages 6-12. *Jack and Jill* is an award-winning magazine for children ages 6-12. It promotes the healthy educational and creative growth of children through interactive activities and articles. The pages are designed to spark a child's curiosity in a wide range of topics through articles, games, and activities. Inside you will find: current real-world topics in articles in stories; challenging puzzles and games; and interactive entertainment through experimental crafts and recipes. Please do not send artwork. "We prefer to work with professional illustrators of our own choosing. Write entertaining and imaginative stories for kids, not just about them. Writers should understand what is funny to kids, what's important to them, what excites them. Don't write from an adult 'kids are so cute' perspective. We're also looking for health and healthful lifestyle stories and articles, but don't be preachy." Estab. 1938. Circ. 40,000.

FICTION Submit complete ms via postal mail; no e-mail submissions. The tone of the stories should be fun and engaging. Stories should hook readers right from the get-go and pull them through the story. Humor is very important! Dialogue should be witty instead of just furthering the plot. The story should convey some kind of positive message. Possible themes could include self-reliance, being kind to others, appreciating other cultures, and so on. There are a million positive messages, so get creative! Kids can see preachy coming from a mile away, though, so please focus on telling a good story over teaching a lesson. The message—if there is one—should come organically from the story and not feel tacked on. Length: 600-800 words. Pays $25 minimum.

NONFICTION Submit complete ms via postal mail; no e-mail submissions. Queries not accepted. We are especially interested in features or Q&As with regular kids (or groups of kids) in the *Jack and Jill* age group who are engaged in unusual, challenging, or interesting activities. No celebrity pieces, please. Length: up to 700 words. Pays $25 minimum.

POETRY Submit via postal mail; no e-mail submissions. Wants light-hearted poetry appropriate for the age group. Mss must be typewritten with poet's contact information in upper-right corner of each poem's page. SASE required. Length: up to 30 lines/poem. Pays $25-50.

HOW TO CONTACT Responds to mss in 3 months. Publishes ms an average of 8 months after acceptance. Accepts queries by mail.

TERMS Buys all rights. Byline given. Pays on publication. 50% freelance written. Guidelines online.

TIPS "We are constantly looking for new writers who can tell good stories with interesting slants—stories that are not full of outdated and time-worn expressions. We like to see stories about kids who are smart and capable but not sarcastic or smug. Problem-solving skills, personal responsibility, and integrity are good topics for us. Obtain current issues of the magazine and study them to determine our present needs and editorial style."

JUNIOR BASEBALL

JSAN Publishing LLC, 14 Woodway Ln., Wilton CT 06897. **E-mail:** publisher@juniorbaseball.com. **Website:** www.juniorbaseball.com. **Contact:** Jim Beecher, editor and publisher. Bimonthly magazine focused on youth baseball players ages 7-17 (including high school) and their parents/coaches. Edited to various reading levels, depending upon age/skill level of feature. Estab. 1996. Circ. 20,000.

NONFICTION Query. Length: 500-1,000 words. Pays $50-100.

HOW TO CONTACT Editorial lead time 3 months. Responds in 2 weeks to queries; in 1 month to mss. Publishes ms an average of 4 months after acceptance. Accepts queries by e-mail.

PHOTOS Photos can be e-mailed in 300 dpi JPEGs. State availability. Captions, identification of subjects required. Offers $10-100/photo; negotiates payment individually.

TERMS Buys all rights. Byline given. Pays on publication. No kill fee. 25% freelance written. Sample copy: $5 or free online.

TIPS "Must be well-versed in baseball! Have a child who is very involved in the sport, or have extensive hands-on experience in coaching baseball at the youth, high school, or higher level. We can always use accurate, authoritative skills information, and good photos to accompany is a big advantage! This magazine is read by experts. No fiction, poems, games, puzzles, etc."

KEYS FOR KIDS DEVOTIONAL

Keys for Kids Ministries, 2060 43rd St. SE, Grand Rapids MI 49508. **E-mail:** editorial@keysforkids.org. **Website:** www.keysforkids.org. **Contact:** Courtney Lasater, editor. Daily devotional featuring stories and Scripture verses for children ages 6-12 that help kids dig into God's Word and apply it to their lives. Please put your name and contact information on the first page of your submission. We strongly prefer receiving submissions via our website. Story length is typically 340-375 words. To see full guidelines or submit a story, please go to www.keysforkids.org/writersguidelines. Estab. 1982. Circ. 50,000 print (not including digital circulation).

FICTION Need short contemporary stories with spiritual applications for kids. Please suggest a key verse and an appropriate Scripture passage, generally 3-10 verses, to reinforce the theme of your story. Length: Up to 375 words. Pays $30.

HOW TO CONTACT Editorial lead time 6-8 months. Responds in 2-4 months. Typically publishes stories 6-9 months after acceptance. Accepts queries by e-mail, online submission form.

TERMS Buys all rights. Byline given. Pays on acceptance. 95% freelance. Sample copy online Guidelines online

LADYBUG

Website: www.cricketmag.com. *Ladybug* magazine is an imaginative magazine with art and literature for young children ages 3-6. Publishes 9 issues/year. Estab. 1990. Circ. 125,000.

FICTION imaginative contemporary stories, original retellings of fairy and folk tales, multicultural stories. Submit via online submissions manager: cricket.submittable.com. Length: up to 800 words. Pays up to 25¢/word.

NONFICTION Seeks "simple explorations of interesting places in a young child's world (such as the library and the post office), different cultures, nature,

and science. These articles can be straight nonfiction, or they may include story elements, such as a fictional child narrator." Submit via online submissions manager: cricketmag.submittable.com. Length: up to 400 words. Pays up to 25¢/word.

POETRY Wants poetry that is "rhythmic, rhyming; serious, humorous." Submit via online submissions manager: cricket.submittable.com. Length: up to 20 lines/poem. Pays up to $3/line ($25 minimum).

HOW TO CONTACT Send submissions to: Art Submissions Coordinator, Cricket Media, 70 E. Lake St., Suite 800, Chicago IL 60601. Please allow 3-6 months response time. Responds in 6 months to mss. Accepts queries by online submission form.

ILLUSTRATION Prefers "bright colors; all media, but uses watercolor and acrylics most often; same size as magazine is preferred but not required." To be considered for future assignments: "Please do not send original artwork. Send postcards, promotional brochures, or color photocopies. Be sure that each sample is marked with your name, address, phone number and website or blog. Art submissions will not be returned."

TERMS Acquires print and digital rights, plus promotional rights. Byline given. Pays on publication. Guidelines available online.

LEADING EDGE MAGAZINE

4087 JKB, Provo UT 84602. **E-mail:** editor@leadingedgemagazine.com; fiction@leadingedgemagazine.com; art@leadingedgemagazine.com; poetry@leadingedgemagazine.com; nonfiction@leadingedgemagazine.com. **Website:** www.leadingedgemagazine.com. **Contact:** Heather White, editor-in-chief. Semiannual magazine covering science fiction and fantasy. "*Leading Edge* is a magazine dedicated to new and upcoming talent in the fields of science fiction and fantasy. We strive to encourage developing and established talent and provide high-quality speculative fiction to our readers." Does not accept mss with sex, excessive violence, or profanity. Accepts unsolicited submissions. Estab. 1981. Circ. 200.

FICTION Needs fantasy, science fiction. Send complete ms with cover letter and SASE. Include estimated word count. Length: up to 15,000 words. Pays 1¢/word; $50 maximum.

NONFICTION Needs essays, expose, interview, reviews. Send complete ms with cover letter and SASE.

Include estimated word count. Length: up to 15,000 words. Pays 1¢/word; $50 maximum.

POETRY Publishes 2-4 poems per issue. Poetry should reflect both literary value and popular appeal and should deal with science fiction- or fantasy-related themes. No e-mail submissions. Cover letter is preferred. Include name, address, phone number, length of poem, title, and type of poem at the top of each page. Please include SASE with every submission. Pays $10 for first 4 pages; $1.50/each subsequent page.

HOW TO CONTACT Responds within 12 months to mss. Publishes ms an average of 2-4 months after acceptance. Accepts queries by mail, e-mail.

ILLUSTRATION Buys 24 illustrations/issue; 48 illustrations/year. Uses b&w artwork only. Works on assignment only. Contact: Art Director. Illustrations only: Send postcard sample with portfolio, samples, URL. Responds only if interested. Samples filed. Credit line given.

TERMS Buys first North American serial rights. Byline given. Pays on publication. No kill fee. 90% freelance written. Single copy: $5.95. "We no longer provide subscriptions, but *Leading Edge* is now available on Amazon Kindle, as well as print-on-demand." Guidelines online.

TIPS "Buy a sample issue to know what is currently selling in our magazine. Also, make sure to follow the writer's guidelines when submitting."

THE LOUISVILLE REVIEW

Spalding University, 851 S. Fourth St., Louisville KY 40203. (502)873-4398. **Fax:** (502)992-2409. **E-mail:** louisvillereview@spalding.edu. **Website:** www.louisvillereview.org. **Contact:** Ellyn Lichvar, managing editor. *The Louisville Review*, published twice/year, prints poetry, fiction, nonfiction, and drama. Has a section devoted to poetry by writers under age 18 (grades K-12) called "The Children's Corner." *The Louisville Review* is 150 pages, digest-sized, flat-spined. Receives about 700 submissions/year, accepts about 10%. Estab. 1976.

FICTION Needs novel excerpts, short stories. Submit complete ms by mail or online submissions manager. Also publishes plays. No word limit, but prefers shorter pieces. Pays contributor's copies.

NONFICTION Needs essays. Submit via online submissions manager. No word limit, but prefers shorter pieces. Pays contributor's copies.

POETRY Accepts submissions via online manager; please see website for more information. "Poetry by children must include permission of parent to publish if accepted. Address those submissions to 'The Children's Corner.'" Reads submissions year round. Has published poetry by Wendy Bishop, Gary Fincke, Michael Burkard, and Sandra Kohler. Pays contributor's copies.

HOW TO CONTACT Responds in 3-6 months to mss. Accepts queries by e-mail.

TERMS Sample copy: $5. Single copy: $8. Subscription: $14/year, $27/2 years, $40/3 years (foreign subscribers add $6/year for s&h). Guidelines online.

MAGIC DRAGON

Association for Encouragement of Children's Creativity, P.O. Box 687, Webster NY 14580. **E-mail:** magicdragonmagazine@gmail.com; info.@magicdragonmagazine.com. **Website:** www.magicdragonmagazine.com. **Contact:** Patricia A. Roesch. Quarterly magazine publishes children's writing and art (no photography). "All work is created by children age 12 and younger (elementary school grades). We consider stories, poems, and artwork. Queries, writing, and art accepted by USPS mail and by e-mail." Nonprofit, educational magazine. Estab. 2005. Circ. 3,500.

Ⓞ Magic Dragon exists solely to encourage creative expression in young children and to support the arts in education.

FICTION Needs adventure, fantasy, historical, humorous. Submit complete ms. Pays 1 contributor's copy.

NONFICTION Needs essays, humor, inspirational, personal experience. Send complete ms. Length: up to 250 words. Pays 1 contributor's copy.

POETRY Length: up to 30 lines/poem. Pays 1 contributor's copy.

HOW TO CONTACT Editorial lead time 3-6 months. Time between acceptance and publication varies. Accepts queries by mail, e-mail.

TERMS No rights purchased. Byline given. Pays contributor's copy on publication. No kill fee. No freelance. Sample: $4. Guidelines available online.

Submit writing as Word document or Word document attachment, 12 point New Times Roman or carefully printed; art as jpeg or original. Include stamped, self-addressed envelope for return of art. Be sure postage is adequate.

TIPS "Artists: Include an SASE with adequate postage with all original artwork. If it's a copy, make sure the colors and copy are the same and the lines are clear. Include an explanation of how you created the art (crayon, watercolor, paper sculpture, etc.)."

MUSE

E-mail: muse@cricketmedia.com. **Website:** www.cricketmag.com. "The goal of *Muse* is to give as many children as possible access to the most important ideas and concepts underlying the principal areas of human knowledge. Articles should meet the highest possible standards of clarity and transparency, aided, wherever possible, by a tone of skepticism, humor, and irreverence." Estab. 1996. Circ. 40,000.

FICTION Needs science fiction. Query with published clips. Length: 1,000-1,600 words

NONFICTION Needs interview, photo feature, profile. entertaining stories from the fields of science, technology, engineering, art, and math. Query by e-mail with published clips. Length: 1,200-1,800 words for features; 500-800 words for profiles and interviews; 100-300 words for photo essays.

HOW TO CONTACT Send submissions to: Art Submissions Coordinator, Cricket Media, 70 E. Lake St., Suite 800, Chicago IL 60601. Accepts queries by e-mail.

ILLUSTRATION Illustrations are by assignment only. PLEASE DO NOT send original artwork. Send postcards, promotional brochures, or color photocopies. Be sure that each sample is marked with your name, address, phone number, and website or blog. Art submissions will not be returned.

NATIONAL GEOGRAPHIC KIDS

National Geographic Society, 1145 17th St. NW, Washington DC 20036. **E-mail:** ashaw@ngs.org. **Website:** www.kids.nationalgeographic.com. **Contact:** Michelle Tyler, editorial assistant. Magazine published 10 times/year. "It's our mission to find fresh ways to entertain children while educating and exciting them about their world." Estab. 1975. Circ. 1.3 million.

○ "We do not want poetry, sports, fiction, or story ideas that are too young—our audience is between ages 6-14."

NONFICTION Needs general interest, humor, interview, technical. Query with published clips and résumé. Length: 100-1,000 words. Pays $1/word for assigned articles.

HOW TO CONTACT Editorial lead time 6+ months. Publishes ms an average of 6 months after acceptance. Accepts queries by mail.

PHOTOS State availability. Captions, identification of subjects, model releases required. Reviews contact sheets, negatives, transparencies, prints. Negotiates payment individually.

TERMS Buys all rights. Makes work-for-hire assignments. Byline given. Pays on acceptance. Offers 10% kill fee. 70% freelance written. Sample copy for #10 SASE. Guidelines online.

TIPS "Submit relevant clips. Writers must have demonstrated experience writing for kids. Read the magazine before submitting."

NATURE FRIEND MAGAZINE

4253 Woodcock Lane, Dayton VA 22821. (540)867-0764. **E-mail:** info@naturefriendmagazine.com; editor@naturefriendmagazine.com; photos@naturefriendmagazine.com. **Website:** www.naturefriendmagazine.com. **Contact:** Kevin Shank, editor. Monthly children's magazine covering creation-based nature. *Nature Friend* includes stories, puzzles, science experiments, and nature experiments. All submissions need to honor God as creator. Estab. 1983. Circ. 8,000.

○ Picture-oriented material and conversational material needed.

NONFICTION Needs how-to. Send complete ms. Length: 250-900 words. Pays 5¢/word.

HOW TO CONTACT Editorial lead time 4 months. Responds in 6 months to mss.

PHOTOS Send photos. Captions, identification of subjects required. Reviews prints. Offers $20-75/photo.

TERMS Buys first rights, buys one-time rights. Byline given. Pays on publication. No kill fee. 80% freelance written. Sample copy: $5, postage paid. Guidelines available on website.

TIPS "We want to bring joy and knowledge to children by opening the world of God's creation to them. We endeavor to create a sense of awe about nature's Creator and a respect for His creation. We'd like to see more submissions on hands-on things to do with a nature theme (not collecting rocks or leaves—real stuff). Also looking for good stories that are accompanied by good photography."

POCKETS

The Upper Room, P.O. Box 340004, Nashville TN 37203. (615)340-7333. **E-mail:** pockets@upperroom. org. **Website:** pockets.upperroom.org. **Contact:** Lynn W. Gilliam, editor. Magazine published 11 times/ year. "*Pockets* is a Christian devotional magazine for children ages 6-12. All submissions should address the broad theme of the magazine. Each issue is built around a theme with material which can be used by children in a variety of ways. Scripture stories, fiction, poetry, prayers, art, graphics, puzzles and activities are included. Submissions do not need to be overtly religious. They should help children experience a Christian lifestyle that is not always a neatly wrapped moral package but is open to the continuing revelation of God's will. Seasonal material, both secular and liturgical, is desired." Estab. 1981.

○ Does not accept e-mail or fax submissions.

FICTION "Stories should contain lots of action, use believable dialogue, be simply written, and be relevant to the problems faced by this age group in everyday life." Submit complete ms by mail. No e-mail submissions. Length: 600-1,000 words.

NONFICTION Picture-oriented, young readers, middle readers: cooking, games/puzzles. Submit complete ms by mail. No e-mail submissions. Length: 400-1,000 words. Pays 14¢/word.

POETRY Both seasonal and theme poems needed. Considers poetry by children. Length: up to 20 lines. Pays $25 minimum.

HOW TO CONTACT Responds in 8 weeks to mss. Publishes ms an average of 1 year after acceptance.

PHOTOS Send 4-6 close-up photos of children actively involved in peacemakers at work activities. Send photos, contact sheets, prints, or digital images. Must be 300 dpi. Pays $25/photo.

TERMS Buys first North American serial rights. Byline given. Pays on acceptance. No kill fee. 60% freelance written. Each issue reflects a specific theme. Guidelines online.

TIPS "Theme stories, role models, and retold scripture stories are most open to freelancers. Poetry is also open. It is very helpful if writers read our writers' guidelines and themes on our website."

RAINBOW RUMPUS

P.O. Box 6881, Minneapolis MN 55406. **Website:** www.rainbowrumpus.org. **Contact:** Liane Bonin Starr, editor in chief and fiction editor. "*Rainbow Rumpus* is the world's only online literary magazine for children and youth with lesbian, gay, bisexual, and transgender (LGBT) parents. We are creating a new genre of children's and young adult fiction. Please carefully read and observe the guidelines on our website." Estab. 2005. Circ. 300 visits/day.

FICTION "Stories should be written from the point of view of children or teens with lesbian, gay, bisexual, or transgender parents or other family members, or who are connected to the LGBT community. Stories featuring families of color, bisexual parents, transgender parents, family members with disabilities, and mixed-race families are particularly welcome." Query editor through website's Contact page. Be sure to select the Submissions category. Length: 800-2,500 words for stories for 4- to 12-year-olds; up to 5,000 words for stories for 13- to 18-year-olds. Pays $300/ story.

ILLUSTRATION Buys 1 illustration/issue. Uses both b&w and color artwork. Reviews ms/illustration packages from artists: Query. Illustrations only: Query with samples. Contact: Beth Wallace, fiction editor. Samples not returned; samples filed depending on the level of interest. Credit line given.

TERMS Buys first North American online rights for mss; may request print anthology and audio or Buys recording rights. Byline given. Pays on publication. Guidelines available online.

TIPS "Emerging writers encouraged to submit. You do not need to be a member of the LGBT community to participate."

SCIENCE WEEKLY

P.O. Box 70638, Chevy Chase MD 20813. (301)680-8804. **E-mail:** info@scienceweekly.com. **Website:** www.scienceweekly.com. **Contact:** Dr. Claude Mayberry, publisher. *Science Weekly* uses freelance writers to develop and write an entire issue on a single science topic. Send résumé only, not submissions. Authors preferred within the greater D.C./Virginia/Maryland area. *Science Weekly* works on assignment only. Estab. 1984. Circ. 200,000.

○ Submit résumé only.

NONFICTION young readers, middle readers (K-6th grade): science/math education, education, problem-solving.

TERMS Pays on publication. Sample copy free online.

❶ SEVENTEEN MAGAZINE

300 W. 57th St., 17th Floor, New York NY 10019. (917)934-6500. **Fax:** (917)934-6574. **E-mail:** mail@ seventeen.com. **Website:** www.seventeen.com. **Contact:** Consult masthead to contact appropriate editor. Monthly magazine covering topics geared toward young adult American women. "We reach 14.5 million girls each month. Over the past 6 decades, *Seventeen* has helped shape teenage life in America. We represent an important rite of passage, helping to define, socialize, and empower young women. We create notions of beauty and style, proclaim what's hot in popular culture, and identify social issues." Estab. 1944. Circ. 2,000,000.

○ *Seventeen* no longer accepts fiction submissions.

NONFICTION Query by mail. Consult masthead to pitch appropriate editor. Length: 200-2,000 words.

HOW TO CONTACT Accepts queries by mail.

ILLUSTRATION *Only interested in agented material.* Buys 10 illustrations/issue; 120 illustrations/year. Works on assignment only. Reviews ms/illustration packages. Illustrations only: Query with samples. Responds only if interested. Samples not returned; samples filed. Credit line given.

PHOTOS Looking for photos to match current stories. Model/property releases required; captions required. Uses color, 8×10 prints; 35mm, 2¼×2¼, 4×5, or 8×10 transparencies. Query with samples or résumé of credits, or submit portfolio for review. Responds only if interested.

TERMS Buys first North American serial rights, first rights, or all rights. Buys exclusive rights for 3 months. Byline sometimes given. Pays on publication. Writer's guidelines for SASE.

TIPS "Send for guidelines before submitting."

SHINE BRIGHTLY

GEMS Girls' Clubs, 1333 Alger St., SE, Grand Rapids MI 49507. (616)241-5616. **Fax:** (616)241-5558. **E-mail:** shinebrightly@gemsgc.org. **Website:** www. gemsgc.org. **Contact:** Kelli Gilmore, managing editor. Monthly magazine from September to May with a double issue for September/October. "Our purpose is to lead girls into a living relationship with Jesus Christ and to help them see how God is at work in their lives and the world around them. Puzzles, crafts, stories, and articles for girls ages 9-14." Estab. 1970. Circ. 13,000.

FICTION Does not want "unrealistic stories and those with trite, easy endings. We are interested in manuscripts that show how real girls can change the world." Needs ethnic, historical, humorous, mystery, religious, slice-of-life vignettes. Believable only. Nothing too preachy. Submit complete ms in body of e-mail. No attachments. Length: 700-900 words. Pays up to $35, plus 2 copies.

NONFICTION Needs humor, inspirational, interview, personal experience, photo feature, religious, travel. Submit complete ms in body of e-mail. No attachments. Length: 100-800 words. Pays up to $35, plus 2 copies.

POETRY Limited need for poetry. Pays $5-15.

HOW TO CONTACT Responds in 2 months to mss. Publishes ms an average of 4 months after acceptance.

ILLUSTRATION Samples returned with SASE. Credit line given.

PHOTOS Purchased with or without ms. Appreciate multicultural subjects. Reviews 5x7 or 8x10 clear color glossy prints. Pays $25-50 on publication.

TERMS Buys first North American serial rights, buys second serial (reprint) rights, buys simultaneous rights. Byline given. Pays on publication. No kill fee. 60% freelance written. Works with new and published/established writers. Sample copy with 9x12 SASE with 3 first class stamps and $1. Guidelines online.

TIPS Writers: "Please check our website before submitting. We have a specific style and theme that deals with how girls can impact the world. The stories should be current, deal with pre-adolescent problems and joys, and help girls see God at work in their lives through humor as well as problem-solving." Prefers not to see anything on the adult level, secular material, or violence. Writers frequently oversimplify the articles and often write with a Pollyanna attitude. An author should be able to see his/her writing style as exciting and appealing to girls ages 9-14. The style can be fun, but also teach a truth. Subjects should be current and important to *SHINE brightly* readers. Use our theme update as a guide. We would like to receive material with a multicultural slant."

SKIPPING STONES

A Multicultural Literary Magazine, Skipping Stones. Inc., P.O. Box 3939, Eugene OR 97403-0939. (541)342-4956. **E-mail:** editor@skippingstones.org. **Website:** www.skippingstones.org. **Contact:** Arun Toké, edi-

MAGAZINES

tor. "*Skipping Stones* is an award-winning multicultural, nonprofit magazine designed to promote cooperation, creativity and celebration of cultural and ecological richness. We encourage submissions by children of color, minorities and under-represented populations. We want material meant for children and young adults/teenagers with multicultural or ecological awareness themes. Think, live and write as if you were a child, tween or teen. We want material that gives insight to cultural celebrations, lifestyle, customs and traditions, glimpse of daily life in other countries and cultures. Photos, songs, artwork are most welcome if they illustrate/highlight the points. Translations are invited if your submission is in a language other than English." Themes may include cultural celebrations, living abroad, challenging disability, hospitality customs of various cultures, cross-cultural understanding, African, Asian and Latin American cultures, humor, international understanding, turning points and magical moments in life, caring for the earth, spirituality, and multicultural awareness. *Skipping Stones* is magazine-sized, saddle-stapled, printed on recycled paper. Published quarterly during the school year (4 issues). Estab. 1988. Circ. 1,200 print, plus online and Web.

FICTION Middle readers, young adult/teens: contemporary, meaningful, humorous. All levels: folktales, multicultural, nature/environment. Multicultural needs include: bilingual or multilingual pieces; use of words from other languages; settings in other countries, cultures or multi-ethnic communities. Needs adventure, ethnic, historical, humorous. multicultural, international, social issues. No suspense or romance stories. Send complete ms. Length: 1,000 words maximum. Pays 6 contributor's copies.

NONFICTION Needs essays, general interest, humor, inspirational, interview, opinion, personal experience, photo feature, travel. All levels: animal, biography, cooking, games/puzzles, history, humorous, interview/profile, multicultural, nature/environment, creative problem-solving, religion and cultural celebrations, sports, travel, social and international awareness. Does not want to see preaching, violence or abusive language. Send complete ms. Length: 1,000 words maximum. Pays 6 contributor's copies.

POETRY Submit up to 5 poems at a time. Considers simultaneous submissions; no previously published poems. Accepts e-mail submissions. Cover letter is preferred. "Include your cultural background, experiences, and the inspiration behind your creation." Time between acceptance and publication is 6-9 months. "A piece is chosen for publication when most of the editorial staff feel good about it." Seldom comments on rejected poems. Publishes multi-theme issues. Responds in up to 4 months. Poems by youth under the age of 19 only. Length: 30 lines maximum. Pays 2 contributor's copies, offers 40% discount for more copies and subscription, if desired.

HOW TO CONTACT Editorial lead time 3-4 months. Responds only if interested. Send nonreturnable samples. Publishes ms an average of 4-8 months after acceptance. Accepts queries by mail, e-mail.

ILLUSTRATION Prefers illustrations by teenagers and young adults. Will consider all illustration packages. Manuscript/illustration packages: Query; submit complete ms with final art; submit tearsheets. Responds in 4 months. Credit line given.

PHOTOS Black & white photos preferred, but color photos with good contrast are welcome. Needs: youth 7-17, international, nature, celebrations. Send photos. Captions required. Reviews 4X6 prints, low-res JPEG files. Offers no additional payment for photos.

TERMS Buys first North American serial rights, non-exclusive reprint, and electronic rights. Byline given. No kill fee. 80% freelance written. Sample: $7. Subscription: $25. Guidelines available online or for SASE.

TIPS "Be original and innovative. Use multicultural, nature, or cross-cultural themes. Multilingual submissions are welcome."

SOUL FOUNTAIN

E-mail: soulfountain@antarcticajournal.com. **Website:** www.antarcticajournal.com/soul-fountain/. **Contact:** Tone Bellizzi, editor. *Soul Fountain* is produced by The Antarctica Journal, a not-for-profit arts project of the Hope for the Children Foundation, committed to empowering young and emerging artists of all disciplines at all levels to develop and share their talents through performance, collaboration, and networking. Digitally publishes poetry, art, photography, short fiction, and essays on the antarcticajournal.com website. Open to all. Publishes quality submitted work, and specializes in emerging voices. Favors visionary, challenging, and consciousness-expanding material. Estab. 1997.

FICTION Submit by e-mail only. No cover letters, please.

POETRY Submit 2-3 poems by e-mail. No cover letters, please. Does not want poems about pets, nature, romantic love, or the occult. Sex and violence themes not welcome. Welcomes poetry by teens.

HOW TO CONTACT Accepts queries by e-mail.

TERMS Guidelines online.

SPARKLE

GEMS Girls' Clubs, 1333 Alger St. SE, Grand Rapids MI 49507. (616)241-5616. **Fax:** (616)241-5558. **E-mail:** sparkle@gemsgc.org. **Website:** www.gemsgc.org. **Contact:** Kelli Gilmore, managing editor; Lisa Hunter, art director/photo editor. Monthly magazine for girls ages 6-9 from October to March. Mission is to prepare young girls to live out their faith and become world-changers. Strives to help girls make a difference in the world. Looks at the application of scripture to everyday life. Also strives to delight the reader and cause the reader to evalute her own life in light of the truth presented. Finally, attempts to teach practical life skills. Estab. 2002. Circ. 9,000.

FICTION Young readers: adventure, animal, contemporary, ethnic/multicultural, fantasy, folktale, health, history, humorous, music and musicians, mystery, nature/environment, problem-solving, religious, recipes, service projects, slice-of-life, sports, suspense/mystery, vignettes, interacting with family and friends. Send complete ms. Length: 100-400 words. Pays $35 maximum.

NONFICTION Young readers: animal, arts/crafts, biography, careers, cooking, concept, games/puzzles, geography, health, history, hobbies, how-to, humor, inspirational, interview/profile, math, multicultural, music/drama/art, nature/environment, personal experience, photo feature, problem-solving, quizzes, recipes, religious, science, social issues, sports, travel. Looking for inspirational biographies, stories from Zambia, and ideas on how to live a green lifestyle. Send complete ms. Length: 100-400 words. Pays $35 maximum.

POETRY Prefers rhyming. "We do not wish to see anything that is too difficult for a first grader to read. We wish it to remain light. The style can be fun but should also teach a truth." No violence or secular material.

HOW TO CONTACT Editorial lead time 3 months. Responds 3 months to mss. Accepts queries by e-mail.

ILLUSTRATION Buys 1-2 illustrations/issue; 8-10 illustrations/year. Uses color artwork only. Works on assignment only. Reviews ms/illustration packages from artists. Send ms with dummy. Illustrations only: send promo sheet. Contact: Sara DeRidder. Responds in 3 weeks only if interested. Samples returned with SASE; samples filed. Credit line given.

PHOTOS Send photos. Identification of subjects required. Reviews at least 5X7 clear color glossy prints, GIF/JPEG files on CD. Offers $25-50/photo.

TERMS Buys first North American serial rights, first rights, one-time rights, second serial (reprint), first rights, second rights. Byline given. Pays on publication. 40% freelance written. Sample copy for 9x13 SAE, 3 first-class stamps, and $1 for coverage/publication cost. Guidelines available for #10 SASE or online.

TIPS "Keep it simple. We are writing to first to third graders. It must be simple yet interesting. Mss should build girls up in Christian character but not be preachy. They are just learning about God and how He wants them to live. Mss should be delightful as well as educational and inspirational. Writers should keep stories simple but not write with a 'Pollyanna' attitude. Authors should see their writing style as exciting and appealing to girls ages 6-9. Subjects should be current and important to *Sparkle* readers. Use our theme as a guide. We would like to receive material with a multicultural slant."

SPIDER

Website: www.cricketmag.com. Monthly reading and activity magazine for children ages 6-9. "*Spider* introduces children to the highest-quality stories, poems, illustrations, articles, and activities. It was created to foster in beginning readers a love of reading and discovery that will last a lifetime. We're looking for writers who respect children's intelligence." Estab. 1994. Circ. 70,000.

FICTION Wants "complex and believable" stories. Needs fantasy, humorous. No romance, horror, religious. Submit complete ms via online submissions manager (cricketmag.submittable.com). Length: 300-1,000 words. Pays up to 25¢/word.

NONFICTION Submit complete ms via online submissions manager (cricketmag.submittable.com). Length: 300-800 words. Pays up to 25¢/word.

POETRY Submit up to 5 poems via online submissions manager (cricketmag.submittable.com). "Poems should be succinct, imaginative, and accessible; we tend to avoid long narrative poems." Length: up to 20 lines/poem. Pays up to $3/line.

HOW TO CONTACT Send submissions to: Art Submissions Coordinator, Cricket Media, 70 E. Lake St., Suite 800, Chicago IL 60601. Responds in 6 months to mss. Accepts queries by online submission form.

ILLUSTRATION "Please do not send original artwork. Send postcards, promotional brochures, or color photocopies. Be sure that each sample is marked with your name, address, phone number and website or blog. Art submissions will not be returned."

TERMS Rights purchased vary. Byline given. Pays on publication. 85% freelance written. Sample copy available online. Guidelines available online.

TIPS "We'd like to see more of the following: engaging nonfiction, fillers, and 'takeout page' activities; folktales, fairy tales, science fiction, and humorous stories. Most importantly, do not write down to children."

STONE SOUP

E-mail: editor@stonesoup.com. **Website:** https://stonesoup.com. **Contact:** Emma Wood, editor. Monthly magazine of writing and art by children age 13 and under, including fiction, poetry, book reviews, and art. We also publish blogposts by children and educators on our site. *Stone Soup*, a digital magazine with a print annual, is the national magazine of writing and art by kids, founded in 1973. Receives 5,000 poetry submissions/year, accepts about 20. Subscription: $24.99/year (U.S.). "We have a preference for writing and art based on real-life experiences; no formula stories or poems. We only publish writing by children up to (and including) age 13. We do not publish writing by adults." Subscription includes downloadable PDFs of each issue as well as more than 15 years of back issues online. Estab. 1973.

FICTION Needs adventure, ethnic, experimental, fantasy, historical, humorous, mystery, science fiction, slice-of-life vignettes, suspense. "We do not like assignments or formula stories of any kind." We only accept submissions through Submittable. Length: 150-5,000 words. Pays in a contributor copy of the print annual (a collection of the years' issues along with bonus content from the blogs), discounted subscription rates.

NONFICTION Needs historical, humor, memoir, personal experience, reviews. Submit complete ms; no SASE. Pays in a contributor copy of the print annual (a collection of the years' issues along with bonus content from the blogs), discounted subscription rates.

POETRY Prefers free verse but considers all kinds. Pays in a contributor copy of the print annual (a collection of the years' issues along with bonus content from the blogs), discounted subscription rates.

HOW TO CONTACT Publishes ms an average of 4 months after acceptance. Accepts queries by e-mail.

PHOTOS

TERMS Buys all rights. Pays on publication. 100% freelance written. View a PDF sample copy online. Guidelines online.

TIPS "All writing we publish is by young people ages 13 and under. We do not publish any writing by adults. We can't emphasize enough how important it is to read a couple of issues of the magazine. You can read stories and poems from past issues online. We have a strong preference for writing on subjects that mean a lot to the author. If you feel strongly about something that happened to you or something you observed, use that feeling as the basis for your story or poem. Stories should have good descriptions, realistic dialogue, and a point to make. In a poem, each word must be chosen carefully. Your poem should present a view of your subject, and a way of using words that are special and all your own."

TC MAGAZINE (TEENAGE CHRISTIAN)

HU Box 10750, Searcy AR 72149. (501)279-4530. **E-mail:** season@harding.edu. **Website:** www.tcmagazine.org. "*TC Magazine* is published by the Mitchell Center for Leadership & Ministry. We are dedicated to the idea that it is not only possible but entirely excellent to live in this world with a vibrant and thriving faith. That, and an awesome magazine." Estab. 1961.

NONFICTION Query or submit complete ms.

HOW TO CONTACT Accepts queries by e-mail.

ILLUSTRATION Works on assignment only. Send ms with dummy. Illustrations only. Responds only if interested.

PHOTOS Buys photos separately. Model/property release required. Uses hi-res color digital photos. E-mail. Responds only if interested.

TERMS Pays on publication. Guidelines available online.

YOUNG RIDER

2030 Main Street, Irvine CA 92614. (949) 855-8822. **Fax:** (949) 855-3045. **E-mail:** yreditor@i5publishing.com. **Website:** www.youngrider.com. "*Young Rider* magazine teaches young people, in an easy-to-read and entertaining way, how to look after their horses properly, and how to improve their riding skills safely."

FICTION young adults: adventure, animal, horses. "We would prefer funny stories, with a bit of conflict, which will appeal to the 13-year-old age group. They should be written in the third person, and about kids." Query. Length: 800-1,000 words. Pays $150.

NONFICTION young adults: animal, careers, famous equestrians, health (horse), horse celebrities, riding. Query with published clips. Length: 800-1,000 words. Pays $200/story.

PHOTOS Buys photos with accompanying ms only. Uses high-res digital images only—in focus, good light. Model/property release required; captions required.

TERMS Byline given. Guidelines available online.

TIPS "Fiction must be in third person. Read magazine before sending in a query. No 'true story from when I was a youngster.' No moralistic stories. Fiction must be up-to-date and humorous, teen-oriented. No practical or how-to articles—all done in-house."

AGENTS & ART REPS

//

This section features listings of literary agents and art reps who either specialize in, or represent a good percentage of, children's writers and/or illustrators. While there are a number of children's publishers who are open to nonagented material, using the services of an agent or rep can be beneficial to a writer or artist. Agents and reps can get your work seen by editors and art directors more quickly. They are familiar with the market and have insights into which editors and art directors would be most interested in your work. Also, they negotiate contracts and will likely be able to get you a better deal than you could get on your own.

Agents and reps make their income by taking a percentage of what writers and illustrators receive from publishers. The standard percentage for agents is 10 to 15 percent; art reps generally take 25 to 30 percent. We have not included any agencies in this section that charge reading fees.

WHAT TO SEND

When putting together a package for an agent or rep, follow the guidelines given in their listings. Most agents open to submissions prefer initially to receive a query letter describing your work. For novels and longer works, some agents ask for an outline and a number of sample chapters, but you should send these only if you're asked to do so. Never fax or e-mail query letters or sample chapters to agents without their permission. Just as with publishers, agents receive a large volume of submissions. It may take them a long time to reply, so you may want to query several agents at one time. It's best, however, to have a complete manuscript considered by only one agent at a time. Always include a self-addressed, stamped envelope (SASE).

For initial contact with art reps, send a brief query letter and self-promo pieces, following the guidelines given in the listings. If you don't have a flier or brochure, send photocopies. Always include a SASE.

For those who both write and illustrate, some agents listed will consider the work of author/illustrators. Read through the listings for details.

As you consider approaching agents and reps with your work, keep in mind that they are very choosy about whom represent. Your work must be high quality and presented professionally to make an impression on them. For more information on approaching agents and additional listings, see *Guide to Literary Agents* (Writer's Digest Books).

AN ORGANIZATION FOR AGENTS

In some listings of agents you'll see references to AAR (The Association of Authors' Representatives). This organization requires its members to meet an established list of professional standards and code of ethics.

The objectives of AAR include keeping agents informed about conditions in publishing and related fields; encouraging cooperation among literary organizations; and assisting agents in representing their author-clients' interests. Officially, members are prohibited from directly or indirectly charging reading fees. They offer writers a list of member agents on their website. They also offer a list of recommended questions an author should ask an agent and other FAQs, all found on their website. They can be contacted at AAR, 676A 9th Ave. #312, New York NY 10036. (212)840-5777. E-mail: aarinc@mindspring. com. Website: www.aar-online.org.

A+B WORKS

Website: http://aplusbworks.com. **Contact:** Amy Jameson, Brandon Jameson.

HOW TO CONTACT Query via online submission form. "Due to the high volume of queries we receive, we can't guarantee a response." Accepts simultaneous submissions.

ADAMS LITERARY

7845 Colony Rd., C4 #215, Charlotte NC 28226. (704)542-1440. **Fax:** (704)542-1450. **E-mail:** info@adamsliterary.com. **Website:** www.adamsliterary.com. **Contact:** Tracey Adams, Josh Adams. Adams Literary is a full-service literary agency exclusively representing children's and young adult authors and artists.
Ⓞ   Temporarily closed to submissions.

HANDLES Represents "the finest children's book and young adult authors and artists."

RECENT SALES *The Cruelty*, by Scott Bergstrom (Feiwel & Friends); *The Little Fire Truck*, by Margery Cuyler (Christy Ottaviano); *Unearthed*, by Amie Kaufman and Meagan Spooner (Disney-Hyperion); *A Handful of Stars*, by Cynthia Lord (Scholastic); *Under Their Skin*, by Margaret Peterson Haddix (Simon & Schuster); *The Secret Horses of Briar Hill*, by Megan Shepherd (Delacorte); *The Secret Subway*, by Shana Corey (Schwartz & Wade); *Impyrium*, by Henry Neff (HarperCollins).

TERMS Agent receives 15% commission on domestic sales; 20% on foreign sales. Offers written contract.

HOW TO CONTACT **Submit through online form on website only.** Send e-mail if that is not operating correctly. All submissions and queries should first be made through the online form on website. Will not review—and will promptly recycle—any unsolicited submissions or queries received by mail. Before submitting work for consideration, review complete guidelines online, as the agency sometimes shuts off to new submissions. Accepts simultaneous submissions. "While we have an established client list, we do seek new talent—and we accept submissions from both published and aspiring authors and artists."

TIPS "Guidelines are posted (and frequently updated) on our website."

ALIVE LITERARY AGENCY

7680 Goddard St., Suite 200, Colorado Springs CO 80920. (719)260-7080. **Fax:** (719)260-8223. **E-mail:** info@aliveliterary.com. **Website:** www.aliveliterary.com. **Contact:** Rick Christian. Alive is the largest, most influential literary agency for inspirational content and authors.

HANDLES This agency specializes in inspirational fiction, Christian living, how-to, and commercial nonfiction. Actively seeking inspirational, literary and mainstream fiction, inspirational nonfiction, and work from authors with established track records and platforms. Does not want to receive poetry, scripts, or dark themes.

TERMS Agent receives 15% commission on domestic sales. Offers written contract; two-month notice must be given to terminate contract.

HOW TO CONTACT "Because all our agents have full client loads, they are only considering queries from authors referred by clients and close contacts. Please refer to our guidelines at http://aliveliterary.com/submissions. Authors referred by an Alive client or close contact are invited to send proposals to submissions@aliveliterary.com." Your submission should include a referral (name of referring Alive client or close contact in the e-mail subject line. In the e-mail, please describe your personal or professional connection to the referring individual), a brief author biography (including recent speaking engagements, media appearances, social media platform statistics, and sales histories of your books), a synopsis of the work for which you are seeking agency representation (including the target audience, sales and marketing hooks, and comparable titles on the market), and the first 3 chapters of your manuscript. Alive will respond to queries meeting the above guidelines within 8-10 weeks.

TIPS Rewrite and polish until the words on the page shine. Endorsements, a solid platform, and great connections may help, provided you can write with power and passion. Hone your craft by networking with publishing professionals, joining critique groups, and attending writers' conferences.

AZANTIAN LITERARY AGENCY

Website: www.azantianlitagency.com. **Contact:** Jennifer Azantian.

HANDLES Stories that explore meaningful human interactions against fantastic backdrops, underrepresented voices, obscure retold fairy tales, quirky middle grade, modernized mythologies, psychological horror, literary science fiction, historical fantasy, magical realism, internally consistent epic fantasy, and spooky stories for younger readers.

HOW TO CONTACT During open submission windows only: send your query letter, 1-2 page synopsis, and first 10-15 pages all pasted in an e-mail (no attachments). Please note in the e-mail subject line if your work was requested at a conference, is an exclusive submission, or was referred by a current client. Accepts simultaneous submissions.

THE BENT AGENCY

19 W. 21st St., #201, New York NY 10010. **E-mail:** info@thebentagency.com. **Website:** www.thebentagency.com. **Contact:** Jenny Bent.

RECENT SALES *Caraval*, by Stephanie Garber (Flatiron); *Rebel of the Sands*, by Alwyn Hamilton (Viking Children's/Penguin BFYR); *The Square Root of Summer*, by Harriet Reuter Hapgood (Roaring Brook/Macmillan); *Dirty Money*, by Lisa Renee Jones (Simon & Schuster); *True North*, by Liora Blake (Pocket Star).

HOW TO CONTACT "Tell us briefly who you are, what your book is, and why you're the one to write it. Then include the first 10 pages of your material in the body of your e-mail. We respond to all queries; please resend your query if you haven't had a response within 4 weeks." Accepts simultaneous submissions.

DAVID BLACK LITERARY AGENCY

335 Adams St., Suite 2707, Brooklyn NY 11201. (718)-852-5500. **Fax:** (718)852-5539. **Website:** www.davidblackagency.com. **Contact:** David Black, owner.

RECENT SALES Some of the agency's best-selling authors include: Erik Larson, Stuart Scott, Jeff Hobbs, Mitch Albom, Gregg Olsen, Jim Abbott, and John Bacon.

HOW TO CONTACT "To query an individual agent, please follow the specific query guidelines outlined in the agent's profile on our website. Not all agents are currently accepting unsolicited queries. To query the agency, please send a 1-2 page query letter describing your book, and include information about any previously published works, your audience, and your platform." Do not e-mail your query unless an agent specifically asks for an e-mail. Accepts simultaneous submissions.

BOND LITERARY AGENCY

4340 E. Kentucky Ave., Suite 471, Denver CO , 80246. (303)781-9305. **Website:** www.bondliteraryagency.com. **Contact:** Sandra Bond. The agency is small, with a select list of writers. Represents adult and young adult fiction, both literary and commercial, including mysteries and women's fiction. Nonfiction interests include narrative, history, science and business.

HANDLES Agency does not represent romance, poetry, young reader chapter books, children's picture books, or screenplays.

RECENT SALES *The Past is Never*, by Tiffany Quay Tyson; *Cold Case: Billy the Kid*, by W.C. Jameson; *Women in Film: The Truth and the Timeline*, by Jill S. Tietjen and Barbara Bridges; Books 7 & 8 in the Hiro Hattori Mystery Series, by Susan Spann.

TERMS No fees.

HOW TO CONTACT Please submit query by e-mail (absolutely no attachments unless requested). No unsolicited mss. "They will let you know if they are interested in seeing more material. No phone calls, please." Accepts simultaneous submissions.

THE BOOK GROUP

20 W. 20th St., Suite 601, New York NY 10011. (212)803-3360. **Website:** www.thebookgroup.com. The Book Group is a full service literary agency located in the heart of Manhattan. Launched in 2015 by publishing industry veterans. The Book Group shares a singular passion: to seek out and cultivate writers, and to serve as their champions throughout their careers. "We represent a wide range of distinguished authors, including critically acclaimed and bestselling novelists, celebrated writers of children's literature, and award-winning historians, food writers, memoirists and journalists."

HANDLES Please do not send poetry or screenplays.

RECENT SALES *This Is Not Over*, by Holly Brown; *Perfect Little World*, by Kevin Wilson; *City of Saints & Thieves*, by Natalie C. Anderson; *The Runaway Midwife*, by Patricia Harman; *Always*, by Sarah Jio; *The Young Widower's Handbook*, by Tom McAllister.

HOW TO CONTACT Send a query letter and 10 sample pages to submissions@thebookgroup.com, with the first and last name of the agent you are querying in the subject line. All material must be in the body of the e-mail, as the agents do not open attachments. "If we are interested in reading more, we will get in touch with you as soon as possible." Accepts simultaneous submissions.

BOOKSTOP LITERARY AGENCY

67 Meadow View Rd., Orinda CA 94563. (925)254-2664. **Fax:** (925)254-1668. **E-mail:** info@bookstopliterary.com. **Website:** www.bookstopliterary.com. Rep-

resents authors and illustrators of books for children and young adults.

HANDLES "Special interest in Hispanic, Asian, American, African-American, and multicultural writers. Also seeking quirky picture books; clever adventure/mystery novels; eye-opening nonfiction; heartfelt middle-grade; unusual teen romance."

TERMS Agent receives 15% commission on domestic sales. Offers written contract, binding for 1 year.

HOW TO CONTACT Send: cover letter, entire ms for picture books; first 10 pages of novels; proposal and sample chapters OK for nonfiction. E-mail submissions: Paste cover letter and first 10 pages of ms into body of e-mail, send to info@bookstoliterary.com. Send sample illustrations only if you are an illustrator. Illustrators: send postcard or link to online portfolio. Do not send original artwork. Accepts simultaneous submissions.

BRADFORD LITERARY AGENCY

5694 Mission Center Rd., #347, San Diego CA 92108. (619)521-1201. **E-mail:** queries@bradfordlit.com. **Website:** www.bradfordlit.com. **Contact:** Laura Bradford, Natalie Lakosil, Sarah LaPolla, Kari Sutherland, Jennifer Chen Tran. "The Bradford Literary Agency is a boutique agency which offers a full range of representation services to authors who are both published and pre-published. Our mission at the Bradford Literary Agency is to form true partnerships with our clients and build long-term relationships that extend from writing the first draft through the length of the author's career."

◑ Picture book writers should contact Natalie only at this agency.

HANDLES Laura Bradford does not want to receive poetry, screenplays, short stories, westerns, horror, new age, religion, crafts, cookbooks, gift books. Natalie Lakosil does not want to receive inspirational novels, memoir, romantic suspense, adult thrillers, poetry, screenplays. Sarah LaPolla does not want to receive nonfiction, picture books, inspirational/spiritual novels, romance, or erotica. Monica Odom does not want to receive genre romance, erotica, military, poetry, or inspirational/spiritual works.

RECENT SALES Sold 115 titles in the last year, including *Snowed In With Murder*, by Auralee Wallace (St. Martin's); *All the Secrets We Keep*, by Megan Hart (Montlake); *The Notorious Bargain*, by Joanna Shupe (Avon); *Allegedly*, by Tiffany Jackson (Katherine Te-

gen Books); *Wives of War*, by Soraya Lane (Amazon); *The Silver Gate*, by Kristin Bailey (Katherine Tegen Books); *Witchtown*, by Cory Putman Oakes (Houghton Mifflin Harcourt); *Under Her Skin*, by Adriana Anders (Sourcebooks); *The Fixer*, by HelenKay Dimon (Avon); *Too Hard To Forget*, by Tessa Bailey (Grand Central); *In A Daze Work*, by Siobhan Gallagher (Ten Speed); *Piper Morgan Makes A Splash*, by Stephanie Faris (Aladdin); *The Star Thief*, by Lindsey Becker (Little, Brown); *Vanguard*, by Ann Aguirre (Feiwel & Friends); *Gray Wolf Island*, by Tracey Neithercott (Knopf); *Single Malt*, by Layla Reyne (Carina Press); *Whiskey Sharp: Unraveled*, by Lauren Dane (HQN).

TERMS Agent receives 15% commission on domestic sales; 25% commission on foreign sales. Offers written contract. Charges for extra copies of books for foreign submissions.

HOW TO CONTACT Accepts e-mail queries only; For submissions to Laura Bradford or Natalie Lakosil, send to queries@bradfordlit.com. For submissions to Sarah LaPolla, send to sarah@bradfordlit.com. For submissions to Kari Sutherland, send to kari@bradfordlit.com. For submissions to Jennifer Chen Tran, send to jen@bradfordlit.com. The entire submission must appear in the body of the e-mail and not as an attachment. The subject line should begin as follows: "QUERY: (the title of the ms or any short message that is important should follow)." For fiction: e-mail a query letter along with the first chapter of ms and a synopsis. Include the genre and word count in your query letter. Nonfiction: e-mail full nonfiction proposal including a query letter and a sample chapter. Accepts simultaneous submissions. Obtains most new clients through queries.

BRANDT & HOCHMAN LITERARY AGENTS, INC.

1501 Broadway, Suite 2310, New York NY 10036. (212)840-5760. **Fax:** (212)840-5776. **Website:** brandthochman.com. **Contact:** Gail Hochman.

HANDLES No screenplays or textbooks.

RECENT SALES This agency sells 40-60 new titles each year. A full list of their hundreds of clients is on the agency website.

TERMS Agent receives 15% commission on domestic sales; 20% commission on foreign sales.

HOW TO CONTACT "We accept queries by e-mail and regular mail; however, we cannot guarantee a response to e-mailed queries. For queries via regular mail, be sure to include a SASE for our reply. Query letters should be no more than 2 pages and should include a convincing overview of the book project and information about the author and his or her writing credits. Address queries to the specific Brandt & Hochman agent whom you would like to consider your work. Agent e-mail addresses and query preferences may be found at the end of each agent profile on the 'Agents' page of our website." Accepts simultaneous submissions. Obtains most new clients through recommendations from others.

TIPS "Write a letter which will give the agent a sense of you as a professional writer—your long-term interests as well as a short description of the work at hand."

M. COURTNEY BRIGGS

Derrick & Briggs, LLP, 100 N. Broadway Ave., 28th Floor, Oklahoma City OK 73102. (405)235-1900. **Fax:** (405)235-1995. **Website:** www.derrickandbriggs.com. "M. Courtney Briggs combines her primary work as a literary agent with expertise in intellectual property, entertainment law, and estates and probate. Her clients are published authors (exclusively), theatres, and a variety of small businesses and individuals."

HOW TO CONTACT

CURTIS BROWN, LTD.

10 Astor Place, New York NY 10003. (212)473-5400. **Fax:** (212)598-0917. **Website:** www.curtisbrown.com. Represents authors and illustrators of fiction, nonfiction, picture books, middle grade, young adult.

RECENT SALES This agency prefers not to share information on specific sales.

TERMS Agent receives 15% commission on domestic sales; 20% on foreign sales. Offers written contract. 75-day notice must be given to terminate contract. Charges for some postage (overseas, etc.).

HOW TO CONTACT Please refer to the "Agents" page on the website for each agent's submission guidelines. Accepts simultaneous submissions. Obtains most new clients through recommendations from others, solicitations, conferences.

BROWNE & MILLER LITERARY ASSOCIATES

(312) 922-3063. **Website:** www.browneandmiller.com. **Contact:** Danielle Egan-Miller, president. Founded in 1971 by Jane Jordan Browne, Browne & Miller Literary Associates is the Chicago area's leading literary agency. Danielle Egan-Miller became president of the agency in 2003 and has since sold hundreds of books with a heavy emphasis on commercial adult fiction.

Her roster includes several New York Times best-selling authors and numerous prize- and award-winning writers. She loves a great story well told.

○ "We are very hands-on and do much editorial work with our clients. We are passionate about the books we represent and work hard to help clients reach their publishing goals."

HANDLES Browne & Miller is most interested in literary and commercial fiction, women's fiction, women's historical fiction, literary-leaning crime fiction, dark suspense/domestic suspense, romance of most subgenres including time travel, Christian/inspirational fiction by established authors, and a wide range of platform-driven nonfiction by nationally-recognized author-experts. "We do not represent children's books of any kind; we do not represent horror, science fiction or fantasy, short stories, poetry, original screenplays,or articles."

HOW TO CONTACT Query via e-mail only; no attachments. Do not send unsolicited mss. Accepts simultaneous submissions.

ANDREA BROWN LITERARY AGENCY, INC.

E-mail: andrea@andreabrownlit.com; caryn@andreabrownlit.com; lauraqueries@gmail.com; jennifer@andreabrownlit.com; kelly@andreabrownlit.com; jennL@andreabrownlit.com; jamie@andreabrownlit.com; jmatt@andreabrownlit.com; kathleen@andreabrownlit.com; lara@andreabrownlit.com; soloway@andreabrownlit.com. **Website:** www.andreabrownlit.com.

○ "Writers should review the large agent bios on the agency website to determine which agent to contact. Please choose only one agent to query. The agents share queries, so a no from one agent at Andrea Brown Literary Agency is a no from all." *E-queries only.*

HANDLES Specializes in all kinds of children's books—illustrators and authors. 98% juvenile books. Considers: nonfiction, fiction, picture books, young adult.

RECENT SALES *The Scorpio Races*, by Maggie Stiefvater (Scholastic); *The Future of Us*, by Jay Asher; *Triangles*, by Ellen Hopkins (Atria); *Crank*, by Ellen Hopkins (McElderry/S&S); *Burned*, by Ellen Hopkins (McElderry/S&S); *Impulse*, by Ellen Hopkins (McElderry/S&S); *Glass*, by Ellen Hopkins (McElderry/S&S); *Tricks*, by Ellen Hopkins (McElderry/S&S); *Fallout*, by Ellen Hopkins (McElderry/S&S); *Perfect*, by Ellen Hopkins (McElderry/S&S); *The Strange Case of Origami Yoda*, by Tom Angleberger (Amulet/Abrams); *Darth Paper Strikes Back*, by Tom Angleberger (Amulet/Abrams); *Becoming Chloe*, by Catherine Ryan Hyde (Knopf); Sasha Cohen autobiography (HarperCollins); *The Five Ancestors*, by Jeff Stone (Random House); *Thirteen Reasons Why*, by Jay Asher (Penguin); *Identical*, by Ellen Hopkins (S&S).

TERMS Agent receives 15% commission on domestic sales; 25% commission on foreign sales. Offers written contract.

HOW TO CONTACT For picture books, submit a query letter and complete ms in the body of the e-mail. For fiction, submit a query letter and the first 10 pages in the body of the e-mail. For nonfiction, submit proposal, first 10 pages in the body of the e-mail. Illustrators: submit a query letter and 2-3 illustration samples (in jpeg format), link to online portfolio, and text of picture book, if applicable. "We only accept queries via e-mail. No attachments, with the exception of jpeg illustrations from illustrators." Visit the agents' bios on our website and choose only one agent to whom you will submit your e-query. Send a short e-mail query letter to that agent with "QUERY" in the subject field. Accepts simultaneous submissions. Obtains most new clients through referrals from editors, clients and agents. Check website for guidelines and information.

KIMBERLEY CAMERON & ASSOCIATES

1550 Tiburon Blvd., #704, Tiburon CA 94920. (415)789-9191. **Website:** www.kimberleycameron. com. **Contact:** Kimberley Cameron.

HANDLES "We are looking for a unique and heartfelt voice that conveys a universal truth."

HOW TO CONTACT Prefers queries via site. Only query one agent at a time. For fiction, fill out the correct submissions form for the individual agent and attach the first 50 pages and a synopsis (if requested) as a Word doc or PDF. For nonfiction, fill out the correct submission form of the individual agent and attach a full book proposal and sample chapters (includes the first chapter and no more than 50 pages) as a Word doc or PDF. Accepts simultaneous submissions. Obtains new clients through recommendations from others, solicitations.

THE CAT AGENCY, INC.

29 Newman Place, Fairfield CT 06825. (917)434-3141. **E-mail:** christy@catugeau.com. **Website:** www. CATugeau.com. **Contact:** Christina Tugeau, agent; Christy T. Ewers, owner/agent. Passionate for over 25 years about kids art and stories and the people who make and share them. We are 'hands on' with our group of artists..encourage interconnections. Now the first mother/daughter agency in the business.. and quite proud of it.

◑　　Accepting limited new artists in the Children's Publishing Industry both domestically and internationally.

HANDLES Actively seeking illustrators and artist/authors (and book ideas from agency artists).

TERMS Receives 25% commission. Contract terms very friendly but exclusive in industry. No fees other than a percentage of work done.

HOW TO CONTACT For first contact, e-mail samples and live website link, with note. No CDs. "Artists responsible for providing samples for portfolios and mailings." Accepts simultaneous submissions. Finds illustrators through recommendations from others, direct contact, conferences, personal search.

TIPS "Do research, read articles on CAT website, study picture books at bookstores, promote yourself a bit to learn the industry. Be professional. Know what you do best, and be prepared to give rep what they need to present you! Do have e-mail and scanning capabilities, too."

CHALBERG & SUSSMAN

115 W. 29th St., Third Floor, New York NY 10001. (917)261-7550. **Website:** www.chalbergsussman.com.

RECENT SALES The agents' sales and clients are listed on their website.

HOW TO CONTACT To query by e-mail, please contact one of the following: terra@chalbergsussman.com, rachel@chalbergsussman.com, nicole@chalbergsussman.com, lana@chalbergsussman.com. To query by regular mail, please address your letter to one agent and include SASE. Accepts simultaneous submissions.

THE CHUDNEY AGENCY

72 N. State Rd., Suite 501, Briarcliff Manor NY 10510. (914)465-5560. **E-mail:** steven@thechudneyagency. com. **Website:** www.thechudneyagency.com. **Contact:** Steven Chudney.

HANDLES "At this time, the agency is only looking for author/illustrators (one individual), who can both write and illustrate wonderful picture books. The author/illustrator must really know and understand the prime audience's needs and wants of the child reader! Storylines should be engaging, fun, with a hint of a life lessons and cannot be longer than 800 words. With chapter books, middle grade and teen novels, I'm primarily looking for quality, contemporary literary fiction: novels that are exceedingly well-written, with wonderful settings and developed, unforgettable characters. I'm looking for historical fiction that will excite me, young readers, editors, and reviewers, and will introduce us to unique characters in settings and situations, countries, and eras we haven't encountered too often yet in children's and teen literature." Does not want most fantasy and no science fiction.

HOW TO CONTACT No snail mail submissions. Queries only. Submission package info to follow should we be interested. For children's picture books, we only want author/illustrator projects. Submit a pdf with full text and at least 5-7 full-color illustrations. Accepts simultaneous submissions.

DON CONGDON ASSOCIATES INC.

110 William St., Suite 2202, New York NY 10038. (212)645-1229. **Fax:** (212)727-2688. **E-mail:** dca@doncongdon.com. **Website:** doncongdon.com.

HANDLES Susan Ramer: "Not looking for romance, science fiction, fantasy, espionage, mysteries, politics, health/diet/fitness, self-help, or sports." Katie Kotchman: "Please do not send her screenplays or poetry."

RECENT SALES This agency represents many best-selling clients such as David Sedaris and Kathryn Stockett.

HOW TO CONTACT "For queries via e-mail, you must include the word 'query' and the agent's full name in your subject heading. Please also include your query and sample chapter in the body of the e-mail, as we do not open attachments for security reasons. Please query only one agent within the agency at a time. If you are sending your query via regular mail, please enclose a SASE for our reply. If you would like us to return your materials, please make sure your postage will cover their return." Accepts simultaneous submissions.

JILL CORCORAN LITERARY AGENCY

2150 Park Place, Suite 100, El Segundo CA 90245. **Website:** jillcorcoranliteraryagency.com. **Contact:** Jill Corcoran.

HANDLES Actively seeking picture books, middle-grade, young adult, crime novels, psyhcological suspense, and true crime. Does not want to receive screenplays, chapbooks, or poetry.

HOW TO CONTACT Please go online to the agency submissions page and submit to the agent you feel would best represent your work. Accepts simultaneous submissions.

CORVISIERO LITERARY AGENCY

275 Madison Ave., at 40th, 14th Floor, New York NY 10016. (646)856-4032. **Fax:** (646)217-3758. **E-mail:** consult@corvisieroagency.com. **Website:** www.corvisieroagency.com. **Contact:** Marisa A. Corvisiero, Founder, Senior Agent, Attorney. "We are a boutique literary agency founded by Marisa A Corvisiero, Esq. This agency is a place where authors can find professional and experienced representation." *Does not accept unsolicited mss.*

HOW TO CONTACT Accepts submissions via QueryManager. Include query letter, 5 pages of complete and polished ms, and a 1-2 page synopsis. For nonfiction, include a proposal instead of the synopsis. Each agent profile on website has a button for direct submissions. Accepts simultaneous submissions.

D4EO LITERARY AGENCY

7 Indian Valley Rd., Weston CT 06883. (203)544-7180. **Fax:** (203)544-7160. **Website:** www.d4eoliteraryagency.com. **Contact:** Bob Diforio.

TERMS Offers written contract, binding for 2 years; automatic renewal unless 60 days notice given prior to renewal date. Charges for photocopying and submission postage.

HOW TO CONTACT Each of these agents has a different submission e-mail and different tastes regarding how they review material. See all on their individual agent pages on the agency website. Obtains most new clients through recommendations from others.

LAURA DAIL LITERARY AGENCY, INC.

121 W. 27th St., Suite 1201, New York NY 10001. (212)239-7477. **E-mail:** literary@ldlainc.com. **Website:** www.ldlainc.com.

HANDLES Specializes in women's fiction, literary fiction, young adult fiction, as well as both practical and idea-driven nonfiction. "Due to the volume of queries and mss received, we apologize for not answering every e-mail and letter. None of us handles children's picture books or chapter books. No New Age. We do not handle screenplays or poetry."

HOW TO CONTACT "If you would like, you may include a synopsis and no more than 10 pages. If you are mailing your query, please be sure to include a self-addressed, stamped envelope; without it, you may not hear back from us. To save money, time and trees, we prefer queries by e-mail to queries@ldlainc.com. We get a lot of spam and are wary of computer viruses, so please use the word 'Query' in the subject line and include your detailed materials in the body of your message, not as an attachment." Accepts simultaneous submissions.

DARHANSOFF & VERRILL LITERARY AGENTS

133 W. 72nd St., Room 304, New York NY 10023. (917)305-1300. **Website:** www.dvagency.com. "We are most interested in literary fiction, narrative nonfiction, memoir, sophisticated suspense, and both fiction and nonfiction for younger readers. Please note we do not represent theatrical plays or film scripts."

RECENT SALES A full list of clients is available on their website.

HOW TO CONTACT Send queries via e-mail. Accepts simultaneous submissions.

LIZA DAWSON ASSOCIATES

(212)465-9071. **Website:** www.lizadawsonassociates. com. **Contact:** Caitie Flum.

HANDLES Multiple agents at this agency represent young adult mss. This agency specializes in readable literary fiction, thrillers, mainstream historicals, women's fiction, young adult, middle-grade, academics, historians, journalists, and psychology.

TERMS Agent receives 15% commission on domestic sales; 20% commission on foreign sales. Offers written contract.

HOW TO CONTACT Query by e-mail only. No phone calls. Each of these agents has their own specific submission requirements, which you can find online at the agency's website. Obtains most new clients through recommendations from others, conferences, and queries.

THE JENNIFER DE CHIARA LITERARY AGENCY

299 Park Ave., 6th Floor, New York NY 10171. (212)739-0803. **E-mail:** jenndec@aol.com. **Website:** www.jdlit.com. **Contact:** Jennifer De Chiara.

TERMS Agent receives 15% commission on domestic sales. Offers written contract.

HOW TO CONTACT Each agent has their own e-mail submission address and submission instructions; check the website for the current updates, as policies do change. Accepts simultaneous submissions. Obtains most new clients through recommendations from others, conferences, query letters.

DEFIORE & COMPANY

47 E. 19th St., 3rd Floor, New York NY 10003. (212)925-7744. **Fax:** (212)925-9803. **Website:** www. defliterary.com.

HANDLES "Please be advised that we are not considering dramatic projects at this time."

TERMS Agent receives 15% commission on domestic sales; 20% commission on foreign sales. Offers written contract; 10-day notice must be given to terminate contract. Charges clients for photocopying and overnight delivery (deducted only after a sale is made).

HOW TO CONTACT Query with SASE or e-mail to submissions@defliterary.com. "Please include the word 'query' in the subject line. All attachments will be deleted; please insert all text in the body of the e-mail. For more information about our agents, their individual interests, and their query guidelines, please visit our 'About Us' page on our website." Accepts simultaneous submissions. Obtains most new clients through recommendations from others.

JOELLE DELBOURGO ASSOCIATES, INC.

101 Park St., Montclair NJ 07042. (973)773-0836. **E-mail:** joelle@delbourgo.com. **Website:** www.delbourgo.com. **Contact:** Joelle Delbourgo. "We are a boutique agency representing a wide range of nonfiction and fiction. Nonfiction: narrative, research-based and prescriptive nonfiction, including history, current affairs, education, psychology and personal development, parenting, science, business and economics, diet and nutrition, and cookbooks. Adult and young adult commercial and literary fiction, some middle grade. We do not represent plays, screenplays, poetry and picture books."

HANDLES "We are former publishers and editors with deep knowledge and an insider perspective. We have a reputation for individualized attention to clients, strategic management of authors' careers, and creating strong partnerships with publishers for our clients." Do not send scripts, picture books, poetry.

RECENT SALES *Prison 865: The Search for Hitler's Death Camp Guards in America*, by Debbie Cenziper (Hachette Books); *Hushed in Death*, by Stephen P. Kelly (Pegasus); *Hypersext: Keeping Our Children Safe in a Sexualized World*, by Jillian P. Roberts PhD with Sara Au (Quarto); *The Griffins of Castle Cary*, by Heather Shumaker (Simon & Schuster Children's); *Biscuit: 50 California-Style Recipes*, by Michael Volpatt (Running Press); *Husbands and Other Sharp Objects*, by Marilyn Simon Rothstein (Lake Union).

TERMS Agent receives 15% commission on domestic sales and 20% commission on foreign sales as well as television/film adaptation when a co-agent is involved. Offers written contract. Charges clients for postage and photocopying.

HOW TO CONTACT It's preferable if you submit via e-mail to a specific agent. Query 1 agent only. No attachments. Put the word "Query" in the subject line. "While we do our best to respond to each query, if you have not received a response in 60 days you may consider that a pass. Please do not send us copies of self-published books unless requested. Let us know if you are sending your query to us exclusively or if this is a multiple submission. For nonfiction, let us know if a proposal and sample chapters are available; if not, you should probably wait to send your query when you have a completed proposal. For fiction and memoir, embed the *first* 10 pages of manuscript into the e-mail after your query letter. Please no attachments. If we like your first pages, we may ask to see your synopsis and more manuscript. Please do not cold call us or make a follow-up call unless we call you." Accepts simultaneous submissions.

TIPS "Do your homework. Do not cold call. Read and follow submission guidelines before contacting us. Do not call to find out if we received your material. No e-mail queries. Treat agents with respect, as you would any other professional, such as a doctor, lawyer or financial advisor."

SANDRA DIJKSTRA LITERARY AGENCY

1155 Camino del Mar, PMB 515, Del Mar CA 92014. **E-mail:** queries@dijkstraagency.com. **Website:** www.dijkstraagency.com. The Dijkstra Agency was established over 35 years ago and is known for guiding the careers of many best-selling fiction and non-fiction authors, including Amy Tan, Lisa See, Maxine Hong Kingston, Chitra Divakaruni, Eric Foner, Marcus Rediker, and many more. "We handle nearly all genres, except for poetry." Please see www.dijkstraagency.com for each agent's interests.

TERMS Works in conjunction with foreign and film agents. Agent receives 15% commission on domestic sales and 20% commission on foreign sales. Offers written contract. No reading fee.

HOW TO CONTACT "Please see guidelines on our website, www.dijkstraagency.com. Please note that we only accept e-mail submissions. Due to the large number of unsolicited submissions we receive, we are only able to respond those submissions in which we are interested." Accepts simultaneous submissions.

TIPS "Remember that publishing is a business. Do your research and present your project in as professional a way as possible. Only submit your work when you are confident that it is polished and ready for prime-time. Make yourself a part of the active writing community by getting stories and articles published, networking with other writers, and getting a good sense of where your work fits in the market."

DONAGHY LITERARY GROUP

(647)527-4353. **E-mail:** stacey@donaghyliterary.com. **Website:** www.donaghyliterary.com. **Contact:** Stacey Donaghy. "Donaghy Literary Group provides full-service literary representation to our clients at every stage of their writing career. Specializing in commercial fiction, we seek middle grade, young adult, new adult and adult novels."

TERMS Agent receives 15% commission on domestic sales; 20% commission on foreign sales. Offers written contract, 30-day notice must be given to terminate contract.

HOW TO CONTACT Visit agency website for "new submission guidelines" Do not e-mail agents directly. This agency only accepts submissions through the QueryManager database system. Accepts simultaneous submissions.

TIPS "Only submit to one DLG agent at a time, we work collaboratively and often share projects that may be better suited to another agent at the agency."

DUNHAM LITERARY, INC.

110 William St., Suite 2202, New York NY 10038. (212)929-0994. **Website:** www.dunhamlit.com. **Contact:** Jennie Dunham.

HANDLES Does not want Westerns, genre romance, poetry.

RECENT SALES *The Bad Kitty Series*, by Nick Bruel (Macmillan); *The Christmas Story*, by Robert Sabuda (Candlewick); *The Gollywhopper Games* and Sequels, by Jody Feldman (HarperCollins); *Foolish Hearts*, by Emma Mills (Macmillan); *Learning Not To Drown*, by Anna Shinoda (Simon & Schuster); *Gangster Nation*, by Tod Goldberg (Counterpoint); *A Shadow All of Light*, by Fred Chappell (Tor).

TERMS Agent receives 15% commission on domestic sales; 20% commission on foreign sales.

HOW TO CONTACT E-mail queries preferred, with all materials pasted in the body of the e-mail. Attachments will not be opened. Paper queries are also accepted. Please include a SASE for response and return of materials. Please include the first 5 pages with the query. Accepts simultaneous submissions. Obtains most new clients through recommendations from others, solicitations.

DUNOW, CARLSON, & LERNER AGENCY

27 W. 20th St., Suite 1107, New York NY 10011. (212)645-7606. **E-mail:** mail@dclagency.com. **Website:** www.dclagency.com.

RECENT SALES A full list of agency clients is on the website.

HOW TO CONTACT Query via snail mail with SASE, or by e-mail. E-mail preferred, paste 10 sample pages below query letter. No attachments. Will respond only if interested. Accepts simultaneous submissions.

DYSTEL, GODERICH & BOURRET LLC

1 Union Square W., Suite 904, New York NY 10003. (212)627-9100. **Fax:** (212)627-9313. **Website:** www.dystel.com.

🖸 "We have discovered many of our most talented authors in the slush pile. We read everything that is sent to us, whether we decide to represent it or not." Dystel & Goderich Literary

Management recently acquired the client list of Bedford Book Works.

HANDLES "We are actively seeking fiction for all ages, in all genres." No plays, screenplays, or poetry.

TERMS Agent receives 15% commission on domestic sales; 19% commission on foreign sales. Offers written contract.

HOW TO CONTACT Query via e-mail and put "Query" in the subject line. "Synopsis, outlines or sample chapters (say, one chapter or the first 25 pages of your manuscript) should either be included below the cover letter or attached as a separate document. We won't open attachments if they come with a blank e-mail." Accepts simultaneous submissions. Obtains most new clients through recommendations from others, solicitations, conferences.

TIPS "DGLM prides itself on being a full-service agency. We're involved in every stage of the publishing process, from offering substantial editing on mss and proposals, to coming up with book ideas for authors looking for their next project, negotiating contracts and collecting monies for our clients. We follow a book from its inception through its sale to a publisher, its publication, and beyond. Our commitment to our writers does not, by any means, end when we have collected our commission. This is one of the many things that makes us unique in a very competitive business."

EDEN STREET LITERARY

P.O. Box 30, Billings NY 12510. **E-mail:** info@edenstreetlit.com. **Website:** www.edenstreetlit.com. **Contact:** Liza Voges. Eden Street represents over 40 authors and author-illustrators of books for young readers from pre-school through young adult. Their books have won numerous awards over the past 30 years. Eden Street prides themselves on tailoring services to each client's goals, working in tandem with them to achieve literary, critical, and commercial success. Welcomes the opportunity to work with additional authors and illustrators. This agency gives priority to members of SCBWI.

🖸 At the moment we are not open to submisssions except to those attending SCBWI conferences where we are attending, if that should change, we will update the information.

RECENT SALES *Dream Dog*, by Lou Berger; *Biscuit Loves the Library*, by Alyssa Capucilli; *The Scraps Book*, by Lois Ehlert; *Two Bunny Buddies*, by Kathryn O. Galbraith; *Between Two Worlds*, by Katherine Kirkpatrick.

HOW TO CONTACT E-mail a picture book ms or dummy; a synopsis and 3 chapters of a MG or YA novel; a proposal and 3 sample chapters for nonfiction. Accepts simultaneous submissions.

JUDITH EHRLICH LITERARY MANAGEMENT, LLC

146 Central Park W., 20E, New York NY 10023. (646)505-1570. **Fax:** (646)505-1570. **E-mail:** jehrlich@judithehrlichliterary.com. **Website:** www.judithehrlichliterary.com. Judith Ehrlich Literary Management LLC, established in 2002 and based in New York City, is a full service agency. "We represent nonfiction and fiction, both literary and commercial for the mainstream trade market. Our approach is very hands on, editorial, and constructive with the primary goal of helping authors build successful writing careers." Special areas of interest include compelling narrative nonfiction, outstanding biographies and memoirs, lifestyle books, works that reflect our changing culture, women's issues, psychology, science, social issues, current events, parenting, health, history, business, and prescriptive books offering fresh information and advice. "We also seek and represent stellar commercial and literary fiction, including romance and other women's fiction, historical fiction, literary mysteries, and select thrillers. Our agency deals closely with all major and independent publishers. When appropriate, we place our properties with foreign agents and co-agents at leading film agencies in New York and Los Angeles."

HANDLES Does not want to receive novellas, poetry, textbooks, plays, or screenplays.

RECENT SALES Fiction: *The Bicycle Spy*, by Yona Zeldis McDonough (Scholastic); *The House on Primrose Pond*, by Yona McDonough (NAL/Penguin); *You Were Meant for Me*, by Yona McDonough (NAL/Penguin); *Echoes of Us: The Hybrid Chronicles*, Book 3 by Kat Zhang (HarperCollins); *Once We Were: The Hybrid Chronicles* Book 2, by Kat Zhang (HarperCollins). Nonfiction: *Listen to the Echoes: The Ray Bradbury Interviews (Deluxe Edition)*, by Sam Weller (Hat & Beard Press); *What are The Ten Commandments?*, by Yona McDonough (Grosset & Dunlap); *Little Author in the Big Woods: A Biography of Laura Ingalls Wilder*, by Yona McDonough (Christy Ottaviano Books/Henry Holt); *Ray Bradbury: The Last Interview: And Other Conversations*, by Sam Weller (Melville House); *Who Was Sojourner Truth?*, by Yona McDonough (Grosset & Dunlap); *Power Branding: Leveraging the Success of the World's Best Brands*, by Steve McKee (Palgrave Macmillan); *Confessions of a Sociopath: A Life Spent Hiding in Plain Sight*, by M.E. Thomas (Crown); *Luck and Circumstance: A Coming of Age in New York and Hollywood and Points Beyond*, by Michael Lindsay-Hogg (Knopf).

HOW TO CONTACT E-query, with a synopsis and some sample pages. The agency will respond only if interested. Accepts simultaneous submissions.

EINSTEIN LITERARY MANAGEMENT

27 W. 20th St., No. 1003, New York NY 10011. (212)221-8797. **E-mail:** info@einsteinliterary.com. **Website:** http://einsteinliterary.com. **Contact:** Susanna Einstein.

HANDLES "As an agency we represent a broad range of literary and commercial fiction, including upmarket women's fiction, crime fiction, historical fiction, romance, and books for middle-grade children and young adults, including picture books and graphic novels. We also handle non-fiction including cookbooks, memoir and narrative, and blog-to-book projects. Please see agent bios on the website for specific information about what each of ELM's agents represents." Does not want poetry, textbooks, or screenplays.

HOW TO CONTACT Please submit a query letter and the first 10 double-spaced pages of your manuscript in the body of the e-mail (no attachments). Does not respond to mail queries or telephone queries or queries that are not specifically addressed to this agency. Accepts simultaneous submissions.

ETHAN ELLENBERG LITERARY AGENCY

155 Suffolk St., #2R, New York NY 10002. (212)431-4554. **E-mail:** agent@ethanellenberg.com. **Website:** ethanellenberg.com.

HANDLES "We are actively looking for established and new writers in a wide range of genres. We are looking for storytellers of all kinds and remain confident that books, in whatever format they are published, will continue to play a key role in our society to entertain and to instruct. We're interested in all kinds of commercial fiction, including thrillers, mysteries, children's, romance, women's fiction, ethnic, science fiction, fantasy and general fiction. We are also interested in literary fiction as long as it has a strong narrative. In nonfiction, we are interested in current affairs, history, health, science, psychology, cookbooks, new age, spirituality, pop culture, adventure, true crime, biography and memoir. We are also open to reviewing other genres and topics, as long as the material is for a trade or general audience and not scholarly." Does not want poetry, short stories, or screenplays.

HOW TO CONTACT For fiction, submit brief query letter, synopsis (1-2 pages), first 50 pages of ms, SASE. For nonfiction, submit brief query letter, book proposal (outline, sample chapters, author bio, etc.), SASE. For picture books, submit query letter, complete ms, color copies of sample illustrations (4-5 examples), SASE. Accepts simultaneous submissions.

EMPIRE LITERARY

115 W. 29th St., 3rd Floor, New York NY 10001. (917)213-7082. **E-mail:** abarzvi@empireliterary.com. **Website:** www.empireliterary.com.

HOW TO CONTACT Please only query one agent at a time. "If we are interested in reading more we will get in touch with you as soon as possible." Accepts simultaneous submissions.

EVATOPIA, INC.

8447 Wilshire Blvd., Suite 401, Beverly Hills CA 90211. **E-mail:** submissions@evatopia.com. **Website:** www.evatopia.com. **Contact:** Margery Walshaw. Evatopia supports writers through consulting, literary management, and publishing services.

HANDLES "All of our staff members have strong writing and entertainment backgrounds, making us sympathetic to the needs of our clients."

TERMS Agent receives 15% commission on domestic sales. Agent receives 15% commission on foreign sales. Offers written contract; 30-day notice must be given to terminate contract.

HOW TO CONTACT Submit via online submission form at www.evatopiaentertainment.com. Accepts simultaneous submissions. Obtains most new clients through recommendations.

TIPS "Remember that you only have 1 chance to make that important first impression. Make your loglines original and your synopses concise. The secret to a screenwriter's success is creating an original story and telling it in a manner that we haven't heard before."

DIANA FINCH LITERARY AGENCY

116 W. 23rd St., Suite 500, New York NY 10011. (917)544-4470. **E-mail:** diana.finch@verizon.net. **Website:** dianafinchliteraryagency.blogspot.com. **Contact:** Diana Finch. A boutique agency in Manhattan's Chelsea neighborhood. "Many of the agency's clients are journalists, and I handle book-related magazine assignments as well as book deals. I am the Chair of the AAR's International Committee, attend overseas book fairs, and actively handle foreign rights to my clients' work."

HANDLES For news about the agency and agency clients, see the agency Facebook page at https://www.facebook.com/DianaFinchLitAg/. "Does not want romance or children's picture books."

RECENT SALES *The Journeys of the Trees*, by Zach St George (W. W. Norton); *Owls of the Eastern Ice*, by Jonathan Slaght (FSG/Scientific American); *Uncolor: on toxins in personal products*, by Ronnie Citron-Fink (Island Press); *Cutting School*, by Professor Noliwe Rooks (The New Press); *Merchants of Men*, by Loretta Napoleoni (Seven Stories Press); *Beyond $15*, by Jonathan Rosenblum (Beacon Press); *The Age of Inequality*, by the Editors of In These Times (Verso Books); *Seeds of Resistance*, by Mark Schapiro (Hot Books/Skyhorse).

TERMS Agent receives 15% commission on domestic sales; 20% commission on foreign sales. Offers written contract. "I charge for overseas postage, galleys, and books purchased, and try to recoup these costs from earnings received for a client, rather than charging outright."

HOW TO CONTACT This agency prefers submissions via its online form. Accepts simultaneous submissions. Obtains most new clients through recommendations from others.

TIPS "Do as much research as you can on agents before you query. Have someone critique your query letter before you send it. It should be only 1 page and describe your book clearly—and why you are writing it—but also demonstrate creativity and a sense of your writing style."

FINEPRINT LITERARY MANAGEMENT

207 W. 106th St., Suite 1D, New York NY 10025. (212)279-1282. **Website:** www.fineprintlit.com.

TERMS Agent receives 15% commission on domestic sales; 20% commission on foreign sales.

HOW TO CONTACT E-query. For fiction, send a query, synopsis, bio, and 30 pages pasted into the e-mail. No attachments. For nonfiction, send a query only; proposal requested later if the agent is interested. Accepts simultaneous submissions. Obtains most new clients through recommendations from others, solicitations.

JAMES FITZGERALD AGENCY

118 Waverly Place, #1B, New York NY 10011. **E-mail:** submissions@jfitzagency.com. **Website:** www.jfitzagency.com. **Contact:** James Fitzgerald. "As an agency, we primarily represent books that reflect the popular culture of today being in the forms of fiction, nonfiction, graphic and packaged books. In order to have your work considered for possible representation, the following information must be submitted. Please submit all information in English even if your manuscript is in another language."

RECENT SALES A full and diverse list of titles are on this agency's website.

HOW TO CONTACT Query via e-mail or snail mail. This agency's online submission guidelines page explains all the elements they want to see when you submit a nonfiction book proposal. Accepts simultaneous submissions.

FLANNERY LITERARY

1140 Wickfield Ct., Naperville IL 60563. **E-mail:** jennifer@flanneryliterary.com. **Website:** flanneryliterary.com. **Contact:** Jennifer Flannery. "Flannery Literary is a Chicago-area literary agency representing writers of books for children and young adults because the most interesting, well-written, and time-honored books are written with young people in mind."

HANDLES This agency specializes in children's and young adult fiction and nonfiction. It also accepts picture books. 100% juvenile books. Actively seeking middle grade and young adult novels. Fewer picture-books. None that rhyme, please

TERMS Agent receives 15% commission on domestic sales; 20% commission on foreign sales. Offers written contract, binding for life of book in print.

HOW TO CONTACT Query by e-mail only. "Multiple queries are fine, but please inform us. Please no attachments. If you're sending a query about a novel, please embed in the e-mail the first 5-10 pages; if it's a picture book, please embed the entire text in the e-mail. We do not open attachments unless they have been requested." Accepts simultaneous submissions. Obtains new clients through referrals and queries.

TIPS "Write an engrossing, succinct query describing your work. We are always looking for a fresh new voice."

FLETCHER & COMPANY

78 Fifth Ave., 3rd Floor, New York NY 10011. **Website:** www.fletcherandco.com. **Contact:** Christy Fletcher. Today, Fletcher & Co. is a full-service literary management and production company dedicated to writers of upmarket nonfiction as well as commercial and literary fiction.

RECENT SALES *The Profiteers*, by Sally Denton; *The Longest Night*, by Andrea Williams; *Disrupted: My Misadventure in the Start-Up Bubble*, by Dan Lyons; *Free Re-Fills: A Doctor Confronts His Addiction*, by Peter Grinspoon, M.D.; *Black Man in a White Coat: A Doctor's Reflections on Race and Medicine*, by Damon Tweedy, M.D.

HOW TO CONTACT Send queries to info@fletcherandco.com. Please do not include e-mail attachments with your initial query, as they will be deleted. Address your query to a specific agent. No snail mail queries. Accepts simultaneous submissions.

FOLIO LITERARY MANAGEMENT, LLC

The Film Center Building, 630 Ninth Ave., Suite 1101, New York NY 10036. (212)400-1494. **Fax:** (212)967-0977. **Website:** www.foliolit.com.

This agency has many agents, and their specialties are listed on the website.

HANDLES No poetry, stage plays, or screenplays.

HOW TO CONTACT Query via e-mail only (no attachments). Read agent bios online for specific submission guidelines and e-mail addresses, and to check if someone is closed to queries. "All agents respond to queries as soon as possible, whether interested or not. If you haven't heard back from the individual agent within the time period that they specify on their bio page, it's possible that something has gone wrong, and your query has been lost–in that case, please e-mail a follow-up."

TIPS "Please do not submit simultaneously to more than one agent at Folio. If you're not sure which of us is exactly right for your book, don't worry. We work closely as a team, and if one of our agents gets a query that might be more appropriate for someone else, we'll always pass it along. It's important that you check each agent's bio page for clear directions as to how to submit, as well as when to expect feedback."

FOUNDRY LITERARY + MEDIA

33 W. 17th St., PH, New York NY 10011. (212)929-5064. **Fax:** (212)929-5471. **Website:** www.foundry-media.com.

HOW TO CONTACT Target one agent only. Send queries to the specific submission e-mail of the agent. For fiction: send query, synopsis, author bio, first 3 chapters—all pasted in the e-mail. For nonfiction, send query, sample chapters, TOC, author bio (all pasted). "We regret that we cannot guarantee a response to every submission we receive. If you do not receive a response within 8 weeks, your submission is not right for our lists at this time." Accepts simultaneous submissions.

TIPS "Consult website for each agent's submission instructions."

FOX LITERARY

110 W. 40th St., Suite 2305, New York NY 10018. **Website:** foxliterary.com. Fox Literary is a boutique agency which represents commercial fiction, along with select works of literary fiction and nonfiction that have broad commercial appeal.

HOW TO CONTACT E-mail query and first 5 pages in body of e-mail. E-mail queries preferred. For snail mail queries, must include an e-mail address for response and no response means no. Do not send SASE. No e-mail attachments. Accepts simultaneous submissions.

REBECCA FRIEDMAN LITERARY AGENCY

E-mail: brandie@rfliterary.com. **Website:** www.rfliterary.com.

RECENT SALES A complete list of agency authors is available online.

HOW TO CONTACT Please submit your brief query letter and first chapter (no more than 15 pages, double-spaced). No attachments. Accepts simultaneous submissions.

FULL CIRCLE LITERARY, LLC

Website: www.fullcircleliterary.com. **Contact:** Stefanie Von Borstel. "Full Circle Literary is a full-service literary agency, offering a full circle approach to literary representation. Our team has diverse experi-

ence in book publishing including editorial, marketing, publicity, legal and rights, which we use collectively to build careers book by book. We work with both award-winning veteran and debut writers and artists and our team has a knack for finding and developing new and diverse talent. Learn more about our agency and submission guidelines by visiting our website." This agency goes deeply into depth about what they are seeking and submission guidelines on their agency website.

HANDLES Actively seeking nonfiction and fiction projects that offer new and diverse viewpoints, and literature with a global or multicultural perspective. "We are particularly interested in books with a Latino or Middle Eastern angle."

TERMS Agent receives 15% commission on domestic sales; 25% commission on foreign sales. Offers written contract which outlines responsibilities of the author and the agent.

HOW TO CONTACT Online submissions only via submissions form online. Please complete the form and submit cover letter, author information and sample writing. For sample writing: fiction please include the first 10 ms pages. For nonfiction, include a proposal with 1 sample chapter. Accepts simultaneous submissions. Obtains most new clients through recommendations from others and conferences.

FUSE LITERARY

Foreword Literary, Inc. dba FUSE LITERARY, P.O. Box 258, La Honda CA 94020. **E-mail:** info@fuseliterary.com. **Website:** www.fuseliterary.com. **Contact:** Contact each agent directly via e-mail. Fuse Literary is a full-service, hybrid literary agency based in San Francisco with offices in New York, Chicago, Dallas, North Dakota and Vancouver. "We blend the tried-and-true methods of traditional publishing with the brash new opportunities engendered by digital publishing, emerging technologies, and an evolving author-agent relationship. Fuse manages a wide variety of clients, from bestsellers to debut authors, working with fiction and nonfiction for children and adults worldwide. We combine technical efficiency with outside-the-covers creative thinking so that each individual client's career is specifically fine-tuned for them. We are not an agency that sells a book and then washes our hands of the project. We realize that our ongoing success directly results from that of our clients, so we remain at their side to cultivate and strategize throughout the many lives of each book, both before and after the initial sale. Innovations, such as our Short Fuse client publishing program, help bridge the gaps between books, growing and maintaining the author's fan base without lag. The partners launched Fuse following tenures at established agencies, bringing with them experience in writing, teaching, professional editing, book marketing, blogging and social media, running high-tech companies, and marketing new technologies. A boutique, collaborative agency, Fuse provides each client with the expertise and forward vision of the group. We pride ourselves on our flexibility and passion for progression in an ever-changing publishing environment. We believe that the agency of the future will not just react to change but will actively create change, pushing markets and advancing formats to provide authors with the best possible outlets for their art."

RECENT SALES Seven-figure and six figure deals for NYT bestseller Julie Kagawa (YA); six-figure deal for debut Melissa D. Savage (MG); six-figure deal for Kerry Lonsdale (suspense); two six-figure audio deals for fantasy author Brian D. Anderson; *First Watch*, by Dale Lucas (fantasy); *This Is What a Librarian Looks Like*, by Kyle Cassidy (photo essay); *A Big Ship at the Edge of the Universe*, by Alex White (sci-fi); Runebinder Chronicles, by Alex Kahler (YA); *Perceptual Intelligence*, by Dr. Brian Boxler Wachler (science); *The Night Child*, by Anna Quinn (literary); *Pay Day*, by Kellye Garrett (mystery); Breakup Bash Series, by Nina Crespo (romance); *America's Next Reality Star*, by Laura Heffernan (women's fiction); *Losing the Girl*, by MariNaomi (graphic novel); *Maggie and Abby's Neverending Pillow Fort*, by Will Taylor (MG); *Idea Machine*, by Jorjeana Marie (how-to).

TERMS "We earn 15% on negotiated deals for books and with our co-agents earn between 20-30% on foreign translation deals depending on the territory; 20% on TV/Movies/Plays; other multimedia deals are so new there is no established commission rate. The author has the last say, approving or not approving all deals." After the initial 90-day period, there is a 30-day termination of the agency agreement clause. No fees.

HOW TO CONTACT E-query an individual agent. Check the website to see if any individual agent has closed themselves to submissions, as well as for a description of each agent's individual submission preferences. (You can find these details by clicking on each agent's photo.) Only accepts e-mailed queries that follow our online guidelines.

GALLT AND ZACKER LITERARY AGENCY

273 Charlton Ave., South Orange NJ 07079. (973)761-6358. **Website:** www.galltzacker.com. **Contact:** Nancy Gallt, Marietta Zacker. "At the Gallt and Zacker Literary Agency we represent people, not projects. We aim to bring to life stories and artwork that help young readers throughout the world become life-long book enthusiasts and to inspire and entertain readers of all ages."

HANDLES "Books for children and young adults." Actively seeking author, illustrators, author/illustrators who create books for young adults and younger readers.

RECENT SALES Rick Riordan's Books (Hyperion); *Trace*, by Pat Cummings (Harper); *What Gloria Heard*, illustrated by Daria Peoples (Bloomsbury); *Gondra's Treasure*, illustrated by Jennifer Black Reinhardt (Clarion/HMH); *Caterpillar Summer*, by Gillian McDunn (Bloomsbury); *It Wasn't Me*, by Dana Alison Levy (Delacorte/Random House); *Namesake*, by Paige Britt (Scholastic); *The Turning*, by Emily Whitman (Harper); *Rot*, by Ben Clanton (Simon & Schuster). *The Year They Fell*, by David Kreizman (Imprint/Macmillan); *Manhattan Maps*, by Jennifer Thermes (Abrams); *The Moon Within*, by Aida Salazar (Scholastic); *Artist in Space*, by Dean Robbins (Scholastic); *Lucy McGee*, by Mary Amato (Holiday House); *Where Are You From?*, by Yamile Saied Méndez (Harper); *The Artist*, by Selina Alko (Scholastic).

TERMS Agent receives 15% commission on domestic sales; 20% commission on foreign sales. Offers written contract; 30-day notice must be given to terminate contract.

HOW TO CONTACT Submit through online submission form on agency website. No e-mail queries, please. Accepts simultaneous submissions. Obtains new clients through submissions, conferences and recommendations from others.

TIPS "Writing and illustrations stand on their own, so submissions should tell the most compelling stories possible—whether visually, in narrative, or both."

GELFMAN SCHNEIDER / ICM PARTNERS

850 7th Ave., Suite 903, New York NY 10019. **Website:** www.gelfmanschneider.com. **Contact:** Jane Gelfman, Deborah Schneider.

HANDLES "Among our diverse list of clients are novelists, journalists, playwrights, scientists, activists & humorists writing narrative nonfiction, memoir, political & current affairs, popular science and popular culture nonfiction, as well as literary & commercial fiction, women's fiction, and historical fiction." Does not currently accept screenplays or scripts, poetry, or picture book queries.

TERMS Agent receives 15% commission on domestic sales; 20% commission on foreign sales; 15% commission on film sales. Offers written contract. Charges clients for photocopying and messengers/couriers.

HOW TO CONTACT Query. Check Submissions page of website to see which agents are open to queries and further instructions. Accepts simultaneous submissions.

THE GERNERT COMPANY

136 E. 57th St., New York NY 10022. (212)838-7777. **E-mail:** info@thegernertco.com. **Website:** www.thegernertco.com. "Our client list is as broad as the market; we represent equal parts fiction and nonfiction."

RECENT SALES *Partners*, by John Grisham; *The River Why*, by David James Duncan; *The Thin Green Line*, by Paul Sullivan; *A Fireproof Home for the Bride*, by Amy Scheibe; *The Only Girl in School*, by Natalie Standiford.

HOW TO CONTACT Please send us a query letter by e-mail to info@thegernertco.com describing the work you'd like to submit, along with some information about yourself and a sample chapter if appropriate. Please indicate in your letter which agent you are querying. Please do not send e-mails directly to individual agents. It's our policy to respond to your query only if we are interested in seeing more material, usually within 4-6 weeks. See company website for more instructions. Accepts simultaneous submissions. Obtains most new clients through recommendations from others, solicitations.

BARRY GOLDBLATT LITERARY LLC

320 7th Ave. #266, Brooklyn NY 11215. **Website:** www.bgliterary.com. **Contact:** Barry Goldblatt; Jennifer Udden.

HANDLES "Please see our website for specific submission guidelines and information on our particular tastes."

RECENT SALES *Trolled*, by Bruce Coville; *Grim Tidings*, by Caitlin Kittridge; *Max at Night*, by Ed Vere.

TERMS Agent receives 15% commission on domestic sales; 20% on foreign and dramatic sales. Offers written contract. 60 days notice must be given to terminate contract.

HOW TO CONTACT "E-mail queries can be sent to query@bgliterary.com and should include the word 'query' in the subject line. To query Jen Udden specifically, e-mail queries can be sent to query.judden@gmail.com. Please know that we will read and respond to every e-query that we receive, provided it is properly addressed and follows the submission guidelines below. We will not respond to e-queries that are addressed to no one, or to multiple recipients. Your e-mail query should include the following within the body of the e-mail: your query letter, a synopsis of the book, and the first 5 pages of your manuscript. We will not open or respond to any e-mails that have attachments. If we like the sound of your work, we will request more from you. Our response time is 4 weeks on queries, 6-8 weeks on full manuscripts. If you haven't heard from us within that time, feel free to check in via e-mail." Accepts simultaneous submissions. Obtains clients through referrals, queries, and conferences.

TIPS "We're a hands-on agency, focused on building an author's career, not just making an initial sale. We don't care about trends or what's hot; we just want to sign great writers."

IRENE GOODMAN LITERARY AGENCY

27 W. 24th St., Suite 700B, New York NY 10010. **E-mail:** miriam.queries@irenegoodman.com, barbara.queries@irenegoodman.com, rachel.queries@irenegoodman.com, kim.queries@irenegoodman.com, victoria.queries@irenegoodman.com, irene.queries@irenegoodman.com, brita.queries@irenegoodman.com. **Website:** www.irenegoodman.com. **Contact:** Brita Lundberg.

HANDLES Commercial and literary fiction and nonfiction. No screenplays, poetry, or inspirational fiction.

TERMS 15% commission.

HOW TO CONTACT Query. Submit synopsis, first 10 pages pasted into the body of the email. E-mail queries only! See the website submission page. No e-mail attachments. Query 1 agent only. Accepts simultaneous submissions.

TIPS "We are receiving an unprecedented amount of e-mail queries. If you find that the mailbox is full, please try again in two weeks. E-mail queries to our personal addresses will not be answered. E-mails to our personal inboxes will be deleted."

DOUG GRAD LITERARY AGENCY, INC.

156 Prospect Park West, #3L, Brooklyn NY 11215. (718)788-6067. **Website:** www.dgliterary.com. **Contact:** Doug Grad. Throughout Doug's editorial career, he was always an author's advocate—the kind of editor authors wanted to work with because of his keen eye, integrity, and talent for developing projects. He was also a skillful negotiator, sometimes to the chagrin of literary agents. For the last 10 years, he has been bringing those experiences to the other side of the table in offering publishers the kind of high-quality commercial fiction and nonfiction that he himself was proud to publish. He has sold award-winning and bestselling authors.

HANDLES Does not want fantasy, young adult, or children's picture books.

RECENT SALES *The Next Greatest Generation*, by Joseph L. Galloway and Marvin J. Wolf (Thomas Nelson); *Game Face: A Lifetime of Hard-Learned Lessons On and Off the Basketball Court*, by Bernard King with Jerome Preisler (Da Capo); Dan Morgan thriller series, by Leo Maloney (Kensington); Cajun Country cozy mystery series, by Ellen Byron (Crooked Lane); *Please Don't Feed the Mayor* and *Alaskan Catch*, by Sue Pethick (Kensington).

TERMS None.

HOW TO CONTACT Query by e-mail first. No sample material unless requested; no printed submissions by mail. Accepts simultaneous submissions.

SANFORD J. GREENBURGER ASSOCIATES, INC.

55 Fifth Ave., New York NY 10003. (212)206-5600. **Fax:** (212)463-8718. **Website:** www.greenburger.com. "Large enough to be a full service agency, including international rights, but small enough to manage and service clients personally, SJGA works closely with authors to edit and fine-tune proposals, refine concepts and ensure that the best work reaches editors. The agents freely share information and expertise, creat-

ing a collaborative partnership unique to the industry. The combined result is reflected in the numerous successes of the agency's authors (including Dan Brown, Patrick Rothfuss, and Robin Preiss Glasser)."

HANDLES No screenplays.

TERMS Agent receives 15% commission on domestic sales; 20% commission on foreign sales. Charges for photocopying and books for foreign and subsidiary rights submissions.

HOW TO CONTACT E-query. "Please look at each agent's profile page for current information about what each agent is looking for and for the correct email address to use for queries to that agent. Please be sure to use the correct query e-mail address for each agent." Obtains most new clients through recommendations from others.

THE GREENHOUSE LITERARY AGENCY

E-mail: submissions@greenhouseliterary.com. **Website:** www.greenhouseliterary.com. **Contact:** Sarah Davies.

"At Greenhouse we aim to establish strong, long-term relationships with clients and work hard to find our authors the very best publisher and deal for their writing. We often get very involved editorially, working creatively with authors where necessary. Our goal is to submit high-quality manuscripts to publishers while respecting the role of the editor who will have their own publishing vision."

HANDLES "We represent authors writing fiction and nonfiction for children and teens. The agency has offices in both the US and UK, and the agency's commission structure reflects this—taking 15% for sales to both US and UK, thus treating both as 'domestic' market." All genres of children's and YA fiction. Very occasionally, a nonfiction proposal will be considered. Does not want to receive picture books texts (ie, written by writers who aren't also illustrators) or short stories, educational or religious/inspirational work, pre-school/novelty material, screenplays. Represents novels and some nonfiction.Considers these fiction areas: juvenile, chapter book series, middle grade, young adult. Does not want to receive poetry, picture book texts (unless by author/illustrators) or work aimed at adults; short stories, educational or religious/inspirational work, pre-school/novelty material, or screenplays.

RECENT SALES *The Preacher Woods*, by Ashley Elston (Disney-Hyperion); *The Science of Breakable Things*, by Tae Keller (Random House); *We Speak in Storms*, by Natalie Lund (Philomel); *When We Wake*, by Elle Cosimano; *Secrets of Topsea* , by Kir Fox & M. Shelley Coats; *The Bigfoot Files*, by Lindsay Eagar (Candlewick); *Wanted: Women Mathematicians*, by Tami Lewis Brown & Debbie Loren Dunn (Disney-Hyperion); *Fake*, by Donna Cooner (Scholastic).

TERMS Agent receives 15% commission on domestic sales; 25% commission on foreign sales. Offers written contract. This agency occasionally charges for submission copies to film agents or foreign publishers.

HOW TO CONTACT Query 1 agent only. Put the target agent's name in the subject line. Paste the first 5 pages of your story after the query. Accepts simultaneous submissions.

TIPS "Before submitting material, authors should visit the Greenhouse Literary Agency website and carefully read all submission guidelines."

KATHRYN GREEN LITERARY AGENCY, LLC

157 Columbus Ave., Suite 510, New York NY 10023. (212)245-4225. **E-mail:** query@kgreenagency.com. **Website:** www.kathryngreenliteraryagency.com. **Contact:** Kathy Green.

HANDLES "Considers all types of fiction but particularly like historical fiction, cozy mysteries, young adult and middle grade. For nonfiction, I am interested in memoir, parenting, humor with a pop culture bent, and history. Quirky nonfiction is also a particular favorite." Does not want to receive science fiction, fantasy, children's picture books, screenplays, or poetry.

RECENT SALES *Jigsaw Jungle*, by Kristin Levine; *Jane, Anonymous*, by Laurie Faria, Stolarz; *To Woo a Wicked Widow*, by Jenna Jaxon.

TERMS Agent receives 15% commission on domestic sales; 20% commission on foreign sales.

HOW TO CONTACT Query by e-mail. Send no attachments unless requested. Do not send queries via regular mail. Responds in 4 weeks. "Queries do not have to be exclusive; however if further material is requested, please be in touch before accepting other representation." Accepts simultaneous submissions. Obtains most new clients through recommendations from others, solicitations, conferences.

JILL GRINBERG LITERARY MANAGEMENT

392 Vanderbilt Ave., Brooklyn NY 11238. (212)620-5883. **Website:** www.jillgrinbergliterary.com. "Our authors are novelists, historians, and scientists; memoirists and journalists; illustrators and musicians, cultural critics and humanitarians. They are passionate about what they write. They have strong, authentic voices, whether they are writing fiction or writing nonfiction. They are brilliant storytellers. Our authors have won the American Book Award, the National Book Award and the Pulitzer Prize, as well as the Printz Award and Newbery Honor award. They appear on The New York Times and international bestseller lists. We don't make a habit of dividing our list by category—our authors transcend category. Our authors write for every audience, picture book to adult. They are not easily boxed or contained within any neat, singular label. They often cross categories, are 'genre busting.' We love books, but we take on authors. Our authors are career authors. We are deeply invested in their careers and in making every book count. We are committed to developing ongoing relationships with writers and have represented a good number of our authors for 10 years plus. We understand the importance of the author–publisher connection and put great focus on matching our authors to the right editors and publishers. We fiercely advocate for our authors while maintaining a strong network of top editors and publishers. We have many years of publicity and marketing experience between us, and we give tremendous thought to positioning. Every project requires a tailored, personalized plan. Every author is a unique. Every author has a different path."

HANDLES "We do not accept unsolicited queries for screenplays."

HOW TO CONTACT "Please send queries via e-mail to info@jillgrinbergliterary.com–include your query letter, addressed to the agent of your choice, along with the first 50 pages of your ms pasted into the body of the e-mail or attached as a doc. or docx. file. We also accept queries via mail, though e-mail is preferred. Please send your query letter and the first 50 pages of your ms by mail, along with a SASE, to the attention of your agent of choice. Please note that unless a SASE with sufficient postage is provided, your materials will not be returned. As submissions are shared within the office, please only query one agent with your project." Accepts simultaneous submissions.

TIPS "We prefer submissions by electronic mail."

HARTLINE LITERARY AGENCY

123 Queenston Dr., Pittsburgh PA 15235-5429. (412)829-2483. **E-mail:** jim@hartlineliterary.com. **Website:** www.hartlineliterary.com. **Contact:** James D. Hart. Many of the agents at this agency are generalists. This agency also handles inspirational and Christian works.

HANDLES "This agency specializes in the Christian bookseller market." We also represent general market, but no graphic sex or language. Actively seeking adult fiction, all genres, self-help, social issues, Christian living, parenting, marriage, business, biographies, narrative non-fiction, creative nonfiction. Does not want to receive erotica, gay/lesbian, horror, graphic violence.

TERMS Agent receives 15% commission on domestic sales. Offers written contract.

HOW TO CONTACT E-query preferred, USPS to the Pittsburgh office. Target one agent only. "All e-mail submissions sent to Hartline Agents should be sent as a MS Word doc attached to an e-mail with 'submission: title, authors name and word count' in the subject line. A proposal is a single document, not a collection of files. Place the query letter in the email itself. Do not send the entire proposal in the body of the e-mail or send PDF files." Further guidelines online. Accepts simultaneous submissions. Obtains most new clients through recommendations from others, and at conferences.

TIPS Please follow the guidelines on our web site www.hartlineliterary for the fastest response to your proposal. E-mail proposals only.

❾ ANTONY HARWOOD LIMITED

103 Walton St., Oxford OX2 6EB, United Kingdom. (44)(018)6555-9615. **Website:** www.antonyharwood. com. **Contact:** Antony Harwood; James Macdonald Lockhart; Jo Williamson.

TERMS Agent receives 15% commission on domestic sales; 20% commission on foreign sales.

HOW TO CONTACT "We are happy to consider submissions of fiction and nonfiction in every genre and category except for screenwriting and poetry. If you wish to submit your work to us for consideration, please send a covering letter, brief outline and the opening 50 pages by e-mail. If you want to post your material to us, please be sure to enclose an SAE or the cost of return postage." Replies if interested. Accepts simultaneous submissions.

RICHARD HENSHAW GROUP

145 W. 28th St., 12th Floor, New York NY 10001. (212)414-1172. **Website:** www.richardhenshawgroup. com. **Contact:** Rich Henshaw.

HANDLES "We specialize in popular fiction and nonfiction and are affiliated with a variety of writers' organizations. Our clients include *New York Times* bestsellers and recipients of major awards in fiction and nonfiction." "We only consider works between 65,000-150,000 words." "We do not represent children's books, screenplays, short fiction, poetry, textbooks, scholarly works or coffee-table books."

TERMS Agent receives 15% commission on domestic sales; 20% commission on foreign sales. No written contract. Charges clients for photocopying and book orders.

HOW TO CONTACT "Please feel free to submit a query letter in the form of an e-mail of fewer than 250 words to submissions@henshaw.com address." No snail mail queries. Accepts simultaneous submissions. Obtains most new clients through recommendations from others, solicitations, conferences.

TIPS "While we do not have any reason to believe that our submission guidelines will change in the near future, writers can find up-to-date submission policy information on our website. Always include a SASE with correct return postage."

HERMAN AGENCY

350 Central Park W., Apt. 41, New York NY 10025. (212)749-4907. **E-mail:** ronnie@hermanagencyinc. com; katia.hermanagency@gmail.com. **Website:** www.hermanagencyinc.com. Literary and artistic agency. Member of SCBWI, Graphic Artists' Guild and Authors' Guild. Some of the illustrators represented: Michael Rex, Troy Cummings, Mike Lester, Geoffrey Hayes. Currently not accepting new clients unless they have been successfully published by major trade publishing houses. **Contact:** Ronnie Ann Herman or Katia Herman. "We are a small boutique literary agency that represents authors and artists for the children's book market. We are only accepting submissions for picture books, middle grade, graphic novels."

○ We are accepting very few new clients. If you do to hear from us within 8 weeks, please understand that that means we are not able to represent your work.

HANDLES Specializes in childrens' books of all genres. Actively seeking author/artist picture books and illustrated readers, series, middle grade. Does not want YA or adult books.

TERMS Agent receives 15% commission. Exclusive contract.

HOW TO CONTACT Exclusive representation required. For first contact, e-mail. Responds in 8-16 weeks. For first contact, artists or author/artists should e-mail a link to their website with bio and list of published books as well as new picture book manuscript or dummy to Ronnie. We will contact you only if your samples are right for us. For first contact, authors of middle-grade should e-mail bio, list of published books and first ten pages. Finds illustrators and authors through recommendations from others, conferences, queries/solicitations. Submit via e-mail only. Accepts simultaneous submissions. Obtains very few clients.

TIPS "Check our website to see if you belong with our agency."

HILL NADELL LITERARY AGENCY

6442 Santa Monica Blvd., Suite 201, Los Angeles CA 90038. (310)860-9605. **E-mail:** queries@hillnadell. com. **Website:** www.hillnadell.com.

TERMS Agent receives 15% commission on domestic and film sales; 20% commission on foreign sales. Charges clients for photocopying and foreign mailings.

HOW TO CONTACT Send a query and SASE. If you would like your materials returned, please include adequate postage. To submit electronically: Send your query letter and the first 5-10 pages to queries@hillnadell.com. No attachments. Due to the high volume of submissions the agency receives, it cannot guarantee a response to all e-mailed queries. Accepts simultaneous submissions.

HOLLOWAY LITERARY

P.O. Box 771, Cary NC 27512. **E-mail:** submissions@ hollowayliteraryagency.com. **Website:** hollowayliteraryagency.com. **Contact:** Nikki Terpilowski. A full-service boutique literary agency located in Raleigh, NC.

HANDLES "Note to self-published authors: While we are happy to receive submissions from authors who have previously self-published novels, we do not represent self-published works. Send us your unpublished manuscripts only." Nikki is open to submissions and is selectively reviewing queries for cozy mysteries with culinary, historical or book/publishing industry themes written in the vein of Jaclyn Brady, Laura Childs, Julie Hyzy and Lucy Arlington; women's fiction with strong magical realism similar to Meena van Praag's *The Dress Shop of Dreams*, Sarah Addison Allen's *Garden Spells, Season of the Dragonflies* by Sarah Creech and Mary Robinette Kowal's Glamourist Series. She would love to find a wine-themed mystery series similar to Nadia Gordon's Sunny McCoskey series or Ellen Crosby's Wine County Mysteries that combine culinary themes with lots of great Southern history. Nikki is also interested in seeing contemporary romance set in the southern US or any wine county or featuring a culinary theme, dark, edgy historical romance, gritty military romance or romantic suspense with sexy Alpha heroes and lots of technical detail. She is also interested in acquiring historical fiction written in the vein of Alice Hoffman, Lalita Tademy and Isabel Allende. Nikki is also interested in espionage, military, political and AI thrillers similar to Tom Clancy, Robert Ludlum, Steve Berry, Vince Flynn, Brad Thor and Daniel Silva. Nikki has a special interest in non-fiction subjects related to governance, politics, military strategy and foreign relations; food and beverage, mindfulness, southern living and lifestyle. Does not want horror, true crime or novellas.

RECENT SALES A list of recent sales are listed on the agency website's "news" page.

HOW TO CONTACT Send query and first 15 pages of ms pasted into the body of e-mail to submissions@ hollowayliteraryagency.com. In the subject header write: (Insert Agent's Name)/Title/Genre. Holloway Literary does accept submissions via mail (query letter and first 50 pages). Expect a response time of at least 3 months. Include e-mail address, phone number, social media accounts, and mailing address on your query letter. Accepts simultaneous submissions.

HSG AGENCY

37 W. 28th St., 8th Floor, New York NY 10001. **E-mail:** channigan@hsgagency.com; jsalky@hsgagency.com; jgetzler@hsgagency.com; sroberts@hsgagency.com; leigh@hsgagency.com. **Website:** hsgagency.com.

Contact: Carrie Hannigan; Jesseca Salky; Josh Getzler; Soumeya Roberts; Leigh Eisenman. Hannigan Salky Getzler (HSG) Agency is a boutique literary agency, formed by Carrie Hannigan, Jesseca Salky and Josh Getzler in 2011. "Our agents have over 40 years combined experience in the publishing industry and represent a diverse list of best-selling and award-winning clients. HSG is a full-service literary agency that through collaborative and client-focused representation manages all aspects of an author's career, from manuscript shaping, to sale and publication, subsidiary rights management, marketing and publicity strategy, and beyond. Our diverse and skilled team represents all types of fiction and non-fiction, for both adults and children, and has strong relationships with every major publisher as well as familiarity with independent and start-up publishers offering a different approach to publishing. Our clients have access to the resources and expertise of every member of our agency team, which includes in-house lawyers and contracts professionals, foreign rights managers, and royalty and accounting specialists. Most importantly, our worth is measured by the success of our clients, and so you will find in each HSG agent not only a staunch advocate but a career-long ally."

HANDLES Carrie Hannigan: In the kidlit world, right now Carrie is looking for humorous books and books with warmth, heart and a great voice in both contemporary and fantasy. She is also open to graphic novels and nonfiction. Jesseca Salky: Jesseca is looking for literary fiction submissions that are family stories (she loves a good mother/daughter tale), have a strong sense of place (where the setting feels like its own character), or a daring or unique voice (think Jamie Quatro), as well as upmarket fiction that can appeal to men and women and has that Tropper/Hornby/Matt Norman quality to it. Josh Getzler: Josh is particularly into foreign and historical fiction; both women's fiction (your Downton Abbey/Philippa Gregory Mashups), straight ahead historical fiction (think Wolf Hall or The Road to Wellville); and thrillers and mysteries (The Alienist, say; or Donna Leon or Arianna Franklin). He'd love a strong French Revolution novel. In nonfiction, he's very interested in increasing his list in history (including micro-histories), business, and political thought–but not screeds. Soumeya Roberts: In fiction, Soumeya is seeking literary and upmarket novels and collections, and also represents realistic young-adult and middle-grade.

She likes books with vivid voices and compelling, well-developed story-telling, and is particularly interested in fiction that reflects on the post-colonial world and narratives by people of color. In nonfiction, she is primarily looking for idea-driven or voice-forward memoirs, personal essay collections, and approachable narrative nonfiction of all stripes. Leigh Eisenman: Leigh seeks submissions in the areas of literary and upmarket commercial fiction for adults, and is particularly drawn to: flawed protagonists she can't help but fall in love with (Holden Caulfield was her first crush); stories that take place in contemporary New York, but also any well-defined, vivid setting; explorations of relationships (including journeys of self-discovery); and of course, excellent writing. On the nonfiction side, Leigh is interested in cookbooks, food/travel-related works, health and fitness, lifestyle, humor/gift, and select narrative nonfiction. Please note that we do not represent screenplays, romance fiction, or religious fiction.

RECENT SALES *A Spool of Blue Thread*, by Anne Tyler (Knopf); *Blue Sea Burning*, by Geoff Rodkey (Putnam); *The Partner Track,* by Helen Wan (St. Martin's Press); *The Thrill of the Haunt*, by E.J. Copperman (Berkley); *Aces Wild*, by Erica Perl (Knopf Books for Young Readers); *Steve & Wessley: The Sea Monster*, by Jennifer Morris (Scholastic); *Infinite Worlds*, by Michael Soluri (Simon & Schuster).

HOW TO CONTACT Please send a query letter and the first 5 pages of your ms (within the e-mail–no attachments please) to the appropriate agent for your book. If it is a picture book, please include the entire ms. If you were referred to us, please mention it in the first line of your query. Please note that we do not represent screenplays, romance fiction, or religious fiction. All agents are open to new clients.

ICM PARTNERS

65 E. 55th St., New York NY 10022. (212)556-5600. **E-mail:** careersny@icmpartners.com. **Website:** www.icmtalent.com. **Contact:** Literary Department. With the most prestigious literary publications department in the world, ICM Partners represents a wide range of writers, including the authors of best-selling fiction, self-help and nonfiction books, as well as journalists who write for prominent newspapers and magazines. In addition to handling the sale of publication rights, ICM Partners' literary agents in New York work closely with a team of agents in Los Angeles dedicated ex-

clusively to seeking out opportunities for film and television adaptations. Its foreign rights department works in partnership with the Curtis Brown agency in England, which sells book and magazine projects in the UK and other English-speaking countries as well foreign language translations throughout the world.

HOW TO CONTACT Accepts simultaneous submissions.

INKLINGS LITERARY AGENCY

3419 Virginia Beach Blvd. #183, Virginia Beach VA 23452. **E-mail:** michelle@inklingsliterary.com. **Website:** www.inklingsliterary.com. Inklings Literary Agency is a full service, hands-on literary agency seeking submissions from established authors as well as talented new authors. "We represent a broad range of commercial and literary fiction as well as memoirs and true crime. We are not seeking short stories, poetry, screenplays, or children's picture books."

TERMS Agent takes 15% domestic, 20% subsidiary commission. Charges no fees.

HOW TO CONTACT E-queries only. To query, type "Query (Agent Name)" plus the title of your novel in the subject line, then please send your query letter, short synopsis, and first 10 pages pasted into the body of the e-mail to query@inklingsliterary.com. Check the agency website to make sure that your targeted agent is currently open to submissions. Accepts simultaneous submissions.

INKWELL MANAGEMENT, LLC

521 Fifth Ave., Suite 2600, New York NY 10175. (212)922-3500. **Fax:** (212)922-0535. **E-mail:** info@inkwellmanagement.com. **Website:** www.inkwellmanagement.com.

TERMS Agent receives 15% commission on domestic sales; 20% commission on foreign sales. Offers written contract.

HOW TO CONTACT "In the body of your e-mail, please include a query letter and a short writing sample (1-2 chapters). We currently accept submissions in all genres except screenplays. Due to the volume of queries we receive, our response time may take up to 2 months. Feel free to put 'Query for [Agent Name]: [Your Book Title]' in the e-mail subject line." Accepts simultaneous submissions. Obtains most new clients through recommendations from others.

TIPS "We will not read mss before receiving a letter of inquiry."

INTERNATIONAL TRANSACTIONS, INC.

P.O. Box 97, Gila NM 88038-0097. (845)373-9696. **Website:** www.intltrans.com. **Contact:** Peter Riva. Since 1975, the company has specialized in international idea and intellectual property brokerage catering to multi-national, multi-lingual, licensing and rights' representation of authors and publishers as well as producing award-winning TV and other media. They have been responsible for over 40 years of production, in both media and product, resulting in excess of $1.6 billion in retail sales and several international historic events (the memorabilia of which are on permanent display in national institutions in America, Germany, and France as well as touring internationally). In 2000 by JoAnn Collins BA, RN joined the company and acts as an Associate Editor specializing in women's voices and issues. In 2013 they created an imprint, published by Skyhorse Publishing, called Yucca Publishing which featured over 40 new and independent voices–exciting additions to the book world. In 2015 they created an imprint, Horseshoe Books, to facilitate out-of-print backlist titles to re-enter the marketplace.

HANDLES "We specialize in large and small projects, helping qualified authors perfect material for publication." Actively seeking intelligent, well-written innovative material that breaks new ground. Does not want to receive material influenced by TV (too much dialogue); a rehash of previous successful novels' themes, or poorly prepared material. Does not want to be sent any material being reviewed by others.

RECENT SALES Averaging 20+ book placements per year.

TERMS Agent receives 15% (25%+ on illustrated books) commission on domestic sales; 20% commission on foreign sales and media rights. Offers written contract; 100-day notice must be given to terminate contract. No additional fees, ever.

HOW TO CONTACT In 2018, we will be extremely selective of new projects. First, e-query with an outline or synopsis. E-queries only. Put "Query: [Title]" in the e-mail subject line. Submissions or emails received without these conditions met are automatically discarded. Obtains most new clients through recommendations from others.

TIPS "'Book'—a published work of literature. That last word is the key. Not a string of words, not a book of (TV or film) 'scenes,' and never a stream of consciousness unfathomable by anyone outside of the writer's coterie. A writer should only begin to get 'interested in getting an agent' if the work is polished, literate and ready to be presented to a publishing house. Anything less is either asking for a quick rejection or is a thinly disguised plea for creative assistance—which is often given but never fiscally sound for the agents involved. Writers, even published authors, have difficulty in being objective about their own work. Friends and family are of no assistance in that process either. Writers should attempt to get their work read by the most unlikely and stern critic as part of the editing process, months before any agent is approached. In another matter: the economics of our job have changed as well. As the publishing world goes through the transition to e-books (much as the music industry went through the change to downloadable music)—a transition we expect to see at 95% within 10 years—everyone is nervous and wants 'assured bestsellers' from which to eke out a living until they know what the new e-world will continue to bring. This makes the sales rate and, especially, the advance royalty rates, plummet. Hence, our ability to take risks and take on new clients' work is increasingly perilous financially for us and all agents."

JABBERWOCKY LITERARY AGENCY

49 W. 45th St., 12th Floor, New York NY 10036. **Website:** www.awfulagent.com. **Contact:** Joshua Bilmes.

○   Each agent at this agency is different in terms of openness to submissions. As of the agency updating this listing, only Eddie Schneider, Sam Morgan and Lisa Rodgers were open to queries. Check the agency website for more info.

HANDLES This agency represents quite a lot of genre fiction (science fiction & fantasy), romance, and mystery; and is actively seeking to increase the amount of nonfiction projects. It does not handle children's or picture books. Book-length material only—no poetry, articles, or short fiction.

RECENT SALES *Alcatraz #5* by Brandon Sanderson; *Aurora Teagarden*, by Charlaine Harris; *The Unnoticeables*, by Robert Brockway; *Messenger's Legacy*, by Peter V. Brett; *Slotter Key*, by Elizabeth Moon. Other clients include Tanya Huff, Simon Green, Jack Campbell, Myke Cole, Marie Brennan, Daniel Jose Older, Jim Hines, Mark Hodder, Toni Kelner, Ari Marmell, Ellery Queen, Erin Tettensor, and Walter Jon Williams.

TERMS Agent receives 15% commission on domestic sales; 20% commission on foreign sales. Offers written contract, binding for 1 year. Charges clients for book purchases, photocopying, international book/ms mailing.

HOW TO CONTACT "We are currently open to unsolicited queries. No e-mail, phone, or fax queries, please. Query with SASE. Please check our website, as there may be times during the year when we are not accepting queries. Query letter only; no manuscript material unless requested." Accepts simultaneous submissions. Obtains most new clients through solicitations, recommendation by current clients.

TIPS "In approaching with a query, the most important things to us are your credits and your biographical background to the extent it's relevant to your work. I (and most agents) will ignore the adjectives you may choose to describe your own work."

JANKLOW & NESBIT ASSOCIATES

285 Madison Ave., 21st Floor, New York NY 10017. (212)421-1700. **Fax:** (212)355-1403. **E-mail:** info@janklow.com. **Website:** www.janklowandnesbit.com.

HOW TO CONTACT Be sure to address your submission to a particular agent. For fiction submissions, send an informative cover letter, a brief synopsis and the first 10 pages. "If you are sending an e-mail submission, please include the sample pages in the body of the e-mail below your query. For nonfiction submissions, send an informative cover letter, a full outline, and the first 10 pages of the ms. If you are sending an e-mail submission, please include the sample pages in the body of the e-mail below your query. For picture book submissions, send an informative cover letter, full outline, and include a picture book dummy and at least one full-color sample. If you are sending an e-mail submission, please attach a picture book dummy as a PDF and the full-color samples as JPEGs or PDFs." Accepts simultaneous submissions. Obtains most new clients through recommendations from others.

TIPS "Please send a short query with first 10 pages or artwork."

HARVEY KLINGER, INC.

300 W. 55th St., Suite 11V, New York NY 10019. (212)581-7068. **Website:** www.harveyklinger.com. **Contact:** Harvey Klinger. Always interested in considering new clients, both published and unpublished.

HANDLES This agency specializes in big, mainstream, contemporary fiction and nonfiction. Great debut or established novelists and in nonfiction, authors with great ideas and a national platform already in place to help promote one's book. No screenplays, poetry, textbooks or anything too technical.

RECENT SALES *Land of the Afternoon Sun*, by Barbara Wood; *I Am Not a Serial Killer*, by Dan Wells; *Me, Myself and Us*, by Brian Little; *The Secret of Magic*, by Deborah Johnson; *Children of the Mist*, by Paula Quinn. Other clients include George Taber, Terry Kay, Scott Mebus, Jacqueline Kolosov, Jonathan Maberry, Tara Altebrando, Alex McAuley, Eva Nagorski, Greg Kot, Justine Musk, Michael Northrup, Nina LaCour, Ashley Kahn, Barbara De Angelis, Robert Patton, Augusta Trobaugh, Deborah Blum, Jonathan Skariton.

TERMS Agent receives 15% commission on domestic sales; 25% commission on foreign sales. Offers written contract. Charges for photocopying mss and overseas postage for mss.

HOW TO CONTACT Use online e-mail submission form on the website, or query with SASE via snail mail. No phone or fax queries. Don't send unsolicited mss or e-mail attachments. Make submission letter to the point and as brief as possible. Accepts simultaneous submissions. Obtains most new clients through recommendations from others.

THE KNIGHT AGENCY

232 W. Washington St., Madison GA 30650. **E-mail:** deidre.knight@knightagency.net. **Website:** http://knightagency.net/. **Contact:** Deidre Knight. The Knight Agency is a full-service literary agency with a focus on genre-based adult fiction, YA, MG and select nonfiction projects. With 9 agents and a full-time support staff, our agency strives to give our clients individualized attention. "Our philosophy emphasizes building the author's entire career, from editorial, to marketing, to subrights and social media. TKA has earned a reputation for discovering vivid, original works, and our authors routinely land bestsellers on the New York Times, USA Today, Publishers Weekly, Los Angeles Times, Barnes & Noble Bestseller and Amazon.com Hot 100 lists. Awards received by clients include the RITA, the Hugo, the Newberry Medal, Goodreads Choice Award, the Lambda, the Christy, and Romantic Times' Reviewer Choice Awards, to name only a few."

HANDLES Actively seeking Romance in all subgenres, including romantic suspense, paranormal romance, historical romance (a particular love of mine), LGBT, contemporary, and also category romance. Occasionally I represent new adult. I'm also seeking women's fiction with vivid voices, and strong concepts (think me before you). Further seeking YA and MG, and select nonfiction in the categories of personal development, self-help, finance/business, memoir, parenting and health. Does not want to receive screenplays, short stories, poetry, essays, or children's picture books.

TERMS 15% Simple agency agreement with open-ended commitment. 15% commission on all domestic sales, 20% on foreign and film.

HOW TO CONTACT E-queries only. "Your submission should include a one page query letter and the first five pages of your manuscript. All text must be contained in the body of your e-mail. Attachments will not be opened nor included in the consideration of your work. Queries must be addressed to a specific agent. Please do not query multiple agents." Accepts simultaneous submissions.

KT LITERARY, LLC

9249 S. Broadway, #200-543, Highlands Ranch CO 80129. **E-mail:** contact@ktliterary.com. **Website:** www.ktliterary.com. **Contact:** Kate Schafer Testerman, Sara Megibow, Renee Nyen, Hannah Fergesen, Hilary Harwell. KT Literary is a full-service literary agency operating out of Highlands Ranch, in the suburbs of Denver, Colorado, where every major publishing house is merely an e-mail or phone call away. We believe in the power of new technology to connect writers to readers, and authors to editors. We bring over a decade of experience in the New York publishing scene, an extensive list of contacts, and a lifetime love of reading to the foothills of the Rocky Mountains.

HANDLES Kate is looking only at young adult and middle grade fiction, especially #OwnVoices, and selective nonfiction for teens and tweens. Sara seeks authors in middle grade, young adult, romance, science fiction, and fantasy. Renee is looking for young adult and middle grade fiction only. Hannah is interested in speculative fiction in young adult, middle grade, and adult. Hilary is looking for young adult and middle grade fiction only. "We're thrilled to be actively seeking new clients with great writing, unique stories, and complex characters, for middle grade, young adult, and adult fiction. We are especially interested in diverse voices." Does not want adult mystery, thrillers, or adult literary fiction.

RECENT SALES *On the Wall*, by Carrie Harris; *The Last Sun*, by K.D. Edwards; *The Odds of Loving Grover Cleveland*, by Rebekah Crane; *Trail of Lightning*, by Rebecca Roanhorse; *Future Lost*, by Elizabeth Briggs; *The Summer of Jordi Perez*, by Amy Spalding; *What Goes Up*, by Wen Baragrey, and many more. A full list of clients and most recent sales are available on the agency website and some recent sales are available on Publishers Marketplace.

TERMS Agent receives 15% commission on domestic sales; 20% commission on foreign sales. Offers written contract; 30-day notice must be given to terminate contract.

HOW TO CONTACT "To query us, please select one of the agents at kt literary at a time. If we pass, you can feel free to submit to another. Please e-mail your query letter and the first 3 pages of your manuscript in the body of the e-mail to either Kate at katequery@ktliterary.com, Sara at saraquery@ktliterary.com, Renee at reneequery@ktliterary.com, Hannah at hannahquery@ktliterary.com, or Hilary at hilaryquery@ktliterary.com. The subject line of your e-mail should include the word 'Query' along with the title of your manuscript. Queries should not contain attachments. Attachments will not be read, and queries containing attachments will be deleted unread. We aim to reply to all queries within 4 weeks of receipt. For examples of query letters, please feel free to browse the About My Query archives on the KT Literary website. In addition, if you're an author who is sending a new query, but who previously submitted a novel to us for which we requested chapters but ultimately declined, please do say so in your query letter. If we like your query, we'll ask for the first 5 chapters and a complete synopsis. For our purposes, the synopsis should include the full plot of the book including the conclusion. Don't tease us. Thanks! We are not accepting snail mail queries or queries by phone at this time. We also do not accept pitches on social media." Accepts simultaneous submissions. Obtains most new clients through query slush pile.

LEVINE GREENBERG ROSTAN LITERARY AGENCY, INC.

307 Seventh Ave., Suite 2407, New York NY 10001. (212)337-0934. **Fax:** (212)337-0948. **E-mail:** submit@lgrliterary.com. **Website:** www.lgrliterary.com.

RECENT SALES **Notorious RBG**, by Irin Carmon and Shana Knizhnik; **Pogue's Basics: Life**, by David Pogue; **Invisible City**, by Julia Dahl; **Gumption**, by Nick Offerman; **All the Bright Places**, by Jennifer Niven.

TERMS Agent receives 15% commission on domestic sales; 20% commission on foreign sales. Offers written contract. Charges clients for out-of-pocket expenses—telephone, fax, postage, photocopying—directly connected to the project.

HOW TO CONTACT E-query to submit@lgrliterary.com, or online submission form. "If you would like to direct your query to one of our agents specifically, please feel free to name them in the online form or in the email you send." Cannot respond to submissions by mail. Do not attach more than 50 pages. "Due to the volume of submissions we receive, we are unable to respond to each individually. If we would like more information about your project, we'll contact you within 3 weeks (though we do get backed up on occasion!)." Accepts simultaneous submissions. Obtains most new clients through recommendations from others.

TIPS "We focus on editorial development, business representation, and publicity and marketing strategy."

LEVY CREATIVE MANAGEMENT

425 E. 58th St., Suite 37F, New York NY 10022. (212)687-6463. **Fax:** (212)661-4839. **E-mail:** info@levycreative.com. **Website:** www.levycreative.com. **Contact:** Sari S. Schorr. Handles illustration, ms/illustration packages. Represents 15 illustrators. International Artist Management Agency headquartered in New York City, one of the leading Artist Management & Illustration agencies representing a small grouping of only award-winning artists.

HANDLES Currently open to illustrators seeking representation. Open to both new and established illustrators.

TERMS Offers written contract. Advertising costs are split: 75% paid by illustrators; 25% paid by rep.

HOW TO CONTACT For first contact, see submission guidelines on website. Accepts simultaneous submissions. Finds illustrators through recommendations from others, word of mouth, competitions.

LKG AGENCY

60 Riverside Blvd., #1101, New York NY 10069. **E-mail:** query@lkgagency.com. **Website:** lkgagency.com. **Contact:** Lauren Galit; Caitlen Rubino-Bradway. The LKG Agency was founded in 2005 and is based on the Upper West Side of Manhattan. "We are a boutique literary agency that specializes in middle grade and young adult fiction, as well as nonfiction, both practical and narrative, with a particular interest in women-focused how-to. We invest a great deal of care and personal attention in each of our authors with the aim of developing long-term relationships that last well beyond the sale of a single book."

HANDLES "The LKG Agency specializes in nonfiction, both practical and narrative, as well as middle grade and young adult fiction." Actively seeking parenting, beauty, celebrity, dating & relationships, entertainment, fashion, health, diet & fitness, home & design, lifestyle, memoir, narrative, pets, psychology, women's focused, middle grade & young adult fiction. Does not want history, biography, true crime, religion, picture books, spirituality, screenplays, poetry any fiction other than middle grade or young adult.

HOW TO CONTACT For nonfiction submissions, please send a query letter to nonfiction@lkgagency.com, along with a TOC and 2 sample chapters. The TOC should be fairly detailed, with a paragraph or 2 overview of the content of each chapter. Please also make sure to mention any publicity you have at your disposal. For middle grade and young adult submissions, please send a query, synopsis, and the three (3) chapters, and address all submissions to mgya@lkgagency.com. On a side note, while both Lauren and Caitlen consider young adult and middle grade, Lauren tends to look more for middle grade, while Caitlen deals more with young adult fiction. Please note: due to the high volume of submissions, we are unable to reply to every one. If you do not receive a reply, please consider that a rejection. Accepts simultaneous submissions.

STERLING LORD LITERISTIC, INC.

115 Broadway, New York NY 10006. (212)780-6050. **Fax:** (212)780-6095. **E-mail:** info@sll.com. **Website:** www.sll.com.

TERMS Agent receives 15% commission on domestic sales; 20% commission on foreign sales. Offers written contract.

HOW TO CONTACT Query via snail mail. "Please submit a query letter, a synopsis of the work, a brief proposal or the first 3 chapters of the manuscript, a brief bio or resume, and SASE for reply. Original artwork is not accepted. Enclose sufficient postage if you wish to have your materials returned to you. We do not respond to unsolicited e-mail inquiries." Accepts simultaneous submissions.

LOWENSTEIN ASSOCIATES INC.

115 E. 23rd St., Floor 4, New York NY 10010. (212)206-1630. **Website:** www.lowensteinassociates.com. **Contact:** Barbara Lowenstein.

HANDLES Barbara Lowenstein is currently looking for writers who have a platform and are leading experts in their field, including business, women's issues, psychology, health, science and social issues, and is particularly interested in strong new voices in fiction and narrative nonfiction. Does not want westerns, textbooks, children's picture books and books in need of translation.

TERMS Agent receives 15% commission on domestic sales; 20% commission on foreign sales. Offers written contract. Charges for large photocopy batches, messenger service, international postage.

HOW TO CONTACT "For fiction, please send us a 1-page query letter, along with the first 10 pages pasted in the body of the message by e-mail to assistant@bookhaven.com. If nonfiction, please send a 1-page query letter, a table of contents, and, if available, a proposal pasted into the body of the e-mail. Please put the word 'QUERY' and the title of your project in the subject field of your e-mail and address it to the agent of your choice. Please do not send an attachment as the message will be deleted without being read and no reply will be sent." Accepts simultaneous submissions. Obtains most new clients through recommendations from others, solicitations, conferences.

TIPS "Know the genre you are working in and read!"

⊙ ANDREW LOWNIE LITERARY AGENCY, LTD.

36 Great Smith St., London SW1P 3BU, England. (44)(207)222-7574. **Fax:** (44)(207)222-7576. **E-mail:** lownie@globalnet.co.uk; david.haviland@andrewlownie.co.uk. **Website:** www.andrewlownie.co.uk.

Contact: Andrew Lownie (nonfiction); David Haviland (fiction). The Andrew Lownie Literary Agency Ltd is one of the UK's leading boutique literary agencies with some 200 nonfiction and fiction authors and is actively building its fiction list through new agent David Haviland. Its authors regularly win awards and appear in the bestseller lists. It prides itself on its personal attention to its clients and specialises both in launching new writers and taking established writers to a new level of recognition. According to Publishers Marketplace, Andrew Lownie has been the top selling non-fiction agent in the world for the last few years. He has also been shortlisted for 'Agent of the Year' at the British Bookseller Awards many times.

HANDLES This agent has wide publishing experience, extensive journalistic contacts, and a specialty in showbiz/celebrity memoir. Actively seeking showbiz memoirs, narrative histories, and biographies. No poetry, short stories, children's fiction, academic, or scripts.

RECENT SALES Sells about fifty books a year, with over a dozen top 10 bestsellers including many number ones, as well as the memoirs of Queen Elizabeth II's press officer Dickie Arbiter, Lance Armstrong's masseuse Emma O'Reilly, actor Warwick Davis, Multiple Personality Disorder sufferer Alice Jamieson, round-the-world yachtsman Mike Perham, poker player Dave 'Devilfish' Ulliott, David Hasselhoff, Sam Faiers and Kirk Norcross from TOWIE, Spencer Matthews from Made in Chelsea, singer Kerry Katona. Other clients: Juliet Barker, Guy Bellamy, Joyce Cary estate, Roger Crowley, Patrick Dillon, Duncan Falconer, Cathy Glass, Timothy Good, Robert Hutchinson, Lawrence James, Christopher Lloyd, Sian Rees, Desmond Seward, Daniel Tammet, Casey Watson and Matt Wilven.

TERMS Agent receives 15% commission on domestic sales; 20% commission on foreign sales. Offers written contract; 30-day notice must be given to terminate contract.

HOW TO CONTACT Query by e-mail only. For nonfiction, submit outline and one sample chapter. For fiction, a synopsis and the first 3 chapters. Accepts simultaneous submissions. Obtains most new clients through recommendations from others and unsolicited through website.

LR CHILDREN'S LITERARY

(312)659-8325. **Website:** www.lrchildrensliterary.com. **Contact:** Loretta Caravette. "LR Children's Literary represents authors and illustrators of children's books. We are interested in all genres–picture books, easy readers and early chapter books, middle grade and YA. Please no fantasy for YA or Middle Grade."

HANDLES "I am very interested in the easy readers and early chapter books. I will take on an author/illustrator combination."

HOW TO CONTACT E-query only. Alert this agent if you are contacting other agencies at the same time. If submitting young adult or middle grade, submit the first 3 chapters and a synopsis. If submitting a picture book, send no more than 2 mss. Illustrations (no more than 5MB) can be sent as .JPG or .PDF formats. Accepts simultaneous submissions.

TIPS "No phone calls please."

GINA MACCOBY LITERARY AGENCY

P.O. Box 60, Chappaqua NY 10514. (914)238-5630. **Website:** www.publishersmarketplace.com/members/ginamaccoby/. **Contact:** Gina Maccoby. Gina Maccoby is a New York literary agent representing authors of literary and upmarket fiction and narrative nonfiction for adults and children, including New York Times bestselling and award-winning titles. First and foremost she is captured by an engaging, compelling voice; across all forms she is looking for strong storytelling and fresh perspectives. Areas of interest in nonfiction include history, biography, current events, long-form journalism, and popular science. In fiction she is looking for upmarket novels, mysteries and thrillers, middle grade, and young adult. Gina served four terms on the Board of Directors of the Association of Authors' Representatives and is a member of both the Royalties and Contracts Committees. She belongs to SCBWI and is a long-time member of the Authors Guild. Prior to establishing her own agency in 1986, she was a literary agent at Russell & Volkening for 6 years where she handled her own clients as well as first serial, foreign and movie rights for the agency. Gina grew up mostly in Northern California and graduated with Honors from Harvard College.

TERMS Agent receives 15% commission on domestic sales; 20-25% commission on foreign sales, which includes subagents commissions. May recover certain costs, such as purchasing books, shipping books overseas by airmail, legal fees for vetting motion picture contracts, bank fees for electronic funds transfers, overnight delivery services.

HOW TO CONTACT Query by e-mail only. Accepts simultaneous submissions. Obtains most new clients through recommendations.

MANSION STREET LITERARY MANAGEMENT

E-mail: querymansionstreet@gmail.com. **Website:** mansionstreet.com. **Contact:** Jean Sagendorph; Michelle Witte.

HANDLES Jean is not interested in memoirs or medical/reference. Typically sports and self-help are not a good fit; also does not represent travel books. Michelle is not interested in fiction or nonfiction for adults.

RECENT SALES *Shake and Fetch*, by Carli Davidson; *Bleed, Blister, Puke and Purge*, by J. Marin Younker; *Spectrum*, by Ginger Johnson; *I Left You a Present* and *Movie Night Trivia*, by Robb Pearlman; *Open Sesame!*, by Ashley Evanson; *Fox Hunt*, by Nilah Magruder; *ABC Now You See Me*, by Kim Siebold.

HOW TO CONTACT Send a query letter and no more than the first 10 pages of your ms in the body of an e-mail. Query one specific agent at this agency. No attachments. You must list the genre in the subject line. If the genre is not in the subject line, your query will be deleted. Accepts simultaneous submissions.

● MARJACQ SCRIPTS LTD

Box 412, 19/12 Crawford St., London W1H 1PJ, United Kingdom. (44)(207)935-9499. **Fax:** (44)(207)935-9115. **E-mail:** enquiries@marjacq.com. **Website:** www.marjacq.com. **Contact:** Submissions: individual agent. Business matters: Guy Herbert.. Founded in 1974 by Jacqui Lyons and the late screenwriter and novelist George Markstein, Marjacq is a full-service literary agency with a diverse range of authors across both fiction and non-fiction for adults, young adults and children. We work closely with our authors at every stage of the process, from editorial guidance and negotiating deals, to long-term career management - including selling their work into as many languages as possible and seeking the best opportunities for adaptation to Film, TV and other media. We are a member of the Association of Authors' Agents (AAA).

HANDLES Actively seeking quality fiction, nonfiction, children's books, and young adult books. Does not want to receive stage plays or poetry.

RECENT SALES 3-book deal for Stuart McBride (HarperCollins UK) (repeated *Sunday Times* #1 bestseller); 3-book deal for Howard Linskey.

TERMS Agent receives 15% commission on direct book sales; 20% on foreign rights, film etc Offers written contract. Services include in-house business affairs consultant. No service fees other than commission. Recharges bank fees for money transfers.

HOW TO CONTACT Submit outline, synopsis, 3 sample chapters, bio, covering letter, SASE. "Do not bother with fancy bindings and folders. Keep synopses, bio, and covering letter short." Accepts simultaneous submissions. Obtains most new clients through recommendations from others, solicitations, conferences.

TIPS "Keep trying! If one agent rejects you, you can try someone else. Perseverance and self-belief are important, but do listen to constructive criticism. Be warned, few agents will give you advice as a non-client. We just don't have the time. Be aware of what is being published. If you show awareness of what other writers are doing in your field/genre, you might be able to see how your book fits in and why an editor/agent might be interested in taking it on. Take care with your submissions. Research the agency and pay attention to presentation: ALWAYS follow the specific agency submission guidelines. Doing so helps the agent assess your work. Join writers groups. Sharing your work is a good way to get constructive criticism. If you know anyone in the industry, use your contacts. A personal recommendation will get more notice than cold calling."

MARLENA AGENCY

278 Hamilton Ave., Princeton NJ 08540. (609)252-9405. **Fax:** (609)252-9408. **E-mail:** marlena@marlenaagency.com. **Website:** www.marlenaagency.com. Represents illustrators including Gerard Dubois, Linda Helton, Paul Zwolak, Serge Bloch, Hadley Hooper, Jean-François Martin, Pierre Mornet, Pep Montserrat, Tomasz Walenta, Istvan Orosz, Javier Jaen, Edmon de Haro, Scott Mckowen, Olimpia Zagnoli, Francesco Bongiorni, Lincoln Agnew, Frederic Benaglia, Natalya Balnova, Nate Kitch, Federico Jordan, Agata Endo Nowicka, Mariko Jesse and Carmen Segovia, Andre da Loba and others.

HANDLES Currently open to illustrators seeking representation. Open to both new and established illustrators.

TERMS Exclusive representation required. Offers written contract.

HOW TO CONTACT For first contact, send tearsheets, photocopies, or e-mail low resolution samples only. Submission guidelines available for #10 SASE. Accepts simultaneous submissions. Finds illustrators through queries/solicitations, magazines and graphic design.

TIPS "Be creative and persistent."

MARSAL LYON LITERARY AGENCY, LLC

PMB 121, 665 San Rodolfo Dr. 124, Solana Beach CA 92075. **E-mail:** jill@marsallyonliteraryagency.com, kevan@marsallyonliteraryagency.com, patricia@marsallyonliteraryagency.com, Deborah@marsallyonliteraryagency.com; shannon@marsallyonliteraryagency.com. **Website:** www.marsallyonliteraryagency.com. Query e-mails: jill@marsallyonliteraryagency.com; kevan@marsallyonliteraryagency.com; deborah@marsallyonliteraryagency.com; shannon@marsallyonliteraryagency.com; patricia@marsallyonliteraryagency.com.

○ Please see our web site and visit the pages for each agent to best match your submission to our agents' interests.

RECENT SALES All sales are posted on Publishers' Marketplace.

HOW TO CONTACT Query by e-mail. Query only one agent at this agency at a time. "Please visit our website to determine who is best suited for your work. Write 'query' in the subject line of your e-mail. Please allow up to several weeks to hear back on your query." Accepts simultaneous submissions.

TIPS "Our agency's mission is to help writers achieve their publishing dreams. We want to work with authors not just for a book but for a career; we are dedicated to building long-term relationships with our authors and publishing partners. Our goal is to help find homes for books that engage, entertain, and make a difference."

MARTIN LITERARY AND MEDIA MANAGEMENT

E-mail: sharlene@martinlit.com. **Website:** www.martinlit.com. **Contact:** Sharlene Martin. "Please see our website at www.martinlit.com for company overview, testimonials, bios of literary managers."

HANDLES This agency has strong ties to film/TV. Sharlene Martin has an overall deal with ITV for un-scripted television, Actively seeking nonfiction that is highly commercial and that can be adapted to film. "We are being inundated with queries and submissions that are wrongfully being submitted to us, which only results in more frustration for the writers. Please review our Submission Page on our website and direct your query accordingly."

RECENT SALES *Taking My Life Back*, by Rebekah Gregory with Anthony Flacco; *Maximum Harm*, by Michele McPhee; *Breakthrough*, by Jack Andraka; *In the Matter of Nikola Tesla: A Romance of the Mind*, by Anthony Flacco; *Honor Bound: My Journey to Hell and Back with Amanda Knox*, by Raffaele Sollecito; *Impossible Odds: The Kidnapping of Jessica Buchanan and Dramatic Rescue by SEAL Team Six*, by Jessica Buchanan, Erik Landemalm and Anthony Flacco; *Walking on Eggshells*, by Lisa Chapman; *Newtown: An American Tragedy*, by Matthew Lysiak; *Publish Your Nonfiction Book*, by Sharlene Martin and Anthony Flacco.

TERMS Agent receives 15% commission on domestic sales. We are exclusive for foreign sales to Taryn Fagerness Agency. Offers written contract, binding for 1 year; 1-month notice must be given to terminate contract. 99% of materials are sent electronically to minimize charges to author for postage and copying.

HOW TO CONTACT Query via e-mail with MS Word only. No attachments on queries; place letter in body of e-mail. Accepts simultaneous submissions. Obtains most new clients through recommendations from others.

TIPS "Have a strong platform for nonfiction. Please don't call. (I can't tell how well you write by the sound of your voice.) I welcome e-mail. I'm very responsive when I'm interested in a query and work hard to get my clients' materials in the best possible shape before submissions. Do your homework prior to submission and only submit your best efforts. Please review our website carefully to make sure we're a good match for your work. If you read my book, *Publish Your Nonfiction Book: Strategies For Learning the Industry, Selling Your Book and Building a Successful Career* (Writer's Digest Books) you'll know exactly how to charm me."

MASSIE & MCQUILKIN

27 W. 20th St., Suite 305, New York NY 10011. **E-mail:** info@lmqlit.com. **Website:** www.lmqlit.com.

HANDLES "Massie & McQuilkin is a full-service literary agency that focuses on bringing fiction and nonfiction of quality to the largest possible audience."

RECENT SALES Clients include Roxane Gay, Peter Ho Davies, Kim Addonizio, Natasha Trethewey, David Sirota, Katie Crouch, Uwen Akpan, Lydia Millet, Tom Perrotta, Jonathan Lopez, Chris Hayes, Caroline Weber.

TERMS Agent receives 15% commission on domestic sales; 20% commission on foreign sales. Offers written contract; 30-day notice must be given to terminate contract. Only charges for reasonable business expenses upon successful sale.

HOW TO CONTACT E-query preferred. Include the word "Query" in the subject line of your e-mail. Review the agency's online page of agent bios (lmqlit.com/contact.html), as some agents want sample pages with their submissions and some do not. If you have not heard back from the agency in 4 weeks, assume they are not interested in seeing more. Accepts simultaneous submissions. Obtains most new clients through recommendations from others, solicitations, conferences.

MARGRET MCBRIDE LITERARY AGENCY

P.O. Box 9128, La Jolla CA 92038. (858)454-1550. **Website:** www.mcbrideliterary.com. The Margret McBride Literary Agency has been in business for almost 40 years and has successfully placed over 300 books with mainstream publishers such as Hachette, Hyperion, HarperCollins, Penguin Random House, Simon & Schuster, Rodale, Macmillan, John Wiley & Sons, Houghton Mifflin Harcourt, Workman and Thomas Nelson. We are always looking for new and interesting projects to get excited about. For information about submitting your work for our consideration, please see our website: www.mcbrideliterary.com."

🖵 Only accepts e-mail queries. No snail mail please.

HANDLES This agency specializes in mainstream nonfiction and some commercial fiction. Actively seeking commercial nonfiction, business, health, self-help. Does not want screenplays, romance, poetry, or children's.

RECENT SALES *Millennial Money*, by Grant Sabatier (Atria/Penguin Random House); *Nimble*, by Baba Prasad (Perigee/Penguin Random House—US and World rights excluding India); *Carefrontation*, by Dr.

Arlene Drake (Regan Arts/Phaidon); *There Are No Overachievers*, by Brian Biro (Crown Business/Penguin Random House); *Cheech Is Not My Real Name*, by Richard Marin (Grand Central Books/Hachette); *Killing It!*, by Sheryl O'Loughlin (Harper Business/HarperCollins); *Scrappy*, by Terri Sjodin (Portfolio/Penguin Random House).

TERMS Agent receives 15% commission on domestic sales; 25% commission on translation rights sales (15% to agency, 10% to sub-agent). Charges for overnight delivery and photocopying.

HOW TO CONTACT Please check our website, as instructions are subject to change. Only e-mail queries are accepted: staff@mcbridelit.com. In your query letter, provide a brief synopsis of your work, as well as any pertinent information about yourself. We recommend that authors look at book jacket copy of professionally published books to get an idea of the style and content that should be included in a query letter. Essentially, you are marketing yourself and your work to us, so that we can determine whether we feel we can market you and your work to publishers. There are detailed nonfiction proposal guidelines on our website, but we recommend author's get a copy of How to Write a Book Proposal by Michael Larsen for further instruction. **Please note: The McBride Agency will not respond to queries sent by mail, and will not be responsible for the return of any material submitted by mail.** Accepts simultaneous submissions.

TIPS "E-mail queries only. Please don't call to pitch your work by phone."

SEAN MCCARTHY LITERARY AGENCY

E-mail: submissions@mccarthylit.com. **Website:** www.mccarthylit.com. **Contact:** Sean McCarthy.

HANDLES Sean is drawn to flawed, multifaceted characters with devastatingly concise writing in YA, and character-driven work or smartly paced mysteries/adventures in MG. In picture books, he looks more for unforgettable characters, off-beat humor, and especially clever endings. He is not currently interested in issue-driven stories or query letters that pose too many questions.

HOW TO CONTACT E-query. "Please include a brief description of your book, your biography, and any literary or relevant professional credits in your query letter. If you are a novelist: Please submit the first 3 chapters of your manuscript (or roughly 25 pages) and a 1-page synopsis in the body of the e-mail or as a Word or PDF attachment. If you are a picture book author: Please submit the complete text of your manuscript. We are not currently accepting picture book manuscripts over 1,000 words. If you are an illustrator: Please attach up to 3 JPEGs or PDFs of your work, along with a link to your website." Accepts simultaneous submissions.

⊙ ANNE MCDERMID & ASSOCIATES, LTD

320 Front St. W., Suite 1105, Toronto ON M5V 3B6, Canada. (647)788-4016. **Fax:** (416)324-8870. **E-mail:** admin@mcdermidagency.com. **Website:** www.mcdermidagency.com. **Contact:** Anne McDermid.

HANDLES The agency represents literary novelists and commercial novelists of high quality, and also writers of nonfiction in the areas of memoir, biography, history, literary travel, narrative science, and investigative journalism. "We also represent a certain number of children's and YA writers and writers in the fields of science fiction and fantasy."

HOW TO CONTACT Query via e-mail or mail with a brief bio, description, and first 5 pages of project only. Accepts simultaneous submissions. *No unsolicited manuscripts.* Obtains most new clients through recommendations from others.

MCINTOSH & OTIS, INC.

353 Lexington Ave., New York NY 10016. (212)687-7400. **Fax:** (212)687-6894. **E-mail:** info@mcintoshandotis.com. **Website:** www.mcintoshandotis.com. **Contact:** Elizabeth Winick Rubinstein. McIntosh & Otis has a long history of representing authors of adult and children's books. The children's department is a separate division.

HANDLES Actively seeking "books with memorable characters, distinctive voices, and great plots."

TERMS Agent receives 15% commission on domestic sales; 20% on foreign sales.

HOW TO CONTACT E-mail submissions only. Each agent has their own e-mail address for subs. For fiction: Please send a query letter, synopsis, author bio, and the first 3 consecutive chapters (no more than 30 pages) of your novel. For nonfiction: Please send a query letter, proposal, outline, author bio, and 3 sample chapters (no more than 30 pages) of the ms. For children's & young adult: Please send a query letter, synopsis and the first 3 consecutive chapters (not to exceed 25 pages) of the ms. Accepts simultaneous

submissions. Obtains clients through recommendations from others, editors, conferences and queries.

HOWARD MORHAIM LITERARY AGENCY

30 Pierrepont St., Brooklyn NY 11201. (718)222-8400. **Fax:** (718)222-5056. **E-mail:** info@morhaimliterary.com. **Website:** www.morhaimliterary.com.

HANDLES Agent Kate McKean represents young adult and middle grade when she is open to submissions. Concerning books for children and teens, she seeks "middle grade and young adult full-length novels only in the areas of: mystery, thriller, horror, romance, LGBTQ issues, contemporary fiction, sports, magical realism, fantasy, and science fiction." Concerning what not to send her, avoid sending the following: "books that feature dragons, angels/demons/Grim Reaper, werewolves/vampires/zombies etc., zany middle grade stories about a character's wacky adventures, stories about bullying, stories that center around orphans or parents who die in car crashes, ghost-teens back to right wrongs. No novels in verse. No picture books or chapter books." Kate McKean is open to many subgenres and categories of YA and MG fiction. Check the website for the most details. Actively seeking fiction, nonfiction, and young adult novels.

HOW TO CONTACT Query via e-mail with cover letter and 3 sample chapters. See each agent's listing for specifics. Accepts simultaneous submissions.

MOVEABLE TYPE MANAGEMENT

244 Madison Ave., Suite 334, New York NY 10016. **E-mail:** achromy@movabletm.com. **Website:** www.movabletm.com. **Contact:** Adam Chromy.

HANDLES Mr. Chromy is a generalist, meaning that he accepts fiction submissions of virtually any kind (except juvenile books aimed for middle grade and younger) as well as nonfiction. He has sold books in the following categories: new adult, women's, romance, memoir, pop culture, young adult, lifestyle, horror, how-to, general fiction, and more.

RECENT SALES *The Wedding Sisters*, by Jamie Brenner (St. Martin's Press); *Rage*, by (AmazonCrossing); *Sons Of Zeus*, by Noble Smith (Thomas Dunne Books); *World Made By Hand And Too Much Magic*, by James Howard Kunstler (Grove/Atlantic Press); *Dirty Rocker Boys*, by Bobbie Brown (Gallery/S&S).

HOW TO CONTACT E-queries only. Responds if interested. For nonfiction: Send a query letter in the body of an e-mail that precisely introduces your topic and approach, and includes a descriptive bio. For journalists and academics, please also feel free to include a CV. Fiction: Send your query letter and the first 10 pages of your novel in the body of an e-mail. Your subject line needs to contain the word "Query" or your message will not reach the agency. No attachments and no snail mail. Accepts simultaneous submissions.

ERIN MURPHY LITERARY AGENCY

824 Roosevelt Trail, #290, Windham ME 04062. **Website:** emliterary.com. **Contact:** Erin Murphy, president; Ammi-Joan Paquette, senior agent; Tricia Lawrence, agent; Tara Gonzalez, associate agent.

○ This agency only represents children's books. "We do not accept unsolicited manuscripts or queries. We consider new clients by referral or personal contact only (such as meeting at writers conferences)."

HANDLES Specializes in children's books only.
TERMS Agent receives 15% commission on domestic sales; 20-30% on foreign sales. Offers written contract. 30 days notice must be given to terminate contract.
HOW TO CONTACT Accepts simultaneous submissions.
TIPS Please do not submit to more than one agent at EMLA at a time.

JEAN V. NAGGAR LITERARY AGENCY, INC.

JVNLA, Inc., 216 E. 75th St., Suite 1E, New York NY 10021. (212)794-1082. **Website:** www.jvnla.com. **Contact:** Jennifer Weltz.

HANDLES This agency specializes in mainstream fiction and nonfiction and literary fiction with commercial potential as well as young adult, middle grade, and picture books. Does not want to receive screenplays.
RECENT SALES *Mort(e)*, by Robert Repino; *The Paying Guests*, by Sarah Waters; *The Third Victim*, by Phillip Margolin; *Every Kind of Wanting*, by Gina Frangello; *The Lies They Tell*, by Gillian French; *Dietland*, by Sarai Walker; *Mr. Rochester*, by Sarah Shoemaker; *Not If I See You First*, by Eric Lindstrom.
TERMS Agent receives 15% commission on domestic sales; 20% commission on foreign sales. Offers written contract. Charges for overseas mailing, messenger services, book purchases, photocopying—all deductible from royalties received.

HOW TO CONTACT "Visit our website to send submissions and see what our individual agents are looking for. No snail mail submissions please!" Accepts simultaneous submissions.
TIPS "We recommend courage, fortitude, and patience: the courage to be true to your own vision, the fortitude to finish a novel and polish it again and again before sending it out, and the patience to accept rejection gracefully and wait for the stars to align themselves appropriately for success."

NELSON LITERARY AGENCY

1732 Wazee St., Suite 207, Denver CO 80202. (303)292-2805. **E-mail:** query@nelsonagency.com. **Website:** www.nelsonagency.com. **Contact:** Kristin Nelson, President. Kristin Nelson established Nelson Literary Agency, LLC, in 2002 and over the last decade of her career, she has represented over thirty-five *New York Times* bestselling titles and many *USA Today* bestsellers. Editors call her "a hard-working bulldog agent that will fight for you." When not busy selling books, she is quite sporty. She attempts to play tennis and golf. She also loves playing Bridge (where she is the youngest person in the club). On weekends, she and her husband can be found in the mountains hiking with their 12-year old rat terrier, Chutney. "I'm looking for a good story well told. How you tell that story doesn't need to fit in a neat little category. For specifics, check out the examples on the Submission Guidelines page, follow the clear directions posted there, then submit a query directly to."

○ Kristin is looking for a good story well told. How you tell that story doesn't need to fit in a neat little category. For those looking for more specifics, the below might be helpful: Young adult and upper-level middle-grade novels in all subgeneres; big crossover novels with one foot squarely in genre (*Wool, The Night Circus, Gone Girl*); literary commercial novels (*Hotel on the Corner of Bitter and Sweet, Major Pettigrew's Last Stand, The Art of Racing in the Rain*); upmarket women's fiction (*Keepsake, My Sister's Keeper, Still Alice*); single-title romance, historicals especially (*Ravishing The Heiress, The Ugly Duchess, The Heir*); lead title or hardcover science fiction and fantasy (*Soulless, Game of Thrones, Old Man's War*).

HANDLES NLA specializes in representing commercial fiction and high-caliber literary fiction. "We represent many popular genre categories, including historical romance, steampunk, and all subgenres of YA." Regardless of genre, "we are actively seeking good stories well told." Does not want nonfiction, memoir, stage plays, screenplays, short story collections, poetry, children's picture books, early reader chapter books, or material for the Christian/inspirational market.

TERMS Agent charges industry standard commission.

HOW TO CONTACT "Please visit our website and carefully read our submission guidelines. We do not accept any queries on Facebook or Twitter. Query by e-mail only. Write the word 'Query' in the e-mail subject line along with the title of your novel. Send no attachments, but please paste the first 10 pages of your novel in the body of the e-mail beneath your query letter." Accepts simultaneous submissions.

TIPS "If you would like to learn how to write an awesome pitch paragraph for your query letter or would like any info on how publishing contracts work, please visit Kristin's popular industry blog Pub Rants: http://nelsonagency.com/pub-rants/."

NEW LEAF LITERARY & MEDIA, INC.

110 W. 40th St., Suite 2201, New York NY 10018. (646)248-7989. **Fax:** (646)861-4654. **Website:** www.newleafliterary.com. "We are a passionate agency with a relentless focus on building our clients' careers. Our approach is big picture, offering a one-stop shop built without silos and access to a variety of services including international sales, film and television, and branding resources for all clients. Our aim is to challenge conformity and re-imagine the marketplace while equipping our clients with the tools necessary to navigate an evolving landscape and succeed."

RECENT SALES *Carve the Mark*, by Veronica Roth (HarperCollins); *Red Queen*, by Victoria Aveyard (HarperCollins); *Lobster is the Best Medicine*, by Liz Climo (Running Press); *Ninth House*, by Leigh Bardugo (Henry Holt); *A Snicker of Magic*, by Natalie Lloyd (Scholastic).

HOW TO CONTACT Send query via e-mail. Please do not query via phone. The word "Query" must be in the subject line, plus the agent's name, i.e.–Subject: Query, Suzie Townsend. You may include up to 5 double-spaced sample pages within the body of the e-mail. No attachments, unless specifically requested. Include all necessary contact information. You will receive an auto-response confirming receipt of your query. "We only respond if we are interested in seeing your work."

PARK LITERARY GROUP, LLC

270 Lafayette St., Suite 1504, New York NY 10012. (212)691-3500. **Fax:** (212)691-3540. **E-mail:** info@ parkliterary.com. **Website:** www.parkliterary.com.

HANDLES The Park Literary Group represents fiction and nonfiction with a boutique approach: an emphasis on servicing a relatively small number of clients, with the highest professional standards and focused personal attention. Does not want to receive poetry or screenplays.

RECENT SALES This agency's client list is on their website. It includes bestsellers Nicholas Sparks, Soman Chainani, Emily Giffin, and Debbie Macomber.

HOW TO CONTACT Please specify the first and last name of the agent to whom you are submitting in the subject line of the e-mail. All materials must be in the body of the e-mail. Responds if interested. For fiction submissions, please include a query letter with short synopsis and the first 3 chapters of your work. Accepts simultaneous submissions.

RUBIN PFEFFER CONTENT

648 Hammond St., Chestnut Hill MA 02467. **E-mail:** info@rpcontent.com. **Website:** www.rpcontent.com. **Contact:** Rubin Pfeffer. Rubin Pfeffer Content is a literary agency exclusively representing children's and young adult literature, as well as content that will serve educational publishers and digital developers. Working closely with authors and illustrators, RPC is devoted to producing long-lasting children's literature: work that exemplifies outstanding writing, innovative creativity, and artistic excellence.

HANDLES High-quality children's fiction and non-fiction, including picture books, middle-grade, and young adult. No manuscripts intended for an adult audience.

HOW TO CONTACT Note: Rubin Pfeffer accepts submissions by referral only. Melissa Nasson is open to queries for picture books, middle-grade, and young adult fiction and nonfiction. To query Melissa, email her at melissa@rpcontent.com, include the query letter in the body of the email, and attach the first 50 pages as a Word doc or PDF. If you wish to query Rubin Pfeffer by referral only, specify the contact information of your reference when submitting. Authors/illustrators should send a query and a 1-3 chapter ms via e-mail (no postal submissions). The query, placed in the body of the e-mail, should include a synopsis of the piece, as well as any relevant information regarding previous publications, referrals, websites, and biographies. The ms may be attached as a .doc or a .pdf file. Specifically for illustrators, attach a PDF of the dummy or artwork to the e-mail. Accepts simultaneous submissions.

PIPPIN PROPERTIES, INC.

(212)338-9310. **E-mail:** info@pippinproperties.com. **Website:** www.pippinproperties.com. **Contact:** Holly McGhee. Pippin Properties, Inc. opened its doors in 1998, and for the past 17 years we have been privileged to help build careers for authors and artists whose work stands the test of time, many of whom have become household names in their own right such as Peter H. Reynolds, Kate DiCamillo, Sujean Rim, Doreen Cronin, Renata Liwska, Sarah Weeks, Harry Bliss, Kate & Jim McMullan, Katherine Applegate, David Small, and Kathi Appelt. We also love to launch new careers for amazing authors and artists such as Jason Reynolds, Anna Kang and Chris Weyant, and Jandy Nelson.

HANDLES "We are strictly a children's literary agency devoted to the management of authors and artists in all media. We are small and discerning in choosing our clientele."

TERMS Agent receives 15% commission on domestic sales; 25% commission on foreign sales. Offers written contract; 30-day notice must be given to terminate contract.

HOW TO CONTACT If you are a writer who is interested in submitting a ms, please query us via e-mail, and within the body of that e-mail please include: the first chapter of your novel with a short synopsis of the work or the entire picture book ms. For illustrators interested in submitting their work, please send a query letter detailing your background in illustration and include links to website with a dummy or other examples of your work. Direct all queries to the agent whom you wish to query and please do not query more than one. No attachments, please. Accepts simultaneous submissions. Obtains most new clients through recommendations from others.

TIPS "Please do not call after sending a submission."

PRENTIS LITERARY

PMB 496 6830 NE Bothell Way, Kenmore WA 98028. **Website:** prentisliterary.com. **Contact:** Autumn Frisse, acquisitions; Terry Johnson, business manager. A boutique author focused agency with a devotion to words and the innovative voices that put those words to good use. The agency has always centered on finding books we are passionate about homes. When Linn Prentis was alive, this was her mission and long before she passed, it indeed has been ours as well. Many a time passion has lead us to love, champion and sell books that defy pat definition. While we obviously are seeking the commercially successful, we also demand good writing which we admire that sparks our passion.

HANDLES Special interest in sci-fi and fantasy, but fiction is what truly interests us. Nonfiction projects have to be something we just can't resist. Actively seeking science fiction/fantasy, POC/intersectional, women's fiction, LBGTQ+, literary fiction, children's fiction, YA, MG, mystery, horror, romance, nonfiction/memoir. Please visit website for comprehensive list. Does not want to "receive books for little kids."

RECENT SALES Sales include The Relic Hunter: A Gina Miyoko Mystery NYT best selling author, Maya Bohnhoff, Substrate Phantoms for Jessica Reisman, Vienna for William Kirby; Hunting Ground, Frost Burned and Night Broken titles in two series for NY Times bestselling author Patricia Briggs (as well as a graphic novel *Homecoming*) and a story collection; with more coming; a duology of novels for A.M. Dellamonica whose first book, *Indigo Springs*, won Canada's annual award for best fantasy, as well as several books abroad for client Tachyon Publications.

TERMS Agent receives 15% commission on domestic sales; 20% commission on foreign sales. Offers written contract; 60-day notice must be given to terminate contract.

HOW TO CONTACT No phone or fax queries. No surface mail. For submission use our submission form posted on our submission page or e-mail acquisitions afrisse@prentisliterary.com. For other business business questions e-mail: tjohnson@prentisliterary.com. Accepts simultaneous submissions. Obtains most new clients through recommendations from others, solicitations.

PROSPECT AGENCY

551 Valley Rd., PMB 377, Upper Montclair NJ 07043. (718)788-3217. **Fax:** (718)360-9582. **Website:** www. prospectagency.com. "Prospect Agency focuses on adult and children's literature, and is currently look-

ing for the next generation of writers and illustrators to shape the literary landscape. We are a small, personal agency that focuses on helping each client reach success through hands-on editorial assistance and professional contract negotiations. We also strive to be on the cutting edge of technologically. The agents here spend a lot of time forming personal relationships with authors and their work. Every agent here has incredibly strong editorial skills, and works directly with clients to balance the goals of selling individual books and managing a career."

HANDLES Handles nonfiction, fiction, picture books, middle grade, young adult. "We're looking for strong, unique voices and unforgettable stories and characters."

TERMS Agent receives 15% on domestic sales, 20% on foreign sales sold directly and 25% on sales using a subagent. Offers written contract.

HOW TO CONTACT All submissions are electronic and must be submitted through the portal at prospectagency.com/submissions. We do not accept any submissions through snail mail. Accepts simultaneous submissions. Obtains new clients through conferences, recommendations, queries, and some scouting.

✪ P.S. LITERARY AGENCY

2010 Winston Park Dr., 2nd Floor, Oakville ON L6H 5R7, Canada. **E-mail:** info@psliterary.com. **Website:** www.psliterary.com. **Contact:** Curtis Russell, principal agent; Carly Watters, senior agent; Maria Vicente, literary agent; Eric Smith; literary agent; Kurestin Armada, associate agent.. The P.S. Literary Agency (PSLA) represents both fiction and nonfiction works to leading publishers in North America, Europe and throughout the World. "We maintain a small but select client list that receives our undivided attention and focused efforts. PSLA seeks to work with clients who are professional and committed to their goals. It is our desire to work with clients for the duration of their careers."

◖ "The P.S. Literary Agency represents both fiction and nonfiction in a variety of categories. Seeking both new and established writers."

HANDLES Actively seeking both fiction and nonfiction. Seeking both new and established writers. Does not want to receive poetry or screenplays.

TERMS Agent receives 15% commission on domestic sales; 25% commission on foreign sales. "We offer a written contract, with 30-days notice to terminate."

HOW TO CONTACT Query letters should be directed to query@psliterary.com. PSLA does not accept or respond to phone, paper, or social media queries. Obtains most new clients through solicitations.

TIPS "Please review our website for the most up-to-date submission guidelines. We do not charge reading fees. We do not offer a critique service."

THE PURCELL AGENCY

E-mail: tpaqueries@gmail.com. **Website:** www.the-purcellagency.com. **Contact:** Tina P. Schwartz. This is an agency for authors of children's and teen literature.

HANDLES This agency also takes juvenile nonfiction for MG and YA markets. At this point, the agency is not considering fantasy, science fiction or picture book submissions.

RECENT SALES *Seven Suspects*, by Renee James; *A Kind of Justice*, by Renee James; *Adventures at Hound Hotel*, by Shelley Swanson Sateren; *Adventures at Tabby Towers*, by Shelley Swanson Sateren; *Keys to Freedom*, by Karen Meade.

HOW TO CONTACT Check the website to see if agency is open to submissions and for submission guidelines. Accepts simultaneous submissions.

RED SOFA LITERARY

(651)224-6670. **E-mail:** dawn@redsofaliterary.com laura@redsofaliterary.com; amanda@redsofaliterary.com; stacey@redsofaliterary.com; erik@redsofaliterary.com; liz@redsofaliterary.com. **Website:** www.red-sofaliterary.com. **Contact:** Dawn Frederick, owner/literary agent; Laura Zats, literary agent; Amanda Rutter, associate literary agent; Stacey Graham, associate literary agent; Erik Hane, associate literary agent; Liz Rahn, subrights agent.

HANDLES Dawn Frederick: "I am always in search of a good work of nonfiction that falls within my categories (see my specific list at our website). I especially love pop culture, interesting histories, social sciences/advocacy, humor and books that are great conversation starters. As for fiction, I am always in search of good YA and MG titles. For YA I will go a little darker on the tone, as I enjoy a good gothic, contemporary or historical YA novel. For MG, I will always want something fun and lighthearted, but would love more contemporary themes too." **Laura Zats:** "Diverse YA of all kinds, I'm looking for all genres here, and am especially interested in settings or characters I haven't seen before and queer romantic relationships if there's a romance. Adult science fiction and fantasy. Please note I have an anthropology degree, I'm interested in well-drawn cultures and subverting traditional Chosen One, quest, and colonial narratives. I will fall on the floor and salivate if your writing reminds me of N.K. Jemisin or Nnedi Okorafor. No white dudes on quests, dreams, or Western ideas of Hell, please. Romance/erotica - I am looking for all settings and subgenres here. Must have verbal consent throughout and a twist to traditional romance tropes. If you send me the next The Hating Game, I will be the happiest agent in all the land. Please no rape, querying anything shorter than 60K, or shifters" **Amanda Rutter:** "Science fiction/fantasy, the non-YA ideas, young adult and middle grade–science fiction/fantasy." **Stacey Graham:** "Middle-grade with a great voice — especially funny and/or spooky, Nonfiction (MG/YA/Adult), Romance, and Mystery with a humorous bent." **Erik Hane:** "Literary fiction, Nonfiction [no memoirs]." These are the things we are not actively seeking: **Dawn:** "Memoirs, it seems everyone ignores this request. I also prefer to represent books that aren't overly sappy, overly romantic, or any type of didactic/moralistic." **Laura:** "Nonfiction, including memoir. Adult mystery/thriller/literary fiction. Fiction without quirky or distinctive hooks. Books that follow or fit in trends." **Amanda:** "I am definitely not a non-fiction person. I rarely read it myself, so wouldn't know where to start where to represent! Also, although I enjoy middle grade fiction and would be happy to represent, I won't take on picture books." **Stacey:** "At this time, I do not want to represent YA, fantasy, sci-fi, or romance." **Erik:** "I definitely don't want to represent fiction that sets out at the start to be 'genre.' I like reading it, but I don't think it's for me as an agent. Bring me genre elements, but I think I'd rather let the classification happen naturally. I also don't want memoir unless you've really, really got something unique and accessible. I also don't want to represent children's lit; that's another thing I really do love and appreciate but don't quite connect with professionally."

TERMS Agent receives 15% commission on domestic sales; 20% commission on foreign sales. Offers written contract.

HOW TO CONTACT Query by e-mail or mail with SASE. No attachments, please. Submit full proposal (for nonfiction especially, for fiction it would be nice) plus 3 sample chapters (or first 50 pages) and any other pertinent writing samples upon request by the specific agent. Do not sent within or attached to the query letter. Pdf/doc/docx is preferred, no rtf documents please. Accepts simultaneous submissions. Obtains new clients through queries, also through recommendations from others, solicitations.

TIPS "Always remember the benefits of building an author platform, and the accessibility of accomplishing this task in today's industry. Most importantly, research the agents queried. Avoid contacting every literary agent about a book idea. Due to the large volume of queries received, the process of reading queries for unrepresented categories (by the agency) becomes quite the arduous task. Investigate online directories, printed guides (like *Writer's Market*), individual agent websites, and more, before beginning the query process. It's good to remember that each agent has a vision of what s/he wants to represent and will communicate this information accordingly. We're simply waiting for those specific book ideas to come in our direction."

REES LITERARY AGENCY

14 Beacon St., Suite 710, Boston MA 02108. (617)227-9014. **E-mail:** lorin@reesagency.com. **Website:** reesagency.com.

TERMS Agent receives 15% commission on domestic sales; 20% commission on foreign sales.

HOW TO CONTACT Consult website for each agent's submission guidelines and e-mail addresses, as they differ. Accepts simultaneous submissions. Obtains most new clients through recommendations from others, conferences, submissions.

REGAL HOFFMANN & ASSOCIATES LLC

242 W. 38th St., Floor 2, New York NY 10018. (212)684-7900. **Fax:** (212)684-7906. **Website:** www.rhaliterary.com. Regal Hoffmann & Associates LLC, a full-service agency based in New York, was founded in 2002. We represent works in a wide range of categories, with an emphasis on literary fiction, outstanding thriller and crime fiction, and serious narrative nonfiction.

HANDLES We represent works in a wide range of categories, with an emphasis on literary fiction, outstanding thriller and crime fiction, and serious narrative nonfiction. Actively seeking literary fiction and narrative nonfiction. Does not want romance, science fiction, poetry, or screenplays.

RECENT SALES *Wily Snare*, by Adam Jay Epstein; *Perfectly Undone*, by Jamie Raintree; *A Sister in My House*, by Linda Olsson; *This Is How It Really Sounds*, by Stuart Archer Cohen; *Autofocus*, by Lauren Gibaldi; *We've Already Gone This Far*, by Patrick Dacey; *A Fierce and Subtle Poison*, by Samantha Mabry; *The Life of the World to Come*, by Dan Cluchey; *Willful Disregard*, by Lena Andersson; *The Sweetheart*, by Angelina Mirabella.

TERMS Agent receives 15% commission on domestic sales; 20% commission on foreign sales. We charge no reading fees.

HOW TO CONTACT Query with SASE or via e-mail to submissions@rhaliterary.com. No phone calls. Submissions should consist of a 1-page query letter detailing the book in question, as well as the qualifications of the author. For fiction, submissions may also include the first 10 pages of the novel or one short story from a collection. Responds if interested. Accepts simultaneous submissions.

TIPS "We are deeply committed to every aspect of our clients' careers, and are engaged in everything from the editorial work of developing a great book proposal or line editing a fiction manuscript to negotiating state-of-the-art book deals and working to promote and publicize the book when it's published. We are at the forefront of the effort to increase authors' rights in publishing contracts in a rapidly changing commercial environment. We deal directly with co-agents and publishers in every foreign territory and also work directly and with co-agents for feature film and television rights, with extraordinary success in both arenas. Many of our clients' works have sold in dozens of translation markets, and a high proportion of our books have been sold in Hollywood. We have strong relationships with speaking agents, who can assist in arranging author tours and other corporate and college speaking opportunities when appropriate."

♻ THE RIGHTS FACTORY

P.O. Box 499, Station C, Toronto ON M6J 3P6, Canada. (416)966-5367. **Website:** www.therightsfactory.com. "The Rights Factory is an international literary agency."

HANDLES Plays, screenplays, textbooks.

HOW TO CONTACT There is a submission form on this agency's website. Accepts simultaneous submissions.

RODEEN LITERARY MANAGEMENT

3501 N. Southport #497, Chicago IL 60657. **E-mail:** info@rodeenliterary.com. **Website:** www.rodeenliterary.com. **Contact:** Paul Rodeen.

HANDLES Actively seeking "writers and illustrators of all genres of children's literature including picture books, early readers, middle-grade fiction and nonfiction, graphic novels and comic books, as well as young adult fiction and nonfiction." This is primarily an agency devoted to children's books.

HOW TO CONTACT Unsolicited submissions are accepted by e-mail only. Cover letters with synopsis and contact information should be included in the body of your e-mail. An initial submission of 50 pages from a novel or a longer work of nonfiction will suffice and should be pasted into the body of your e-mail. Accepts simultaneous submissions.

ANDY ROSS LITERARY AGENCY

767 Santa Ray Ave., Oakland CA 94610. (510)238-8965. **E-mail:** andyrossagency@hotmail.com. **Website:** www.andyrossagency.com. **Contact:** Andy Ross. "I opened my literary agency in 2008. Prior to that, I was the owner of the legendary Cody's Books in Berkeley for 30 years. My agency represents books in a wide range of nonfiction genres including: narrative nonfiction, science, journalism, history, popular culture, memoir, and current events. I also represent literary, commercial, historical, crime, upmarket women's fiction, and YA fiction. For nonfiction, I look for writing with a strong voice, robust story arc, and books that tell a big story about culture and society by authors with the authority to write about their subject. In fiction, I like stories about real people in the real world. No vampires and trolls, thank you very much. I don't represent poetry, science fiction, paranormal, and romance. Authors I represent include: Daniel Ellsberg, Jeffrey Moussaieff Masson, Anjanette Delgado, Elisa Kleven, Tawni Waters, Randall Platt, Mary Jo McConahay, Gerald Nachman, Michael Parenti, Paul Krassner, Milton Viorst, and Michele Anna Jordan. I am a member of the Association of Author Representatives (AAR). Check out my website and blog."

HANDLES "This agency specializes in general nonfiction, politics and current events, history, biography, journalism and contemporary culture as well as literary, commercial, and YA fiction." Does not want to receive poetry.

RECENT SALES ~~See my website.~~

TERMS Agent receives 15% commission on domestic sales; 20% commission on foreign sales or other deals made through a sub-agent. Offers written contract.

HOW TO CONTACT Queries should be less than half page. Please put the word "query" in the title header of the e-mail. In the first sentence, state the category of the project. Give a short description of the book and your qualifications for writing. Accepts simultaneous submissions.

SADLER CHILDREN'S LITERARY

(815)209-6252. **Website:** www.sadlerchildrensliterary. com. **Contact:** Jodell Sadler. "Sadler Children's Literary is an independent literary agency, serving aspiring authors and illustrators and branding careers through active media and marketing management in the field of children's literature."

HANDLES Actively seeks picture book author-illustrators or illustrators interested in picture book writing, or illustrators of MG illustrated titles or graphic novels. Please place this in the subject line when you query. Does not want fantasy. "It's not for me. I'm open to KidLit categories from board books to YA novels. My particular focus is on picture books from author-illustrators."

RECENT SALES *Snow Beast* and *Dog Adoption Day* (Roaring Brook Press, Macmillan, 2017, 2018) by author-illustrator, Phil Gosier; *Mr. McGinty's Monarchs* (Sleeping Bear Press, 2016) by Linda Vander Heyden.

TERMS Standard rate. Provided on contract.

HOW TO CONTACT "E-mail submissions only from conferences and events, including participation in webinars and webinar series courses at KidLitCollege. Your subject line should read 'Code provided—(Genre) Title_by_Author' and specifically addressed to me. I prefer a short letter: Hook (why my agency), pitch for you project, and bio (brief background and other categories you work in). All submissions in body of the e-mail, no attachments. Query and complete picture book text; first 10 pages for longer genre category. If you are an illustrator or author-illustrator, I encourage you to contact me, and please send a link to your online portfolio." Accepts simultaneous submissions. "I only obtain clients through writing conferences and SCBWI, Writer's Digest, and KidLitCollege. com webinars and events."

VICTORIA SANDERS & ASSOCIATES

(212)633-8811. **E-mail:** queriesvsa@gmail.com. **Website:** www.victoriasanders.com. **Contact:** Victoria Sanders.

HANDLES Various agents at this agency handle juvenile books, such as young adult and picture books.

TERMS Agent receives 15% commission on domestic sales; 20% commission on foreign/film sales. Offers written contract.

HOW TO CONTACT Authors who wish to contact us regarding potential representation should send a query letter with the first 3 chapters (or about 25 pages) pasted into the body of the message to queriesvsa@gmail.com. We will only accept queries via e-mail. Query letters should describe the project and the author in the body of a single, 1-page e-mail that does not contain any attached files. Important note: Please paste the first 3 chapters of your manuscript (or about 25 pages, and feel free to round up to a chapter break) into the body of your e-mail." Accepts simultaneous submissions.

TIPS "Limit query to letter (no calls) and give it your best shot. A good query is going to get a good response."

WENDY SCHMALZ AGENCY

402 Union St., #831, Hudson NY 12534. (518)672-7697. **E-mail:** wendy@schmalzagency.com. **Website:** www.schmalzagency.com. **Contact:** Wendy Schmalz.

HANDLES Not looking for picture books, science fiction or fantasy.

TERMS Agent receives 15% commission on domestic sales; 20% on foreign sales; 25% for Asia.

HOW TO CONTACT Accepts only e-mail queries. Paste synopsis into the e-mail. Do not attach the ms or sample chapters or synopsis. Replies to queries only if they want to read the ms. If you do not hear from this agency within 2 weeks, consider that a no. Accepts simultaneous submissions. Obtains clients through recommendations from others.

SUSAN SCHULMAN LITERARY AGENCY LLC

454 W. 44th St., New York NY 10036. (212)713-1633. **E-mail:** susan@schulmanagency.com. **Website:** www.publishersmarketplace.com/members/schulman/. **Contact:** Susan Schulman. "A literary agency specializes in representing foreign rights, motion picture, television and allied rights, live stage including com-

mercial theater, opera and dance adaptations, new media rights including e-book and digital applications, and other subsidiary rights on behalf of North American publishers and independent literary agents. The agency also represents its own clients domestically and internationally in all markets. The agency has a particular interest in fiction and nonfiction books for, by and about women and women's issues and interests. The agency's areas of focus include: commercial and literary fiction and nonfiction, specifically narrative memoir, politics, economics, social issues, history, urban planning, finance, law, health, psychology, body/mind/spirit, and creativity and writing."

HANDLES "We specialize in books for, by and about women and women's issues including nonfiction self-help books, fiction, and theater projects. We also handle the film, television. and allied rights for several agencies as well as foreign rights for several publishing houses." Actively seeking new nonfiction. Considers plays. Does not want to receive poetry, television scripts or concepts for television.

RECENT SALES Sold 70 titles in the last year; hundreds of subsidiary rights deals.

TERMS Agent receives 15% commission on domestic sales; 20% commission on foreign sales. Offers written contract; 30-day notice must be given to terminate contract.

HOW TO CONTACT "For fiction: query letter with outline and three sample chapters, resume and SASE. For nonfiction: query letter with complete description of subject, at least one chapter, resume and SASE. Queries may be sent via regular mail or e-mail. Please do not submit queries via UPS or Federal Express. Please do not send attachments with e-mail queries Please incorporate the chapters into the body of the e-mail." Accepts simultaneous submissions. Obtains most new clients through recommendations from others, solicitations, conferences.

TIPS "Keep writing!" Schulman describes her agency as "professional boutique, long-standing, eclectic."

SELECTIC ARTISTS

9 Union Square, #123, Southbury CT 06488. **E-mail:** christopher@selectricartists.com. **Website:** www.selectricartists.com. **Contact:** Christopher Schelling. "Selectric Artists is an agency for literary and creative management founded and run by Christopher Schelling. Selectric's client list includes best-selling and critically-acclaimed authors in many genres, as

well as a few New York pop-rock musicians. Schelling has been an agent for over twenty years and previously held executive editor positions at Dutton and HarperCollins."

HOW TO CONTACT E-mail only. Consult agency website for status on open submissions. Accepts simultaneous submissions.

SERENDIPITY LITERARY AGENCY, LLC

305 Gates Ave., Brooklyn NY 11216. **E-mail:** rbrooks@serendipitylit.com; info@serendipitylit.com. **Website:** www.serendipitylit.com; facebook.com/serendipitylit. **Contact:** Regina Brooks.

○ "Authors who have a hook, platform, and incredible writing are ideal. Must be willing to put efforts into promotion."

TERMS Agent receives 15% commission on domestic sales; 20% commission on foreign sales. Offers written contract; 2-month notice must be given to terminate contract. Charges clients for office fees, which are taken from any advance.

HOW TO CONTACT Check the website, as there are online submission forms for fiction, nonfiction and juvenile. Website will also state if we're temporarily closed to submissions to any areas. Accepts simultaneous submissions. Obtains most new clients through conferences, referrals.

TIPS "See the books *Writing Great Books For Young Adults* and *You Should Really Write A Book: How To Write Sell And Market Your Memoir*. We are looking for high concept ideas with big hooks. If you get writer's block try possibiliteas.co, it's a muse in a cup."

THE SEYMOUR AGENCY

475 Miner St., Canton NY 13617. (239) 398-8209. **E-mail:** nicole@theseymouragency.com; julie@theseymouragency.com. **Website:** www.theseymouragency.com.

TERMS Agent receives 12-15% commission on domestic sales.

HOW TO CONTACT Accepts e-mail queries. Check online for guidelines. Accepts simultaneous submissions.

SPENCERHILL ASSOCIATES

8131 Lakewood Main St., Building M, Suite 205, Lakewood Ranch FL 34202. (941)907-3700. **E-mail:** submission@spencerhillassociates.com. **Website:** www.spencerhillassociates.com. **Contact:** Karen Solem,

Nalini Akolekar, Amanda Leuck, Sandy Harding, and Ali Herring.

HANDLES "We handle mostly commercial women's fiction, historical novels, romance (historical, contemporary, paranormal, urban fantasy), thrillers, and mysteries. We also represent Christian fiction only—no nonfiction." No nonfiction, poetry, children's picture books, or scripts.

RECENT SALES A full list of sales and clients is available on the agency website.

TERMS Agent receives 15% commission on domestic sales; 20% commission on foreign sales. Offers written contract; 3-month notice must be given to terminate contract.

HOW TO CONTACT "We accept electronic submissions only. Please send us a query letter in the body of an e-mail, pitch us your project and tell us about yourself: Do you have prior publishing credits? Attach the first three chapters and synopsis preferably in .doc, rtf or txt format to your email. Send all queries to submission@spencerhillassociates.com. Or submit through the QueryManager link on our website. We do not have a preference for exclusive submissions, but do appreciate knowing if the submission is simultaneous. We receive thousands of submissions a year and each query receives our attention. Unfortunately, we are unable to respond to each query individually. If we are interested in your work, we will contact you within 12 weeks." Accepts simultaneous submissions.

THE SPIELER AGENCY

27 W. 20 St., Suite 302, New York NY 10011. (212)757-4439, ext. 1. **Fax:** (212)333-2019. **Website:** thespieleragency.com. **Contact:** Joe Spieler.

TERMS Agent receives 15% commission on domestic sales. Charges clients for messenger bills, photocopying, postage.

HOW TO CONTACT "Before submitting projects to the Spieler Agency, check the listings of our individual agents and see if any particular agent shows a general interest in your subject (e.g. history, memoir, YA, etc.). Please send all queries either by e-mail or regular mail. If you query us by regular mail, we can only reply to you if you include a SASE." Accepts simultaneous submissions. Obtains most new clients through recommendations, listing in *Guide to Literary Agents*.

STIMOLA LITERARY STUDIO

308 Livingston Ct., Edgewater NJ 07020. **E-mail:** info@stimolaliterarystudio.com. **Website:** www.stimolaliterarystudio.com. **Contact:** Rosemary B. Stimola. "A full service literary agency devoted to representing authors and author/illustrators of fiction and nonfiction, pre-school through young adult, who bring unique and substantive contributions to the industry."

HANDLES Actively seeking remarkable middle grade, young adult fiction, and debut picture book author/illustrators. No institutional books.

TERMS Agent receives 15% commission on domestic sales; 20% (if subagents are employed) commission on foreign sales. Offers written contract, binding for all children's projects. 60 days notice must be given to terminate contract.

HOW TO CONTACT Query via e-mail as per submission guidelines on website. Author/illustrators of picture books may attach text and sample art. A PDF dummy is preferred. Accepts simultaneous submissions. While unsolicited queries are welcome, most clients come through editor, agent, client referrals.

TIPS Agent is hands-on, no-nonsense. May request revisions. Does not line edit but may offer suggestions for improvement before submission. Well-respected by clients and editors. "A firm but reasonable deal negotiator."

STONESONG

270 W. 39th St. #201, New York NY 10018. (212)929-4600. **E-mail:** editors@stonesong.com. **Website:** stonesong.com.

HANDLES Does not represent plays, screenplays, picture books, or poetry.

RECENT SALES *Sweet Laurel*, by Laurel Gallucci and Claire Thomas; *Terrain: A Seasonal Guide to Nature at Home*, by Terrain; *The Prince's Bane*, by Alexandra Christo; *Deep Listening*, by Jillian Pransky; *Change Resilience*, by Lior Arussy; *A Thousand Words*, by Brigit Young.

HOW TO CONTACT Accepts electronic queries for fiction and nonfiction. Submit query addressed to a specific agent. Include first chapter or first 10 pages of ms. Accepts simultaneous submissions.

THE STRINGER LITERARY AGENCY LLC

P.O. Box 111255, Naples FL 34108. **E-mail:** mstringer@stringerlit.com. **Website:** www.stringerlit.com.

Contact: Marlene Stringer. This agency focuses on commercial fiction for adults and teens.

HANDLES This agency specializes in fiction. "We are an editorial agency, and work with clients to make their manuscripts the best they can be in preparation for submission. We focus on career planning, and help our clients reach their publishing goals. We advise clients on marketing and promotional strategies to help them reach their target readership. Because we are so hands-on, we limit the size of our list; however, we are always looking for exceptional voices and stories that demand we read to the end. You never know where the next great story is coming from." This agency is seeking thrillers, crime fiction (not true crime), mystery, women's fiction, single title and category romance, fantasy (all subgenera), earth-based science fiction (no space opera, aliens, etc.), and YA/teen. Does not want to receive picture books, MG, plays, short stories, or poetry. This is not the agency for inspirational romance or erotica. No space opera. The agency is not seeking nonfiction as of this time (2016).

RECENT SALES *The Conqueror's Wife*, by Stephanie Thornton; *When I'm Gone*, by Emily Bleeker; *Magic Bitter, Magic Sweet*, by Charlie N. Holmberg; *Belle Chasse*, by Suzanne Johnson; *Chapel of Ease*, by Alex Bledsoe; *Wilds of the Bayou*, by Susannah Sandlin; *Summit Lake*, by Charlie Donlea; The Jane Doe Series, by Liana Brooks; *The Mermaid's Secret*, by Katie Schickel; *The Sutherland Scandals*, by Anna Bradley; *Fly By Night*, by Andrea Thalasinos; The Joe Gale Mystery Series, by Brenda Buchanan; The Kate Baer Series, by Shannon Baker; Los Nephilim Series, by T. Frohock; The Dragonsworn Series, by Caitlyn McFarland; *The Devious Dr. Jekyll*, by Viola Carr; *The Dragon's Price*, by Bethany Wiggins; The Otter Bite Romance Series, by Maggie McConnell; *Machinations*, by Haley Stone; Film Rights to *Wreckage*, by Emily Bleeker.

TERMS Standard commission. "We do not charge fees."

HOW TO CONTACT Electronic submissions through website submission form only. Please make sure your ms is as good as it can be before you submit. Agents are not first readers. For specific information on what we like to see in query letters, refer to the information at www.stringerlit.com under the heading "Learn." Accepts simultaneous submissions. Obtains new clients through referrals, submissions, conferences.

TIPS "If your ms falls between categories, or you are not sure of the category, query and we'll let you know if we'd like to take a look. We strive to respond as quickly as possible. If you have not received a response in the time period indicated on website, please re-query."

THE STROTHMAN AGENCY, LLC

63 E. 9th St., 10X, New York NY 10003. **E-mail:** info@strothmanagency.com. **Website:** www.strothmanagency.com. **Contact:** Wendy Strothman, Lauren MacLeod. The Strothman Agency, LLC is a highly selective literary agency operating out of New York and Nashville, TN dedicated to advocating for authors of significant books through the entire publishing cycle. Recent Strothman Agency authors have won the Pulitzer Prize for Biography, the National Book Critics Circle Award for Non-Fiction, the Lincoln Prize, and many other awards. Clients have appeared on New York Times bestsellers lists, on National Book Award Long Lists, and two were Finalists for the Pulitzer Prize in History.

HANDLES Specializes in history, science, biography, politics, narrative journalism, nature and the environment, current affairs, narrative nonfiction, business and economics, young adult fiction and nonfiction, and middle grade fiction and nonfiction. "The Strothman Agency seeks out scholars, journalists, and other acknowledged and emerging experts in their fields. We specialize in history, science, narrative journalism, nature and the environment, current affairs, narrative nonfiction, business and economics, young adult fiction and nonfiction, middle grade fiction and nonfiction. We are not signing up projects in romance, science fiction, picture books, or poetry."

TERMS Agent receives 15% commission on domestic sales; 20% commission on foreign sales. Offers written contract; 30-day notice must be given to terminate contract.

HOW TO CONTACT Accepts queries only via e-mail. See submission guidelines online. Accepts simultaneous submissions. "All e-mails received will be responded to with an auto-reply. If we have not replied to your query within 6 weeks, we do not feel that it is right for us." Accepts simultaneous submissions. Obtains most new clients through recommendations from others.

EMMA SWEENEY AGENCY, LLC

245 E 80th St., Suite 7E, New York NY 10075. **E-mail:** info@emmasweeneyagency.com. **Website:** www.emmasweeneyagency.com.

HANDLES Does not want erotica.

HOW TO CONTACT "We accept only electronic queries, and ask that all queries be sent to queries@emmasweeneyagency.com rather than to any agent directly. Please begin your query with a succinct (and hopefully catchy) description of your plot or proposal. Always include a brief cover letter telling us how you heard about ESA, your previous writing credits, and a few lines about yourself. We cannot open any attachments unless specifically requested, and ask that you paste the first 10 pages of your proposal or novel into the text of your e-mail." Accepts simultaneous submissions.

TALCOTT NOTCH LITERARY

31 Cherry St., Suite 100, Milford CT 06460. (203)876-4959. **Fax:** (203)876-9517. **E-mail:** editorial@talcottnotch.net. **Website:** www.talcottnotch.net. **Contact:** Gina Panettieri, President.

HANDLES "We are most actively seeking projects featuring diverse characters and stories which expand the reader's understanding of our society and the wider world we live in."

RECENT SALES Agency sold 65 titles in the last year, including *The Widower's Wife* , by Cate Holahan (Crooked Lane Books); *Tier One*, by Brian Andrews and Jeffrey Wilson (Thomas & Mercer) and *Beijing Red*, written as Alex Ryan (Crooked Lane Books); *Firestorm*, by Nancy Holzner (Berkley Ace Science Fiction); *The New Jersey Mob*, by Scott Deitche (Rowman and Littlefield); *The Homeplace*, by Kevin Wolf (St. Martin's Press); *The Goblin Crown*, by Robert Hewitt Wolfe (Turner Publishing); *The Unprescription for Autism*, by Janet Lintala (Amacom); *Disintegration*, by Richard Thomas (Random House/Alibi); *Red Line*, by Brian Thiem (Crooked Lane Books); and more.

TERMS Agent receives 15% commission on domestic sales; 20% commission on foreign sales. Offers written contract, binding for 1 year.

HOW TO CONTACT Query via e-mail (preferred) with first 10 pages of the ms pasted within the body of the e-mail, not as an attachment. Accepts simultaneous submissions.

TIPS "Know your market and how to reach them. A strong platform is essential in your book proposal. Can you effectively use social media/Are you a strong networker: Are you familiar with the book bloggers in your genre? Are you involved with the interest-specific groups that can help you? What can you do to break through the 'noise' and help present your book to your readers? Check our website for more tips and information on this topic."

THOMPSON LITERARY AGENCY

115 W. 29th St., Third Floor, New York NY 10001. (347)281-7685. **Website:** thompsonliterary.com. **Contact:** Meg Thompson, founder.

HANDLES The agency is always on the lookout for both commercial and literary fiction, as well as young adult and children's books. "Nonfiction, however, is our specialty, and our interests include biography, memoir, music, popular science, politics, blog-to-book projects, cookbooks, sports, health and wellness, fashion, art, and popular culture." "Please note that we do not accept submissions for poetry collections or screenplays, and we only consider picture books by established illustrators."

HOW TO CONTACT "For fiction: Please send a query letter, including any salient biographical information or previous publications, and attach the first 25 pages of your manuscript. For nonfiction: Please send a query letter and a full proposal, including biographical information, previous publications, credentials that qualify you to write your book, marketing information, and sample material. You should address your query to whichever agent you think is best suited for your project." Accepts simultaneous submissions.

THREE SEAS LITERARY AGENCY

P.O. Box 444, Sun Prairie WI 53590. (608)834-9317. **E-mail:** queries@threeseaslit.com. **Website:** threeseasagency.com. **Contact:** Michelle Grajkowski, Cori Deyoe.

HANDLES "We represent more than 50 authors who write romance, women's fiction, science fiction/fantasy, thrillers, young adult and middle grade fiction, as well as select nonfiction titles. Currently, we are looking for fantastic authors with a voice of their own." 3 Seas does not represent poetry or screenplays.

RECENT SALES REPRESENTS Bestselling authors, including Jennifer Brown, Katie MacAlister, Kerrelyn Sparks, and C.L. Wilson.

TERMS Agent receives 15% commission on domestic sales; 20% commission on foreign sales. Offers written contract.

HOW TO CONTACT E-mail queries only; no attachments, unless requested by agents. For fiction, please e-mail the first chapter and synopsis along with a cover letter. Also, be sure to include the genre and the number of words in your manuscript, as well as pertinent writing experience in your query letter. For nonfiction, e-mail a complete proposal, including a query letter and your first chapter. For picture books, query with complete text. Accepts simultaneous submissions. Obtains most new clients through recommendations from others, conferences.

○ TRANSATLANTIC LITERARY AGENCY

2 Bloor St. E., Suite 3500, Toronto ON M4W 1A8, Canada. (416)488-9214. **E-mail:** info@transatlanticagency.com. **Website:** transatlanticagency.com. The Transatlantic Agency represents adult and children's authors of all genres, including illustrators. We do not handle stage plays, musicals or screenplays. Please review the agency website and guidelines carefully before making any inquiries, as each agent has their own particular submission guidelines.

HANDLES "In both children's and adult literature, we market directly into the US, the United Kingdom and Canada." Represents adult and children's authors of all genres, including illustrators. Does not want to receive picture books, musicals, screenplays or stage plays.

RECENT SALES Sold 250 titles in the last year.

TERMS Agent receives 15% commission on domestic sales; 20% commission on foreign sales. Offers written contract; 45-day notice must be given to terminate contract. This agency charges for photocopying and postage when it exceeds $100.

HOW TO CONTACT Always refer to the website, as guidelines will change, and only various agents are open to new clients at any given time. Obtains most new clients through recommendations from others.

S○OTT TREIMEL NY

434 Lafayette St., New York NY 10003. (212)505-8353. **E-mail:** general@scotttreimelny.com. **Website:** scotttreimelny.blogspot.com; www.scotttreimelny.com. **Contact:** Chris Hoyt.

HANDLES This agency specializes in tightly focused segments of the trade and institutional markets, representing both authors and illustrators of books for children and teens.

RECENT SALES *Misunderstood Shark*, by Ame Dyckman (Scholastic); *Crimson*, by Arthur Slade (Harp-

erCanada); *Willa and the Bear*, by Philomena O'Neill (Sterling); *Wee Beastie Series*, by Ame Dyckman (Simon & Schuster); *A Bike Like Sergio's*, by Maribeth Boelts (Candlewick); *Lucky Jonah*, by Richard Scrimger (HarperCanada); *Other Word-ly*, by Yee-Lum Mak (Chronicle); *The Passover Cowboy*, by Barbara Diamond Golden (Apples & Honey Press); *Dandy*, by Ame Dyckman (Little Brown); *You Don't Want a Unicorn*, by Ame Dyckman (Little Brown); *Par-Tay*, by Eloise Greenfield (Alazar Press); *The Women Who Caught the Babies*, by Eloise Greenfield (Alazar Books); *Pupunzel*, by Maribeth Boelts (Random House); *The Fairy Dog Mother*, by Maribeth Boelts (Random House); *Flickers*, by Arthur Slade (HarperCanada).

TERMS Agent receives 15% commission on domestic sales; 20% commission on foreign sales. Offers verbal or written contract, standard terms. Only charges fees for books needed to sell subsidiary rights—foreign, film, etc.

HOW TO CONTACT No longer accepts unsolicited submissions. Wants—via e-mail only—queries from writers recommended by his clients and/or editor pals or that he has met at conferences. Accepts simultaneous submissions.

TIPS "We look for dedicated authors and illustrators able to sustain longtime careers in our increasingly competitive field. I want fresh, not derivative story concepts with overly familiar characters. We look for gripping stories, characters, pacing, and themes. We read for an authentic (to the age) point-of-view, and look for original voices. We spend significant time hunting for the best new work, and do launch debut talent each year. It is best not to send warm-up manuscripts or those already seen all over town."

TRIADA US

P.O. Box 561, Sewickley PA 15143. (412)401-3376. **E-mail:** uwe@triadaus.com; brent@triadaus.com; laura@triadaus.com; lauren@triadaus.com; amelia@triadaus.com. **Website:** www.triadaus.com. **Contact:** Dr. Uwe Stender, President. Triada US was founded by Dr. Uwe Stender over twelve years ago. Since then, the agency has built a high-quality list of fiction and nonfiction for kids, teens, and adults. Triada US titles are consistently critically acclaimed and translated into multiple languages.

HANDLES Actively seeking fiction and non-fiction across a broad range of categories of all age levels.

RECENT SALES *The Hemingway Thief*, by Shaun Harris (Seventh Street); *Finder's Fee*, by Summer Heacock (Mira); *Not Perfect*, by Elizabeth LaBan (Lake Union);

Sometime After Midnight, by L. Philips (Viking); *The Diminished,* by Kaitlyn Sage Patterson (Harlequin Teen); *A Short History of the Girl Next Door,* by Jared Reck (Knopf); *Chaotic Good,* by Whitney Gardner (Knopf); *Project Pandora,* by Aden Polydoros (Entangled Teen); *Skulls!,* by Blair Thornburgh (Atheneum).

TERMS Triada US retains 15% commission on domestic sales and 20% commission on foreign and translation sales. Offers written contract; 30-day notice must be given prior to termination.

HOW TO CONTACT E-mail queries preferred. Please paste your query letter and the first 10 pages of your ms into the body of a message e-mailed to the agent of your choice. Please note: a rejection from 1 Triada US agent is a rejection from all. Obtains most new clients through submission inbox (query letters and requested mss), client referrals, and conferences.

TRIDENT MEDIA GROUP

41 Madison Ave., 36th Floor, New York NY 10010. (212)333-1511. **E-mail:** info@tridentmediagroup.com. **Website:** www.tridentmediagroup.com. **Contact:** Ellen Levine.

HANDLES Actively seeking new or established authors in a variety of fiction and nonfiction genres.

HOW TO CONTACT Submit through the agency's online submission form on the agency website. Query only one agent at a time. If you e-query, include no attachments. Accepts simultaneous submissions.

TIPS "If you have any questions, please check FAQ page before e-mailing us."

THE UNTER AGENCY

23 W. 73rd St., Suite 100, New York NY 10023. (212)401-4068. **E-mail:** jennifer@theunteragency.com. **Website:** www.theunteragency.com. **Contact:** Jennifer Unter.

HANDLES This agency specializes in children's, nonfiction, and quality fiction.

RECENT SALES A full list of recent sales/titles is available on the agency website.

HOW TO CONTACT Send an e-query. There is also an online submission form. If you do not hear back from this agency within 3 months, consider that a no. Accepts simultaneous submissions.

UPSTART CROW LITERARY

244 Fifth Avenue, 11th Floor, New York NY 10001. **Website:** www.upstartcrowliterary.com. **Contact:** Danielle Chiotti, Alexandra Penfold.

HOW TO CONTACT Submit a query and 20 pages pasted into an e-mail. Accepts simultaneous submissions.

WELLS ARMS LITERARY

Website: www.wellsarms.com. Wells Arms Literary represents children's book authors and illustrators to the trade children's book market.

HANDLES "We focus on books for young readers of all ages: board books, picture books, readers, chapter books, middle grade, and young adult fiction." Actively seeking middle grade, young adult, magical realism, contemporary, romance, fantasy. "We do not represent to the textbook, magazine, adult romance or fine art markets."

HOW TO CONTACT E-query. Put "query" and your title in your e-mail subject line addressed to info@wellsarms.com. Accepts simultaneous submissions.

WERNICK & PRATT AGENCY

Website: www.wernickpratt.com. **Contact:** Marcia Wernick; Linda Pratt; Emily Mitchell. "Wernick & Pratt Agency provides each client with personal attention and the highest quality of advice and service that has been the hallmark of our reputations in the industry. We have the resources and accumulated knowledge to assist clients in all aspects of their creative lives including editorial input, contract negotiations, and subsidiary rights management. Our goal is to represent and manage the careers of our clients so they may achieve industry wide and international recognition, as well as the highest level of financial potential."

◑ Dedicated to children's books.

HANDLES "Wernick & Pratt Agency specializes in children's books of all genres, from picture books through young adult literature and everything in between. We represent both authors and illustrators. We do not represent authors of adult books." Wants people who both write and illustrate in the picture book genre; humorous young chapter books with strong voice, and which are unique and compelling; middle grade/YA novels, both literary and commercial. No picture book mss of more than 750 words, or mood pieces; work specifically targeted to the educational market; fiction about the American Revolution, Civil War, or World War II unless it is told from a very unique perspective.

HOW TO CONTACT Submit via e-mail only to submissions@wernickpratt.com. "Please indicate to which agent you are submitting." Detailed submission guidelines available on website. "Submissions will only be responded to further if we are interested in them. If you do not hear from us within 6 weeks of your submission, it should be considered declined." Accepts simultaneous submissions.

○ WESTWOOD CREATIVE ARTISTS, LTD.

386 Huron St., Toronto ON M5S 2G6, Canada. (416)964-3302. **E-mail:** wca_office@wcaltd.com. **Website:** www.wcaltd.com. Westwood Creative Artists is Canada's largest literary agency. It's also one of the oldest and most respected. "Situated in Toronto's Annex neighbourhood, our staff of 11 includes 6 full-time book agents who are supported by an in-house international rights agent and an outstanding network of twenty-four international co-agents. We take great pride in the enthusiastic response to our list from publishers around the world and in the wide praise our writers receive from Canadian and international critics. We are honored that many of the writers we represent have won and been shortlisted for such esteemed prizes as the Man Booker Prize, the Nobel Prize, and the Scotiabank Giller Prize."

HANDLES "We take on children's and young adult writers very selectively. The agents bring their diverse interests to their client lists, but are generally looking for authors with a mastery of language, a passionate, expert or original perspective on their subject, and a gift for storytelling." "Please note that WCA does not represent screenwriters, and our agents are not currently seeking poetry or children's picture book submissions."

HOW TO CONTACT E-query only. Include credentials, synopsis, and no more than 10 pages. No attachments. Accepts simultaneous submissions.

TIPS "We will reject outright complete, unsolicited manuscripts, or projects that are presented poorly in the query letter. We prefer to receive exclusive submissions and request that you do not query more than one agent at the agency simultaneously. It's often best if you approach WCA after you have accumulated some publishing credits."

WHIMSY LITERARY AGENCY, LLC

49 N. 8th St., 6G, Brooklyn NY 11249. (212)674-7162. **E-mail:** whimsynyc@aol.com. **Contact:** Jackie Meyer. Whimsy Literary Agency LLC, specializes in nonfiction books and authors that educate, entertain, and inspire people.

HANDLES "Whimsy looks for non-fiction projects that are concept- and platform-driven. We seek books that educate, inspire, and entertain." Actively seeking experts in their field with integrated and established platforms.

TERMS Agent receives 15% commission on domestic sales; 20% commission on foreign sales. Offers written contract.

HOW TO CONTACT Send your proposal via e-mail to whimsynyc@aol.com (include your media platform, table of contents with full description of each chapter). First-time authors: "We appreciate proposals that are professional and complete. Please consult the many fine books available on writing book proposals. We are not considering poetry, or screenplays. Please Note: Due to the volume of queries and submissions, we are unable to respond unless they are of interest to us." Accepts simultaneous submissions. Obtains most new clients through recommendations from others, solicitations.

WRITERS HOUSE

21 W. 26th St., New York NY 10010. (212)685-2400. **Fax:** (212)685-1781. **Website:** www.writershouse.com.

HANDLES This agency specializes in all types of popular fiction and nonfiction, for both adult and juvenile books as well as illustrators. Does not want to receive scholarly, professional, poetry, plays, or screenplays.

TERMS Agent receives 15% commission on domestic sales. Agent receives 20% commission on foreign sales. Offers written contract, binding for 1 year. Agency charges fees for copying mss/proposals and overseas airmail of books.

HOW TO CONTACT Individual agent email addresses are available on the website. "Please e-mail us a query letter, which includes your credentials, an explanation of what makes your book unique and special, and a synopsis. Some agents within our agency have different requirements. Please consult their individual Publisher's Marketplace (PM) profile for details. We respond to all queries, generally within six to eight weeks." If you prefer to submit my mail, address it to an individual agent, and please include SASE for our reply. (If submitting to Steven Malk: Writers House, 7660 Fay Ave., #338H, La Jolla, CA 92037.) Accepts simultaneous submissions. Obtains most new clients through recommendations from authors and editors.

TIPS "Do not send mss. Write a compelling letter. If you do, we'll ask to see your work. Follow submission guidelines and please do not simultaneously submit your work to more than one Writers House agent."

CLUBS & ORGANIZATIONS

Contacts made through organizations such as the ones listed in this section can be quite beneficial for children's writers and illustrators. Professional organizations provide numerous educational, business, and legal services in the form of newsletters, workshops, or seminars. Organizations can provide tips about how to be a more successful writer or artist, as well as what types of business cards to keep, health and life insurance coverage to carry, and competitions to consider.

An added benefit of belonging to an organization is the opportunity to network with those who have similar interests, creating a support system. As in any business, knowing the right people can often help your career, and important contacts can be made through your peers. Membership in a writer's or artist's organization also shows publishers you're serious about your craft. This provides no guarantee your work will be published, but it gives you an added dimension of credibility and professionalism.

Some of the organizations listed here welcome anyone with an interest, while others are only open to published writers and professional artists. Organizations such as the Society of Children's Book Writers and Illustrators (SCBWI, www.scbwi.org) have varying levels of membership. SCBWI offers associate membership to those with no publishing credits, and full membership to those who have had work for children published. International organizations such as SCBWI also have regional chapters throughout the US and the world. Write or call for more information regarding any group that interests you, or check the websites of the many organizations that list them. Be sure to get information about local chapters, membership qualifications, and services offered.

AMERICAN ALLIANCE FOR THEATRE & EDUCATION

718 7th St. NW, Washington DC 20001. (202)909-1194. **E-mail:** info@aate.com. **Website:** www.aate.com. Purpose of organization: to promote standards of excellence in theatre and drama education. "We achieve this by assimilating quality practices in theatre and theatre education, connecting artists, educators, researchers, and scholars with each other, and by providing opportunities for our members to learn, exchange, and diversify their work, their audiences, and their perspectives." Membership cost: $115 annually for individual in US and Canada, $220 annually for organization, $60 annually for students, and $70 annually for retired people, $310 annually for University Departmental memberships; add $30 outside Canada and US Holds annual conference (July or August). Contests held for unpublished play reading project and annual awards in various categories. Awards plaque and stickers for published playbooks. Publishes list of unpublished plays deemed worthy of performance and stages readings at conference. Contact national office at number above or see website for contact information for Playwriting Network Chairpersons.

AMERICAN SOCIETY OF JOURNALISTS AND AUTHORS

355 Lexington Ave., 15th Floor, New York NY 10017. (212)997-0947. **Website:** www.asja.org. Qualifications for membership: "Need to be a professional freelance nonfiction writer. Refer to website for further qualifications." Membership cost: Application fee—$50; annual dues—$210. Group sponsors national conferences. Professional seminars online and in person around the country. Workshops/conferences open to nonmembers. Publishes a newsletter for members that provides confidential information for nonfiction writers. **Contact:** Holly Koenig, interim executive director.

ARIZONA AUTHORS' ASSOCIATION

6939 East Chaparral Rd., Paradise Valley AZ 85253. (602)510-8076. **E-mail:** azauthors@gmail.com. **Website:** www.azauthors.com. Since 1978, Arizona Authors' Association has served to offer professional, educational and social opportunities to writers and authors and serves as an informational and referral network for the literary community. Members must be authors, writers working toward publication, agents, publishers, publicists, printers, illustrators, etc. Az Authors' publishes a bimonthly newsletter and the renown annual *Arizona Literary Magazine*. The Association sponsors the international Arizona Literary Contest including poetry, essays, short stories, new drama writing, novels, and published books with cash prizes and awards bestowed at a Fall ceremony. Winning entries are published or advertised in the *Arizona Literary Magazine*. First and second place winners in poetry, essay and short story categories are entered in the annual Pushcart Prize. Learn more online. **Contact:** Lisa Aquilina, President.

THE AUTHORS GUILD, INC.

31 E. 32nd St., 7th Floor, New York NY 10016. (212)563-5904. **Fax:** (212)564-5363. **E-mail:** staff@authorsguild.org. **Website:** www.authorsguild.org. Purpose of organization: to offer services and materials intended to help authors with the business and legal aspects of their work, including contract problems, copyright matters, freedom of expression, and taxation. Guild has 8,000 members. Qualifications for membership: Must be book author published by an established American publisher within 7 years or any author who has had 3 works (fiction or nonfiction) published by a magazine or magazines of general circulation in the last 18 months. Associate membership also available. Different levels of membership include: associate membership with all rights except voting available to an author who has a firm contract offer or is currently negotiating a royalty contract from an established American publisher. "The Guild offers free contract reviews to its members. The Guild conducts several symposia each year at which experts provide information, offer advice, and answer questions on subjects of interest and concern to authors. Typical subjects have been the rights of privacy and publicity, libel, wills and estates, taxation, copyright, editors and editing, the art of interviewing, standards of criticism, and book reviewing. Transcripts of these symposia are published and circulated to members. The *Authors Guild Bulletin*, a quarterly journal, contains articles on matters of interest to writers, reports of Guild activities, contract surveys, advice on problem clauses in contracts, transcripts of Guild and League symposia, and information on a variety of professional topics. Subscription included in the cost of the annual dues. **Contact:** Mary Rasenberger, executive director.

☾ CANADIAN SOCIETY OF CHILDREN'S AUTHORS, ILLUSTRATORS AND PERFORMERS

720 Bathurst St., Suite 503, Toronto, Ontario M5S 2R4, Canada. (416)515-1559. **E-mail:** office@canscaip.org. **Website:** www.canscaip.org. Purpose of organization: development of Canadian children's culture and support for authors, illustrators, and performers working in this field. Qualifications for membership: Members: professionals who have been published (not self-published) or have paid public performances/records/tapes to their credit. Friends: share interest in field of children's culture. Sponsors workshops/conferences. Manuscript evaluation services; publishes newsletter: includes profiles of members; news round-up of members' activities countrywide; market news; news on awards, grants, etc; columns related to professional concerns. **Contact:** Helena Aalto, administrative director.

LEWIS CARROLL SOCIETY OF NORTH AMERICA

11935 Beltsville Dr., Beltsville MD 20705. **E-mail:** secretary@lewiscarroll.org. **Website:** www.lewiscarroll.org. "We are an organization of Carroll admirers of all ages and interests and a center for Carroll studies." Qualifications for membership: "An interest in Lewis Carroll and a simple love for Alice (or the Snark for that matter)." Membership cost: $35 (regular membership), $50 (foreign membership), $100 (sustaining membership). The Society meets twice a year—in spring and in fall; locations vary. Publishes a semi-annual journal, *Knight Letter*, and maintains an active publishing program. **Contact:** Sandra Lee Parker, secretary.

GRAPHIC ARTISTS GUILD

32 Broadway, Suite 1114, New York NY 10004. (212)791-3400. **Fax:** 212-791-0333. **E-mail:** admin@gag.org. **Website:** www.graphicartistsguild.org. Purpose of organization: "To promote and protect the economic interests of member artists. It is committed to improving conditions for all creators of graphic arts and raising standards for the entire industry." Qualification for full membership: 50% of income derived from the creation of graphic artwork. Associate members include those in allied fields and students. Initiation fee: $30. Full memberships: $200; student membership: $75/year. Associate membership: $170/year. Publishes *Graphic Artists Guild Handbook, Pricing and Ethical Guidelines* (members receive a copy as part of their membership). **Contact:** Patricia McKiernan, executive director.

HORROR WRITERS ASSOCIATION

P.O. Box 56687, Sherman Oaks CA 91413. 1-818-220-3965. **E-mail:** hwa@horror.org; membership@horror.org. **Website:** www.horror.org. Purpose of organization: To encourage public interest in horror and dark fantasy and to provide networking and career tools for members. Qualifications for membership: Complete membership rules online at www.horror.org/memrule.htm. At least one low-level sale is required to join as an affiliate. Nonwriting professionals who can show income from a horror-related field may join as an associate (booksellers, editors, agents, librarians, etc.). To qualify for full active membership, you must be a published, professional writer of horror. Membership cost: $69 annually. Holds annual Stoker Awards Weekend and HWA Business Meeting. Publishes monthly newsletter focusing on market news, industry news, HWA business for members. Sponsors awards. We give the Bram Stoker Awards for superior achievement in horror annually. Awards include a handmade Stoker trophy designed by sculptor Stephen Kirk. Awards open to nonmembers. **Contact:** Brad Hodson, Administrator.

INTERNATIONAL READING ASSOCIATION

P.O. Box 8139, Newark DE 19714. (302)731-1600. **E-mail:** councils@reading.org. **Website:** www.reading.org. The International Reading Association seeks to promote high levels of literacy for all by improving the quality of reading instruction through studying the reading process and teaching techniques; serving as a clearinghouse for the dissemination of reading research through conferences, journals, and other publications; and actively encouraging the lifetime reading habit. Its goals include professional development, advocacy, partnerships, research, and global literacy development. Sponsors annual convention. Publishes a newsletter called "Reading Today." Sponsors a number of awards and fellowships. More information online.

INTERNATIONAL WOMEN'S WRITING GUILD

International Women's Writing Guild, 5 Penn Plaza, 19th Floor, PMB# 19059, New York NY 10001. (917)720-6959. **E-mail:** iwwgquestions@gmail.com. **Website:** www.iwwg.wildapricot.org. IWWG is a network for the personal and professional empowerment of women through writing. Open to any woman connected to the written word regardless of professional portfolio. IWWG sponsors several annual conferences in all areas of the U.S. The major event, held in the summer, is a week-long conference attracting hundreds of women writers from around the globe. **Contact:** Marj Hahne, Interim Director of Operations.

LITERARY MANAGERS AND DRAMATURGS OF THE AMERICAS

P.O. Box 604074, Bayside NY 11360. (800)680-2148. **E-mail:** info@lmda.org. **Website:** www.lmda.org. LMDA is a not-for-profit service organization for the professions of literary management and dramaturgy. Student Membership: $30/year. Open to students in dramaturgy, performing arts and literature programs, or related disciplines. Proof of student status required. Includes national conference, New Dramaturg activities, local symposia, job phone, and select membership meetings. Individual Membership: $75/year. Open to full-time and part-time professionals working in the fields of literary management and dramaturgy. All privileges and services including voting rights and eligibility for office. Institutional Membership: $200/year. Open to theaters, universities, and other organizations. Includes all privileges and services except voting rights and eligibility for office. Publishes a newsletter featuring articles on literary management, dramaturgy, LMDA program updates, and other articles of interest. Spotlight sponsor membership $500/year; Open to theatres, universities, and other organizations; includes all priviledges for up to six individual members, plus additional promotional benefits.

THE NATIONAL LEAGUE OF AMERICAN PEN WOMEN

Pen Arts Building, 1300 17th St. N.W., Washington D.C. 20036-1973. (202)785-1997. **Fax:** (202)452-6868. **E-mail:** contact@nlapw.org. **Website:** www.americanpenwomen.org. Purpose of organization: to promote professional female work in art, letters, and music since 1897. Qualifications for membership: An applicant must show "proof of sale" in each chosen category—art, letters, and music. Levels of membership include: Active, Associate, International Affiliate, Members-at-Large, Honorary Members (in one or more of the following classifications: Art, Letters, and Music). Holds workshops/conferences. Publishes magazine 4 times/year titled *The Pen Woman*. Sponsors various contests in areas of Art, Letters, and Music. Awards made at Biennial Convention. Biannual scholarships awarded to non-Pen Women for mature women. Awards include cash prizes—up to $1,000. Specialized contests open to nonmembers. **Contact:** Nina Brooks, corresponding secretary.

NATIONAL WRITERS ASSOCIATION

10940 S. Parker Rd., #508, Parker CO 80138. **E-mail:** natlwritersassn@hotmail.com. **Website:** www.nationalwriters.com. Association for freelance writers. Qualifications for membership: associate membership—must be serious about writing; professional membership—must be published and paid writer (cite credentials). Sponsors workshops/conferences: TV/screenwriting workshops, NWAF Annual Conferences, Literary Clearinghouse, editing and critiquing services, local chapters, National Writer's School. Open to nonmembers. Publishes industry news of interest to freelance writers; how-to articles; market information; member news and networking opportunities. Sponsors poetry contest; short story contest; article contest; novel contest. Awards cash for top 3 winners; books and/or certificates for other winners; honorable mention certificate places 5-10. Contests open to nonmembers.

NATIONAL WRITERS UNION

256 W. 38th St., Suite 703, New York NY 10018. (212)254-0279. **Fax:** (212)254-0673. **E-mail:** nwu@nwu.org. **Website:** www.nwu.org. Advocacy for freelance writers. Qualifications for membership: "Membership in the NWU is open to all qualified writers, and no one shall be barred or in any manner prejudiced within the Union on account of race, age, sex, sexual orientation, disability, national origin, religion, or ideology. You are eligible for membership if you have published a book, a play, three articles, five poems, one short story, or an equivalent amount of newsletter, publicity, technical, commer-

cial, government, or institutional copy. You are also eligible for membership if you have written an equal amount of unpublished material and you are actively writing and attempting to publish your work." Holds workshops throughout the country. Members only section on website offers rich resources for freelance writers. Skilled contract advice and grievance help for members.

PEN AMERICAN CENTER

588 Broadway, Suite 303, New York NY 10012. (212)334-1660. **E-mail:** info@pen.org. **Website:** www.pen.org. An association of writers working to advance literature, to defend free expression, and to foster international literary fellowship. PEN welcomes to its membership all writers and those belonging to the larger literary community. We ask that writers have at least one book published or be writers with proven records as professional writers; playwrights and screenwriters should have at least one work produced in a professional setting. Others should have achieved recognition in the literary field. Editors, literary agents, literary scouts, publicists, journalists, bloggers, and other literary professionals are all invited to join as Professional Members. If you feel you do not meet these guidelines, please consider joining as an Advocate Member. Candidates for membership may be nominated by a PEN member or they may nominate themselves with the support of two references from the literary community or from a current PEN member. PEN members receive a subscription to the PEN journal, the PEN Annual Report, and have access to medical insurance at group rates. Members living in the New York metropolitan and tri-state area, or near the Branches, are invited to PEN events throughout the year. Membership in PEN American Center includes reciprocal privileges in PEN American Center branches and in foreign PEN Centers for those traveling abroad. Application forms are available online. PEN American Center is the largest of the 141 centers of PEN International, the world's oldest human rights organization and the oldest international literary organization. PEN International was founded in 1921 to dispel national, ethnic, and racial hatreds and to promote understanding among all countries. PEN American Center, founded a year later, works to advance literature, to defend free expression, and to foster international literary

fellowship. The Center has a membership of 3,400 distinguished writers, editors, and translators. In addition to defending writers in prison or in danger of imprisonment for their work, PEN American Center sponsors public literary programs and forums on current issues, sends prominent authors to inner-city schools to encourage reading and writing, administers literary prizes, promotes international literature that might otherwise go unread in the United States, and offers grants and loans to writers facing financial or medical emergencies.

PUPPETEERS OF AMERICA, INC.

Sabathani Community Center, 310 East 38th St., Suite 127, Minneapolis MN 55409. (888)568-6235. **E-mail:** membership@puppeteers.org; execdir@puppeteers.org. **Website:** www.puppeteers.org. Purpose of organization: to promote the art and appreciation of puppetry as a means of communications and as a performing art. The Puppeteers of America boasts an international membership. There are 9 different levels of membership, from family to youth to library to senior and more. See the website for all details. Costs are $35-90 per year.

SCIENCE-FICTION AND FANTASY WRITERS OF AMERICA, INC.

P.O. Box 3238, Enfield CT 06083. **Website:** www.sfwa.org. Purpose of organization: to encourage public interest in science fiction literature and provide organization format for writers/editors/artists within the genre. Qualifications for membership: at least 1 professional sale or other professional involvement within the field. Different levels of membership include: active—requires 3 professional short stories or 1 novel published; associate—requires 1 professional sale; or affiliate—which requires some other professional involvement such as artist, editor, librarian, bookseller, teacher, etc. Workshops/conferences: annual awards banquet, usually in April or May. Open to nonmembers. Publishes quarterly journal, the *SFWA Bulletin*. Sponsors Nebula Awards for best published science fiction or fantasy in the categories of novel, novella, novelette, and short story. Awards trophy. Also presents the Damon Knight Memorial Grand Master Award for Lifetime Achievement, and, beginning in 2006, the Andre Norton Award for Outstanding Young Adult Science Fiction or Fantasy Book of the Year.

SOCIETY OF CHILDREN'S BOOK WRITERS AND ILLUSTRATORS

4727 Wilshire Blvd #301, Los Angeles CA 90010. (323)782-1010. **Fax:** (323)782-1892. **E-mail:** scbwi@scbwi.org; membership@scbwi.org. **Website:** www.scbwi.org. Purpose of organization: to assist writers and illustrators working or interested in the field. Qualifications for membership: an interest in children's literature and illustration. Membership cost: $80/year. Plus one time $95 initiation fee. Different levels of membership include: P.A.L. membership—published by publisher listed in SCBWI Market Surveys; full membership—published authors/illustrators (includes self-published); associate membership—unpublished writers/illustrators. Holds 100 events (workshops/conferences) worldwide each year. National Conference open to nonmembers. Publishes bi-monthly magazine on writing and illustrating children's books. Sponsors annual awards and grants for writers and illustrators who are members. **Contact:** Stephen Mooser, president; Lin Oliver, executive director.

SOCIETY OF ILLUSTRATORS

128 E. 63rd St., New York NY 10065. (212)838-2560. **Fax:** (212)838-2561. **E-mail:** info@societyillustrators.org. **Website:** www.societyillustrators.org. "Our mission is to promote the art and appreciation of illustration, its history, and evolving nature through exhibitions, lectures, and education. Annual dues for nonresident illustrator members (those living more than 125 air miles from SI's headquarters): $300. Dues for resident illustrator members: $500 per year; resident associate members: $500. Artist members shall include those who make illustration their profession and earn at least 60% of their income from their illustration. Associate members are those who earn their living in the arts or who have made a substantial contribution to the art of illustration. This includes art directors, art buyers, creative supervisors, instructors, publishers, and like categories. The candidate must complete and sign the application form, which requires a brief biography, a listing of schools attended, other training and a résumé of his or her professional career. Candidates for illustrators membership, in addition to the above requirements, must submit examples of their work." **Contact:** Anelle Miller, executive director.

SOCIETY OF MIDLAND AUTHORS

P.O. Box 10419, Chicago IL 60610. **Website:** www.midlandauthors.com. Purpose of organization: create closer association among writers of the Middle West; stimulate creative literary effort; maintain collection of members' works; encourage interest in reading and literature by cooperating with other educational and cultural agencies. Qualifications for membership: membership by invitation only. Must be author or co-author of a book demonstrating literary style and published by a recognized publisher and be identified through residence with Illinois, Indiana, Iowa, Kansas, Michigan, Minnesota, Missouri, Nebraska, North Dakota, Ohio, South Dakota or Wisconsin. Open to students (if authors). Membership cost: $40/year dues. Different levels of membership include: regular—published book authors; associate, nonvoting—not published as above but having some connection with literature, such as librarians, teachers, publishers and editors. Program meetings held 5 times a year, featuring authors, publishers, editors, or the like individually or on panels. Usually second Tuesday of October, November, February, March, and April. Also holds annual awards dinner in May. Publishes a newsletter focusing on news of members and general items of interest to writers. Sponsors contests. "Annual awards in six categories, given at annual dinner in May. Monetary awards for books published that premiered professionally in previous calendar year. Send SASE to contact person for details." Categories include adult fiction, adult nonfiction, juvenile fiction, juvenile nonfiction, poetry, biography. No picture books. Contest open to nonmembers. **Contact:** Meg Tebo, president.

SOCIETY OF SOUTHWESTERN AUTHORS

Fax: (520)751-7877. **E-mail:** wporter202@aol.com. **Website:** www.ssa-az.org. Purpose of organization: to promote fellowship among professional and associate members of the writing profession, to recognize members' achievements, to stimulate further achievement, and to assist persons seeking to become professional writers. Qualifications for membership: Professional Membership: proof of publication of a book, articles, TV screenplay, etc. Associate Membership: proof of desire to write, and/or become a professional. Self-published authors may receive status of Professional Membership at the discretion of the board of directors. Membership cost: see website. Sometimes this organization hosts writing events, such as its cosponsorship of the Arizona Writing Workshops in Phoenix and Tucson in November 2014.

⊙ TEXT & ACADEMIC AUTHORS ASSOCIATION (TAA)

TAA, P.O. Box 367, Fountain City WI 54629. (727)563-0020. **E-mail:** info@taaonline.net. **Website:** www.taaonline.net. TAA's overall mission is "To support textbook and academic authors in the creation of top-quality educational and scholarly works that stimulate the love of learning and foster the pursuit of knowledge." Qualifications for membership: all authors and prospective authors are welcome. Membership cost: $20-$200. Workshops/conferences: June each year. Newsletter focuses on all areas of interest to textbook and academic authors.

THEATRE FOR YOUNG AUDIENCES/USA

c/o The Theatre School, 2350 N. Racine Ave., Chicago IL 60614. (773)325-7981. **Fax:** (773)325-7920. **E-mail:** info@tyausa.org. **Website:** tyausa.org. Purpose of organization: to promote theater for children and young people by linking professional theaters and artists together; sponsoring national, international, and regional conferences and providing publications and information. Also serves as US Center for International Association of the Theatre for Children and Young People. Different levels of memberships include: organizations, individuals, students, retirees, libraries. *TYA Today* includes original articles, reviews, and works of criticism and theory, all of interest to theater practitioners (included with membership). Publishes *Marquee*, a directory that focuses on information on members in US.

VOLUNTEER LAWYERS FOR THE ARTS

1 E. 53rd St., 6th Floor, New York NY 10022. (212)319-2787, ext. 1. **Fax:** (212)752-6575. **E-mail:** vlany@vlany.org. **Website:** www.vlany.org. Purpose of organization: Volunteer Lawyers for the Arts is dedicated to providing free arts-related legal assistance to low-income artists and not-for-profit arts organizations in all creative fields. Over 1,000 attorneys in the New York area donate their time through VLA to artists and arts organizations un-

able to afford legal counsel. Everyone is welcome to use VLA's Art Law Line, a legal hotline for any artist or arts organization needing quick answers to arts-related questions. VLA also provides clinics, seminars, and publications designed to educate artists on legal issues that affect their careers. Members receive discounts on publications and seminars as well as other benefits.

⊙ WRITERS' FEDERATION OF NEW BRUNSWICK

P.O. Box 4528, Rothesay, New Brunswick E2E 5X2, Canada. (506)224-0364. **E-mail:** info@wfnb.ca. **Website:** www.wfnb.ca. Purpose of organization: "to promote New Brunswick writing and to help writers at all stages of their development." Qualifications for membership: interest in writing. Membership cost: $50 basic annual membership; $5, high school students; $50, institutional membership. Holds workshops/conferences. Publishes a newsletter with articles concerning the craft of writing, member news, contests, markets, workshops, and conference listings. Sponsors annual literary competition, $20-$35 entry fee for members, $25-$40 for nonmembers. Categories: fiction, nonfiction, poetry, children's literature. **Contact:** Cathy Fynn, executive director.

⊙ WRITERS' FEDERATION OF NOVA SCOTIA

1113 Marginal Rd., Halifax, Nova Scotia B3H 4P7, Canada. (902)423-8116. **Fax:** (902)422-0881. **E-mail:** director@writers.ns.ca. **Website:** www.writers.ns.ca. Purpose of organization: "to foster creative writing and the profession of writing in Nova Scotia; to provide advice and assistance to writers at all stages of their careers; and to encourage greater public recognition of Nova Scotian writers and their achievements." Regional organization open to anybody who writes. Currently has 800+ members. Offerings include resource library with over 2,500 titles, promotional services, workshop series, annual festivals, mentorship program. Publishes *Eastword*, a bimonthly newsletter containing "a plethora of information on who's doing what; markets and contests; and current writing events and issues." Members and nationally known writers give readings that are open to the public. Additional information online.

WRITERS' GUILD OF ALBERTA

11759 Groat Rd. NW, Edmonton, Alberta T5M 3K6, Canada. (780)422-8174. **E-mail:** mail@writersguild. ca. **Website:** writersguild.ca. Purpose of organization: to support, encourage, and promote writers and writing, to safeguard the freedom to write and to read, and to advocate for the well-being of writers in Alberta. Currently has over 1,000 members. Offerings include retreats/conferences; monthly events; bimonthly magazine that includes articles on writing and a market section; weekly electronic bulletin with markets and event listings; and the Stephan G. Stephansson Award for Poetry (Alberta residents only). Holds workshops/conferences. Publishes a newsletter focusing on markets, competitions, contemporary issues related to the literary arts (writing, publishing, censorship, royalties etc.). Sponsors annual literary awards in 5 categories (novel, nonfiction, children's literature, poetry, drama). Awards include $1,500. Open to nonmembers. **Contact:** Carol Holmes.

CONFERENCES & WORKSHOPS

Writers and illustrators eager to expand their knowledge of the children's publishing industry should consider attending one of the many conferences and workshops held each year. Whether you're a novice or seasoned professional, conferences and workshops are great places to pick up information on a variety of topics and network with experts in the publishing industry, as well as with your peers.

Listings in this section provide details about what conference and workshop courses are offered, where and when they are held, and the costs. Some of the national writing and art organizations also offer regional workshops throughout the year. Write, call, or visit websites for information.

Members of the Society of Children's Book Writers and Illustrators (SCBWI) can find information on conferences in national and local SCBWI newsletters. Nonmembers may attend SCBWI events as well. (Some SCBWI regional events are listed in this section.) For information on SCBWI's annual national conferences and all of their regional events, check their website (scbwi.org) for a complete calendar of conferences and happenings.

AGENTS & EDITORS CONFERENCE

Writers' League of Texas, 611 S. Congress Ave., Suite 200 A-3, Austin TX 78704. (512)499-8914. **Website:** www.writersleague.org/38/conference. **Contact:** Michael Noll, program director. Annual conference held in summer. 2018 dates: June 29-July 1. "This standout conference gives each attendee the opportunity to become a publishing insider. Meet more than 25 top agents, editors, and industry professionals through one-on-one consultations and receptions. Get tips and strategies for revising and improving your manuscript from keynote speakers and presenters (including award-winning and best-selling writers)." Discounted rates are available at the conference hotel.

COSTS Registration for the 2018 conference: $409 for Writers' League members and $469 for non-members through April 2, 2018. Registrations through April 2 include a one-on-one consultation with an agent or editor. After April 2: $449 for members and $409 for non-members, with consultations available for individual purchase.

ADDITIONAL INFORMATION Register before April 3 to receive a free consultation with an agent or editor.

ALASKA WRITERS CONFERENCE

Alaska Writers Guild, P.O. Box 670014, Chugiak AK 99567. **E-mail:** alaskawritersguild.awg@gmail.com. **Website:** alaskawritersguild.com. Annual event held in the fall—usually September. Duration: 2 days. There are many workshops and instructional tracks. Sometimes teams up with SCBWI and Alaska Pacific University to offer courses at the event. Literary agents are in attendance each year to hear pitches and meet writers.

Ⓠ Manuscript critiques available. Note also that the Alaska Writers Guild has many events and meetings each year, not just the annual conference.

AMERICAN CHRISTIAN WRITERS CONFERENCES

P.O. Box 110390, Nashville TN 37222. (800)219-7483 or (615)331-8668. **E-mail:** acwriters@aol.com. **Website:** www.acwriters.com. **Contact:** Reg Forder, director. ACW hosts a dozen annual two-day writers conferences and mentoring retreats across America taught by editors and professional freelance writers.

These events provide excellent instruction, networking opportunities, and valuable one-on-one time with editors. Open to all forms of Christian writing (fiction, nonfiction, and scriptwriting). Conferences are held between March and November during each year. Special rates are available at the host hotel (usually a major chain like Holiday Inn).

COSTS Costs vary and may depend on type of event (conference or mentoring retreat).

ADDITIONAL INFORMATION E-mail or call for conference brochures.

ANNUAL SPRING POETRY FESTIVAL

City College, 160 Convent Ave., New York NY 10031. (212)650-6356. **Website:** www.ccny.cuny.edu/poetry/festival. Workshops geared to all levels. Open to students. Write for more information. Site: Theater B of Aaron Davis Hall.

ANTIOCH WRITERS' WORKSHOP

Antioch Writers' Workshop, c/o Antioch University Midwest, 900 Dayton St., Yellow Springs OH 45387. (937)769-1803. **E-mail:** info@antiochwritersworkshop.com. **Website:** www.antiochwritersworkshop.com. **Contact:** Sharon Short, director. Programs are offered year-round; annual conference held in summer. Average attendance: 80. Workshop concentrations: fiction, poetry, personal essay, and memoir. Site: Antioch University Midwest in the Village of Yellow Springs. Literary agents attend. Writers of all levels (beginner to advanced) are warmly welcomed to discover their next steps on their writing paths—whether that's developing craft or preparing to submit for publication. An agent and an editor will be speaking and available for meetings with attendees. Accommodations are available at local hotels and bed-and-breakfasts.

ADDITIONAL INFORMATION The easiest way to contact this event is through the website's contact form.

ATLANTA WRITERS CONFERENCE

Atlanta Writers Club, Westin Atlanta Airport Hotel, 4736 Best Rd., Atlanta GA 30337. **E-mail:** awconference@gmail.com. **Website:** www.atlantawritersconference.com/about. **Contact:** George Weinstein. Annual conference held in spring. 2018 dates: May 4-5. Literary agents and editors are in attendance to take pitches and critique ms samples and query letters. Conference offers a screenwriting workshop, instructional sessions with local authors, and separate question-and-answer panels with the agents and editors. Site: Westin Airport Atlanta Hotel. A block of rooms is reserved at the conference hotel. Booking instructions will be sent in the registration confirmation e-mail.

COSTS Manuscript critiques are $170 each (2 spots/waitlists maximum). Pitches are $70 each (2 spots/waitlists maximum). There's no charge for waitlists unless a spot opens. Query letter critiques are $70 (1 spot maximum). Other workshops and panels may also cost extra; see website. The "all activities" option is $620 and includes 2 manuscript critiques, 2 pitches, and 1 of each remaining activity.

ADDITIONAL INFORMATION A free shuttle runs between the airport and the hotel.

BIG SUR WRITING WORKSHOP

Henry Miller Library, Hwy. 1, Big Sur CA 93920. (831)667-2574. **E-mail:** writing@henrymiller.org. **Website:** bigsurwriting.wordpress.com. Annual workshop focusing on children's writing (picture books, middle-grade, and young adult). Held every spring in Big Sur Lodge in Pfeiffer State Park. Cost of workshop includes meals, lodging, workshop, and Saturday evening reception. This event is helmed by the literary agents of the Andrea Brown Literary Agency. All attendees meet with at least 2 faculty members to have their work critiqued.

○ Full editorial schedule and much more available online. The Lodge is located 25 miles south of Carmel in Big Sur's Pfeiffer State Park, 47225 Hwy. 1, Big Sur CA 93920.

BOOKS-IN-PROGRESS CONFERENCE

Carnegie Center for Literacy and Learning, 251 W. Second St., Lexington KY 40507. (859)254-4175. **E-mail:** ccll1@carnegiecenterlex.org. **Website:** carnegiecenterlex.org. **Contact:** Laura Whitaker, program director. This is an annual writing conference at the Carnegie Center for Literacy and Learning in Lexington, Kentucky. It typically happens in June. "Each conference will offer writing and publishing workshops and includes a keynote presentation." Literary agents are flown in to meet with writers and hear

pitches. Website is updated several months prior to each annual event. See website for list of area hotels.

○ "Personal meetings with faculty (agents and editors) are only available to full conference participants. Limited slots available. Please choose only one agent; only one pitching session per participant."

CAPE COD WRITERS CENTER ANNUAL CONFERENCE

P.O. Box 408, Osterville MA 02655. (508)420-0200. **E-mail:** writers@capecodwriterscenter.org. **Website:** www.capecodwriterscenter.org. **Contact:** Nancy Rubin Stuart, executive director. Announcing the 56th broad-based literary conference August 2-5, 2018 at the Resort and Conference Center at Hyannis, MA. Workshops in fiction, nonfiction, poetry, memoir, mystery, thrillers, writing for children, social media, screenwriting, promotion, pitches and queries, agent meetings and ms mentorship with agents, editors and faculty. Resort and Conference Center of Hyannis, Massachusetts.

COSTS Costs vary, depending on the number of courses selected, beginning at $125. Several scholarships are available.

CELEBRATION OF SOUTHERN LITERATURE

Southern Lit Alliance, 301 E. 11th St., Suite 301, Chattanooga TN 37403. (423)267-1218. **Fax:** (866)483-6831. **Website:** www.southernlitalliance.org. Biennial conference held in odd-numbered years. "The Celebration of Southern Literature stands out because of its unique collaboration with the Fellowship of Southern Writers, an organization founded by towering literary figures like Eudora Welty, Cleanth Brooks, Walker Percy, and Robert Penn Warren to recognize and encourage literature in the South. The Fellowship awards 11 literary prizes and inducts new members, making this event the place to discover up-and-coming voices in Southern literature. The Southern Lit Alliance's Celebration of Southern Literature attracts more than 1,000 readers and writers from all over the United States. It strives to maintain an informal atmosphere where conversations will thrive, inspired by a common passion for the written word. The Southern Lit Alliance (formerly the Arts & Education Council) started as one of 12 pilot agencies founded by a Ford Foundation grant in 1952. The Alliance is the only organization of the 12 still in existence. The Southern

Lit Alliance celebrates Southern writers and readers through community education and innovative literary arts experiences."

CLARKSVILLE WRITERS CONFERENCE

1123 Madison St., Clarksville TN 37040. (931)551-8870. **E-mail:** artsandheritage@cdelightband.net. **Website:** www.artsandheritage.us/writers. **Contact:** Ellen Kanervo. Annual conference held in the summer at Austin Peay State University. Features a variety of presentations on fiction, nonfiction, and more. Past presenting authors include Tom Franklin, Frye Gaillard, William Gay, Susan Gregg Gilmore, Will Campbell, John Seigenthaler Sr., Alice Randall, George Singleton, Alanna Nash, and Robert Hicks. "Our presentations and workshops are valuable to writers and interesting to readers."

COSTS Costs available online; prices vary depending on how long attendees stay and if they attend the banquet dinner.

ADDITIONAL INFORMATION Multiple literary agents are flown in to the event every year to meet with writers and take pitches.

CONFERENCE FOR WRITERS & ILLUSTRATORS OF CHILDREN'S BOOKS

Book Passage, 51 Tamal Vista Blvd., Corte Madera CA 94925. (415)927-0960, ext. 401. **E-mail:** plivingston@bookpassage.com. **Website:** www.bookpassage.com. Conference for writers and illustrators geared toward beginner and intermediate levels. Sessions cover such topics as the nuts and bolts of writing and illustrating, publisher's spotlight, market trends, developing characters, finding a voice, and the author–agent relationship.

GOTHAM WRITERS' WORKSHOP

writingclasses.com, 555 Eighth Ave., Suite 1402, New York NY 10018. (212)974-8377. **Fax:** (212)307-6325. **E-mail:** contact@gothamwriters.com. **Website:** www. writingclasses.com. Offers craft-oriented creative writing courses in general creative writing, fiction writing, screenwriting, nonfiction writing, article writing, stand-up comedy writing, humor writing, memoir writing, novel writing, children's book writing, playwriting, poetry, songwriting, mystery writing, science fiction writing, romance writing, television writing, article writing, travel writing, and busi-ness writing, as well as classes on freelancing, selling your screenplay, blogging, writing a nonfiction book proposal, and getting published. Also, the workshop offers a teen program, private instruction, and a mentoring program. Classes are held at various schools in New York as well as online. Online classes are held throughout the year. Agents and editors participate in some workshops.

ADDITIONAL INFORMATION See the website for courses, pricing, and instructors.

HAMPTON ROADS WRITERS CONFERENCE

Hampton Roads Writers, P.O. Box 56228, Virginia Beach VA 23456. (757)639-6146. **E-mail:** hrwriters@cox.net. **Website:** hamptonroadswriters.org. Annual conference held in September. 2018 dates: September 13-15. Workshops cover fiction, nonfiction, memoir, poetry, lyric writing, screenwriting, and the business of getting published. A bookshop, 3 free contests with cash prizes, free evening networking social, and many networking opportunities will be available. Multiple literary agents are in attendance each year to meet with writers and hear ten-minute pitches. Much more information available on the website.

COSTS Costs vary. There are discounts for members, for early bird registration, for students, and more.

HIGHLAND SUMMER CONFERENCE

P.O. Box 7014, Radford University, Radford VA 24142. **E-mail:** tburriss@radford.edu; rbderrick@radford.edu. **Website:** tinyurl.com/q8z8ej9. **Contact:** Dr. Theresa Burriss; Ruth Derrick. The Highland Summer Writers' Conference is a 4-day lecture-seminar workshop combination conducted by well known guest writers. It offers the opportunity to study and practice creative and expository writing within the context of regional culture. The course is graded on a pass/fail basis for undergraduates and with letter grades for graduate students. It may be taken twice for credit. The evening readings are free and open to the public. Services at a reduced rate for continuing education credits or to simply participate.

HIGHLIGHTS FOUNDATION FOUNDERS WORKSHOPS

814 Court St., Honesdale PA 18431. (877)288-3410. **Fax:** (570)253-0179. **E-mail:** klbrown@highlights-foundation.org. **Website:** highlightsfoundation.org. 814 Court St.Honesdale PA 18431. (570)253-1192. **Fax:**

(570)253-0179. **E-mail:** contact@highlightsfoundation.org. **Website:** www.highlightsfoundation.org. **Contact:** Kent Brown, director. Workshops geared toward those interested in writing and illustrating for children, intermediate and advanced levels. Classes offered include: Writing Novels for Young Adults, Biography, Nonfiction Writing, Writing Historical Fiction, Wordplay: Writing Poetry for Children, Heart of the Novel, Nature Writing for Kids, Visual Art of the Picture Book, The Whole Novel Workshop, and more (see website for updated list). Workshops held near Honesdale, PA. Workshops limited to between 8 and 14 people. Cost of workshops range from $695 and up. Cost of workshop includes tuition, meals, conference supplies and private housing. Call for application and more information. **Contact:** Kent L. Brown, Jr.. Offers more than three dozen workshops per year. Duration: 3-7 days. Attendance: limited to 10-14. Genre-specific workshops and retreats on children's writing, including fiction, nonfiction, poetry, and promotions. "Our goal is to improve, over time, the quality of literature for children by educating future generations of children's authors." Retreat center location: Highlights Founders' home in Boyds Mills, Pennsylvania. Coordinates pickup at local airport. Offers overnight accommodations. Participants stay in guest cabins on the wooded grounds surrounding Highlights Founders' home adjacent to the house/conference center.

"Applications will be reviewed and accepted on a first-come, first-served basis. Applicants must demonstrate specific experience in the writing area of the workshop they are applying for—writing samples are required for many of the workshops."

COSTS Prices vary based on workshop. Check website for details.

ADDITIONAL INFORMATION Some workshops require pre-workshop assignment. Brochure available for SASE, by e-mail, on website, by phone, by fax. Accepts inquiries by phone, fax, e-mail, SASE. Editors attend conference.

HOUSTON WRITERS GUILD CONFERENCE

Writefest Houston, Houston Writers Guild, P.O. Box 42255, Houston TX 77242. (281)736-7168. **E-mail:** info@houstonwritersguild.org. **Website:** houstonwritersguild.org. This annual conference, organized by the Houston Writers Guild, happens in the spring and has concurrent sessions and tracks on the craft and business of writing. Each year, multiple agents are in attendance taking pitches from writers.

Starting in 2018, the Houston Writers Guild has teamed up with Writespace Houston to enhance the conference. The festival, Writefest, is now a weeklong event with various tracks of sessions during the weekday evenings as well as during the weekend of the festival. Literary journals as well as publishing companies and agents are featured.

COSTS Costs are different for members and nonmembers. Costs depend on how many days and events you sign up for.

ADDITIONAL INFORMATION The conference dates for 2018 are April 30 through May 6; Each year the conference takes place either the last weekend of April or the first weekend of May depending on venue availability.

The Guild also hosts a conference the last weekend of September called Indiepalooza. This conference focuses on marketing and branding for all authors and specific presentations and sessions for authors who are self-publishing.

IOWA SUMMER WRITING FESTIVAL

The University of Iowa, 250 Continuing Education Facility, University of Iowa, Iowa City IA 52242. (319)335-4160. **Fax:** (319)335-4039. **E-mail:** iswfestival@uiowa.edu. **Website:** www.iowasummerwritingfestival.org. Annual festival held in June and July. More than 100 workshops and more than 50 instructors. Workshops are 1 week or a weekend. Attendance is limited to 12 people per class, with more than 1,500 participants throughout the summer. Offers courses across the genres: novel, short story, poetry, essay, memoir, humor, travel, playwriting, screenwriting, writing for children, and women's writing. Held at the University of Iowa campus. Speakers have included Marvin Bell, Lan Samantha Chang, John Dalton, Hope Edelman, Katie Ford, Patricia Foster, Bret Anthony Johnston, and Barbara Robinette Moss. Accommodations available at area hotels. Information on overnight accommodations available by phone or on website.

ADDITIONAL INFORMATION Brochures are available in February. Inquire via e-mail or on website. "Register early. Classes fill quickly."

IWWG SPRING BIG APPLE CONFERENCE

(917)720-6959. **E-mail:** iwwgquestions@iwwg.org. **Website:** www.iwwg.org. One- or two-day annual conference held in New York in Spring. Includes writing workshops, new-authors panel discussing publishing trends, book fair, agents panel, and one-on-one pitch sessions.

JAMES RIVER WRITERS CONFERENCE

2319 E. Broad St., Richmond VA 23223. (804)433-3790. **E-mail:** info@jamesriverwriters.org. **Website:** www.jamesriverwriters.org. **Contact:** Katharine Herndon. Nonprofit supporting writers in the Richmond, VA, area and beyond. Annual conference held in October. The event has master classes, agent pitching, critiques, panels, and more. Previous attending speakers include Ellen Oh, Margot Lee Shetterly, David Baldacci, Jeannette Walls, Adriana Trigiani, Jacqueline Woodson, and more.

- The James River Writers conference is frequently recognized for its friendly atmosphere and southern hospitality.

COSTS Check website for updated pricing.

KENTUCKY WRITERS CONFERENCE

Southern Kentucky Book Fest, WKU South Campus, 2355 Nashville Rd., Bowling Green KY 42101. (270)745-4502. **E-mail:** sara.volpi@wku.edu. **Website:** www.sokybookfest.org. **Contact:** Sara Volpi. This event is entirely free to the public. 2018 date: April 20-21. Duration: 2 days. Part of the 2-day Southern Kentucky Book Fest. Authors who will be participating in the Book Fest on Saturday will give attendees at the conference the benefit of their wisdom on Friday (16 sessions available). For the first time, additional workshops will be offered on Saturday! Free workshops on a variety of writing topics will be presented. Sessions run for 75 minutes, and the day begins at 9 a.m. and ends at 3:30 p.m. The conference is open to anyone who would like to attend, including high school students, college students, teachers, and the general public. Registration will open online in February.

- Since the event is free, interested attendees are asked to register in advance. Information on how to do so is on the website.

KINDLING WORDS EAST

Website: www.kindlingwords.org. Annual retreat held early in the year near Burlington, Vermont. 2017 dates: January 26-29. A retreat with three strands: writer, illustrator, and editor; professional level. Intensive workshops for each strand, and an open schedule for conversations and networking. Registration limited to approximately 70. Hosted by the four-star Inn at Essex (room and board extra). Participants must be published by a CCBC listed publisher, or if in publishing, occupy a professional position. Registration opens August 1 or as posted on the website, and fills quickly. Check website to see if spaces are available, to sign up to be notified when registration opens each year, or for more information. Inquire via contact form on the website.

KINDLING WORDS WEST

Website: www.kindlingwords.org. Annual retreat specifically for children's book writers held in spring out west. 2017 dates: March 21-28. 2017 location: Marble Falls, Texas. Kindling Words West is an artist's colony–style week with workshops by gifted teachers followed by a working retreat. Participants gather just before dinner to have white-space discussions; evenings include fireside readings, star gazing, and songs. Participants must be published by CBC-recognized publisher.

LA JOLLA WRITERS CONFERENCE

P.O. Box 178122, San Diego CA 92177. **E-mail:** akuritz@san.rr.com. **Website:** www.lajollawritersconference.com. **Contact:** Jared Kuritz, director. Annual conference held in fall. 2017 dates: October 27-29. Conference duration: 3 days. Attendance: 200 maximum. The LaJolla Writers Conference covers all genres and both fiction and nonfiction as well as the business of writing. "We take particular pride in educating our attendees on the business aspect of the book industry and have agents, editors, publishers, publicists, and distributors teach classes. There is unprecedented access to faculty. Our conference offers lecture sessions that run for 50 minutes and workshops that run for 110 minutes. Each block period is dedicated to either workshop or lecture-style classes, with 6-8 classes on various topics available each block. For most workshop classes, you are encouraged to bring written work for review. Literary agents from prestigious agencies such as the Andrea Brown

Literary Agency, the Dijkstra Agency, the McBride Agency, Full Circle Literary Group, the Zimmerman Literary Agency, the Van Haitsma Literary Agency, the Farris Literary Agency, and more have participated in the past, teaching workshops in which they are familiarized with attendee work. Late night and early bird sessions are also available. The conference creates a strong sense of community, and it has seen many of its attendees successfully published."

COSTS $395 for full 2017 conference registration (doesn't include lodging or breakfast).

LEAGUE OF UTAH WRITERS' ANNUAL WRITER'S CONFERENCES

Spring Conference and Quills Conference, 1042 East Fort Union Blvd. #443, Midvale UT 84047. (385)434-0355. **E-mail:** president@leagueofutahwriters.org. **Website:** https://www.leagueofutahwriters.com. **Contact:** Johnny Worthen. The annual Spring Conference presented by League of Utah Writers includes a full day of workshops and presentations focused on improving your skills as a writer. Please join us! The Quills Conference is an intermountain west professional writer's weekend. Come learn from industry professionals what you need to be successful in writing and publishing. This two day event is packed with presentations on poetry, prose and screenwriting and includes dining with an award-winning catering staff at the beautiful University Marriott adjacent to the University of Utah campus. Conference meals include Friday dinner and Saturday lunch. Awards banquet is optional. Register for the appropriate ticket if you wish to attend the Saturday night banquet where the 2018 Quill Awards will be announced.

○ The Spring Conference is held at Salt Lake Community College Student Ctr. The Quills Conference is held at Salt Lake City Marriott University Park.

COSTS Spring Conference is $50 for members. Quills Conference is $250 for members.

MIDWEST WRITERS WORKSHOP

(765)282-1055. **E-mail:** midwestwriters@yahoo.com. **Website:** www.midwestwriters.org. **Contact:** Jama Kehoe Bigger, director. Annual workshop held in July in east central Indiana. Writer workshops geared toward writers of all levels, including craft and business sessions. Topics include most genres. Faculty/speakers have included Joyce Carol Oates, George Plimpton, Clive Cussler, Haven Kimmel, William Kent Krueger, William Zinsser, John Gilstrap, Lee Martin, Jane Friedman, Chuck Sambuchino, and numerous best-selling mystery, literary fiction, young adult, and children's authors. Workshop also includes agent pitch sessions, ms evaluation, query letter critiques, and social media tutoring. Registration tentatively limited to 240.

COSTS $155-400. Most meals included.

ADDITIONAL INFORMATION Offers scholarships. See website for more information. Keep in touch with the MWW at facebook.com/midwestwriters and twitter.com/midwestwriters.

MISSOURI WRITERS' GUILD CONFERENCE

St. Louis MO **E-mail:** mwgconferenceinfo@gmail.com. **Website:** www.missouriwritersguild.org. **Contact:** Tricia Sanders, vice president/conference chair. Annual conference held in spring. 2017 dates: May 5-7. Writer and illustrator workshops geared to all levels. Open to students. "Gives writers the opportunity to hear outstanding speakers and to receive information on marketing, research, and writing techniques." Agents, editors, and published authors in attendance.

ADDITIONAL INFORMATION The primary contact individual changes every year, because the conference chair changes every year. See the website for contact info.

MONTROSE CHRISTIAN WRITERS' CONFERENCE

Montrose Bible Conference, 218 Locust St., Montrose PA 18801. (570)278-1001 or (800)598-5030. **Fax:** (570)278-3061. **E-mail:** mbc@montrosebible.org. **Website:** www.montrosebible.org. "Annual conference held in July. Offers workshops, editorial appointments, and professional critiques. We try to meet writing needs, for beginners and advanced, covering fiction, poetry, and writing for children. It is small enough to allow personal interaction between attendees and faculty. Speakers have included William Petersen, Mona Hodgson, Jim Watkins, and Bob Hostetler." Held in Montrose. Will meet planes in Binghamton, New York, and Scranton, Pennsylvania. On-site accommodations: room and board $360-490/conference, including food (2018 rates). RV court available.

COSTS Tuition is $195.

ADDITIONAL INFORMATION "Writers can send work ahead of time and have it critiqued for a small fee." The attendees are usually church related. The writing has a Christian emphasis. Conference information available in April. For brochure, visit website, e-mail, or call. Accepts inquiries by phone or e-mail.

MOUNT HERMON CHRISTIAN WRITERS CONFERENCE

P.O. Box 413, Mount Hermon CA 95041. **E-mail:** info@mounthermon.org. **Website:** writers.mounthermon.org. Annual professional conference. 2017 dates: April 7-11. Average attendance: 450. Sponsored by and held at the 440-acre Mount Hermon Christian Conference Center near San Jose, California, in the heart of the coastal redwoods. "We are a broad-ranging conference for all areas of Christian writing, including fiction, nonfiction, fantasy, children's, teen, young adult, poetry, magazines, inspirational, and devotional writing. This is a working, how-to conference, with Major Morning tracks in all genres (including a track especially for teen writers), and as many as 20 optional workshops each afternoon. Faculty-to-student ratio is about 1 to 6. The bulk of our more than 70 faculty members are editors and publisher representatives from major Christian publishing houses nationwide." Speakers have included T. Davis Bunn, Debbie Macomber, Jerry Jenkins, Bill Butterworth, Dick Foth, and others.

MUSE AND THE MARKETPLACE

Grub Street, 162 Boylston St., 5th Floor, Boston MA 02116. (617)695-0075. **E-mail:** info@grubstreet.org. **Website:** museandthemarketplace.com. Grub Street's national conference for writers. Held held in the late spring, such as early May. 2017 dates: May 5-7. Conference duration: 3 days. Average attendance: 400. Dozens of agents are in attendance to meet writers and take pitches. The conference has workshops on all aspects of writing. Boston Park Plaza Hotel.

○ The Muse and the Marketplace is designed to give aspiring writers a better understanding of the craft of writing fiction and nonfiction, to prepare them for the changing world of publishing and promotion, and to create opportunities for meaningful networking. On all 3 days, prominent and nationally recognized established and emerging authors lead sessions on the craft of writing—the "muse" side of things—while editors, literary agents, publicists, and other industry professionals lead sessions on the business side—the "marketplace."

NORTH CAROLINA WRITERS' NETWORK FALL CONFERENCE

P.O. Box 21591, Winston-Salem NC 27120. (336)293-8844. **E-mail:** mail@ncwriters.org. **Website:** www.ncwriters.org. Annual conference held in November in different North Carolina venues. Average attendance: 250. This organization hosts 2 conferences: 1 in the spring and 1 in the fall. Each conference is a weekend full of workshops, panels, book signings, and readings (including open mic). There will be a keynote speaker, a variety of sessions on the craft and business of writing, and opportunities to meet with agents and editors. Special rates are usually available at the conference hotel, but attendees must make their own reservations. **COSTS** Approximately $250 (includes 4 meals).

NORTHERN COLORADO WRITERS CONFERENCE

407 Cormorant Court, Fort Collins CO 80525. (970)227-5746. **E-mail:** april@northerncoloradowriters.com. **Website:** www.northerncoloradowriters.com. Annual conference held in Fort Collins. 2017 dates: May 5-6. Duration: 2-3 days. The conference features a variety of speakers, agents, and editors. There are workshops and presentations on fiction, nonfiction, screenwriting, children's books, marketing, magazine writing, staying inspired, and more. Previous agents who have attended and taken pitches from writers include Jessica Regel, Kristen Nelson, Rachelle Gardner, Andrea Brown, Ken Sherman, Jessica Faust, Gordon Warnock, and Taylor Martindale. Each conference features more than 30 workshops from which to choose from. Previous keynotes include Chuck Sambuchino, Andrew McCarthy, and Stephen J. Cannell. Conference hotel may offer rooms at a discounted rate.
COSTS Prices vary depending on a number of factors. See website for details.

ODYSSEY FANTASY WRITING WORKSHOP

P.O. Box 75, Mont Vernon NH 03057. (603)673-6234. **E-mail:** jcavelos@odysseyworkshop.org. **Website:** www.odysseyworkshop.org. **Contact:** Jeanne Cavelos. Saint Anselm College, 100 Saint Anselm Dr., Manchester NH 03102 Annual workshop held in June (through July). Conference duration: 6 weeks. Average attendance: 15. A workshop for fantasy, science fiction, and horror writers that combines an intensive learning and writing experience with in-depth feedback on students' mss. Held on the campus of Saint Anselm College in Manchester, New Hampshire. Speakers have included George R.R. Martin, Elizabeth Hand, Jane Yolen, Catherynne M. Valente, Holly Black, and Dan Simmons. Most students stay in Saint Anselm College apartments to get the full Odyssey experience. Each apartment has 2 bedrooms and can house a total of 2 to 3 people (with each bedroom holding 1 or 2 students). The apartments are equipped with kitchens, so you may buy and prepare your own food, which is a money-saving option, or you may eat at the college's Coffee Shop or Dining Hall. Wireless internet access and use of laundry facilities are provided at no cost. Students with cars will receive a campus parking permit.

Since its inception in 1996, the Odyssey Writing Workshop has become one of the most highly respected workshops for writers of fantasy, science fiction, and horror in the world. Top authors, editors and agents have served as guests at Odyssey. Fifty-nine percent of graduates have gone on to be professionally published. Among Odyssey's graduates are *New York Times* bestsellers, Amazon bestsellers, and award winners.

COSTS $2,025 tuition, $195 textbook, $892 housing (double room), $1,784 housing (single room), $40 application fee, $600 food (approximate), $950 optional processing fee to receive college credit.

ADDITIONAL INFORMATION Students must apply and include a writing sample. Application deadline: April 8. Students' works are critiqued throughout the 6 weeks. Workshop information available in October. For brochure/guidelines, send SASE, e-mail, visit website, or call.

OHIO KENTUCKY INDIANA CHILDREN'S LITERATURE CONFERENCE

Northern Kentucky University, 405 Steely Library, Highland Heights KY 41099. (859)572-6620. **Fax:** (859)572-5390. **E-mail:** smithjen@nku.edu. **Website:** www.dearbornhighlandsarts.org/oki-conference-registration. **Contact:** Jennifer Smith. Annual conference held in November for writers and illustra-

tors, geared toward all levels. Open to all. Emphasizes multicultural literature for children and young adults. Contact Jennifer Smith for more information.

COSTS $85; includes registration/attendance at all workshop sessions, continental breakfast, lunch, and author/illustrator signings. Manuscript critiques are available for an additional cost. E-mail or call for more information.

OKLAHOMA WRITERS' FEDERATION, INC. ANNUAL CONFERENCE

9800 South Hwy. 137, Miami OK 74354. **Website:** www.owfi.org. Annual conference held first weekend in May, just outside Oklahoma City. Writer workshops geared toward all levels. "The goal of the conference is to create good stories with strong bones. We will be exploring cultural writing and cultural sensitivity in writing." Several literary agents are in attendance each year to meet with writers and hear pitches.

COSTS Costs vary depending on when registrants sign up. Cost includes awards banquet and famous author banquet. Three extra sessions are available for an extra fee. Visit the event website for more information and a complete faculty list.

OUTDOOR WRITERS ASSOCIATION OF AMERICA ANNUAL CONFERENCE

615 Oak St., Suite 201, Missoula MT 59801. (406)728-7434. **E-mail:** info@owaa.org. **Website:** owaa.org. **Contact:** Jessica Seitz, conference and membership coordinator. Outdoor communicator workshops geared toward all levels. Annual three-day conference includes craft improvement seminars and newsmaker sessions. 2017 dates: June 24-26. Site: Duluth, Minnesota. Cost includes attendance at all workshops and meals.

COSTS Before April 28, $225 for members and $425 for non-members. After April 28, $249 for members and $449 for non-members. Single-day rates are also available.

OZARK CREATIVE WRITERS, INC. CONFERENCE

P.O. Box 9076, Fayetteville AR 72703. **E-mail:** ozarkcreativewriters1@gmail.com. **Website:** www.ozarkcreativewriters.com. The annual event is held in October at the Inn of the Ozarks, in the resort town of Eureka Springs, Arkansas. Approximately 200 writers attend each year; many also enter the creative writing competitions. Open to professional and amateur writers, workshops are geared toward all levels and all forms of the creative process and literary arts; sessions sometimes also include songwriting. Includes presentations by best-selling authors, editors, and agents. Offering writing competitions in all genres.

○ A full list of sessions and speakers is online. The conference usually has agents and/or editors in attendance to meet with writers.

PACIFIC COAST CHILDREN'S WRITERS WHOLE-NOVEL WORKSHOP: FOR ADULTS AND TEENS

P.O. Box 244, Aptos CA 95001. **Website:** www.childrenswritersworkshop.com. Annual conference held in fall. 2018 dates: Sept. 28-30. Offers semi-advanced through published writers an editor and/or agent critique on their full novel or 15-page partial. (The latter may include mid-book and synopsis critiques.) Focus is on craft as a marketing tool. Team-taught master classes (open clinic ms critiques) explore topics such as "Story Architecture and Arcs." Offers continuous close contact with faculty, who have included Andrea Brown (agent, president of Andrea Brown Literary) and Simon Boughton (vice president/executive editor of 3 Macmillan imprints). Attendance: 16 maximum. For the most critique options and early bird discount, submit e-application in May (dates on website); regisgtration is open until all places are filled. Content: character-driven upper middle-grade and young adult novels. Collegial; highly hands-on. Reading peer mss before master class observations and discussions maximizes learning. Usually at least one enrollee lands a book deal with faculty. A concurrent workshop is open to teens, who give adults smart target-reader feedback.

COSTS Visit website for tiered fees (includes lodging, meals), schedule, and more; e-mail Director Nancy Sondel via the contact form.

PENNWRITERS CONFERENCE

P.O. Box 685, Dalton PA 18414. **E-mail:** conference-co@pennwriters.org; info@pennwriters.org. **Website:** pennwriters.org/conference. The Mission of Pennwriters, Inc., is to help writers of all levels, from the novice to the award-winning and multi-published, improve and succeed in their craft. The annual Pennwriters conference is held every year in May in Penn-

sylvania, switching between locations—Lancaster in even numbered years and Pittsburgh in odd numbered years. 2017 dates: May 19-21 at the Pittsburgh Airport Marriott. Literary agents are in attendance to meet with writers. Costs vary. Pennwriters members in good standing get a slightly reduced rate.

○ As the official writing organization of Pennsylvania, Pennwriters has 8 different areas with smaller writing groups that meet. Each of these areas sometimes has their own, smaller event during the year in addition to the annual writing conference.

ADDITIONAL INFORMATION Sponsors contest. Published authors judge fiction in various categories. Agent/editor appointments are available on a first-come, first-served basis.

PHILADELPHIA WRITERS' CONFERENCE

P.O. Box 7171, Elkins Park PA 19027. (215)619-7422. **E-mail:** info@pwcwriters.org. **Website:** pwcwriters.org. Annual conference held in June. Duration: 3 days. Average attendance: 160-200. Conference covers many forms of writing: novel, short story, genre fiction, nonfiction book, magazine writing, blogging, juvenile, poetry. See website for details. Hotel may offer discount for early registration.

○ Offers 14 workshops, usually 4 seminars, several "manuscript rap" sessions, a Friday Roundtable Forum Buffet with speaker, and the Saturday Annual Awards Banquet with speaker. Attendees may submit mss in advance for criticism by the workshop leaders and are eligible to submit entries in more than 10 contest categories. Cash prizes and certificates are given to first and second place winners, plus full tuition for the following year's conference to first place winners.

ADDITIONAL INFORMATION Accepts inquiries by e-mail. Agents and editors attend the conference. Many questions are answered online.

PIKES PEAK WRITERS CONFERENCE

Pikes Peak Writers, P.O. Box 64273, Colorado Springs CO 80962. (719)244-6220. **E-mail:** registrar@pikespeakwriters.com. **Website:** www.pikespeakwriters.com/ppwc. Annual conference held in April. 2017 dates: April 28-30. Conference duration: 3 days. Average attendance: 300. Workshops, presentations, and panels focus on writing and publishing mainstream and genre fiction (romance, science fiction/fantasy, suspense/thrillers, action/adventure, mysteries, children's, young adult). Agents and editors are available for meetings with attendees on Saturday. Speakers have included Jeff Lindsay, Rachel Caine, and Kevin J. Anderson. Marriott Colorado Springs holds a block of rooms at a special rate for attendees until late March. **COSTS** $395-465 (includes all 7 meals). **ADDITIONAL INFORMATION** Readings with critiques are available on Friday afternoon. Registration forms are online; brochures are available in January. Send inquiries via e-mail.

PNWA SUMMER WRITERS CONFERENCE

Writers' Cottage, 317 NW Gilman Blvd. Suite 8, Issaquah WA 98027. (425)673-2665. **E-mail:** pnwa@pnwa.org. **Website:** www.pnwa.org. Annual conference held in July. 2017 dates: July 20-23. Duration: 4 days. Average attendance: 400. Attendees have the chance to meet agents and editors, learn craft from authors, and uncover marketing secrets. Speakers have included J.A. Jance, Sheree Bykofsky, Kimberley Cameron, Jennie Dunham, Donald Maass, Jandy Nelson, Robert Dugoni, and Terry Brooks.

ROCKY MOUNTAIN FICTION WRITERS COLORADO GOLD CONFERENCE

Rocky Mountain Fiction Writers, Denver Renaissance Hotel, Denver CO **E-mail:** conference@rmfw.org. **Website:** www.rmfw.org. **Contact:** Pamela Nowak and Susan Brooks. Annual conference held in September. Duration: 3 days. Average attendance: 400+. Themes include general fiction, genre fiction, contemporary romance, mystery, science fiction/fantasy, mainstream, young adult, screenwriting, short stories, and historical fiction, as well as marketing and career management. 2018 keynote speakers are Kate Moretti, James Scott Bell, and Christopher Paolini. Past speakers have included Diana Gabaldon, Sherry Thomas, Lori Rader-Day, Ann Hood, Robert J. Sawyer, Jeffery Deaver, William Kent Krueger, Margaret George, Jodi Thomas, Bernard Cornwell, Terry Brooks, Dorothy Cannell, Patricia Gardner Evans, Diane Mott Davidson, Constance O'Day, and Connie Willis. Approximately 16 acquiring editors and agents attend annually. Special rates will be available at conference hotel.

COSTS Available on website.
ADDITIONAL INFORMATION Pitch appointments available at no charge. Add-on options include agent and editor critiques, master classes, pitch coaching, query letter coaching, special critiques, and more.

SAN DIEGO STATE UNIVERSITY WRITERS' CONFERENCE

SDSU College of Extended Studies, 5250 Campanile Dr., San Diego State University, San Diego CA 92182. (619)594-2099. **Fax:** (619)594-8566. **E-mail:** sdsuwritersconference@mail.sdsu.edu. **Website:** ces.sdsu.edu/writers. Annual conference held in January. 2017 dates: January 20-22. Conference duration: 2.5 days. Average attendance: 350. Covers fiction, nonfiction, scriptwriting, and e-books. Held at the San Diego Marriott Mission Valley Hotel. Each year the conference offers a variety of workshops for the beginner and advanced writers. This conference allows writers to choose which workshops best suit their needs. In addition to the workshops, editor reading appointments and agent/editor consultation appointments are provided so attendees may meet with editors and agents one-on-one to discuss specific questions. A reception is offered Saturday immediately following the workshops, offering attendees the opportunity to socialize with the faculty in a relaxed atmosphere. In previous years, approximately 60 faculty members have attended. Attendees must make their own travel arrangements. A conference rate for attendees is available at the event hotel (Marriott Mission Valley Hotel). **COSTS** $495-549. Extra costs for consultations.

2019 SAN FRANCISCO WRITERS CONFERENCE

Hyatt Regency Embarcadero, San Francisco CA 94111. (925)420-6223. **E-mail:** barbara@sfwriters.org; www.sfwriters.org. **Website:** sfwriters.org. **Contact:** Barbara Santos, marketing director. 2019 dates: February 14-17. Annual conference held President's Day weekend in February. Average attendance: 700. "More than 100 top authors, respected literary agents, and major publishing houses are at the event so attendees can make face-to-face contact with all the right people. Writers of nonfiction, fiction, poetry, and specialty writing (children's books, lifestyle books, etc.) will all benefit from the event. There are important sessions on marketing, self-publishing, technology, and trends in the publishing industry. Plus, there's an optional session called Speed Dating with Agents where attendees can meet with literary agents. Past speakers have included Jane Smiley, Debbie Macomber, Clive Cussler, Guy Kawasaki, Jennifer Crusie, R.L. Stine, Lisa See, Steve Berry, and Jacquelyn Mitchard. Best-selling authors, agents and several editors from traditional publishing houses participate each year, and many will be available for meetings with attendees." The Hyatt Regency Embarcadero offers a discounted SFWC rate (based on availability). Call directly: (415) 788-1234. Across from the Ferry Building in San Francisco, the hotel is located so that everyone arriving at the Oakland or San Francisco airport can take the BART to the Embarcadero exit, directly in front of the hotel.

○ Attendees can take educational sessions and network with presenters from the publishing world. Free editorial and PR consults, exhibitor hall, pitching and networking opportunities available throughout the four-day event. Also several free sessions offered to the public. See website for details or sign up for the SFWC Newsletter for updates.

COSTS Full registration is $895 (as of the 2018 event) with early bird registration discounts through February 1.

ADDITIONAL INFORMATION "Present yourself in a professional manner, and the contacts you will make will be invaluable to your writing career. Fliers, details, and registration information are online."

SANTA BARBARA WRITERS CONFERENCE

27 W. Anapamu St., Suite 305, Santa Barbara CA 93101. (805)568-1516. **E-mail:** info@sbwriters.com. **Website:** www.sbwriters.com. Annual conference held in June. 2017 dates: June 18-23. Average attendance: 200. Covers fiction, nonfiction, journalism, memoir, poetry, playwriting, screenwriting, travel writing, young adult, children's literature, humor, and marketing. Speakers have included Ray Bradbury, William Styron, Eudora Welty, James Michener, Sue Grafton, Charles M. Schulz, Clive Cussler, Fannie Flagg, Elmore Leonard, and T.C. Boyle. Agents will appear on a panel; in addition, there will be an agents and editors day that allows writers to pitch their projects in one-on-one meetings. Hyatt Santa Barbara.

COSTS Early conference registration is $575, and regular registration is $650.

ADDITIONAL INFORMATION Register online or contact for brochure and registration forms.

SCBWI—AUSTIN CONFERENCE

E-mail: austin@scbwi.org. **Website:** austin.scbwi.org. **Contact:** Samantha Clark, regional advisor. Annual conference features a faculty of published authors and illustrators. Past years have featured National Book Award winner William Alexander, Caldecott Honors Liz Garton Scanlon and Molly Idle, *New York Times* best-selling author Cynthia Leitich Smith, and more. Editors and agents are in attendance to meet with writers. The schedule consists of keynotes and breakout sessions with tracks for writing (picture book and novel), illustrating, and professional development.

COSTS Costs vary for members, students and non-members, and discounted early-bird pricing is available. Visit website for full pricing options.

○ SCBWI—CANADA EAST

E-mail: canadaeast@scbwi.org; almafullerton@almafullerton.com. **Website:** www.canadaeast.scbwi.org. **Contact:** Alma Fullerton, regional advisor. Writer and illustrator events geared toward all levels. Usually offers one event in spring and another in the fall. Check website for updated information.

SCBWI—CENTRAL-COASTAL CALIFORNIA; FALL CONFERENCE

P.O. Box 1500, Simi Valley CA 93062. **E-mail:** cencal@scbwi.org. **Website:** cencal.scbwi.org. **Contact:** Mary Ann Fraser, regional advisor. Annual conference held in October. Geared to all levels. Speakers include editors, authors, illustrators, and agents. Fiction and nonfiction picture books, middle-grade, and young adult novels, and magazine submissions addressed. There is an annual writing contest in all genres plus illustration display. For fees and other information, e-mail or visit website.

SCBWI—COLORADO/WYOMING (ROCKY MOUNTAIN); EVENTS

E-mail: rmc@scbwi.org. **Website:** www.rmc.scbwi.org. **Contact:** Todd Tuell and Lindsay Eland, regional advisors. SCBWI Rocky Mountain chapter (Colorado/Wyoming) offers special events, schmoozes, meetings, and conferences throughout the year. Major events: Fall Conference (annual, September); Summer

Retreat, "Big Sur in the Rockies" (bi- and tri-annual). More info on website.

SCBWI—EASTERN NEW YORK; FALLING LEAVES MASTER CLASS RETREAT

Silver Bay NY **E-mail:** easternny@scbwi.org. **Website:** easternny.scbwi.org; scbwieasternny.weebly.com/falling-leaves.html. **Contact:** Nancy Castaldo, regional advisor. P.O. Box 159, Valatie NY 12184 Annual master class retreat hosted by SCBWI Eastern New York and held in November in Silver Bay on Lake George. Holds ms and portfolio critiques, question-and-answer and speaker sessions, intensives, and more, with respected authors and editors. Theme varies each year between picture books, novels, and nonfiction. Applications accepted June 15 through August 15. See website for more information.

SCBWI—MID-ATLANTIC; ANNUAL FALL CONFERENCE

P.O. Box 3215, Reston VA 20195. **E-mail:** midatlantic@scbwi.org. **Website:** midatlantic.scbwi.org/. **Contact:** Ellen R. Braaf, regional advisor. For updates and details, visit website. Registration limited to 250. Conference fills quickly. Includes continental breakfast and boxed lunch. Optional craft-focused workshops and individual consultations with conference faculty are available for additional fees.

🎧 This conference takes place in October. Previous conferences have been held in Sterling, Virginia.

SCBWI—NEW ENGLAND; WHISPERING PINES WRITER'S RETREAT

West Greenwich RI **E-mail:** whisperingpinesretreat@yahoo.com. **Website:** newengland.scbwi.org; www.whisperingpinesretreat.org. **Contact:** Kristin Russo and Pam Vaughan, event codirectors. Three-day retreat (with stays overnight) held annually in mid-to-late March. 2017 dates: March 17-19. Offers the opportunity to work intimately with professionals in an idyllic setting. Attendees will work with others who are committed to quality children's literature in small groups and will benefit from a 30-minute one-on-one critique with a mentor. Also includes mentors' presentations and an intimate question-and-answer session, Team Kid Lit Jeopardy with prizes, and more. Retreat limited to 32 full-time participants.

SCBWI—NEW JERSEY;

ANNUAL SUMMER CONFERENCE

New Jersey NJ **Website:** newjersey.scbwi.org. **Contact:** Cathleen Daniels, regional advisor. This weekend conference is held in the summer. Highlights include multiple one-on-one critiques; "how to" workshops for every level; first page sessions; agent pitches; and interaction with the faculty of editors, agents, art director, and authors. On Friday, attendees can sign up for writing intensives or register for illustrators' day with the art directors. Published authors attending the conference can sign up to participate in the bookfair to sell and autograph their books; illustrators have the opportunity to display their artwork. Attendees have the option to participate in group critiques after dinner on Saturday evening and attend a mix-and-mingle with the faculty on Friday night. Meals are included with the cost of admission. Conference is known for its high ratio of faculty to attendees and interaction opportunities.

SCBWI WINTER CONFERENCE ON WRITING AND ILLUSTRATING FOR CHILDREN

4727 Wilshire Blvd #301, Los Angeles CA 90010. (323)782-1010. **Fax:** (323)782-1892. **E-mail:** scbwi@scbwi.org. **Website:** www.scbwi.org. **Contact:** Stephen Mooser. Annual conference held in February. Average attendance: 1,000. Conference is to promote writing and illustrating for children (picture books, middle-grade, and young adult) and to give participants an opportunity to network with professionals. Covers financial planning for writers, marketing your book, art exhibitions, and more. The winter conference is held in Manhattan.

COSTS See website for current cost and conference information.

ADDITIONAL INFORMATION SCBWI also holds an annual summer conference in August in Los Angeles.

SOUTH CAROLINA WRITERS WORKSHOP

4711 Forest Dr., Suite 3, P.M.B. 189, Columbia SC 29206. **E-mail:** scwwliaison@gmail.com. **Website:** www.myscwa.org. Conference held in October at the Metropolitan Conference Center in Columbia. Held almost every year. Conference duration: 3 days. Features critique sessions, open mic readings, and presentations from agents and editors. More than 50 different workshops for writers to choose from, dealing with all subjects of writing craft, writing business, getting an agent, and more. Agents will be in attendance.

SOUTH COAST WRITERS CONFERENCE

Southwestern Oregon Community College, P.O. Box 590, 29392 Ellensburg Ave., Gold Beach OR 97444. (541)247-2741. **Fax:** (541)247-6247. **E-mail:** scwc@socc.edu. **Website:** www.socc.edu/scwriters. **Contact:** Karim Shumaker. Annual conference held Presidents' Day weekend in February. 2017 dates: February 17-18. Conference duration: 2 days. Covers fiction, poetry, children's, nature, screenwriting, songwriting, and marketing. 2017 keynote speaker: Jamie Duclos-Yourdon. Presenters include C. Lill Ahrens, Jennifer Burns Bright, Bill Cameron, Nina Kiriki Hoffman, Rita Hosking, Janet Sumner Johnston, Vinnie Kinsella, Michael Lamanna, and Bruce Holland Rogers. List of local motels that offer discounts to conference participants is available on request.

COSTS Friday workshop cost is $55. Saturday conference cost is $60 before January 31 and $70 after. Fish fry lunch is $14 if purchased in advance, or $15 at the door.

SOUTHEASTERN WRITERS ASSOCIATION—ANNUAL WRITERS WORKSHOP

E-mail: purple@southeasternwriters.org. **Website:** www.southeasternwriters.org. Annual four-day workshop, held in Epworth By The Sea, St. Simons Island, Georgia. Open to all writers. 2018 dates: June 8-12. Tuition includes 3 free evaluation conferences with instructors (minimum two-day registration). Offers contests with cash prizes. Manuscript deadlines: May 15 for both contests and evaluations. Lodging at Epworth and throughout St. Simons Island. Visit website for more information.

○ Instruction offered for novel writing, short fiction, young adult, humor, columns, poetry, memoir, and self-publishing. Includes agent in residence, publisher in residence, and photographer for author head shots.

COSTS Cost of workshop: $445 for 4 days or lower prices for daily tuition or early bird special. (See website for tuition pricing.)

SPACE COAST WRITERS GUILD ANNUAL CONFERENCE

P.O. Box 262, Melbourne FL 32902. **E-mail:** stilley@scwg.org. **Website:** www.scwg.org. Conference held along the east coast of central Florida in the last weekend of January, though necessarily every year. Check website for up-to-date information. Conference duration: 2 days. Average attendance: 150+. This conference is hosted in Florida and features a variety of presenters on all topics. Critiques are available for a price, and agents in attendance will take pitches from writers. Previous presenters have included Debra Dixon, Davis Bunn (writer), Ellen Pepus (agent), Jennifer Crusie, Chuck Sambuchino, Madeline Smoot, Mike Resnick, Christina York, Ben Bova, and Elizabeth Sinclair. The conference is hosted in a beachside hotel, with special room rates available.

COSTS Check website for current pricing.

STEAMBOAT SPRINGS WRITERS CONFERENCE

A Day For Writers, Steamboat Springs Arts Council, Eleanor Bliss Center for the Arts at the Depot, P.O. Box 774284, Steamboat Springs CO 80477. (970)879-9008. **E-mail:** info@steamboatwriters.com. **Website:** www.steamboatwriters.com. **Contact:** Barbara Sparks. 1001 13th St., Steamboat Springs CO 80487. Annual event will be Saturday July 28, 2018. Instructors Rachel Weaver and John Cotter. Workshops geared toward intermediate levels. Open to professionals and amateurs alike. Average attendance: 35-40 (registration limited, conference fills quickly). Optional pre-conference gathering Friday night. Meet-and-greet buffet social followed by Five Minutes of Fame session for conference participants to share their work. 2018 instructors Rachel Weaver and John Cotter will each lead 2 workshops.

○ "Our conference emphasizes instruction within the seminar format. Novices and polished professionals benefit from the individual attention and camaraderie which can be established within small groups. A pleasurable and memorable learning experience is guaranteed by the relaxed and friendly atmosphere of the old train depot."

COSTS $60 early registration; $75 after May 27. Registration fee includes continental breakfast and luncheon.

◑ SURREY INTERNATIONAL WRITERS' CONFERENCE

SiWC, 151-10090 152 St., Suite 544, Surrey BC V3R 8X8, Canada. **E-mail:** kathychung@siwc.ca. **Website:** www.siwc.ca. **Contact:** Kathy Chung, proposals contact and conference coordinator. Annual professional development writing conference outside Vancouver, Canada, held every October. Writing workshops geared toward beginner, intermediate, and advanced levels. More than 80 workshops and panels, on all topics and genres, plus pre-conference master classes. Blue Pencil and agent/editor pitch sessions included. Different conference price packages available. Check the conference website for more information. This event has many literary agents in attendance taking pitches. Annual fiction writing contest open to all with $1,000 prize for first place. Conference registration opens in early June every year. Register early to avoid disappointment as the conference is likely to sell out.

TEXAS WRITING RETREAT

Navasota TX **E-mail:** paultcuclis@gmail.com. **Website:** www.texaswritingretreat.com. **Contact:** Paul Cuclis, coordinator. The Texas Writing Retreat is an intimate event with a limited number of attendees. 2017 dates: January 11-16. Held on a private residence ranch an hour outside of Houston, the retreat has an agent and editor in attendance teaching. All attendees get to pitch the attending agent. Meals, excursions, and amenities are included. This is a unique event that combines craft sessions, business sessions, time for writing, relaxation, and more. The retreat is not held every year; it's best to check the website.

COSTS Costs vary per event. There are different pricing options for those staying on-site versus commuters.

◐ THE UNIVERSITY OF WINCHESTER WRITERS' FESTIVAL

University of Winchester, Winchester Hampshire S022 4NR, United Kingdom. (44)(0)1962-827238. **E-mail:** judith.heneghan@winchester.ac.uk. **Website:** www.writersfestival.co.uk. **Contact:** Judith Heneghan, festival director. The 36th Winchester Writers' Festival (2017) takes place on June 16-18 at the University of Winchester, offering inspiration, learning, and networking for new and emerging writers working in all forms and genres. Choose from 18 day-long workshops and 28 talks, plus book up to 4 one-to-one appointments per attendee with leading literary agents, commissioning editors, and award-winning authors to help you harness your creative ideas, turn them into marketable work, and pitch to publishing professionals. If you cannot attend, you may still enter one of our nine writing competitions. Enjoy a creative writing weekend in Winchester, the oldest city in England. Only one hour from London. To view festival details, including all the competition details, please go to the official event website. Booking opens in February. On-site student single ensuite accommodation available. Also, a range of hotels and bed and breakfasts nearby in the city.

COSTS See festival program.

ADDITIONAL INFORMATION Lunch, and tea/coffee/cake included in the booking cost. Dinner can be booked separately. All dietary needs catered for.

TMCC WRITERS' CONFERENCE

Truckee Meadows Community College, 7000 Dandini Blvd., Reno NV 89512. (775)673-7111. **E-mail:** wdce@tmcc.edu. **Website:** wdce.tmcc.edu. Annual conference held in April. 2017 date: April 8. Average attendance: 150. Conference focuses on strengthening mainstream/literary fiction and nonfiction works and how to market them to agents and publishers. Site: Truckee Meadows Community College in Reno. "There is always an array of speakers and presenters with impressive literary credentials, including agents and editors." Speakers have included Chuck Sambuchino, Sheree Bykofsky, Andrea Brown, Dorothy Allison, Karen Joy Fowler, James D. Houston, James N. Frey, Gary Short, Jane Hirschfield, Dorrianne Laux, and Kim Addonizio. Literary agents are on site to take pitches from writers. Contact the conference manager to learn about accommodation discounts.

ADDITIONAL INFORMATION "The conference is open to all writers, regardless of their level of experience. Brochures are available online and mailed in January. Send inquiries via e-mail."

UNICORN WRITERS CONFERENCE

17 Church Hill Rd., Redding CT 06896, USA. (203)938-7405. **E-mail:** unicornwritersconference@gmail.com. **Website:** www.unicornwritersconference.com. **Contact:** Jan L. Kardys, chair. This writers conference draws upon its close proximity to New York

and pulls in over 40 literary agents and 15 major New York editors to pitch each year. There are manuscript review sessions (40 pages equals 30 minutes with an agent/editor), query/manuscript review sessions, and 6 different workshops every hour. Cost: $325, includes all workshops and 3 meals. Held at Reid Castle, Purchase, New York. Directions available on event website.

○ "The forty pages for manuscript reviews are read in advance by your selected agents/editors, but follow the submission guidelines on the website. Check the genre chart for each agent and editor before you make your selection."

COSTS $325 includes all workshops (6 every hour to select on the day of the conference), gift bag, and 3 meals. Additional cost for manuscript reviews: $60 each.

ADDITIONAL INFORMATION The first self-published authors will be featured on the website, and the bookstore will sell their books at the event.

UNIVERSITY OF WISCONSIN AT MADISON WRITERS INSTITUTE

21 N. Park St., Madison WI 53715. (608)265-3972. E-mail: laurie.scheer@wisc.edu. **Website:** uwwritersinstitute.wisc.edu. Annual conference. 2018 dates: April 12-15. Conference on fiction and nonfiction held at the University of Wisconsin at Madison. Guest speakers are published authors and publishing executives. Agents and publishing companies take pitches. Theme: Pathway to Publication.

COSTS $250-375, depending on discounts and if you attend one day or multiple days.

WESLEYAN WRITERS CONFERENCE

Wesleyan University, 294 High St., Room 207, Middletown CT 06459. (860)685-3604. **Fax:** (860)685-2441. **E-mail:** agreene@wesleyan.edu. **Website:** www.wesleyan.edu/writing/conference. **Contact:** Anne Greene, director. Annual conference held in June. 2017 dates: June 14-18. Average attendance: 100. Focuses on the novel, fiction techniques, short stories, poetry, screenwriting, nonfiction, literary journalism, memoir, mixed media work, and publishing. The conference is held on the campus of Wesleyan University, in the hills overlooking the Connecticut River. Features a faculty of award-winning writers, seminars, and readings of new fiction, poetry, nonfiction, and

mixed media forms—as well as guest lectures on a range of topics including publishing. Both new and experienced writers are welcome. Participants may attend seminars in all genres. Speakers have included Esmond Harmsworth (Zachary Shuster Harmsworth), Daniel Mandel (Sanford J. Greenburger Associaties), Amy Williams (ICM and Collins McCormick), and many others. Agents will be speaking and available for meetings with attendees. Participants are often successful in finding agents and publishers for their mss. Wesleyan participants are also frequently featured in the anthology *Best New American Voices*. Meals are provided on campus. Lodging is available on campus or in town.

ADDITIONAL INFORMATION Ms critiques are available but not required.

WHIDBEY ISLAND WRITERS' CONFERENCE

(360)331-0307. **E-mail:** http://writeonwhidbey.org. **Website:** http://writeonwhidbey.org. P.O. Box 1289, Langley, WA 98260. (360)331-6714. **E-mail:** writers@whidbey.com. **Website:** www.writeonwhidbey.org. **Writers Contact:** Conference Director. Three days focused on the tools you need to become a great writer. Learn from a variety of award-winning children's book authors and very experienced literary agents. Variety of preconference workshops and conference topics. Conference held in early spring. Registration limited to 290. Cost: $395; early bird and member discounts available. Registration includes workshops, fireside chats, book-signing reception, various activities, and daily luncheons. The conference offers consultation appointments with editors and agents. Registrants may reduce the cost of their conference by volunteering. See the website for more information. "The uniquely personal and friendly weekend is designed to be highly interactive." Annual conference held in early spring. Registration limited to 290. Registration includes workshops, fireside chats, book-signing reception, various activities, and daily luncheons. The conference offers consultation appointments with editors and agents. Registrants may reduce the cost of their conference by volunteering. See the website for more information. "The uniquely personal and friendly weekend is designed to be highly interactive." There are a variety of sessions on topics such as fiction, craft, poetry, platform, agents, screenwriting, and much more. Topics are varied, and there is something for all writers. Multiple agents and editors are in attendance. The schedule and faculty change every year, and those changes are reflected online

COSTS Cost: $395; early bird and member discounts available

WILLAMETTE WRITERS CONFERENCE

2108 Buck St., West Linn OR 97068. (503)305-6729. **Fax:** (503)344-6174. **Website:** willamettewriters.com/wwcon/. Annual conference held in August. 2015 dates: Aug. 7-9. Conference duration: 3 days. Average attendance: 600. "Willamette Writers is open to all writers, and we plan our conference accordingly. We offer workshops on all aspects of fiction, nonfiction, marketing, the creative process, screenwriting, etc. Also, we invite top-notch inspirational speakers for keynote addresses. We always include at least 1 agent or editor panel and offer a variety of topics of interest to both fiction and nonfiction writers and screenwriters." Agents will be speaking and available for meetings with attendees. If necessary, arrangements can be made on an individual basis through the conference hotel. Special rates may be available. 2015 location is the Lloyd Center DoubleTree Hotel.

◯ An extensive list literary agents and editors, plus Hollywood film managers, agents and producers, will be on hand to listen to pitches.

COSTS Pricing schedule available online.

ADDITIONAL INFORMATION Brochure/guidelines are available for a catalog-sized SASE.

WINTER POETRY & PROSE GETAWAY

Murphy Writing of Stockton University, 35 S. Dr. Martin Luther King Blvd., Atlantic City NJ 08401, USA. (609)626-3596. **E-mail:** info@murphywriting.com. **Website:** www.stockton.edu/wintergetaway. **Contact:** Amanda Murphy. Annual January conference at the Jersey Shore. January 13-16, 2017. "This is not your typical writers conference. Advance your craft and energize your writing at the Winter Getaway. Enjoy challenging and supportive workshops, insightful feedback, and encouraging community. Choose from small, intensive workshops in memoir, novel, young adult, nonfiction, screenwriting, and poetry." Room packages at the historic Stockton Seaview Hotel are available.

◯ "At most conferences, writers listen to talks and panels and sit in sessions where previously written work is discussed. At the Get-

away, they write. Most workshops are limited to 10 or fewer participants. By spending the entire weekend in one workshop, participants will venture deeper into their writing, making more progress than they thought possible."

COSTS See website or call for current fee information.

ADDITIONAL INFORMATION Previous faculty has included Julianna Baggott, Christian Bauman, Laure-Anne Bosselaar, Kurt Brown, Mark Doty (National Book Award winner), Stephen Dunn (Pulitzer Prize winner), Dorianne Laux, Carol Plum-Ucci, James Richardson, Mimi Schwartz, Terese Svoboda, and more.

WOMEN WRITING THE WEST

8547 E. Araphoe Rd., Box J-541, Greenwood Village CO 80112-1436. **E-mail:** conference@womenwritingthewest.org; shanna@shannahatfield.com. **Website:** www.womenwritingthewest.org. 2018 conference dates: October 25-28; Location: Walla Walla, Washington. "Women Writing the West is a nonprofit association of writers, editors, publishers, agents, booksellers, and other professionals writing and promoting the women's West. As such, women writing their stories in the American West in a way that illuminates them authentically. In addition, the organization provides support, encouragement, and inspiration to all women writing about any facet of the American West. Membership is open to all interested persons worldwide, including students. WWW membership also allows the choice of participation in our marketing marvel, the annual WWW Catalog of Author's Books. An annual conference is held every fall. The event covers research, writing techniques, multiple genres, marketing/promotion, and more. Agents and editors share ideas in a panel format as well as meeting one-on-one for pitch sessions with attendees. Conference location changes each year. The blog and social media outlets publish current WWW activities, features market research, and share articles of interest pertaining to American West literature and member news. WWW annually sponsors the WILLA Literary Award, which is given in several categories for outstanding literature featuring women's stories, set in the West. The winner of a WILLA literary Award receives a cash award and a trophy at the annual conference. Contest is open to non-members. See website for location and accommodation details.

COSTS See website. Discounts available for members, and for specific days only.

WRITEAWAYS

E-mail: writeawaysinfo@gmail.com. **Website:** https://www.writeaways.com. **Contact:** Mimi Herman. "We created Writeaways—writing getaways—to help you find the time you need to write. We provide writing instruction, fabulous food and company in beautiful places, and an inspiring place for you to take a writing vacation with your muse. We pamper you while providing rigorous, supportive assistance to help you become the best writer possible. We have week-long workshops in France and Italy, and weekend-plus-optional-retreat programs in North Carolina." North Carolina: The Whitehall, Camden, North Carolina. France: Chateau du Pin, near Champtocé-sur Loire (18 miles west of Angers). Italy: Villas Cini and Casanova, near Bucine, between Siena and Arezzo.

○ For 2018, consider these dates: Workshop by the River (NC): May 4-6 and Aug. 3-5; Retreat by the River (NC): May 6-9, Aug. 5-7; France (Chateau du Pin): Oct. 8-15; Italy (Villas Cini and Casanova): Oct. 17-24; The Grand Tour (France and Italy back to back): Oct. 8-24.

COSTS North Carolina workshop: $395 single room/bath, $345 shared bath. North Carolina retreat: $160/night; $145/night workshop participants. France and Italy: $2,350 single room, $2,100 shared rooms. The Grand Tour (France and Italy): $4,200 each single room, $4,000 each shared room.

WRITE-BY-THE-LAKE WRITER'S WORKSHOP & RETREAT

21 N. Park St., 7th Floor, Madison WI 53715. (608)262-3447. **E-mail:** christine.desmet@wisc.edu. **Website:** www.dcs.wisc.edu/lsa/writing. **Contact:** Christine DeSmet, director. Open to all writers and students; 12 or more workshops for all levels. Includes classes for full novel critique and one master class for 50 pages. Usually held the third week of June on the University of Wisconsin-Madison campus (second week in 2018). Registration limited to 15 each section; fewer in master classes. Writing facilities available; computer labs, wifi in all buildings and on the outdoor lakeside terrace. E-mail for more information. "Registration opens every January for following June."

COSTS $395 before May 15; $445 after that. Additional cost for master classes and college credits. Cost includes instruction, welcome luncheon, and pastry/coffee each day.

○ WRITE CANADA

The Word Guild, Suite 226, 245 King George Rd., Brantford Ontario N3R 7N7, Canada. **E-mail:** write-canada@thewordguild.com. **Website:** thewordguild.com/events/write-canada. Annual conference in Ontario for Christian writers of all types and at all stages. Conference duration: 3 days. Offers solid instruction, stimulating interaction, exciting challenges, and worshipful community.

○ "Write Canada is the nation's largest Christian writers' conference held annually. Each year hundreds of writers and editors—authors, journalists, columnists, bloggers, poets and playwrights—gather to hone their craft. Over the past three decades, Write Canada has successfully equipped writers and editors, beginner to professional, from all across North America."

WRITE IN THE HARBOR

Website: continuingedtacoma.com/writeintheharbor. 3993 Hunt St., Gig Harbor WA 98335. (253)460-2424. **Website:** continuingedtacoma.com/writeintheharbor. Annual conference held in fall. Offers workshops geared toward beginner, intermediate, advanced, and professional levels. Includes welcome reception, keynote speaker, and several presenters. Registration limited to 150. Cost of conference: $129 after August 1; $159 after September 16. Write for more information. Annual conference held in fall. Offers workshops geared toward beginner, intermediate, advanced, and professional levels. Includes welcome reception, keynote speaker, and several presenters. Registration limited to 80.

COSTS See website.

WRITE ON THE SOUND

WOTS, City of Edmonds Arts Commission, Frances Anderson Center, 700 Main St., Edmonds WA 98020. (425)771-0228. **E-mail:** wots@edmondswa.gov. **Website:** www.writeonthesound.com. **Contact:** Laurie Rose, Conference Organizer or Frances Chapin, Edmonds Arts Commission Mgr. Small, affordable annual conference focused on the craft of writing. Held the first weekend in October. 2018 dates: October 5-7. Conference duration: 3 days. Average attendance: 275. Features over 30 presenters, keynote, writing contest, ms critique appts, roundtable discussions, book signing reception, onsite bookstore, and opportunity to network with faculty and attendees. Edmonds is located just north of Seattle on the Puget Sound. Best Western Plus/Edmonds Harbor Inn is a conference partner.

⬤ Past attendee says, "I came away from every session with ideas to incorporate into my own writer's toolbox. The energy was wonderful because everyone was there for a single purpose: to make the most of a weekend for writers, whatever the level of expertise. I can't thank all the organizers, presenters, and volunteers enough for a wonderful experience."

COSTS $85-285 (not including optional fees).

ADDITIONAL INFORMATION Schedule posted on website late spring/early summer. Registration opens mid-July. Attendees are required to select the sessions when they register. Waiting lists for conference and manuscript appointments are available.

WRITE-TO-PUBLISH CONFERENCE

WordPro Communication Services, 9118 W. Elmwood Dr., Suite 1G, Niles IL 60714. (847)296-3964. **E-mail:** lin@writetopublish.com. **Website:** www.writetopublish.com. **Contact:** Lin Johnson, director. Annual conference. 2018 dates: June 13-16. Average attendance: 175. Conference is focused on the Christian market and includes classes for writers at all levels. Open to high school students. Site: Wheaton College, Wheaton, Illinois (Chicago area). [This is not a function of Wheaton College.] Campus residence hall rooms available. See the website for current information and costs.

COSTS See the website for current costs.

ADDITIONAL INFORMATION Conference information available in late January or early February. For details, visit website, or e-mail brochure@writetopublish.com. Accepts inquiries by e-mail, phone.

WRITING AND ILLUSTRATING FOR YOUNG READERS CONFERENCE

1480 E. 9400 S., Sandy UT 84093. **E-mail:** staff@wifyr.com. **Website:** www.wifyr.com. Brigham Young University, 348 Harman Continuing Education Bldg.Provo UT 84602-1532. (801)442-2568. **Fax:** (801)422-0745. **E-mail:** cw348@byu.edu. **Website:** http://wifyr.byu.edu. Annual workshop held in June. Five-day workshop designed for people who want to write for children or teenagers. Participants focus on a single market during daily four-hour morning writing workshops: picture books, book-length fiction (novels), fantasy/science fiction, nonfiction, mystery, beginning writing or illustration. Afternoon workshop sessions feature a variety of topics of interest to writers for all youth ages. Workshop cost: $439— includes all workshop and breakout sessions plus a banquet on Thursday evening. Afternoon-only registration available; participants may attend these sessions all five days for a fee of $109. Attendance at the Thursday evening banquet is included in addition to the afternoon mingle, plenary, and breakout sessions. Annual workshop held in June. 2017 dates: June 12-16. Duration: 5 days. Average attendance: more than 100. Learn how to write, illustrate, and publish in the children's and young adult markets. Beginning and advanced writers and illustrators are tutored in a small-group workshop setting by published authors and artists and receive instruction from and network with editors, major publishing house representatives, and literary agents. Afternoon attendees get to hear practical writing and publishing tips from published authors, literary agents, and editors. Site: Waterford School in Sandy, UT. Speakers have included John Cusick, Stephen Fraser, Alyson Heller, and Ruth Katcher. A block of rooms is available at the Best Western Cotton Tree Inn in Sandy, UT, at a discounted rate. This rate is good as long as there are available rooms.

⬤ Guidelines and registration are on the website.

ADDITIONAL INFORMATION There is an online form to contact this event.

WRITING FOR THE SOUL

Jerry B. Jenkins Christian Writers Guild, P.O. Box 88288, Black Forest CO 80908. (866)495-7551. **Fax:** (719)494-1299. **E-mail:** jerry@jerryjenkins.com. **Website:** www.jerryjenkins.com. Conferences as announced, covering fiction, nonfiction, and online writing. Nationally known, best-selling authors as keynote speakers, hosted by Jerry B. Jenkins. See website for pricing, locations, dates, and accommodations.

WYOMING WRITERS CONFERENCE

Cheyenne WY **E-mail:** president@wyowriters.org. **Website:** wyowriters.org. **Contact:** Chris Williams. This is a statewide writing conference for writers of Wyoming and neighboring states. Each year, multiple published authors, editors, and literary agents are in attendance to meet with writers and take pitches.

CONTESTS, AWARDS & GRANTS

Publication is not the only way to get your work recognized. Contests and awards can also be great ways to gain recognition in the industry. Grants, offered by organizations like the Society of Children's Book Writers and Illustrators (SCBWI), offer monetary recognition to writers, giving them more financial freedom as they work on projects.

When considering contests or applying for grants, be sure to study guidelines and requirements. Regard entry deadlines as gospel and follow the rules to the letter.

Note that some contests require nominations. For published authors and illustrators, competitions provide an excellent way to promote your work. Your publisher may not be aware of local competitions such as state-sponsored awards—if your book is eligible, have the appropriate person at your publishing company nominate or enter your work for consideration.

To select potential contests and grants, read through the listings that interest you, then send for more information about the types of written or illustrated material considered and other important details. A number of contests offer information through websites given in their listings.

If you are interested in knowing who has received certain awards in the past, check your local library or bookstores or consult *Children's Books: Awards & Honors*, compiled and edited by the Children's Book Council (www.cbcbooks.org). Many bookstores have special sections for books that are Caldecott and Newbery Medal winners. Visit the American Library Association website, www.ala.org, for information on the Caldecott, Newbery, Coretta Scott King, and Printz Awards. Visit www.hbook.com for information on The Boston Globe-Horn Book Award. Visit www.scbwi.org/awards.htm for information on The Golden Kite Award.

JANE ADDAMS CHILDREN'S BOOK AWARDS

Jane Addams Peace Association, 777 United Nations Plaza, 6th Floor, New York NY 10017. (212)652-8830. **E-mail:** info@janeaddamspeace.org. **Website:** www.janeaddamspeace.org. **Contact:** Heather Palmer, co-chair. The Jane Addams Children's Book Awards are given annually to the children's books published the preceding year that effectively promote the cause of peace, social justice, world community, and the equality of the sexes and all races as well as meeting conventional standards for excellence. Books eligible for this award may be fiction, poetry, or nonfiction. Books may be any length. Entries should be suitable for ages 2-12. See website for specific details on guidelines and required book themes. Deadline: December 31. Judged by a national committee of WILPF members concerned with children's books and their social values is responsible for making the changes each year.

○ ALCUIN SOCIETY AWARDS FOR EXCELLENCE IN BOOK DESIGN IN CANADA

The Alcuin Society, P.O. Box 3216, Stn. Terminal, Vancouver BC V6B 3X8, Canada. (604)732-5403. **E-mail:** awards@alcuinsociety.com; info@alcuinsociety.com. **Website:** www.alcuinsociety.com. **Contact:** Leah Gordon. The Alcuin Society Awards for Excellence in Book Design in Canada is the only national competition for book design in Canada. Winners are selected from books designed and published in Canada. Awards are presented annually at appropriate ceremonies held each year. Winning books are exhibited nationally and internationally at the Tokyo, Frankfurt, and Leipzig Book Fairs, and are Canada's entries in the international competition in Leipzig, "Book Design from all over the World" in the following spring. Submit previously published material from the year before the award's call for entries. Submissions made by the publisher, author or designer (Canadian). Deadline: March 1. Prizes: 1st, 2nd, 3rd, and Honourable Mention in each category (at the discretion of the judges). Judged by professionals and those experienced in the field of book design.

AMERICAS AWARD

Website: http://claspprograms.org/americasaward. **Contact:** Denise Woltering. The Américas Award encourages and commends authors, illustrators, and publishers who produce quality children's and young adult books that portray Latin America, the Caribbean, or Latinos in the United States. Up to 2 awards (for primary and secondary reading levels) are given in recognition of US published works of fiction, poetry, folklore, or selected nonfiction (from picture books to works for young adults). The award winners and commended titles are selected for their (1) distinctive literary quality; (2) cultural contextualization; (3) exceptional integration of text, illustration and design; and (4) potential for classroom use. To nominate a copyright title from the previous year, publishers are invited to submit review copies to the committee members listed on the website. Publishers should send 8 copies of the nominated book. Deadline: January 4. Prize: $500, plaque and a formal presentation at the Library of Congress, Washington DC.

AMERICA & ME ESSAY CONTEST

Farm Bureau Insurance, P.O. Box 30400, Lansing MI 48909. **E-mail:** lfedewa@fbinsmi.com. **Website:** FarmBureauInsurance.com. **Contact:** Lisa Fedewa. Focuses on encouraging students to write about their personal Michigan heroes: someone who lives in the state and who has encouraged them, taught them important lessons, and helped them pursue their dreams. Open to Michigan eighth graders. Contest rules and entry form available on website. Encourages Michigan youth to recognize the heroes in their communities and their state. Deadline: November 18. Prize: $1,000, plaque, and medallion for top 10 winners. Home office volunteers.

AMERICAN ASSOCIATION OF UNIVERSITY WOMEN AWARD IN JUVENILE LITERATURE

4610 Mail Service Center, Raleigh NC 27699-4610. (919)807-7290. **E-mail:** michael.hill@ncdcr.gov. **Website:** www.ncdcr.gov. **Contact:** Michael Hill, awards coordinator. Annual award. Book must be published during the year ending June 30. Submissions made by author, author's agent or publisher. SASE for contest rules. Author must have maintained either legal residence or actual physical residence, or a combination of both, in the state of North Carolina for 3 years immediately preceding the close of the contest period. Only published work (books) eligible. Recognizes the year's best work of juvenile literature by a North Carolina resident. Deadline: July 15. Prize: Awards a cup to the winner and winner's name inscribed on a plaque displayed within the North Carolina Office of Archives and History. Judged by three-judge panel.

○ Competition receives 10-15 submissions per category.

HANS CHRISTIAN ANDERSEN AWARD

Nonnenweg 12, Postfach Basel CH-4009, Switzerland. **E-mail:** liz.page@ibby.org. **E-mail:** ibby@ibby.org. **Website:** www.ibby.org. **Contact:** Liz Page, director. The Hans Christian Andersen Award, awarded every two years by the International Board on Books for Young People (IBBY), is the highest international recognition given to an author and an illustrator of children's books. The Author's Award has been given since 1956, the Illustrator's Award since 1966. Her Majesty Queen Margrethe II of Denmark is the Patron of the Hans Christian Andersen Awards. The awards are presented at the biennial congresses of IBBY. Awarded to an author and to an illustrator, living at the time of the nomination, who by the outstanding value of their work are judged to have made a lasting contribution to literature for children and young people. The complete works of the author and of the illustrator will be taken into consideration in awarding the medal, which will be accompanied by a diploma. Candidates are nominated by National Sections of IBBY in good standing. Prize: Awards medals according to literary and artistic criteria. Judged by the Hans Christian Andersen International Jury.

ARIZONA LITERARY CONTEST AND BOOK AWARDS

Arizona Authors' Association, 6939 East Chaparral Rd., Paradise Valley AZ 85253-7000. (602)554-8101. **E-mail:** azauthors@gmail.com. **Website:** www.azauthors.com. **Contact:** Lisa Aquilina, president. Arizona Authors' Association sponsors annual literary competition in poetry, short story, essay, unpublished novels, and published books (fiction, nonfiction, and children's literature) and Arizona Book of the Year. Cash prizes awarded ($500 Book of the Year) from Green Pieces Press and 1st, 2nd, and 3rd place in seven categories ($150, $75 and $50, respectively) from Vignetta Syndicate LLC. New category in 2017, New Drama Writing, with a grand prize of $250. All category winners are published in the *Arizona Literary Magazine*. NEW PRIZE in 2018 for Unpublished Novel category. Winner receives a standard, traditional publishing contract through IngramElliott Book Publishers. NEW CATEGORY in 2018 - Published Cookbooks! Must have 2017 or 2018 copyright date at time of submission. Poetry, short story, essay, and new drama writing submissions must be unpublished. Work must have been published in the current or immediate past calendar year. Considers simultaneous submissions. Entry form and guidelines available on website or upon request. Deadline: July 2. Begins accepting submissions January 1. Finalists notified by Labor Day weekend. Prizes: Grand Prize, Arizona Book of the Year Award: $500. All categories except new drama writing: 1st Prize: $150 and publication; 2nd Prize: $75 and publication; 3rd Prize: $50 and publication. New drama writing grand prize $250 and publication. Features in *Arizona Literary Magazine* can be taken instead of money and publication. 1st and 2nd prize winners in poetry, essay, and short story are nominated for the Pushcart Prize. Judged by nationwide published authors, editors, literary agents, and reviewers. Winners announced at an awards dinner and ceremony held the first Saturday in November.

○ Competition receives approximately 1,500+ entries per year. Submissions welcome from authors worldwide. All entries must be written in English.

MARILYN BAILLIE PICTURE BOOK AWARD

The Canadian Children's Book Centre, 40 Orchard View Blvd., Suite 217, Toronto ON M4R 1B9, Canada. (416)975-0010, ext. 222. **Fax:** (416)975-8970. **E-mail:** meghan@bookcentre.ca. **Website:** www.bookcentre.ca. **Contact:** Meghan Howe. The Marilyn Baillie Picture Book Award honors excellence in the illustrated picture book format. To be eligible, the book must be an original work in English, aimed at children ages 3-8, written and illustrated by Canadians. Books published in Canada or abroad are eligible. Eligible genres include fiction, non-fiction and poetry. Books must be published between Jan. 1 and Dec. 31 of the previous calendar year. New editions or re-issues of previously published books are not eligible for submission. Send 5 copies of title along with a completed submission form. Deadline: mid-December annually. Prize: $20,000.

MILDRED L. BATCHELDER AWARD

Website: http://www.ala.org/alsc/awardsgrants/. The Batchelder Award is given to the most outstanding children's book originally published in a language other than English in a country other than the United States, and subsequently translated into English for publication in the US. Visit website for terms and criteria of award. The purpose of the award, a citation to an American publisher, is to encourage international exchange of quality children's books by recognizing US publishers of such books in translation. Deadline: December 31.

JOHN AND PATRICIA BEATTY AWARD

E-mail: tbronzan@sonoma.lib.ca.us. **Website:** http://www.cla-net.org/?page=113. **Contact:** Tiffany Bronzan, award chair. The California Library Association's John and Patricia Beatty Award, sponsored by Baker & Taylor, honors the author of a distinguished book for children or young adults that best promotes an awareness of California and its people. Must be a children's or young adult books published in the previous year, set in California, and highlight California's cultural heritage or future. Send title suggestiosn to the committee members. Deadline: January 31. Prize: $500 and an engraved plaque. Judged by a committee of CLA members, who select the winning title from books published in the United States during the preceding year.

✪ THE GEOFFREY BILSON AWARD FOR HISTORICAL FICTION FOR YOUNG PEOPLE

The Canadian Children's Book Centre, 40 Orchard View Blvd., Suite 217, Toronto ON M4R 1B9, Canada. (416)975-0010, ext. 222. **Fax:** (416)975-8970. **Website:** www.bookcentre.ca. **Contact:** Meghan Howe. Awarded annually to reward excellence in the writing of an outstanding work of historical fiction for young readers, by a Canadian author, published between Jan 1 and Dec 31 of the previous calendar year. Open to Canadian citizens and/or permanent residents of Canada.Books must be published between January 1 and December 31 of the previous year. Books must be first foreign or first Canadian editions. Autobiographies are not eligible. Jury members will consider the following: historical setting and accuracy, strong character and plot development, well-told, original story, and stability of book for its intended age group. Send 5 copies of the title along with a completed submission form. Deadline: mid-December annually. Prize: $5,000.

THE IRMA S. AND JAMES H. BLACK AWARD

Bank Street College of Education, 610 W. 112th St., New York NY 10025-1898. (212)875-4458. **Fax:** (212)875-4558. **E-mail:** kfreda@bankstreet.edu. **Website:** http://bankstreet.edu/center-childrens-literature/irma-black-award/. **Contact:** Kristin Freda. Award give to an outstanding book for young children—a book in which text and illustrations are inseparable, each enhancing and enlarging on the other to produce a singular whole. Entries must have been published during the previous calendar year. Publishers submit books. Submit only one copy of each book. Does not accept unpublished mss. Deadline: mid-December. Prize: A scroll with the recipient's name and a gold seal designed by Maurice Sendak. Judged by a committee of older children and children's literature professionals. Final judges are first-, second-, and third-grade classes at a number of cooperating schools.

✪ BOROONDARA LITERARY AWARDS

City of Boroondara, 340 Camberwell Rd., Camberwell VIC 3124, Australia. **E-mail:** bla@boroondara.vic.gov.au. **Website:** www.boroondara.vic.gov.au/literary-awards. Contest for unpublished work in 2 categories: Young Writers who live, go to school or work in the City of Boroondara: 5th-6th grade (Junior), 7th-9th grade (Middle), and 10th-12th grade (Senior), prose and poetry on any theme; and Open Short Story from residents of Australia (1,500-3,000 words). Deadline: 5pm on August 28. Prizes: Young Writers, Junior: 1st Place: $150; 2nd Place: $100; 3rd Place: $50. Young Writers, Middle and Senior: 1st Place: $600; 2nd Place: $400; 3rd Place: $200. Open Short Story: 1st Place: $1,500; 2nd Place: $1000; 3rd Place $500.

BOSTON GLOBE-HORN BOOK AWARDS

The Boston Globe, Horn Book, Inc., 300 The Fenway, Palace Road Building, Suite P-311, Boston MA 02115. (617)278-0225. **Fax:** (617)278-6062. **E-mail:** bghb@hbook.com; info@hbook.com. **Website:** www.hbook.

com/bghb/. Offered annually for excellence in literature for children and young adults (published June 1-May 31). Categories: picture book, fiction and poetry, nonfiction. Judges may also name up to 2 honor books in each category. Books must be published in the US, but may be written or illustrated by citizens of any country. The Horn Book Magazine publishes speeches given at awards ceremonies. Guidelines for submitting books online. Submit a book directly to each of the judges. See www.hbook.com/bghb-submissions for details on submitting, as well as contest guidelines. Deadline: May 15. Prize: $500 and an engraved silver bowl; honor book recipients receive an engraved silver plate. Judged by a panel of 3 judges selected each year.

☼ ANN CONNOR BRIMER BOOK AWARD

(902)490-2742. **Website:** www.atlanticbookawards.ca/. **Contact:** Laura Carter, Atlantic Book Awards Festival Coordinator. In 1990, the Nova Scotia Library Association established the Ann Connor Brimer Award for writers residing in Atlantic Canada who have made an outstanding contribution to writing for Atlantic Candian young people. Author must be alive and residing in Atlantic Canada at time of nomination. Book intended for youth up to the age of 15. Book in print and readily available. Fiction or nonfiction (except textbooks). Book must have been published within the previous year. Prize: $2,000. Two shortlisted titles: $250 each.

CALIFORNIA YOUNG PLAYWRIGHTS CONTEST

Playwrights Project, 3675 Ruffin Rd., Suite 330, San Diego CA 92123-1870. (858)384-2970. **Fax:** (858)384-2974. **E-mail:** write@playwrightsproject.org. **Website:** www.playwrightsproject.org/programs/contest/. **Contact:** Cecelia Kouma, executive director. The California Young Playwrights Contest is open to Californians under age 19. Every year young playwrights submit original scripts to the contest. Every writer who requests feedback receives an individualized script critique. Selected writers win script readings or full professional productions in Plays by Young Writers festival. Distinguished artists from major theatres select festival scripts and write comments to the playwrights. Submissions are required to be unpublished and not produced professionally. Submissions made by the author. SASE for contest rules and entry form.

Scripts must be a minimum of 10 standard typewritten pages. Scripts will *not* be returned. If requested, entrants receive detailed evaluation letter. Guidelines available online. Deadline: June 1. Prize: Scripts will be produced in spring at a professional theatre in San Diego. Writers submitting scripts of 10 or more pages receive a detailed script evaluation letter upon request. Judged by professionals in the theater community, a committee of 5-7; changes somewhat each year.

☼ CANADIAN TALES SHORT STORY COMPETITION

Red Tuque Books, Unit #6, 477 Martin St., Penticton BC V2A 5L2, Canada. (778)476-5750. **Fax:** (778)476-5750. **E-mail:** dave@redtuquebooks.ca. **Website:** www.redtuquebooks.ca. **Contact:** David Korinetz, contest director. Offered annually for unpublished works. Check the guidelines on the website. Purpose of award is to promote Canada and Canadian publishing. Stories require a Canadian element. There are three ways to qualify. They can be written by a Canadian, written about Canadians, or take place somewhere in Canada. Deadline: December 31. Prize: 1st Place: $500; 2nd Place: $150; 3rd Place: $100; and 10 prizes of $25 will be given to honorable mentions. All 13 winners will be published in an anthology. They will each receive a complimentary copy. Judged by Canadian authors/publishers in the appropriate genre. Acquires first print rights. Contest open to anyone.

☼   This contest switches genre every 3 years. 2016 is for Fantasy/Science Fiction, 2017 is for Mystery/Horror, and 2018 is for Romance/Humor/Inspirational.

CASCADE WRITING CONTEST & AWARDS

Oregon Christian Writers, 1075 Willow Lake Road N., Keizer Oregon 97303. **E-mail:** cascade@oregonchristianwriters.org. **E-mail:** cascade@oregonchristianwriters.org. **Website:** http://oregonchristianwriters.org/. **Contact:** Marilyn Rhoads and Julie McDonald Zander. The Cascade Awards are presented at the annual Oregon Christian Writers Summer Conference (held at the Red Lion on the River in Portland, Oregon, each August) attended by national editors, agents, and professional authors. The contest is open for both published and unpublished works in the following categories: contemporary fiction book, historical fiction book, speculative fiction book, nonfiction book, memoir book, young adult/middle grade fiction book, young adult/middle grade nonfiction book, children's chapter book and picture book (fiction and nonfiction), poetry, devotional, article, column, story, or blog post. Two additional special Cascade Awards are presented each year: the Trailblazer Award to a writer who has distinguished him/herself in the field of Christian writing; and a Writer of Promise Award for a writer who demonstrates unusual promise in the field of Christian writing. For a full list of categories, entry rules, and scoring elements, visit website. Guidelines and rules available on the website. Entry forms will be available on the first day for entry. Annual multi-genre competition to encourage both published and emerging writers in the field of Christian writing. Deadline: March 31. Submissions period begins February 14. Prize: Award certificate and pin presented at the Cascade Awards ceremony during the Oregon Christian Writers Annual Summer Conference. Finalists are listed in the conference notebook and winners are listed online. Cascade Trophies are awarded to the recipients of the Trailblazer and Writer of Promise Awards. Judged by published authors, editors, librarians, and retail book store owners and employees. Final judging by editors, agents, and published authors from the Christian publishing industry.

CHILDREN'S AFRICANA BOOK AWARD

Outreach Council of the African Studies Association, c/o Rutgers University -Livingston campus, 54 Joyce Kilmer Ave., Piscataway NJ 08854, USA. (703)549-8208; (301)585-9136. **E-mail:** africaaccess@aol.com. **E-mail:** Harriet@AfricaAccessReview.org. **Website:** www.africaaccessreview.org. **Contact:** Brenda Randolph, chairperson. The Children's Africana Book Awards are presented annually to the authors and illustrators of the best books on Africa for children and young people published or distributed in the U.S. The awards were created by the Outreach Council of the African Studies Association (ASA) to dispel stereotypes and encourage the publication and use of accurate, balanced children's materials about Africa. The awards are presented in 2 categories: Young Children and Older Readers. Entries must have been published in the calendar year previous to the award. Work submitted for awards must be suitable for children ages 4-18; a significant portion of books' content must be about Africa; must by copyrighted in the calendar year prior to award year; must be published or distributed in the US. Books should be suitable for children and young adults, ages 4-18. A significant portion of the book's content should be about Africa. Deadline: January 31 of the award year. Judged by African Studies and Children's Literature scholars. Nominated titles are read by committee members and reviewed by external African Studies scholars with specialized academic training.

CHILDREN'S BOOK GUILD AWARD FOR NONFICTION

E-mail: theguild@childrensbookguild.org. **Website:** www.childrensbookguild.org. Annual award. "One doesn't enter. One is selected. Our jury annually selects one author for the award." Honors an author or illustrator whose total work has contributed significantly to the quality of nonfiction for children. Prize: Cash and an engraved crystal paperweight. Judged by a jury of Children's Book Guild specialists, authors, and illustrators.

CHRISTIAN BOOK AWARD® PROGRAM

Evangelical Christian Publishers Association, 5801 S. McClintock Dr, Suite 104, Tempe AZ 85283. (480)966-3998. **Fax:** (480)966-1944. **E-mail:** info@ecpa.org. **Website:** www.ecpa.org. **Contact:** Stan Jantz, ED. The Evangelical Christian Publishers Association (ECPA) recognizes quality and encourages excellence by presenting the ECPA Christian Book Awards® (formerly known as Gold Medallion) each year. Categories include Christian Living, Biography & Memoir, Faith & Culture, Children, Young People's Literature, Devotion & Gift, Bibles, Bible Reference Works, Bible Study, Ministry Resources and New Author. All entries must be evangelical in nature and submitted through an ECPA member publisher. Books must have been published in the calendar year prior to the award. Publishing companies submitting entries must be ECPA members in good standing. See website for details. The Christian Book Awards® recognize the highest quality in Christian books and is among the oldest and most prestigious awards program in Christian publishing. Submission period runs September 1-30. Judged by experts, authors and retailers with years of experience in their field.

○ Book entries are submitted by ECPA member publishers according to criteria including date of publication and category.

◑ THE CITY OF VANCOUVER BOOK AWARD

Cultural Services Dept., Woodward's Heritage Building, 111 W. Hastings St., Suite 501, Vancouver BC V6B 1H4, Canada. (604)871-6634. **Fax:** (604)871-6005. **E-mail:** marnie.rice@vancouver.ca; culture@vancouver.ca. **Website:** https://vancouver.ca/people-programs/city-of-vancouver-book-award.aspx. The annual City of Vancouver Book Award recognizes authors of excellence of any genre who contribute to the appreciation and understanding of Vancouver's history, unique character, or the achievements of its residents. The book must exhibit excellence in one or more of the following areas: content, illustration, design, format. The book must not be copyrighted prior to the previous year. Submit four copies of book. See website for details and guidelines. Deadline: May 18. Prize: $3,000. Judged by an independent jury.

◑ CLA YOUNG ADULT BOOK AWARD

1150 Morrison Dr.,, Suite 400, Ottawa ON K2H 8S9, Canada. (613)232-9625. **Fax:** (613)563-9895. **E-mail:** cshea@cbvrsb.ca. **Website:** www.cla.ca. **Contact:** Carmelita Cechetto-Shea, chair. This award recognizes an author of an outstanding English language Canadian book which appeals to young adults between the ages of 13 and 18. To be eligible for consideration, the following must apply: it must be a work of fiction (novel, collection of short stories, or graphic novel), the title must be a Canadian publication in either hardcover or paperback, and the author must be a Canadian citizen or landed immigrant. The award is given annually, when merited, at the Canadian Library Association's annual conference. Deadline: December 31. Prize: $1,000.

COLORADO BOOK AWARDS

Colorado Humanities & Center for the Book, 7935 E. Prentice Ave., Suite 450, Greenwood Village CO 80111. (303)894-7951. **Fax:** (303)864-9361. **E-mail:** bess@coloradohumanities.org. **Website:** www.coloradohumanities.org. **Contact:** Bess Maher. An annual program that celebrates the accomplishments of Colorado's outstanding authors, editors, illustrators, and photographers. Awards are presented in at least ten categories including anthology/collection, biography, children's, creative nonfiction, fiction, history, nonfiction, pictorial, poetry, and young adult. To be eligible for a Colorado Book Award, a primary contributor to the book must be a Colorado writer, editor, illustrator, or photographer. Current Colorado residents are eligible, as are individuals engaged in ongoing literary work in the state and authors whose personal history, identity, or literary work reflect a strong Colorado influence. Authors not currently Colorado residents who feel their work is inspired by or connected to Colorado should submit a letter with his/her entry describing the connection. Deadline: January 9.

CWW ANNUAL WISCONSIN WRITERS AWARDS

Council for Wisconsin Writers, 4964 Gilkeson Rd, Waunakee WI 53597. **E-mail:** karlahuston@gmail.com. **Website:** www.wiswriters.org. **Contact:** Geoff Gilpin, president and annual awards co-chair; Karla Huston, secretary and annual awards co-chair; Sylvia Cavanaugh, annual awards co-chair; Edward Schultz, annual awards co-chair, Erik Richardson, annual awards co-chair. Offered annually for work published by Wisconsin writers during the previous calendar year. Nine awards: Major Achievement (presented in alternate years); short fiction; short nonfiction; nonfiction book; poetry book; fiction book; children's literature; Lorine Niedecker Poetry Award; Christopher Latham Sholes Award for Outstanding Service to Wisconsin Writers (presented in alternate years); Essay Award for Young Writers. Open to Wisconsin residents. Entries may be submitted via postal mail only. See website for guidelines and entry forms. Deadline: January 31. Submissions open on November 1. Prizes: First place prizes: $500. Honorable mentions: $50. List of judges available on website.

MARGARET A. EDWARDS AWARD

50 East Huron St., Chicago IL 60611-2795. (312)280-4390 or (800)545-2433. **Fax:** (312)280-5276. **E-mail:** yalsa@ala.org. **Website:** www.ala.org/yalsa/edwards. **Contact:** Nichole O'Connor. Annual award administered by the Young Adult Library Services Association (YALSA) of the American Library Association (ALA) and sponsored by *School Library Journal* magazine. Awarded to an author whose book or books, over a period of time, have been accepted by young adults as an authentic voice that continues to illuminate their experiences and emotions, giving insight into their lives. The book or books should enable them to understand themselves, the world in which they live, and their relationship with others and with society. The book

or books must be in print at the time of the nomination. Submissions must be previously published no less than 5 years prior to the first meeting of the current Margaret A. Edwards Award Committee at Midwinter Meeting. Nomination form is available on the YALSA website. Deadline: December 1. Prize: $2,000. Judged by members of the Young Adult Library Services Association.

SHUBERT FENDRICH MEMORIAL PLAYWRITING CONTEST

Pioneer Drama Service, Inc., P.O. Box 4267, Englewood CO 80155. (303)779-4035. **Fax:** (303)779-4315. **E-mail:** editors@pioneerdrama.com. **E-mail:** submissions@pioneerdrama.com. **Website:** www.pioneerdrama.com. **Contact:** Brian Taylor, acquisitions editor. Annual competition that encourages the development of quality theatrical material for educational, community and children's theatre markets. Previously unpublished submissions only. Only considers mss with a running time between 20-120 minutes. Open to all writers not currently published by Pioneer Drama Service. Guidelines available online. No entry fee. Cover letter, SASE for return of ms, and proof of production or staged reading must accompany all submissions. Deadline: Ongoing contest; a winner is selected by June 1 each year from all submissions received the previous year. Prize: $1,000 royalty advance in addition to publication. Judged by editors.

DOROTHY CANFIELD FISHER CHILDREN'S BOOK AWARD

Midstate Library Service Center, Dorothy Canfield Fisher Book Award Committee, c/o Vermont Department of Libraries, 109 State St., Montpelier VT 05609. (802)828-6954. **E-mail:** grace.greene@state.vt.us. **Website:** www.dcfaward.org. **Contact:** Mary Linney, chair. Annual award to encourage Vermont children to become enthusiastic and discriminating readers by providing them with books of good quality by living American or Canadian authors published in the current year. E-mail for entry rules. Titles must be original work, published in the U.S., and be appropriate to children in grades 4-8. The book must be copyrighted in the current year. It must be written by an American author living in the U.S. or Canada, or a Canadian author living in Canada or the U.S. Deadline: December of year book was published. Prize: Awards a scroll presented to the winning author at an award ceremony. Judged by children, grades 4-8, who vote for their favorite book.

◑ THE NORMA FLECK AWARD FOR CANADIAN CHILDREN'S NON-FICTION

The Canadian Children's Book Centre, 40 Orchard View Blvd., Suite 217, Toronto ON M4R 1B9, Canada. (416)975-0010 ext. 222. **Fax:** (416)975-8970. **E-mail:** meghan@bookcentre.ca. **Website:** www.bookcentre.ca. **Contact:** Meghan Howe. The Norma Fleck Award was established by the Fleck Family Foundation to recognize and raise the profile of exceptional nonfiction books for children. Offered annually for books published between January 1 and December 31 of the previous calendar year. Open to Canadian citizens and/or permanent residents. Books must be first foreign or first Canadian editions. Nonfiction books in the following categories are eligible: culture and the arts, science, biography, history, geography, reference, sports, activities, and pastimes. Deadline: mid-December annually. Prize: $10,000. The award will go to the author unless 40% or more of the text area is composed of original illustrations, in which case the award will be divided equally between author and illustrator.

FLICKER TALE CHILDREN'S BOOK AWARD

Morton Mandan Public Library, 609 W. Main St., Mandan ND 58554. **E-mail:** laustin@cdln.info. **Website:** www.ndla.info/flickertale. **Contact:** Linda Austin. Award gives children across the state of North Dakota a chance to vote for their book of choice from a nominated list of 20: 4 in the picture book category; 4 in the intermediate category; 4 in the juvenile category (for more advanced readers); 4 in the upper grade level nonfiction category. Also promotes awareness of quality literature for children. Previously published submissions only. Submissions nominated by librarians and teachers across the state of North Dakota. Deadline: April 1. Prize: A plaque from North Dakota Library Association and banquet dinner. Judged by children in North Dakota.

DON FREEMAN ILLUSTRATOR GRANTS

4727 Wilshire Blvd Suite 301, Los Angeles CA 90010. (323)782-1010. **Fax:** (323)782-1892. **E-mail:** grants@scbwi.org; sarahbaker@scbwi.org. **Website:** www.scbwi.org. **Contact:** Sarah Baker. The grant-in-aid is available to both full and associate members of the SCBWI who, as artists, seriously intend to make picture books their chief contribution to the field of children's literature. Applications and prepared materials are available in October. Grant awarded and announced in August. SASE for award rules and entry forms. SASE for return of entries. Enables picture book artists to further their understanding, training, and work in the picture book genre. Deadline: March 31. Submission period begins March 1. Prize: Two grants of $1,000 each awarded annually. One grant to a published illustrator and one to a pre-published illustrator.

THEODOR SEUSS GEISEL AWARD

Association for Library Service to Children, Division of the American Library Association, 50 E. Huron, Chicago IL 60611. (800)545-2433. **E-mail:** alscawards@ala.org. **Website:** www.ala.org. The Theodor Seuss Geisel Award is given annually to the author(s) and illustrator(s) of the most distinguished American book for beginning readers published in English in the United States during the preceding year. The award is to recognize the author(s) and illustrator(s) who demonstrate great creativity and imagination in his/her/their literary and artistic achievements to engage children in reading. Terms and criteria for the award are listed on the website. Entry will not be returned. Deadline: December 31. Prize: Medal, given at awards ceremony during the ALA Annual Conference.

✪ JOHN GLASSCO TRANSLATION PRIZE

Literary Translators' Association of Canada, 620-03 Concordia University, 1455 boul. de Maisonneuve Ouest, Montréal QC H3G 1M8, Canada. (514)848-2424, ext. 8702. **E-mail:** info@attlc-ltac.org. **Website:** attlc-ltac.org/john-glassco-translation-prize. **Contact:** Glassco Prize Committee. Offered annually for a translator's first book-length literary translation into French or English, published in Canada during the previous calendar year. The translator must be a Canadian citizen or permanent resident. Eligible genres include fiction, creative nonfiction, poetry, and children's books. Deadline: July 31. Prize: $1,000.

GOLDEN KITE AWARDS

Society of Children's Book Writers and Illustrators (SCBWI), SCBWI Golden Kite Awards, 8271 Bev-

erly Blvd., Los Angeles CA 90048-4515. (323)782-1010. **Fax:** (323)782-1892. **E-mail:** bonniebader@sbcwi.org. **Website:** www.scbwi.org. Given annually to recognize excellence in children's literature in 4 categories: fiction, nonfiction, picture book text, and picture book illustration. Books submitted must be published in the previous calendar year. Both individuals and publishers may submit. Submit 4 copies of book. Submit to one category only, except in the case of picture books. Must be a current member of the SCBWI. Deadline: December 1. Prize: One Golden Kite Award Winner and one Honor Book will be chosen per category. Winners and Honorees will receive a commemorative poster also sent to publishers, bookstores, libraries, and schools; a press release; an announcement on the SCBWI website; and on SCBWI Social Networks.

✪ GOVERNOR GENERAL'S LITERARY AWARDS

Canada Council for the Arts, 150 Elgin St., P.O. Box 1047, Ottawa ON K1P 5V8, Canada. (800)263-5588, ext. 5573. **Website:** ggbooks.ca. The Canada Council for the Arts provides a wide range of grants and services to professional Canadian artists and art organizations in dance, media arts, music, theatre, writing, publishing, and the visual arts. Books must be first edition literary trade books written, translated, or illustrated by Canadian citizens or permanent residents of Canada and published in Canada or abroad in the previous year. In the case of translation, the original work must also be a Canadian-authored title. For complete eligibility criteria, deadlines, and submission procedures, please visit the website at www.canadacouncil.ca. The Governor General's Literary Awards are given annually for the best English-language and French-language work in each of 7 categories, including fiction, non-fiction, poetry, drama, young people's literature (text), young people's literature (illustrated books), and translation. Deadline: Depends on the book's publication date. See website for details. Prize: Each GG winner receives $25,000. Non-winning finalists receive $1,000. Publishers of the winning titles receive a $3,000 grant for promotional purposes. Evaluated by fellow authors, translators, and illustrators. For each category, a jury makes the final selection.

GUGGENHEIM FELLOWSHIPS

John Simon Guggenheim Memorial Foundation, 90 Park Ave., New York NY 10016. (212)687-4470. **E-mail:** fellowships@gf.org. **Website:** www.gf.org. Often characterized as "midcareer" awards, Guggenheim Fellowships are intended for men and women who have already demonstrated exceptional capacity for productive scholarship or exceptional creative ability in the arts. Fellowships are awarded through two annual competitions: one open to citizens and permanent residents of the United States and Canada, and the other open to citizens and permanent residents of Latin America and the Caribbean. Candidates must apply to the Guggenheim Foundation in order to be considered in either of these competitions. The Foundation receives between 3,500 and 4,000 applications each year. Although no one who applies is guaranteed success in the competition, there is no prescreening: all applications are reviewed. Approximately 200 Fellowships are awarded each year. Deadline: September 15.

HACKNEY LITERARY AWARDS

4650 Old Looney Mill Rd, Birmingham AL 35243. **E-mail:** info@hackneyliteraryawards.org. **Website:** www.hackneyliteraryawards.org. **Contact:** Myra Crawford, PhD, executive director. Offered annually for unpublished novels, short stories (maximum 5,000 words), and poetry (50 line limit). Guidelines on website. Deadline: September 30 (novels), November 30 (short stories and poetry). Prize: $5,000 in annual prizes for poetry and short fiction ($2,500 national and $2,500 state level). 1st Place: $600; 2nd Place: $400; 3rd Place: $250; plus $5,000 for an unpublished novel. Competition winners will be announced on the website each March.

THE MARILYN HALL AWARDS FOR YOUTH THEATRE

P.O. Box 148, Beverly Hills CA 90213. **Website:** www.beverlyhillstheatreguild.com. **Contact:** Candace Coster, competition coordinator. The Marilyn Hall Awards consist of 2 monetary prizes for plays suitable for grades 6-8 (middle school) or for plays suitable for grades 9-12 (high school). The 2 prizes will be awarded on the merits of the play scripts, which includes its suitability for the intended audience. The plays should be approximately 45-75 minutes in length. There is no production connected to any of the prizes, though a staged reading is optional at the discretion of the BHTG. Unpublished submissions only. Authors must be U.S. citizens or legal residents and must sign entry form personally. Deadline: The last day of February. Submission period begins January 15. Prize: 1st Prize: $700; 2nd Prize: $300.

AURAND HARRIS MEMORIAL PLAYWRITING AWARD

The New England Theatre Conference, Inc., 215 Knob Hill Dr., Hamden CT 06518. **Fax:** (203)288-5938. **E-mail:** mail@netconline.org. **E-mail:** mail@netconline.org. **Website:** www.netconline.org. Offered annually for an unpublished full-length play for young audiences. Guidelines available online or for SASE. Open to all. All scripts submitted by email *only*. Deadline: May 1.

ERIC HOFFER AWARD

Hopewell Publications, LLC, P.O. Box 11, Titusville NJ 08560-0011. **Fax:** (609)964-1718. **E-mail:** info@hopepubs.com. **Website:** www.hofferaward.com. **Contact:** Dawn Shows, EHA Coordinator. Annual contest for previously published books. Recognizes excellence in independent publishing in many unique categories: Art (titles capture the experience, execution, or demonstration of the arts); Poetry (all styles); Chapbook (40 pages or less, artistic assembly); General Fiction (nongenre-specific fiction); Commercial Fiction (genre-specific fiction); Children (titles for young children); Young Adult (titles aimed at the juvenile and teen markets); Culture (titles demonstrating the human or world experience); Memoir (titles relating to personal experience); Business (titles with application to today's business environment and emerging trends); Reference (titles from traditional and emerging reference areas); Home (titles with practical applications to home or home-related issues, including family); Health (titles promoting physical, mental, and emotional well-being); Self-help (titles involving new and emerging topics in self-help); Spiritual (titles involving the mind and spirit, including relgion); Legacy Fiction and Nonfiction (titles over 2 years of age that hold particular relevance to any subject matter or form); E-book Fiction; E-book Nonfiction. Open to any writer of published work within the last 2 years, including categories for older books. This contest recognizes excellence in independent publishing in many unique categories. Also awards the Montaigne Medal for most though-provoking book, the Da Vinci Eye for best cover, and the First Horizon Award for best new authors. Results published in the US Review of Books. Deadline: January 21. Grand Prize: $2,500; honors (winner, runner-up, honorable mentions) in each category, including the Montaigne Medal (most thought-provoking), da Vinci Art (cover art), First Horizon (first book), and Best in Press (small, academic, micro, self-published).

MARILYN HOLLINSHEAD VISITING SCHOLARS FELLOWSHIP

University of Minnesota, 113 Anderson Library, 222 21st Ave. South, Minneapolis MN 55455. **Website:** http://www.lib.umn.edu/clrc/awards-grants-and-fellowships. Marilyn Hollinshead Visiting Scholars Fund for Travel to the Kerlan Collection is available for research study. Applicants may request up to $1,500. Send a letter with the proposed purpose and plan to use specific research materials (manuscripts and art), dates, and budget (including airfare and per diem). Travel and a written report on the project must be completed and submitted in the previous year. Deadline: June 1.

⊙ AMELIA FRANCES HOWARD-GIBBON ILLUSTRATOR'S AWARD

1150 Morrison Drie, Suite 400, Ottawa ON K 2H859, Canada. (613)232-9625. **Fax:** (613)563-9895. **Website:** www.bookcentre.ca. **Contact:** Diana Cauthier. Annually awarded to an outstanding illustrator of a children's book published in Canada during the previous calendar year. The award is bestowed upon books that are suitable for children up to and including age 12. To be eligible for the award, an illustrator must be a Canadian citizen or a permanent resident of Canada, and the text of the book must be worthy of the book's illustrations. Deadline: November 30. Prize: A plaque and a check for $1,000 (CAD).

THE JULIA WARD HOWE/ BOSTON AUTHORS AWARD

The Boston Authors Club, The Boston Authors Club, 36 Sunhill Lane, Newton Center MA 02459. **E-mail:** bostonauthors@aol.com;. **Website:** www.boston-authorsclub.org. **Contact:** Alan Lawson. This annual award honors Julia Ward Howe and her literary friends who founded the Boston Authors Club in 1900. It also honors the membership over 110 years, consisting of novelists, biographers, historians, gover-

nors, senators, philosophers, poets, playwrights, and other luminaries. There are 2 categories: trade books and books for young readers (beginning with chapter books through young adult books). Authors must live or have lived (college counts) within a hundred 100-mile radius of Boston within the last 5 years. Subsidized books, cook books and picture books are not eligible. Deadline: January 15. Prize: $1,000. Judged by the members.

CAROL OTIS HURST CHILDREN'S BOOK PRIZE

Westfield Athenaeum, 6 Elm St., Westfield MA 01085. (413)568-7833. **Fax:** (413)568-0988. **Website:** www.westath.org. **Contact:** Pamela Weingart. The Carol Otis Hurst Children's Book Prize honors outstanding works of fiction and nonfiction, including biography and memoir, written for children and young adults through the age of eighteen that exemplify the highest standards of research, analysis, and authorship in their portrayal of the New England Experience. The prize will be presented annually to an author whose book treats the region's history as broadly conceived to encompass one or more of the following elements: political experience, social development, fine and performing artistic expression, domestic life and arts, transportation and communication, changing technology, military experience at home and abroad, schooling, business and manufacturing, workers and the labor movement, agriculture and its transformation, racial and ethnic diversity, religious life and institutions, immigration and adjustment, sports at all levels, and the evolution of popular entertainment. The public presentation of the prize will be accompanied by a reading and/or talk by the recipient at a mutually agreed upon time during the spring immediately following the publication year. Books must have been copyrighted in their original format during the calendar year, January 1 to December 31, of the year preceding the year in which the prize is awarded. Any individual, publisher, or organization may nominate a book. See website for details and guidelines. Deadline: December 31. Prize: $500.

INSIGHT WRITING CONTEST

Insight Magazine, 55 W. Oak Ridge Dr., Hagerstown MD 21740-7390. **Fax:** (301)393-4055. **E-mail:** insight@rhpa.org. **Website:** www.insightmagazine.org. **Contact:** Omar Miranda, editor. Annual contest for writers in the categories of student short story, general short story, and student poetry. Unpublished submissions only. General category is open to all writers; student categories must be age 22 and younger. Deadline: July 31. Prizes: Student Short and General Short Story: 1st Prize: $250; 2nd Prize: $200; 3rd Prize: $150. Student Poetry: 1st Prize: $100; 2nd Prize: $75; 3rd Prize: $50.

INTERNATIONAL LITERACY ASSOCIATION CHILDREN'S AND YOUNG ADULT'S BOOK AWARDS

P.O. Box 8139, 800 Barksdale Rd., Newark DE 19714-8139. (302)731-1600, ext. 221. **E-mail:** kbaughman@reading.org. **E-mail:** committees@reading.org. **Website:** www.literacyworldwide.org. **Contact:** Kathy Baughman. The ILA Children's and Young Adults Book Awards are intended for newly published authors who show unusual promise in the children's and young adults' book field. Awards are given for fiction and nonfiction in each of three categories: primary, intermediate, and young adult. Books from all countries and published in English for the first time during the previous calendar year will be considered. See website for eligibility and criteria information. Entry should be the author's first or second book. Deadline: January 15. Prize: $1,000.

⊙ THE IODE JEAN THROOP BOOK AWARD

The Lillian H. Smith Children's Library, 239 College St., 4th St., Toronto ON M5T 1R5, Canada. (905)522-9537. **E-mail:** mcscott@torontopubliclibrary.ca; iodeontario@bellnet.ca. **Website:** www.iodeontario.ca. **Contact:** Martha Scott. Each year, the Municipal Chapter of Toronto IODE presents an award intended to encourage the publication of books for children between the ages of 6-12 years. The award-winner must be a Canadian citizen, resident in Toronto or the surrounding area, and the book must be published in Canada. Deadline: December 31. Prize: Award and cash prize of $2,000. Judged by a selected committee.

JEFFERSON CUP AWARD

P.O. Box 56312, Virginia Beach VA 23456. (757)689-0594. **Website:** www.vla.org. **Contact:** Lauri Newell, current chairperson. The Jefferson Cup honors a distinguished biography, historical fiction, or American history book for young people. The Jefferson Cup Committee's goal is to promote reading about America's past; to encourage the quality writing of

United States history, biography, and historical fiction for young people; and to recognize authors in these disciplines. Deadline: January 31.

THE EZRA JACK KEATS BOOK AWARD FOR NEW WRITER AND NEW ILLUSTRATOR

University of Southern Mississippi, de Grummond Children's Literature Collection, 118 College Dr., #5148, Hattiesburg MS 39406-0001. **Website:** https://www.degrummond.org/. Annual award to an outstanding new author and new illustrator of children's books that portray universal qualities of childhood in our multicultural world. Many past winners have gone on to distinguished careers, creating books beloved by parents, children, librarians and teachers around the world. Writers and illustrators must have had no more than 3 books previously published. Prize: $3,000 honorarium for each winner. Judged by a distinguished selection committee of early childhood education specialists, librarians, illustrators and experts in children's literature.

EZRA JACK KEATS/KERLAN MEMORIAL FELLOWSHIP

University of Minnesota Libraries, 113 Elmer L. Andersen Library, 222 21st Ave. S, Minneapolis MN 55455. **E-mail:** asc-clrc@umn.edu. **Website:** https://www.lib.umn.edu/clrc/awards-grants-and-fellowships. This fellowship from the Ezra Jack Keats Foundation will provide $1,500 to a talented writer and/or illustrator of children's books who wishes to use the Kerlan Collection for the furtherance of his or her artistic development. Special consideration will be given to someone who would find it difficult to finance a visit to the Kerlan Collection. The Ezra Jack Keats Fellowship recipient will receive transportation costs and a per diem allotment. See website for application deadline and for digital application materials. Winner will be notified in February. Study and written report must be completed within the calendar year. Deadline: January 30.

KENTUCKY BLUEGRASS AWARD

Website: www.kasl.us. The Kentucky Bluegrass Award is a student choice program. The KBA promotes and encourages Kentucky students in kindergarten through grade 12 to read a variety of quality literature. Each year, a KBA committee for each grade category chooses the books for the four Master Lists (K-2, 3-5, 6-8 and 9-12). All Kentucky public and private schools, as well as public libraries, are welcome to participate in the program. To nominate a book, see the website for form and details. Deadline: March 1. Judged by students who read books and choose their favorite.

CORETTA SCOTT KING BOOK AWARDS

50 E. Huron St., Chicago IL 60611-2795. (800)545-2433. **E-mail:** olos@ala.org. **Website:** www.ala.org/csk. **Contact:** Office for Diversity, Literacy and Outreach Services. The Coretta Scott King Book Awards are given annually to outstanding African American authors and illustrators of books for children and young adults that demonstrate an appreciation of African American culture and universal human values. The award commemorates the life and work of Dr. Martin Luther King, Jr., and honors his wife, Mrs. Coretta Scott King, for her courage and determination to continue the work for peace and world brotherhood. Must be written for a youth audience in one of three categories: preschool-4th grade; 5th-8th grade; or 9th-12th grade. Book must be published in the year preceding the year the award is given, evidenced by the copyright date in the book. See website for full details, criteria, and eligibility concerns. Purpose is to encourage the artistic expression of the African American experience via literature and the graphic arts, including biographical, historical and social history treatments by African American authors and illustrators. Deadline: December 1. Judged by the Coretta Scott King Book Awards Committee.

✪ THE STEPHEN LEACOCK MEMORIAL MEDAL FOR HUMOUR

149 Peter St. N., Orillia ON L3V 4Z4, Canada. (705)326-9286. **E-mail:** bettewalkerca@gmail.com. **Website:** www.leacock.ca. **Contact:** Bette Walker, award committee, Stephen Leacock Associates. The Leacock Associates awards the prestigious Leacock Medal for the best book of literary humor written by a Canadian and published in the current year. The winning author also receives a cash prize of $15,000 thanks to the generous support of the TD Financial Group. 2 runners-up are each awarded a cash prize of $1,500. Deadline: December 31. Prize: $15,000.

LEAGUE OF UTAH WRITERS CONTEST

The League of Utah Writers, The League of Utah Writers, P.O. Box 64, Lewiston UT 84320. (435)755-7609. **E-mail:** luwcontest@gmail.com; luwriters@gmail.com. **Website:** www.luwriters.org. Open to any writer, the LUW Contest provides authors an opportunity to get their work read and critiqued. Multiple categories are offered; see website for details. Entries must be the original and unpublished work of the author. Winners are announced at the Annual Writers Round-Up in September. Those not present will be notified by e-mail. Deadline: June 15. Submissions period begins March 15. Prize: Cash prizes are awarded. Judged by professional authors and editors from outside the League.

✪ MARSH AWARD FOR CHILDREN'S LITERATURE IN TRANSLATION

The English-Speaking Union, Dartmouth House, 37 Charles St., London En W1J 5ED, United Kingdom. 020 7529 1590. **E-mail:** emma.coffey@esu.org. **Website:** www.marshchristiantrust.org; www.esu.org. **Contact:** Emma Coffey, education officer. The Marsh Award for Children's Literature in Translation, awarded biennially, was founded to celebrate the best translation of a children's book from a foreign language into English and published in the UK. It aims to spotlight the high quality and diversity of translated fiction for young readers. The Award is administered by the ESU on behalf of the Marsh Christian Trust. Submissions will be accepted from publishers for books produced for readers from 5 to 16 years of age. Guidelines and eligibility criteria available online.

MCKNIGHT ARTIST FELLOWSHIPS FOR WRITERS, LOFT AWARD(S) IN CHILDREN'S LITERATURE/ CREATIVE PROSE/POETRY

The Loft Literary Center, 1011 Washington Ave. S., Suite 200, Open Book, Minneapolis MN 55415. (612)215-2575. **Fax:** (612)215-2576. **E-mail:** loft@loft.org. **Website:** www.loft.org. **Contact:** Bao Phi. "The Loft administers the McKnight Artists Fellowships for Writers. Five $25,000 awards are presented annually to accomplished Minnesota writers and spoken word artists. Four awards alternate annually between creative prose (fiction and creative nonfiction) and poetry/spoken word. The fifth award is presented in children's literature and alternates annually for writing for ages 8 and under and writing for children older than 8." The awards provide the writers the opportunity to focus on their craft for the course of the fellowship year. Prize: $25,000.

○ THE VICKY METCALF AWARD FOR LITERATURE FOR YOUNG PEOPLE

The Writers' Trust of Canada, 460 Richmond St. W., Suite 600, Toronto ON M5V 1Y1, Canada. (416)504-8222. **E-mail:** info@writerstrust.com. **Website:** www.writerstrust.com. **Contact:** Amanda Hopkins. The Vicky Metcalf Award is presented to a Canadian writer for a body of work in children's literature at The Writers' Trust Awards event held in Toronto each fall. Open to Canadian citizens and permanent residents only. Prize: $25,000.

MILKWEED PRIZE FOR CHILDREN'S LITERATURE

Milkweed Editions, 1011 Washington Ave. S., Suite 300, Minneapolis MN 55415. (612)332-3192. **Fax:** (612)215-2550. **E-mail:** editor@milkweed.org. **Website:** www.milkweed.org. Milkweed Editions will award the Milkweed Prize for Children's Literature to the best mss for young readers that Milkweed accepts for publication during the calendar year by a writer not previously published by Milkweed. All mss for young readers submitted for publication by Milkweed are automatically entered into the competition. Seeking full-length fiction between 90-200 pages. Does not consider picture books or poetry collections for young readers. Recognizes an outstanding literary novel for readers ages 8-13 and encourage writers to turn their attention to readers in this age group. Prize: $10,000 cash prize in addition to a publishing contract negotiated at the time of acceptance. Judged by the editors of Milkweed Editions.

MINNESOTA BOOK AWARDS

The Friends of the Saint Paul Public Library, 1080 Montreal Ave., Suite 2, St. Paul MN 55116. (651)222-3242. **Fax:** (651)222-1988. **E-mail:** mnbookawards@thefriends.org. **Website:** www.mnbookawards.org. A year-round program celebrating and honoring Minnesota's best books, culminating in an annual awards ceremony. Recognizes and honors achievement by members of Minnesota's book and book arts community. All books must be the work of a Minnesota author or primary artistic creator (current Minnesota resident who maintains a year-round residence in Minnesota). All books must be published within the calendar year prior to the Awards presentation. Deadline: Books should be entered by 5 p.m. on the third Friday in November.

NATIONAL BOOK AWARDS

The National Book Foundation, 90 Broad St., Suite 604, New York NY 10004. (212)685-0261. **E-mail:** nationalbook@nationalbook.org; agall@nationalbook.org. **Website:** www.nationalbook.org. **Contact:** Amy Gall. The National Book Foundation and the National Book Awards celebrate the best of American literature, expand its audience, and enhance the cultural value of great writing in America. The contest offers prizes in 4 categories: fiction, nonfiction, poetry, and young people's literature. Books should be published between December 1 and November 30 of the past year. Submissions must be previously published and must be entered by the publisher. General guidelines available on website. Interested publishes should phone or e-mail the Foundation. Deadline: Submit entry form, payment, and a copy of the book by July 1. Prize: $10,000 in each category. Finalists will each receive a prize of $1,000. Judged by a category specific panel of 5 judges for each category.

NATIONAL OUTDOOR BOOK AWARDS

921 S. 8th Ave., Stop 8128, Pocatello ID 83209. (208)282-3912. **E-mail:** wattron@isu.edu. **Website:** www.noba-web.org. **Contact:** Ron Watters. Nine categories: History/biography, outdoor literature, instructional texts, outdoor adventure guides, nature guides, children's books, design/artistic merit, natural history literature, and nature and the environment. Additionally, a special award, the Outdoor Classic Award, is given annually to books which, over a period of time, have proven to be exceptionally valuable works in the outdoor field. Application forms and eligibility requirements are available online. Applications for the Awards program become available in early June. Deadline: August 23. Prize: Winning books are promoted nationally and are entitled to display the National Outdoor Book Award (NOBA) medallion.

NATIONAL WRITERS ASSOCIATION NONFICTION CONTEST

The National Writers Association, 10940 S. Parker Rd., #508, Parker CO 80134. **E-mail:** natlwritersassn@hotmail.com. **Website:** www.nationalwriters.com. Only unpublished works may be submitted. Judging of entries will not begin until the contest ends. Nonfiction in the following areas will be accepted: articles—submission should include query letter, 1st page of manuscript, separate sheet citing 5 possible markets; essay—the complete essay and 5 possible markets on separate sheet; nonfiction book proposal including query letter, chapter by chapter outline, first chapter, bio, and market analysis. Those unsure of proper manuscript format should request Research Report #35. The purpose of the National Writers Association Nonfiction Contest is to encourage the writing of nonfiction and recognize those who excel in this field. Deadline: December 31. Prize: 1st-5th place awards. Other winners will be notified by March 31st. 1st Prize: $200 and Clearinghouse representation if winner is book proposal; 2nd Prize: $100; 3rd Prize: $50; 4th-10th places will receive a book. Honorable Mentions receive a certificate. Judging will be based on originality, marketability, research, and reader interest. Copies of the judges evaluation sheets will be sent to entrants furnishing an SASE with their entry.

NATIONAL WRITERS ASSOCIATION SHORT STORY CONTEST

10940 S. Parker Rd., #508, Parker CO 80134. **E-mail:** natlwritersassn@hotmail.com. **Website:** www.nationalwriters.com. Any genre of short story manuscript may be entered. All entries must be postmarked by July 1. Contest opens April 1. Only unpublished works may be submitted. All manuscripts must be typed, double-spaced, in the English language. Maximum length is 5,000 words. Those unsure of proper manuscript format should request Research Report #35. The entry must be accompanied by an entry form (photocopies are acceptable) and return SASE if you wish the material and rating sheets returned. Submissions will be destroyed, otherwise. Receipt of entry will not be acknowledged without a return postcard. Author's name and address must appear on the first page. Entries remain the property of the author and may be submitted during the contest as long as they are not published before the final notification of winners. Final prizes will be awarded in June. The purpose of the National Writers Assn. Short Story Contest is to encourage the development of creative skills, recognize and reward outstanding ability in the area of short story writing. Prize: 1st Prize: $250; 2nd Prize: $100; 3rd Prize: $50; 4th-10th places will receive a book. 1st-3rd place winners may be asked to grant one-time rights for publication in *Authorship* magazine. Honorable Mentions receive a certificate. Judging will be based on originality, marketability, research, and reader interest. Copies of the judges evaluation sheets will be sent to entrants furnishing an SASE with their entry.

NATIONAL YOUNGARTS FOUNDATION

2100 Biscayne Blvd., Miami FL 33137. (305)377-1140. **Fax:** (305)377-1149. **E-mail:** info@nfaa.org; apply@youngarts.org. **Website:** www.youngarts.org. The National YoungArts Foundation (formerly known as the National Foundation for Advancement in the Arts) was established in 1981 by Lin and Ted Arison to identify and support the next generation of artists and to contribute to the cultural vitality of the nation by investing in the artistic development of talented young artists in the visual, literary, design and performing arts. Each year, there are approximately 11,000 applications submitted to YoungArts from 15-18 year old (or grades 10-12) artists, and from these, approximately 700 winners are selected who are eligible to participate in programs in Miami, New York, Los Angeles, and Washington D.C. (with Chicago and other regions in the works). YoungArts provides these emerging artists with life-changing experiences and validation by renowned mentors, access to significant scholarships, national recognition and other opportunities throughout their careers to help ensure that the nation's most outstanding emerging artists are encouraged to pursue careers in the arts. See website for details about applying. Prize: Cash awards up to $10,000.

JOHN NEWBERY MEDAL

Association for Library Service to Children, Division of the American Library Association, 50 E. Huron, Chicago IL 60611. (800)545-2433, ext. 2153. **Fax:** (312)280-5271. **E-mail:** alscawards@ala.org. **Website:** www.ala.org. The Newbery Medal is awarded annually by the American Library Association for the most distinguished contribution to American literature for children. Previously published submissions only; must be published prior to year award is given. SASE for award rules. Entries not returned. Medal awarded at Caldecott/Newbery banquet during ALA annual conference. Deadline: December 31. Judged by Newbery Award Selection Committee.

NEW ENGLAND BOOK AWARDS

1955 Massachusetts Ave., #2, Cambridge MA 02140. (617)547-3642. **Fax:** (617)547-3759. **E-mail:** nan@neba.org. **Website:** www.newenglandbooks.org/programs/awards-scholarships/new-england-book-awards/. **Contact:** Nan Sorensen, administrative coordinator. All books must be either written by a New England based author or be set in New England. Eligible books must be published between September 1, 2017 and August 31, 2018 in either hardcover or paperback. Submissions made by New England booksellers; publishers. Submit written nominations only; actual books should not be sent. $25 fee per title for non-member submissions. Award is given to a specific title, fiction, non-fiction, children's. The titles must be either about New England, set in New England or by an author residing in the New England. The titles must be hardcover, paperback original or reissue that was published between September 1 and August 31. Entries must be still in print and available. Deadline: June 8. Prize: Winners will receive $250 for literacy to a charity of their choice. Judged by NEIBA membership.

NEW VOICES AWARD

Website: www.leeandlow.com. Open to students. Annual award. Lee & Low Books is one of the few minority-owned publishing companies in the country and has published more than 100 first-time writers and illustrators. Winning titles include *The Blue Roses*, winner of a Patterson Prize for Books for Young People; *Janna and the Kings*, an IRA Children's Book Award Notable; and *Sixteen Years in Sixteen Seconds*, selected for the Texas Bluebonnet Award Masterlist. Submissions made by author. SASE for contest rules or visit website. Restrictions of media for illustrators: The author must be a writer of color who is a resident of the U.S. and who has not previously published a children's picture book. For additional information, send SASE or visit Lee & Low's website. Encourages writers of color to enter the world of children's books.

Deadline: September 30. Prize: $1,000 and standard publication contract (regardless of whether or not writer has an agent) along with an advance against royalties; New Voices Honor Award: $500 prize. Judged by Lee & Low editors.

NORTH AMERICAN INTERNATIONAL AUTO SHOW HIGH SCHOOL POSTER CONTEST

Detroit Auto Dealers Association, 1900 W. Big Beaver Rd., Troy MI 48084-3531, USA. (248)643-0250. **Fax:** (248)283-5148. **E-mail:** sherp@dada.org. **Website:** www.naias.com. **Contact:** Sandy Herp. Open to students. Annual contest. Submissions made by the author and illustrator. Entrants must be Michigan high school students enrolled in grades 10-12. Winning posters may be displayed at the NAIAS and reproduced in the official NAIAS program, which is available to the public, international media, corporate executives and automotive suppliers. Winning posters may also be displayed on the official NAIAS website at the sole discretion of the NAIAS. Contact Detroit Auto Dealers Association (DADA) for contest rules and entry forms or retrieve rules from website. Deadline: November. Prize: Chairman's Award: $1,000; State Farm Insurance Award: $1,000; Designer's Best of Show (Digital and Traditional): $500; Best Theme: $250; Best Use of Color: $250; Most Creative: $250. A winner will be chosen in each category from grades 10, 11 and 12. Prizes: 1st place in 10, 11, 12: $500; 2nd place: $250; 3rd place: $100. Judged by an independent panel of recognized representatives of the art community.

NORTHERN CALIFORNIA BOOK AWARDS

Northern California Book Reviewers Association, c/o Poetry Flash, 1450 Fourth St. #4, Berkeley CA 94710. (510)525-5476. **E-mail:** ncbr@poetryflash.org; editor@poetryflash.org. **Website:** www.poetryflash.org. **Contact:** Joyce Jenkins, executive director. Annual Northern California Book Award for outstanding book in literature, open to books published in the current calendar year by Northern California authors. NCBR presents annual awards to Bay Area (northern California) authors annually in fiction, nonfiction, poetry and children's literature. Previously published books only. Must be published the calendar year prior to spring awards ceremony. Submissions nominated by publishers; author or agent could also nominate published work. Send 3 copies of the book to attention: NCBR. Encourages writers and stimulates interest in books and reading. Deadline: December 28. Prize: $100 honorarium and award certificate. Judging by voting members of the Northern California Book Reviewers.

○ NOVA WRITES COMPETITION FOR UNPUBLISHED MANUSCRIPTS

Writers' Federation of Nova Scotia, 1113 Marginal Rd., Halifax NS B3H 4P7. (902)423-8116. **Fax:** (902)422-0881. **E-mail:** programs@writers.ns.ca. **Website:** www.writers.ns.ca. **Contact:** Robin Spittal, communications and development officer. Annual program designed to honor work by unpublished writers in all 4 Atlantic Provinces. Entry is open to writers unpublished in the category of writing they wish to enter. Prizes are presented in the fall of each year. Categories include: short form creative nonfiction, long form creative nonfiction, novel, poetry, short story, and writing for children/young adult novel. Judges return written comments when competition is concluded. Page lengths and rules vary based on categories. See website for details. Anyone resident in the Atlantic Provinces since September 1st immediately prior to the deadline date is eligible to enter. Only one entry per category is allowed. Each entry requires its own entry form and registration fee. Deadline: December 13. Prizes vary based on categories. See website for details.

OHIOANA BOOK AWARDS

Ohioana Library Association, 274 E. First Ave., Suite 300, Columbus OH 43201-3673. (614)466-3831. **Fax:** (614)728-6974. **E-mail:** ohioana@ohioana.org. **Website:** www.ohioana.org. **Contact:** David Weaver, executive director. Writers must have been born in Ohio or lived in Ohio for at least 5 years, but books about Ohio or an Ohioan need not be written by an Ohioan. Finalists announced in May and winners in July. Winners notified by mail in early summer. Offered annually to bring national attention to Ohio authors and their books, published in the last year. (Books can only be considered once.) Categories: Fiction, nonfiction, juvenile, poetry, and books about Ohio or an Ohioan. Deadline: December 31. Prize: $1,000 cash prize, certificate, and glass sculpture. Judged by

a jury selected by librarians, book reviewers, writers and other knowledgeable people.

OKLAHOMA BOOK AWARDS

200 NE 18th St., Oklahoma City OK 73105. (405)521-2502. **Fax:** (405)525-7804. **E-mail:** connie.armstrong@libraries.ok.gov. **Website:** www.odl.state.ok.us/ocb. **Contact:** Connie Armstrong, executive director. This award honors Oklahoma writers and books about Oklahoma. Awards are presented to best books in fiction, nonfiction, children's, design and illustration, and poetry books about Oklahoma or books written by an author who was born, is living or has lived in Oklahoma. SASE for award rules and entry forms. Winner will be announced at banquet in Oklahoma City. The Arrell Gibson Lifetime Achievement Award is also presented each year for a body of work. Previously published submissions only. Submissions made by the author, author's agent, or entered by a person or group of people, including the publisher. Must be published during the calendar year preceding the award. Deadline: January 10. Prize: Awards a medal. Judging by a panel of 5 people for each category, generally a librarian, a working writer in the genre, booksellers, editors, etc.

ORBIS PICTUS AWARD FOR OUTSTANDING NONFICTION FOR CHILDREN

1111 W. Kenyon Rd., Urbana IL 61801-1096. (217)328-3870. **Fax:** (217)328-0977. **E-mail:** elementary@ncte.org. **Website:** www.ncte.org/awards/orbispictus. The NCTE Orbis Pictus Award promotes and recognizes excellence in the writing of nonfiction for children. Orbis Pictus commemorates the work of Johannes Amos Comenius, *Orbis Pictus—The World in Pictures* (1657), considered to be the first book actually planned for children. Submissions should be made by an author, the author's agent, or by a person or group of people. Must be published in the calendar year of the competition. Deadline: November 1. Prize: A plaque given at the NCTE Elementary Section Luncheon at the NCTE Annual Convention in November. Up to 5 honor books awarded. Judged by members of the Orbis Pictus Committee.

OREGON BOOK AWARDS

925 SW Washington St., Portland OR 97205. (503)227-2583. **Fax:** (503)241-4256. **E-mail:** la@literary-arts.org. **Website:** www.literary-arts.org. **Contact:** Susan Denning, director of programs and events. The an-

nual Oregon Book Awards celebrate Oregon authors in the areas of poetry, fiction, nonfiction, drama and young readers' literature published between August 1 and July 31 of the previous calendar year. Awards are available for every category. See website for details. Entry fee determined by initial print run; see website for details. Entries must be previously published. Oregon residents only. Accepts inquiries by phone and e-mail. Finalists announced in January. Winners announced at an awards ceremony in November. List of winners available in April. Deadline: August 26. Prize: Grant of $2,500. (Grant money could vary.) Judged by writers who are selected from outside Oregon for their expertise in a genre. Past judges include Mark Doty, Colson Whitehead and Kim Barnes.

OREGON LITERARY FELLOWSHIPS

925 S.W. Washington, Portland OR 97205. (503)227-2583. **E-mail:** susan@literary-arts.org. **Website:** www.literary-arts.org. **Contact:** Susan Moore, Director of programs and events. Oregon Literary Fellowships are intended to help Oregon writers initiate, develop, or complete literary projects in poetry, fiction, literary nonfiction, drama, and young readers literature. Writers in the early stages of their career are encouraged to apply. The awards are merit-based. Guidelines available in February for SASE. Accepts inquiries by e-mail, phone. Oregon residents only. Recipients announced in January. Deadline: Last Friday in June. Prize: $3,000 minimum award, for approximately 8 writers and 2 publishers. Judged by out-of-state writers

THE ORIGINAL ART

128 E. 63rd St., New York NY 10065. (212)838-2560. **Fax:** (212)838-2561. **E-mail:** kim@societyillustrators.org; info@societyillustrators.org. **Website:** www.societyillustrators.org. **Contact:** Kate Feirtag, exhibition director. The Original Art is an annual exhibit created to showcase illustrations from the year's best children's books published in the US. For editors and art directors, it's an inspiration and a treasure trove of talent to draw upon. Previously published submissions only. Request "call for entries" to receive contest rules and entry forms. Works will be displayed at the Society of Illustrators Museum of American Illustration in New York City October-November annually. Deadline: July 18. Judged by 7 professional artists and editors.

HELEN KEATING OTT AWARD FOR OUTSTANDING CONTRIBUTION TO CHILDREN'S LITERATURE

CSLA, 10157 SW Barbur Blvd. #102C, Portland OR 97219. (503)244-6919. **Fax:** (503)977-3734. **E-mail:** sharper1@kent.edu. **Website:** www.cslainfo.org. **Contact:** S. Meghan Harper, awards chair. Annual award given to a person or organization that has made a significant contribution to promoting high moral and ethical values through children's literature. Recipient is honored in July during the conference. Awards certificate of recognition, the awards banquet, and one-night's stay in the hotel. A nomination for an award may be made by anyone. An application form is available online. Elements of creativity and innovation will be given high priority by the judges.

PATERSON PRIZE FOR BOOKS FOR YOUNG PEOPLE

The Poetry Center at Passaic County Community College, One College Blvd., Paterson NJ 07505. (973)684-6555. **Fax:** (973)523-6085. **E-mail:** mgillan@pccc.edu. **Website:** www.pccc.edu/poetry. **Contact:** Maria Mazziotti Gillan, executive director. Award for a book published in the previous year in each age category (Pre-K-Grade 3, Grades 4-6, Grades 7-12). Deadline: February 1. Prize: $500.

THE KATHERINE PATERSON PRIZE FOR YOUNG ADULT AND CHILDREN'S WRITING

Hunger Mountain, Vermont College of Fine Arts, 36 College St., Montpelier VT 05602. (802)828-8517. **E-mail:** hungermtn@vcfa.edu. **Website:** www.hungermtn.org. **Contact:** Samantha Kolber, Managing Editor. The annual Katherine Paterson Prize for Young Adult and Children's Writing honors the best in young adult and children's literature. Submit young adult or middle grade mss, and writing for younger children, short stories, picture books, poetry, or novel excerpts, under 10,000 words. Guidelines available on website. Deadline: March 8. Prize: $1,000 and publication for the first place winner; $100 each and publication for the three category winners. Judged by a guest judge every year. The 2016 judge is Rita Williams-Garcia, author of Newbery Honor-winning novel, *One Crazy Summer*.

PENNSYLVANIA YOUNG READERS' CHOICE AWARDS PROGRAM

Pennsylvania School Librarians Association, 134 Bisbing Road, Henryville PA 18332. **E-mail:** pyrca.psla@gmail.com. **Website:** www.psla.org. **Contact:** Alice L. Cyphers, co-coordinator. Submissions nominated by a person or group. Must be published within 5 years of the award—for example, books published in 2013 to present are eligible for the 2018-2019 award. Check the Program wiki at pyrca.wikispaces.com for submission information. View information at the Pennsylvania School Librarians' website or the Program wiki. Must be currently living in North America. The purpose of the Pennsylvania Young Reader's Choice Awards Program is to promote the reading of quality books by young people in the Commonwealth of Pennsylvania, to encourage teacher and librarian collaboration and involvement in children's literature, and to honor authors whose works have been recognized by the students of Pennsylvania. Deadline: September 15. Prize: Framed certificate to winning authors. Four awards are given, one for each of the following grade level divisions: K-3, 3-6, 6-8, YA. Judged by children of Pennsylvania (they vote).

PEN/PHYLLIS NAYLOR WORKING WRITER FELLOWSHIP

E-mail: awards@pen.org. **Website:** www.pen.org/awards. **Contact:** Arielle Anema, Literary Awards Coordinator. Offered annually to an author of children's or young-adult fiction. The Fellowship has been developed to help writers whose work is of high literary caliber but who have not yet attracted a broad readership. The Fellowship is designed to assist a writer at a crucial moment in his or her career to complete a book-length work-in-progress. Candidates have published at least one novel for children or young adults which have been received warmly by literary critics, but have not generated sufficient income to support the author. Writers must be nominated by an editor or fellow author. See website for eligibility and nomination guidelines. Deadline: Submissions open during the summer of each year. Visit PEN.org/awards for up-to-date information on deadlines. Prize: $5,000.

PLEASE TOUCH MUSEUM BOOK AWARD

Memorial Hall in Fairmount Park, 4231 Avenue of the Republic, Philadelphia PA 19131. (215)578-5153. **Fax:** (215)578-5171. **E-mail:** hboyd@pleasetouchmuseum.org. **Website:** www.pleasetouchmuseum.org. **Contact:** Heather Boyd. This prestigious award has recognized and encouraged the publication of high quality books. The award was exclusively created to recognize and encourage the writing of publications that help young children enjoy the process of learning through books, while reflecting PTM's philosophy of learning through play. The awards to to books that are imaginative, exceptionally illustrated, and help foster a child's life-long love of reading. To be eligible for consideration, a book must be distinguished in text, illustration, and ability to explore and clarify an idea for young children (ages 7 and under). Deadline: October 1. Books for each cycle must be published within previous calendar year (September-August). Judged by a panel of volunteer educators, artists, booksellers, children's authors, and librarians in conjunction with museum staff.

PNWA LITERARY CONTEST

Pacifc Northwest Writers Association, PMB 2717, 1420 NW Gilman Blvd., Suite 2, Issaquah WA 98027. (452)673-2665. **Fax:** (452)961-0768. **E-mail:** pnwa@pnwa.org. **Website:** www.pnwa.org. Annual literary contest with 12 different categories. See website for details and specific guidelines. Each entry receives 2 critiques. Winners announced at the PNWA Summer Conference, held annually in mid-July. Deadline: February 20. Prize: 1st Place: $600; 2nd Place: $300; 3rd Place: $100. Judged by an agent or editor attending the conference.

POCKETS FICTION-WRITING CONTEST

P.O. Box 340004, Nashville TN 37203-0004. (615)340-7333. **Fax:** (615)340-7267. **E-mail:** pockets@upperroom.org. **Website:** www.pockets.upperroom.org. **Contact:** Lynn W. Gilliam, senior editor. Designed for 6- to 12-year-olds, *Pockets* magazine offers wholesome devotional readings that teach about God's love and presence in life. The content includes fiction, scripture stories, puzzles and games, poems, recipes, colorful pictures, activities, and scripture readings. Freelance submissions of stories, poems, recipes, puzzles and games, and activities are welcome. Stories should be 750-1,000 words. Multiple submissions are permitted. Past winners are ineligible. The primary purpose of *Pockets* is to help children grow in their relationship with God and to claim the good news of the gospel of Jesus Christ by applying it to their daily lives. *Pockets* espouses respect for all human beings and for God's creation. It regards a child's faith journey as an integral part of all of life and sees prayer as undergirding that journey. Deadline: August 15. Submission period begins March 15. Prize: $500 and publication in magazine.

EDGAR ALLAN POE AWARD

1140 Broadway, Suite 1507, New York NY 10001. (212)888-8171. **E-mail:** mwa@mysterywriters.org. **Website:** www.mysterywriters.org. Mystery Writers of America is the leading association for professional crime writers in the United States. Members of MWA include most major writers of crime fiction and nonfiction, as well as screenwriters, dramatists, editors, publishers, and other professionals in the field. Categories include: Best Novel, Best First Novel by an American Author, Best Paperback/E-Book Original, Best Fact Crime, Best Critical/Biographical, Best Short Story, Best Juvenile Mystery, Best Young Adult Mystery, Best Television Series Episode Teleplay, and Mary Higgins Clark Award. Purpose of the award: Honor authors of distinguished works in the mystery field. Previously published submissions only. Submissions should be made by the publisher. Work must be published/produced the year of the contest. Deadline: November 30. Prize: Awards ceramic bust of "Edgar" for winner; certificates for all nominees. Judged by active status members of Mystery Writers of America (writers).

MICHAEL L. PRINTZ AWARD

Young Adult Library Services Association, Division of the American Library Association, 50 E. Huron, Chicago IL 60611. (800)545-2433. **Fax:** (312)280-5276. **E-mail:** yalsa@ala.org. **Website:** www.ala.org/yalsa/printz. **Contact:** Nichole O'Connor, program officer for events and conferences. The Michael L. Printz Award annually honors the best book written for teens, based entirely on its literary merit, each year. In addition, the Printz Committee names up to 4 honor books, which also represent the best writing in young adult literature. The award-winning book can be fiction, nonfiction, poetry or an anthology, and can be a work of joint authorship or editorship. The books must be published between January 1 and December 31 of the preceding year and be designated by its publisher as being either a young adult book or one published for the age range that YALSA defines as young adult, e.g. ages 12 through 18. Deadline: December 1. Judged by an award committee.

PURPLE DRAGONFLY BOOK AWARDS

Story Monsters LLC, 4696 W Tyson St, Chandler AZ 85226-2903. (480)940-8182. **Fax:** (480)940-8787. **E-mail:** linda@storymonsters.com. **Website:** www.dragonflybookawards.com. **Contact:** Cristy Bertini, contest coordinator. The Purple Dragonfly Book Awards are designed with children in mind. Awards are divided into 54 distinct subject categories, ranging from books on the environment and cooking to sports and family issues. The Purple Dragonfly Book Awards are geared toward stories that appeal to children of all ages. We now offer new Marketing/Promotion Categories: Book Trailer, Bookmark, Flyer, Media Kit, and Press Release. The awards are open to books published in any calendar year and in any country that are available for purchase. Books entered must be printed in English. Traditionally published, partnership published and self-published books are permitted, as long as they fit the above criteria. Submit materials to: Cristy Bertini, Attn: Dragonfly Book Awards, 1271 Turkey St., Ware, MA 01082. Deadline: May 1. The grand prize winner will receive a $500 cash prize, a certificate commemorating their accomplishment, 100 Grand Prize seals, a one-hour marketing consulting session with Linda F. Radke, a news release announcing the winners sent to a comprehensive list of media outlets, and a listing on the Dragonfly Book Awards website. All first-place winners of categories will be put into a drawing for a $100 prize. In addition, each first-place winner in each category receives a certificate commemorating their accomplishment, 25 foil award seals, and mention on Dragonfly Book Awards website. All winners receive certificates and are listed in Story Monsters Ink magazine. Judged by industry experts with specific knowledge about the categories over which they preside.

QUILL AND SCROLL WRITING, PHOTO AND MULTIMEDIA CONTEST AND BLOGGING COMPETITION

School of Journalism, Univ. of Iowa, 100 Adler Journalism Bldg., Iowa City IA 52242-2004. (319)335-3457.

Fax: (319)335-3989. **E-mail:** quill-scroll@uiowa.edu. **E-mail:** quill-scroll@uiowa.edu. **Website:** quilland-scroll.org. **Contact:** Jeffrey Browne, contest director. Entries must have been published in a high school or professional newspaper or website during the previous year, and must be the work of a currently enrolled high school student, when published. Open to students. Annual contest. Previously published submissions only. Submissions made by the author or school media adviser. Deadline: February 5. Prize: Winners will receive *Quill and Scroll*'s National Award Gold Key and, if seniors, are eligible to apply for one of the scholarships offered by *Quill and Scroll*. All winning entries are automatically eligible for the International Writing and Photo Sweepstakes Awards. Engraved plaque awarded to sweepstakes winners.

● THE RED HOUSE CHILDREN'S BOOK AWARD

Red House Children's Book Award, 123 Frederick Road, Cheam, Sutton, Surrey SM1 2HT, United Kingdom. **E-mail:** info@rhcba.co.uk. **Website:** www.red-housechildrensbookaward.co.uk. **Contact:** Sinead Kromer, national coordinator. The Red House Children's Book Award is the only national book award that is entirely voted for by children. A shortlist is drawn up from children's nominations and any child can then vote for the winner of the three categories: Books for Younger Children, Books for Younger Readers and Books for Older Readers. The book with the most votes is then crowned the winner of the Red House Children's Book Award. Deadline: December 31.

TOMÁS RIVERA MEXICAN AMERICAN CHILDREN'S BOOK AWARD

Dr. Jesse Gainer, Texas State University, 601 University Drive, San Marcos TX 78666-4613. (512)245-2357. **E-mail:** riverabookaward@txstate.edu. **Website:** www.riverabookaward.org. **Contact:** Dr. Jesse Gainer, award director. Texas State University College of Education developed the Tomas Rivera Mexican American Children's Book Award to honor authors and illustrators who create literature that depicts the Mexican American experience. The award was established in 1995 and was named in honor of Dr. Tomas Rivera, a distinguished alumnus of Texas State University. The book will be written for younger children, ages pre-K to 5th grade (awarded in even years), or older children, ages 6th grade to 12 grade (awarded in odd years). The text and illustrations will be of highest quality. The portrayal/representations of Mexican Americans will be accurate and engaging, avoid stereotypes, and reflect rich characterization. The book may be fiction or non- fiction. See website for more details and directions. Deadline: November 1.

◎ ROCKY MOUNTAIN BOOK AWARD: ALBERTA CHILDREN'S CHOICE BOOK AWARD

Box 42, Lethbridge AB T1J 3Y3, Canada. (403)381-0855. **Website:** www.rmba.info. **Contact:** Michelle Dimnik, contest director. Annual contest. No entry fee. Awards: Gold medal and author tour of selected Alberta schools. Judging by students. Canadian authors and/or illustrators only. Submit entries to Richard Chase. Previously unpublished submissions only. Submissions made by author's agent or nominated by a person or group. Must be published within the 3 years prior to that year's award. Register before January 20th to take part in the Rocky Mountain Book Award. SASE for contest rules and entry forms. Purpose of contest: "Reading motivation for students, promotion of Canadian authors, illustrators and publishers." Gold Medal and sponsored visit to several Alberta Schools or Public Libraries. Judged by students.

◎ SASKATCHEWAN BOOK AWARDS

315-1102 8th Ave., Regina SK S4R 1C9, Canada. (306)569-1585. **E-mail:** director@bookawards.sk.ca. **Website:** www.bookawards.sk.ca. **Contact:** Courtney Bates-Hardy, executive director. Saskatchewan Book Awards celebrates, promotes, and rewards Saskatchewan authors and publishers worthy of recognition through 14 awards, granted on an annual or semiannual basis. Awards: Fiction, Nonfiction, Poetry, Scholarly, First Book, Prix du Livre Français, Regina, Saskatoon, Indigenous Peoples' Writing, Indigenous Peoples' Publishing, Publishing in Education, Publishing, Children's Literature/Young Adult Literature, Book of the Year. November 1. Prize: $2,000 (CAD) for all awards except Book of the Year, which is $3,000 (CAD). Juries are made up of writing and publishing professionals from outside of Saskatchewan.

 ♻ Saskatchewan Book Awards is the only provincially focused book award program in Saskatchewan and a principal ambassador for

Saskatchewan's literary community. Its solid reputation for celebrating artistic excellence in style is recognized nationally.

SCBWI MAGAZINE MERIT AWARDS

4727 Wilshire Blvd., Suite 301, Los Angeles CA 90010. (323)782-1010. **Fax:** (323)782-1892. **E-mail:** grants@scbwi.org. **Website:** www.scbwi.org. **Contact:** Stephanie Gordon, award coordinator. The SCBWI is a professional organization of writers and illustrators and others interested in children's literature. Membership is open to the general public at large. All magazine work for young people by an SCBWI member—writer, artist or photographer—is eligible during the year of original publication. In the case of co-authored work, both authors must be SCBWI members. Members must submit their own work. Requirements for entrants: 4 copies each of the published work and proof of publication (may be contents page) showing the name of the magazine and the date of issue. Previously published submissions only. For rules and procedures see website. Must be a SCBWI member. Recognizes outstanding original magazine work for young people published during that year, and having been written or illustrated by members of SCBWI. Deadline: December 15 of the year of publication. Submission period begins January 1. Prize: Awards plaques and honor certificates for each of 4 categories (fiction, nonfiction, illustration and poetry). Judged by a magazine editor and two "full" SCBWI members.

SHEEHAN YA BOOK PRIZE

Elephant Rock Books, P.O. Box 119, Ashford CT 06278. **E-mail:** elephantrockbooksya@gmail.com. **Website:** elephantrockbooks.com/ya.html. **Contact:** Jotham Burrello and Amanda Hurley. Elephant Rock is a small independent publisher. Their first YA book, *The Carnival at Bray* by Jessie Ann Foley was a Morris Award Finalist, and Printz Honor Book. Runs contest every other year. Check website for details. Guidelines are available on the website: http://www.elephantrockbooks.com./about.html#submissions. "Elephant Rock Books' teen imprint is looking for a great story to follow our critically acclaimed novel, *The Carnival at Bray*. We're after quality stories with heart, guts, and a clear voice. We're especially interested in the quirky, the hopeful, and the real. We are not particularly interested in genre fiction and prefer standalone novels, unless you've got the next *Hunger Games*. We seek writers who believe in the transformative power of a great story, so show us what you've got." Deadline: July 1. Prize: $1,000 as an advance. Judges vary year-to-year.

SKIPPING STONES BOOK AWARDS

E-mail: editor@SkippingStones.org. **Website:** www.skippingstones.org. **Contact:** Arun N. Toke', Exec. Editor. Open to published books, publications/magazines, educational videos, and DVDs. Annual awards. Submissions made by the author or publishers and/or producers. Send request for contest rules and entry forms or visit website. Many educational publications announce the winners of our book awards. The winning books and educational videos/DVDs are announced in the July-September issue of *Skipping Stones* and also on the website. In addition to announcements on social media pages, the reviews of winning titles are posted on website. *Skipping Stones* multicultural magazine has been published for over 28 years. Recognizes exceptional, literary and artistic contributions to juvenile/children's literature, as well as teaching resources and educational audio/video resources in the areas of multicultural awareness, nature and ecology, social issues, peace, and nonviolence. Deadline: February 28. Prize: Winners receive gold honor award seals, attractive honor certificates, and publicity via multiple outlets. Judged by a multicultural selection committee of editors, students, parents, teachers, and librarians.

SKIPPING STONES YOUTH AWARDS

P.O. Box 3939, Eugene OR 97403-0939. (541)342-4956. **Fax:** (541)342-4956. **E-mail:** editor@skippingstones.org. **Website:** www.skippingstones.org. **Contact:** Arun N. Toké. Annual awards to promote creativity as well as multicultural and nature awareness in youth. Cover letter should include name, address, phone, and e-mail. Entries must be unpublished. Length: 1,000 words maximum; 30 lines maximum for poems. Open to any writer between 7 and 17 years old. Guidelines available by SASE, e-mail, or on website. Accepts inquiries by e-mail or phone. Results announced in the October-December issue of *Skipping Stones*. Winners notified by mail. For contest results, visit website. Everyone who enters receives the issue which features the award winners. Deadline: June 25. Prize: Publication in the autumn issue of *Skipping Stones*, honor certificate, subscription to magazine, plus 5 multicultural and/or nature books. Judged by editors and reviewers at *Skipping Stones* magazine.

SKIPPING STONES YOUTH HONOR AWARDS

P.O. Box 3939, Eugene OR 97403-0939. (541)342-4956. **E-mail:** editor@SkippingStones.org. **Website:** www. SkippingStones.org. **Contact:** Arun N. Toké, editor. Now celebrating its 29th year, *Skipping Stones* is a winner of N.A.M.E.EDPRESS, Newsstand Resources, Writer and Parent's Choice Awards. Open to students. Annual awards. Submissions made by the author. The winners are published in the October-December issue of *Skipping Stones*. Everyone who enters the contest receives the Autumn issue featuring Youth Awards. SASE for contest rules or download from website. Entries must include certificate of originality by a parent and/or teacher and a cover letter that included cultural background information on the author. Submissions can either be mailed or e-mailed. Up to ten awards are given in three categories: (1) Compositions (essays, poems, short stories, songs, travelogues, etc.): Entries should be typed (double-spaced) or neatly handwritten. Fiction or nonfiction should be limited to 1,000 words; poems to 30 lines. Non-English writings are also welcome. (2) Artwork (drawings, cartoons, paintings or photo essays with captions): Entries should have the artist's name, age and address on the back of each page. Send the originals with SASE. Black & white photos are especially welcome. Limit: 8 pieces. (3) Youth Organizations: Describe how your club or group works to: (a) preserve the nature and ecology in your area, (b) enhance the quality of life for low-income, minority or disabled or (c) improve racial or cultural harmony in your school or community. Use the same format as for compositions. Recognizes youth, 7 to 17, for their contributions to multicultural awareness, nature and ecology, social issues, peace and nonviolence. Also promotes creativity, self-esteem and writing skills and to recognize important work being done by youth organizations. Deadline: June 25. Judged by *Skipping Stones* staff.

KAY SNOW WRITING CONTEST

Willamette Writers, Willamette Writers, 2108 Buck St., West Linn OR 97068. (503)305-6729. **Fax:** (503)344-6174. **E-mail:** reg@willamettewriters.com. **Website:** www.willamettewriters.org. Willamette Writers is the largest writers' organization in Oregon and one of the largest writers' organizations in the United States. It is a non-profit, tax-exempt Oregon corporation led by volunteers. Elected officials and directors administer an active program of monthly meetings, special seminars, workshops, and an annual writing conference. Continuing with established programs and starting new ones is only made possible by strong volunteer support. See website for specific details and rules. There are six different categories writers can enter: Adult Fiction, Adult Nonfiction, Poetry, Juvenile Short Story, Screenwriting, and Student Writer. The purpose of this annual writing contest, named in honor of Willamette Writer's founder, Kay Snow, is to help writers reach professional goals in writing in a broad array of categories and to encourage student writers. Deadline: April 23. Submission deadline begins January 15. Prize: One first prize of $300, one second place prize of $150, and a third place prize of $50 per winning entry in each of the six categories. Student first prize is $50, $20 for second place, $10 for third.

SOCIETY OF MIDLAND AUTHORS AWARD

Society of Midland Authors, Society of Midland Authors, P.O. Box 10419, Chicago IL 60610-0419. **E-mail:** marlenetbrill@comcast.net. **Website:** www.midlandauthors.com. **Contact:** Marlene Targ Brill, awards chair. Since 1957, the Society has presented annual awards for the best books written by Midwestern authors. The Society began in 1915. The contest is open to any title published within the year prior to the contest year. Open to adult and children's authors/poets who reside in, were born in, or have strong ties to a Midland state, which includes Illinois, Indiana, Iowa, Kansas, Michigan, Minnesota, Missouri, Nebraska, North Dakota, South Dakota, Ohio, and Wisconsin. The Society of Midland Authors (SMA) Award is presented to one title in each of 6 categories: adult nonfiction, adult fiction, adult biography and memoir, children's nonfiction, children's fiction, and poetry. There may be honor book winners as well. Books and entry forms must be mailed to the 3 judges in each category; for a list of judges and the entry and payment forms, visit the SMA website. Do not mail books to the society's P.O. box. The fee can be sent to the SMA P.O. box or paid via Paypal. Deadline: The first Saturday in January for books from the previous year. Prize: $500 and a plaque that is awarded at the SMA banquet in May in Chicago. Honorary winners receive a plaque. Check the SMA website for each year's judges.

STORY MONSTER APPROVED BOOK AWARDS

Story Monsters LLC, 4696 W. Tyson St., Chandler AZ 85226. (480)940-8182. **Fax:** (480)940-8787. **E-mail:** linda@storymonsters.com. **E-mail:** cristy@storymonsters.com. **Website:** www.dragonflybookawards.com. **Contact:** Cristy Bertini. Recognizes and honors accomplished authors in the field of children's literature who inspire, inform, teach, or entertain. A Story Monsters seal of approval on your book tells teachers, librarians, and parents they are giving children the very best. Offered on an annual basis, we have expanded our program to include 23 distinct categories which cover a variety of genres and target ages. Guidelines available online. Send submissions to Cristy Bertini, Attn.: Dragonfly Book Awards, 1271 Turkey St., Ware, MA 01082. Deadline: December 1. The Book of the Year winner will receive an advertorial, which includes a feature interview and a full-page ad in Story Monsters Ink® magazine (a $1,600 value), a certificate commemorating their accomplishment, and 50 Story Monsters Approved! seals. All books earning a Story Monsters Approved! Gold Medal Honor receive a gold medal, a certificate, and 25 award seals. All books earning a Story Monsters Approved! designation receive a certificate and 15 award seals. All winners are listed in a news release sent to a comprehensive list of media outlets, on the Dragonfly Book Awards website, and in Story Monsters Ink® magazine. Our judging panel includes industry experts in specific fields as well as experts in education and publishing.

SYDNEY TAYLOR MANUSCRIPT COMPETITION

Association of Jewish Libraries, Sydney Taylor Manuscript Award Competition, 204 Park St., Montclair NJ 07042-2903. **E-mail:** stmacajl@aol.com. **Website:** www.jewishlibraries.org/main/Awards/SydneyTaylorManuscriptAward.aspx. **Contact:** Aileen Grossberg. This competition is for unpublished writers of juvenile fiction. Material should be for readers ages 8-13. The manuscript should have universal appeal and reveal positive aspects of Jewish life that will serve to deepen the understanding of Judaism for all children. Download rules and forms from website. Must be an unpublished fiction writer or a student; also, books must range from 64-200 pages in length. "AJL assumes no responsibility for publication, but hopes this cash incentive will serve to encourage new

writers of children's stories with Jewish themes for all children." To encourage new fiction of Jewish interest for readers ages 8-13. Deadline: September 30. Prize: $1,000. Judging by qualified judges from within the Association of Jewish Libraries.

SYDNEY TAYLOR BOOK AWARD

E-mail: chair@sydneytaylorbookaward.org. **Website:** www.sydneytaylorbookaward.org. **Contact:** Ellen Tilman, chair. The Sydney Taylor Book Award is presented annually to outstanding books for children and teens that authentically portray the Jewish experience. Deadline: November 30. Cannot guarantee that books received after November 30 will be considered. Prize: Gold medals are presented in 3 categories: younger readers, older readers, and teen readers. Honor books are awarded in silver medals, and notable books are named in each category. Winners are selected by a committee of the Association of Jewish Libraries. Each committee member must receive an individual copy of each book that is to be considered.

Please contact the chair for submission details.

TD CANADIAN CHILDREN'S LITERATURE AWARD

The Canadian Children's Book Centre, 40 Orchard View Blvd., Suite 217, Toronto ON M4R 1B9, Canada. (416)975-0010, ext. 222. **Fax:** (416)975-8970. **E-mail:** meghan@bookcentre.ca. **Website:** www.bookcentre.ca. **Contact:** Meghan Howe. The TD Canadian Children's Literature Award is for the most distinguished book of the year. All books, in any genre, written and illustrated by Canadians and for children ages 1-12 are eligible. Only books published in Canada are eligible for submission. Books must be published between January 1 and December 31 of the previous calendar year. Open to Canadian citizens and/or permanent residents of Canada. Deadline: mid-December. Prizes: Two prizes of $30,000, 1 for English, 1 for French. $20,000 will be divided among the Honour Book English titles and Honour Book French titles, to a maximum of 4; $2,500 shall go to each of the publishers of the English and French grand-prize winning books for promotion and publicity.

TORONTO BOOK AWARDS

City of Toronto c/o Toronto Arts & Culture, Cultural Partnerships, City Hall, 9E, 100 Queen St. W., Toronto ON M5H 2N2, Canada. **E-mail:** shan@toronto.ca. **Website:** www.toronto.ca/book_awards. The Toronto Book Awards honor authors of books of literary or artistic merit that are evocative of Toronto. There are no separate categories; all books are judged together. Any fiction or nonfiction book published in English for adults and/or children that are evocative of Toronto are eligible. To be eligible, books must be published between January 1 and December 31 of previous year. Deadline: April 30. Prize: Each finalist receives $1,000 and the winning author receives $10,000 ($15,000 total in prize money available).

VEGETARIAN ESSAY CONTEST

The Vegetarian Resource Group, P.O. Box 1463, Baltimore MD 21203. (410)366-VEGE. **Fax:** (410)366-8804. **E-mail:** vrg@vrg.org. **Website:** www.vrg.org. Write a 2-3 page essay on any aspect of veganism/vegetarianism. Entrants should base their paper on interviewing, research, and/or personal opinion. You need not be a vegetarian to enter. Three different entry categories: age 14-18; age 9-13; and age 8 and under. Prize: $50.

VFW VOICE OF DEMOCRACY

Veterans of Foreign Wars of the U.S., National Headquarters, 406 W. 34th St., Kansas City MO 64111. (816)968-1117. **E-mail:** kharmer@vfw.org. **Website:** https://www.vfw.org/VOD/. The Voice of Democracy Program is open to students in grades 9-12 (on the Nov. 1 deadline), who are enrolled in a public, private or parochial high school or home study program in the United States and its territories. Contact your local VFW Post to enter (entry must not be mailed to the VFW National Headquarters, only to a local, participating VFW Post). Purpose is to give high school students the opportunity to voice their opinions about their responsibility to our country and to convey those opinions via the broadcast media to all of America. Deadline: November 1. Prize: Winners receive awards ranging from $1,000-30,000.

● WESTERN AUSTRALIAN PREMIER'S BOOK AWARDS

State Library of Western Australia, Perth Cultural Centre, 25 Francis St., Perth WA 6000, Australia. (61)(8)9427-3151. **E-mail:** premiersbookawards@slwa.wa.gov.au. **Website:** pba.slwa.wa.gov.au. **Contact:** Karen de San Miguel. Annual competition for Australian citizens or permanent residents of Australia, or writers whose work has Australia as its primary focus. Categories: children's books, digital narrative, fiction, nonfiction, poetry, scripts, writing for young adults, West Australian history, and Western Australian emerging writers. Submit 5 original copies of the work to be considered for the awards. All works must have been published between January 1 and December 31 of the prior year. See website

for details and rules of entry. Deadline: January 31. Prize: Awards $25,000 for Premier's Prize; awards $15,000 each for the Children's Books, Digital Narrative, Fiction, and Nonfiction categories; awards $10,000 each for the Poetry, Scripts, Western Australian History, Western Australian Emerging Writers, and Writing for Young Adults; awards $5,000 for People's Choice Award.

WESTERN HERITAGE AWARDS

National Cowboy & Western Heritage Museum, 1700 NE 63rd St., Oklahoma City OK 73111-7997. (405)478-2250. **Fax:** (405)478-4714. **Website:** www.nationalcowboymuseum.org. **Contact:** Jessica Limestall. The National Cowboy & Western Heritage Museum Western Heritage Awards were established to honor and encourage the legacy of those whose works in literature, music, film, and television reflect the significant stories of the American West. Accepted categories for literary entries: western novel, nonfiction book, art book, photography book, juvenile book, magazine article, or poetry book. Previously published submissions only; must be published the calendar year before the awards are presented. Requirements for entrants: The material must pertain to the development or preservation of the West, either from a historical or contemporary viewpoint. Literary entries must have been published between December 1 and November 30 of calendar year. Five copies of each published work must be furnished for judging with each entry, along with the completed entry form. Works recognized during special awards ceremonies held annually at the museum. There is an autograph party preceding the awards. Awards ceremonies are sometimes broadcast. The WHA are presented annually to encourage the accurate and artistic telling of great stories of the West through 16 categories of western literature, television, film and music; including fiction, nonfiction, children's books and poetry. See website for details and category definitions. Deadline: November 30. Prize: Awards a Wrangler bronze sculpture designed by famed western artist, John Free. Judged by a panel of judges selected each year with distinction in various fields of western art and heritage.

WESTERN WRITERS OF AMERICA

271CR 219, Encampment WY 82325. (307)329-8942. **E-mail:** wwa.moulton@gmail.com. **Website:** www.westernwriters.org. **Contact:** Candy Moulton, executive director. Eighteen Spur Award categories in various aspects of the American West. Send entry form with your published work. Accepts multiple submissions, each with its own entry form, available on our website. The nonprofit Western Writers of America has promoted and honored the best in Western literature with the annual Spur Awards, selected by panels of judges. Awards, for material published last year, are given for works whose inspirations, image and literary excellence best represent the reality and spirit of the American West. Deadline: January 4.

JACKIE WHITE MEMORIAL NATIONAL CHILDREN'S PLAY WRITING CONTEST

1800 Nelwood Dr., Columbia MO 65202-1447. (573)874-5628. **E-mail:** jwmcontest@cectheatre.org. **Website:** www.cectheatre.org. **Contact:** Tom Phillips. Annual contest that encourages playwrights to write quality plays for family audiences. Previously unpublished submissions only. Submissions made by author. Play may be performed during the following season. All submissions will be read by at least 3 readers. Author will receive a written evaluation of the script. Guidelines available online. Deadline: June 1. Prize: $500 with production possible. Judging by current and past board members of CEC and by non-board members who direct plays at CEC.

LAURA INGALLS WILDER MEDAL

50 E. Huron, Chicago IL 60611. (800)545-2433. **E-mail:** alscawards@ala.org. **Website:** www.ala.org/alsc/awards-grants/bookmedia/wildermedal. Award offered every 2 years. The Wilder Award honors an author or illustrator whose books, published in the US, have made, over a period of years, a substantial and lasting contribution to literature for children. The candidates must be nominated by ALSC members. Medal presented at Newbery/Caldecott banquet during annual conference. Judging by Wilder Award Selection Committee.

WILLA LITERARY AWARD

E-mail: jcpeone@gmail.com. **Website:** www.women-writingthewest.org. **Contact:** Carmen Peone. The WILLA Literary Award honors the year's best in published literature featuring women's or girls' stories set in the West. Women Writing the West (WWW), a nonprofit association of writers and other professionals writing and promoting the Women's West, underwrites and presents the nationally recognized award annually (for work published between January 1 and December 31). The award is named in honor of Pulitzer Prize winner Willa Cather, one of the country's foremost novelists. The award is given in 8 categories: historical fiction, contemporary fiction, original softcover fiction, creative nonfiction, scholarly nonfiction, poetry, children's fiction and nonfiction and young adult fiction/nonfiction. Entry forms available on the website. Deadline: November 1–February 1. Prize: $150 and a trophy. Finalist receives a plaque. Both receive digital and sticker award emblems for book covers. Notice of Winning and Finalist titles mailed to more than 4,000 booksellers, libraries, and others. Award announcement is in early August, and awards are presented to the winners and finalists at the annual WWW Fall Conference. Also, the eight winners will participate in a drawing for 2 two week all expenses paid residencies donated by Playa at Summer Lake in Oregon. Judged by professional librarians not affiliated with WWW.

RITA WILLIAMS YOUNG ADULT PROSE PRIZE CATEGORY

Soul-Making Keats Literary Competition, The Webhallow House, 1544 Sweetwood Dr., Broadmoor Village CA 94015-2029. (650)756-5279. **Fax:** (650)756-5279. **E-mail:** soulkeats@mail.com. **Website:** www.soulmakingcontest.us. **Contact:** Eileen Malone. For writers in grades 9-12 or equivalent age. Up to 3,000 words in prose form of choice. Complete rules and guidelines available online. Deadline: November 30 (postmarked). Prize: $100 for first place; $50 for second place; $25 for third place. Judged (and sponsored) by Rita Wiliams, an Emmy-award winning investigative reporter with KTVU-TV in Oakland, California.

PAUL A. WITTY OUTSTANDING LITERATURE AWARD

P.O. Box 8139, Newark DE 19714-8139. (800)336-7323. **Fax:** (302)731-1057. **Website:** www.reading.org. **Contact:** Marcie Craig Post, executive director. This award recognizes excellence in original poetry or prose written by students. Elementary and secondary students whose work is selected will receive an award. Deadline: February 2. Prize: Not less than $25 and a citation of merit.

WORK-IN-PROGRESS GRANT

Society of Children's Book Writers and Illustrators (SCBWI), 8271 Beverly Blvd., Los Angeles CA 90048. (323)782-1010. **E-mail:** grants@scbwi.org; wipgrant@scbwi.org. **Website:** www.scbwi.org. Six grants—one designated specifically for picture book text, chapter book/early readers, middle grade, young adult fiction, nonfiction, and multicultural fiction or nonfiction—to assist SCBWI members in the completion of a specific project. Open to SCBWI members only. Deadline: March 31. Open to submissions on March 1.

WRITE NOW

Indiana Repertory Theatre, 140 W. Washington St., Indianapolis IN 46204. 480-921-5770. **E-mail:** info@writenow.co. **Website:** www.writenow.co. The purpose of this biennial workshop is to encourage writers to create strikingly original scripts for young audiences. It provides a forum through which each playwright receives constructive criticism and the support of a development team consisting of a professional director and dramaturg. Finalists will spend approximately one week in workshop with their development team. At the end of the week, each play will be read as a part of the Write Now convening. Guidelines available online. Deadline: August 15.

WRITER'S DIGEST SELF-PUBLISHED BOOK AWARDS

Writer's Digest, 10151 Carver Road, Suite 300, Blue Ash OH 45242. (715)445-4612, ext. 13430. **E-mail:** writersdigestselfpublishingcompetition@fwmedia.com. **Website:** www.writersdigest.com. **Contact:** Nicole Howard. Contest open to all English-language, self-published books for which the authors have paid the full cost of publication, or the cost of printing has been paid for by a grant or as part of a prize. Categories include: Mainstream/Literary Fiction, Genre Fiction, Nonfiction, Inspirational (spiritual/new age), Life Stories (biographies/autobiographies/family histories/memoirs), Children's Books, Reference Books (directories/encyclopedias/guide books), Poetry, and Middle-Grade/Young Adult Books. Judges reserve the right to re-categorize entries. Judges reserve the right to withhold prizes in any category. All winners will be notified in October. Entrants must send a printed and bound book. Entries will be evaluated on content, writing quality, and overall quality of production and appearance. No handwritten books are accepted. Books must have been published within the past 5 years from the competition deadline. Books which have previously won awards from *Writer's Digest* are not eligible. Early bird deadline: April 2. Prizes: Grand Prize: $8,000, a trip to the Writer's Digest Conference, promotion in *Writer's Digest*, 10 copies of the book will be sent to major review houses, and a guaranteed review in *Midwest Book Review*; 1st Place (9 winners): $1,000 and promotion in *Writer's Digest*; Honorable Mentions: $50 worth of Writer's Digest Books and promotion on writersdigest.

com. All entrants will receive a brief commentary from one of the judges.

WRITER'S DIGEST SELF-PUBLISHED E-BOOK AWARDS

Writer's Digest, 10151 Carver Road, Suite 300, Blue Ash OH 45242. (715)445-4612, ext. 13430. **E-mail:** writersdigestselfpublishingcompetition@fwmedia.com. **Website:** www.writersdigest.com. **Contact:** Nicole Howard. Contest open to all English-language, self-published e-books for which the authors have paid the full cost of publication, or the cost of publication has been paid for by a grant or as part of a prize. Categories include: Mainstream/Literary Fiction, Genre Fiction, Nonfiction (includes reference books), Inspirational (spiritual/new age), Life Stories (biographies/autobiographies/family histories/memoirs), Children's Books, Poetry, and Middle-Grade/Young Adult Books. Judges reserve the right to re-categorize entries. Judges reserve the right to withhold prizes in any category. All winners will be notified by December 31. Entrants must enter online. Entrants may provide a file of the book or submit entry by the Amazon gifting process. Acceptable file types include: .epub, .mobi, .ipa. Word processing documents will not be accepted. Entries will be evaluated on content, writing quality, and overall quality of production and appearance. Books must have been published within the past 5 years from the competition deadline. Books which have previously won awards from *Writer's Digest* are not eligible. Early bird deadline: August 1; Deadline: September 4. Prizes: Grand Prize: $5,000, promotion in *Writer's Digest*, $200 worth of Writer's Digest Books, and more; 1st Place (9 winners): $1,000 and promotion in *Writer's Digest*; Honorable Mentions: $50 worth of Writer's Digest Books and promotion on writersdigest.com. All entrants will receive a brief commentary from one of the judges.

WRITERS-EDITORS NETWORK INTERNATIONAL WRITING COMPETITION

CNW Publishing, P.O. Box A, North Stratford NH 03590-0167. **E-mail:** contestentry@writers-editors.com. **E-mail:** info@writers-editors.com. **Website:** www.writers-editors.com. **Contact:** Dana K. Cassell, executive director. Annual award to recognize publishable talent. New categories and awards for 2018: Nonfiction (unpublished or self-published; may be an article, blog post, essay/opinion piece, column, nonfiction book chapter, children's article or book chapter); fiction (unpublished or self-published; may be a short story, novel chapter, Young Adult [YA] or children's story or book chapter); poetry (unpublished or self-published; may be traditional or free verse poetry or children's verse). Guidelines available online. Open to any writer. Maximum length: 4,000 words. Accepts inquiries by e-mail, phone and mail. Entry form online. Results announced May 31. Winners notified by mail and posted on website. Results available for SASE or visit website. Deadline: March 15. Prize: 1st Place: $150 plus one year Writers-Editors membership; 2nd Place: $100; 3rd Place: $75. All winners and Honorable Mentions will receive certificates as warranted. Most Promising entry in each category will receive a free critique by a contest judge. Judged by editors, librarians, and writers.

○ WRITERS' GUILD OF ALBERTA AWARDS

Writers' Guild of Alberta, Percy Page Centre, 11759 Groat Rd., Edmonton AB T5M 3K6, Canada. (780)422-8174. **Fax:** (780)422-2663. **E-mail:** mail@writersguild.ca. **Website:** writersguild.ca. **Contact:** Executive Director. Offers the following awards: Wilfrid Eggleston Award for Nonfiction; Georges Bugnet Award for Fiction; Howard O'Hagan Award for Short Story; Stephan G. Stephansson Award for Poetry; R. Ross Annett Award for Children's Literature; Gwen Pharis Ringwood Award for Drama; Jon Whyte Memorial Essay Award; James H. Gray Award for Short Nonfiction. Eligible entries will have been published anywhere in the world between January 1 and December 31 of the current year. The authors must have been residents of Alberta for at least 12 of the 18 months prior to December 31. Unpublished mss, except in the drama and essay categories, are not eligible. Anthologies are not eligible. Works may be submitted by authors, publishers, or any interested parties. Deadline: December 31. Prize: Winning authors receive $1,500; short piece prize winners receive $700.

WRITERS' LEAGUE OF TEXAS BOOK AWARDS

Writers' League of Texas, 611 S. Congress Ave., Suite 200A-3, Austin TX 78704. (512)499-8914. **Fax:** (512)499-0441. **E-mail:** sara@writersleague.org. **Website:** www.writersleague.org. **Contact:** Sara Kocek. Open to Texas authors of books published the previous year. To enter this contest, you must be a Texas author. "Texas author" is defined as anyone who (whether currently a resident or not) has lived in Texas for a period of 3 or more years. This contest is open to indie or self-published authors as well as traditionally-published authors. Deadline: February 28. Open to submissions October 7. Prize: $1,000 and a commemorative award.

WRITING CONFERENCE WRITING CONTESTS

P.O. Box 664, Ottawa KS 66067-0664. (785)242-2947. **Fax:** (785)242-2473. **E-mail:** jbushman@writingconference.com. **E-mail:** support@studentq.com. **Website:** www.writingconference.com. **Contact:** John H. Bushman, contest director. Unpublished submissions only. Submissions made by the author or teacher. Purpose of contest: To further writing by students with awards for narration, exposition and poetry at the elementary, middle school, and high school levels. Deadline: January 8. Prize: Awards plaque and publication of winning entry in The Writers' Slate online, April issue. Judged by a panel of teachers.

YEARBOOK EXCELLENCE CONTEST

100 Adler Journalism Building, Iowa City IA 52242-2004. (319)335-3457. **Fax:** (319)335-3989. **E-mail:** quill-scroll@uiowa.edu. **Website:** www.quilland-scroll.org. **Contact:** Jeff Browne, executive director. High school students who are contributors to or staff members of a student yearbook at any public or private high school are invited to enter the competition. Awards will be made in each of the 18 divisions. There are two enrollment categories: Class A: more than 750 students; Class B: 749 or less. Winners will receive Quill and Scroll's National Award Gold Key and, if seniors, are eligible to apply for one of the Edward J. Nell Memorial or George and Ophelia Gallup scholarships. Open to students whose schools have Quill and Scroll charters. Previously published submissions only. Submissions made by the author or school yearbook adviser. Must be published in the 12-month span prior to contest deadline. Visit website for list of current and previous winners. Purpose is to recognize and reward student journalists for their work in yearbooks and to provide student winners an opportunity to apply for a scholarship to be used freshman year in college for students planning to major in journalism. Deadline: November 1.

● THE YOUNG ADULT FICTION PRIZE

Victorian Premier's Literary Awards, State Government of Victoria, The Wheeler Centre, 176 Little Lonsdale Street, Melbourne VIC 3000, Australia. (61)(3)90947800. **E-mail:** vpla@wheelercentre.com. **Website:** http://www.wheelercentre.com/projects/victorian-premier-s-literary-awards-2016/about-the-awards. **Contact:** Project Officer. Visit website for guidelines and nomination forms. Prize: $25,000.

YOUNG READER'S CHOICE AWARD

E-mail: hbray@missoula.lib.mt.us. **Website:** www.pnla.org. **Contact:** Honore Bray, president. The Pacific Northwest Library Association's Young Reader's Choice Award is the oldest children's choice award in the U.S. and Canada. Nominations are taken only from children, teachers, parents and librarians in the Pacific Northwest: Alaska, Alberta, British Columbia, Idaho, Montana and Washington. Nominations will not be accepted from publishers. Nominations may include fiction, nonfiction, graphic novels, anime, and manga. Nominated titles are those published 3 years prior to the award year. Deadline: February 1. Books will be judged on popularity with readers. Age appropriateness will be considered when choosing which of the three divisions a book is placed. Other considerations may include reading enjoyment; reading level; interest level; genre representation; gender representation; racial diversity; diversity of social, political, economic, or religions viewpoints; regional consideration; effectiveness of expression; and imagination. The Pacific Northwest Library Association is committed to intellectual freedom and diversity of ideas. No title will be excluded because of race, nationality, religion, gender, sexual orientation, political or social view of either the author or the material.

THE YOUTH HONOR AWARDS

Skipping Stones Youth Honor Awards, Skipping Stones Magazine, Skipping Stones Magazine, P.O. Box 3939, Eugene OR 97403, USA. (541)342-4956. **E-mail:** info@skippingstones.org. **E-mail:** editor@skippingstones.org. **Website:** www.skippingstones.org. **Contact:** Arun N. Toke, Editor and Publisher. *Skipping Stones* is an international, literary, and multicultural, children's magazine that encourages cooperation, creativity, and celebration of cultural and linguistic diversity. It explores stewardship of the ecological and social webs that nurture us. It offers a forum for communication among children from different lands and backgrounds. *Skipping Stones* expands horizons in a playful, creative way. This is a non-commercial, non-profit magazine with no advertisements. In its 28th year. Original writing and art from youth, ages 7 to 17, should be typed or neatly handwritten. The entries should be appropriate for ages 7 to 17. Prose under 1,000 words; poems under 30 lines. Word limit: 1,000. Poetry: 30 lines. Non-English and bilingual writings are welcome. To promote multicultural, international and nature awareness. Deadline: June 25. Prize: An Honor Award Certificate, a subscription to Skipping Stones and five nature and/or multicultural books. They are also invited to join the Student Review Board. Everyone who enters the contest receives the autumn issue featuring the ten winners and other noteworthy entries. Editors and interns at the *Skipping Stones* magazine

○ Youth awards are for children only; you must be under 18 years of age to qualify.

ANNA ZORNIO MEMORIAL CHILDREN'S THEATRE PLAYWRITING COMPETITION

University of New Hampshire, Department of Theatre and Dance, PCAC, 30 Academic Way, Durham NH 03824. (603)862-3038. **Fax:** (603)862-0298. **E-mail:** mike.wood@unh.edu. **Website:** cola.unh.edu/theatre-dance/program/anna-zornio-childrens-theatre-playwriting-award. **Contact:** Michael Wood. Offered every 4 years for unpublished well-written plays or musicals appropriate for young audiences with a maximum length of 60 minutes. May submit more than 1 play, but not more than 3. Honors the late Anna Zornio, an alumna of The University of New Hampshire, for dedication to and inspiration of playwriting for young people, K-12th grade. Deadline: March 1, 2021. Prize: $500.

PUBLISHERS & THEIR IMPRINTS

//

The publishing world is in constant transition. With all the buying, selling, reorganizing, consolidating, and dissolving, it's hard to keep publishers and their imprints straight. To help make sense of these changes, here's a breakdown of major publishers (and their divisions)—who owns whom and which imprints are under each company umbrella. Keep in mind that this information changes frequently. The website of each publisher is provided to help you keep an eye on this ever-evolving business.

HACHETTE BOOK GROUP

www.hachettebookgroup.com

GRAND CENTRAL PUBLISHING
Forever
Forever Yours
Grand Central Life & Style
Twelve
Vision

HACHETTE AUDIO

HACHETTE BOOKS
Black Dog & Leventhal
Jericho Books

HACHETTE NASHVILLE
Center Street
Faith Words

LITTLE, BROWN AND COMPANY
Back Bay Books

Jimmy Patterson

Lee Boudreaux Books

Mulholland Books

LITTLE, BROWN BOOKS FOR YOUNG READERS

LB Kids

Poppy

ORBIT

Redhook

Yen Press

PERSEUS

Avalon Travel

Basic Books

Da Capo

PublicAffairs

Running Press

HARPERCOLLINS

www.harpercollins.com

ADULT

Amistad

Anthony Bourdain Books

Avon

Avon Impulse

Avon Inspire

Avon Red

Bourbon Street Books

Broadside Books

Custom House

Dey Street

Ecco Books

Harper Books

Harper Business

Harper Design

Harper Luxe

Harper Paperbacks

Harper Perennial

Harper Voyager

Harper Wave

HarperAudio

HarperCollins 360

HarperElixir

HarperLegend

HarperOne

William Morrow

William Morrow Paperbacks

Witness

CHILDREN'S

Amistad

Balzer + Bray

Greenwillow Books

HarperAudio

HarperCollins Children's Books

HarperFestival

HarperTeen

HarperTeen Impulse

Katherine Tegen Books

Walden Pond Press

CHRISTIAN PUBLISHING

Bible Gateway

Blink

Editorial Vida

FaithGateway

Grupo Nelson

Nelson Books

Olive Tree

Thomas Nelson

Tommy Nelson

W Publishing Group

WestBow Press

Zonderkidz

Zondervan

Zondervan Academic

HARLEQUIN

Carina Press

Harlequin Books

Harlequin TEEN

HQN Books

Kimani Press

Love Inspired

MIRA Books

Worldwide Mystery

HARPERCOLLINS AUSTRALIA

HARPERCOLLINS CANADA

Collins

Harper Avenue

Harper Perennial

Harper Weekend

HarperCollins Canada

Patrick Crean Editions

HARPERCOLLINS INDIA

HARPERCOLLINS NEW ZEALAND

HARPERCOLLINS UK

4th Estate

Avon

Carina

Collins

Harper Audio

Harper Voyager

Harper360

HarperCollins Children's Books

HarperFiction

HarperImpulse

HarperNonFiction

Mills & Boon

MIRA

MIRA Ink

The Borough Press

Times Books

William Collins

MACMILLAN PUBLISHERS

us.macmillan.com

DISTRIBUTED PUBLISHERS

Bloomsbury USA and Walker & Company

The College Board

Drawn and Quarterly

Entangled Publishing

Graywolf Press

Guinness World Records

Media Lab Books

Page Street Publishing Co.

Papercutz

Rodale

FARRAR, STRAUS AND GIROUX

Faber and Faber Inc.

Farrar, Straus and Giroux Books for Young Readers

FSG Originals

Hill and Wang

North Point Press

Sarah Crichton Books

Scientific American

FIRST SECOND

FLATIRON BOOKS

HENRY HOLT & CO.

Henry Holt Books for Young Readers

Holt Paperbacks

Metropolitan Books

Times Books

MACMILLAN AUDIO

MACMILLAN CHILDREN'S

Farrar, Straus & Giroux for Young Readers

Feiwel & Friends

Henry Holt Books for Young Readers

Imprint

Kingfisher

Macmillan Children's Publishing Group

Priddy Books

Roaring Brook Press

Square Fish

Tor Children's

PICADOR

QUICK AND DIRTY TIPS

ST. MARTIN'S PRESS

Griffin

Let's Go

Minotaur Books

St. Martin's Press Paperbacks

Thomas Dunne Books

Truman Talley Books

TOR/FORGE

Starscape

Tor Teen Books

PENGUIN RANDOM HOUSE

www.penguinrandomhouse.com

CROWN PUBLISHING GROUP

Amphoto Books

Broadway Books

Clarkson Potter

Convergent Books

Crown

Crown Archetype

Crown Business

Crown Forum

Harmony Books

Hogarth

Image Catholic Books

Pam Krauss Books

Potter Craft

Potter Style

Ten Speed Press

Three Rivers Press

Tim Duggan Books

WaterBrook Multnomah

Watson-Guptill

KNOPF DOUBLEDAY PUBLISHING GROUP

Alfred A. Knopf

Anchor Books

Doubleday

Everyman's Library

Nan A. Talese

Pantheon Books

Schocken Books

Vintage Books

Vintage Espanol

PENGUIN

Avery

Berkley

Blue Rider Press

DAW

Dial Books for Young Readers

Dutton

Dutton Children's Books

Firebird

Frederick Warne

G.P. Putnam's Sons

G.P. Putnam's Sons Books for Young Readers

Grosset & Dunlap

InterMix

Kathy Dawson Books

Nancy Paulsen Books

Penguin

Penguin Audio

Peguin Classics

Penguin Press

Penguin Workshop

Penguin Young Readers

Philomel

Plume

Portfolio

Price Stern Sloan

Puffin

Razorbill

Riverhead

Speak

TarcherPerigee

Viking Books

Viking Children's Books

PENGUIN RANDOM HOUSE PUBLISHING GROUP

Alibi

Ballantine Books

Bantam

Delacorte Press

Dell

Del Rey

Del Rey/LucasBooks

The Dial Press

Flirt

Hydra

Loveswept

Lucas Books

One World

The Modern Library

Penguin Random House Trade Group

Penguin Random House Trade Paperbacks

Presidio Press

Random House

Spiegel & Grau

PENGUIN RANDOM HOUSE CHILDREN'S BOOKS

Alfred A. Knopf

Crown

Delacorte Press

Doubleday

Dragonfly Books

Ember

Kids@Random (RH Children's Books)

Golden Books

Laurel-Leaf Books

Now I'm Reading!

The Princeton Review

Random House Books for Young Readers

Schwartz & Wade Books

Sylvan Learning

Wendy Lamb Books

Yearling Books

RANDOM HOUSE AUDIO/LIVING LANGUAGE

Books on Tape

Living Language

Listening Library

Penguin Random House Audio Publishing

RH Large Print

RH INTERNATIONAL

Penguin Random House Australia

The Penguin Random House Group (UK)

Penguin Random House Grupo Editorial (Argentina)

Penguin Random House Grupo Editorial (Chile)

Penguin Random House Grupo Editorial (Colombia)

Penguin Random House Grupo Editorial (Mexico)

Penguin Random House Grupo Editorial (Peru)

Penguin Random House Grupo Editorial (Portugal)

Penguin Random House Grupo Editorial (Spain)

Penguin Random House Grupo Editorial (Uruguay)

Penguin Random House India

Penguin Random House New Zealand

Penguin Random House of Canada

Penguin Random House Struik (South Africa)

Transworld Ireland

Verlagsgruppe Penguin Random House

SIMON & SCHUSTER

www.simonandschuster.com

SIMON & SCHUSTER ADULT PUBLISHING

Adams Media

Atria

Emily Bestler Books

Enliven

Folger Shakespeare Library

Free Press

Gallery

Howard

Jeter Publishing

North Star Way

Pocket

Pocket Star

Scout Press

Scribner

Simon & Schuster

Threshold

Touchstone

SIMON & SCHUSTER CHILDREN'S PUBLISHING

Aladdin

Atheneum

Simon & Schuster Books for Young Readers

Beach Lane Books

Little Simon

Margaret K. McElderry

Paula Wiseman Books

Saga Press

Salaam Reads

Simon Pulse

Simon Spotlight

SIMON & SCHUSTER AUDIO PUBLISHING

Pimsleur

Simon & Schuster Audio

SIMON & SCHUSTER INTERNATIONAL

Simon & Schuster Australia

Simon & Schuster Canada

Simon & Schuster UK

GLOSSARY OF INDUSTRY TERMS

Common terminology and lingo.

///

AAR. Association of Authors' Representatives.

ABA. American Booksellers Association.

ABC. Association of Booksellers for Children.

ADVANCE. A sum of money a publisher pays a writer or illustrator prior to the publication of a book. It is usually paid in installments, such as one half on signing the contract, one half on delivery of a complete and satisfactory manuscript. The advance is paid against the royalty money that will be earned by the book.

ALA. American Library Association.

ALL RIGHTS. The rights contracted to a publisher permitting the use of material anywhere and in any form, including movie and book club sales, without additional payment to the creator.

ANTHOLOGY. A collection of selected writings by various authors or gatherings of works by one author.

ANTHROPOMORPHIZATION. The act of attributing human form and personality to things not human (such as animals).

ASAP. As soon as possible.

ASSIGNMENT. An editor or art director asks a writer, illustrator, or photographer to produce a specific piece for an agreed-upon fee.

B&W. Black and white.

BACKLIST. A publisher's list of books not published during the current season but still in print.

BEA. BookExpo America.

BIENNIALLY. Occurring once every two years.

BIMONTHLY. Occurring once every two months.

BIWEEKLY. Occurring once every two weeks.

BOOK PACKAGER. A company that draws all elements of a book together, from the initial concept to writing and marketing strategies, then sells the book package to a book publisher and/or movie producer. Also known as book producer or book developer.

BOOK PROPOSAL. Package submitted to a publisher for consideration, usually consisting of a synopsis and outline as well as sample chapters.

BUSINESS-SIZE ENVELOPE. Also known as a #10 envelope. The standard size used in sending business correspondence.

CAMERA-READY. Refers to art that is completely prepared for copy camera platemaking.

CAPTION. A description of the subject matter of an illustration or photograph; photo captions include persons' names where appropriate. Also called cutline.

CBC. Children's Book Council.

CLEAN-COPY. A manuscript free of errors that needs no editing; it is ready for typesetting.

CLIPS. Samples, usually from newspapers or magazines, of a writer's published work.

CONCEPT BOOKS. Books that deal with ideas, concepts and large-scale problems, promoting an understanding of what's happening in a child's world. Most prevalent are alphabet and counting books, but also includes books dealing with specific concerns facing young people (such as divorce, birth of a sibling, friendship, or moving).

CONTRACT. A written agreement stating the rights to be purchased by an editor, art director, or producer and the amount of payment the writer, illustrator, or photographer will receive for that sale.

CONTRIBUTOR'S COPIES. The magazine issues sent to an author, illustrator, or photographer in which her work appears.

CO-OP PUBLISHER. A publisher that shares production costs with an author but, unlike subsidy publishers, handles all marketing and distribution. An author receives a high percentage of royalties until her initial investment is recouped, then standard royalties. (Children's Writer's & Illustrator's Market does not include co-op publishers.)

COPY. The actual written material of a manuscript.

COPYEDITING. Editing a manuscript for grammar usage, spelling, punctuation, and other general style.

COPYRIGHT. A means to legally protect an author's/illustrator's/photographer's work. This can be shown by writing the creator's name and the year of the work's creation.

COVER LETTER. A brief letter, accompanying a complete manuscript, especially useful if responding to an editor's request for a manuscript. May also accompany a book proposal.

CUTLINE. See caption.

DIVISION. An unincorporated branch of a company.

DUMMY. A loose mock-up of a book showing placement of text and artwork.

ELECTRONIC SUBMISSION. A submission of material by e-mail or Web form.

FINAL DRAFT. The last version of a polished manuscript ready for submission to an editor.

FIRST NORTH AMERICAN SERIAL RIGHTS. The right to publish material in a periodical for the first time, in the U.S. or Canada.

F&GS. Folded and gathered sheets. An early, not-yet-bound copy of a picture book.

FLAT FEE. A one-time payment.

GALLEYS. The first typeset version of a manuscript that has not yet been divided into pages.

GENRE. A formulaic type of fiction, such as horror, mystery, romance, fantasy, suspense, thriller, science fiction, or western.

GLOSSY. A photograph with a shiny surface, as opposed to one with a matte finish.

GOUACHE. Opaque watercolor with an appreciable film thickness and an actual paint layer.

HALFTONE. Reproduction of a continuous tone illustration with the image formed by dots produced by a camera lens screen.

HARD COPY. The printed copy of a computer's output.

HARDWARE. Refers to all the mechanically integrated components of a computer that are not software—circuit boards, transistors and the machines that are the actual computer.

HI-LO. High interest, low reading level.

HOME PAGE. The first page of a website.

IBBY. International Board on Books for Young People.

IMPRINT. Name applied to a publisher's specific line of books.

IRA. International Reading Association.

IRC. International Reply Coupon. Sold at the post office to enclose with text or artwork sent to a recipient outside your own country to cover postage costs when replying or returning work.

KEYLINE. Identification of the positions of illustrations and copy for the printer.

LAYOUT. Arrangement of illustrations, photographs, text and headlines for printed material.

LGBTQ. Lesbian/gay/bisexual/trans/queer.

LINE DRAWING. Illustration done with pencil or ink using no wash or other shading.

MASS MARKET BOOKS. Paperback books directed toward an extremely large audience sold in supermarkets, drugstores, airports, newsstands, online retailers, and bookstores.

MECHANICALS. Paste-up or preparation of work for printing.

MIDDLE-GRADE OR MID-GRADE. See middle reader.

MIDDLE READER. The general classification of books written for readers approximately ages nine to twelve. Often called middle-grade or mid-grade.

MS (MSS). Manuscript(s).

MULTIPLE SUBMISSIONS. See simultaneous submissions.

NCTE. National Council of Teachers of English.

NEW ADULT (NA). Novels with characters in their late teens or early twenties who are exploring what it means to be an adult.

ONE-TIME RIGHTS. Permission to publish a story in periodical or book form one time only.

PACKAGE SALE. The sale of a manuscript and illustrations/photos as a "package" paid for with one check.

PAYMENT ON ACCEPTANCE. The writer, artist, or photographer is paid for her work at the time the editor or art director decides to buy it.

PAYMENT ON PUBLICATION. The writer, artist, or photographer is paid for her work when it is published.

PICTURE BOOK. A type of book aimed at preschoolers to eight-year-olds that tells a story using a combination of text and artwork, or artwork only.

PRINT. An impression pulled from an original plate, stone, block, screen, or negative; also a positive made from a photographic negative.

PROOFREADING. Reading text to correct typographical errors.

QUERY. A letter to an editor or agent designed to capture interest in an article or book you have written or propose to write. (See the article "Before Your First Sale.")

READING FEE. Money charged by some agents and publishers to read a submitted manuscript. (Children's Writer's & Illustrator's Market does not include agencies that charge reading fees.)

REPRINT RIGHTS. Permission to print an already published work whose first rights have been sold to another magazine or book publisher.

RESPONSE TIME. The average length of time it takes an editor or art director to accept or reject a query or submission, and inform the creator of the decision.

RIGHTS. The bundle of permissions offered to an editor or art director in exchange for printing a manuscript, artwork, or photographs.

ROUGH DRAFT. A manuscript that has not been checked for errors in grammar, punctuation, spelling, or content.

ROUGHS. Preliminary sketches or drawings.

ROYALTY. An agreed percentage paid by a publisher to a writer, illustrator, or photographer for each copy of her work sold.

SAE. Self-addressed envelope.

SASE. Self-addressed, stamped envelope.

SCBWI. The Society of Children's Book Writers and Illustrators.

SECOND SERIAL RIGHTS. Permission for the reprinting of a work in another periodical after its first publication in book or magazine form.

SEMIANNUAL. Occurring every six months or twice a year.

SEMIMONTHLY. Occurring twice a month.

SEMIWEEKLY. Occurring twice a week.

SERIAL RIGHTS. The rights given by an author to a publisher to print a piece in one or more periodicals.

SIMULTANEOUS SUBMISSIONS. Queries or proposals sent to several publishers at the same time. Also called multiple submissions. (See the article "Before Your First Sale.")

SLANT. The approach to a story or piece of artwork that will appeal to readers of a particular publication.

SLUSH PILE. Editors' term for their collections of unsolicited manuscripts.

SOFTWARE. Programs and related documentation for use with a computer.

SOLICITED MANUSCRIPT. Material that an editor has asked for or agreed to consider before being sent by a writer.

SPAR. Society of Photographers and Artists Representatives.

SPECULATION (SPEC). Creating a piece with no assurance from an editor or art director that it will be purchased or any reimbursements for material or labor paid.

SUBSIDIARY RIGHTS. All rights other than book publishing rights included in a book contract, such as paperback, book club, and movie rights.

SUBSIDY PUBLISHER. A book publisher that charges the author for the cost of typesetting, printing and promoting a book. Also called a vanity publisher. (Note: Children's Writer's & Illustrator's Market does not include subsidy publishers.)

SYNOPSIS. A summary of a story or novel. Usually a page to a page and a half, single-spaced, if part of a book submission.

TABLOID. Publication printed on an ordinary newspaper page turned sideways and folded in half.

TEARSHEET. Page from a magazine or newspaper containing your printed art, story, article, poem or photo.

THUMBNAIL. A rough layout in miniature.

TRADE BOOKS. Books sold in bookstores and through online retailers, aimed at a smaller audience than mass market books, and printed in smaller quantities by publishers.

TRANSPARENCIES. Positive color slides; not color prints.

UNSOLICITED MANUSCRIPT. Material sent without an editor's, art director's, or agent's request.

VANITY PUBLISHER. See subsidy publisher.

WORK-FOR-HIRE. An arrangement between a writer, illustrator, or photographer and a company under which the company retains complete control of the work's copyright.

YA. See young adult.

YOUNG ADULT. The general classification of books written for readers approximately ages twelve to sixteen. Often referred to as YA.

YOUNG READER. The general classification of books written for readers approximately ages five to eight.

GENERAL INDEX

SUBJECT INDEX

AGE LEVEL INDEX

YOUNG READERS

WD WRITER'S DIGEST

Is Your Manuscript Ready?

Trust 2nd Draft Critique Service to prepare your writing to catch the eye of agents and editors. You can expect:

- Expert evaluation from a hand-selected, professional critiquer
- Know-how on reaching your target audience
- Red flags for consistency, mechanics, and grammar
- Tips on revising your manuscript and query to increase your odds of publication

Visit WritersDigestShop.com/2nd-draft for more information.

THE PERFECT COMPANION TO *WRITER'S MARKET*

The Writer's Market Guide to Getting Published

Learn exactly what it takes to get your work into the marketplace, get it published, and get paid for it!

Available from WritersDigestShop.com and your favorite book retailers.

To get started, join our mailing list: **WritersDigest.com/enews**

FOLLOW US ON:

 Find more great tips, networking and advice by following **@writersdigest**

 And become a fan of our Facebook pag **facebook.com/writersdigest**